WINDOWS 2000

Windows 2000 Administration

WINDOWS 2000

Windows 2000 Administration

GEORGE **SPALDING**

Osborne/**McGraw-Hill**

Berkeley   New York   St. Louis   San Francisco
Auckland   Bogotá   Hamburg   London   Madrid
Mexico City   Milan   Montreal   New Delhi   Panama City
Paris   São Paulo   Singapore   Sydney
Tokyo   Toronto

Osborne/**McGraw-Hill**
2600 Tenth Street
Berkeley, California 94710
U.S.A.

For information on translations or book distributors outside the U.S.A., or to arrange bulk purchase discounts for sales promotions, premiums, or fundraisers, please contact Osborne/**McGraw-Hill** at the above address.

Windows 2000 Administration

1234567890 DOC DOC 019876543210

ISBN 0-07-882582-2

Publisher	**Proofreader**
Brandon A. Nordin	Karen Mead
Associate Publisher and	**Indexer**
Editor-in-Chief	Valerie Robbins
Scott Rogers	**Computer Designers**
Acquisitions Editor	Jani Beckwith
Wendy Rinaldi	E. A. Pauw
Project Editor	**Illustrators**
Patty Mon	Robert Hansen
Acquisitions Coordinator	Michael Mueller
Monika Faltiss	Beth Young
Technical Editor	**Series Design**
Chris Branson	Peter F. Hancik
Copy Editor	
Peter Weverka	

This book was composed with Corel VENTURA™ Publisher.

Information has been obtained by Osborne/**McGraw-Hill** from sources believed to be reliable. However, because of the possibility of human or mechanical error by our sources, Osborne/**McGraw-Hill**, or others, Osborne/**McGraw-Hill** does not guarantee the accuracy, adequacy, or completeness of any information and is not responsible for any errors or omissions or the results obtained from use of such information.

To Cyrille Fortier, Jr. (Grandpa Cy),
the only father I've known for the last 20 years,
who still believes that everything I do
is smoke and mirrors.

About the Author

For over 25 years, George Spalding has been helping individuals on four continents realize their full potential by simplifying complex topics and motivating people to acquire new skills. After his appointment to the faculty of Yale University in 1972, he spent several years as a consultant to the White House on technical presentations and White House conferences. During that same period, he coordinated technical presentations for members of the president's cabinet, the Smithsonian Institution, the National Institutes of Health, and the Federal Bureau of Investigation.

Enthralled by the young field of local area networking, George installed his first LAN in 1983. Certified as a CNE (Certified NetWare Engineer) and CNI (Certified NetWare Instructor), he cut his computer networking teeth consulting and teaching Novell NetWare in the 3.x and 4.x environments for several years. Immediately grasping the incredible potential of Microsoft's new Windows NT, George quickly added that to his repertoire, certifying first as an MCT (Microsoft Certified Trainer) and next as an MCSE (Microsoft Certified Systems Engineer) and an MCP+I (Microsoft Certified Professional + Internet). George has been both consulting and teaching Windows NT 4.0 and NT security for the last four years in the United States and Europe. In fact, since 1992, George has personally trained more than 10,000 people on various versions of Microsoft Windows.

After his continuing love/hate relationship with Windows NT 4.0, George became convinced that the next version of NT was going to set the benchmark for both desktop and network operating systems for the new millennium. He has been running and studying what is now Windows 2000 since the beta 1 release of NT 5.0. While ordinarily a skeptic, George is proud of what Microsoft has achieved and thankful to be able to share his knowledge through the pages of this book.

His keen blend of quick wit and high-tech humor make George a much sought after presenter. His speaking credentials include keynote presentations at the 1998 Pacific Rim HDI Conference in Sydney, the 1999 and 2000 Support Services Conference, the Midwest launch of Windows 2000, and the 2000 NT/2000 MIS Security Conference. He will also be presenting Windows 2000 sessions at the 2000 Fall Comdex show.

A sampling of George's clients include 3M, Arthur Andersen, BellSouth, Boeing, NASA, Cargill, Carnegie Mellon University, C.I.A., DataCard, Defense Information Systems Agency (DISA), Deloitte and Touche, Federal Reserve Bank, Glaxo Wellcome, Help Desk Institute, Intel Corporation, Lucent Technologies, Miller Brewing, M.I.T., Nabisco Foods, Owens-Corning, Panama Canal Commission, Pfizer Pharmaceutical, Rollerblade, Inc., Shiva, SMC, Sylvania, Target, The Halifax, Toro, Upjohn Pharmaceutical, West Group, and Westinghouse.

CONTENTS

ACKNOWLEDGMENTS

t seems cliched to say that, even though my name is on the cover, there are so many people to thank. But it's so true.

I must begin with my wife, Mary Kay, whose indulgence and caring support throughout this process have been unwavering. I love you, dear. And to my children and grandchildren who went on with their lives (as they should) without me, because I was always "upstairs writing," you make me more proud each day.

Next my heartfelt thanks to Jim Ginther, Jr., and Dave Fletcher of MindSharp Learning Center in the Twin Cities, without whose support in scheduling flexibility, equipment, and lab time, this book would not have been possible.

Kudos to Jane Holcombe for a great Chapter 5, to Kenton Gardinier for the bulk of the material in Chapters 13 and 14, to Cliff Jacobson and Daniel Webster for hours of additional research and in-depth expertise, to Robert Myhre for several of the listed scripts, and to the MCTs and consultants of Microsoft (especially Paul Adare and Joern Wettern) whose commitment to knowledge and quality has greatly enhanced my own expertise.

And finally, to the folks at Osborne, Peter Weverka and Nancy Crumpton, who fixed my words, to Monika Faltiss, who kept me on schedule (no small task), to Patty Mon, who kept me focused (an even bigger task), and to the most industry-savvy editor in the business, Wendy Rinaldi, who was assertive and incisive (and could firmly kick my butt) when it was called for and laid off when she knew I couldn't take any more. You are the best team in technical publishing today. I have no idea how I lucked into you guys on my first book, but thank God I did. You guided me through the process like the pros you are, and your involvement has created a much better product. Thank you.

—George Spalding

INTRODUCTION

▼

As you should expect, every effort was made to remove errors from this document, but I'm sure several remain. Since I used the released version of Windows 2000 for nearly all research and screenshots, time was very short. For any errors you may find, I apologize in advance and would love to know about them to correct future editions. You may contact me at gspalding@mindsharp.com. As an introduction, let's take a quick look at each chapter.

Chapter 1 takes us on a brief tour of what's new in Windows 2000. It's a Win2K overview with brief explanations. I felt that many readers would appreciate one place to look for a list of all the new features in Microsoft's finest product to date.

Chapter 2 goes deep into the installation and upgrade processes for Windows 2000 Professional clients. Special attention is paid to the needs of the corporate network administrators, with the last half of the chapter focusing on the three kinds of Win2K unattended installations: command line, Sysprep, and RIPrep.

Chapter 3 deals with installing the Windows 2000 Server and upgrading from the Windows NT 4.0 Server environment. In-depth discussions of hardware requirements and in-place upgrades of existing network services are also included.

Chapter 4 explores the new, and largely uncharted, Microsoft Management Console. You will learn how to administer your network from within a single administrative tool (using taskpads) and create read only, limited function (user mode) MMCs for delegated administrators.

Chapter 5 delves into the supported file systems of Windows 2000: FAT16, FAT32, and NTFSv5. Dynamic volumes and Win2K fault tolerance are discussed, along with Dfs and its completely new replication topology.

Chapter 6 tackles the essential network services in Windows 2000: DNS, DHCP, and WINS. The Win2K dynamic DNS is the brave new world in name resolution with dynamic updates, SRV records, incremental zone transfer, and AD-integrated zones. DHCP becomes a more integrated part of the whole Windows 2000 network architecture with DNS integration and server authorization. And we still need WINS for backward compatibility and downlevel name resolution.

Chapter 7 introduces the new concepts of Routing and Remote Access in Windows 2000 Server. RADIUS and the Internet Authentication Service, RRAS policies and profiles, Internet connection sharing, NAT routing, and demand-dial interface are discussed.

Chapter 8 begins the discussion of Active Directory with the basics of X.500 Directory Services. It then proceeds to explain the place of each of the Active Directory building blocks: forest, domains, organizational units, and trusts in the big AD design picture. Finally, each type of leaf object is enumerated along with some of the ramifications and specific Active Directory structure decisions.

Chapter 9 focuses on the installation of the Active Directory, its requirements and preferences. What to do before upgrading an NT 4.0 domain controller and precautions to take during the upgrade cycle are listed as well. This chapter also includes a detailed discussion of each step in the Active Directory Installation Wizard and the consequences of certain selections.

Chapter 10 takes the next step in the Active Directory process and explains in detail how to configure and manage the Active Directory. Creating, modifying, and deleting domains and OUs, configuring sites, AD replication, and editing the schema are all elaborated.

Chapter 11 delves deeper into the day-to-day administration of the Active Directory with a discussion of how to manage the AD common objects: users, groups, printers, and folders. Details on creating, modifying, deleting, copying, moving, and finding common objects are located here. Also, a detailed explanation of Win2K group types and scope and their deployment options is included.

Chapter 12 hones in specifically on the Active Directory clients. Joining domains, creating, modifying, deleting, and moving the AD computer accounts, configuring the logon process, and managing downlevel legacy clients are discussed in detail.

Chapter 13 explains the intricacies of Windows 2000 authentication and network identification. Topics include all supported authentication protocols: LM, NTLM, NTLMv2, Kerberos v5, smart cards, and PKI. Remote access authentication and new security mechanisms in RRAS are also discussed.

Chapter 14 discusses the implementation of Windows 2000 security. Active Directory object and property security settings are detailed as well as recommendations for the file system and the Registry.

Chapter 15 examines the various backup tools and disaster recovery strategies that should be employed on a Windows 2000 Active Directory domain as well as on member servers or standalone workgroup servers. The built-in tools for Active Directory recovery are also detailed.

Chapter 16 points out the pros and cons of a variety of different migration strategies. The assumption is made that you are currently running an NT 4.0 domain with an assortment of Microsoft clients. Each NT 4.0 domain model is examined, and migration recommendations are provided. Client migration is examined independent of the discussion of the domain migration strategies.

I realize many of you will not read this book straight through from cover-to-cover but rather will pick and choose the topics that interest you. I hope that the reference quality of the book will serve you with high-quality, accurate information. I trust that your journey into the vastness of Windows 2000 will treat you and your organization well. Until the next time.

—George Spalding

CHAPTER 1

Windows 2000 Overview

The Windows 2000 operating system is one of the largest developments in the network computing industry in the last ten years. It's a large development as well for the business consumer of computing technology. Windows 2000 redefines integration. Which means that it's big. Really big. So big that, at first, Windows 2000 is a bit frightening, a little overwhelming, hard to get your arms all the way around, impossible to take in all at once. But be patient and stick it out because, after the initial "You must be kidding," your fear will turn to excitement, to anticipation, and, finally, to joy as you realize that Microsoft has truly delivered a first-generation product that, while not perfect, is just too good not to use.

JUST HOW IMPORTANT *IS* WINDOWS 2000 TO THE MICROSOFT CORPORATION?

In previous rollouts of Microsoft operating systems, there were always the older versions to pump cash into the enterprise and the nebulous promise, "We were working toward 'Cairo,' the great OS of the future." Skeptics chided, "Don't use any Microsoft OS until Service Pack 3." And, unfortunately, they were right. Until now.

Windows 2000 is the realization of the promises that we've been hearing from Microsoft for most of the 1990s. It's the product designed to take the disparate strides in development that have occurred over the last four years and bring them together under a single banner. It's put up or shut up time for the folks from Redmond and they've bet the farm on this one. Windows 2000 has to work—and work well—right out of the box. And much to the surprise of skeptics everywhere, including myself, it does.

WINDOWS 2000 PRODUCT CATEGORIES

Windows 2000 comes in four sizes: Workstation and Small, Medium, and Large Servers. Unlike NT 4.0, the feature set found in Win2K Professional (Workstation) and the Server products are not totally identical. Win2K Professional is focused on and configured specifically for the end user. Win2K Pro will take over the desktop and laptop market in a few months. The reason? It has Plug and Play, Power Management, and a slew of really cool, neat, and helpful features that actually work. Also, every business computer will ship with Win2K.

Windows 2000 Professional

Windows 2000 Professional replaces Windows NT 4.0 Workstation. Win2K Pro supports one or two processors and up to 4GB of RAM. It requires a minimum of 685MB of disk space (1GB recommended).

The reality-based hardware requirements for desktop computers are:

▼   Pentium II, 300 MHz

■   64MB RAM (128MB strongly recommended)

■   PC 98- or NetPC-compliant

▲   PXE Boot ROM support for Remote OS Install

For notebooks, the hardware requirements are:

▼   Pentium II, 233MHz

■   64MB RAM (128MB strongly recommended)

▲   A recent BIOS upgrade

Win2K Pro contains a number of new, user-oriented features, including:

▼   Personalized menus (the menu items you never click don't show up)

■   Much cleaner and simpler dialog boxes (don't show 'em anything you don't have to)

■   Offline folders and Synchronization Manager (a Briefcase that actually works)

▲   Hibernate mode (copy the entire contents of RAM to disk and shut down)

Since by far the most commonly installed version of Win2K Pro is the Intel single processor version, extra time and effort has been spent tweaking this version for maximum performance.

Windows 2000 Server

Windows 2000 Server replaces Windows NT 4.0 Server. Win2K Server supports one to four processors. It can handle up to 4GB of RAM and requires 685MB of minimum disk space, with a minimum 1GB volume recommended by Microsoft. Based on the future needs of a growing Active Directory, inevitable Service Packs, additional services, directory-enabled applications, and support tools you might wish to add, 2GB is my minimum recommendation for the volume holding the OS (disk space is cheap) with another 3GB for the Active Directory.

All versions of Win2K Server include the Win2K Terminal Service. It replaces Windows NT 4.0 Server, Terminal Server Edition (based on the Citrix Winframe product). More on that later.

The reality-based minimum hardware requirements are:

▼   Pentium II, 400MHz

▲   256MB RAM (more strongly recommended)

Windows 2000 Advanced Server

Windows 2000 Advanced Server replaces Windows NT 4.0 Server, Enterprise Edition. Win2K AS supports up to eight processors and up to 8GB of RAM. Any RAM over 4GB requires an Intel Pentium III Xeon chip (don't buy one with less than 2MB L2 cache or you're wasting the considerable money you sweated bullets to get approved).

Here's the scoop on this mondo RAM stuff. Windows 2000 is a 32-bit operating system, as was Windows NT 4.0. Its 32-bit (2^{32}) addressing provides a 4GB virtual address space no matter how you cut it. Period. End of discussion. You just can't invent memory or addresses. All processors since the 386 have used 32-bit addressing, giving them a maximum of 4GB of RAM. So long as NT could address 4GB and the chips could address 4GB, we were in sync and life was good. But technology never rests when there's money to be made. The Intel Xeon chip supports 36-bit (2^{36}) PAE (Physical Address Extensions) memory addressing, which means that addressable memory (RAM) can reach 64GB. However, Win2K still uses 32-bit addressing. For the time being, Microsoft has stop-gapped this apparent mismatch by going back to its roots. Conceptually, in the same way that later versions of DOS and Win 3.*x* were able to use memory above their 1MB address limit by calling it Extended Memory and loading HIMEM.SYS in the CONFIG.SYS file at bootup, Win2K AS utilizes its 4GB virtual address space and then "extends" its reach into the higher addresses with a "window" to acquire another 2GB for system files and processes. What once was old is new again. Brand new applications written (using APIs) just for this platform can reach all the way to 64GB. This will all sort itself out in a year or so after Intel releases its 64-bit Itanium chip and Microsoft follows with its 64-bit port of Win2K. But I digress.

Win2K Advanced Server includes:

▼   Terminal Services (replaces Windows NT 4.0 Server, Terminal Server Edition)

▲   Two Server Clustering Service (replaces Cluster Server) and Load Balancing Service (replaces WLBS)

The reality-based minimum hardware requirements are:

▼   Pentium III, 500MHz, (2MB L2 cache strongly recommended)

■   256MB RAM (256MB recommended per processor)

▲   685 disk space at minimum; 4GB OS/AD volume recommended

Windows 2000 Datacenter Server

Windows 2000 Datacenter Server is the brand-new "XXL" version of NT technology. This "big, honkin'" version supports up to 32 processors and up to 64GB of RAM (see the preceding section, "Windows 2000 Advanced Server," for details on memory). Win2K Datacenter Server will not ship with the rest of the Windows 2000 products. Look for a ship date of summer 2000.

Win2K Datacenter Server includes:

▼ Terminal Services (replaces Windows NT 4.0 Server, Terminal Server Edition)

▲ Four Server Clustering Service (replaces Cluster Server) and Load Balancing Service (replaces WLBS)

The reality-based minimum hardware requirements are:

▼ Pentium III, 500MHz, (2MB L2 cache strongly recommended)

■ 512MB RAM (256MB recommended per processor)

▲ 1GB disk space at minimum; 5GB OS/AD volume recommended

Get all the latest hardware compatibility specs at www.microsoft.com/hwtest/hcl.

DOMAINS, TRUSTS, AND THE ACTIVE DIRECTORY

Of all the changes and improvements made in Windows 2000, the single most important is the addition of the Active Directory (AD). Nearly every facet of the OS now revolves around the AD. The next generation of BackOffice products will depend on the AD, the first being Exchange 2000, which is shirking its own active directory system to depend instead completely on the Win2K AD. The Active Directory is the central repository for all the objects that make up our enterprise: domains, organizational units, users, groups, computers, printers, and so on. Using some of the tenants of the X.500 directory services specification, the hierarchical AD removes many of the shortcomings of the NT 4.0 flat domain structure. In combination with DNS, DHCP, and other services, the AD can make running a Win2K network easier, more efficient, and more fun—that's right, fun. When was the last time you had fun running your network?

Active Directory

The Active Directory is new in Windows 2000, although earlier versions of the AD have existed for several years in Exchange. The Active Directory is an "X.500-like" hierarchical database of all objects in the entire enterprise. Figure 1-1 shows a basic Active Directory structure. AD objects include users, groups, computers, domain controllers, printers, contacts, shared folders, and organizational units. The Win2K AD must use TCP/IP as its network protocol.

The Win2K Active Directory uses a basic top-down hierarchical model. At the top is a single forest of one or more trees, which must contain at least one (root) domain, which must contain at least one organizational unit (OU), and several other containers.

The recommended size limitation for the initial Win2K release is one million objects per domain. (However, lab tests have run the number of objects all the way up to 10 million without failure.)

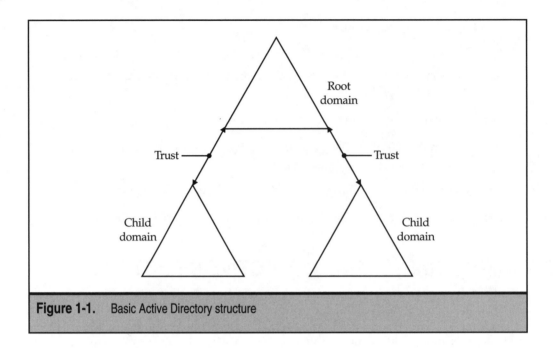

Figure 1-1.   Basic Active Directory structure

By default, all Win2K computers can use the AD. Computers running DOS, Windows 3.*x*, Windows 95/98, and NT 3.51 or NT 4.0 (legacy or "downlevel" clients) can still log on to a Win2K domain (domain controller), but will be unable to take advantage of any features of the Active Directory. Windows 95/98 computers require a new Directory Services add-on client (dsclient.exe) that ships with Win2K Server to interact with the AD. No add-on AD client is available for Win 3.*x*, DOS, or NT 3.51. NT 4.0, Service Pack 7 contains a Windows 2000 AD client for NT 4.0. Direct upgrades to Win2K Pro are possible from Windows 95/98, NT 3.51, and NT 4.0. Even after the AD add-on client is installed for downlevel clients, functionality remains limited.

Domains

The basic concept and the name "domain" stay the same, but the architecture (to protect the innocent) changes from the NT 4.0 "flat" domain model (all domains are equal) to a hierarchical domain model (a parent domain with child domains under it). The parent (or root) domain and all of its child domains are defined as a single domain tree. Multiple trees in the same AD become a forest.

The Win2K domain is the major building block for the Active Directory. It partitions the AD in terms of replication, inheritance, and security.

Naming Contexts

In Windows 2000, domains are named in accordance with the Internet's DNS (Domain Name System) standard (RFCs 1034 & 1035). For example, in a Win2K AD, suppose the root domain in a tree is called "bigcompany.com," as in Figure 1-2, which shows an example of Active Directory naming. In this case, the marketing "child" domain under it is named "mktg.bigcompany.com"; the production "child" domain is called "prod.bigcompany.com", and so on.

Each parent, or root, domain must have a separate naming context. Each naming context (root domain) begins a new tree within the forest. Microsoft chose this naming convention to allow DNS to be used for all Win2K name resolutions.

Recommendation: 1 DNS server per site.

Global Catalog

The Global Catalog (GC) is new in Windows 2000. With thousands or hundreds of thousands of objects in a single directory, it could be difficult and time-consuming to locate a specific object in the AD database. To facilitate finding objects, the AD provides an index

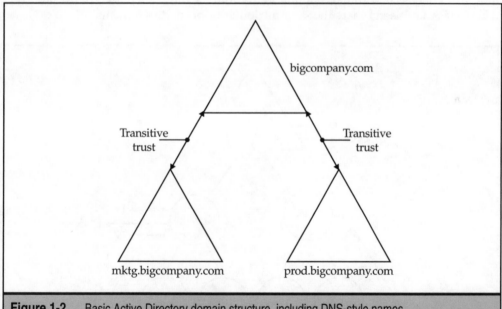

Figure 1-2.   Basic Active Directory domain structure, including DNS-style names

of objects called the Global Catalog. The Global Catalog is basically a search engine to help users and applications find objects published in the AD.

The Global Catalog, which can only exist on a domain controller (DC), contains a listing of every object in every domain in the entire forest, but it does not contain every property of every object. Figure 1-3 illustrates a domain with Global Catalog Servers. Users can search for objects by a predefined set of searchable criteria. For example, you can locate a user by logon ID, first name, last name, e-mail address, or organization.

By default, only one Global Catalog server exists in the entire forest, on the first DC created in the forest. Because the GC contains a list of every object in every domain in the forest, its replication is forest-wide. The Global Catalog also contains the names of all AD groups and the membership lists of each Universal group.

Recommendation: 1 Global Catalog server per site.

Forest

An AD forest defines the outside boundaries, or the perimeter, of the Win2K Active Directory. Another name for the forest could be the enterprise. There is a single forest in the Active Directory. Within it are trees, and within the trees are domains. Using the Global Catalog, all objects within the forest can be located quickly. The forest allows for easy movement of objects within its boundaries. Within the forest, all objects of the same type (object class; i.e., users) share the same attributes or properties (schema).

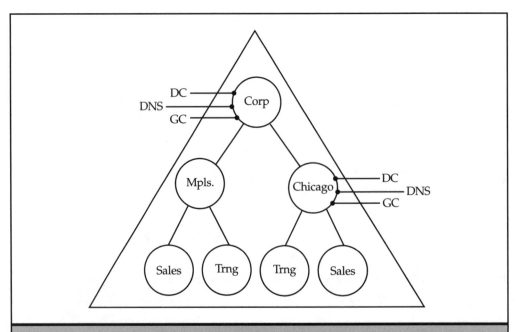

Figure 1-3.   A single Win2K domain with organizational units, domain controllers, Global Catalog Servers, and Domain Name Servers

Two forests (a future merger perhaps?) cannot be combined in the initial release of Windows 2000. A nontransitive, LSA, uni-directional NT 4.0-style trust can exist between domains in two separate Win2K forests.

Trusts

In NT 4.0, LSA trusts are manually established in one direction between two NT domains. NT 4.0 trusts are nontransitive. For communication to occur, a separate and discrete trust must be established between each domain in each direction.

In Windows 2000, Kerberos trusts are automatically established in both directions (trust has always been a two-way street) between the parent and child domains as each new child domain is added to the tree. Figure 1-4 demonstrates Win2K trusts. These Kerberos trusts are also transitive, so communication can pass from one domain to another and then on to another without an administrator intervening or the creation of explicit trusts.

Windows 2000 still supports explicit (NT 4.0-style) trusts for backward-compatibility with existing NT 4.0 domains, connections to domains in other forests, and cross-link, or convenience, trusts between Win2K domains.

Organizational Units

Organizational units (OUs) are new in Windows 2000. Figure 1-5 shows a Win2K domain with OUs. OUs exist within a domain. In essence, OUs are subdomains that contain AD objects. These objects are grouped by similar function or geographical location. OUs exist primarily for the purpose of delegating administrative authority and group policy application. An OU can contain nearly any AD object, including another OU.

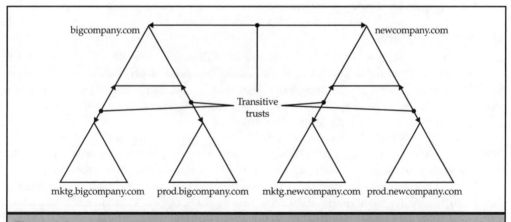

Figure 1-4.   AD forest with two root domains, four child domains, and transitive trusts

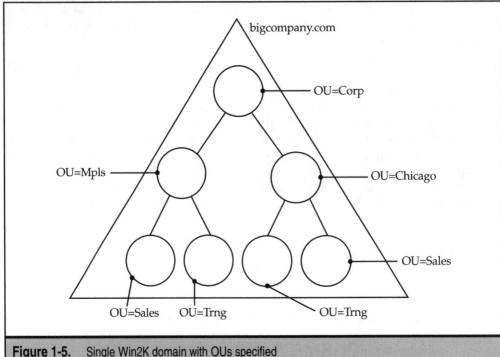

Figure 1-5.   Single Win2K domain with OUs specified

OUs are the major unit of administration in the Windows 2000 Active Directory. For the first time in a Microsoft product, they truly allow for administrative authority to be delegated. By default, OUs inherit their permissions and group policies from their parent.

Domain Controllers

Unlike the master-slave PDC/BDC relationship of domain controllers (DCs) in NT 4.0, where only the Primary Domain Controller could be updated, all domain controllers in Win2K are masters and all can accept updates at any time. This "multi-master" replication model allows for increased availability and fault tolerance. Figure 1-6 demonstrates a Win2K domain with multiple domain controllers.

Again unlike NT 4.0, the decision whether a Win2K Server will be a DC is made *after* the Server installation is complete. Any Win2K Server can be promoted to a domain controller and any Win2K domain controller can be demoted to a standalone or member Server.

Win2K DCs default to mixed (4.0 PDC/BDC) mode. Mixed mode allows all existing NT 4.0 functionality to be maintained (specifically, PDC/BDC replication). Win2K DCs can switch to native mode when all DCs in a given domain are upgraded to Win2K. The switch from mixed to native mode is irreversible for that specific domain.

Recommendation: 1 domain controller per site.

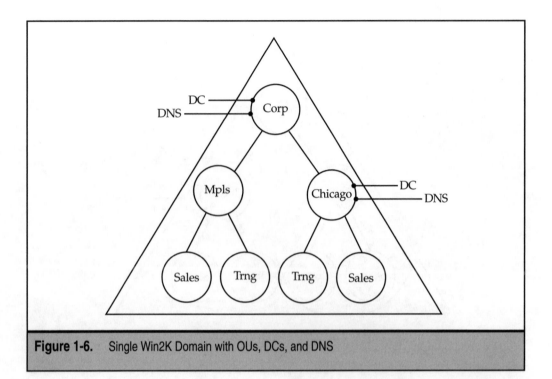

Figure 1-6.   Single Win2K Domain with OUs, DCs, and DNS

Sites

Sites are new in Windows 2000, but may be familiar to Exchange administrators from NT 4.0. Forests, trees, domains, and OUs are all logical elements of the Active Directory, but a site is a physical boundary defined within the AD. Sites are defined as one or more well-connected IP subnets. Figure 1-7 shows a Win2K domain with multiple sites. "Well-connected" means a reasonably fast and reliable connection. "Reasonably fast" could mean anything from 128K in a small company, to 1.5Mbps (T-1) in a medium-sized firm, to 10 or even 100 Mbps in a large organization. "Reliable" means that the connection stays up. In other words, a site contains the computers that are near me, the "chips" in the neighborhood.

By default, an entire forest has only one site. Sites are used to control domain replication, facilitate faster user logons, and improve response to most queries and searches by users and directory-aware applications. Sites only contain computers. Administrators must manually create and configure all sites, site links, and site link bridges.

In case you weren't counting, the recommendations for each site are:

▼   1 domain controller

■   1 DNS server

▲   1 Global Catalog server

And with the wonders of modern technology, they can all be on the same computer.

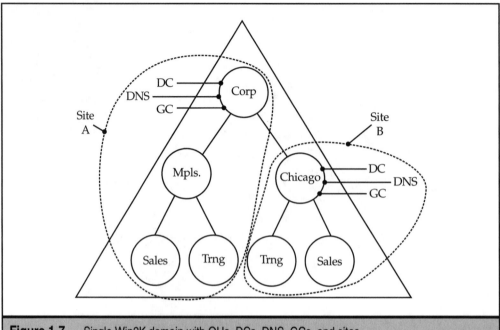

Figure 1-7. Single Win2K domain with OUs, DCs, DNS, GCs, and sites

Domain Replication

In NT 4.0, the default PDC to BDC replication interval is every five minutes. This is configurable in the PDC Registry.

In Windows 2000, DCs from the same domain that are also located in the same site replicate changes every five minutes by default. Replication traffic is uncompressed within a site. By default, DCs from the same domain located on different sites replicate every three hours. Intersite replication traffic is fully compressed to 15 percent of its original size. DCs from different domains do not replicate their AD, but do replicate their Global Catalog.

The KCC (Knowledge Consistency Checker) automatically configures replication so that no DC in the same site is ever more than three hops from the DC that originates a change. Intersite replication uses a "bridgehead" server model.

The unit of domain replication in NT 4.0 between the PDC and all BDCs is the entire object (same with Exchange 5.5). For example, if a user changes his or her password in NT

4.0, the entire user object and all of its properties is sent from the PDC to each BDC to update the security accounts database (SAM) during the next replication cycle.

However, if a user changes his or her password in Windows 2000, the user object is updated on the domain controller to which the user happens to be connected. Next, only the password and GUID (AD identifying information) are sent to all other replication partners in the user's domain during the next replication cycle and to their partners during the next cycle, and so on.

FILE SYSTEMS AND STORAGE MANAGEMENT

Windows 2000 supports every file system that Microsoft has ever created—and then some: FAT16, FAT32, NTFSv4, NTFSv5, Dfs, and so on. This means we can dual-boot Win2K with Windows 95, 98, or NT 4.0, but doing so is not recommended. The end-user can now encrypt the data on the notebook hard disk. But the greatest positive impact for the average network administrator will be the addition of dynamic disks. Volumes can be created, extended, and configured online without rebooting the system. Cool!

Distributed File System (Dfs)

Available for NT 4.0, the distributed file system (Dfs) is significantly enhanced in Windows 2000. Figure 1-8 shows the distributed file system (Dfs) allows a user to see a limited, logical view of the file system rather than the actual physical file system with its many server lists and their weird, confusing names. The Dfs root can be published in the AD for fault tolerance.

Used in conjunction with file replication service (FRS), multiple data replicas can be located close to the user for better performance and additional fault tolerance. Win2K, NT 4.0, and Windows 98 include Dfs client software; Windows 95 Dfs client software is available for downloading.

File Replication Service (FRS)

Replacing NT 4.0's directory replication service, the Win2K file replication service (FRS) is new in Windows 2000. FRS allows admin-designated files to be replicated to multiple computers within a domain. FRS is integral in domain replication as well. Each domain controller contains the Shared System Volume which, by default, is known as "sysvol." Any file placed on the sysvol of any domain controller will be replicated to every other domain controller in the same domain. Examples of such files are Group Policy Templates, logon scripts, NT 4.0 system policy files, company phone directories, etc. Using FRS in conjunction with Dfs can place multiple replicas of the same data in locations that are geographically close to the user.

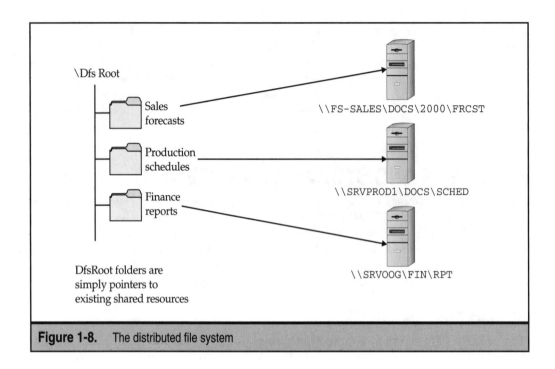

Figure 1-8. The distributed file system

CD-ROM File System (CDFS)

CD-ROM File System (CDFS) is the same as NT 4.0. It is read-only and is maintained for backward compatibility.

Universal Disk File System (UDFS)

The successor to CDFS, universal disk file system (UDFS) is targeted to CD and DVD media. Win2K supports read but not write at this time. Win2K implementation meets existing standards: ISO 13346, ECMA 167, and OSTA UDF from the Optical Storage Technology Association (www.osta.org). Full DVD functionality with your specific hardware may still require a third-party driver.

FAT16 (File Allocation Table, 16-bit)

FAT16 is unchanged. This *is* your father's file system. Released in 1983, FAT16 remains the least secure, most vulnerable, and most widely-installed file system in the history of computers. It is maintained in Win2K for backward-compatibility, ease of upgrade, and interoperability with legacy systems.

FAT16 supports volumes up to 2GB in Windows 9*x* and volumes up to 4GB in NT 4.0 and Win2K.

FAT32 (File Allocation Table, 32-bit)

FAT32 is the new, improved version of your father's file system. New suit, no tie, new haircut, wireless digital phone, and a multifunctional digital watch, but the same old dad. FAT32 ships with Windows 95 OSR2 and later, Windows 98, and Win2K.

Usually installed on disk volumes of 2GB and greater, Windows 95/98 can use it to create volumes up to 2TB (that's 2 terabytes, or roughly 2 trillion bytes). FAT32 also stores data more efficiently by using a much smaller cluster size than FAT16.

In Win2K, however, Microsoft chose to limit the maximum size of new FAT32 volumes to 32GB. If you're upgrading existing volumes from Win 9x, it will support (read/write) larger volumes. (How many of you have volumes larger than 32GB on your current Win 9x desktop?)

FAT32 still has absolutely no security features.

NTFS v4 (NT File System, version 4)

Windows 2000 automatically upgrades all existing NT 4.0 NTFS (NT file system) volumes to NTFS v5 format during installation. Therefore, maintaining a true NTFSv4 file system on a Win2K machine without jumping through ludicrous "noops" (nerd hoops) is impossible.

Even though Microsoft specifically recommends *not* dual-booting with Win2K, some will choose to wander aimlessly through a weekend of CDs and pizza. If you insist on maintaining a dual-boot with NT 4.0, you must have Service Pack 4 or higher on your NT 4.0 installation prior to the Win2K installation. Without it, you can't interact with the file system after you install Win2K. Windows NT 4+SP4 includes a new ntfs.sys that allows some limited interoperability (read and write) between NT4 and Win2K.

NTFS v5 (NT File System, version 5)

Major changes abound in the NTFS (NT File System) v5 file system in Win2K. We finally get disk quotas for NTFS to limit the amount of disk space that is available to a user on a volume. Offline folders is an exciting new feature whereby traveling users can "sync up" their data with a corporate server. New Volume Management technology from Veritas creates two types of disks: basic and dynamic. Dynamic disks allow us to change or configure volumes without rebooting. The encrypting file system (EFS) is part of NTFSv5 and protects files on the disk by encrypting them with the user's special key. The addition of mount points with dynamic disks allows the "mounting" of a separate volume under a folder on a different volume. A new indexing service speeds up performance on all Win2K-supported file systems, especially NTFS. A first-time concept for Microsoft, hierarchical storage management (HSM) technology will migrate infrequently used files to another storage medium.

Windows File Protection

The system files necessary to run Windows 2000 are not even displayed in Windows Explorer by default. The system files, if damaged or deleted, recopy themselves back to their correct location automatically from the DLL cache. If the DLL cache is deleted or corrupted, the system file checker (sfc.exe) command line utility will recopy the files from the Server CD to the DLL cache. In NT 4.0, we would have had to do a repair with the ERD or a complete reinstall to resolve these situations.

Disk Quotas

NTFS v5 supports disk quotas ('bout time). Quotas are configured per-user, per-volume, based on file ownership by the user's SID (security ID). Administrators can configure exactly when users are warned (threshold) and what they can do when they reach their quotas.

Disk quotas can be activated by group policies. Applications will see only the available space for the logged-on user when checking for disk space during setup. Disk quotas also apply to the print spool file. This prevents the user from spooling the print job that ate Cleveland.

Offline Folders

Also referred to as "client-side caching," the offline folders feature is designed to allow users to seamlessly work with server-based documents on a traveling notebook computer. This is the Briefcase that actually works.

Folders flagged to work offline are copied, or "cached," onto the notebook before disconnecting from the network. Documents are automatically synchronized with the server-based version upon the notebook's return to the network. Conflicts are displayed so that the user can resolve them. Synchronization settings are controlled by the Synchronization Manager. Documents cannot be merged. Offline folders can be used in conjunction with Folder Redirection.

Folder Redirection

A number of desktop-related folders can be redirected using a Group Policy function called Folder Redirection. The basic premise is simple. When a user logs on, the folders appear as they normally would on the user's desktop but in actuality reside on a central server somewhere else. The user is unaware of the folder's true location and the user experience is unchanged. The folders eligible for redirection are My Documents, My Pictures, Application Data, Start Menu, and Desktop. Redirected folders can be used in conjunction with offline folders to create a seamless experience for the mobile user.

Volume Management

Completely new in Windows 2000, there are now two kinds of disks: basic and dynamic. Basic disks, which are managed by ftdisk.sys as in NT 4.0, operate the same way they did in NT 4.0. They cannot be extended online; a reboot is required. Dynamic disks, which are managed by new LVM from Veritas (www.veritas.com), create a number of new possibilities. After the entire physical disk is converted to dynamic, volumes can be extended online, and NTFS-formatted stripes and mirrors can be created, broken, and recovered without taking the volume offline or rebooting the system. Moreover, there is no limit to the number of logical volumes on a dynamic disk. Dynamic volumes are designed for servers only and are disabled on notebooks. Dynamic volumes are transparent to applications.

At least 1MB of unpartitioned space is required on each physical hard disk to upgrade from a basic to a dynamic disk.

Recommendation: From now on, leave at least 10MB of unpartitioned (not unformatted or unused) space on every physical disk you partition and format. Period. No one will miss it. No one will know. It could save you hours, even days of effort down the pike. We'll call it the "CYA area."

Following are the volume types on a dynamic disk:

▼ **Simple volume (no fault tolerance)**   A single volume on a single physical disk.

■ **Spanned volume (no fault tolerance)**   Contains disk space from two or more physical disks (Volume Sets in NT 4.0).

■ **Striped volume (no fault tolerance)**   Stripes data across a single volume created from free space on two to 32 disks (RAID 0 – Stripe Sets in NT 4.0).

■ **Mirrored volumes (fault tolerant)**   Creates two identical, continuously updated copies of a simple volume on two physical disks (Disk Mirroring in NT 4.0).

▲ **RAID-5 volumes (fault tolerant)**   Stripes data and recovery information across a single volume created from free space on up to 32 disks (three disks minimum). Includes detailed parity information for data recovery in case of drive failure (Stripe Sets with Parity in NT 4.0).

Volume Mount Points

Using dynamic volumes, you can mount a volume to an empty directory on an existing NTFSv5 volume, a drive letter, or both. Mount points can be used to mount volumes existing on the local computer only.

EFS (Encrypting File System)

On NTFSv5 volumes, files can be encrypted on the disk. To be used by any application, the files must be decrypted. Only the user (the logged-on user who performed the encryption) and the Recovery Agent (required) can decrypt the files. This feature was designed to protect data on notebooks and home directories on servers. You cannot encrypt and compress the same file.

Designated Recovery Agents (by default, the administrator) can recover encrypted data for an entire domain (using AD and Certificate Server). Recovery becomes essential when a user leaves the company. In certain situations deleting local users could leave encrypted files unrecoverable.

Chkdsk

The new chkdsk is faster and more scaleable. The progress indicator is now accurate. New options to skip most of the index verification (/I) and cycle checking (/C) speed up the checking process considerably. The bigger the system, the bigger the improvement.

Defrag

Win2K defrag is an MMC snap-in from Executive Software, the folks who have been writing Diskeeper since NT 3.51. The somewhat hobbled version included with Windows 2000 only defragments local volumes, so no remote operations are possible. No scripting is possible because defrag is a manual local operation done one volume at a time. Works with NTFS, FAT16, and FAT32. More functionality is available with the full Diskeeper product from Executive Software.

Indexing Service

The new Win2K indexing service builds indices of the file system to make full-text and property searches of all supported files on the system go faster. It runs on FAT16, FAT32, and NTFS volumes, but is optimized for NTFS v5. NTFS v5 uses a new feature called the change journal that actually keeps track of changes to the volume on a real-time basis. The Win2K indexing service uses the NTFS v5 change journal to build its index at blinding speed.

Indexing service ships with all versions of Win2K and is fully integrated with all Windows 2000 features. It is fully configurable and gives us a much more full-featured and efficient solution than the NT 4.0 Find Fast.

Hierarchical Storage Management (HSM)

The hierarchical storage management (HSM) concept is simple. Take my least recently used (LRU) files and migrate them from my disk to another storage medium while still keeping a reference (a pointer) to the file on the NTFS directory. This way, space is available on my disk system for the files that folks need to retrieve. While we're at it, let's make all this happen without human intervention based on certain conditions being met.

Based on technology from HighGround Systems (www.highground.com), here's the way it works: When disk free space reaches a minimum threshold (say, 10 percent), make LRU files into pointers to another medium (a tape), and keep migrating files until disk free space reaches a maximum threshold (say, 20 percent). When files are requested (read), data is automatically brought back to the disk (assuming that the tape cartridge resides in some kind of supported automated changer). The migrated status of the file is reflected by the file's icon (a small clock is added to the icon).

All Win2K Servers ship with RSS (Remote Storage Server) provided by Seagate Software. The current release supports only two tiers of storage, online (disk) as the first tier and tape as the second tier. Other tiers will be possible (CDs, WORMs, and so on) in future versions. RSS uses RSM (Removable Storage Manager) for device support.

Removable Storage Manager (RSM)

In Win2K, Microsoft is trying to create a common device interface for all types of storage hardware. That device is called Removable Storage Manager (RSM). RSM includes broad support for media changers of all types (tape changers, jukeboxes and so on). The goal is for all future storage-aware applications to write to a single (intermediate) storage platform interface (RSM) and for storage hardware vendors to create drivers for the RSM platform in order to create completely vendor-independent storage solutions.

Backup

We can finally back up to something besides tape. Win2K Backup (ntbackup.exe) can write to a file, a Zip drive, a writable CD, and other hard drives and volumes, as well as tape. It supports all the new file system features (EFS, dynamic volumes, and so on) and all Win2K file systems (FAT16, FAT32, and NTFS). Tape changers are supported via RSM. It's even integrated with Active Directory.

Now here's a surprise: Win2K Backup is where you create your Win2K Emergency Repair Disk, which no longer contains a copy of the registry.

New Storage Interfaces

Win2K supports all the latest (and fastest) interfaces for I/O devices. USB (Universal Serial Bus) supports up to 127 devices and runs at 12 Mbps. The IEEE 1394 standard supports up to 63 devices and runs at 400 Mbps today, and many times that speed tomorrow. I_2O (IIO) Intelligent I/O from Intel offloads the I/O processing from the main CPU to another processor on the system to improve throughput. Fibre Channel (currently supporting 1000 Mbps and 126 devices with an arbitrated loop) will allow for speeds across the wire that are currently beyond our imagination for the applications of tomorrow such as full-motion video and storage area networks.

NETWORK SERVICES

Win2K institutes a wealth of changes in networking, the most significant being the requirement for TCP/IP. With IP required, DNS moves into a pivotal role in any Win2K network. Basically, the Win2K DNS does what it has always done (Internet name resolution), some of what WINS used to do (locating network services), and what the Active Directory needs it to do (direct queries to the right machine on the right site)—a huge job. AD can't install without a DNS, and, looking toward the future, IPv6 will require a dynamic DNS server as well, even on a small network, because no one can remember a 128-bit IP address. DHCP keeps up with the Joneses by integrating with DNS. The remaining network services upgrade from NT 4.0, in some cases bringing separate, independent products into a common fold. Get ready for the RFC cascade.

Domain Name Service (DNS)

DNS is greatly enhanced in Windows 2000. Win2K Active Directory requires the use of DNS to perform all name resolution; in fact, the Active Directory cannot even install without an existing Win2K-level DNS Server online. Microsoft wants to make NetBIOS, WINS and Computer Browsing obsolete. The name resolution mechanism Microsoft has chosen to replace them all is the Internet's Domain Name Service.

In Win2K, DNS must support the use of SRV records (RFC 2052), which means that Win2K services must register their locations with DNS. Win2K DNS must support Dynamic Updates (RFC 2136) from the DHCP Server and DHCP client, which means that, as a computer boots, the DHCP Server registers its existence with DNS, and then the client continues to register services as they load. Secure dynamic updates (RFC 2137) are also supported with Active Directory. The Win2K DNS utilizes (IXFR) incremental zone transfer (RFC 1995). NT 4.0 transferred the entire zone (AXFR), but Win2K sends just the changes as long as IXFR is supported by the receiving DNS. BIND 8.2.1 also supports SRV records, dynamic updates, and incremental zone transfer.

In Win2K, DNS can achieve fault tolerance by integrating its primary zones into the AD, which then replicates the zones to each DC during the normal replication cycle.

WINS (Windows Internet Name Service)

As in NT 4.0, NetBIOS name resolution is achieved by using WINS. All downlevel clients continue to use WINS, as they have in the past, to locate other computers and services. WINS will be required until all NetBIOS naming and applications using NetBIOS APIs have been purged from the network (don't hold your breath). WINS is also used if the DNS lookup fails to produce a name resolution. One enhancement over the NT 4.0 version of WINS is the ability to delete expired records from the WINS database.

Computer Browsing

The Computer Browsing service operates the same way it did in NT 4.0. Although not needed at all by Win2K-level clients, downlevel clients still use it as an adjunct to WINS. Even in full Win2K native mode, the Master Browser role still exists in one DC per domain, the PDC Emulator (Operations Master), for backward compatibility.

Dynamic Host Configuration Protocol (DHCP)

Dynamic Host Configuration Protocol (DHCP) is substantially enhanced in Windows 2000. In Win2K, a DHCP Server must be "authorized" in order to lease IP addresses, which prevents any administrator from creating a rogue Win2K DHCP server that could distribute duplicate addresses. As previously mentioned, Win2K DHCP servers are fully integrated with Win2K DNS. Win2K DHCP now supports superscopes, allowing one set of configuration options to apply to multiple scopes of addresses. Additional option classes (i.e., remote boot images) are also supported, as are multicast scopes for future applications.

If DHCP is unavailable, Win2K will automatically assign addresses to facilitate network connectivity in the 169.254.*x.x* range. A wonderful feature for a "mom & pop" network but downright annoying in a corporate environment.

Remote Installation Services (RIS)

The Remote Installation Services (RIS) is new in Windows 2000. Figure 1-9 demonstrates how Remote Install works. With the appropriate hardware or boot options on the workstation, RIS allows the remote installation of the Win2K Professional OS with little user intervention.

A true remote installation requires hardware that is NetPC-compliant, has PXE Boot ROM (PreBoot Execution Environment) on the NIC, or has a supported NIC with a RI boot disk to achieve full remote install functionality. RIS uses DHCP to locate the RI Server.

In the corporate environment, RIS can provide incredible savings and true dock-to-desk functionality without a stop along the way to configure the equipment.

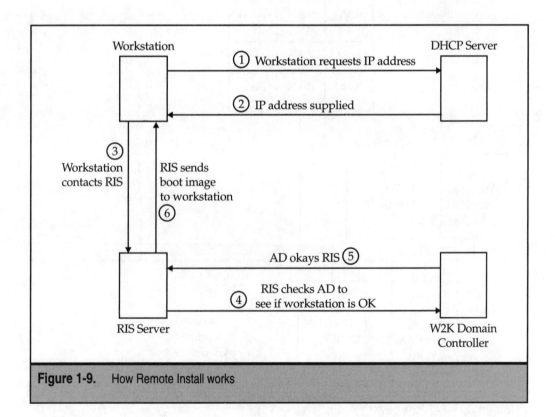

Figure 1-9.   How Remote Install works

Terminal Services (TS)

Enhanced in Windows 2000, Terminal Services (TS) allows multiple "terminal sessions" to exist on a single Win2K Server. Utilizing technology originally developed by Citrix Systems (www.citrix.com) for NT 3.51, NT 4.0 shipped a Microsoft version called Windows NT Server 4.0, Terminal Server Edition that required a separate kernel to achieve multi-user capability.

In Win2K, Terminal Services is simply an additional service that is included with all versions of Win2K Server. Figure 1-10 illustrates how Terminal Services work. TS allows

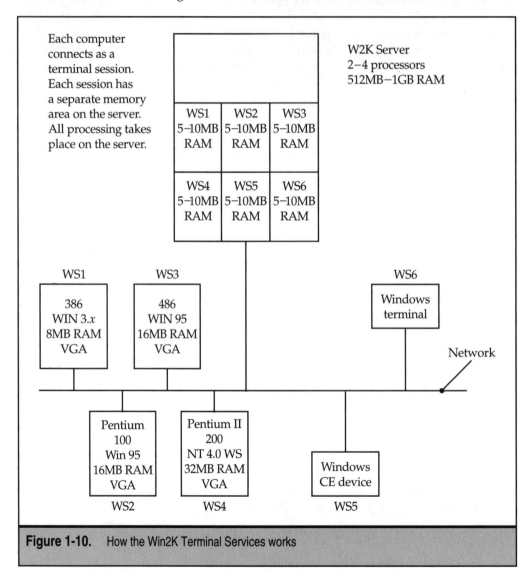

Figure 1-10.   How the Win2K Terminal Services works

all levels of Windows clients, from Win 3.*x*, Win 9*x*, NT, Win2K, and WinCE, to access the server through individual terminal sessions. Shadowing of existing sessions is also supported in this version. Existing applications (exactingly) written to the Win32 specifications should run unchanged in Terminal Services sessions. Terminal Services are now part of the core product, which means no more special service packs for the Terminal Server Edition. Each TS client must be licensed in addition to the OS.

TS requires additional Terminal Services client access licenses for the Server as well, but two free licenses are included for remote administration.

Cluster Service

The Cluster Service has been enhanced in Windows 2000. Win2K Advanced Server (AS) and Datacenter Server (DCS) include the Windows Cluster Service. Win2K AS provides the traditional two-server failover while Win2K DCS provides a four-server, cascading failover, clustering solution that is designed to handle mission-critical situations. Figure 1-11 shows the Win2K AS Clustering Service configuration. The Cluster Service replaces the NT 4.0, Windows NT Server 4.0, Enterprise Edition, which provided a two-server, failover, clustering solution for mission-critical applications. Cluster Service is now part of the core product, which means no more special service packs for "Enterprise Editions."

The usual implementation would contain two fairly large servers (primary/secondary) and a large external SCSI disk array (see the Hardware Compatibility List at www.microsoft.com/hwtest/hcl). Applications must be cluster-aware to operate successfully in a fail-over cluster. Currently, Microsoft offers only two applications that run

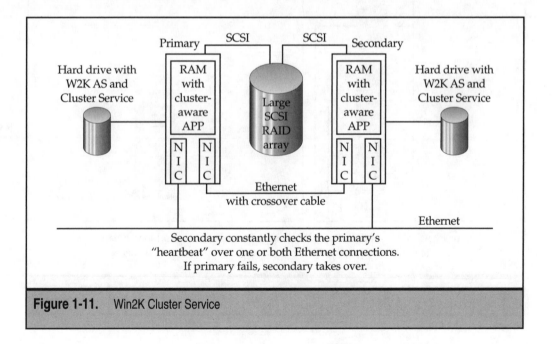

Figure 1-11. Win2K Cluster Service

on a cluster, Exchange 5.5, Enterprise Edition and SQL Server 7.0, Enterprise Edition. The next versions of each of these, Exchange 2000 and SQL 2000, will also be cluster-aware. Third-party vendors are beginning to get on the bandwagon.

Load Balancing Service

Using technology originally acquired from Valence Research in June, 1998, Convoy Cluster software was made available to users of Windows NT Server 4.0, Enterprise Edition, in January, 1999. Now integrated into Windows 2000 Advanced Server and Datacenter Server, the Load Balancing Service allows up to 32 servers to function as a single virtual entity. To do this, the Load Balancing Service automatically allocates an incoming user request to the most available server. Figure 1-12 demonstrates the Win2K Load Balancing Service. The Load Balancing Service is now part of the core product, which means no more special service packs for "Enterprise Editions."

A key element of Microsoft's implementation of load balancing is that it can only succeed if the data on the computers involved is static. For example, suppose you have a busy Web site that runs IIS where nerds can register to win T-shirts, palm pilots, and

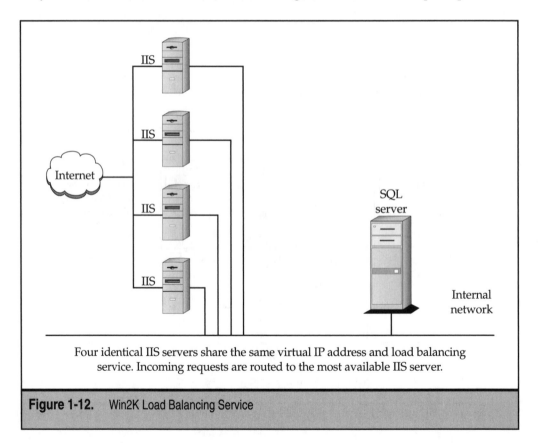

Four identical IIS servers share the same virtual IP address and load balancing service. Incoming requests are routed to the most available IIS server.

Figure 1-12.   Win2K Load Balancing Service

other cool stuff. You keep this registration data on a separate SQL Server box. You decide to upgrade your site to four IIS servers with load balancing. Figure 1-12 shows how it would look.

REMOTE ACCESS

Remote access has expanded greatly in Windows 2000. Microsoft has made significant strides toward increased security, VPNs, vendor-independence, and support for Internet standards. However, I'd like to apologize in advance for the flood of RFCs and acronyms I am about to foist upon the unsuspecting. I'm afraid the CRAG (Completely Random Acronym Generator) works overtime in the field of data communications.

Routing and Remote Access Service (RRAS)

The Windows 2000 Routing and Remote Access Service (RRAS) is enhanced in nearly every aspect over NT 4.0 RAS and RRAS. The most obvious is the requirement for stronger (than NT 4.0) access permissions to logon using RRAS.

The Routing section of Win2K RRAS allows static routes to be assigned to dial-in clients. It also supports both RIP and OSPF routing protocols and multiprotocol routing using IP, IPX, and AppleTalk.

The Remote Access part of Win2K RRAS supports a completely new concept of remote access policies and profiles—a concept that dramatically increases both the security and configurability of remote access in Win2K. In addition, Win2K RRAS offers much stronger permissions than NT 4.0 RAS, support for ATM (Asynchronous Transfer Mode), new standards of compliance (RADIUS), and new VPN support (IPSec and L2TP).

Extensible Authentication Protocol (EAP)

Specified in RFC 2284, the Extensible Authentication Protocol (EAP) allows the exact authentication method to be negotiated by the dial-in client and the RRAS server. EAP probably won't change your life today, but it creates the hooks (APIs) by which developers can add new authentication methods to Win2K—even hooks we haven't thought of yet.

In Win2K, EAP supports:

▼ Token cards (SecurID, Fortezza, and so on), the physical cards that provide the user with a password that may change with each use or each minute.

■ MD5-CHAP (Message Digest 5 Challenge Handshake Authentication Protocol), which provides 128-bit encryption for logon IDs and passwords.

▲ TLS (Transport Layer Security), which is used by smart cards and biometric devices (i.e., retina scanners, fingerprint readers, and so on), and, in the not too distant future, DNA readers?

Remote Authentication Dial-In User Service (RADIUS)

Specified in RFCs 2138 and 2139, the Remote Authentication Dial-In User Service (RADIUS) is designed as a large-scale, vendor-independent, distributed dial-in service. The key word here is "distributed." The basic concept is that large and geographically diverse companies require secure authentication from their employees all over the world. However, rather than lease high-speed lines and create their own private networks (*¡mucho dinero!*), they use the Internet. After attaching to the Internet, they connect to the RRAS server at the edge of their corporate intranet. The RRAS server is functioning as the RADIUS client, the RADIUS client then forwards the client request to the RADIUS server on the corporate intranet that authenticates the login requests using Internet Authentication Service (IAS), and the employees' activity is logged. Since RADIUS is vendor-independent, any or all of the pieces in this scenario could be Win2K.

Internet Protocol Security (IPSec)

First specified in RFC 1825 and later refined in RFC 2401, Internet Protocol Security (IPSec) uses cryptographic services to ensure secure private communications over IP networks such as the Internet. IPSec encrypts each IP packet by using a shared private key (SA–Security Association) that is negotiated by the communicating partners (clients) at the beginning of each TCP session.

In Win2K, IPSec is configurable by user, group, application, domain, site, and forest using IPSec Policy Manager (MMC snap-in) in group policies.

Point-to-Point Tunneling Protocol (PPTP)

Specified in RFC 2637 and introduced with NT 4.0, the Point-to-Point Tunneling Protocol (PPTP) actually "tunnels," or encapsulates, and encrypts one type of packet inside a normal IP packet to establish reasonably secure communications (VPN) over IP networks. Tunneling is like placing a private letter in a secured pouch with a padlock on it. The recipient has the key. PPTP supports normal IP only. PPTP does not support virtual circuits, header compression, or tunnel authentication. PPTP uses PPP for encryption.

Layer Two Tunneling Protocol (L2TP)

Specified in RFC 2661, the Layer Two Tunneling Protocol (L2TP) represents a big step forward in the quest for secure communications over the Internet. L2TP is an enhanced version of PPTP. It supports IP, Frame Relay PVCs (permanent virtual circuits), X.25 VCs, and ATM VCs over an IP network. L2TP supports header compression, which makes it faster than PPTP. It also supports tunnel authentication. L2TP can use IPSec for encryption.

Bandwidth Allocation Protocol (BAP)

Specified in RFC 2125, the Bandwidth Allocation Protocol (BAP) does exactly what its name implies: it allocates bandwidth dynamically. The assumption is that you have one or more connections with multiple links (two or more ISDN lines), with multiple links being the key factor here. BAP will monitor a connection's bandwidth utilization on each link, and, if the utilization drops below a pre-configured percentage, BAP will drop one of the links and make it available for another connection.

BAP settings are configurable in Win2K remote access policies.

Remote Access Policies

New in Win2K, remote access policies are shared between IAS and RRAS and cooperate with the AD to provide secure access. Remote access policies are stored, by connection, on the RRAS server. There are three components of a remote access policy:

▼ **Conditions**   These must be met or a connection will be refused (correct time of day, user groups, caller ID, IP address).

■ **Permissions**   Both the AD user account *and* the remote access policy must grant the user dial-in permission.

▲ **Profiles**   Settings for authentication and encryption protocols must be applied to each connection. If the connection settings don't match the user's dial-in settings or the profile settings, the connection is denied.

Multiple remote access policies are allowed, but can actually block each other if they are not carefully configured.

MANAGEMENT

Managing a Windows 2000 corporate network has been drastically improved over NT 4.0 (there was a lot of room for improvement), but the reporting capabilities are still missing in this release. Microsoft has given us good tools to create and configure our servers, but few tools to analyze, document, and troubleshoot what we've already done. Wisely, I believe, Microsoft has left the field wide open for third-party vendors to create a wealth of tools that the Win2K enterprise administrator will cry for. The most prominent addition to the Win2K management functionality is the implementation of group policies. With group policy objects, Microsoft is getting closer to its goal of "zero administration" of the desktop, increased ROI (return on investment), and a dramatically reduced TCO (total cost of ownership) in the corporate network.

Microsoft Management Console (MMC)

Microsoft's common framework for snap-in management applications used in the past with IIS 4.0, SQL 7.0, SMS 2.0 and NT 4.0, SP4 SCM. All Win2K administrative tools are run from Microsoft Management Console (MMC), even shortcuts to non-MMC tools. Snap-ins are interoperable, transferring data supplied to MMC between snap-in modules. Individual consoles can be customized and saved as .msc files either in read/write (Author mode), which allows changes to the tool itself, or read-only mode (User mode), which does not allow changes. In conjunction with specific rights and permissions, the read-only User mode enables truly delegated administration to a subdomain or OU. (See detailed information on the MMC in Chapter 4.)

Intellimirror

Primarily a concept rather than a technology, Intellimirror encompasses a number of different technologies from Win2K. Group policies will reconfigure the workstation's registry and security settings as well as deploy applications. Offline folders allow a traveling user to work with server-based folders on the road. Folder redirection connects the user to specific server-based folders transparently. The folders are displayed on the desktop as if they were local.

Group Policies

Administering every desktop in the organization from a central location seems like a simple plan, but realizing the dream of a "no touch" solution is more complex. From its early beginnings as a "cache the whole workstation" idea, Microsoft has refined each associated technology involved to achieve a truly innovative and workable solution. It's true, administrators can't just push a magic button and configure 10,000 desktops, but users can simply log on and have every option configured on their machine, whether they travel from one node to another within a building or around the world.

Group policies are applied to either computers or users first by site, then domain, and then OU (SDOU). Figure 1-13 shows how group policies are applied.

Group Policy objects (GPOs) can include all or some of the following:

▼ **Administrative templates** Basically the same as NT 4.0 system policies, these write changes to the workstation registry. The difference in Win2K is that the registry changes reverse themselves when the policy is removed.

■ **Scripts** Startup/shutdown scripts for computers; logon/logoff scripts for users.

■ **Disk Quotas** Limits on disk usage on a per user, per volume basis.

■ **Security templates** Settings for user rights, services, group membership, registry settings, file system access, registry access, and so on.

■ **Folder Redirection** Redirection of specific folders from the user's desktop to a remote server.

▲ **Application deployment**   Assigning applications to users or computers; publishing applications to users. Defined as the "software follows me" approach.

Windows Script Host (WSH)

Microsoft took a lot of well-deserved criticism for the lack of scripting capabilities in NT 4.0 (after all, real admins run scripts). In response to the critics, Microsoft had two options: either create yet another new scripting language for Win2K (Don't need it! Got enough already!), or create a new script interpreter that understands all the popular existing scripting languages (Works for me!). The script interpreter option won and Microsoft named it Windows Script Host (WSH). The WSH will execute ASCII text files in the following scripting languages (syntax):

Batch files (.bat or .cmd)	Perl
VBScript	TCL
JScript	REXX
CScript	Python

Soon additional services for UNIX (not included with Win2K Server) will add the capability to interpret UNIX shell scripts as well (see www.interix.com).

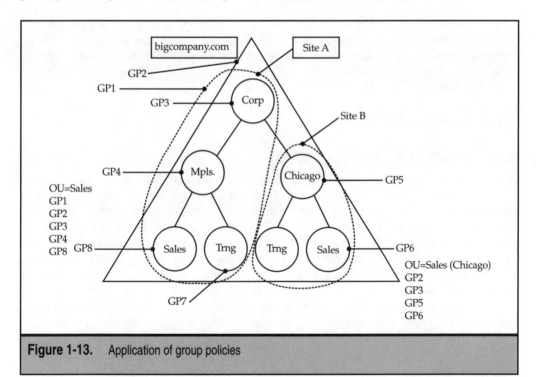

Figure 1-13.   Application of group policies

Win2K Groups

Groups in Win2K have expanded greatly from NT 4.0. This expansion becomes more than a little frustrating seeing as the NT 4.0 group structure is already far more complex than any other NOS (network operating system). Microsoft created the Win2K group structure to accommodate large, multidomain enterprises. I doubt that many of the small or medium-sized single domain environments that most of us inhabit will ever use all of the group capabilities that exist in Win2K, nor should they.

Win2K has two types of groups in the Active Directory:

▼ Distribution (e-mail only for use with Exchange 2000)

▲ Security (like NT 4.0 groups, used as a security principal and also for messaging)

In addition to a group type, each Win2K group has a scope of influence:

▼ **Domain Local**   Based in AD; applied to resources within its own domain; members from any domain

■ **Global**   Based in AD; can join groups in any domain; members only from its own domain

▲ **Universal**   Based in GC; applied to any domain; members from any domain (available in Native mode only)

Once we switch a Win2K domain to Native mode, Universal groups are supported, and Domain Local and Global groups can be nested. The nesting of groups is necessary in large enterprises because of a 5,000 member limit on a single group. Also in Native mode, administrators can promote a Domain Local or a Global group to a Universal group, if desired.

In addition to the AD-based groups, each non-DC Win2K computer still has a local SAM database with local users and local groups for authentication and access control when a domain is not involved.

System Preparation Tool (Sysprep)

The biggest problem associated with "cloning" installations in NT 4.0 was the propagation of duplicate SIDs. However, System Preparation Tool (Sysprep) strips the identifying information and the SIDs out of an existing Win2K install. Using a third-party disk imaging tool (check out Ghost at www.symantec.com or Drive Image Pro at www.powerquest.com), the remaining "90 percent installed" image is stored (in a binary copy) on a server or CD, from which it can then be distributed to any number of computers. The image can include installed applications as well. Rebooting the newly imaged computer will begin a mini-install that requests user and computer identifying information and generates unique SIDs. Even this inconvenience can be avoided by creating a sysprep.inf file to complete the install.

Setup Manager

We were able to perform scripted installs in NT 4.0, but had to create the scripts from scratch in ASCII text with a strange and wondrous syntax. The NT 4.0 Resource Kit contains a utility called Setup Manager that helps write the unattend.txt files for NT 4.0 scripted installs. The Win2K Setup Manager, which is shown in Figure 1-14, literally creates the unattend.txt answer file for scripted installations for you. After you have installed a Win2K computer normally, simply point the Setup Manager to that PC and Setup Manager creates a script to duplicate that installation. Cool.

Windows Installer Service

New in Windows 2000, the Windows Installer service is a great feature. The Installer service allows programmers of future applications (Office 2000, for example) to create packages (.msi files) for unattended remote installations. Here's how it works: The user initiates the setup process (either by running setup.msi or clicking an assigned app), the Installer service loads, and the Installer service completes the installation based on the settings in the .msi file. The Installer service runs in the security context of the system, not the security context of the current user, so remote installations won't "bomb out" because the user lacks rights or permissions. For non-.msi apps, Win2K ships with WinInstallLE from Seagate, which repackages existing installs for remote deployment.

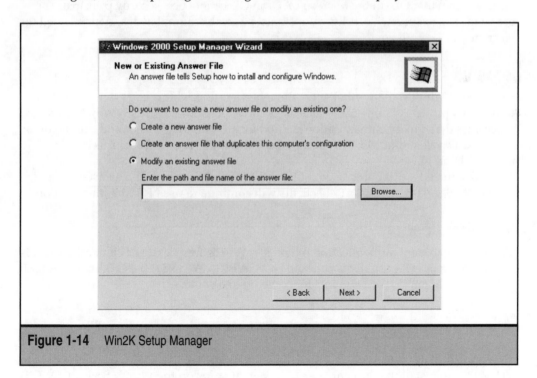

Figure 1-14   Win2K Setup Manager

In conjunction with group policies, the Installer also manages application changes, patches, upgrades, and even uninstalls. But the coolest feature is self-healing, resilient apps. For example, suppose a user, while cleaning his or her hard drive, deletes a number of files ending in .dll because these files "are never used" (this really does happen, you know, at other people's companies). In Win2K, if the apps were assigned to the user in group policies, the next time the user runs Word 2000, the Win2K Installer service automatically checks for the files it needs, discovers the missing .dll files, installs them from the server, and opens Word 2000. Try *that* in NT 4.0!

SECURITY

There are lots of improvements on the security front: phasing out NTLM authentication and NetBIOS, implementing Kerberos v5, file encryption, PKI (Public Key Infrastructure) support, and WFP (Windows File Protection), just to name a few. The most important and encouraging development is the obvious shift in Microsoft's thinking toward security. It has been given a higher priority. The folks in Redmond have finally realized that they can't ship an "enterprise" OS without a significant focus on security.

One important difference to note between Novell's NDS and the Microsoft AD is that, in NDS, an OU can (and often does) become a security principal; that is, an OU can be granted permissions to other objects in the tree that will then be inherited by all the objects (users, groups) within that OU. In the Microsoft AD, an OU cannot be a security principal. Therefore, in the Microsoft AD, security groups must be created, populated, and maintained for the granting of permissions.

Kerberos v5

Named for Kerberos, the mythological three-headed dog who guards the gates of Hell, Kerberos v5 provides dramatically increased authentication integrity to Win2K. Kerberos v5 becomes the primary authentication method for all computers, users, and trust accounts in Win2K. Developed at M.I.T. as part of the Athena project, Kerberos specifications are listed in RFC 1510.

Win2K includes Kerberos client software for Win2K only. Existing DOS, Win 3.*x*, Win95, Win98, NT 3.51, and NT 4.0 clients will continue to use NTLM authentication.

NTLM Authentication

NTLM (NT-LanMan) authentication remains in Win2K for backward compatibility. It is unchanged from NT 4.0. Clients running DOS, Win 3.*x*, Win95/98, NT 3.51, and NT 4.0 will require LM and NTLM support for some time to come.

NTLMv2

A new, more secure authentication protocol now exists called NTLMv2. Win2K computers support NTLMv2 natively. For existing Win 9*x* clients, the only way to move up to NTLMv2 is to install the dsclient.exe software that ships on the Win2K Server CD. This add-on will also make them AD-aware. As for NT, you can make sure that all of our NT 4.0 clients and servers are currently running Service Pack 4 or higher. NTLMv2 was initially released as part of NT 4.0, SP4.

Encrypting File System (EFS)

On NTFS v5 volumes, files can be encrypted on the disk. To be used by any application, the files must be decrypted. Only the user (the logged-on user who performed the encryption) and the Recovery Agent (required) can decrypt the files. Encryption is designed to protect data on notebooks and home directories on servers. You cannot encrypt and compress the same file. Encrypting File System (EFS) uses 128-bit encryption in the U.S. and Canada, and host of the rest of the world.

Designated Recovery Agents (by default, the administrator) can recover encrypted data for an entire domain (using AD and Certificate Server). An effective recovery strategy is essential in case users leave the company or their local account is accidentally deleted.

X.509 Certificates and Certificate Server

Win2K fully supports X.509 v3 Certificates for PKI (public key infrastructure) security and digital signatures. These certificates are used in secure Internet communications today. When you check out of an online store and establish a secure connection, here is what happens: The public key of a certificate-issuing authority (Verisign), which is contained in a certificate already in your browser, is presented to the private key of the vendor's Web server for an encryption algorithm that establishes the secure session.

In Win2K, the certificate-issuing authority can be a third party such as Verisign or Entrust, or a highly protected Win2K Server running Certificate Server.

Certificate Mapping

X.509 certificates are not the property of Microsoft, but are an industry standard. This allows for the mapping of a user's certificate for authentication on another system. The concept of single sign-on, even to a foreign OS like UNIX, moves one step closer to reality with the mapping of a standard X.509 certificate. A certificate is assigned to a user when they logon to Win2K, an application being run on Win2K by that user needs data from a UNIX host, the X.509 certificate is used to authenticate the application (service) to the UNIX host so that it can retrieve the data. The entire process is transparent to the user.

Smart Card Support

Smart cards actually contain a limited-capability processor and a small amount of memory. They can be programmed to hold a user's private key and a digital certificate that contains the user's public key. With the addition of a smart card reader, a Win2K computer can use the smart card to authenticate users and provide encryption services. The main advantage of the smart card is that all the user's encryption keys and logon information stay with the user on the card—they never reside on the hard drive or floppy drive of any computer. Smart Card readers are available today for both desktop and notebook computers.

Access Control List (ACL) Permissions

NTFS has always had fourteen possible permissions for each folder and file. For each permission there is an individual Allow or Deny option (On/Off; 1/0). In NT 4.0, to control the access permissions and auditing of files and folders, only six permissions were exposed in the interface for use in the ACL Editor.

In Win2K (and NT 4.0, SP4 + SCM), all fourteen permissions are exposed in the interface, each with a separate Allow or Deny option, as shown in Figure 1-15. Strangely, however, in NT 4.0 there is a No Access permission that doesn't exist in Win2K. In Win2K, Full Control – [Deny] – equals the NT 4.0 No Access.

Secondary Logon Service

Secondary Logon Service enables a logged-on user to run an application as though he or she were a different user. For example, an admin can log on with a restricted account but run administrative tools as a privileged account. Secondary Logon Service is similar to the su command in UNIX and the su.exe program in the Windows NT Server 4.0 Resource Kit. The feature is a great tool for scripting because individual lines in the script can run at different levels of privilege. The command line tool is runas.

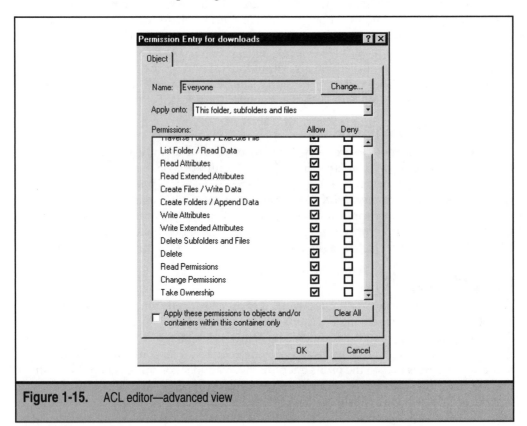

Figure 1-15.   ACL editor—advanced view

MIGRATION TOOLS

Win2K is barely out the door and folks are already lining up to help you migrate to Windows 2000 from NT 4.0 and NetWare. Individual machine upgrades may be quite easy, but a complete NT domain or NDS tree migration is a whole different ball game. Planning, testing, planning, testing, and—oh, yeah—more planning and more testing along with a great migration tool will make for a successful upgrade, a well-performing network, happy users, and happy management.

Domain Migrator (DM)

Licensed from Mission Critical Software, Domain Migrator (DM) is an important addition to the Win2K toolkit. DM ships with Win2K Server as an MMC snap-in. It allows the migration of any and all objects from NT 3.51, NT 4.0, and Win2K domains in any combination or direction. Since it is included with all Win2K servers, check this one out before laying out the one-time cash and learning curve for the third-party tools. If your enterprise has less than 1000 users, check this one out. DM should be able to handle most small to medium-sized NT to Win2K migrations.

Active Directory Connector (ADC)

Included with Win2K, the Active Directory Connector (ADC) provides ongoing, real-time synchronization of user and group objects between the Win2K AD and the existing AD running on Exchange Server 5.5 (requires SP2). Synchronization can be established in both directions, if desired. Upgrading to Exchange 2000 obsoletes the ADC. Watch out for the creation of new SIDs if you create the Win2K user accounts with the ADC. New SIDs can mean loss of access to resources.

Systems Management Server (SMS 2.0)

The existing version of Systems Management Server (SMS 2.0) can package an upgrade of Win2K Pro to existing SMS 2.0 client workstations. Expect a future SMS release to have tighter integration into Win2K and the Active Directory.

Microsoft Directory Synchronization Services

In January 2000, Microsoft announced a licensing agreement with FastLane Technologies (www.fastlane.com) to include its DM/Consolidator data-migration technology in the upcoming Microsoft File Migration Utility (MSFMU). The technology serves companies migrating from a Novell NetWare environment to Windows 2000. In addition, through integration with Microsoft Directory Synchronization Services (MSDSS), MSFMU can assign an appropriate security access setting in Windows 2000 automatically to each file it moves. Both MSDSS and MSFMU will be available in the upcoming release of Microsoft Services for NetWare version 5 (slated for Summer 2000).

Third-Party Migration Tools

A number of companies are already in competition for your Win2K migration business. Most of the products are similar in scope and capability but use different technologies to achieve the desired results. Listed below are the ones that deserve a closer look at this time.

OnePoint EA

Mission Critical Software (www.missioncritical.com) offers a complete suite of systems administration and operations management software called OnePoint EA that is compatible with NT and Win2K. The component focused on Windows 2000 migration is the OnePoint Domain Administrator. One of the problems with the Mission Critical suite is that the strongest tool (Domain Migrator) was sold to Microsoft. Mission Critical has had to rebuild its toolkit in the wake of that sale.

Domain Administrator's features are:

▼ Automated discovery and assessment of data

■ Automated Active Directory OU population

■ Automated migration to Windows NT 4.0 or Windows 2000 from NetWare

▲ Automated domain consolidation and reconfiguration

DM/Suite

FastLane Technologies (www.fastlanetech.com) also offers a suite of systems management and domain administration tools called DM/Suite. The component that focuses on migration to Windows 2000 is called DM/Manager. A mature product with a potential downside. It uses a proprietary scripting language called "final." Could be a steep learning curve prior to the migration with little payback after the migration.

FastLane DM/Manager's features are:

▼ Automates any domain reconfiguration

■ Is intuitive and step-by-step

■ Integrates with centralized management

▲ Automates iterative migration processes

Microsoft has licensed DM/Consolidator from EastLane for use in its upcoming services for NetWare 5.0.

DirectManage

Entevo (www.entevo.com) offers a suite of tools called DirectManage that offers "comprehensive directory management, before, during, and after Windows 2000." The migration tool specializing in Windows 2000 migration is called DirectMigrate. The good news about the Entevo product is that it uses VBScript to automate the migration. Many organizations already possess expertise in Visual Basic so this could be a plus.

DirectMigrate 2000's features are:

▼ Support for all migration scenarios

■ Integral migration process management

▲ Comprehensive functionality

Enterprise Suite

Aelita Software Group (www.aelita.net) has a full-featured set of migration and management tools called the Enterprise Suite. It contains seven separate tools but those directly related to domain migration are:

▼ Virtuosity is a database-driven management utility that comprises comprehensive auditing, reporting, and domain clean-up tools.

■ Domain Migration Wizard helps move you from a multidomain structure to a single domain as well as create an Active Directory structure and test it in a controlled environment.

▲ Delegation Manager allows you to delegate administrative tasks on the network.

GENERAL FEATURES

There are so many areas of improvement in Windows 2000 that some just fall under the "miscellaneous" category. Some of these new features, like language independence, will make the international market much happier. Administrators the world over will love Service Pack slip-streaming, fewer reboots, and advanced printing support. End-users will find their lives made easier with the network connections wizard, personalized menus, task scheduler, plug and play configuration, and advanced power options. In short, there is a little something for everyone in this section.

Language Independence

Utilizing a language .dll, each Win2K domain can have a separate language of administration. Each Win2K workstation can have an independent language for system prompts. Most importantly, the OS itself is totally independent of language, which means that all service packs can now release simultaneously worldwide. The only remaining geographic versioning is now based on encryption strength, 128-bit in the U.S. and Canada, and 40-bit for the rest of the world.

Service Pack Slip-Streaming

Win2K service packs will support slip-streaming. In addition to the normal, fully installed update with a service pack, server-based installation files can also be updated directly with the new, compressed files contained in the Win2K service packs. This way, all new installs from server-based source files will, in fact, be the latest version when they install. Service pack slip-streaming will save lots of time and trouble for scripted installs.

Fewer Reboots

Of the nearly fifty reboots needed to configure every option of NT Server 4.0, approximately seven remain in Win2K. The reboots which do remain are for fairly important functions like changing the computer name (causes DNS registration), adding or removing Active Directory, etc. Most important, is what does NOT force a reboot: adding new services, adding network protocols, reconfiguring the disk, etc. Administrators will be cheering with joy (it could happen) instead of screaming and pulling their hair out.

Advanced Printing Support

IPP (Internet Printing Protocol) allows the transmission of files for printing directly to a URL, browser-based printing management, as well as the ability to download and install print drivers over an intranet or the Internet. In Win2K, printer objects can be published in the AD and the GC for easy searching.

Network Connections Wizard

Instead of going to one place for dial-up and another for LAN connections, all network connections (dial-up, LAN, VPN, and so on) are set up and configured within a single Control Panel wizard. The wizard makes it so easy, you'll wonder why it ever seemed hard. Based on your initial selections and the current configuration of the computer, the wizard walks you through the process of setting up any kind of network connection: LAN, dialup, Internet, VPN and direct cable.

Personalized Menus

For each user, the Start menu, Programs menu, and subsequent submenus that emanate from the Start menu initially display all possible choices. But after a few days only shortcuts that the user has accessed recently are displayed. The onscreen menu displays a tiny chevron to indicate that additional options exist but are not being displayed. A click on the chevron or simply hovering on the menu for five seconds will display all shortcuts. It's really a great feature once you get used to it, but a little freaky at first. I foresee a lot of "Where'd all my stuff go?" calls to the help desk. It can be configured (turned off) from the Taskbar Properties.

Task Scheduler

Win2K ships with an upgraded graphical Task Scheduler with which a user can schedule scripts and programs to run once or at specific intervals in the future. The "at" command line utility is still available for use in scripts. The Task Scheduler in Win2K replaces "winat" from the NT Server 4.0 Resource Kit, a graphical version of the at scheduler.

Windows Driver Model (WDM)

The goal of the Windows Driver Model (WDM) is to provide common device drivers for both Win98 and Win2K, thus allowing extensive device support in Windows 2000.

The WDM includes the new I/O standards IEEE 1394 and USB, the power management option ACPI, and common drivers for sound cards, video capture boards, DVDs, digital cameras, scanners, mice, keyboards, and so on. It's quite compatible with the newer technology.

However, due to significant differences between the architecture of Win98 and Win2K, the Windows Driver Model does *not* include file systems, video graphics adapters, network interface cards, and storage devices. These types of devices have separate drivers for Win98 and Win2K.

Plug and Play (PNP) Support

The Plug and Play (PNP) specification is five years old, and because most of us use hardware that is less than five years old (your switch to Win2K probably forced you to buy new hardware anyway), PNP has a good chance of working as it was designed. Plug in the card and it works. Period. No configuration. Win2K is the second architecture and the third generation of PNP for Microsoft. My testing indicates that they really got it right this time.

The PNP spec requires that interface cards identify themselves to the Configuration Manager and then allow themselves to be dynamically configured based on available resources in the system. The OS then automatically loads the correct drivers and you're in business.

PNP also works with removable devices (PC Cards) by allowing the hot-swapping of devices while the system is on.

Power Options

A number of new power options are available in Windows 2000:

▼ ACPI (advanced configuration and power interface) is an open industry specification co-developed by Intel, Microsoft, and Toshiba. Its primary goal is to enable operating system directed power management (OSPM), whereby all power activities are managed by the OS. ACPI supports "Wake On LAN" and "OnNow."

■ ACPI uses a different HAL.

■ ACPI is the single Win2K feature most likely to require a BIOS upgrade.

■ Standby, or sleep, mode requires minimal battery usage while the system remains on.

▲ Hibernate mode copies the entire contents of the PC's RAM to available disk space, then shuts the system completely off. A restart copies the disk "memory" back into RAM and you're up and running. Hibernate does not require a special suspend partition and is totally controlled by Win2K.

SUMMARY

Windows 2000 is one small step in computing history, but one giant leap for Microsoft. With Windows 2000, Microsoft has stepped out of the enterprise networking shadows to present a viable and attractive competitor to Novell's dominance in the directory services market. No longer can it be said that Microsoft writes desktop operating systems and office suites but doesn't understand enterprise networks. By dumping its dependence on NetBIOS and incorporating existing and emerging Internet standards, Windows 2000 sets the stage for the next generation of network management.

CHAPTER 2

Implementing Clients on a Windows 2000 Network

Chapter 2 outlines the benefits of the Windows 2000 installation procedures and provides detailed documentation of each type of attended installation from a normal installation of Win2K Pro, to an upgrade from Windows 98, to an upgrade from NT 4.0 Workstation. From the network administration point of view, we describe the three methods of performing unattended installations: command line with answer file, the System Preparation Tool (Sysprep) with a third-party cloning tool, and the new Remote Installation Service and its Remote Installation Preparation Wizard (RIPrep). We also look closely at the new Win2K tools associated with unattended installations.

WINDOWS 2000 PROFESSIONAL

Windows 2000 Professional is without a doubt the best desktop operating system I have ever seen. I seldom gush over Microsoft products. I take what they say with a grain of salt and then test it all myself. But this product is as close as I have ever come to perfection on the desktop. As we move forward through our discussions of the nitty-gritty details of this mammoth product known as Windows 2000, you will realize that Microsoft has truly outdone themselves with Win2K Pro. It does it all with speed, robustness, and reliability that is unprecedented in Microsoft's history. If you are not using this operating system on your desktop or especially your laptop, then read the installation/upgrade instructions in this chapter and get with the program.

Hardware Requirements

The Microsoft Web site declares that Win2K Pro can run on a Pentium 133 with 64MB RAM and at least 700MB of free disk space. And it can. It will run faster with 128MB RAM, and you'll like it even better with a PII 300 or 400. Microsoft has announced support for 95 percent of all hardware and peripherals shipped after January 1, 1998, which means that the newer equipment will work flawlessly with Win2K (see the next section for a discussion of BIOS) and some of the older computers and peripherals may have some problems. As you will see later in this chapter, a DHCP-PXE (Preboot eXecution Environment) boot ROM on the embedded network interface card will also prove beneficial.

Check out www.microsoft.com/windows2000/compatible for more information on hardware compatibility issues and www.microsoft.com/hwtest/hcl for the up-to-date Hardware Compatibility List (HCL) for Windows 2000.

Notebook Computers Are Special

Dynamic volumes (see Chapter 5) are not supported on notebook computers. That's probably because the hardware configuration, especially removable hard drives, can be changed so easily in a notebook. Advanced Configuration and Power Interface (ACPI) and Advanced Power Management (APM) are supported. The newest of these standards, ACPI, is an open industry specification co-developed by Intel, Microsoft, and Toshiba. Its mission is to enable operating system directed power management (OSPM), whereby all power activities are managed by the OS. ACPI specifications list a "good" BIOS date of July 1, 1998, which means that if your computer has a BIOS dated prior to July 1, 1998, it should be upgraded. BIOS upgrades are available from the computer vendor's Web site. For more information on whether your computer's BIOS should be upgraded, look in the biosinfo.inf file on the \I386 folder of the Server or Professional CD. This installation information file was last updated on 11/14/99 and contains a list of all the computer BIOS configurations that work and don't work with ACPI and APM as of that date. It then lists the registry hacks that the Setup program needs to perform to make the Win2K installation a success. Look for updates to this file in later service packs.

Installing Windows 2000 Professional

Since the Windows 2000 Professional product will be predominantly used and, potentially, installed by the end user community, Microsoft has done a great deal to simplify, clarify, and automate the installation process. Unlike most network administrators (and authors), end users may install Win2K only once. Even in the first-time installation, Win2K Pro tends to shine. The on-screen prompts are clear and complete, and the general comfort level of the user should be enhanced by the interface. The other advantage is that Microsoft has chosen a marketing-free installation interface. We are not chided to register the software or told about the newest, latest, and greatest features. It just installs—and quite nicely at that.

Setup Disks

In Win2K, the Setup program is no longer responsible for creating the bootable setup floppies. And, in Win2K, four setup floppies are needed to boot Win2K instead of the three floppies required in NT 4.0. You can create the four Win2K setup floppies by running either makeboot.exe or makebt32.exe, either of which can be found on the Win2K Professional CD in the \BOOTDISK folder. You'll need four blank, formatted, high-density (1.44MB) floppies. As in NT 4.0, after the setup floppies are created, they enable you to begin an installation on a computer on which no OS has been installed or to execute a repair on a Win2K system that cannot boot (see Chapter 15 for information on the emergency repair process). If your computer can boot from a CD, the exact same functionality can be achieved by booting up with the Professional CD in the CD-ROM drive. And booting up with the CD is much faster than booting from four floppies.

Booting from a CD

When booting from a CD, the first screen displays the message, "Setup is inspecting your computer's hardware configuration" on a black background. Next, a DOS-like blue screen appears (not the BSOD—Blue Screen of Death). Windows 2000 Setup proceeds to install a number of device drivers, especially ones that control disks and I/O channels, so that it can continue. The various driver filenames flash by on the status bar at the bottom of the screen.

Welcome to Setup

Soon the Welcome to Setup screen appears. Press ENTER to set up Windows 2000, R for repair, or F3 to Quit. So far, the process is no different from an NT 4.0 Workstation installation.

License Agreement

The Windows 2000 Licensing Agreement appears. It is similar to the NT 4.0 installation agreement, except you can now press F8 immediately to agree to the terms without having to press the PGDN key 13 times.

Disk and Volume Configuration

Setup searches for previous versions of Windows and then displays the current disk and volume configuration. As in NT 4.0, you can place the Win2K installation on an existing volume, create a new partition from unpartitioned space, or even delete and re-create a partition. If you create a new partition using Setup, Win2K reserves either a 4MB or 8MB unpartitioned area (depending on the size of the partition) at the end of the disk. The unpartitioned area will be needed if you wish to convert the disk to dynamic later on. (Chapter 5 offers more information on dynamic volumes.) If you use an existing partition that's already FAT, Setup gives you the option of converting it to NTFS. If the existing partition is already NTFS, Setup simply proceeds with the installation.

Due to limitations in the NT 4.0 Setup program, the installation partition was limited in NT 4.0 to 4GB, but no such limit appears in the Win2K installation program. You may select or create a partition of up to 32GB and choose to format it either in NTFSv5 or FAT (any partition over 2GB will automatically format in FAT32). If you create a partition larger than 32GB, you can format it only with NTFSv5. During an upgrade, Win2K can use an existing FAT32 volume larger than 32GB if there is one, but it cannot create FAT32 volumes larger than 32GB. The largest NTFS volume size is the incredible, and still theoretical limit, of 16EB (exabytes). Your best option is to create partitions and format them with NTFS during the installation process. Choosing FAT now and converting the partition to NTFS after the installation may result in a less-than-optimal cluster size and default file system security. The conversion utility changes the volume cluster size to 512 bytes when converting to NTFS, whereas natively formatted NTFS creates 4KB clusters, which are much more efficient and increase performance (see Chapter 5 for more information on disk cluster sizes).

Setup then formats the new partition (an approximate time estimate is one minute per gigabyte), checks it for errors, and proceeds to copy all the installation files it will need to the volume that you just specified on the computer's hard drive.

When the process is complete, the system reboots automatically in a graphical mode, and you see some attractive screens like the one in Figure 2-1.

Next, after a slight pause (the system asks you to wait and even says "please"), the Welcome to the Windows 2000 Setup Wizard screen appears for about ten seconds. Then the Installing Devices screen appears, and Setup begins detecting and installing the drivers for the devices that are present on your computer. It's Plug and Play at its finest. The

Figure 2-1.   The new graphical bootup screen

on-screen caption mentions that your screen may flicker. And it will flicker, or blink on and off, several times. Don't worry. This is normal.

Regional Settings

After the devices are installed, you get the Regional Settings dialog box. Here, you can make choices about language (click the Advanced button to get code page conversion tables), numbers, currency, time, date, input locales (multiple locale settings for input languages, different keyboard layouts, and hot-key settings for switching between them). These choices make installing in languages other than English easier. They also handle date, time, and currency displays. The locale defaults are English (United States) for the system, English (United States) for the user, and the U.S. keyboard layout. Those of you in the United States can simply click the Next button. The only piece of Win2K that doesn't change when you choose a different language is the opening logon dialog box, which always appears in English.

Personalize Your Software

The Personalize Your Software screen appears. Enter your name, enter your organization, and click Next.

Your Product Key

The Your Product Key screen appears, as shown in Figure 2-2. As in Windows 98, enter the 25-character product key from the CD case. Type carefully! Mercifully, the product key is checked immediately for accuracy instead of six screens later. The product key is especially important in Win2K because, in order to perform maintenance on this installation, the same CD (or installation point) with the same product key must be used.

Computer Name and Admin Password

Next is the Computer Name and Administrator Password screen shown in Figure 2-3. Win2K automatically creates a unique, 15-character computer name by taking the first word in the organization's name (that you entered two screens back) and appending a completely random set of letters and numbers to it. The purpose of the auto-generated name is to make certain that remote installation services see unique computer names on the network (required by NetBIOS, WINS, and DNS). The unique names actually remove one of the issues from scripted Win2K OS installations.

I strongly recommend changing the computer name to something meaningful and developing a scalable naming strategy for all workstations before installing. Win2K workstation computer names can be changed after installation.

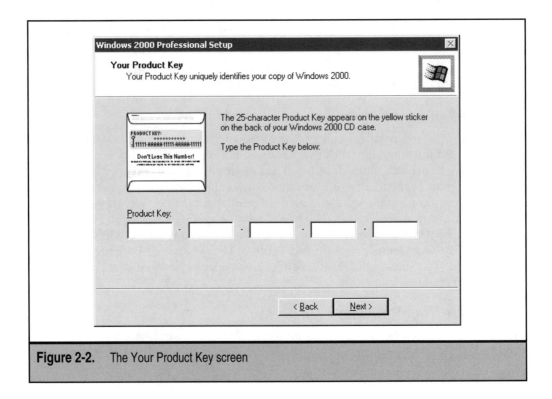

Figure 2-2.   The Your Product Key screen

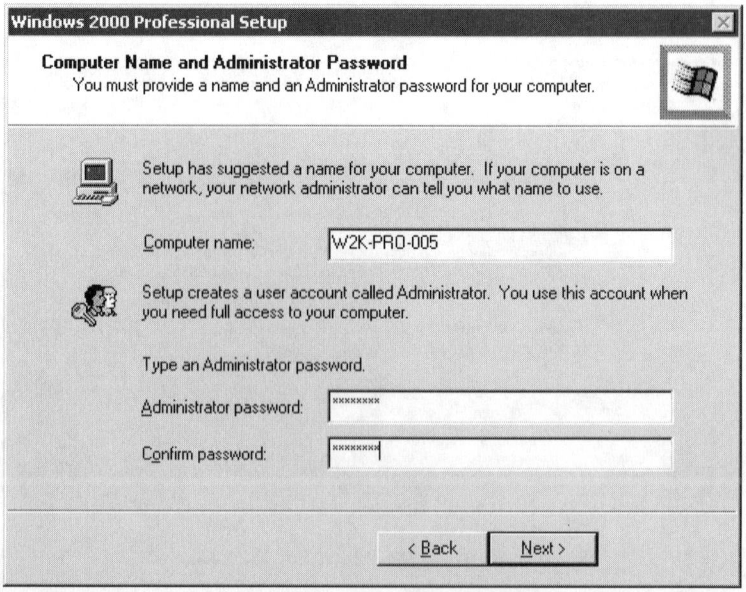

Figure 2-3.   Computer Name and Administrator Password screen

Enter a secure password (one that is complex in nature and consists of 11 characters) for the Administrator account—the local Administrator account held in the local security account database (SAM) database of this (and only this) computer. The password you enter is *not* the password of the domain administrator. Click Next.

Date and Time

The Date and Time Settings screen appears. Enter the correct date, time, and time zone for this workstation. The time zone is especially important since the time itself will be synchronized from the authenticating Win2K domain controller (DC). Decide whether to adjust for daylight saving time twice a year in April and October. Click Next.

Networking Settings

The Networking Settings screen appears. Setup automatically installs the required networking components. When the components are installed, you are asked to select either Typical or Custom settings as shown in Figure 2-4.

TYPICAL VS. CUSTOM SETTINGS   According to the on-screen caption, Typical settings create "network connections using the Client for Microsoft Networks, File and Print Sharing for Microsoft Networks, and the TCP/IP transport protocol with automatic

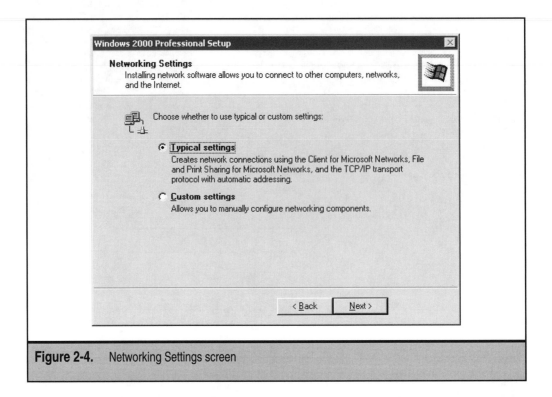

Figure 2-4. Networking Settings screen

addressing." So if you want the standard Microsoft networking client software that most of us use, at least to get through the installation, then Typical settings work for you. If File and Print Sharing must be enabled on this workstation, perhaps because the computer will have a network printer attached, will serve as a print server for a direct connect printer, or will need to share its folders and files, then the Typical settings can be checked.

Typical settings also sets the TCP/IP parameters to automatic addressing, which means that the TCP/IP settings will default to using Dynamic Host Configuration Protocol (DHCP). In other words, this workstation is going to be a DHCP client, which is usually not a problem but one nagging issue needs addressing here. If, for any reason, the client DHCP broadcast fails to receive an address from a DHCP server at this time, the network interface card (NIC) will be assigned an "automatic IP address" in the 169.254.*x.x* range. This new feature in Win2K can drive a network administrator absolutely crazy because once this automatic address is assigned, it doesn't want to let go. Also, if you happen to have two NICs in the computer during installation, be sure to select Custom settings here and read the description of each NIC carefully so you know which NIC you are configuring. Choosing Typical settings with two network cards will result in one receiving a DHCP-assigned address (Setup decides which one) and the other receiving an "automatic" 169.254.*x.x* address. To get around this problem, you can select Custom settings and make the necessary configuration changes, script the installation, or use RIS (see the section "Unattended Installations," later in this chapter).

Workgroup or Computer Domain

The Workgroup or Computer Domain screen appears. If you select No, This Computer Is Not on a Network, or Is on a Network Without a Domain, Setup defaults to the workgroup name WORKGROUP. You are welcome to enter any workgroup name you like. Because a workgroup has been selected, Setup understands that this computer will stand alone and is ready to move forward. If you select Yes, Make This Computer a Member of the Following Domain, enter the name of the domain to which this workstation will belong. Click Next and provide the userID and password of an account from that domain with the power to add computer accounts. Adding computer accounts is one of the administrative tasks that can be delegated to others using the Delegation of Control Wizard (see Chapter 11).

Installing Components

Next, the Installing Components screen appears. This step is the final file copy process of the installation. All the remaining required components are copied, installed, and configured. The components will take several minutes to install.

Performing Final Tasks

When all the components have been installed and configured, the Performing Final Tasks screen appears. This is the last screen. When performing final tasks, Setup does the following:

▼ Installs Start menu items

■ Registers components

■ Saves settings

▲ Removes any temporary files

Finishing these final tasks can take quite a while. When the final tasks are done, the Completing the Windows 2000 Setup Wizard screen appears. Remove the CD that may still be in the drive and click the Finish button. Then wait while the system restarts.

The First Restart after the Installation

After the installation is complete and the system has been restarted, regardless of whether you elected to place the computer account in a domain or a workgroup, the Welcome to the Network Identification Wizard screen appears. Click Next.

If you selected No, This Computer Is Not on a Network, or Is on a Network Without a Domain during setup, then the Users of This Computer screen appears, as shown in Figure 2-5, on first bootup giving you two options:

▼ **Users Must Enter a Username and Password to Use This Computer.** This is equivalent to the NT 4.0 Workstation local logon. You must know the name and password of a user in the local SAM database in order to log on.

▲ **Windows Always Assumes the Following User Has Logged on to This Computer.** Selecting this option will enable this workstation to start without user interaction. The system will be configured at each startup as if the selected user has logged on, which is equivalent to the NT 4.0 autoadminlogon registry option in the Winlogon key. In NT 4.0, we had to configure this manually by editing the registry, which is exactly what happens in Win2K as well, only we now have a GUI to make it easier. The registry key is `HKLM\SOFTWARE\Microsoft\Windows NT\CurrentVersion\Winlogon`. The values to look for are `AutoAdminLogon`; a value of 1 is ON and 0 is OFF. `DefaultDomainName` should be equal to the computer name in this example, and `DefaultUserName` is equal to the user selected. The good news is that the `DefaultPassword` value (the user's password) is no longer displayed in clear text the way it was in NT 4.0. Microsoft again opts for greater security in Win2K.

If, on the other hand, you selected Yes, Make This Computer a Member of the Following Domain, then the User Account screen appears on first bootup enabling you, if you so choose, to add a new user account and password to the local SAM database at this time. It

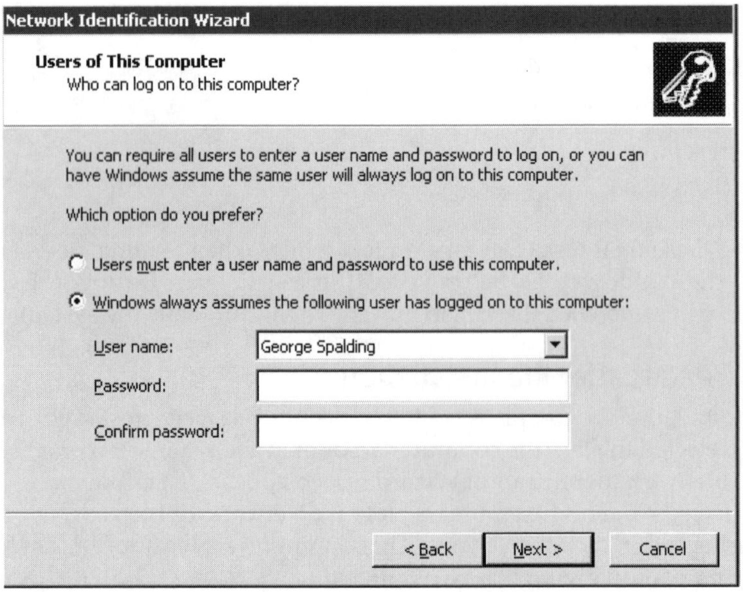

Figure 2-5. Users of This Computer screen

is important to note that you are not adding this user account to the Active Directory domain but rather to the local SAM database of users on this computer.

UPGRADING CLIENTS IN WINDOWS 2000

Because Win2K is fully backward-compatible with the older legacy Microsoft operating systems, administrators have several client options as they move forward with upgrades to Windows 2000:

▼   Do nothing. Upgrade the servers and domain controllers in the back room. Work out the design of your Active Directory structure. The clients will keep logging on the same way they did before. The users won't even know you've upgraded the domain to the Active Directory. This option may also be necessary if one of the important applications in your organization is incompatible with Win2K. You might just have to spend your time leaning harder on the software vendor to obtain upgrade packs or updated versions of software.

■   Add the Directory Services client to Win 9x. It's quick, painless, easy to do. Once Directory Services client is installed, the Win 9x users can search the AD, and you can strengthen the logon security in both Win 9x and NT 4.0.

▲   Migrate all your Win 9x and NT 4.0 clients to Windows 2000 Professional. The only real drawback here is application compatibility. Test it. Test it. Test it. If you don't, it's gonna come back and whack you in the head like a boomerang! If the apps fail the compatibility tests, see the first bullet.

Sticking with Windows 95 and 98 Clients

From the first day of a Windows 2000 enterprise, Windows 95 and Windows 98 users can log on to the servers and domain controllers using the exact same methods they use right now to log onto their NT 4.0 domains. Nothing has to change at the client computer for logging onto a Win2K Active Directory domain in either mixed or native mode, if we don't require any increase in functionality. There is no requirement for the Win 9x clients to upgrade in order to basically do what they have always done. However, we are not upgrading to Windows 2000 so we can do what we've always done. We want more. And to get the full functionality of the Windows 2000 Active Directory and Group Policies, we'll have to upgrade our legacy clients—maybe not tomorrow, but soon…very soon.

Windows 9x Directory Services Client

Let's say that you've decided against upgrading your Win 9x computers to Win2K at this time. Perhaps you are going to wait until the end of the lease period for each computer and switch to Win2K Pro when you upgrade to the new hardware. Perhaps you're going to focus all your resources on developing the Active Directory structure and your

BackOffice strategy. Whatever the reason, Windows 2000 provides an interim solution for AD availability to Win 9*x* clients: a Directory Services client (dsclient.exe) that ships on the Server CD. You find it in the \CLIENTS\WIN9X folder. You must execute this file on the Win 9*x* computer you wish to upgrade. The DS client extension for Win 9*x* includes the following capabilities:

▼ Ability to log on to a domain controller "closest" to the client (site affinity)

■ Ability to change passwords on any Win2K domain controller instead of the PDC

■ Allows scripting to Active Directory

■ Provides a Dfs client for access to Windows 2000 distributed file system

■ Allows the user to change personal information properties (for example, phone numbers and addresses) on their AD user object

▲ Takes advantage of the more secure authentication features available in NTLMv2

The Directory Services client extension for Win 9*x* has the following limitations:

▼ No Kerberos support for Win 9*x* clients

■ No Group Policy support

▲ No IPSEC/L2TP support

The dsclient.exe file is about 3MB so it won't fit on a floppy, but the installation takes only about 60 seconds. Double-clicking on the file brings up an installation wizard with only four screens: the Welcome screen, the Ready to Install screen, the Installation screen, and the Completed screen for a total of two Nexts and one Finish. There are no configuration decisions to make, no questions to answer; you just keep clicking Next. After the installation, you must restart the Win 9*x* computer. After restarting, there is absolutely no noticeable difference in the bootup or logon process. In fact, you might find yourself thinking that the installation didn't work. If you're like me, you're looking for the On switch or a new client to install from the Control Panel | Network icon, but dsclient is an add-on, not a replacement. Click Start | Find | People, and you realize that you are suddenly, but seamlessly, able to search the Active Directory for objects from Windows 98 just as if you were running Win2K, as shown in Figure 2-6.

Upgrading from Windows 95 or 98 to Windows 2000 Professional

Boot into Windows 95 or 98. Insert the Windows 2000 Professional CD. Autoplay informs you that the CD contains a newer version of Windows and asks, "Would you like to upgrade to Windows 2000?" Click Yes.

The Welcome to the Windows 2000 Setup Wizard screen appears, enabling you to choose Upgrade to Windows 2000 (Recommended) or Install a New Copy of Windows 2000 (Clean Install). Choose Upgrade and Click Next to upgrade. When you choose to

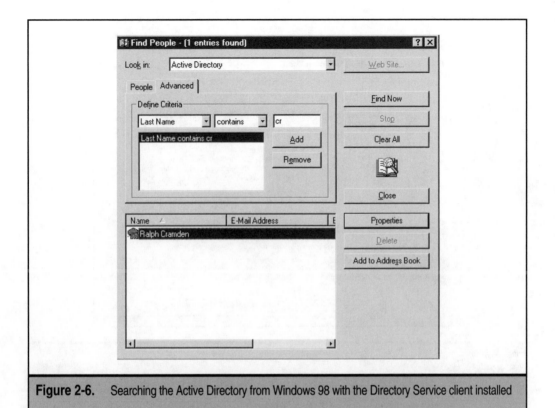

Figure 2-6.   Searching the Active Directory from Windows 98 with the Directory Service client installed

upgrade, you are, of course, also choosing to lose your old installation of Windows 95 or 98. The Win2K upgrade will install in the same \WINDOWS folder that housed the previous Win9x install, and Win2K will delete any Win9x files. The Profiles folder is migrated to the Documents and Settings folder. Choosing Clean Install will allow you to install this copy of Win2K Professional either in the same folder as the original (not recommended) or in a different folder, which creates the possibility of a dual-boot configuration.

The Windows 2000 License Agreement is next. Select I Accept This Agreement to Continue. Click Next. The Your Product Key screen appears. Enter the 25-character product key carefully. Click Next. Thankfully, the product key is checked for accuracy immediately so you'll know whether you've entered it correctly. The product key is specific to the actual CD. It is not generic in any way.

As shown in Figure 2-7, the Preparing to Upgrade to Windows 2000 screen even provides a hyperlink to the Windows Compatibility Web site, but you must, of course, be connected to the Internet during the upgrade for it to function. If your computer is not connected or if you wish to look for compatibility information from time to time, here's the link to the Microsoft Windows 2000 compatibility Web site: www.microsoft.com/windows2000/upgrade/compat/default.asp. Another Web site with application compatibility information is http://windowsupdate.microsoft.com.

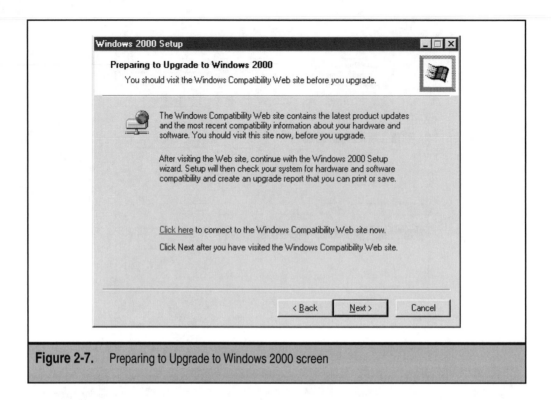

Figure 2-7.   Preparing to Upgrade to Windows 2000 screen

The Provide Upgrade Packs screen appears as shown in Figure 2-8. The screen prompts inform you that some existing programs may need upgrade packs to work with Win2K. This is your first chance to add them. If you select Yes, I Have Upgrade Packs, you are given an opportunity to browse and add those files to the upgrade pack list. You can skip this screen by selecting No, I Don't Have Any Upgrade Packs and clicking Next, and Setup will generate a report later of any applications on your system that may require upgrade packs. These upgrade packs are obtainable only from the software manufacturer of the legacy application. Upgrade packs may contain updated replacement application files and/or scripts for installing them. Click Next.

The Upgrading to the Windows 2000 NTFS File System screen appears. This screen is asking if you would like your FAT16 or FAT32 volumes upgraded to NTFSv5. If you select Yes, Upgrade My Drive, then all your existing FAT volumes will be upgraded to NTFSv5, and you will no longer be able to run any operating system but Windows 2000 on this computer. Click Next.

Setup begins examining your system, and then, as shown in Figure 2-9, the Preparing an Upgrade Report screen appears. Setup examines the existing programs on your entire drive, creates the upgrade report, and prepares to install Win2K. If Setup determines that it requires updated driver files to work with Win2K, it will request them at this time. You can elect to click Next and provide the files later, if you wish. Click Next.

The Upgrade Report screen appears. This screen is designed to report a summary of known Windows 2000 compatibility issues with the devices or applications that it has

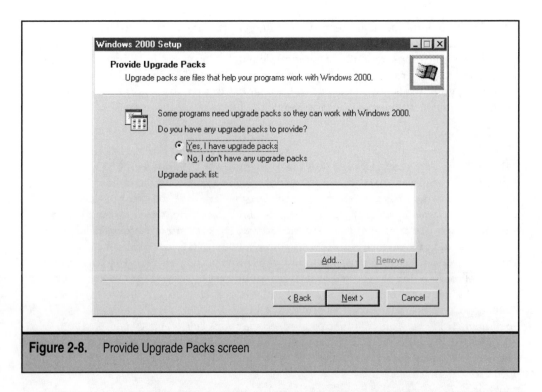

Figure 2-8.   Provide Upgrade Packs screen

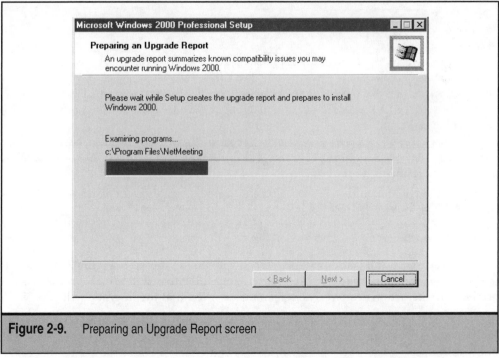

Figure 2-9.   Preparing an Upgrade Report screen

located on your system. Near the bottom of the report in the General Information section (there's even a link to help you get there), Setup gives you the bad news (if any) that some devices or applications may not be compatible with your new Win2K installation and, in some cases, that your Recycle Bin won't be saved and you'll lose your deleted files. From this screen, you can also print the report for later use or save the report as a text file. Click Next. A sample Windows 98 upgrade report file follows:

```
Upgrade Report
--------------
Reliability and quality are key design goals of Windows 2000.
Microsoft realizes that compatibility issues with devices and
programs can compromise these goals if you are not given the best
information available. During Windows 2000 testing of certain devices
and programs, Microsoft found some compatibility problems you might
encounter after you upgrade to Windows 2000. This report describes
those problems. In most cases, new software updates from the hardware
or software vendor can correct these problems. If you are concerned
about the results of this report, you should not upgrade to Windows
2000 until these problems are corrected.
For more information about product compatibility with Windows 2000,
you should contact your hardware or software manufacturer. You can
also visit http://www.microsoft.com/windows2000/compatible for
additional information.
Contents:
  Hardware
Hardware
--------
This section of the report describes hardware compatibility issues.
Incompatible Hardware
The following hardware may not support Windows 2000 without
additional files. Please see the Microsoft Windows 2000 Hardware
Compatibility List at
http://www.microsoft.com/windows2000/compatible/ for a list of
compatible hardware. (Some of the following entries might be software
that is registered as hardware.)
Display adapters
  Standard PCI Graphics Adapter
You can continue with the upgrade, but the hardware may not work
until you supply the additional files.
```

The Ready to Install Windows 2000 screen appears, as shown in Figure 2-10, informing you that Setup now has all the necessary information to install Win2K Pro. This is the last human interaction needed. The screen informs you that the upgrade will take 35–50

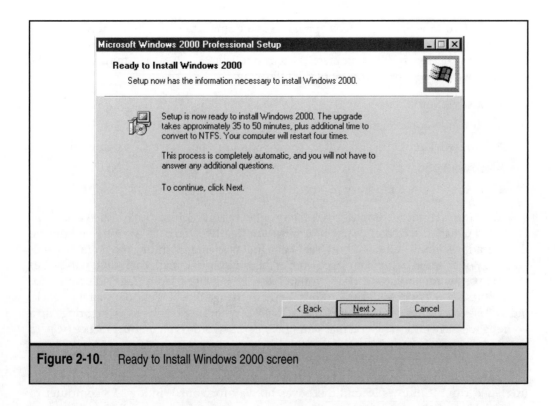

Figure 2-10.   Ready to Install Windows 2000 screen

minutes (an accurate estimate), that your system will restart four times, and that there will be no more questions for you to answer so the upgrade is completely automatic from here. The next human interaction necessary is the Password Creation screen after the upgrade is finished.

Click Next. The system copies its necessary installation files and then restarts automatically. Setup examines the disks, deletes the Windows 98 system files that are no longer needed, and copies the temporary Win2K setup files to its installation folder. Then Setup initializes the configuration, and the system restarts again.

Windows 2000 Professional starts. If you have told Setup to upgrade the drive, it will now convert the FAT volumes to NTFS. After the NTFS file system conversion, the system restarts again. (See the section "Converting FAT to NTFSv5," later in this chapter.) If you elected not to upgrade the drive, this step is skipped.

Windows 2000 Professional starts up with an attractive blue GUI screen and asks you to "Please wait." Then the Installing Devices screen appears and automatically installs the necessary devices. The screen prompts inform you that your screen may flicker for a few seconds. Somewhere during the first half of the progress bar, the screen will almost definitely flicker, which is normal operation. Don't be concerned.

The Networking Settings screen appears and automatically installs the necessary networking components. Then the Installing Components screen appears and automatically copies all the necessary files and installs them into Win2K. The Performing Final Tasks screen appears. These tasks consist of the following:

▼ Installs Start menu items

■ Registers components

■ Upgrades program and system settings (not present in an NT 4.0 upgrade)

■ Saves settings

▲ Removes any temporary files

When the upgrade is complete, the system again restarts automatically. The Win2K Pro Password Creation screen appears, informing you that two accounts were created during the upgrade: Administrator and the User Name that was entered during the original installation of Windows 98. Setup has placed both of these accounts in the local SAM database but with no password, and now it needs you to create a single password that will be used for both of these new Windows 2000 accounts. You can change them individually later by clicking the Users and Passwords icon in Control Panel. Accepting a blank password brings up a warning message informing you that setting blank passwords is an unsafe practice (way to go, Microsoft!) and asking "Are you sure this is what you want to do?" Setup will let you accept blank passwords by responding Yes to this warning message.

A normal logon box now appears. Enter your username and password. Since we just upgraded from Windows 98 and there was no way for your Windows 98 computer to "join" a domain, this computer is not currently a member of a domain. You are now logging on to the local workstation. By default, depending on permissions, rights, and policies, any Authenticated User can join their computer to the domain if they know how. Right-click My Computer on the workstation desktop and select Properties. Click on the Network Identification tab, click the Network ID button, and follow along with the wizard. (Toto, I don't think we're in Kansas anymore.)

First-time Win2K Pro users get the inevitable Welcome message and a new cartoon balloon on the Start menu telling you to Click on the Start Button.

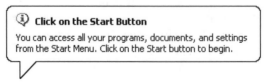

The shortcuts that were present on your original Windows 98 desktop are still on your Win2K desktop. The screen resolution is the same, and the background and wallpaper stay the same as well, though some nice new ones are available to choose from in Win2K Pro. The contents of the \PROFILES folder has migrated to the Documents and Settings folder.

Converting FAT to NTFSv5

Since Windows 95 and 98 can be installed only on FAT volumes, the option to change to NTFS, whether selected during the upgrade or using the conversion utility (convert.exe) after the upgrade, is truly a "conversion" of the drive not a re-format of the volume. When converting the FAT volumes to NTFS, all the existing data is retained. If you chose to delete the partition during setup, then the data is lost, and you executed a native format in FAT or NTFS. There are at least two problems with converting FAT volumes to NTFSv5.

First, the cluster size created in a FAT volume can range from 512 bytes to 32KB versus a 4KB cluster in native NTFS, which makes native NTFSv5 much more efficient. But in a Win 9*x* upgrade scenario, retaining the existing configuration is not a selectable option. The conversion utility will change the cluster size to 512 bytes whether you choose FAT or NTFS.

Second, and much more serious, the default security permissions do not get applied when converting the boot partition from FAT to NTFS, which means that after you've converted the boot partition from FAT to NTFS, the access permissions for the entire volume are set to Everyone has Full Control, just as they were before the conversion. In NT 4.0, the solution to this was fixacls.exe in the NT 4.0 Resource Kit. Win2K provides a different method for applying the permissions after the conversion.

To apply default security to a Win2K Professional workstation NTFS boot partition:

▼ Log on as the local Administrator.

▲ Go to a command prompt and type:

```
Secedit /configure /db c:\winnt\temp\tmp.mdb /cfg
c:\winnt\inf\defltwk.inf /areas filestore
```

Pardon the word wrap; the preceding is a single entry. Assuming that Windows 2000 Professional is installed in the C:\WINNT directory, this command as written will apply the default NTFS permissions to the C:\WINNT and \Program Files folders only. The User Documents and Settings folder is not affected. For any Win2K Professional workstations and especially laptops, I strongly recommend that this option be executed for any NTFSv5 boot partitions that have been converted from FAT.

Application Compatibility Issues

The Win 9*x* operating system will upgrade to Win2K without as much as a hiccup, but the legacy desktop applications are another matter altogether. Microsoft is completely aware of the potential for problems in this area, and that's why they created a new technology called "upgrade packs" to alleviate the problem. This new "upgrade pack" technology places the responsibility for legacy desktop application compatibility squarely on the shoulders of the third-party software manufacturers. They now have a clearly defined channel to bring the updated files to their registered customers, at little or no cost, that will allow their existing applications to run successfully with Win2K. Microsoft has given them options and then stepped back. Unfortunately, in the short term, the most profitable option is probably the brand new "Runs with Windows 2000" version. This, of course, is not free. Their loyal customer base has to pay the full upgrade price to get the application, which might be great for a short-term gain, but I hope that the long-term relationship with the customer would prove more valuable than the quick buck. So search those vendor Web sites and e-mail them frequently if no upgrade pack exists for your software. You never know; they may just be waiting until somebody asks for an upgrade pack.

THE APPLICATION COMPATIBILITY TOOL   Located in the \SUPPORT folder of the Professional or Server CD, apcompat.exe reminds those of us a little long in the tooth of the utility called setver.exe that started shipping way back in 1991 with DOS 5.0. The Application Compatibility Tool, as you can see in Figure 2-11, enables us to determine if a specific application will run in Windows 2000. If not, we can select a downlevel OS to see if it will run at that OS level. When we find an operating system that seems to suit the legacy application (for example, Windows 98), we can set that OS level on that application. In this way, every time the application is launched, it is told that this isn't Windows 2000 at all, it's really Windows 98. Basically, we are lying to the application in order to get it to load correctly. The tool also allows us to make changes in the configuration of certain OS parameters on this installation on Win2K.

Just exactly what is the reason we have to go through this charade? Back in the Windows 95 days, Microsoft wasn't nearly as strict and wasn't nearly as clear about just ex-

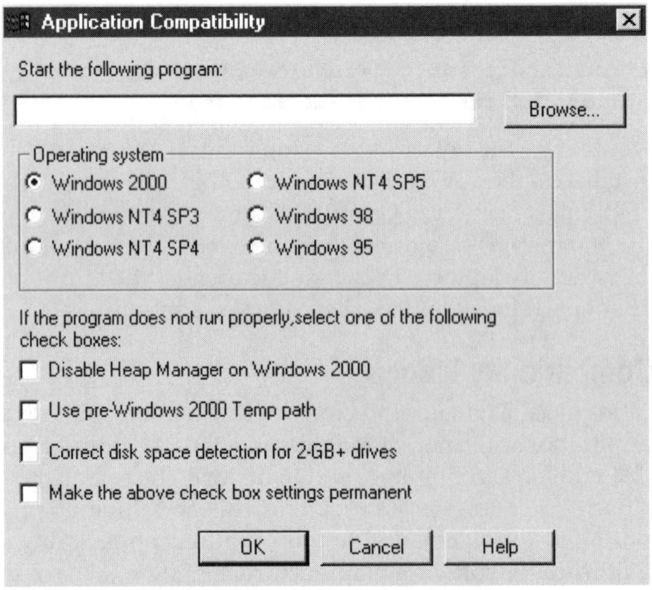

Figure 2-11.   The Application Compatibility Tool

actly what the Win32 specification could be used for. Many developers weren't writing code for the uncertain future that Microsoft was predicting and speculating about. They needed to sell their applications immediately. Because of this situation, they wrote the applications more to the Windows 95 and, subsequently, Windows 98 reality than to the Win32 specification. For their part, Microsoft, as you would expect them to, kept improving the Win32 specification and added hundreds of APIs (application programming interfaces) that gave the developers more power to make Windows work for them. At the same time, Microsoft was alerting the developers about Win2K and how closely the Win32 spec was being adhered to. Thus, due in part to Microsoft's incessant warnings and in part to the continual delays in shipping Win2K, the newest applications appear to work flawlessly with Win2K. The older legacy products don't. They need to be patched, upgraded, or lied to.

Upgrading from Windows NT 4.0

From an NT 4.0 workstation, insert the Windows 2000 Professional CD. Autoplay brings up a message stating that this CD contains a newer version of Windows than the one you currently running and asks if you would like to upgrade to Windows 2000? Click Yes.

The Welcome to the Windows 2000 Setup Wizard screen appears, enabling you to choose Upgrade to Windows 2000 (Recommended) or Install a New Copy of Windows 2000 (Clean Install). Choose Upgrade and click Next to upgrade. When you choose to upgrade, you are, of course, also choosing to wipe out your old installation of NT 4.0 Workstation. The Win2K upgrade will install in the same \WINNT folder that housed the previous NT 4.0 installation and, Win2K will delete any NT 4.0 files. If you wish to maintain a dual-boot configuration with both NT 4.0 and Win2K, you must choose Clean Install and put the Win2K files in a different folder. For dual-boot to function, the current NT 4.0 installation must be patched at Service Pack 4 or higher.

The License Agreement comes up next. Select I Accept This Agreement to continue. Click Next. Then the Your Product Key screen appears. Enter the 25-character product key carefully. Click Next. Thankfully, the product key is checked for accuracy immediately so you'll know whether you've entered it correctly. The product key is specific to the actual CD. It is not generic in any way. This could prove problematic when loading additional services later on.

The Upgrading to the Windows 2000 NTFS File System screen may appear. You will get this screen if your NT system is installed on a FAT volume or if your NT 4.0 installation is patched at Service Pack 3 or lower. This screen, if it appears, is the last human interaction necessary to upgrade an NT 4.0 workstation to Windows 2000 Professional. The Win2K Pro upgrade will proceed automatically from this point.

The system copies all the necessary installation files and then executes the first of several automatic restarts. Upon reboot, a DOS blue screen appears, and Setup looks for previous versions of Windows, deletes legacy files it no longer needs, and proceeds to copy all necessary files to the installation folder. Setup initializes your Windows 2000 configuration and then again restarts automatically. The system restarts in GUI mode and asks you to wait. After a few minutes, the Installing Devices screen appears. The screen warns you that your screen may flicker during this part of the installation. Your screen will flicker. Do not be concerned. It is not a problem; it is normal operation.

The Networking Settings screen appears. If your networking settings are already configured, it will assume the existing settings; if not, it will opt for an automatic assignment of the IP address (DHCP). Next, the Installing Components screen appears. More files are copied. More components are installed. Then the Performing Final Tasks screen appears. The final tasks consist of the following:

▼   Installs Start menu items

■   Registers components

■   Saves settings

▲   Removes any temporary files

When the final tasks are complete (they tend to take over 10 minutes), the system restarts automatically. The elapsed time from inserting the CD to a completely installed Windows 2000 Professional workstation is approximately 45–50 minutes.

Application Compatibility Issues

At this time, there appear to be no significant compatibility issues with current applications running on NT 4.0. The registry structure and the basic architecture of Windows NT 4.0 is fundamentally unchanged in Windows 2000. Therefore, if an application has been written in such a way as to install and run successfully in NT 4.0, it should install and run successfully in Windows 2000. Why all the "waffle" words like "appear to be" and "should"? Because it's just too early to be 100 percent definitive about every application that organizations will attempt to run on this new platform. Obviously, these legacy applications will not know about the Active Directory, but most desktop applications, even the new ones, never will. They need to know about the registry, the SAM, and the file system. And, as far as desktop applications are concerned, these remain unchanged.

UNATTENDED INSTALLATIONS

The goal of nearly every widespread deployment of client workstations is the conservation of the scarcest of technical resources—people. For this reason, the folks at Microsoft have focused a great deal of energy and talent on the goal of truly unattended installations. And they've come up with three different ways to approach the problem:

▼   A simple unattended installation that can be launched at a command line or booted from a CD

■   A disk image or "cloned" installation that takes advantage of existing third-party disk imaging applications

▲ A remote installation service that utilizes new ROM chips in the network cards or specially created boot floppies to initialize and install a brand new computer

We will discuss each of these methods in the sections that follow, but first, a number of important files and utilities are essential as we move forward with the concept of unattended installations. You can find them all on the Win2K Professional, Server, or Advanced Server CD, under the SUPPORT\TOOLS folder. They are located inside a file named deploy.cab. deploy.cab is a zipped "cabinet" file and can be extracted using WinZip, or simply by double-clicking on the file in Win2K. Expand the deploy.cab file and copy its contents into a single folder on your hard drive. Inside deploy.cab are several crucial files, including:

▼ **Setup Manager** (setupmgr.exe, setupmgx.dll)   The tool designed to create answer files for each separate type of unattended installation

■ **System Preparation Tool** (sysprep.exe, setupcl.exe)   The tool designed to prepare a reference computer for cloning

■ **Deployment Tools help file** (deptool.chm—"chm" stands for compiled html)   Contains a wealth of information about the various tools described in this section

■ **Unattend.doc**   Contains 142 pages of voluminous information on creating unattended installation files for use in all types of Win2K installations

▲ **Readme.txt**   Contains late-breaking release notes including specific hardware incompatibility issues

None of these files is installed by default. For even more information about unattended installations, check out this Web site: www.microsoft.com/technet/win2000/dguide/append-c.asp.

Using Setup Manager to Create an Answer File

What is an answer file? It's really a simple concept if you just think of an attended installation (you sitting at the keyboard entering the data) as a series of questions where you supply the answers. Think of a fully automated unattended installation as a series of questions where all the answers come from a text file (a script-like file) that was created in advance of the installation—that file is called the *answer file*. It has a very specific syntax and script format. In NT 4.0, we had to create this script by hand or use the Resource Kit utility Setup Manager. In Win2K, the Setup Manager can now create answer files for all three different types of unattended installations. We'll start with an installation that duplicates a Win2K Professional workstation that already exists. We will always refer to this computer as the *reference computer*. The first example is a simple answer file that can be used at the command line for a network installation or with a floppy for a hands-free CD installation.

Duplicating an Existing Computer for an Unattended Windows 2000 Installation

Click Start | Run, type **setupmgr**, and click OK. The Welcome to the Windows 2000 Setup Manager Wizard screen appears. Click Next. Then the New or Existing Answer File screen appears offering three options:

▼ Create a New Answer File

■ Create an Answer File that Duplicates This Computer's Configuration

▲ Modify an Existing Answer File

For this example, we will select the second option: Create an Answer File that Duplicates This Computer's Configuration. Click Next. The Product to Install screen appears, asking what kind of installation we are trying to automate and offering three options:

▼ Windows 2000 Unattended Installation

■ Sysprep Install

▲ Remote Installation Services

For our test, we will select the first option, Windows 2000 Unattended Installation. Click Next.

The Platform screen asks whether the remote installation is going to be Win2K Professional or Win2K Server. We select Win2K Professional. Click Next.

The User Interaction Level screen, shown in Figure 2-12, now gives us five options:

▼ **Provide Defaults** The answer file provides the values that will become the defaults. The user can change any values we supply.

■ **Fully Automated** A totally hands-free installation in which all answers are provided by the answer file.

■ **Hide Pages** Setup hides the pages from the user that have been answered in the answer file.

■ **Read Only** The user cannot change any answers that were supplied by the answer file.

▲ **GUI Attended** Only the text-mode portion of the Windows setup is automated.

In our example, we will select the second option, Fully Automated. Click Next.

The License Agreement screen appears. Since the user will be unable to accept the terms of the license in a fully automated setup, the installer creating the answer file must accept them now. Click I Accept the Terms and then click Next.

The Customize the Software screen appears. Enter the username and the organization and click Next. The Computer Names screen appears. Here we can add each computer

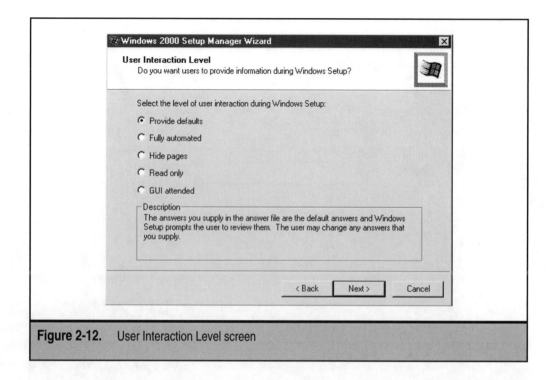

Figure 2-12.   User Interaction Level screen

name we want to create manually by entering the name in the Computer Name textbox and clicking Add. If we enter more than one computer name, a UDF file will be created automatically. Uniqueness Definition Files (UDF) files allow the installation to retrieve most of its information from the answer file and a few pieces (like computer names) from the UDF file. We can also import computer names from a text file where the names have been entered in a one-computer-name-per-line format. Or, finally, we can enable the Automatically Generate Computer Names Based on the Organization Name option and let Setup create the computer names for us based on the organization we entered earlier. I strongly recommend against this last option strictly from a network management point of view. I believe that administrators need to know what the computers on their network are called to facilitate quick response in case of problems. We will enter a single computer name and click Next.

As shown in Figure 2-13, the Administrator Password screen is next. Since we have chosen a fully automated setup, we must now enter the local Administrator password (local SAM) for the system we are going to install. Enter and confirm the Administrator password. We also have the option of logging in automatically as the Administrator after the installation when the computer restarts. And when we select this option, we can determine how many times we can automatically log on. Select the desired options and click Next.

Next, the Display Settings screen appears. The settings displayed are those currently selected on the reference computer. You can modify them or customize them here, if you

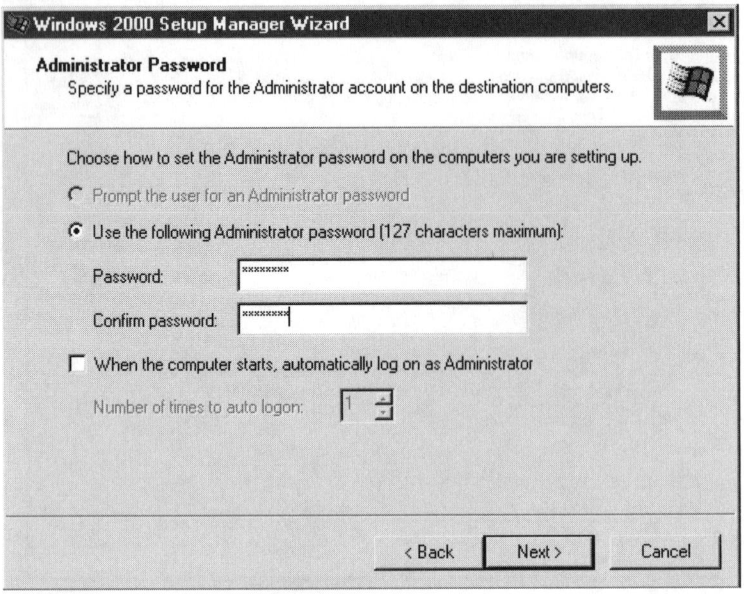

Figure 2-13. Administrator Password screen

wish. Click Next. The Network Settings screen appears with the familiar Typical versus Custom settings options discussed earlier in this chapter. If the reference computer has a statically assigned IP address, the default will be Custom. If, on the other hand, the reference computer is configured to use DHCP, the default will be Typical. Make your selections and then click Next.

If we selected Custom in the last screen, the Number of Network Adapters screen appears, enabling us to choose to configure more than one NIC per workstation. Since this will be a rare occurrence in a network workstation, we will take the default, One Network Adapter, and click Next.

The Networking Components screen appears. This screen appears only if we selected Custom in the Network Settings screen. Here we can configure the TCP/IP properties of the computer we wish to install by highlighting Internet Protocol (TCP/IP) and clicking Properties. In the next screen, we can specify a static IP address, if we wish, and the IP addresses of several DNS and WINS servers through the Advanced button. For our example, we will use a static IP address. When finished, click Next.

The Workgroup or Domain screen comes up, giving us a choice of having our new workstation belong to a workgroup or domain. And if we specify a domain, we can also create a computer account in the domain (assuming it hasn't been pre-created). If we wish to create a new computer account, we must provide the credentials (username and password) of a user with the power to create a computer account. When complete, click Next.

The Time Zone screen pops up, defaulting to the time zone of the reference computer. Click Next. The Additional Settings screen appears, giving us two options: Yes, Edit the Additional Settings, or No, Do Not Edit the Additional Settings. Selecting Yes, Edit the Additional Settings gives us seven more screens to configure dealing with the following topics:

- ▼ **Telephony**   The settings for remote access.

- ■ **Regional Settings**   The settings for dates, time, and currency.

- ■ **Languages**   You can add support for additional languages.

- ■ **Browser and Shell Settings**   The settings for Internet Explorer.

- ■ **Installation Folder**   Install Win2K Professional in a different folder.

- ■ **Install Printers**   Specify the name of a network printer to install the first time the user logs on.

- ▲ **Run Once**   You may enter one or more commands that will run only the first time the system is restarted after installation.

If you selected No, Do Not Edit the Additional Settings or you have completed editing the additional settings, you now come to the Distribution Folder screen where you can create a new distribution folder or modify an existing one. In our example, we will choose not to use a distribution folder but rather to install from a CD. The Answer File Name screen now appears, enabling us to select a location and name for the answer file we have just created. The screen also tells us that if we are installing from a CD, we must name the file winnt.sif and copy it to a floppy disk. Click Next. Then the Completing the Windows 2000 Setup Manager Wizard screen appears. Click Finish. We're done.

To use the answer file we've created, we rename it winnt.sif and copy it to a blank, formatted, nonbootable floppy disk. Take the floppy disk and the Win2K Professional CD to a new computer and insert the CD and reboot. As soon as the computer begins to boot from the CD, insert the floppy in drive A. Do not put the floppy into the computer before rebooting because, as we all know, it won't boot. After the reboot, the computer will install Win2K Professional in about 35 minutes without any further human intervention. Remove the floppy disk after the installation is complete.

FULLY AUTOMATED INSTALLATION ANSWER FILE   This section contains an answer file for a fully automated installation of a Win2K Professional workstation. This script is the end product—the result of the wizard we just completed. This is the text file created by Setup Manager when we selected Windows 2000 Unattended Installation. The script below does the following:

- ▼ Places the OS files in the \WINNT folder.

- ■ Sets the administrator password to "password."

- Sets the time zone to U.S. Central Time.
- Sets the display to 800 × 600.
- Joins the bigcompany.com domain using the administrator's credentials.
- Loads the Microsoft Client and TCP/IP.
- Sets the IP address to 192.168.3.100.
- ▲ Sets the DNS server address to 192.169.3.254 on Adapter1.

```
;FULLY AUTOMATED Win2K PROFESSIONAL INSTALLATION ANSWER FILE
;SetupMgrTag
[Data]
 AutoPartition=1
 MsDosInitiated="0"
 UnattendedInstall="Yes"

[Unattended]
 UnattendMode=FullUnattended
 OemSkipEula=Yes
 OemPreinstall=No
 TargetPath=\WINNT

[GuiUnattended]
 AdminPassword=password
 AutoLogon=Yes
 AutoLogonCount=1
 OEMSkipRegional=1
 TimeZone=20
 OemSkipWelcome=1

[UserData]
 FullName="George Spalding"
 OrgName=GSA
 ComputerName=w2k-pro-009

[Display]
 BitsPerPel=24
 Xresolution=800
 YResolution=600
 Vrefresh=60

[RegionalSettings]
 LanguageGroup=1
[Identification]
```

```
JoinDomain=BIGCOMPANY
DomainAdmin=administrator
DomainAdminPassword=password

[Networking]
 InstallDefaultComponents=No

[NetAdapters]
 Adapter1=params.Adapter1

[params.Adapter1]
 INFID=*

[NetClients]
 MS_MSClient=params.MS_MSClient

[NetServices]
 MS_SERVER=params.MS_SERVER

[NetProtocols]
 MS_TCPIP=params.MS_TCPIP

[params.MS_TCPIP]
 DNS=No
 UseDomainNameDevolution=No
 EnableLMHosts=Yes
 AdapterSections=params.MS_TCPIP.Adapter1

[params.MS_TCPIP.Adapter1]
 SpecificTo=Adapter1
 DHCP=No
 IPAddress=192.168.3.100
 SubnetMask=255.255.255.0
 DNSServerSearchOrder=192.168.3.254
 WINS=No
 NetBIOSOptions=0
```

COMMAND-LINE OPTIONS   The answer file provided in the previous section, with one addition, can also be used as a command-line option as well. Add the following section and values to the file:

```
[SetupMgr]
  DistFolder={enter the folder name where the distribution
```

```
                    files were copied}
DistShare={enter the share name for the distribution folder}
```

Use winnt.exe when initiating the installation from outside of NT. The correct syntax for the command line is as follows:

```
winnt [/s:sourcepath] [/t:drive] [/u:answer_filename]
```

Use winnt32.exe when initiating the installation from inside NT. The correct syntax for the command line is as follows:

```
winnt32 [/s:sourcepath] [/t:drive] [/u:answer_filename]
```

This command line enables a completely hands-free installation or upgrade of Win2K from an existing NT 4.0 computer.

The System Preparation Tool (sysprep.exe)

One of the major challenges in maintaining an NT 4.0 network was the installation of the NT 4.0 Workstation clients. The installation took almost an hour, and that didn't even begin to take into account the numerous applications that were needed on every desktop. A single NT 4.0 Workstation installation, including applications, could take 2–3 hours of an installer's time. The solution was the binary image copying or "cloning" of full installations. Cloning basically takes a binary snapshot of an entire volume on a reference computer. The reference computer is configured exactly as we want it: applications and drivers are installed until it's perfect. Then we clone it. We copy this cloned image to a CD or a server hard drive. Then, when we wish to install another workstation, we boot the new computer with a DOS floppy, connect to the server where the image is located, run the "reverse clone" or restore program, and copy the image from the server to the new computer's hard drive. Thousands of companies have saved millions of hours using this installation method.

Several problems are inherent with cloning. The first is hardware. If the reference computer has different hardware (including disk, video, or network) than the new computer, then those devices will not function on the new computer because no device driver for them is present. In addition, there was no opportunity for the installation program to identify the devices and load new drivers because it was never run. This problem generates the need for a large number of hardware-specific images to be stored on servers or CDs. And this also means that the installer must know exactly which image to choose when bringing the image down to the new machine.

The second problem is the computer name. Each computer cloned from the reference computer will be installed with the same name as the reference computer. All computer names must be unique on a Microsoft network. The computer names must be manually changed immediately after the installation to avoid problems.

The third problem is the network configuration settings. If the reference computer has a static IP address assigned, then each cloned computer will have that same IP address. Since all IP addresses must be unique, this could be a serious problem. The resolution, as you probably already know, is to simply configure the reference computer to use DHCP for its IP address and other TCP/IP configuration parameters.

The last problem is specific to NT: duplicate security IDs (SIDs). When NT installs normally, it creates a unique SID for each computer and its subsequent local user and group accounts. In a cloned installation, each computer receives the SID of the reference computer, and the local user and group accounts receive the SIDs of the users and groups on the reference computer. The design of NT is to guarantee the uniqueness of SIDs across all computers, domains, users, and groups. The manufacturers of the "cloning" software (Symantec's Ghost and PowerQuest's Drive Image Pro) shipped an additional tool (GhostWalk and SIDChanger) that would run through the newly installed computer, change all the existing SIDs to newly generated unique SIDs, and update all the access control lists (ACLs) that contained the old SIDs to the new SIDs. But this caused an extra step (and not a particularly fast one) in a process that was supposed to eliminate steps and save time. Plus Microsoft was not happy about supporting installations that had not been through the hardware identification portion of its Setup program.

Enter Windows 2000. Microsoft knew that cloning was too good an idea to get rid of, but they also knew they didn't want to be in the cloning business. So they invented the System Preparation Tool or just "Sysprep" for short. Sysprep is designed to run on a reference computer, creating a "cloneable" image. Installers then use a third-party copying utility (Ghost or Drive Image Pro) to copy the Sysprep image to a remote server. Then the image is downloaded (restored) onto a new computer. When the new computer is restarted, it will boot into a mini-Setup program, which only takes a few minutes to complete. The mini-Setup program allows the installer to uniquely identify (computer name, username, and organization) the new computer and, by default, automatically generates new unique SIDs for this computer.

Before executing Sysprep, the sysprep.exe and setupcl.exe files must be copied to a folder called \SYSPREP on the root directory of the reference computer. Sysprep can be run with any of the following five switches:

▼ **-quiet**   Will not display on-screen messages.

■ **-pnp**   Forces Plug and Play to refresh at the next restart, which solves the hardware-specific image problem. One Sysprep image coupled with Plug and Play will install all of the correct drivers for the hardware on the target computer. Very cool.

■ **-reboot**   Forces a reboot after the image is installed, which then brings up the Mini-Setup Wizard.

■ **-nosidgen**   Does not generate new SIDs.

▲ **-defeat**   Install will not stop to ask for new product key.

You can use multiple switches in a single command. For example:

```
C:\sysprep\sysprep.exe -quiet -pnp -reboot -defeat
```

When Sysprep is launched, the following warning appears:

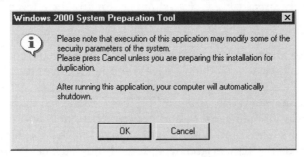

After Sysprep is run, the system shuts down and is ready for cloning. At this point, the installer reboots the system with a floppy and copies the image to a remote server installation point.

Before leaving the System Preparation Tool section, let's recap the steps necessary to use Sysprep:

1. Prepare and configure the reference computer. This step is your shot to install everything but the kitchen sink.

2. Expand deploy.cab on the Server or Professional CD and copy sysprep.exe and setupcl.exe to the C:\SYSPREP folder on the reference computer.

3. Run sysprep.exe on the reference computer, being careful to include the necessary switches.

4. Boot the reference computer with a boot floppy that includes networking software and the third-party imaging application.

5. Start the disk imaging application and create the image. Store it on a remote server hard drive. Share the installation point.

6. Boot a new computer with a floppy with networking components and the disk imaging software. Connect to the remote server and restore (download) the image to the new computer's hard drive.

7. Remove the floppy and reboot the new computer.

8. Complete the Mini-Setup Wizard.

Creating a sysprep.inf File

In the last section, we discussed the System Preparation Tool, which created an image that booted into a mini-Setup that took only a few minutes to execute, but unfortunately, those minutes require that a person be present, which can be a significant problem given the time constraints and geographical dispersal of a widespread deployment. So Microsoft took the concept of the answer file discussed earlier and applied it to the mini-Setup of the Sysprep installation. The result is sysprep.inf—the answer file that fully automates the mini-Setup portion of a Sysprep installation, which follows a reboot of a computer cloned with a Sysprep image.

To create the sysprep.inf file, click Start | Run, type **setupmgr**, and click OK. The Welcome to the Windows 2000 Setup Manager Wizard screen appears. Click Next. The New or Existing Answer File screen appears, offering three options:

▼ Create a New Answer File.

■ Create an Answer File That Duplicates This Computer's Configuration.

▲ Modify an Existing Answer File.

For this example, we will select the second option: Create an Answer File That Duplicates This Computer's Configuration. Click Next. The Product to Install screen appears, asking what kind of installation we are trying to automate and offering three options:

▼ Windows 2000 Unattended Installation

■ Sysprep Install

▲ Remote Installation Services

For this example, we will select the second option: Sysprep Install. Click Next.

The Platform screen asks whether the Sysprep image is going to be Windows 2000 Professional or Windows 2000 Server. We select Windows 2000 Professional. Click Next. Then the License Agreement screen appears, giving us the opportunity to fully automate the installation. No user input is required in a fully automated installation, so the user will be unable to accept the license. The installer must accept it here. To accept the terms of the license agreement, select Yes, Fully Automate the Installation. Choosing No means that the end user must accept the terms. Click Next.

The Customize the Software screen asks for the name and organization. Enter the information and click Next. Then the Computer Name screen appears. This is the name that will be given by default to each computer installed from this image.

The Administrator Password screen is next. Since we have chosen a fully automated setup, we must now enter the local Administrator password for the system we are going to install. Enter and confirm the Administrator password. We also have the option of logging in automatically as the Administrator after the install when the computer restarts. And when we select this option, we can determine how many times we can automatically log on. Click Next.

Next, the Display Settings screen appears. The settings displayed are those currently selected on the reference computer. You can modify or customize them here. Click Next. The Network Settings screen appears with the familiar Typical versus Custom settings options discussed earlier. If the reference computer has a statically assigned IP address, the default will be Custom. If, on the other hand, the reference computer is configured to use DHCP, the default will be Typical. Make your selections and then click Next. As you can see by the next two screens, there is little available to customize in the Custom settings.

If we selected Custom settings in the previous step, the Number of Network Adapters screen appears, enabling us to choose to configure more than one NIC per workstation. Since this will be a rare occurrence in a workstation, we will take the default, one network adapter, and click Next.

The Networking Components screen appears only if we selected Custom in the Network Settings screen. The only component available is the Client for Microsoft Networks. Here we can add a Client Service for NetWare, but that's about it. We cannot configure the TCP/IP settings from here. When finished, click Next.

The Workgroup or Domain screen comes up, giving us a choice of having our new workstation belong to a workgroup or domain. And if we specify a domain, we can also create a computer account in the domain (assuming it hasn't been pre-created). If we wish to create a computer account, we must provide the credentials (that is, the username and password) of a user with the power to create a computer account. When complete, click Next.

The Time Zone screen pops up, defaulting to the time zone of the reference computer. Click Next. Then the Additional Settings screen appears, giving us two options: Yes, Edit the Additional Settings, or No, Do Not Edit the Additional Settings. Selecting Yes, Edit the Additional Settings gives us five more screens to configure, dealing with the following topics:

▼ **Telephony**   The settings for remote access.

■ **Regional Settings**   The settings for dates, time, and currency.

■ **Languages**   You can add support for additional languages.

■ **Install Printers**   Specify a name of a network printer to install the first time the user logs on.

▲ **Run Once**   You may enter one or more commands that will run only the first time the system is restarted after installation.

If you selected No, Do Not Edit the Additional Settings or you have completed editing the additional settings, you now come to the Sysprep Folder screen. Here you can create a new Sysprep folder, modify an existing one, or choose not to create one at all. In our example, we will choose not to create a Sysprep folder.

The OEM (Original Equipment Manufacturer) Duplicator String screen appears, as shown in Figure 2-14. You can enter a description of this particular Sysprep image, which will be placed in the registry (HKLM\SYSTEM\Setup) of the installed computer. This will enable troubleshooting at a later time. We will be able to check which Sysprep image was used to create the installation. Click Next.

The Answer File Name screen now appears, enabling us to select a location and name for the answer file we have just created. The default name is sysprep.inf. It must be located in the Sysprep folder in the root directory. Click Next. Finally, the Completing the Windows 2000 Setup Manager Wizard screen appears. Click Finish. We're done.

THE SYSPREP.INF FILE   This section contains the sysprep.inf answer file created by the Setup Manager.

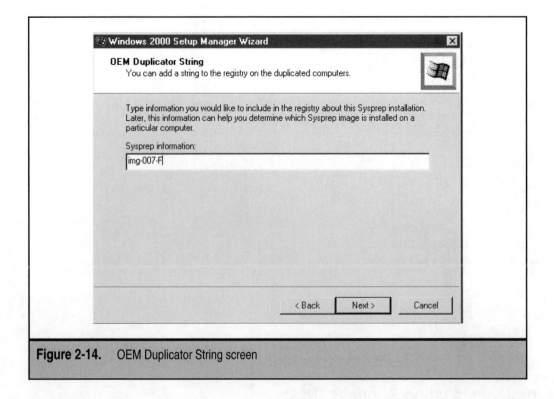

Figure 2-14.   OEM Duplicator String screen

```
;FULLY AUTOMATED SYSPREP.INF FILE FOR AUTOMATING THE MINI-SETUP
;SetupMgrTag
[Unattended]
 OemSkipEula=Yes
 TargetPath=\WINNT

[GuiUnattended]
 AdminPassword=password
 AutoLogon=Yes
 AutoLogonCount=1
 OEMSkipRegional=1
 OEMDuplicatorstring=img-007-F
 TimeZone=20
 OemSkipWelcome=1

[UserData]
 FullName="George Spalding"
 OrgName=GSA
 ComputerName=w2k-pro-011
```

```
[Display]
 BitsPerPel=24
 Xresolution=640
 YResolution=480
 Vrefresh=60

[RegionalSettings]
 LanguageGroup=1

[SetupMgr]
 DistShare=win2000dist

[Identification]
 JoinDomain=BIGCOMPANY
 DomainAdmin=administrator
 DomainAdminPassword=password

[Networking]
 InstallDefaultComponents=No

[NetClients]
 MS_MSClient=params.MS_MSClient
```

Remote Installation Services (RIS)

Remote Installation Services (RIS—pronounced "rizz") is a fairly large concept involving a number of disparate pieces with strange sounding names and even stranger sounding acronyms. The concept is simple: create a special server to hold images of client computers. When a new computer requests an image, send it on down. But the reality feels a lot more complex. Let the weird acronyms roll.

You must install and configure RIS on a domain member server on a dedicated NTFSv5 volume. Where do you get the images? The first one is a gimme; it comes with the RI server installation. For more images, you'll need the Remote Installation Preparation Wizard or RIPrep. RIPrep creates remote installation images, including applications, shortcuts, and so on. RIPrep uses an existing Win2K Pro computer as its reference computer. Next, you'll need client computers with a DHCP-PXE boot ROM on the network card. If you don't have DHCP-PXE boot ROMs on the NICs, then you'll have to create boot floppies using the Remote Boot Disk Generator or RBDG. That's all the pieces unless you want to use Setup Manager to create an additional remboot.sif answer file and associate it with an existing image. Now, let's slow it down a bit and start with the RI server.

Installing the Remote Installation Server

RIS has some unique requirements. First, it can run successfully only on a domain member server, so it requires the Active Directory; standalone workgroup servers will not work. Second, an authorized Win2K DHCP member server must be up and reachable on the network. Third, the RIS server must be authorized by the DHCP console (choose Administrative Tools | DHCP, select DHCP and then right-click and choose Add Server). And, last, but most important, we install the service. The member server designated as the RI server must have a dedicated NTFSv5 volume large enough to hold all the images (estimated at 250MB each) that you will need. The dedicated volume cannot be the system or boot partition and cannot be moved later.

On the domain member server where you wish to install RIS, click Start | Settings | Control Panel | Add/Remove Programs. Click on Add/Remove Windows Components. After a few moments, the Windows Components listing appears. Scroll down and check the box next to Remote Installation Service. Click OK. The Windows Components Wizard begins to copy files; you'll need the original installation Server CD. When the Windows Components Wizard is finished, you'll have to restart the computer.

After the restart is complete, log on to the member server. You now receive a Configure Your Server screen telling you to finish setup. Click on Finish Setup, and you are taken to the Add/Remove Programs screen, as shown in Figure 2-15, with Configure Remote Installation Services highlighted. Click the Configure button to continue.

This starts the Remote Installation Services Setup Wizard. Click Next.

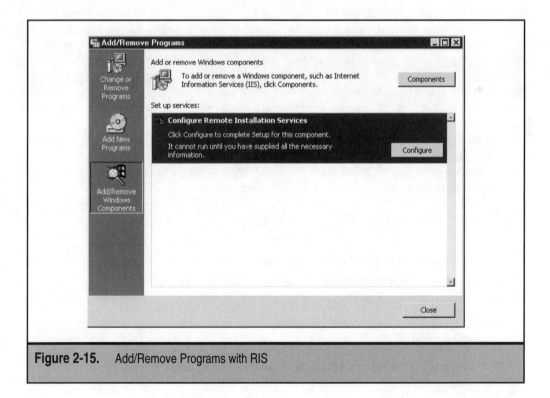

Figure 2-15. Add/Remove Programs with RIS

If the computer is not a member server, if no domain controllers are available, if there is no DHCP service running on the network, or if this computer has not been authorized in the DHCP console, you will receive a Domain Unavailable message:

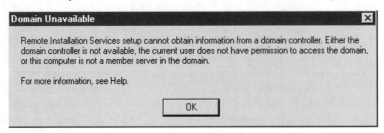

Click OK and correct the problem. The Remote Installation Folder Location screen appears, displaying a default folder location on the first local volume that meets its criteria. You can change the location here if you wish. The remote installation folder cannot be moved later. Click Next.

The Installation Source File Location screen appears. During the installation, all the necessary installation files for Windows 2000 Professional will be copied to the remote installation folder creating the first image. The wizard is asking where it will find those installation files.

The Initial Settings screen appears, asking if you would like this RI server to start supporting clients the minute it is operational. The default setting is off. You can change it here or later on. Then the Windows Installation Image Folder Name screen appears. Setup is asking for the name of the folder where the first image will be placed. Click Next.

The Friendly Description and Help Text screen appears, as shown in Figure 2-16. Setup is asking for the name of the image that is displayed to the installing user by the Client Installation Wizard. The help text provides further explanations to assist the installer in determining which remote installation image to select.

The Review Settings screen provides the last opportunity to go back and change what we have selected. Click Finish.

As shown in Figure 2-17, the Remote Installation Services Setup Wizard now completes the following tasks:

▼ Creating the remote installation folder

■ Copying files needed by the services

■ Copying Windows installation files (which takes a while)

■ Updating Client Installation Wizard screen files

■ Creating unattended Setup answer file

■ Creating remote installation services

■ Updating the registry

■ Creating Single-Instance-Store volume

▲ Starting the required remote installation services

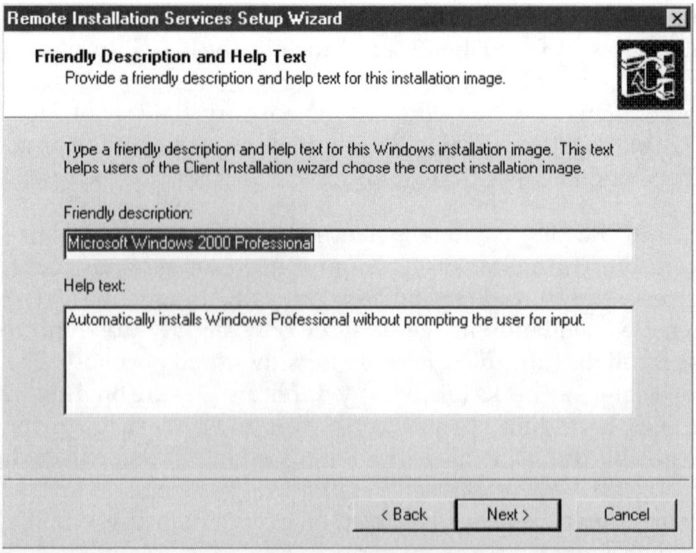

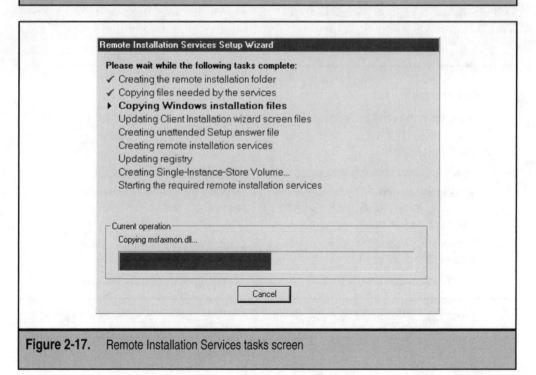

Figure 2-16. Friendly Description and Help Text screen

Figure 2-17. Remote Installation Services tasks screen

When the wizard is finished, click Done. The remote installation service is now installed and configured. This is basically the back end of the process.

Additional services added to the RI server include the Boot Information Negotiations Layer (BINL), which listens for client requests, passes the correct files, and even creates the computer account in the Active Directory, if necessary; the Trivial File Transfer Protocol Daemon (TFTPD), which downloads the initial files to begin the remote installation process; and the Single-Instance-Store (SIS) service discussed in the next section.

SINGLE-INSTANCE-STORE (SIS)   Single-Instance-Store is an incredible new technology pioneered by Microsoft. The name says it all: only one instance of any file is stored on this volume. Its purpose is to alleviate the potential for using mountains of disk space installing multiple remote installation images that are only slightly different from each other and contain nearly all the same files. Files are initially stored normally. Then, every so often, the SIS groveler agent checks to see if any duplicate files are on the volume. If it finds duplicates, it copies the original file into the SIS store and leaves a link in its place. If a new RIPrep image contains duplicate files, they are copied into the store to reduce disk space usage.

This technology could have been enabled on every volume in Win2K, but Microsoft decided it would be a great experiment to put it only on the remote installation volume. Single-Instance-Store is also the reason why the RIS volume must be a totally dedicated NTFSv5 volume and cannot be the system or boot partition.

SYSPREP IMAGING VERSUS RIPREP IMAGING   Sysprep technology involves the creation of workstation images and then their restoration to new client computers. The RIPrep

Sysprep Imaging	RIPrep Imaging
Separate imaging tool must be purchased from a third party. Image can include installed applications.	Included with Win2K Server. Image can include applications.
Does not require Active Directory.	Requires Active Directory.
Images can be stored on various media, including CDs, any UNC share on any local or remote server.	Images must be stored on the RI server.
DHCP recommended (Sysprep does not strip static IP addresses).	DHCP required.
Can partition client hard drive.	Cannot partition client hard drive.

Table 2-1.   Sysprep Imaging versus RIPrep Imaging

technology involves the creation of workstation images and then their restoration to new client computers. Table 2-1 lists some of the differences.

RIPrep

The Remote Installation Preparation Wizard (riprep.exe) is the tool used to create additional images of existing computers for use with RI servers. In other words, like the third-party cloning tools, with RIPrep, we can create the perfect Win2K Pro workstation with applications, shortcuts, everything you want to add, then create a RIPrep image, and have it automatically install onto the client workstations using the remote installation service.

First, we must copy riprep.exe and the imirror.dll file from the RI server to a floppy disk or a single folder on the Windows 2000 Professional workstation designated as the reference computer. Then launch riprep.exe. The Welcome to the Remote Installation Preparation Wizard screen appears. Click Next. The Server Name screen requires the name of the existing RI server you wish to use in support of this remote installation image. Enter the server name and then click Next.

The Folder Name screen asks you to name the folder where you would like to place the remote installation image on the RI server. Enter the folder name and then click Next. The Friendly Description and Help Text screen appears. The text entered here will be displayed to the user by the Client Installation Wizard when the user logs on to perform the installation. Click Next.

As shown in Figure 2-18, if other programs or services are currently running, the Programs or Services are Running screen will appear, strongly suggesting that you close all programs and stop all unnecessary services before proceeding. If no programs are currently running, this screen does not appear. Click Next.

Next, the Review Settings screen appears, giving you an opportunity to change anything you've entered before you finish. Click Next. The Completing the Remote Installation Preparation Wizard screen appears. It offers one last chance to go back. Click Next. Remote Installation Preparation Wizard must now complete the following tasks:

▼ Verify Windows version

■ Analyze partitions

■ Copy partition information

■ Copy files to server (the entire Win2K Professional installation is copied across the network to the RI server, including applications and other folders, which takes a while)

■ Copy and update registry information

▲ Shut down the computer

A new remote installation image now appears on the SIS volume of the RI server in the \REMOTEINSTALL\SETUP\ENGLISH\IMAGES folder.

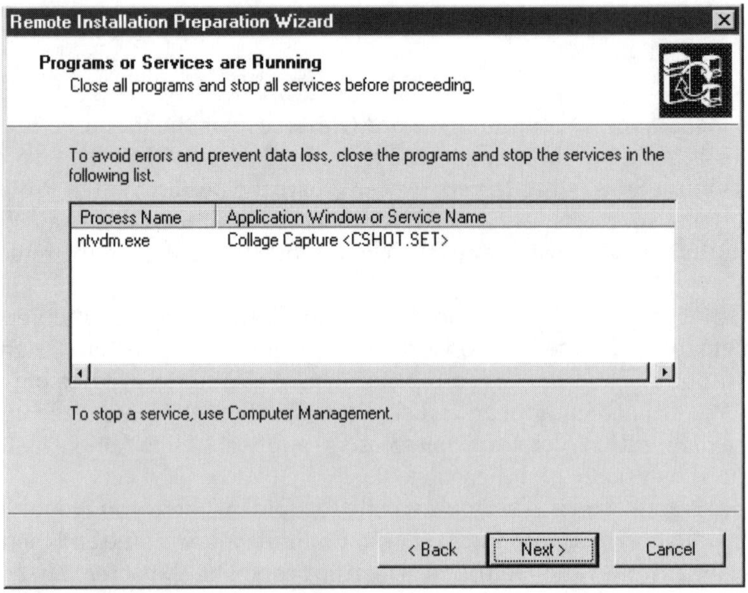

Figure 2-18. Programs or Services are Running screen

The reference computer that was used to create the RIPrep image restarts and begins to run a mini-Setup. If desired, this process can be automated using the sysprep.inf file discussed earlier. The mini-Setup includes the:

▼ Welcome screen
■ License Agreement
■ Regional Settings options
■ Personalize your Software entries
■ Computer Name and Administrator Password screen
■ Date and Time Settings
■ Networking Settings (Typical versus Custom)
■ Networking Components
■ Workgroup or Computer Domain options
■ Performing Final Tasks screen
■ Completion screen
▲ Automatic restart at the end

This mini-Setup is run simply to make the reference computer into a normal working computer again. The RIPrep process removed much of its identifying information in order to create a generic image.

Client Installation Wizard

OK. Let's recap. You've got an RI server. You've got the initial Win2K Pro image created during the RI server configuration. And you have any additional RIPrep images that you've created since the RIS installation also stored on the RI server. Now how does this actually work? Well, it all depends—on your hardware. If your computer has a DHCP-PXE (Preboot eXecution Environment) boot ROM on the network card, it will automatically, upon startup, retrieve an IP address for itself and the IP address of an RI server. This means that your PC possesses four possible boot options in its BIOS:

▼ Diskette drive A

■ Hard-disk drive C

■ CD-ROM device

▲ Network boot

Your computer will use the network boot option when all the rest have been tried and have failed or if this option has been moved up in the BIOS Boot Device Priority list. If the AD computer account has been prestaged in the domain (that is, a domain computer account was created and the GUID was entered in the Managed computer section), then the installation begins immediately. If the computer account has not yet been created, the user is presented with a logon screen by the Client Installation Wizard.

But what about all the computers that we currently own today that do not have a DHCP-PXE boot ROM on the network card? The RI server provides the Remote Boot Disk Generator (rbfg.exe) utility, as shown in Figure 2-19, to create a boot floppy for remote installation. The technology for this floppy is licensed from 3Com. On the RI server, launch rbfg.exe. The rbfg informs you that only specific network cards are supported for remote installations and displays a list for your review as shown in Figure 2-20. You cannot add to the list; you can only review it. If you do not have one of those supported NICs, you cannot use this method of unattended installation for this computer. The newly created floppy disk has only one file visible, risdisk.

After creating the floppy disk (using rbfg.exe), insert it in drive A of the computer you wish to install and reboot. Assuming your computer seeks the diskette drive A for its bootup, the screen then informs you that you are booting from the Windows 2000 Remote Installation Boot Floppy. Your network card type, node address, and a small DHCP and TFTP prompt are displayed. Then you are instructed to Press F12 for Network Service Boot. Have your fingers ready because you've got only a couple of seconds before the boot moves on and this option is no longer functional. Press F12.

The Client Installation Wizard screen appears, informing you that it will need a username, password, and domain to complete this wizard. Press ENTER. The next screen requests your username, password, and domain. Enter the information and press ENTER.

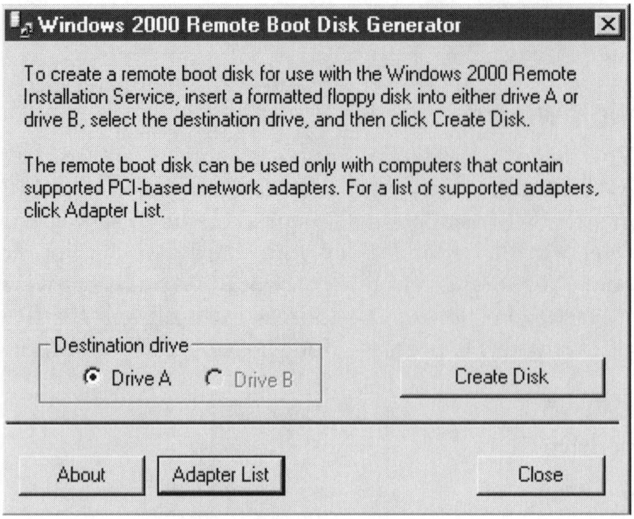

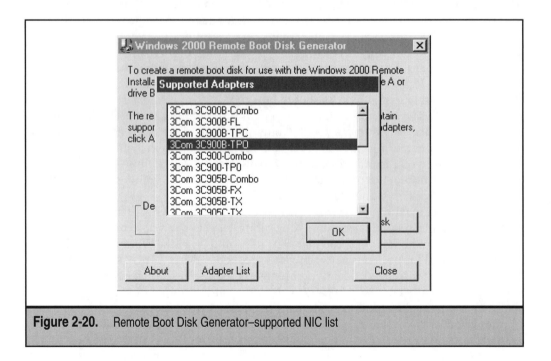

Figure 2-19.   Remote Boot Disk Generator

Figure 2-20.   Remote Boot Disk Generator–supported NIC list

The next screen displays the names of the operating systems (images) available for installation. This is the text entered on the Friendly Description and Help Text screen during RIPrep. Select one and press ENTER.

A flashing warning screen appears, informing you that all data on the hard drive will be deleted! One of the drawbacks of using RIS is that it takes the entire hard drive of the client and creates a single volume. No other options are available. Press ENTER to continue. A summary screen then appears, telling you what the computer account name will be (that is, the username plus a 1 as in "Administrator1"); the GUID it will use for the domain computer account, and the name of the RI server supporting this computer. Remove the boot floppy and press ENTER to begin Setup.

The fully automated installation takes about 30 minutes, including a complete drive format. No human intervention is requested or required.

Creating a Remote Installation Services Answer File

Both the original installation of the RI server and each RIPrep image created their own answer files to automate the installation of each specific image, but it is conceivable that you will want to create an answer file of your own and associate it with an existing RIPrep image. This section provides the instructions to create your own remote installation answer file.

Click Start | Run, type **setupmgr**, and click OK. The Welcome to the Windows 2000 Setup Manager Wizard screen appears. Click Next. The New or Existing Answer File screen appears, offering three options:

▼   Create a New Answer File

■   Create an Answer File that Duplicates This Computer's Configuration

▲   Modify an Existing Answer File

For this example, we will select the second option, Create an Answer File that Duplicates This Computer's Configuration. Click Next. Then the Product to Install screen appears, asking what kind of installation are we trying to automate and offering three options:

▼   Windows 2000 Unattended Installation

■   Sysprep Install

▲   Remote Installation Services

For our test, we will select the third option, Remote Installation Services. Click Next. The User Interaction Level screen gives five options:

▼   **Provide Defaults**   The answer file provides the values that will become the defaults. The user can change any values we supply.

■   **Fully Automated**   A totally hands-free installation, all answers are provided by the answer file.

■ **Hide Pages**   Setup hides the pages from the user that have been answered in
the answer file.

■ **Read Only**   The user cannot change any answers that were supplied by the
answer file.

▲ **GUI Attended**   Only the Text mode portion of the Windows setup is automated.

In our example, we will select the second option, Fully Automated. Click Next. The
License Agreement screen appears. Since the user will be unable to accept the terms of the
license in a fully automated setup, the installer creating the answer file must accept them.
Click I Accept the Terms and then Next.

The Administrator Password screen is next. Since we have chosen a fully automated
setup, we must now enter the local Administrator password for the system we are going
to install. Enter and confirm the Administrator password. We also have the option of logging in automatically as the Administrator after the installation when the computer restarts. And when we select this option, we can determine how many times we can
automatically log on. Click Next.

Next, the Display Settings screen appears. The settings displayed are those currently
selected on the reference computer. You can modify or customize them here. Click Next.
Then the Network Settings screen appears with the familiar Typical versus Custom settings options discussed earlier in this chapter. If the reference computer has a statically
assigned IP address, the default will be Custom. If, on the other hand, the reference computer is configured to use DHCP, the default will be Typical. Make your selection and
then click Next.

If you selected Custom in the last screen, the Number of Network Adapters screen appears, allowing you to choose to configure more than one NIC per workstation. Since this
will be a rare occurrence in a workstation, let's take the default, One Network Adapter,
and click Next. The Networking Components screen appears. This screen appears only if
we selected Custom in the Network Settings screen. Here we can configure the TCP/IP
properties of the computer we wish to install by highlighting Internet Protocol (TCP/IP)
and clicking Properties. In the next screen, we can specify a static IP address, if we wish,
and several DNS and WINS servers through the Advanced button. For our example, we
will use a static IP address. When finished, click Next.

The Time Zone screen pops up, defaulting to the time zone of the reference computer.
Click Next. Then the Additional Settings screen appears, giving us two options: Yes, Edit the
Additional Settings, or No, Do Not Edit the Additional Settings. Selecting Yes, Edit the Ad-
ditional Settings gives us seven more screens to configure dealing with the following topics:

▼ **Telephony**   The settings for remote access.

■ **Regional Settings**   Settings for dates, time, and currency.

■ **Languages**   You can add support for additional languages.

■ **Browser and Shell Settings**   Settings for Internet Explorer.

■ **Installation Folder**   Install Win2K Professional in a different folder.

- ■ **Install Printers** Specify a name of a network printer to install the first time the user logs on.

- ▲ **Run Once** You may enter one or more commands that will run only the first time the system is restarted after installation.

If you selected No, Do Not Edit the Additional Settings or you have completed editing the additional settings, you now come to the Setup Information File Text screen. Here you can edit the description string and provide additional help text. When finished, click Next.

The Answer File Name screen now appears, enabling us to select a location and name for the answer file we have just created. The default name for the file is remboot.sif, and the default location is C:\WIN2000DIST. The folder must already exist before you can click Next. The Completing the Windows 2000 Setup Manager Wizard screen appears. Click Finish. We're done.

THE REMOTE INSTALLATION ANSWER FILE This section contains the remboot.sif answer file created by the Setup Manager.

```
;FULLY AUTOMATED REMOTE INSTALLATION IMAGE ANSWER FILE
;SetupMgrTag
[Data]
 AutoPartition=1
 MsDosInitiated="1"
 UnattendedInstall="Yes"
 floppyless="1"
 OriSrc="\\%SERVERNAME%\RemInst\%INSTALLPATH%"
 OriTyp="4"
 LocalSourceOnCD=1

[SetupData]
 OsLoadOptions="/noguiboot /fastdetect"
 SetupSourceDevice="\Device\LanmanRedirector\%SERVERNAME%\RemInst
 \%INSTALLPATH%"

[Unattended]
 UnattendMode=FullUnattended
 OemSkipEula=Yes
 OemPreinstall=No
 TargetPath=\WINNT
 FileSystem=LeaveAlone
 NtUpgrade=No
 OverwriteOemFilesOnUpgrade=No

[GuiUnattended]
```

```
 AdminPassword=password
 AutoLogon=Yes
 AutoLogonCount=1
 OEMSkipRegional=1
 TimeZone=20
 OemSkipWelcome=1

[UserData]
 FullName="%USERFULLNAME%"
 OrgName="%ORGNAME%"
 ComputerName=%MACHINENAME%

[Display]
 BitsPerPel=24
 Xresolution=640
 YResolution=480
 Vrefresh=60

[RegionalSettings]
 LanguageGroup=1

[SetupMgr]
 DistFolder=C:\win2000dist
 DistShare=win2000dist

[Identification]
 JoinDomain=%MACHINEDOMAIN%
 DoOldStyleDomainJoin=Yes

[Networking]
 InstallDefaultComponents=No
 ProcessPageSections=Yes

[NetAdapters]
 Adapter1=params.Adapter1

[params.Adapter1]
 INFID=*

[NetClients]
 MS_MSClient=params.MS_MSClient

[NetServices]
```

```
MS_SERVER=params.MS_SERVER

[NetProtocols]
MS_TCPIP=params.MS_TCPIP

[params.MS_TCPIP]
DNS=No
UseDomainNameDevolution=No
EnableLMHosts=Yes
AdapterSections=params.MS_TCPIP.Adapter1

[params.MS_TCPIP.Adapter1]
SpecificTo=Adapter1
DHCP=No
IPAddress=192.168.2.90
SubnetMask=255.255.255.0
DNSServerSearchOrder=192.168.2.20
WINS=No
NetBIOSOptions=0

[RemoteInstall]
Repartition=Yes

[OSChooser]
Description="Windows Professional - Standard Installation"
Help="This will install Windows Professional in a standard
  ;configuration."
LaunchFile="%INSTALLPATH%\%MACHINETYPE%\templates\startrom.com"
ImageType=Flat
Version="5.0"
```

The Image Type and Version statements under [OSChooser] are the key elements for this file to work with RIS.

```
[OSChooser]

ImageType=Flat

Version="5.0"
```

For RIS to function correctly, the Image Type value must be set to Flat, indicating that the image is CD-based. The value of Version must be set to "5.0" indicating that this is the Windows 2000 OS.

ASSOCIATING THE RI ANSWER FILE WITH AN EXISTING IMAGE   This task must be performed from the existing RI server itself. On the RI server, go to Administrative Tools | Active Directory Users and Computers, select the RI server name, and right-click Properties. Then select the Remote Install tab and then the Images tab on the Advanced Settings screen. Click the Add button. You can then decide to associate a new answer file to an existing image as shown in Figure 2-21. Remember, by doing this, you are removing the old answer file from the image.

SUMMARY

After a close look at the installation process, you have to give Microsoft a lot of credit. They have been listening closely to their corporate customers. We wanted a simplified, time-saving installation procedure, and we got one. The actual installations aren't much shorter than NT 4.0 or 98 installations, but the key factor is that the amount of human interaction with the setup process is drastically reduced. When you boil it down, that is exactly what we were looking for. The three different options for unattended installation coupled with the automatic hardware detection of Plug and Play make the Windows 2000 installation picture a rosy one indeed.

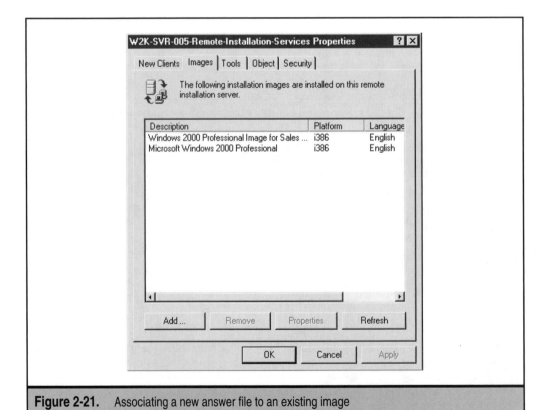

Figure 2-21.   Associating a new answer file to an existing image

CHAPTER 3

Installing Windows 2000 Server

C hapter 3 focuses on the details, issues, and configuration options surrounding a new installation of Windows 2000 Server and Advanced Server. Scripted and unattended installations and upgrading from an NT 4.0 Member Server to a Windows 2000 Server are also covered in this chapter.

HARDWARE REQUIREMENTS

Before you install the Windows 2000 Server, you need an idea of what it will eventually be used for. Will it be a domain controller? Will it be the first domain controller in the forest? Will it be used to house the Operations Masters or the Global Catalog? Will it be an SQL server? An Exchange 5.5 Server? An Exchange 2000 Server? An SMS Server? A Notes/ Domino Server? The eventual role of the Win2K server is paramount in deciding how you will configure the hardware. (For more on hardware considerations for domain controllers, see Chapter 9.)

Upgrading Major Services In Place

Early testing reveals great news for people who must upgrade systems that are already in place: it works. Let's take the most popular applications one at a time. The assumption in the following cases is that a complete full backup has been performed and verified, and that the restore has been tested. Just in case. I'm really not looking for e-mails that tell me entire Exchange organizations just bit the dust and companies are going bankrupt because someone didn't verify the backup.

Exchange Server

An in-place upgrade from an NT 4.0 Server housing an Exchange 5.5 Server works well. The host system must be running NT 4.0 Server SP4 and Exchange 5.5 SP3. Your biggest problem may be your existing two-year-old hardware, which doesn't have enough horsepower to run both Exchange and Win2K together. More details about hardware requirements appear later in this section. Another upgrade path for Exchange involves, first, installing Win2K Active Directory, then using the Active Directory Connector (which ships with Win2K) and your existing Exchange 5.5 organization to populate your new Win2K Active Directory database, and then installing Exchange 2000.

SQL Server

SQL Server and OLAP Services require a machine with even more horsepower than Exchange, so you may have to purchase additional hardware or at least increase the amount of RAM. Databases love RAM. Large data-warehousing applications running on NT 4.0 already use 1 or 2GB of RAM. So don't be stingy with the RAM. But an in-place upgrade of SQL 7.0 running on NT 4.0 Server SP4 does complete successfully. SQL Server 6.5 is not supported on Win2K.

Notes and Domino R5

Notes and Domino R5 run successfully on Win2K Server. From a hardware perspective, what is good enough for Win2K should be good enough for R5. You may have to increase the amount of RAM because Win2K requires a minimum of 256MB for itself and Notes requires about 1MB of RAM for every three users. Domino R5 supports up to four processors, as does Win2K Server. A Notes and Domino R5 Server running on an NT 4.0 Server with Service Pack 4 can be successfully upgraded in place. Never use NT 4.0 Service Pack 6 on a Notes/Domino Server. It breaks.

Systems Management Server

Systems Management Server (SMS) 2.0 requires NT 4.0 Server (PDC, BDC, or member server) with SP4, IE 4.01, SMS Service Pack 1, MDAC 2.0 SP1, and SQL Server 7.0. Just released, Service Pack 2 for SMS 2.0 is strongly recommended for use with Win2K. In most cases, SMS 2.0 running on NT 4.0 requires a big, honkin' computer with a whole lotta horsepower. Depending on the size of the organization and the placement of the SMS SQL database, these installations can range from a single Pentium Pro 200 with 512MB of RAM to multiple computers running quad PII 450's with 1GB of RAM each. As a rule, SMS is even more resource-intensive than Win2K. If SMS runs well, Win2K will do just fine. In-place upgrades of NT 4.0 Servers running SMS 2.0 to Win2K are successful.

Microsoft Proxy Server

To run successfully on Windows 2000, Proxy Server 2.0 requires an update (msp2wizi.exe). The Update wizard is available on the Technet "Service Packs CD 3" CD and the Microsoft Web site. In order to run the wizard, you also need access to the Proxy Server 2.0 installation files. You can either install Proxy Server 2.0 directly on a Windows 2000 server or perform an in-place upgrade from an NT 4.0 server. Either way, the Update wizard contains all the fixes incorporated in Microsoft Proxy Server 2.0 Service Pack 1. More detailed information is available in the release notes that accompany the Update wizard.

Microsoft Cluster Server

With regard to Microsoft Cluster Server in NT 4.0, Enterprise Edition, performing a "rolling" upgrade is recommended. You must have NT 4.0 Server, Enterprise Edition, SP4 or higher. Do an in-place upgrade on one node first and confirm that communication is still working with the other node. Then, assuming it is working, try moving all the resources from the old NT 4.0 node to the new Win2K node. If that works, upgrade the remaining NT 4.0 node.

General Hardware Recommendations

Let's check the minimum hardware requirements for Win2K itself to make sure everything will work reasonably well. The minimum RAM for a Win2K Server or Advanced Server is 256MB. Five hundred and twelve megabytes will work better, but you can live with 256MB for simple file and print services. Applications or services that are already installed may increase the RAM requirement substantially. The processor should be a Pentium II or III (no Celerons, please). Processor speed should be no lower than 400MHz and preferably higher. Up to four processors are supported with Win2K Server; eight processors are supported with Win2K Advanced Server. Busy Win2K domain controllers, Exchange, SQL, SMS, and Notes servers operate much more efficiently with two or more processors. If you have to choose between spending money on a faster processor or upgrading the RAM, go with more RAM every time. Win2K can get by with a lesser processor as long as there is plenty of RAM. Dedicated, single-function servers running network services such as DNS, DHCP, or WINS can operate on as little as a PII 200 with 256MB RAM.

Disk space, I believe, is the biggest problem, especially for NT 4.0 to Win2K upgrades. The Windows 2000 base OS requires about 700MB of free space. Support tools require around 20MB, the Resource Kit around 60MB, and first Service Pack around 100MB. You'd better allow at least 1GB for the OS—and that's before you install any BackOffice applications. By the way, let's not forget the swap file and the memory.dmp file, which require another 512MB. The Active Directory can require another 2 to 3GB (see Chapter 9). In our current NT 4.0 environment, the question is whether you have enough free disk space on an existing NT 4.0 Member Server. If you don't, either install more disk space *before* you attempt to install Win2K Server or go shopping for a whole new box.

BIOS Problems

All PCs have one or more BIOS chips. BIOS chips contain instructions that allow the operating system to talk to the hardware. The date of your BIOS is displayed every time you boot up. Microsoft has committed to supporting equipment manufactured after January 1, 1998, but the ACPI power control specification lists the "good" BIOS date as July 1, 1998. The computer you bought in September 1998 could easily have a BIOS date of April 1998. But enough about dates. What should you do? Prior to installing Win2K, go to your computer vendor's support site, download the latest BIOS upgrade for your model of computer, and apply it.

Early field testing reveals a specific problem. The Setup program identifies your hardware when Win2K installs and loads the drivers appropriate for what it thinks it sees. If the Setup program misidentifies your network card, your NIC won't work until you reinstall the card. If the Setup program misidentifies your modem, your modem won't work. But if it misidentifies your BIOS, your computer won't work. I don't want to leave you with the impression that Win2K misidentifies hardware. Quite the contrary, from my own experience it does a fantastic job. But the BIOS date is beyond the control of Win2K. Only so much backward-compatibility is possible without stagnation. The moral: Update your BIOS before you install.

WINDOWS 2000 SERVER INSTALLATION PROCEDURES

After you slip the Win2K Server CD into the drive on an NT 4.0 Server, you get several options, one of which is to perform a "clean install" as if an OS had never been installed on your computer. This section covers performing a brand-new installation of Windows 2000—a clean install, not an upgrade. Upgrading from an NT 4.0 member server is covered later in this chapter.

Installing from a CD or Network

Windows 2000 Server can be installed from a CD or from a network share point. Because most computers can now boot from a CD, installing from a CD is often the easiest way to install Win2K. But there is a new wrinkle to consider: the product key. Early testing indicates that, depending on the type of licensing program your corporation has with Microsoft (we're talking things like "Select License," not Per Server vs. Per Seat), the product key in the registry will be tied to a specific CD disk. In this case, installing from a CD in a corporate environment without a Select License may prove problematic for troubleshooting down the road.

Setup Disks

In NT 4.0 default setup, the installation or upgrade process created the three setup disks (floppies) that you needed to perform an installation or a repair. You could elect not to create these disks by using a /b option when executing the winnt.exe for a new installation (on the NT 4.0 CD) or the winnt32.exe for an upgrade (in the \WINNT\SYSTEM32 folder). NT 4.0 setup gave you the option of creating these disks later by running winnt or winnt32 with the /ox switch.

In Win2K, the Setup program is no longer responsible for creating the bootable setup floppies. And, in Win2K, four setup floppies are needed to boot Win2K. You can create them by running either makeboot.exe or makebt32.exe, which is found on the Win2K Server CD in the \BOOTDISK folder. You'll need four blank, formatted, high- density (1.44MB) floppies. As in NT 4.0, the setup floppies after they are created allow you to begin an installation on a computer on which no OS has been installed or execute a repair on a Win2K system that cannot boot (see Chapter 15 for information on the Emergency Repair process). If your computer can boot from a CD, the exact same functionality can be achieved by booting up with the Server CD in the CD-ROM drive. And booting up with the Server CD is much faster than using the four floppies.

Starting Out

As we begin to explain the steps necessary in the installation of Windows 2000 Server, we might as well tell you how long all this may take. Therefore, from time to time throughout this section, you will see "Time xx:xx min." This is how much time has elapsed in a relatively normal installation accepting most of the defaults.

Time 00:00 min. (Performed on a 400MHz, uni-processor, 256MB RAM, IDE)

When booting from a CD, the first screen is black and displays this message: "Setup is inspecting your computer's hardware configuration..." Next, a DOS-like blue screen appears (not the BSOD). Windows 2000 Setup proceeds to install a number of potential device drivers, especially controlling disks and I/O channels, so that it can continue. The various driver file names flash by on the status bar at the bottom of the screen.

Welcome to Setup

Soon the Welcome to Setup screen appears, as shown in Figure 3-1. Press ENTER to set up Windows 2000, R for Repair, or F3 to Quit. So far, the process is no different from an NT 4.0 installation.

License Agreement

The Windows 2000 Licensing Agreement appears. It is very similar to the NT 4.0 installation agreement, except you can now press F8 immediately to agree to the terms without having to press the PGDN key thirteen times.

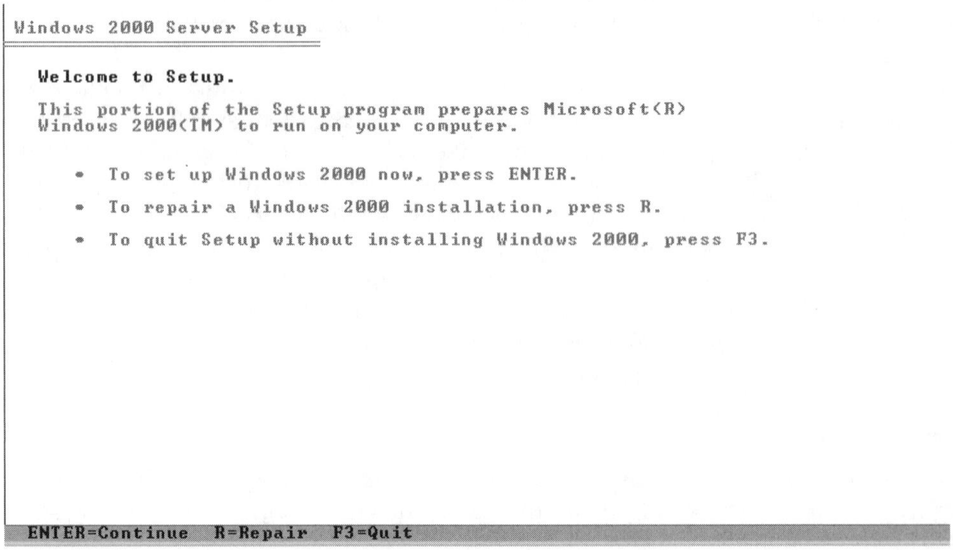

```
Windows 2000 Server Setup

   Welcome to Setup.

   This portion of the Setup program prepares Microsoft(R)
   Windows 2000(TM) to run on your computer.

       •   To set up Windows 2000 now, press ENTER.

       •   To repair a Windows 2000 installation, press R.

       •   To quit Setup without installing Windows 2000, press F3.
```

ENTER=Continue   R=Repair   F3=Quit

Figure 3-1.   The Welcome to Setup screen

Disk and Volume Configuration

Setup searches for previous versions of Windows and then displays the current disk and volume configuration. As in NT 4.0, you can place the Win2K installation on an existing volume, create a new partition from unpartitioned space, or even delete a partition. Notice that, if you create a new partition, Win2K setup reserves an 8MB partition at the end of the disk. The 8MB partition will be needed if you convert the disk to dynamic later on. (Chapter 5 offers more information on dynamic disks.) If you use an existing partition that's FAT, Setup gives you the option of converting it to NTFS. If the existing partition is already NTFS, Setup simply proceeds with the installation.

Due to limitations in the NT 4.0 setup program, the installation partition was limited in NT 4.0 to 4GB, but no such limit appears in the Win2K installation program. You may select or create a partition of up to 32GB and choose to format it either in NTFSv5 or FAT (any partition over 2GB will automatically format in FAT32). If you create a partition larger than 32GB, you can only format it with NTFSv5. During an upgrade, Win2K can use an existing FAT32 volume larger than 32GB, if there is one. It cannot create FAT32 volumes larger than 32GB. The largest NTFS volume size is the incredible and still theoretical limit of 16EB (exabytes). Your best option is to create partitions and format them with NTFS during the installation process. Choosing FAT now and converting the partition to NTFS later may result in a less-than-optimal cluster size. The conversion utility changes the cluster size to 512 bytes, whereas NTFS natively creates 4K clusters (see Chapter 5 for details), which increases storage efficiency and read-write performance.

Setup then formats the new partition (the rough time estimate is one minute per gigabyte), checks it for errors, and proceeds to copy all the installation files it will need to the volume that you just specified on the computer's hard drive.

Time 00:13 min. (including 4GB volume format)

When the process is complete, the system reboots automatically in a graphical mode and you see some very pretty screens like the one in Figure 3-2.

Installing Devices

Next, after a slight pause (the system asks you to wait and even says "please"), the Welcome to the Windows 2000 Setup Wizard screen appears for about ten seconds. Then the Installing Devices screen automatically appears and Setup begins detecting and installing the drivers for the devices that are present on your computer. Plug and Play at its finest. The on-screen caption mentions that your screen may flicker. And flicker it will, several times. Don't be alarmed. This is a normal operation.

Time 00:20 min.

Regional Settings

After the devices are installed, you get the Regional Settings dialog box shown in Figure 3-3. Here, you can make choices about language (click the Advanced button to get code

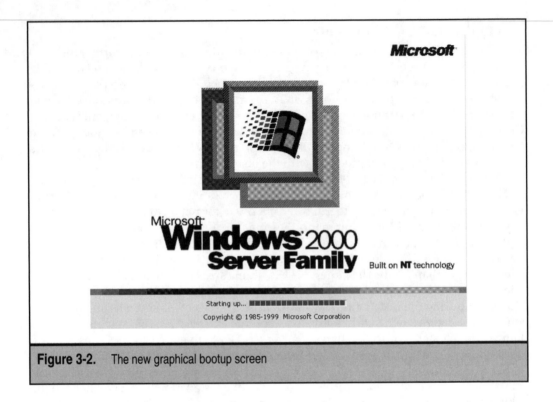

Figure 3-2.   The new graphical bootup screen

page conversion tables), numbers, currency, time, date, input locales (multiple locale settings for input languages, different keyboard layouts, and hot key settings for switching
between them). These choices make installing in languages other than English easier.
They also handle date, time, and currency displays. The locale defaults are English
(United States) for the system, English (United States) for the user, and the U.S. keyboard
layout. Those of you in the U.S. can simply click the Next button. The only piece of Win2K
that doesn't change when you choose a different language is the opening logon dialog
box, which always appears in English.

Personalize Your Software

The Personalize Your Software screen appears. Enter your name, enter your organization, and click Next.

Your Product Key

The Your Product Key screen appears, as shown in Figure 3-4. As in Windows 98, enter
the 25-character product key from the CD case. Type carefully! Thankfully, the product
key is checked immediately for accuracy instead of six screens later. The product key is

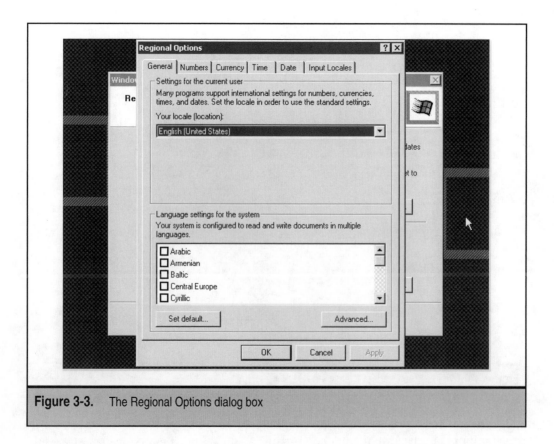

Figure 3-3.   The Regional Options dialog box

especially important in Win2K, because, in order to perform maintenance on this installation, the same CD (or installation point) with the same product key must be used.

Licensing Modes

Next comes the Licensing Modes screen. As in NT 4.0, this is where you enter the number of client access licenses that were purchased. Per Server refers to the number of concurrent connections that this server will support, in which case each connection must have its own client access license (CAL). Per Seat refers to large enterprise clients in which each computer must have its own CAL. No change here from NT 4.0.

Computer Name and Admin Password

Next is the Computer Name and Administrator Password screen shown in Figure 3-5. Win2K automatically creates a unique, 15-character computer name by taking the first word in the organization's name and appending a completely random set of letters and numbers to it. The purpose of the auto-generated name is to make certain that remote installation services see unique computer names on the network (required by NetBIOS,

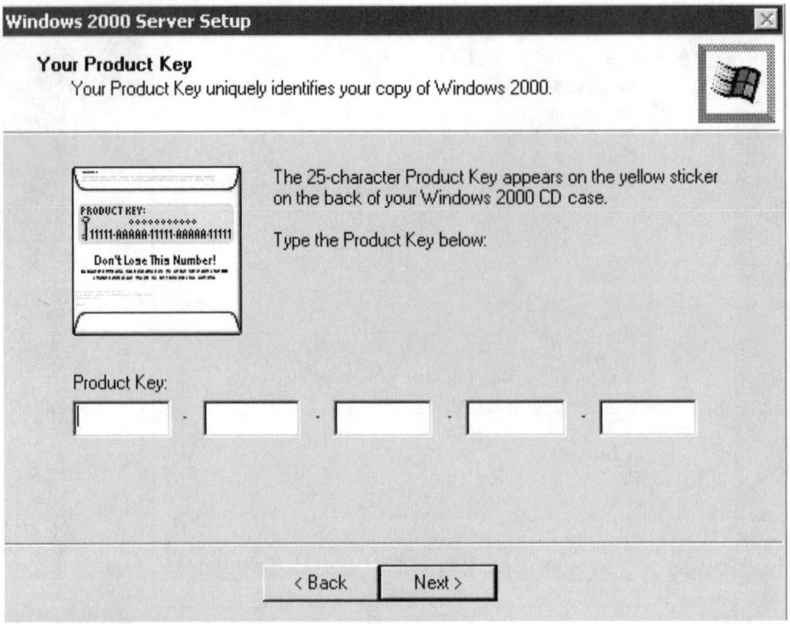

Figure 3-4. The Your Product Key screen

WINS, and DNS). The unique names actually remove one of the issues from scripted Win2K OS installations. A random name might be okay (but hard to intuit) for Win2K Professional workstations, but random names are certainly *not* okay for servers.

For the servers, please change the computer name to something meaningful. I strongly recommend developing a naming strategy for all servers before installing. Computer names can be changed after installation for workstations and member servers, but not for DCs. You can only change the name of a DC computer after it has been demoted to a member server.

Enter a secure password for the Administrator account—the local Administrator account held in the local SAM database of this (and only this) server. The password you enter is *not* the password of the domain administrator. Nor is this the administrator password used in DS Restore mode or the Recovery Console. Click Next.

Windows 2000 Components

The Windows 2000 Components screen, a major screen for configuring the server, appears. If you wish, all the services can be installed after the installation has been com-

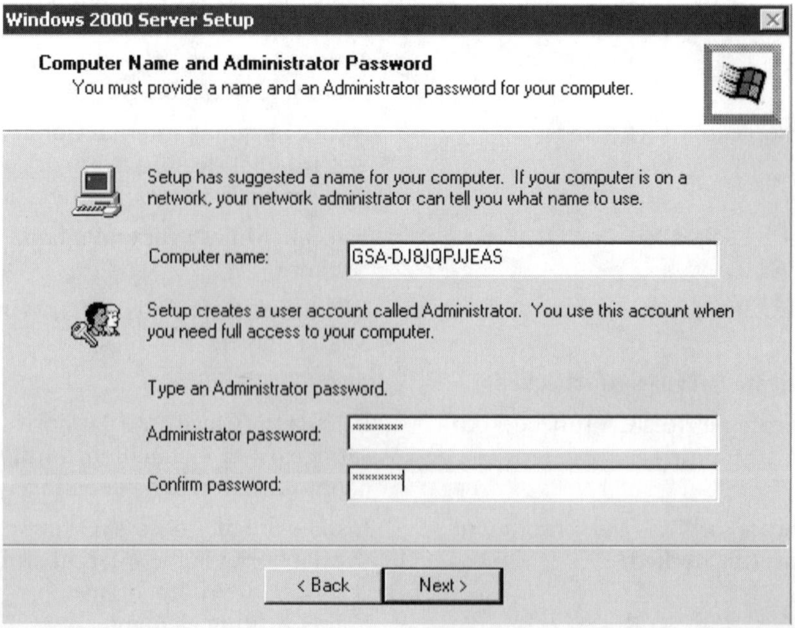

Figure 3-5. The Computer Name and Administrator Password screen

pleted. However, some services may conflict with others. For instance, cluster service cannot be used on the same computer as Terminal Services Application server mode. Certificate services (CS) must be removed from a member server in order to promote it to a domain controller. CS can be reinstalled after the promotion, but you are switching from a standalone CA to an enterprise CA, so you are starting from square one again in terms of configuration and no existing certificates can be renewed. The following table lists the available Win2K components. These components can be added during the initial installation or later, after the install, by using Add/Remove Programs from the Control Panel. After selecting the appropriate components to install, click Next.

Accessories and Utilities (checked)

Accessibility Wizard (checked)	Creates additional options in the keyboard, sound, display, mouse, and system to accommodate people with special needs.

Accessories (checked)	WordPad, Windows Explorer, Synchronization Manager, Paint, Notepad, Image Viewer, Command Prompt, Calculator, Address Book.
Communications (checked)	HyperTerminal, Internet Connection Wizard, NetMeeting, Network and Dial-up Connections, Phone Dialer.
Games (checked)	Freecell, Minesweeper, Pinball, Solitaire.
Multimedia (checked)	CD Player, Sound Recorder, Windows Media Player.
Certificate Services (unchecked)	
Certificate services CA (unchecked)	Installs the Certificate Authority (CA) service. After installation, additional configuration will be necessary.
Certificate services Web enrollment support (unchecked)	Installs the files necessary for accessing the network via the Internet and using a certificate (enrollment) as the authenticating element.
Cluster Service (unchecked) Advanced Server only	Loads the service necessary to create a two-server fail-over cluster.
Indexing Service (checked)	Loads by default but is disabled. This service indexes files and folders on the Win2K file systems.
Internet Information Services (IIS) (Partially checked)	
Common Files (checked)	The essential files needed to load and run the Internet Information Services.
Documentation (checked)	The online documentation for IIS.
File Transfer Protocol (FTP) Server (unchecked)	The TCP/IP service designed to allow this computer to house files, in designated folders, that users from the network can download.
FrontPage 2000 Server Extensions (checked)	Installed on an IIS Web server to allow remote editing and modifications to Web pages hosted on the server.
Internet Information Services Snap-In (checked)	IIS Management Tool usable in the Microsoft Management Console.

Internet Services Manager (HTML) (checked)	IIS Management Tool reachable through a browser.
NNTP Service (unchecked)	Network News Transfer Protocol. Necessary if the server will be used to house Internet newsgroups (Usenet).
SMTP Service (checked)	Simple Mail Transport Protocol. Checked here because it can be used by domain replication and the Certificate Server.
Visual InterDev RAD Remote Deployment Support (unchecked)	Developers might need this if they are involved with Visual InterDev.
World Wide Web Server (checked)	WWW Publishing Service. The Web server.
Management and Monitoring Tools (unchecked)	
Connection Manager Components	Used in conjunction with Routing and Remote Access Service (RRAS). The connection manager is responsible for updating dial-in client address books.
Network Monitor Tools	Network Monitor provides an excellent tool for viewing network activity and packet analysis. A poor man's "sniffer."
Simple Network Management Protocol (SNMP)	Also used in conjunction with RRAS, SNMP provides a common protocol for intelligent network devices to communicate to a central network-monitoring console.
Message Queuing Services (unchecked)	Used in conjunction with transaction-based applications. The Message Queuing Services ensures that a complete transaction is either fully completed or safely rolled back.
Networking Services (unchecked by default, but even when checked, not all individual services are checked. The status listed for each Networking Services service assumes that Networking Services has been checked for install.)	

COM Internet Services Proxy (checked)	Software that supports distributed applications using HTTP to communicate through IIS. An application using COM needs to talk to another component located on another network. The COM Internet Services Proxy allows the Internet to provide that connection.
Domain Name System (DNS) (checked)	Installs the DNS server service. Allows this computer to become a DNS server.
Dynamic Host Configuration Protocol (DHCP (checked)	Installs the DHCP server service. DHCP leases IP addresses and provides TCP/IP-related settings to clients.
Internet Authentication Service (checked)	Used in conjunction with RRAS. This is the authentication service used by RADIUS.
QoS Admission Control Service (checked)	Quality of Service (QoS) establishes bandwidth priority for specific applications. The QoS Admission Control Service controls the bandwidth and network resources on an assigned subnet.
Simple TCP/IP Services (checked)	A few little TCP/IP elements that we never really see: echo, daytime, discard, quote of the day (qotd), and character generator.
Site Server ILS Services (unchecked)	Internet Locator Service. Supports telephony application features such as caller ID, conference calls, video conferencing, and faxing. Also assists in finding users to connect to NetMeeting.
Windows Internet Name Service (WINS) (checked)	WINS is the NetBIOS name resolution service. It is installed by default in Win2K for backward-compatibility with downlevel clients.

Other Network File and Print Services (unchecked)

File Services for Macintosh	Allows Macintosh computers on the network to view a NetBIOS share on a Win2K server as a Macintosh-native UAM volume.
Print Services for Macintosh	Allows Macintosh computers on the network to utilize a Win2K-installed printer.
Print Services for Unix	The Line Printer daemon service that allows a Unix system on the same network to use Win2K-installed printers.
Remote Installation Services (RIS) (unchecked)	RIS controls the entire remote installation process. While not required, it is recommended that RIS be on a dedicated server. RIS requires a separate dedicated volume to allow it to implement its Single-Instance-Store (SIS) technology. This volume holds all the files for remote installations of Win2K Professional workstations. Recommendations are for a minimum volume size of 1GB.
Remote Storage Service (RSS) (unchecked)	When implemented, RSS migrates the least recently used (LRU) files from your disk and moves them onto tape while still maintaining an entry for the file in the volume directory.
Script Debugger (checked)	A service that checks each script that is run for correct syntax. If a script error occurs, the debugger pops on the screen to display the exact point of the error.

Terminal Services (unchecked)

Client Creator Files	Loads the files needed to create a set of floppy disks for installing Terminal Services (TS) Client software. You can create either 16-bit TS client disks for Windows for Workgroups 3.11 or 32-bit client disks for Win 9x and NT.
Enable Terminal Services	As the name declares, checking this enables Terminal Services.
Terminal Services Licensing (unchecked)	Required to run Terminal Services in Application Server mode. Not required if you are only using Remote Administration mode.

Windows Media Services (unchecked)

Windows Media Services	Used to create, manage, and deliver media content over an intranet or the Internet. Includes the Windows Media Encoder and the Windows Media Administrator. Can be installed later.
Windows Media Services Admin	The Windows Media Administrator.

Date & Time

The Date and Time Settings screen appears. Enter the correct date, time, and time zone for this server. Decide whether to adjust for daylight savings time twice a year in April and October. Click Next.

Terminal Services

If you selected Terminal Services in the Components screen, you now must decide which mode you would prefer, Remote administration mode or Application server mode, as shown in Figure 3-6.

In Application Server mode, applications can be deployed and managed from a central location. After an application has been deployed using TS, clients can connect by remote access, LAN, or WAN. Clients can be Windows-based (client files available in Win2K Server), Windows CE-based (client obtained from a hardware vendor), or even non-Windows-based (client requires a Citrix Metaframe add-on). You cannot operate in this mode if you are loading Cluster Services.

Licensing is required to deploy a Terminal Services-enabled server as an application server. Each client must have the TS Client Access License (CAL) as well as a Windows 2000 Server CAL. Each copy of Windows 2000 Professional includes a Terminal Services CAL, but not a Windows 2000 Server CAL.

TS Remote Administration mode allows any server running Windows 2000 Server to be administrated remotely with full access to all administrative tools. Remote adminis-

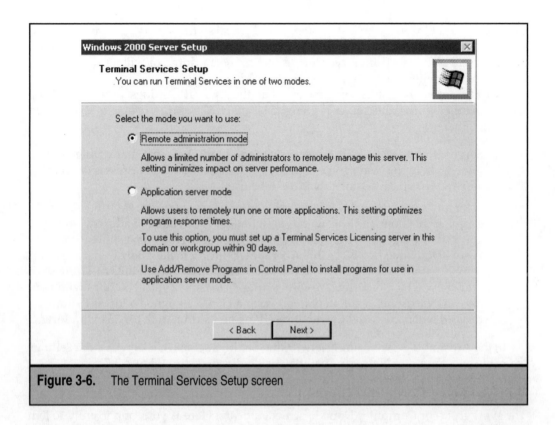

Figure 3-6.   The Terminal Services Setup screen

tration can be performed from any client device, including DOS, Win 9x, and NT 4.0. Win2K Terminal Services includes two per-server connections just for Remote Administration. A TS CAL is not required to connect to Terminal Services in Remote Administration mode, but a Win2K Server CAL is required.

Networking Settings

Click Next. The Networking Settings screen appears. Setup automatically installs the required networking components based on your choices in the Components selection screen. Installing the components can take a couple of minutes if you accept the defaults or many minutes if you checked a number of networking components. When the components are installed, you are asked to select either Typical or Custom settings.

Time 00:25 min. (accepting the default components)

TYPICAL VS. CUSTOM SETTINGS   According to the onscreen caption, Typical settings create "network connections using the Client for Microsoft Networks, File and Print Sharing for Microsoft Networks, and the TCP/IP transport protocol with automatic addressing." If you want the standard Microsoft networking client software that most of us certainly use at least to get through the installation, then Typical settings work for you. If File and Print sharing must be enabled, perhaps because the computer will have a network printer attached, will serve as a print server for a direct connect printer, or will need to share its folders and files, then this setting must be checked.

TCP/IP automatic addressing means that the TCP/IP settings default to using DHCP. In other words, this server is going to be a DHCP client. A couple of issues need addressing here:

▼ Servers shouldn't be DHCP clients; servers should have manually assigned IP addresses. In this way, you can predict and document the addresses of your servers. So typical settings should not be used.

▲ If for any reason the DHCP broadcast fails to receive an address from a DHCP server at this time, the NIC will be assigned an "automatic IP address" in the 169.254.*x.x* range. This new feature in Win2K can drive you absolutely crazy. Also, if you have two NICs in the computer during installation, be sure to select Custom Settings here and read the description of each NIC carefully so you know which NIC you are configuring. Choosing Typical Settings with two network cards will result in one receiving a DHCP-assigned address (Setup decides which one) and the other receiving an "automatic" 169.254.*x.x* address.

In the Advanced Server setup, Networking Settings screen, click on Custom settings to enable and configure Network Load Balancing during setup (Figure 3-7).

Workgroup or Computer Domain

The Workgroup or Computer Domain screen appears. Here is your opportunity to join an existing domain and become a member server during the actual installation. If you select workgroup, Setup defaults to the workgroup name WORKGROUP. You are welcome to enter any workgroup name you like. Because a workgroup has been selected, Setup understands that this computer will stand alone and is ready to move forward. To select a domain, enter the name of the domain to which this server will belong. Click Next and provide the userID and password of an account from that domain with the power to add computer accounts. Adding computer accounts is one of the administrative tasks that can be delegated to others using the Delegation of Control Wizard (see Chapter 11).

Installing Components

Next, the Installing Components screen appears. This step is the final file copy of the install. All the remaining components needed are copied, installed, and configured. The Components will take several minutes to install.

Time 00:33 min.

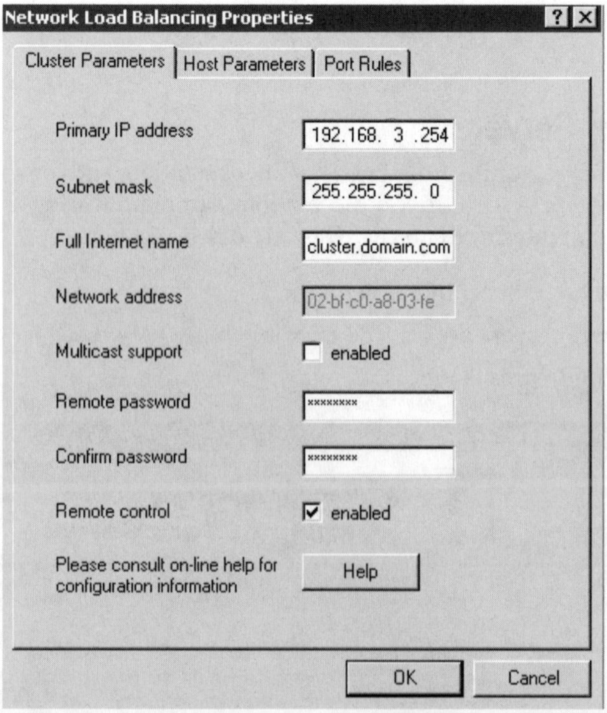

Figure 3-7. Load Balancing options

Performing Final Tasks

When all the components have been installed and configured, the Performing Final Tasks screen appears. Thankfully, it is the last screen. Setup installs the Start menu items, registers all components (in the registry), saves current settings, and removes any temporary files it needed. Finishing these final tasks can take quite a while. When the final tasks are done, the Completing the Windows 2000 Setup Wizard screen appears. Remove CDs that may still be in drives and click the Finish button. Then wait while the system restarts.

Time 00:42 min. (installation complete)

Please note that the time it takes to install Win2K varies depending on the hardware components used and the additional options you chose. The timed Win2K installation presented in this chapter was quite simple because, for the most part, default choices were taken. Choosing additional components and services can lengthen the installation substantially.

Configuring Your Server

After you install, reboot for the first time after an installation, and log in, you always see a Configure Your Server screen. If you did not join a domain during the installation, the screen presents you with three choices. They are discussed here.

▼   This is the only server in my network.

■   One or more servers are already running in my network.

▲   I will configure this server later.

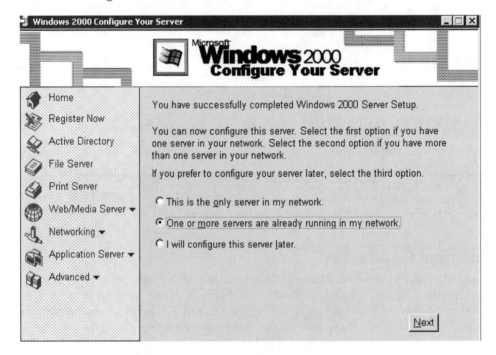

"This Is the Only Server in My Network"

Choosing "This is the only server in my network" tells Setup to do the following: "...automatically configure this server as a domain controller and set up Active Directory,

DHCP, and DNS on your network." You will find links to the Help program so that you can learn more about Active Directory, DHCP, and DNS. The screen warns against going further if these services are already running on the network. Clicking Show More Details informs you that the server will be assigned a static IP address in the 10.*x.x.x* range, that the server will be limited to one subnet, and that you need to reconfigure if you want to add routing services. Thankfully, the screens allow you to back out without proceeding in all cases.

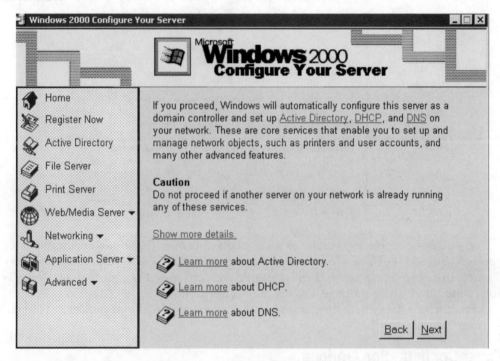

I am sure that these choices are available for very small (one server) installations (Small Business Server, here we come), where the owner of a shoe repair shop is performing the Win2K Server and Active Directory installation. However, being able to click a single button to create a domain and configure the two primary network services is both very cool and a little scary. Clicking Next asks the user to input a domain name (shoerepairworld.local), automatically installs and configures all necessary components, runs the Active Directory Installation Wizard (*dcpromo*) in unattended mode, installs and configures DNS and DHCP, loads the domain administrative tools, and, finally, restarts the computer. Assuming the Server CD is in the drive, all the user has to do is enter the domain name.

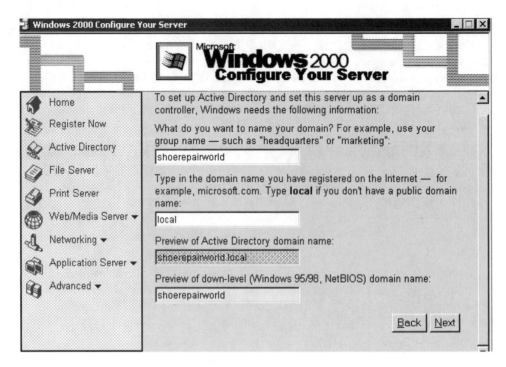

When the server comes back up, it's a domain controller. The domain administrator account has used the local administrator password. DS Restore Mode and the Recovery Console use a blank password. DNS is running and configured as a root server. DHCP is fully configured with a scope of 254 addresses (10.*x.x.x*).

You can only hope that knowledgeable admins are making these choices in your enterprise. You can only hope...

Other Configuration Options

The other two options on the Configure Your Server screen are:

▼   One or more servers are already running in my network.

▲   I will configure this server later.

Both take you to a relatively innocuous screen with links to the Help program and the Microsoft Web site, where you can check out the latest walkthroughs. You can also keep this screen from reappearing by clearing the Show This Screen at Startup check box.

Additional Service Configuration after Installation

If you selected additional components during the installation, some need configuring in order to be fully functional. In this case, the Configure Your Server screen appears with only one choice: Finish Setup. Clicking Finish Setup takes you to the Add/Remove Programs application in Control Panel, where services that require additional configuration are listed. These components definitely require additional configuration:

▼ **Remote Installation Service (RIS)** The Configure button brings up a wizard to help you install RIS. This computer must be a member server in an Active Directory domain. Win2K DHCP and DNS servers must be active on the network. You must have either a CD or a share containing the installation files for Win2K Professional. And there must be a dedicated volume on this computer that is *not* the system or boot partition to host the Single-Instance-Store (SIS) used by RIS. (See Chapter 2 for more information on configuring RIS.)

■ **Message Queuing Service** Configures itself after you click the Configure button. Click Finish when it's done.

▲ **Certificate Services** Clicking Configure brings up choices as to the type of Certificate Authority (CA) you want to install and requests the necessary identifying information. (See Chapter 13 for more configuration options.)

SCRIPTED INSTALLATIONS

On the Win2K Server CD, under the Support\Tools folder, you'll find a file named deploy.cab. *deploy.cab* is a zipped file and can be extracted using a normal copy of WinZip. Inside it are several files, including Setup Manager and unattend.doc. Unattend.doc contains the complete reference (142 pages' worth) for creating unattended installation files for use in all types of Win2K installations. These files also become available after installing RIS.

For even more information about unattended installations, check out this Web site: www.microsoft.com/technet/ win2000/dguide/append-c.asp.

Sample Script

Following is a sample script for installing a Win2K Member Server. This script does the following:

▼ Converts the existing partition to NTFS.

■ Places the OS files in the \WINNT folder.

■ Adds 50 per-server client access licenses.

■ Sets the administrator password to "password."

■ Sets the time zone to U.S. Central Time.

■ Sets the display to 800 × 600.

■ Joins the bigcompany.com domain using the administrator's credentials.

■ Loads the Microsoft Client and TCP/IP.

▲ Sets the IP address to 192.168.3.1 and the DNS server address to 192.168.3.254 on Adapter1.

One way to install Win2K server in a completely unattended fashion is to save this script as a text file named winnt.sif and copy it to a floppy disk. Boot the computer to be installed with the Win2K Server CD, and, after Setup starts, insert the floppy in the drive. The Win2K server installation will proceed without user intervention. It will get all the necessary answers from the "answer" file you provided on the floppy. You must remove the floppy disk when you are requested to do so.

```
;UNATTEND.TXT           ;answer file for unattended Win2K Server install
[Unattended]
UnattendMode=DefaultHide
OemPreinstall = no
NoWaitAfterTextMode = 1
NoWaitAfterGUIMode = 1
FileSystem = ConvertNTFS     ;other option is LeaveAlone
ExtendOEMPartition = 0       ;changing this value to '1' takes
                             ;entire drive during conversion to NTFS
ConfirmHardware = no
NtUpgrade = no
Win31Upgrade = no
TargetPath = \WINNT
OverwriteOemFilesOnUpgrade = no
[UserData]
FullName = "Your Name"          ;Registration information
OrgName = "Your Company Name"    ;Registration information
ProductId = "11111-11111-11111-11111-11111" ;Product Key
ComputerName = "YourComputerName" ;Insert computer name between
                                  ;quotes, avoid spaces
[LicenseFilePrintData]
Automode=PERSERVER               ;licensing is per server,
                                 ;Other option is PERSEAT.
AutoUsers=50                     ;not required for 'per seat'
[GuiUnattended]
OemSkipWelcome = 1
OEMBlankAdminPassword = 1
AdminPassword=password
TimeZone = 020                   ;check time zone list in
                                 ;unattend.doc on install CD
AdvServerType = SERVERNT
AutoLogon = Yes                  ;turns on autologon
AutoLogonCount = 1               ;sets autologon to once only
[GuiRunOnce]
```

```
;"complete local path of file to run the first time you logon"
[Display]
ConfigureAtLogon = 0
BitsPerPel = 4
XResolution = 800
YResolution = 600
VRefresh = 60
AutoConfirm = 1
[Networking]
;InstallDefaultComponents = Yes
[Network]
DetectAdapters = DetectAdaptersSection
InstallProtocols = ProtocolsSection
[Identification]
;JoinWorkgroup=WORKGROUP          ;workgroup name does not require
  ;quote marks lines following are options to join the domain
  ;BIGCOMPANY
JoinDomain = BIGCOMPANY
CreateComputerAccountInDomain = Yes
DomainAdmin = administrator
DomainAdminPassword = password
[DetectAdaptersSection]
DetectCount = 1
[NetAdapters]
Adapter1="Adapter1"
[NetClients]                     ;Other clients could be added
                                 ;to this section
MS_MSClient="MS_MSClient"
[NetProtocols]
MS_TCPIP="MS_TCPIP"
[NetServices]
MS_Server="MS_Server"
[NetOptionalComponents]
DNS=1
[Adapter1]
InfID="*"
[MS_TCPIP]
AdapterSections="Adapter1.tcpip"
[Adapter1.tcpip]
SpecificTo="Adapter1"
DHCP = No
DNS=Yes
DNSDomain=bigcompany.com
SubnetMask=255.255.255.0
```

```
DNSServerSearchOrder=192.168.3.254    ;REMOVE ';' at beginning of line
                                      ;to set during setup
IPAddress=192.168.3.1                 ;REMOVE ';' at beginning of line
                                      ;to set during setup
                               ;also change line above to read DHCP = No
```

A number of additional sample scripts are available on the Microsoft Web site and in the unattend.doc file discussed earlier.

UPGRADING FROM AN NT 4.0 SERVER TO A WINDOWS 2000 SERVER

Most of us will at some point perform an upgrade from an NT 4.0 Server to a Win2K Server. You may approach this with some trepidation. But Microsoft has gone out of its way to make this particular experience as painless as possible.

The Upgrade Screens

If the CD autoplay mechanism doesn't display the CD Welcome screen, click the setup.exe file on the CD to display it. A dialog box informs you, "This CD-ROM contains a newer version of Windows than the one you are presently using." The dialog box asks, "Would you like to upgrade to Windows 2000?" Click Yes to upgrade.

Once again, as a point of reference, we will provide estimated elapsed times for the Win2K upgrade.

> **Time: 00:00 min. (performed on a 300MHz, uniprocessor, 128MB RAM, IDE; this computer does not meet Microsoft's minimum RAM specification, but many existing NT 4.0 servers do match these specs)**

As shown in Figure 3-8, you must next decide if you want to *upgrade* to Windows 2000 or perform a *clean install*. If you are upgrading your NT 4.0 Member Server, PDC, or BDC, select upgrade to Windows 2000. Otherwise, install a new copy of Windows 2000.

The License Agreement appears. You must accept the terms of the agreement by clicking I Accept This Agreement. Click Next to continue.

The Your Product Key screen appears. As in Windows 98, enter the 25-character product key on the CD case. Type carefully! Thankfully, the product key is checked immediately for accuracy and you don't have to wait for six screens to pass before you find out you typed it incorrectly.

You may see the Select Special Options screen, where Language Options, Advanced Installation Options, and Accessibility Options are configured.

Setup checks for sufficient disk space for the upgrade. There must be at least 575MB free on the boot partition. If any volumes on your computer are currently formatted as FAT, Setup gives you an opportunity to convert the volume(s) to the NTFS file system as

Figure 3-8. The Upgrade or Clean Install screen

part of the upgrade process. The onscreen prompt shown in Figure 3-9 also warns you that upgrading the volume to NTFS will make it unavailable to other operating systems such as DOS and Win 9x. Please note that all of your current volumes formatted in NTFSv4 will be automatically upgraded to NTFSv5 without warning. Upgrading automatically is not a problem if Win2K will be the only operating system used to boot this computer.

But if you wish to maintain a dual-boot scenario with NT 4.0 and Win2K, you must install NT 4.0, Service Pack 4 or higher on your NT 4.0 installation prior to installing Win2K. Service Pack 4 includes a new NTFS.SYS file that allows NT 4.0 to interact with an NTFSv5 volume. One other step is necessary to maintain a dual-boot: When you are asked whether you want to upgrade your current system or perform a clean install, you must choose a clean install and place the files in a different directory than your current NT 4.0 installation.

Setup now checks for applications, devices, and services that may be incompatible with Windows 2000. If any exist, they are displayed and Setup provides a Have Disk button so you can add drivers or additional files if you wish.

If Setup determines that certain applications are already installed on your system, the Directory of Applications for Windows 2000 screen shown in Figure 3-10 appears. The

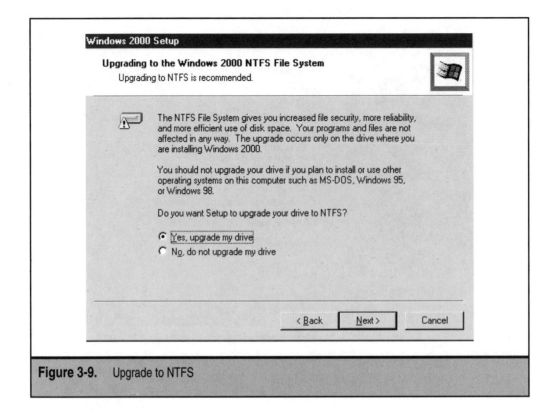

Figure 3-9. Upgrade to NTFS

Directory of Applications button takes you to a link at Microsoft's Web site where the latest application-compatibility information is available. Obviously, the link to the Web site only functions if the computer you are upgrading is connected to the Internet. In case it isn't, here's the URL behind the button: www.microsoft.com/windows2000/upgrade/compat/search/default.asp.

Setup now copies a few necessary files and the system restarts automatically. From this point on in the NT 4.0 upgrade process, no human intervention is either needed or possible.

Time: 00:03 min.

Unattended Upgrade

"Look Ma, no hands!" So it can continue, Windows 2000 Setup proceeds to install, without any further human intervention, a number of potential device drivers that control disk and I/O channels. Various driver file names are displayed on the status bar across the bottom of the screen. Then Windows 2000 starts in a DOS-like blue screen.

The Application Compatibility Tool

Also on the Win2K Server CD in the \Support folder is an application compatibility tool named APCOMPAT.EXE.

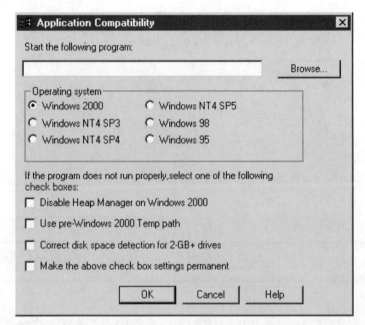

This tool allows you to run a specific legacy application right from the tool, and, if it doesn't run, make certain real-time adjustments in the Operating System, and then run it again to see if the problem is fixed. After you've made changes in parameters that allow the legacy app to run, you can make those changes permanent with one more mouse-click.

Setup now examines the disks, deletes any outdated files, creates a list of new files to be copied, copies all the necessary files for upgrade, initializes and saves the configuration, and restarts the computer again.

Time: 00:11 min.

Windows 2000 starts in a graphical mode this time. If Setup converts a FAT volume to NTFS, it displays a black text window, checks the file system, and converts it to NTFS.

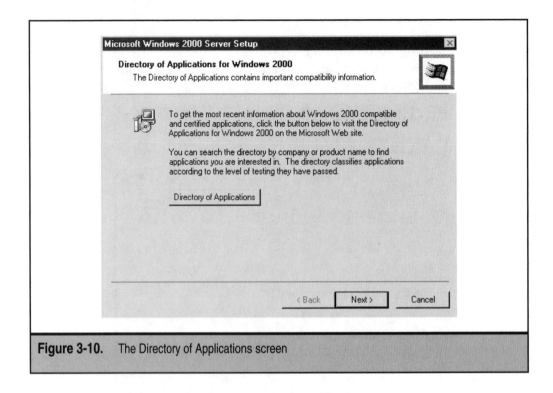

Figure 3-10. The Directory of Applications screen

Setup then restarts the system again. If the existing NT volume was already NTFS, this step is skipped.

Still in graphical mode, Windows 2000 brings up another pretty blue screen. After a brief pause, the Installing Devices screen appears. Here, Setup detects and installs the drivers for all the devices on your computer.

Time: 00:21 min.

The Networking Settings screen appears and installs all the necessary networking components, drivers, protocols, and services.

Time: 00:28 min.

Next comes the Installing Components screen. Setup copies files, updates existing services (IIS), configures all the default components, and installs the standard accessories and management tools.

Time: 00:42 min.

Lastly, the Performing Final Tasks screen appears. Setup installs the Start menu items, registers components in the registry, saves settings, and removes any temporary files that it installed.

Time: 00:59 min. (upgrade complete)

The upgrade is now complete and the system restarts automatically. Remember that how much time the installation or upgrade requires depends on the hardware components involved and the software elements that were installed or upgraded. The last human intervention required occurred at 3 minutes into the upgrade. After that, it's Miller Time. Depending on the services that were installed on the NT 4.0 server prior to the upgrade, you may not be finished just yet.

The First Reboot after Upgrade

Assuming the NT 4.0 Server was not a PDC, the same Configure Your Server screen offers the same three choices described earlier in this chapter under "Configuring Your Server." Do not select the "This is the only server in my network" option if you want this computer to remain a standalone or member server.

If common network services such as WINS, DHCP, or DNS were installed on the NT 4.0 server prior to the upgrade, the first reboot after the upgrade is quite slow and will no doubt yield this familiar message: "One or more services failed to start. Check Event Viewer for details." Actually, the NT 4.0 services were indeed upgraded to Win2K versions during the Installing Components phase of the upgrade process, but the JET databases used by WINS and DHCP, for instance, were not upgraded. However, the first restart tries to load the WINS and DHCP services, fails, and then executes an automatic upgrade on any JET database that the system needs. You need to do nothing to make this happen. It's done automatically. The next reboot will be much faster and will not display any error messages. Be sure to check the Event Viewer System Log because you can view this amazing sequence of events in the log by just following the chronological sequence.

If the system was previously a PDC, then *dcpromo* begins automatically with the Active Directory Installation. It is covered in detail in Chapter 9.

Because Setup never gave you an opportunity to select which services or components you wanted, let's look at what you get. Upgraded versions of standard NT services that are now running are:

▼ Alerter
■ Computer Browser
■ DHCP client
■ Distributed Transaction Coordinator (DTC)
■ DNS client

- Event Log
- License Logging Service, Messenger
- NTLM Security Support Provider
- Plug and Play
- Print Spooler
- Protected Storage
- RPC
- Security Accounts Manager (SAM)
- Server
- TCP/IP NetBIOS Helper
- ▲ Workstation

New Win2K services that are now running as a result of the upgrade are:

- ▼ COM+ Event System
- Distributed File System (Dfs)
- Distributed Link Tracking Client
- FTP Publishing Service (FTP Server)
- IIS Admin
- IPSec Policy Agent
- Logical Disk Manager
- Network Connections
- Remote Registry Service
- Removable Storage
- RunAs (secondary logon) Service
- System Event Notification
- Task Scheduler
- Windows Management Instrumentation (WMI)
- ▲ World Wide Web Publishing Service (IIS Web Server)

If you had previously installed other network services such as WINS, DNS, DHCP, and so on, they are also upgraded and running at this time.

Basically, the same user profile is used with a few upgrades to the new UI in Win2K. You have the same desktop, the same icons, and the same wallpaper. The colors may be different, but all in all the new arrangement is very comfortable for the user.

NT to Win2K upgrades may also be scripted by changing the unattend.txt parameter NtUpgrade=No to NtUpgrade=Yes in the script file.

SUMMARY

Microsoft has done an exceptional job of making what used to be a long and laborious installation process relatively painless. The company has actively searched for ways to make our lives easier—and it's worked. The installation of the OS and most of the services is smooth and reliable. The configuration of complex services is now wizard-driven and straightforward. Microsoft has published and continues to update application compatibility information so that you can plan your upgrade strategies from an informed position. Hats off to Microsoft for this achievement.

CHAPTER 4

Microsoft Management Console

Chapter 4 focuses on the number one tool for administering a Windows 2000 enterprise: the Microsoft Management Console (MMC). Since its inception in the NT 4.0 timeframe the MMC has grown into an administration and management tool so powerful it dwarfs its rivals.

The MMC is actually the Swiss Army Knife of management tools. You name it, it has it. "Twenty tools in one," an ad for the MMC would read. Admins need to understand both the basic and advanced functionality of this tool. In many cases, the MMC is the only tool available to accomplish key administrative tasks in Windows 2000.

MICROSOFT MANAGEMENT CONSOLE (MMC) STRUCTURE

Microsoft took a lot of well-deserved criticism with NT 4.0 because admins had to open a different tool for nearly every task. To create or manage domain users and groups in NT 4.0, you had to go to User Manager for Domains; for local users on member servers or workstations, User Manager; for computer domain accounts, Server Manager; for scheduling tasks, you went to the command prompt. And to make matters worse, Microsoft assigned tasks that didn't seem to fit together to the same tools. To set account policies, for example, you had to go to User Manager for Domains, but that was also where you went to set user rights, set the audit policy for the entire domain, and—get this—set the trust relationships between domains. To set the ACLs on an object, you went to the object itself. Go to Server Manager to configure directory replication. NT 4.0 was very confusing. Being able to go directly to the right tool, the first time, to accomplish a specific task was a matter of perverted pride among NT gurus (me among them).

As NT 4.0 matured, several Microsoft products began to use the MMC as their management tool of choice: SQL 7.0, IIS 4.0, Proxy 2.0, Service Pack 4 Security Configuration Editor. In Windows 2000, the MMC is the default administrative tool. Nearly all Win2K administration can be accomplished in one spot—the MMC.

Understanding the Snap-In Concept

The Microsoft Management Console (MMC) is designed as a framework on which to build tools and utilities for managing computers, systems, networks, and complex services such as the Active Directory. Created to allow the ultimate in extensibility, the MMC is basically an empty shell, as demonstrated in Figure 4-1. The MMC without a snap-in or two can do nothing. The snap-in modules provide the MMC with all of its power and functionality. There are no limits to exactly what a snap-in can do. Existing modules perform everything from relatively simple local tasks such as defragging a disk

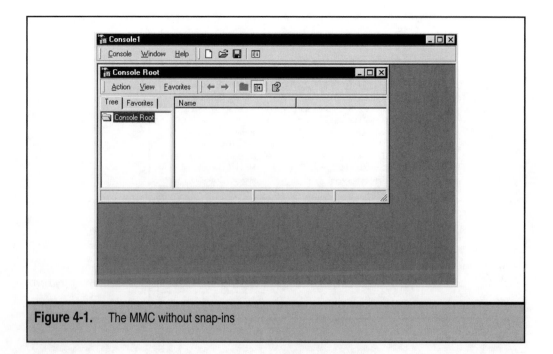

Figure 4-1. The MMC without snap-ins

volume to complex enterprise-wide functions such as managing domains and trusts and moving objects between domains within the Active Directory. Other than disk and storage management utilities from Executive Software, Veritas, and HighGround, Windows 2000 ships with snap-ins created solely by Microsoft. In the future, look for more third-party vendors to provide snap-ins for managing their Win2K-level products. Possibly, these third parties will supply both an independent, standalone management tool and an MMC snap-in. In so doing, third parties will meet Microsoft's requirement for MMC functionality and provide a more vendor-specific management tool.

Adding snap-ins to the MMC is a piece of cake. Click the Start button, choose Run, type **MMC**, and click OK. An empty console window appears (see Figure 4-1). At the top left of the window, click Console to make the drop-down menu appear.

Click the Add/Remove Snap-In command (or press CTRL-M). When the Add/Remove Snap-in dialog box appears, click Add to open the Add Standalone Snap-in dialog box shown in Figure 4-2. It lists all the available standalone snap-ins that you may add to your "empty" console screen. Simply highlight the snap-in you want to load and click the Add button (or double-click).

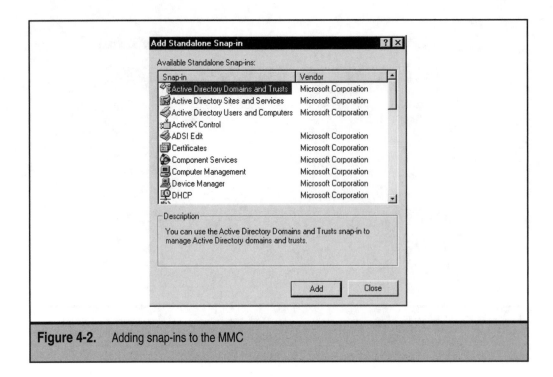

Figure 4-2. Adding snap-ins to the MMC

Every snap-in you add now appears in the Add/Remove Snap-in box. You may add as many snap-ins as desired to your MMC console but you may add only one at a time, standard Windows "list grabbing" functionality (SHIFT, click top & bottom of list or CTRL, click desired items) doesn't work here. When you have completed adding the snap-ins, close the "Add Standalone Snap-in" box and click OK on the "Add/Remove Snap-in" box. Your selections now appear in the Main Console window or console tree.

Snap-In Extensions

You may also choose to load extensions for certain snap-in modules. *Snap-in extensions,* as the name implies, extend the capabilities of snap-in modules. In Figure 4-3, for example, three extensions for the Active Directory Users and Computers snap-in appear: Group Policy, RAS Dialin - User Node Extension, and Terminal Services - Extension. Each snap-in module has its unique set of available extensions, and they can change depending on which of the OS services have been installed. Some snap-ins have no extensions at all. Notice in Figure 4-3 that the default setting is to "add all extensions." Click the Add

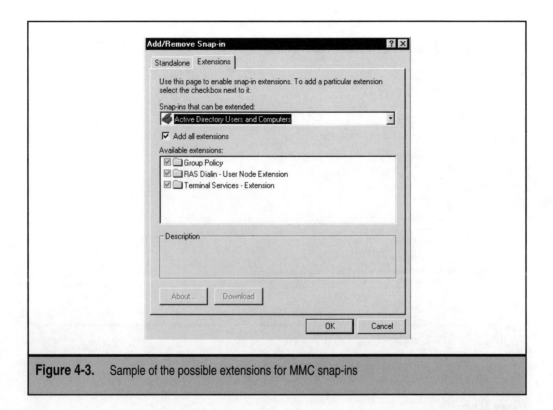

Figure 4-3.   Sample of the possible extensions for MMC snap-ins

All Extensions check box and you are assured by default of receiving the maximum functionality from the snap-in module.

Menu Options

The MMC contains three basic menus: Action, View, and Favorites. We'll discuss the Action and View menus in this section and the Favorites menu in the following section.

Action Menu

The Action menu lists the actions that are currently available to you. Which actions appear depends on what object in the console currently has the focus (in other words, which object is highlighted). Therefore, the Action menu may offer different choices each time you access it. In addition, most of the same choices are available to you by right-clicking the desired object and choosing a command from the context menu, as shown in Figure 4-4.

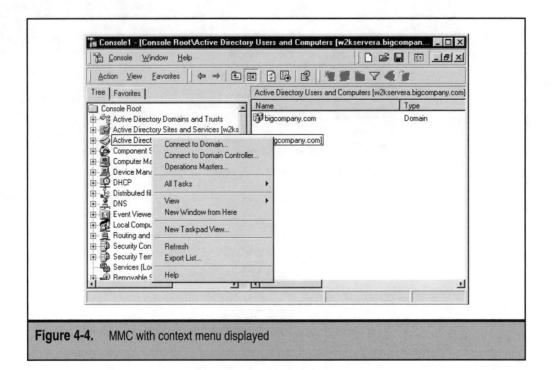

Figure 4-4.   MMC with context menu displayed

View Menu

To obtain the full functionality of the MMC, it is usually necessary for an admin to turn on the Advanced Features option on the View menu. The Advanced Features option is similar to a Show Hidden Files command. Suddenly AD containers that were not there before appear and you discover that every object has a Security Tab on its Properties sheet that wasn't there before either. To fully manage the AD and its security features, you need to check the Advanced Features option.

Checking Users, Groups, and Computers as containers simply allows them to be viewed in the "console" window pane on the left as well as in the "details" pane on the right.

Filter options allow an admin to decide which types of objects are displayed. If you don't care for Microsoft's default filtering options, you may even create your own filter on the fly. In addition, filter options allow you to establish the maximum number of objects to display in each folder. In large environments, establishing a maximum number of objects prevents long waits during the MMC invocation.

As shown in Figure 4-5, the Customize View options give administrators the ability to show or hide each element of the MMC. You can even hide the View menu which is the function we're actually using. If you shoot yourself in the foot by removing the View menu and then wish to go back and customize the view, you can access it from the Customize View option on the System menu (the little hammer icon next to the Console menu).

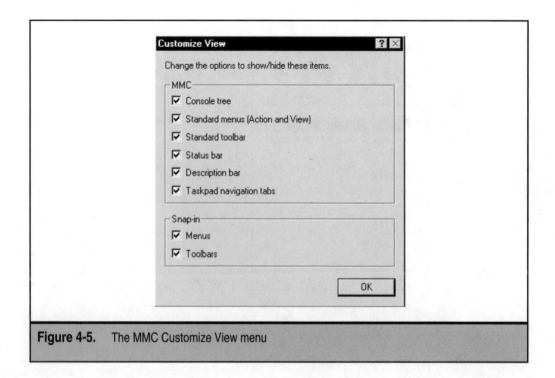

Figure 4-5.   The MMC Customize View menu

ORGANIZING SNAP-INS

One of the problems with a tool that provides as much flexibility as the MMC is that its very flexibility can be its downfall. Adding ten or twenty, even thirty snap-ins to a single console is a fabulous capability but can make for a very crowded and confusing interface. The MMC version (1.2) included with Win2K includes a simple but incredibly effective solution to this problem—the Favorites tab.

Favorites Tab

After the console tree is populated with all the desired snap-ins, you may wish to add certain snap-in views to the Favorites tab. The Favorites tab works much the same way as the Favorites menu in Internet Explorer. Simply highlight a snap-in, click the Favorites menu, and choose Add to Favorites. The current view of the selected item in the console tree is then saved to the Favorites tab. As in IE, you can organize your favorites by creating folders and placing snap-in views in specific folders. In Figure 4-6, for example, four folders have been created on the Favorites tab to hold the different snap-in views. When the MMC holds a large number of snap-ins and they seem to blend together and get lost on the screen, the Favorites concept of organizing them into functional folders proves especially helpful to admins.

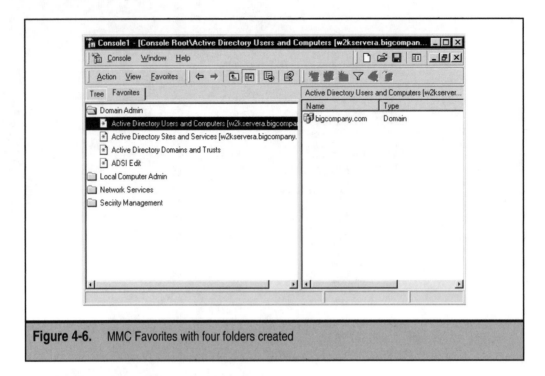

Figure 4-6. MMC Favorites with four folders created

Adding Multiple Instances of the Same Snap-In

As you become adept with the MMC functions, you may wish to load more than one instance or copy of the same snap-in. For example, an admin who has several domains to manage finds it cumbersome and time-consuming to constantly switch between domains in the Active Directory Users and Computers snap-in, so the admin adds one snap-in for each domain, as shown in Figure 4-7. At each Active Directory Users and Computers snap-in present in the Console, the admin connects to a different domain and saves the settings. From now on, the admin can administer multiple domains from the same tool with both domains visible at once. Save the console under DomMnge.msc. Pretty cool.

Here's one more and then you will have to use your imagination to find ways of using multiple instances of the same snap-in. What if you were charged with monitoring the event logs on an entire department's computers? Open a new console, load one copy of the event viewer snap-in *for each computer* you need to manage, save the console as eviewers.msc, and voilà—you've created a tool for monitoring event logs on every machine in the department, as shown in Figure 4-8. A number of snap-ins are computer specific, so you have to select a computer to "point at" or "focus on" with the snap-in when you install it. In Author mode, this "focus" can be changed at any time.

Figure 4-9 shows a completed MMC console with the key administrative snap-ins for managing a typical Windows 2000 domain controller and the Active Directory. This console allows an administrator of a single domain to accomplish nearly every administrative task from his or her Win2K workstation. The default available snap-ins are listed in the next section.

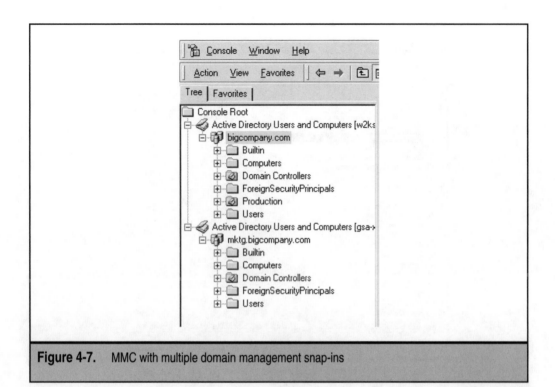

Figure 4-7.   MMC with multiple domain management snap-ins

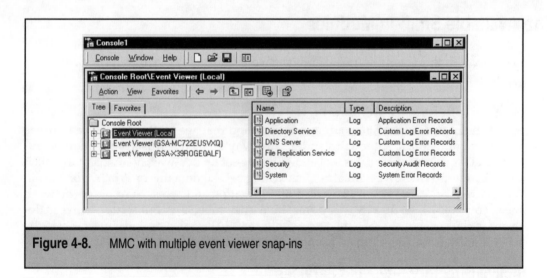

Figure 4-8.   MMC with multiple event viewer snap-ins

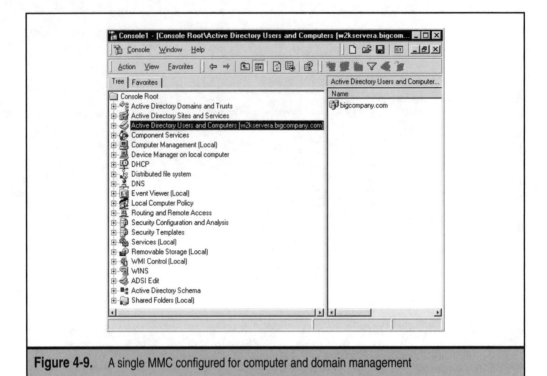

Figure 4-9. A single MMC configured for computer and domain management

The Available Snap-In Modules

Windows 2000 ships with a large number of available snap-ins. Look for even more in the near future as third-party software and hardware vendors begin to weigh in with management and configuration tools for their own products.

Active Directory Domains and Trusts

AD Domains and Trusts allow admins to view and manage all the domains and trusts within an entire forest. Although standard two-way, transitive trusts are configured automatically during *dcpromo*, this tool allows you to set up one-way, nontransitive explicit trusts between Win2K AD domains and existing NT 4.0 domains or Win2K domains in other Active Directory forests. To speed up replication and access to resources between them, you can also set up a two-way, transitive trust, called a *cross-link trust*, between domains in the same forest that are deep within trees. AD Domains and Trusts is also the tool used to transfer the Domain Naming Operations Master role to another DC.

Active Directory Sites and Services

Used primarily to control Active Directory replication, the Active Directory Sites and Services utility manages sites, replication server objects (separate from the computer account), subnets, site links, site link bridges, NTDS settings, and connection objects between servers. You can manage the logical topology of the Active Directory and schedule the replication of the entire forest. Using this tool, you can define the different sites (a well-connected network location), assign subnets to sites, and then use site links to connect it all together. This is also the tool used to specify that a DC will also be a Global Catalog server.

Active Directory Users and Computers

Active Directory Users and Computers is the Big Kahuna. This is where you work with organizational units (OUs), Group Policy object (GPO) links and settings, security and distribution groups, user accounts, computer accounts, shared folders and printers (published in AD), Active Directory permissions, and a host of other objects and tasks. This is the tool used to transfer the PDC Emulator, RID Master, and Infrastructure Master roles to other DCs. The majority of Active Directory administration requires this tool.

ActiveX Control

ActiveX Control allows you to add an already compiled and registered ActiveX Control to your MMC window. A useful way to utilize this snap-in is to write an ActiveX Control that connects to a database of system information, such as one made by SMS. This data could then be displayed by the ActiveX Control within your MMC window.

Certificates

The Certificates snap-in allows you to view details about X.509 certificates, request certificates, find certificates, and view certificate authorities. This tool can manage certificates for a user account, a service account (the services on a particular computer such as the NETLOGON service), or a computer account.

Component Services

Intended for programmers, the Component Services snap-in allows you to view and manage different COM+ settings. You can view the Distributed Transaction Coordinator (DTC)—the client-side part of MTS, the Microsoft Transaction Server—and see a list of transactions and/or statistics about the transactions. You can also view IIS in-process and out-of-process applications or modify the transactional status of a component.

Computer Management

The Computer Management snap-in is essentially a collection of other snap-ins. It has three main categories:

▼ **System Tools**   Device Manager, Event Viewer, Local Users and Groups (disabled on DCs), Performance Logs and Alerts, Shared Folders, System Information

■ **Storage**   Disk Defragmenter, Disk Management, Removable Storage Management

▲ **Services and Applications**   DNS, Indexing Service, Internet Information Services, Services, Telephony, WMI Control

Each of these snap-ins is covered individually later in this section.

Device Manager

Device Manager presents a graphical display of all detected and installed hardware and the associated hardware drivers. Here you can set Plug and Play settings, update drivers, view system resource usage, and resolve hardware conflicts. Similar to the Device Manager in Windows 95/98, this snap-in has a couple of additional features. For example, you can re-scan the Plug and Play devices for hardware changes and turn on or off parameters such as IRQ steering. One "gotcha" is the View Hidden Devices setting. When troubleshooting any kind of device-related problem, be sure you view hidden devices to get a complete picture of what is really happening.

DHCP

The DHCP snap-in lets you authorize (required before it functions, Enterprise Admin only) a DHCP server in the AD. This tool also allows for the creation of new DHCP scopes. You can also define and configure scope options such as Default Gateway and DNS servers. With the DHCP snap-in, you can even configure whether the DHCP server or the client computer is in charge of updating the DNS A and PTR records when granting a lease. Completely new in Win2K DHCP is support for superscopes and multicast scopes.

Disk Defragmenter

Finally a built-in defragmenter! Disk Defragmenter works on FAT16, FAT32, and NTFS volumes on the local machine. Only one instance can be run at a time, and it is designed to be run manually (no built-in scheduling). Disk Defragmenter cannot move the system files, defragment the pagefile, or defragment the Master File Table (MFT), a dynamically grown area that is used to hold the NTFS database of file-to-sector mapping. Disk Defragmenter is intended to be a simple way to retain good input/output performance on data files, and system performance can be enhanced by using some of the features provided by third-party defragmentation utilities. Disk Defragmenter was developed by Executive Software, the makers of Diskeeper.

Disk Management

A replacement for Disk Administrator in NT 4.0, the Disk Management utility allows you to use the new dynamic disk functions in Windows 2000. For example, in a hot-swappable, hard-drive machine, it can re-scan and detect new hard drives. You can also use Disk Management for remote administration to connect to another Windows 2000 machine and manage its disks remotely. After the disks have been changed to dynamic, all disk and volume management is handled without rebooting.

Distributed File System

The Distributed File System snap-in allows you to create new Dfsroots, create new Dfs links (child nodes), and manage the existing Dfs configuration.

DNS

The DNS snap-in is used to manage the new DNS server service that is included with Windows 2000. Using this utility, you can test the DNS server, configure DNS settings, create new DNS zones, and change the DNS zone type and properties.

Event Viewer

Replacing the Event Viewer from NT 4.0, the new Event Viewer snap-in allows you to view and manage event logs such as the Application, Security, and System logs, as in NT 4.0, and you can also view and manage other logs as well, such as Directory Service, DNS Server, and File Replication Service. To use Event Viewer as a centralized, event-viewing tool, you can view the logs on a remote computer and have multiple snap-ins in the MMC that point to different computers.

Fax Service Management

You can use the Fax Service Management tool to configure your computer (and other computers on the network) to send and receive faxes. You can also configure permissions, storage locations, and fax devices.

Folder

Use the Folder snap-in to create a folder hierarchy within the MMC interface (Favorites) to hold other snap-ins. For example, you could have folders for each department in your company and put tools that connect to computers in that department within each folder.

Front Page Server Extensions

Use the Front Page Server Extensions snap-in from within the Internet Information Services snap-in to manage performance settings, permissions settings, and author upload settings.

Group Policy

The Group Policy snap-in links to an existing Group Policy object (GPO) and lets you modify any of its settings, including its permissions. However, the snap-in does not allow the user to select another GPO after it has been added to the MMC console, so you will need to add and configure one of these snap-ins for each GPO you wish to manage within the MMC window.

Indexing Service

Use the Indexing Service snap-in to manage the file system search catalogs on a computer. With it, you can define directories to be included in the search and query the catalogs. This utility affects the file system only. Use multiple snap-ins to connect to each computer you want to administer. The indexing service replaces Find Fast in NT 4.0.

Internet Authentication Service (IAS)

Use the IAS tool to configure your settings for the Remote Authentication Dial-In User Service (RADIUS). It will configure the settings for authorization, authentication, and accounting of your dial-up and virtual private network (VPN) users.

Internet Information Services

Internet Information Services (IIS) has replaced the ISM (Internet Service Manager) from previous versions of IIS. It offers roughly the same functionality as IIS 4.0 does. IIS 5.0 is included with Windows 2000 and installed by default.

IP Security Policy Management

Use IP Security Management to manage the secure communication between computers over TCP/IP. This tool can manage the IPSec policy settings (IP encryption) on a local computer, on a remote computer, or at the domain level.

Link to Web Address

Use the Link to Web Address option to add a URL to be invoked within the MMC. The Web page is displayed in the right pane of the MMC window. The option can be very useful for documentation or intranet-based documentation files. For example, you can point to an internal "User account creation standards" URL.

Local Users and Groups

The Local Users and Groups tool is used to manage users and groups in the local SAM database on a member server or workstation. This option is disabled on domain controllers. A domain controller only uses a separate local mini-SAM in the DS Restore mode and the Recovery Console.

Performance Logs and Alerts

The Performance Logs and Alerts snap-in replaces the Log and Alert views in the Performance Monitor tool in NT 4.0. It does not, however, offer the Chart or Report view. The Report view is completely gone, and the functionality of the Chart view is now under an ActiveX object (you can add it as an ActiveX snap-in) called System Monitor Control.

There's a lot of new functionality within the Log and Alert settings. The NT 4.0-style log files are now called Counter Logs and you can specify how many counters you want to log within an object. You can specify that multiple logs be recorded on a specific schedule with automatic, date-based filenames. You can configure *multiple* events—send a message, start a log to capture data—to occur when an alert threshold is met. A new category of logs called Trace Logs allows you to capture lower-level system data, such as a process thread creation.

One anomaly bears mentioning: With the NT 4.0 Performance Monitor, both physical and logical disk monitoring had to be enabled at the command line with `diskperf -y` or `diskperf -ye` for RAID and then a reboot. However, the objects and counters were always visible in PerfMon even if disk monitoring was not enabled (the disk-activity results would simply show all zeroes).

This behavior changes in Windows 2000. The physical disk object and its counters are enabled by default and are also visible in PerfMon. The logical disk object, however, is hidden in PerfMon because it is not enabled by default. Microsoft chose to hide this object to spare us from seeing all zeroes in the disk performance results simply because we forgot to enable logical disk monitoring at the command line. In order to enable the monitoring of the logical disk object and its counters *and* make the logical disk object visible in PerfMon, go to the command prompt and type:

```
diskperf -yv
```

The system returns the following confirmation:

```
Both Logical and Physical Disk Performance counters on this system
            are now set to start at boot.
```

A reboot will enable both the physical and logical disk objects.

QoS Admission Control

A network control snap-in, the QoS Admission Control tool works with the subnet bandwidth management (SBM) and quality of service (QoS) to configure how, when, and who can use subnet resources. The tool offers settings for data transfer rate, duration, and whether the user can send or receive data. Quality of Service is discussed in Chapter 6 on Network Services.

Removable Storage Management

Use the Removable Storage Management tool to work with removable media such as backup tapes, optical disks, and robotic tape libraries. This snap-in will label and track your media and organize it into media pools.

Routing and Remote Access

The Routing and Remote Access snap-in is used to configure and manage the new Win2K Remote Access Policies and Profiles. This snap-in also allows you to install Routing and Remote Access by clicking the Configure and Enable Routing and Remote Access option on the server object.

Security Configuration and Analysis

Use the Security Configuration and Analysis snap-in to view, analyze, and configure local computer security information. This tool is similar to the Security Configuration Manager (SCM) that was available with NT 4.0 SP4. Use it to create a database of security settings that can be used for future comparisons.

Security Templates

Use the Security Templates tool to create security templates that you can apply to a GPO to define a computer's security settings. You can define things such as event log settings and file and registry ACL permissions. You can even restrict local group membership. Used in conjunction with the Security Configuration and Analysis tool.

Services

Use the Services snap-in to manage a local or remote computer's services. As in NT 4.0, you can configure the logon context and startup options of the service, but you can also configure recovery options when a service fails, create custom names for the services, and view service dependencies.

Shared Folders

The Shared Folders snap-in replaces most of Server Manager from NT 4.0. Use it to manage sharing on a local or remote computer, list files in use, list users connected (and disconnect them), and configure services for Macintosh computers.

System Information

Much like the System Information program in Windows 98 and NT Diagnostics in NT 4.0, the System Information snap-in provides very detailed information about either a local or remote computer. As a display-only tool, it can export this information into a text file, but you will need Device Manager to actually modify device settings.

Telephony

The Telephony snap-in will control the Telephony Application Programming Interface (TAPI) to add telecommunications with voice, data, and video. You can use it to connect over a LAN, the Internet, or a regular phone line.

Terminal Services Configuration

Using Terminal Services Configuration, you can configure connections to terminal services such as encryption level, logon settings, connection times permitted, user disconnect options, and mapping of client resources to their session (such as a printer attached to the client machine).

WINS

Updated from NT 4.0, the WINS snap-in has new features including a consistency check that you can perform on a schedule, set up the server to back up during system shutdown, limit the number of requests the server can handle at one time, and other administrative functions. One key new feature is the ability for an admin to delete an expired record from the WINS database.

WMI Control

Use the Windows Management Instrumentation (WMI) to access your managed enterprise environment. Here you can adjust user and group access, log settings, scripting settings, and the user account used to manage WMI.

CONSOLE OPTIONS

So far our discussions have centered around creating your own consoles and expanding or reconfiguring them at any time. Microsoft calls this *Author mode*, the ability to create and change the console contents and settings. But Author mode is only the beginning. What if you wish to create an MMC console with specific tools and snap-ins and send it to someone in such a way that the recipient cannot change the console? Microsoft uses the term *User mode* to describe the ability to use the snap-ins in a console but without modifying the contents of a console. From the Console menu, choose Options to get to the Options screen shown in Figure 4-10. From there, you can choose which mode to use.

The on-screen descriptions best describe the four choices for console mode. They are described in the following pages.

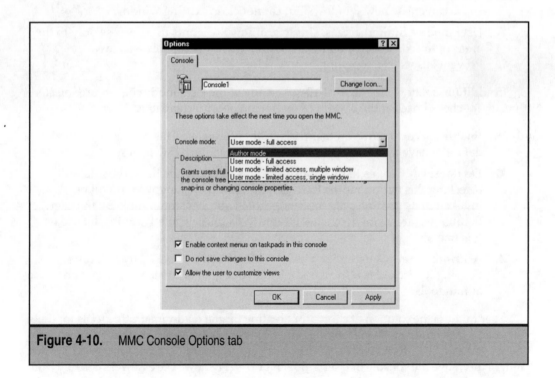

Figure 4-10.   MMC Console Options tab

Author Mode

Author mode, according to the description, "Grants users full access to all MMC functionality, including the ability to add or remove snap-ins, create new windows, create taskpad views and tasks, and view all portions of the console tree." Users may be restricted from entering Author mode via Group Policy. In the Group Policy snap-in or extension, navigate to \User Configuration\Administrative Templates\Windows Components\Microsoft Management Console. There, you will find a large number of settings and restrictions for the MMC, including the following: Restrict the user from entering Author mode.

User Mode

User mode offers three distinct options. Each one gives the user a diminishing level of flexibility, as follows:

▼ **User mode—full access**   "Grants users full access to all window management commands and to the console tree provided. Prevents users from adding or removing snap-ins or changing console properties."

■ **User mode—limited access, multiple window**   "Grants users access only to the areas of the console tree that were visible when the console was saved. Users can create new windows but cannot close existing windows."

▲ **User mode—limited access, single window**   "Grants users access only to the areas of the console tree that were visible when the console was saved. Prevents users from opening new windows."

In addition, as shown in Figure 4-10, when any of the User mode choices are selected, three more check boxes at the bottom of the screen become available:

▼ **Enable context menus on taskpads in this console**   This option is enabled by default. Leave it checked. We'll discuss taskpads in a few pages.

■ **Do not save changes to this console**   This option is unchecked by default. Checking this option means that each time the tool is invoked, it will be invoked in its pristine state, unchangeable and uncustomizeable by the user. Because we are trying to create useable tools for delegated admins, let's leave this one off.

▲ **Allow the user to customize views**   This option is checked by default. Leaving it checked is also a good idea if your goal is efficient, customized admin tools.

User mode is the solution of choice for creating targeted administrative tools for delegated administrators. In Author mode, you can include the snap-ins that admins genuinely need and then focus each snap-in on the appropriate domain, OU, or computer, and, finally, save the console in User mode. Figure 4-11 shows the eviewers console from an earlier discussion saved in User mode—limited access, single window. Notice that the

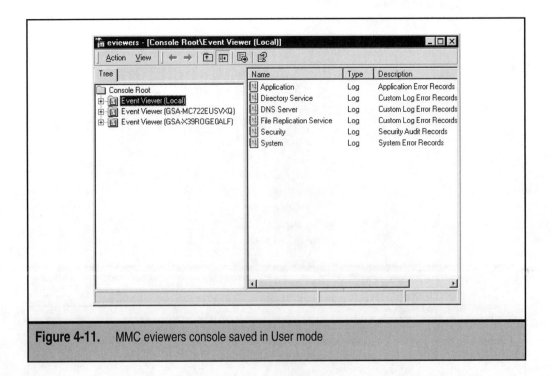

Figure 4-11.   MMC eviewers console saved in User mode

entire menu bar on the top is missing, making it impossible to add anything to this console. User mode creates a tool to be used, not modified or extended.

Administrative Tools

In NT 4.0 Server, clicking the Start button, choosing Programs, and choosing Administrative Tools leads you to a list of separate utilities such as User Manager/User Manager for Domains, Server Manager, Event Viewer, and Performance Monitor, as shown in Figure 4-12. These standalone NT utility programs are each separate and discrete. They have no relationship with each other and, in fact, they have very little in common. If you need to perform domain/server administration from an NT 4.0 workstation or a Win 9x computer, you must load the server tools onto that workstation from the NT 4.0 Server CD at \CLIENTS\SRVTOOLS\WINNT or WIN95\I386. At this location on the CD you will find, as a separate file, each individual tool you will need to perform NT server/domain administration from a Win 9x or NT workstation.

In Windows 2000 Server, clicking the Start button, choosing Programs, and choosing Administrative Tools brings up a list of MMC snap-ins, as shown in Figure 4-13. They may not look like MMC snap-ins because each one is individually wrapped as its own separate MMC console, but don't be confused because all are snap-ins, tried and true. You can't change or add to these administrative tool consoles in any way because they've

Figure 4-12. NT 4.0 PDC Administrative Tools menu

Figure 4-13. Win2K Administrative Tools menu

been saved by Microsoft in User mode—limited access, single window and you can't customize views or save changes.

As we add more services to the Win2K server or domain controller, more administrative tools are added to the list, as shown in Figure 4-14. These dedicated tools are stored as read-only .msc files in the \%WINNT%\SYSTEM32 folder along with the MMC.EXE file itself. If you need to administer a Win2K domain structure from a Win2K Professional workstation, you must load the *adminpak.msi* from the Win2K Server or Advanced Server CD at \I386. This single, self-installing file loads all the necessary tools for administering a Win2K domain and/or server. It installs all of the shipping snap-ins to the \%WINNT%\ SYSTEM32 folder so that they will be available for an admin to place in the MMC console. In addition, *adminpak.msi* adds a full complement of Active Directory and server administration tools to the Administrative Tools menu of the Win2K Professional workstation.

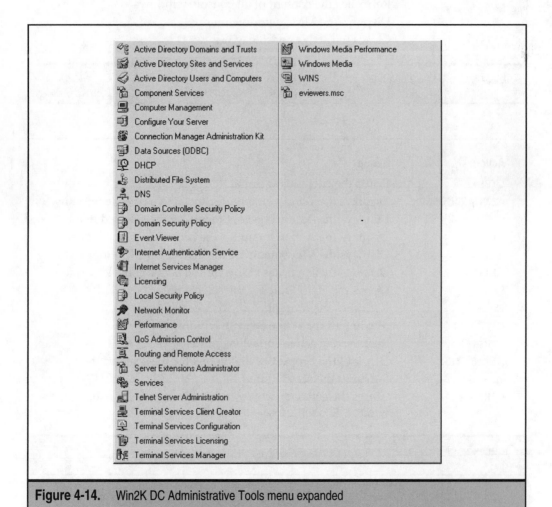

Figure 4-14.   Win2K DC Administrative Tools menu expanded

Keyboard Shortcuts

In addition to the GUI functionality, the MMC offers a number of keyboard shortcuts. They are explained in Table 4-1 and 4-2.

Action	Result
CTRL+O	Opens a saved console
CTRL+N	Opens a new console
CTRL+S	Saves the open console
CTRL+M	Adds or removes a console item
CTRL+W	Opens a new window
F5	Refreshes the content of all console windows
ALT+SPACEBAR	Displays the MMC window menu
ALT+F4	Closes the active console window

Table 4-1.   MMC Main Window Keyboard Shortcuts

Action	Result
CTRL+P	Prints the current page or active pane
ALT+MINUS SIGN	Displays the Window menu for the active console window
SHIFT+F10	Displays the Action shortcut menu for the selected item
ALT+A	Displays the Action menu for the active console window
ALT+V	Displays the View menu for the active console window
ALT+F	Displays the Favorites menu for the active console window
F1	Opens the Help topic for the selected item
F5	Refreshes the content of all console windows
CTRL+F10	Maximizes the active console window
CTRL+F5	Restores the active console window
ALT+ENTER	Displays the Properties dialog box for the selected item
F2	Renames the selected item
CTRL+F4	Closes the active console window. If only one console window is open, closes the whole console.

Table 4-2.   MMC Console Window Keyboard Shortcuts

Taskpads and Tasks

A taskpad view, which appears in the console pane of the MMC window, allows you to create shortcuts, called tasks, that can run everything from wizards, scripts, and programs, to external DOS commands, to snap-ins, to Web pages. All the while, the tasks continue to operate from inside the MMC. Tasks can be very powerful indeed, especially if scripting or batch-file programming are among your talents. The ability to execute a script to replicate AD changes immediately is an excellent use of the task functionality. For example, as shown in Figure 4-15, suppose that, while you are in the MMC, you want the ability to edit the logon scripts for the domain; highlight the domain name, right-click, choose New Taskpad View, complete the wizard, continue with the New Task wizard, and enter the appropriate information.

When complete, simply double-clicking the icon will load Notepad and the logon script for editing , as shown in Figure 4-16. You never leave the MMC. This is but one example of the kind of power that the MMC provides for network administrators who are willing to take a little time up front to save a lot of time down the road.

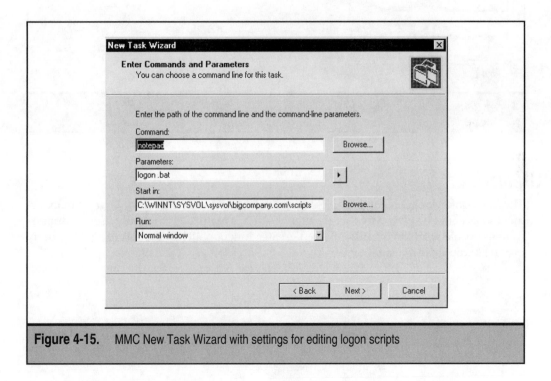

Figure 4-15.   MMC New Task Wizard with settings for editing logon scripts

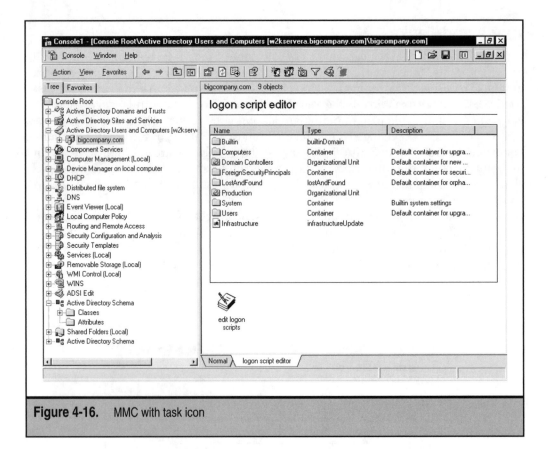

Figure 4-16.   MMC with task icon

SUMMARY

The Microsoft Management Console began its life as an experiment to see if all management tools could be placed in a single interface. It has matured into a truly useful administrative console with the promise of even greater functionality in the future as third-party products ship their management and configuration tools as MMC snap-in modules.

CHAPTER 5

Implementing the Windows 2000 File Systems

Chapter 5 will cover some disk fundamentals as well as the details of the three major file systems available in Windows 2000. Windows 2000 is backward-compatible with all previous Microsoft operating systems. It also features the new NTFS version 5 (NTFSv5) and significant performance-enhancing storage technologies such as Intelligent I/O (I_2O), Fiber Channel, and IEEE 1394 (Firewire).

Windows 2000's full support of I_2O-capable storage cards relieves the server's CPU by offloading processing to the microprocessor on I_2O-capable storage cards. By layering into the SCSI stack, Windows 2000 Server takes advantage of the 1-gigabit-per-second data transfer rate of Fiber Channel, an ANSI and OSI open standard using common transport protocols over copper and fiber-optic cabling. Commonly known as Firewire, IEEE 1394 is a standard for high-speed peripheral connections. Look for it primarily on Storage Area Networks (SANs) providing high-speed connectivity to a centralized bank of incredibly large storage devices and also connecting to multimedia devices, providing a single connection for audio/visual data and control.

DISK FUNDAMENTALS

To administer Windows 2000, you do not normally need to understand the physical operation of disks (and their various components such as motor, platters, cylinders, heads, and so on) nor the encoding schemes used to place data on the surface of the platters. However, to enhance both troubleshooting skills and to aid in selecting a file system, it is useful for an administrator to understand some of the more technical aspects of the organization of disks: the logical structure and the role this logical structure plays in the operating system's ability to store and retrieve data. In this section, we will examine the fundamentals of the logical structure of disks and its role in the bootup of the operating system.

Defining Logical Disk Elements

It is the logical structure that allows an operating system to boot up and to store and retrieve data. This discussion starts with sectors. A hard drive system is divided into sectors within the tracks on both sides of every platter that makes up the physical structure. Strictly speaking, the sectors and tracks are part of the low-level format of a disk (sometimes referred to as the "physical format"). The tracks are "overlaid" by the logical structure, which is placed on the disk by an operating system's partitioning and format program. The details of this logical structure vary according to the operating system used. In the world of IBM PC compatibles (yes, that term lives on nearly 20 years after the introduction), each sector holds 512 bytes of data.

Master Boot Record (MBR)

The first sector on a physical disk is the master boot record (MBR), which is created when a disk is first partitioned. It contains executable code (the master boot code), the disk signature, and the partition table for that physical disk—all within one 512-byte sector.

Partition Table

The partition table takes up only 64 bytes of the MBR, and within these few bytes, the type and location of partitions on the hard disk are identified. The partition table can define up to four partitions, with each defining entry only 16 bytes long. The types of partitions defined in the partition table are limited to *primary*, of which there can be up to four, and *extended*, of which there can be only one. Remember, only a total of four partitions can be defined in the partition table.

Partitions

Each primary partition has as its first sector the boot sector, containing executable code and data placed there by the operating system that formatted the disk.

Of the partitions defined in a partition table, only one can be marked as active, and it must be a primary partition. This primary partition is used during the bootup process, described later in this chapter. For now, we'll stay with partitions.

Many of us have seen and worked with disks in the past that appeared to be partitioned into more than four partitions. If done with only a pre-Windows 2000 Microsoft operating system, this trick can be performed by taking advantage of the extended partition's ability to have more than one logical drive volume assigned to it. The additional information to define these logical drive volumes is kept on disk within the volumes themselves, in an extended boot record, containing an extended partition table. We won't go too deep here, except to say that the extended partition table of each logical volume contains information about both the current volume and the next volume. We can see that locating these extended volumes involves a search by the operating system that begins in the partition table of the MBR and continues through the extended partition table of each logical volume, until the desired logical volume is reached.

Clusters

Space for files in all the disk file systems supported by Windows 2000 is allocated in clusters (also known as "file allocation units"), which consist of one or more sectors. The efficiency of Windows 2000's file systems in regard to clusters varies, with FAT16 winning the prize for the most wasted space because it requires clusters to be as large as 64KB (see Table 5-1 for information on FAT16 cluster sizes, later in this chapter). FAT32 has more reasonable cluster sizes, allowing 4KB clusters for partitions as large as 8GB (see Table 5-2). The NTFS file system of NT and Windows 2000 has cluster sizing similar to FAT32, with that file system's many other benefits, such as security and recoverability (described later in this chapter).

Windows 2000 File System Components

Windows 2000 supports Microsoft's proprietary file system, NTFS, in a new version 5 (NTFSv5), as well as FAT16 and FAT32. In this section, we will discuss these file systems under Windows 2000, as well as a "quasi" file system, Distributed File System (Dfs).

Support for FAT16 and FAT32 is included in Windows 2000 for backward-compatibility with previous Microsoft and non-Microsoft products. Previously, FAT16 was simply known as the FAT file system. Since the advent of FAT32, with Windows 95 OEM Service Release 2 (OSR2), we often use the term "FAT16" to refer to this venerable file system with its roots in the early IBM PC days. Before we discuss the details of these file systems, let's define a few terms that apply to all three of the Win2K-supported file systems.

Clusters

Cluster is the more popular term for file allocation unit, the minimum space that can be allocated to a file or directory. Even on NTFS volumes, space is allocated in clusters. Tables in the following sections define the default cluster sizes of disk volumes formatted with these three file systems.

ALLOCATION OF CLUSTERS   The File Allocation Table (FAT) is where the FAT file systems get their names. The FAT is a list of entries, stored near the beginning of a disk, having a one-to-one mapping with the data clusters on disk. The operating system uses the File Allocation Table when saving and retrieving files.

NTFS uses a mostly relational database structure to store files and directories on disk. It also allocates space in clusters and tracks the cluster usage within the Master File Table (MFT), the core of this file system.

Directory Structure

On both FAT16 and FAT32, a directory, also called a "folder," is a special disk storage area that is used by the operating system to store the location of files and child directories (subdirectories or subfolders). Think of a FAT disk directory as a tiny flat-file database with each record holding just 32 bytes of data. Each record of this little database is a directory entry, storing information about a single directory or file. The location of a file or directory is recorded in the directory entry as a reference to the starting cluster number of the file or directory. Along with the cluster number, the following information is stored in a FAT16 directory entry: filename, file extension, date and time of creation or modification, size, and attributes. FAT32 directories hold the same information, with an additional field to accommodate the larger cluster values. When retrieving a file or directory, the operating system locates the appropriate directory entry and then, using the starting cluster value, looks in the File Allocation Table to find out where all the pieces to the file or directory are located. Therefore, every file or directory access involves two lookup tables, the directory and the FAT.

NTFS does not have the FAT files system's inefficient lookup method; instead, it stores a directory as an index of filenames prefixed with a path. Indexing and sorting of filenames makes NTFS more efficient at locating files. Directories are stored in the Master

File Table (MFT), treated as files, and managed as a hierarchical structure within the mostly relational database design of the file system.

EIGHT-DOT-THREE (8.3) FILENAMES   Beginning with the early days of DOS, we lived within the constraints of filenames that could have only a maximum of eight characters in the filename itself, separated by a period from an extension with a maximum of three characters. This filename constraint remained entrenched through all the versions of DOS and Windows 3.x but was broken with the introduction of Windows NT and Windows 95.

LONG FILENAMES   The FAT directory structure was designed to accommodate only 8.3 DOS-style file names. Therefore, Windows 95, Windows 98, Windows NT, and Windows 2000 have a scheme for getting around this limit in order to store long filenames on FAT volumes. They all use multiple directory entries for directories or files containing a long filename. Simply stated, the standard directory information and an 8.3 alias name is stored in a primary directory entry, and one additional, or secondary, directory is allocated to store each of the 13 characters of the filename. For this reason, the 512-entry hard-coded limit of the root directory of a FAT16 volume can be exhausted by 256 or fewer entries. Why only 13 characters per directory entry when each is 32 bytes long? Because in NT and Windows 2000, each character is stored as a Unicode character, which requires 2 bytes; therefore, 26 bytes are actually used for each of the 13 characters of a filename.

NTFS is more flexible in its ability to store long filenames. It never had the constraints of the 8.3 filenames as in FAT file systems. From its inception, NTFS was designed to hold long filenames. For this reason, NTFS is capable of holding a nearly infinite number of files in its root directory. For backward-compatibility with older applications, NTFS stores a converted 8.3 alias for each long filename.

WINDOWS 2000 FILE SYSTEMS

Each volume of your Windows 2000 installation has the potential of one of the three file systems: FAT16, capable of volumes up to 2GB; FAT32, capable of volumes up to 32GB; and NTFSv5, capable of volumes up to 16 exabytes (a really big volume).

FAT16 Details

When a FAT16 volume is formatted, the size of the volume determines the default cluster size. The cluster number cannot exceed a value that can be represented by 16 bits and must be a power of two. A user can specify a different cluster size if the volume is formatted with the Format program from the command prompt. Table 5-1 shows the default cluster sizes for FAT16 volumes.

FAT 16 Volume Size	Cluster Size
0MB–32MB	512 bytes
33MB–64MB	1KB
65MB–128MB	2KB
129MB–255MB	4KB
256MB–511MB	8KB
512MB–1,023MB	16KB
1,024MB–2,047MB	32KB
2,048MB–4,095MB	64KB

Table 5-1. FAT16 Default Cluster Sizes

FAT32 Details

Windows 2000 now supports the FAT32 file system first introduced with Windows 95 OSR2. While Windows 98 theoretically supports FAT32 volumes up to 2TB (terabytes), Windows 2000 will format FAT32 volumes only up to 32GB in size. Table 5-2 lists the default cluster sizes for FAT32 under Windows 2000. The maximum file size for FAT32 is 4GB less 2 bytes. Windows 2000 can utilize FAT32 volumes greater than 32GB when upgrading a system from Windows 98 that has had larger volumes created before the upgrade. This limit is by design. The recommended file system for Windows 2000 is NTFS.

Microsoft implemented FAT32 with few changes to the existing FAT16 architecture in order to remain compatible with existing software and device drivers. One of the most significant changes was the use of 4 bytes to store cluster values as opposed to FAT16's use of 2 bytes, or 16 bits, for cluster values—hence, the *16* in *FAT16* and the *32* in *FAT32*. Therefore, internal and on-disk data structures and application programming interfaces (APIs) had to be revised, expanded, or disabled to support this new file system and to protect it from damage from MS-DOS FAT16–based disk utilities.

With all this talk about cluster size, I'll bet you're wondering how to see the cluster size of a volume. If you like to work from the GUI, the Windows 2000 Defragmentation Tool's defragmentation report will give you this information, as shown in Figure 5-1. More on using this tool later.

FAT32 Volume Size	Default Cluster Size
Less than 8GB	4KB
Greater than or equal to 8GB, and less than 16GB	8KB
Greater than or equal to 16GB, and less than 32GB	16KB
Greater than or equal to 32GB	32KB

Table 5-2. FAT32 Default Cluster Sizes

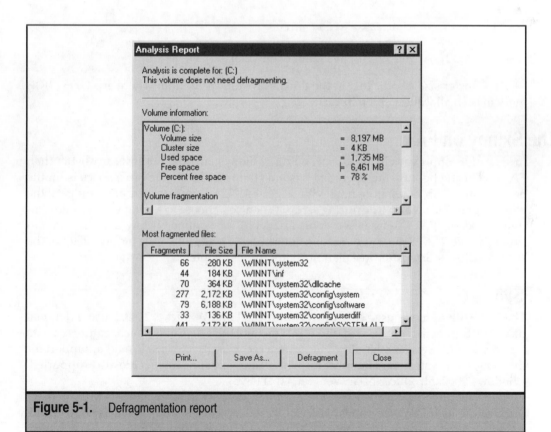

Figure 5-1. Defragmentation report

Since most administrators are comfortable with the command prompt, I suggest you open a command prompt and run good ole chkdsk on a volume (chkdsk *d*:). Following is the output from running this command on a FAT32 volume:

```
The type of the file system is FAT32.
Volume Serial Number is 6017-69CB
Windows is verifying files and folders...
0 percent completed.
50 percent completed..
100 percent completed...
File and folder verification is complete.
Windows has checked the file system and found no problem.
1,453,019,136 bytes total disk space.
 4,096 bytes in 1 files.
1,453,010,944 bytes available on disk.

 4,096 bytes in each allocation unit.
 354,741 total allocation units on disk.
 354,739 allocation units available on disk.
```

The cluster size is indicated in the third line from the bottom. There are 4,096 (4KB) bytes in each allocation unit (cluster).

The Skinny on FAT

In spite of its improved cluster sizes, the FAT32 file system does not scale any better than FAT16. During bootup, the operating system computes how much free space is on the boot volume. This takes more time with larger FAT32 volumes, so the bigger it gets, the worse it gets. This is also true during setup. When you choose to format volumes in Windows 2000 as "FAT," they will default to FAT16 for volumes below 2GB in size and FAT32 above 2GB. Read more reasons not to bother with FAT in Windows 2000 in the section "Cluster Size After Installation," later in this chapter.

NTFSv5

The NTFS file system is used solely by Windows NT and Windows 2000. It uses relational database, transaction processing, and object technologies to provide such features as data security and file system reliability. File system recovery, large storage media, support for the POSIX subsystem, and support for object-oriented applications are also supported. Windows 2000 introduces NTFS version 5 (NTFSv5).

New features in NTFSv5 include support for Hierarchical Storage Management through the use of reparse points, disk quotas, encryption, sparse files, Distributed Link Tracking, the Distributed File System (Dfs), NTFS directory junctions, volume mount points, Indexing Service, and the change journal.

As with the other file systems, NTFS uses clusters to allocate disk space to files and directories. Although the default cluster size depends on the volume size, an administrator can specify a cluster size when formatting a volume. The Disk Management Tool allows a user to specify a cluster size only up to 4KB. Windows 2000 supports file compression but not on volumes with cluster sizes above 4KB. Therefore, the default NTFS cluster size for Windows 2000 never exceeds 4KB (see Table 5-3). When using FORMAT from the command line, a user can specify any of the cluster sizes supported by NTFS, which includes 512 bytes, 1KB, 2KB, 4KB, 8KB, 16KB, 32KB, and 64KB.

Shared Folders in Active Directory

Windows 2000 allows us to share folders as standard, old fashioned SMB (Server Message Blocks) shares. In addition, a share can be published in Active Directory. Once published, a user using the Active Directory search tools can locate the Shared Folder object from anywhere in the Active Directory without depending on their memory or the browser service to locate the share, or on special logon files to make a connection. See the discussion on Shared Folder objects in Chapter 11.

Enhancements to File Sharing

Three important enhancements to File Sharing in Windows 2000 are improved, more flexible management through the Computer Management snap-in, offline files, and the ability to optionally publish shared folders in Active Directory.

ADMINISTERING SHARES THROUGH COMPUTER MANAGEMENT   Of course, you can still use Explorer to create folder shares, but Computer Management is a much more powerful and flexible tool. If you have the required permissions, you may create and manage shares on the local computer or connect a remote computer and do the same. Computer Management has wizards for multi-step tasks, such as creating shares. The Create Shared Folders Wizard allows for the creation of the folder itself. Access the File Sharing Console through Computer Management | System Tools | Shared Folders (Figure 5-2).

NTFSv5 Volume size	Default Cluster size
512MB or less	512 bytes
513MB–1,024MB	1KB
1,025MB–2,048MB	2KB
Greater than 2,048MB	4KB

Table 5-3.   NTFSv5 Default Cluster Sizes

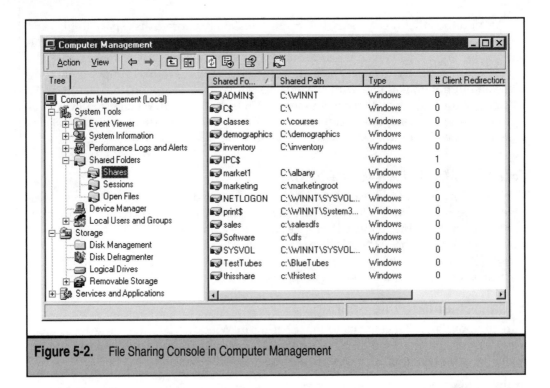

Figure 5-2. File Sharing Console in Computer Management

Published folders can be found in Active Directory using Start Menu | Search | For Files or Folders by anyone having adequate permissions.

Note that before a Shared Folder object can be created in AD, the actual NTFS folder must be shared in the exact same way as you did it in NT 4.0. In Windows Explorer, right-click the folder you wish to share and choose Sharing. Click the radio button next to Share This Folder, type the share name, set the permissions if necessary, and click OK. The folder is now shared using the traditional SMB sharing protocol. Or, if you prefer, type the following at the command line:

```
net share sharename=drive:path
```

In the MMC (Microsoft Management Console) Active Directory Users and Computers, choose the organizational unit (OU) where you would like the Shared Folder object to appear, right-click, and choose New | Shared Folder. The New Object – Shared Folder dialog box appears. Fill in the name that you want displayed in the Active Directory. Then complete the network path with the UNC name (*server**share*) of the preexisting shared folder on a Win2K, NT, or other Microsoft OS–based computer. The AD Shared Folder object now appears in the MMC under the OU.

Offline Files

Another important enhancement to File Sharing in Windows 2000 is offline files, which finally achieves what Briefcase promised and more. Working with network files offline is actually possible due to an enhancement to the network redirector, rather than a file system feature, but I like to talk about it with file systems. There are two sides to offline files: the server side and the client side.

When you create shared folders at the server, you can specify the caching mode for the files and programs in the share. This is the server side of offline files, and these are your choices for the caching mode, configurable for each share (see Figure 5-3):

▼ **Manual Caching for Documents**   In this case, the user will have to manually specify any documents they want to work with offline.

■ **Automatic Caching for Documents**   Open files in a share operating in this mode will automatically be downloaded to the local client's offline cache and be available for offline work.

▲ **Automatic Caching for Programs**   All files and programs within the folder are made available offline, not just those the user has opened.

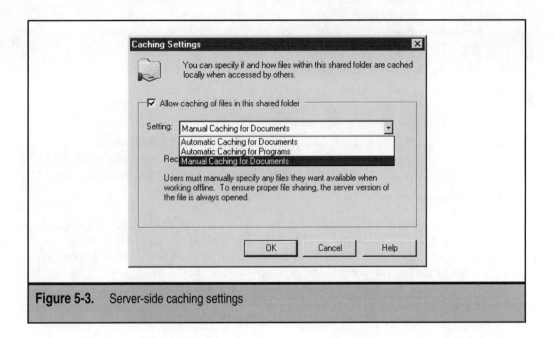

Figure 5-3.   Server-side caching settings

USING OFFLINE FILES   When you create a shared folder through the GUI, caching is turned on, and the default mode is Manual Caching for Documents. To disable caching on existing shares, you must go into the properties of the share and clear the Allow Caching of Files in This Shared Folder check box.

The command-line utility, NET SHARE, enables you to create and share, set permissions on the share, and disable caching, all in one operation using the following syntax:

```
net share sharename=drive:path /cache:manual
```

Actually, you can use this command to do much more than that! For more information about NET SHARE, open a command prompt in Windows 2000 and type:

net share /?

On the client side of things, the access to Offline Files settings is available through Explorer I Tools I Folder Options I Offline Files. These settings are system-wide, and you will find that, by default, this option is turned on for Windows 2000 Professional computers and turned off for Win2K Servers. Once enabled, you can select the following settings (Figure 5-4):

▼   Enable Offline Files.

■   Synchronize All Offline Files Before Logging Off.

■   Enable Reminders. If this setting is selected, you configure the frequency in which you will receive balloon reminders from 1 to 9,999 minutes. These reminders appear when a server to which you are attached for file sharing goes offline.

■   Place Shortcut to Offline Files Folder on the Desktop.

■   Amount of Disk Space to Use for Temporary Offline Files. This setting is expressed as a percentage of disk space, as well as the actual MB or GB. It is set at 10 percent by default.

■   Delete Files (button). This allows you to delete the locally stored, offline versions of files. You can choose to delete only the temporary offline files, or both the temporary offline files and the files that are always available offline.

▲   View Files (button).

On the client side, these offline files are stored in the Client Side Cache, %SYSTEMROOT%\CSC, a hidden folder. You can create a shortcut to it, as indicated in the settings listed previously; and you can look at the folder and see the files, but not what they are. This folder has the potential to *grow*, so if you would like to move this folder, the utility cachemov.exe, available in the Win2K Resource Kit, will do the trick.

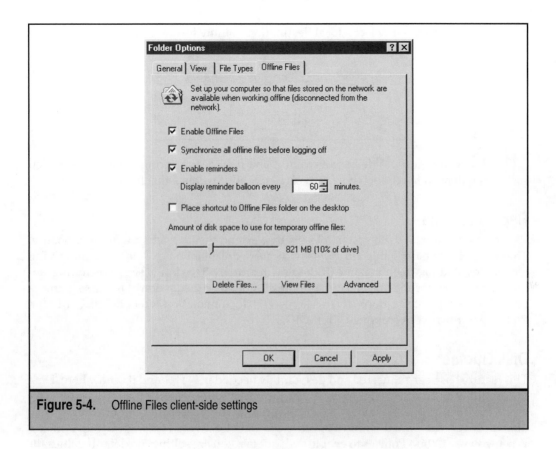

Figure 5-4.   Offline Files client-side settings

Go to a command prompt and type **cachemov**. The Offline Files Cache Mover v1.0 screen appears.

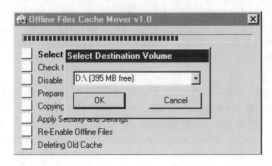

You are prompted to select a local destination volume for the cache. Select a volume and click OK. You may get an error message.

Click OK. If you try to delete this folder, you may get a sharing violation, in which case you will need to reboot before you can successfully delete this folder.

Reparse Points

Reparse points are new file system objects that extend the I/O subsystem functionality. These objects have definable attributes with user-controlled data. This is an underlying technology that has been in some of the new features offered in NTFSv5 including Remote Storage Server and volume mount points. A detailed discussion of Reparse Points is beyond the scope of this book. Even Microsoft's documentation refers the reader to the Platform Software Development Kit (SDK).

Disk Quotas

This feature has been requested and desperately needed in NTFS, and it is now here. Disk quotas allow an administrator to limit the amount of space a specific user may utilize on an NTFSv5 volume. Disk quotas are configured on a per user, per volume basis. Disk quotas for servers located within a specific OU can be activated through Group Policies. When you use Group Policies to enable disk quotas, you are setting the default values for every volume on each server in the container. The built-in Administrators group is not affected by disk quotas. To alter the default quotas for individual users, you must go to the Properties of the specific volume, click the Quota tab and then the Quota Entries button. This will give you a list of users and their current quota usage. You can now configure different quotas for individual users by right-clicking on the specific user.

Applications checking for sufficient disk space during setup will use the amount returned by the available quota of the installing user, not the amount of space actually available on the disk.

USING DISK QUOTAS   To enable disk quotas on an individual volume in My Computer or Windows Explorer, right-click on the volume. Select Properties | Quota (Figure 5-5). Be careful because when enabling disk quotas on an individual volume, the defaults limit the disk space for each user to 1KB each. Be sure and change this quota to something more realistic.

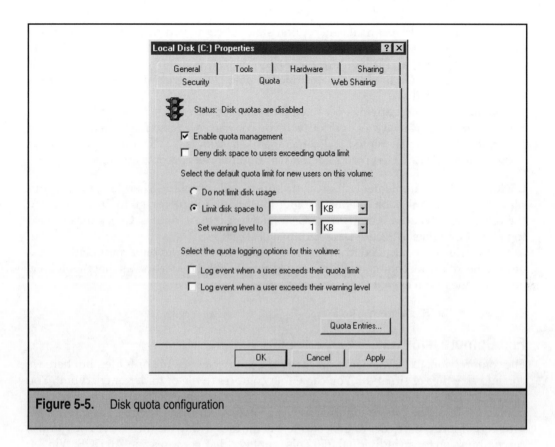

Figure 5-5.   Disk quota configuration

Encrypting File System (EFS)

The new encryption capabilities of NTFSv5 provide enhanced security for files and folders on NTFS volumes. Through the Encrypting File System (EFS), Windows 2000 stores data in encrypted form using 56-bit DES (Data Encryption Standard) encryption, even providing security when the storage media are removed from a Windows 2000 system. It uses a strong public key–based cryptographic scheme to encrypt files and folders. The owner initiates the encryption by placing their key in the Data Decryption Field (DDF), and after that, decryption and encryption happen transparently when the user reads or writes to an encrypted file. Should a user leave the company while their files are still encrypted, Win2K provides the data recovery agent. The recovery agent decryption key is placed in the Data Recovery Field (DRF) of each encrypted file or folder. By default, the administrator (acting as the data recovery agent) transparently uses this key to decrypt an encrypted file.

An encrypted file retains its encryption state when moved or renamed, regardless of the encrypted state of the destination folder. So you could move an encrypted file to an unencrypted folder, and it would remain encrypted. If you move an unencrypted file to an encrypted folder, the file remains unencrypted. Also, renaming does not change a file's encrypted status.

On the other hand, copying encrypted files is a little different because EFS follows the rule that encryption always takes priority. If you copy an encrypted file to an unencrypted folder, it will remain encrypted as long as the file system is NTFS. And, if you copy an unencrypted file to an encrypted folder, it will automatically become encrypted.

USING EFS EFS is implemented as an attribute of a file or folder. Therefore, to encrypt a file or folder, right-click on the file or folder in Windows Explorer, go to Properties, and then click the Advanced button on the General tab next to Attributes. Check the box next to Encrypt Contents to Secure Data and then click OK.

EFS can also be controlled from the command line using the cipher command. For example, the following command will encrypt the \SECURE folder and all of its subfolders and continue to run even if there are errors:

```
cipher /E /S:secure /I /F
```

File Compression

File compression, like EFS, is implemented as an attribute of a file or folder, but here we run into an either-or situation. You can either compress a file or folder or encrypt it. You cannot do both. Once the attribute is set for compression, NTFS automatically compresses the files. You can set compression on a folder or an entire volume, which does not actually compress the folder or the volume, but the files within the directory. You can also set compression for an individual file. This is unlike "disk compression" in DOS, Win 3.*x*, and Win 9*x*, which was really pretty scary, because it compressed an entire volume into a large file, making it appear to be an actual drive as long as certain drivers were loaded.

If you are using file compression, it is important to understand the effect moving and copying a file can have on the compression attribute of the file. This has not changed since Windows NT 4.0, but it is worth a short recap here. In all cases, except one, the file or folder being moved or copied takes on the compression attribute of the new parent folder. The only exception is when a file or folder is moved between folders on the same NTFS partition. In this case, the original compression status remains with the file.

Sparse Files

NTFSv5 Sparse File Support allows programs to create very large files that consume very little disk space. When the sparse file attribute is set, the I/O subsystem will not allocate to disk large strings of data composed of zeros (nonmeaningful data). Only meaningful data will consume disk space. When a file with the sparse attribute set is read from disk, the file is re-assembled to contain the meaningful data that was stored to disk as well as the nonmeaningful data. This requires an application that is sparse file–aware and knows how to set the sparse file attribute. This feature is for use with *really* big files (that is, 1TB or more).

Distributed Link Tracking

The Distributed Link Tracking service of NTFSv5 allows client applications to track files or OLE embedded objects, referenced by shortcuts and OLE links, that have been renamed or moved locally or within a domain. Client applications that take advantage of this service can use it to locate objects that have been moved or renamed since the program made a reference, or link, to the object. For example, if a user creates a shortcut to a data file formatted with NTFSv5 from within Windows 2000, and the file is subsequently moved to another volume with NTFSv5 under Windows 2000 within the same domain, the tracking service will find the file.

The types of changes tracked include:

▼ Renaming the link source

■ Moving the link source within the same volume

■ Moving the link source between two volumes on the same computer

■ Moving the link source between two computers in the same domain

■ Moving a volume from one computer to another in the same domain

■ Renaming a computer within a domain

▲ Changing a network share under which the link source is shared

Volume Mount Points

Volume mount points, also referred to as "junctions," allow you to expand an existing NTFSv5 volume onto another volume or volumes within the same computer. Sounds a little like the old volume sets, doesn't it? Well, not quite. With volume mount points, you select or create an empty folder anywhere on an existing NTFSv5 volume on the same computer and then have it point to a complete volume within the same computer, beginning at the root node of the target volume's file system. This target volume can have any of the supported file systems (FAT16, FAT32, NTFS, CDFS, and UDFS).

These junctions are not visible to applications that have not been written to see them (most are not). This allows users to use junction points to reroute applications or users accessing a local NTFS directory to any other directory. You can even have a junction point to a volume that does not have a drive letter assigned to it, so you are not confined to the 26 drive letters.

Universal Disk File System (UDFS)

The successor to CDFS (Compact Disk File System), UDFS is targeted at CD and DVD media. W2K supports read but not write at this time. W2K implementation meets existing standards: ISO 13346, ECMA 167, and OSTA UDF from the Optical Storage Technology Association (www.osta.org).

We also have the ability to create extended volumes on dynamic disks in Windows 2000. So, why would you want to use mount points as opposed to just extending volumes?

▼ An extended volume cannot be reversed. Mount points are reversible, without damage.

■ When you create mount points, you are also not limited to hard disks. You can mount a CD to an empty folder on your hard disk.

▲ Only mount points allow you to enforce disk quotas on each mounted volume separately.

Since the mount point itself must be hosted on an NTFSv5 volume, you can set security on mount points through explorer.exe or cacls.exe (or xcacls.exe from the Win2K Resource Kit). You may also share a mount point as you would any folder. You may also view the free space of a mounted volume through Windows Explorer, Disk Management, or a command-line utility.

USING MOUNT POINTS   Use the Disk Management snap-in or the command-line tool, mountvol.exe, to create a mount point. To use the Disk Management snap-in, follow these steps:

1. In the Disk Management snap-in, select and right-click on unallocated space on any physical drive in the system (the disk need not be dynamic).

2. Select Create Partition. The Welcome to Create Partition Wizard screen appears.

3. Click Next. The Select Partition Type screen appears. Select Primary or Extended partition.

4. Click Next. The Specify Partition Size screen appears, defaulting to the maximum space available. Enter the size of the partition you wish to create.

5. Click Next. The Assign Drive Letter or Path screen appears (Figure 5-6). You can either assign a drive letter to the new volume or mount this volume to an empty folder on an existing NTFSv5 volume. Enter the drive and folder location you created earlier.

6. Click Next. The Format Partition screen appears, giving you the option to format this partition with any of the three supported file systems.

7. Click Next. The Completing the Create Partition Wizard screen appears, giving you one last chance to click back and change the settings.

8. Click Finish.

You may get an error message after you have finished the wizard, ignore it. Your volume is mounted, but it is unformatted. The mount worked; the format did not. Now right-click the new volume and format it normally.

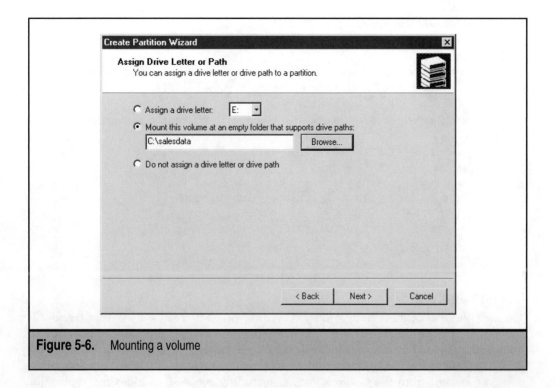

Figure 5-6.   Mounting a volume

If you are a die-hard command-line geek, mountvol.exe, may cure you of this addic-tion. This tool comes with Windows 2000; no need to install it separately. The syntax of the command requires that you provide the volume name. If you are still not scared away, then open up a command prompt on the Windows 2000 computer on which you want to create the mount point and run "mountvol" without any parameters. It will give you the syntax for the command as well as the GUID of all the volumes in the computer. If you are still with me on this, then you should have no trouble piecing together the com-mand now.

The following is sample output from the mountvol command with the volume name information for a computer.

```
Creates, deletes, or lists a volume mount point.

MOUNTVOL [drive:]path VolumeName
MOUNTVOL [drive:]path /D
MOUNTVOL [drive:]path /L


   path  Specifies the existing NTFS directory where the mount
```

```
point will reside.
VolumeName Specifies the volume name that is the target of the mount
point.
/D Removes the volume mount point from the specified directory.
/L Lists the mounted volume name for the specified directory.

Possible values for VolumeName along with current mount points are:

\\?\Volume{827f3225-e79e-11d3-9f8f-806d6172696f}\
C:\

\\?\Volume{54571917-e7e6-11d3-8037-00104b9495d2}\
D:\

\\?\Volume{7d806ec2-e7a7-11d3-8036-806d6172696f}\
R:\
```

Change Journal

Through the use of the Change Journal, Windows 2000 creates a log that tracks file changes (additions, deletions, and modifications) for each NTFS volume. Only applications written to read the Change Journal are affected by the Change Journal. They use the change log to track what has occurred on a particular volume. Various storage applications can benefit from the Change Journal including file system indexing, replication managers, remote storage, and incremental backup applications.

Indexing Service

Based on Index Server from NT 4.0 IIS, another service available only on NTFSv5 is the Indexing Service, which provides full file system content indexing capabilities to Windows 2000 Server. It indexes all files available on a file system, allowing them to be located based on their content or attributes. Users can take advantage of Indexing Service, which is fully integrated with Windows Explorer, through the Find Files or Folders dialog present throughout the Windows 2000 GUI. Its search engine has the uncanny ability to find documents in just about any format: text in a Word document, statistics on an Excel spreadsheet, or the content of an HTML page. You can also use it to index Internet content through Web-based query forms. One of the applications that takes advantage of the Change Log, Indexing Service automatically provides updates, index creation and optimization, and crash recovery. This is a very cool service.

Indexing Service is installed by default but not turned on by default. Once turned on, you can configure Indexing Service to operate on a per file or per directory basis. It takes full advantage of other enhancements to NTFSv5 and also features full integration with the Windows 2000 Hierarchical Storage Management (HSM) feature, providing for the indexing of content archived through HSM.

USING INDEXING SERVICE   Turn on Indexing Service by right-clicking on Start and then select Search. In the left pane of the Search Results window (Figure 5-7), click on Search Options. In the Search Options box, click on Indexing Service.

Each file or directory has indexing settings, available through the Advanced button in its Properties dialog in Explorer. You can access a volume's indexing settings in the Properties of the volume.

By default, indexing is turned on at the volume level. This is configurable through Explorer on the Properties dialog for each volume.

Removable Storage Service (RSS)

Windows 2000 Server provides Removable Storage Service (RSS), Microsoft's implementation of Hierarchical Storage Management. Using RSS, administrators can automate such tasks as mounting and dismounting media. RSS gives Windows 2000 a common interface to robotic media changers and media libraries. Multiple applications can share local libraries and tape or disk drives and control removable media within a single system. The Windows 2000 Backup Utility now has support for RSS.

Figure 5-7.   Turning on the Indexing Service

Single-Instance-Store (SIS)

Single-Instance-Store (SIS) is a new technology for minimizing the use of disk space by having only one instance of any unique file per volume. Pioneered by Microsoft, SIS could have been applied to any NTFSv5 volume under Windows 2000, other than the system or boot volumes. It is turned on only in the remote installation volume of a Remote Installation server. The way it works is that at an interval, a component called the "SIS groveler" checks to see if any duplicate files are on the volume. When it finds a duplicate file, it ensures that a copy of the file exists in the SIS store and then deletes the original file leaving a link in its place. In this way, SIS drastically reduces the disk space necessary to store duplicate files.

NTFSv4 to NTFSv5

When upgrading an NT 4.0 computer with volumes formatted in NTFSv4, the Windows 2000 upgrade process will automatically convert all the NTFS volumes to NTFSv5 without a hint. The only you time you will see an option to upgrade your volumes is in reference to existing FAT volumes, not the NTFS volumes. If the existing partition is already NTFS, Setup simply proceeds with the installation and the upgrade to NTFSv5. Thus, you may suddenly find yourself with NTFSv5 volumes that you hadn't planned on, volumes that are totally incompatible with locally installed versions of Windows previous to Windows NT 4.0 SP 4. This cannot be avoided; take it into consideration when you plan your installations.

Dual-Booting Windows NT with Windows 2000

While clients connecting to an NTFS volume over the network are not affected by the changes made to NTFS in Windows 2000, users trying to dual-boot between previous versions of NT and Windows 2000 need to understand some compatibility issues. To begin with, dual-booting between these operating systems is not recommended. The ability to successfully dual-boot a system with both Windows 2000 and Windows NT using NTFS on a basic system partition depends on Windows NT 4.0 being at a minimum of the Service Pack 4 (SP4) level before the installation of Windows 2000. Windows NT 4.0 SP4 has a special NTFS driver that allows Windows NT 4.0 to mount volumes formatted with NTFSv5. If Windows NT 4.0 SP4 is being used, then any basic volumes formatted with NTFS can be read, but the new features of NTFSv5 will not be available to them, nor any volumes on dynamic disks.

Let's turn the preceding scenario around. You cannot install NT 4.0 on a Windows 2000 computer with NTFSv5 on the system/boot partition(s). As stated previously, NT 4.0 needs to be at least at the SP 4 level to work with NTFSv5. Remember that this kind of dual-boot is not supported or recommended. However, here's where third-party partitioning software comes into play. For more information on partitioning software see: www.powerquest.com.

In addition, Windows NT 4.0 disk utilities such as chkdsk and autochk do not work on volumes formatted with NTFSv5 used in Windows 2000.

Cluster Size After Installation

Tests have shown that when Windows 2000 is installed on an existing 2GB FAT16 partition and the partition is converted to NTFS during the installation, the resulting cluster size is 512 bytes.

In another test, a 4GB FAT volume was created during installation. Although Windows 2000 supports FAT16 volumes up to 4GB, it cannot create a FAT16 volume greater than 2GB during setup. Therefore, a message appears explaining that since the selected volume size was over 2GB, Setup would create a FAT32 partition. Once Windows 2000 was installed, the cluster size on this FAT32 partition was 4KB. Good so far. Then the partition was converted to NTFSv5, and once the conversion was complete, the newly converted NTFSv5 volume had a cluster size of 512 bytes. Remember, the default cluster size of an NTFSv5 volume is 4KB. This very small cluster size of 512 bytes after conversion could cause performance problems on a large hard drive (and what else do we have these days?). This looks like a major shortcoming of the conversion utility and a good reason to not use FAT at all, even if you plan to convert to NTFS later.

If you have decided to ignore the previously given advice and want to convert a volume from FAT anything to NTFSv5, open a command prompt and run the following command:

```
convert d: /fs:ntfs
```

Substitute an appropriate drive letter for *d*.

The most common usage of the FAT-to-NTFS conversion is during a Win 9*x* upgrade.

Bootup

An understanding of the PC bootup process is important to fully comprehend the basic versus dynamic disk discussion later in this chapter. Specific elements of the physical disk and logical volumes are used during the startup of the computer: the master boot record (MBR), the boot sector on the active partition, and the Win2K startup files, just to name a few.

When an IBM-compatible computer starts, the following occurs:

1. An instruction stored in the CPU loads the power-on-self test (POST) from BIOS.

2. The BIOS searches for a boot device.

3. The BIOS loads the first physical sector of the boot device into memory. On a hard drive, this sector will be the MBR; on a floppy drive, it will be the boot sector (in which case, skip Step 4).

4. Code in the MBR loads the boot sector of the active partition, transferring CPU execution to that code.

5. Depending on the operating system, the executable boot code in the boot sector loads the OS startup code into memory. From this point on, what happens depends on the operating system.

6. In the case of Windows 2000, NTLDR (the NT Loader) is the startup code, controlling the startup process until it loads and initializes the Windows 2000 kernel.

Since our Intel systems still actually start up in good old-fashioned real mode, NTLDR switches the processor into 32-bit flat memory mode and then works in this mode as a 32-bit program. NTLDR continues with the following:

1. Starts the mini-file system (built into its own code) needed to access the file system on the system volume.

2. Reads the boot.ini file, displaying the bootstrap loader screen with the operating system selection menu.

3. Accepts your operating system selection or uses the default selection if the timeout period expires before you make a selection. If you select an operating system other than Windows 2000, NTLDR loads bootsect.dos, which contains the boot sector that was on the partition when you installed Windows 2000. If you select Windows 2000, NTLDR runs ntdetect.com, a hardware detection program.

4. If you press F8 at this point, you can access troubleshooting and advanced options. If you do not interrupt the startup and allow Windows 2000 to continue loading, it starts in the configuration in use when Windows 2000 was last shut down.

The New Order: Basic Disks vs. Dynamic Disks

Windows 2000 works with hard drive systems in two different modes: basic and dynamic. In this section, we will define these storage types. They are separate from the file system type format used on the disk. In Windows 2000, both basic and dynamic disks can contain any combination of FAT16, FAT32, and NTFSv5 partitions or volumes. Basic uses the term "partitions," and dynamic uses the term "volume".

Windows 2000 cannot alter the early steps of the bootup process, so to configure disks in a nonstandard way, it must enable the nonstandard disk configuration beyond the boot process. Because of this, you cannot start up Windows 2000 from a spanned, striped, or RAID-5 volume, all of which reside on dynamic disks. We will discuss these new technologies later in this chapter. Since these volumes are not registered in the MBR's partition table, they cannot be part of the startup process.described in "Bootup," which is not to say that the system partition cannot reside on a dynamic volume; it simply means that the volume must be a simple or mirrored volume.

Volume Size Limits

As in NT, Windows 2000's practical partition size limit for an NTFS partition or volume is 2 terabytes (2,199,023,255,522 bytes). This new limit is also, theoretically, applied to FAT32 in

Windows 2000. The problem is that the Format Tool of Windows 2000 has a maximum size limit for FAT32 volumes of 32GB. The theory here is that FAT should be used only on a workstation; on a server, you need the security of NTFS and probably some of the other features, also. Therefore, Microsoft has added this 32GB FAT32 limit to Windows 2000.

Windows 2000's maximum size limit for FAT16 volumes is 4GB. If you are using FAT16 for downlevel compatibility with legacy operating systems, be sure to keep the FAT16 volume size under 2GB to comply with the maximum partition size limits of those operating systems. Like NT 4.0, the Windows 2000 installation program has the same 2GB limit for creating a FAT16 volume during installation.

Basic Disks

Basic disks refers to disks partitioned into either primary or extended partitions, with the partition information stored in the partition table in the manner used for many years. This is compatible with our legacy Microsoft operating systems. If the system is set to boot up from a basic disk, the partition containing the hardware-specific files (ntldr, ntdetect.com, boot.ini) used to load Windows 2000 is known as the "system partition." The partition containing the Windows 2000 operating system files, located in the %SYSTEMROOT% and %SYSTEMROOT%\SYSTEM32 folders, is referred to as the "boot partition." This convention was also used in Windows NT. And yes, I know it is logically backwards. Live with it.

Under Windows 2000, basic disks can also be part of NT-style striped or fault-tolerant sets if, and only if, they were created by a previous installation of NT. This is because Windows 2000 can create primary or extended partitions only on basic disks. All the fancy, multi-disk schemes in Win2K are supported only on dynamic disks using the Disk Management snap-in. Disk Management in Windows 2000 can also convert a basic disk to a dynamic disk. By default, Windows 2000 manages disks as basic disks, until an administrator converts a disk to dynamic.

Basic fault-tolerant sets (mirrored sets and disk striping with parity) on a Windows 2000 system, upgraded from Windows NT 4.0, use the master boot record to store simple partition information, storing extended configuration information regarding the fault-tolerant sets on the first track of the disk.

SUMMARY OF BASIC DISK BENEFITS   Although basic disks seem to be the "old order," there are benefits to staying with basic disks.

▼   They are the only way to go if you want to dual-boot (at least on the physical disk hosting the primary active partition).

■   They can be managed with pre-Windows 2000 disk management tools.

▲   You understand them and trust them.

Dynamic Disks

A dynamic disk is a physical disk that is managed through the MMC Disk Management Console. A dynamic disk can contain only volumes—dynamic volumes—and cannot contain partitions or logical drives. Dynamic disks are not accessible by locally installed

MS-DOS, Windows 95, Windows 98, or Windows NT. Dynamic disks contain simple volumes, spanned volumes, mirrored volumes, striped volumes, and RAID-5 volumes. Disk and volume management on dynamic disks can be performed without having to re-start the operating system. However, the conversion from basic to dynamic does require a reboot.

Dynamic disk volume information is stored in a database at the end of each dynamic disk. Windows 2000 always saves space for this database if the volume is created during setup. The database on each dynamic disk in a Windows 2000 system replicates across all dynamic disks for fault-tolerance. Because the information about the disks is contained on the disks, they can be moved to another Windows 2000 computer without losing this information. All dynamic disks in a computer are members of the same Disk group.

If a system is configured to boot up from a dynamic disk, the volume containing the hardware-specific files (ntldr, boot.ini, and ntdetect.com) used to load Windows 2000 is known as the "system volume." The volume containing the Windows 2000 operating system files, located in the %SYSTEMROOT% and %SYSTEMROOT%\SYSTEM32 folders, is referred to as the "boot volume."

SIMPLE VOLUMES   On a dynamic disk, a simple volume contains the space from only a single physical disk. When converting from basic disks, each primary partition and each logical drive in an extended partition becomes a simple volume. These converted volumes retain their original size and cannot be extended as part of spanned volumes.

SPANNED VOLUMES   A spanned volume can include disk space from two or more disks (up to 32 physical disks). These are the dynamic disk versions of the volume sets of NT 4.0.

MIRRORED VOLUMES   A mirrored volume is made up of two identical copies of a simple volume, each on separate physical hard disks. These provide fault-tolerance and are the equivalent to the mirrored sets created in NT 4.0.

STRIPED VOLUMES   A striped volume contains the area of free space from 2 to 32 physical hard disks, combined into a single volume. Data is written in 64KB chunks to the members of a striped volume in a (would you believe it?) stripe. This is *not* fault-tolerance but does provide improved read performance. If a single physical hard disk in a striped volume fails, the entire striped volume is unusable until the drive is replaced, the striped volume re-created, and a backup restored to the volume.

RAID-5 VOLUMES   A RAID-5 volume is a fault-tolerant configuration made up of equally sized areas from 3 to 32 physical hard disks. The operating system writes data sequentially in 64KB chunks across all members of the RAID-5 volume, a software implementation of the RAID-5 specification. Within each stripe, parity information is available, which can be used to reconstruct the entire volume should one of the hard disks in the RAID-5 volume fail. If this should happen, access to the volume continues, with just a loss of performance, as the volume manager uses an algorithm to re-create the data on the failed member. Once the failed hard disk is replaced, an administrator, using Disk Management, right-clicks on the replaced disk and selects the Reactivate Disk command from the context menu. This will cause the volume manager to regenerate the data onto the new disk.

The recommendation for heavily used Windows 2000 servers and domain controllers is to use the hardware implementation of RAID-5. It will not only increase performance but will enable hot swappable drives and will simplify administration.

DISK GROUPS   Dynamic disks are associated with Disk groups. A Disk group is a collection of dynamic disks managed together. Each disk in a Disk group stores replicas of the same configuration data. This configuration data is stored in a 1MB region at the end of each dynamic disk, which is why we can move multiple disk volumes without losing data. Presently, Windows 2000 allows only one Disk group per computer. Microsoft Technet article Q222189 refers to the use of Veritas LDM-Pro to manage multiple Disk groups.

CLUSTER SERVICE AND DYNAMIC DISKS   Dynamic disks cannot be read by the Windows 2000 Advanced Server Cluster Service; therefore, these disks are unavailable to programs or services in the server cluster. Once Cluster Service is installed, the option to upgrade these disks to dynamic is unavailable in Disk Management. If disks are converted to dynamic before Cluster Service is installed, the configuration wizard does not detect the dynamic disks as available for use in the server cluster and generates an error. Refer to Knowledge Base Article Q237853. This is limited to the disks on the shared disk bus that can be brought online on any of the nodes in the server cluster. Other local drives on the cluster server allow the dynamic disk conversion and support dynamic disk functionality.

SUMMARY OF DYNAMIC DISK BENEFITS   Dynamic disks represent the wave of the future in the area of server-based file systems. The key benefits of dynamic disks are:

- ▼ Only way to create fault-tolerant volumes in Windows 2000.
- ■ Most disk management functions can take effect without a reboot.
- ▲ Volume info is stored on the disk itself rather than in the registry, which helps when recovering from a failed system or when moving disks between machines.

DYNAMIC DISK GOTCHAS   When basic disks are converted to dynamic disks, the underlying partition sizes are retained. There are two problems with this: one is that you may actually not be able to complete the conversion because the existing partitions do not leave the 4MB to 8MB of free unallocated space needed for the dynamic disk database. Second, converted dynamic volumes cannot be extended. Therefore, when converting from basic disks to dynamic disks, Microsoft recommends the following:

1. For disks other than system or boot partitions, back up or copy all basic disk data to another dynamic disk.
2. Delete all basic partitions on the basic disk.
3. Convert the basic disk to dynamic.
4. Create the dynamic volume and then copy or restore the files back to the new dynamic volume.

It is also important to remember that dynamic disks are treated in a nonstandard way by Windows 2000. Other operating systems cannot run on these machines, and it may even be difficult to wipe all traces of dynamic disks from a system. Let's look at some scenarios where this could be a problem.

SCENARIO ONE   Let's say you have been working with Windows 2000 in a test lab. You converted a basic disk to dynamic. Now you would like to wipe out that hard drive and use the computer for some other purposes, say installing Windows NT Workstation 4.0 so that you can test upgrade scenarios. If you rely on your old standby (the DOS or Windows 9x bootable floppy with fdisk) to wipe out the hard drive, you are in for a surprise. It may look like wiping out the hard drive went OK until you attempt to install a new operating system, *even Windows 2000*. That's when you need to resort to another trusty friend, your favorite third-party partitioning tool. These applications have tools for "nuking" the hard drive so that you can get back to a kosher-looking system without the nonstandard stuff placed on the disk for dynamic disks. (See the section "FDISK/MBR" later in this chapter.)

SCENARIO TWO   In your test lab, again, you have a Windows 2000 system with a dynamic disk. You want to continue working with this installation of Windows 2000, but you want to create another volume on the hard drive. Creating this other volume should be done in Disk Manager, but old habits die hard. You boot to DOS or Windows 9x and use fdisk to add a partition to this dynamic disk, which is a very bad move. fdisk gets very confused, and if you manage to get it to create a partition, you will be even sorrier. Windows 2000 will not boot up after such a change, but if you are lucky, you can use fdisk to remove the partition you created.

The moral is: if you are going with dynamic disks, do not mix and match your disk management tools. Use only those tools that understand dynamic disks, whether the tools are from Microsoft or third parties. For more information, see the section "Disk Utilities," later in this chapter.

SCENARIO THREE   During a Windows 2000 installation, you use an existing partition. When you use an existing partition during installation, you live with the boundaries of that partition in addition to the file system conversion issues that we have already addressed. These boundaries might not leave you enough unpartitioned free space on the disk to later convert to dynamic. So what should you do? If, you want the *option* to be able to convert to a dynamic disk after installation, then create a new partition during setup, even if it means removing an existing partition (but clean installations are always the best). Then, Windows 2000 Setup reserves either a 4MB or 8MB (depending on the size of the partition) unpartitioned area at the end of the disk. The unpartitioned area will be needed if you wish to convert the disk to dynamic later on. This is a good thing.

Caching Controllers

In Win2K, hardware write caching is disabled on the disk controllers of all domain controllers. While this may seem like a performance nightmare, it is the only way to ensure the integrity of the Active Directory database and log files in case of a power outage. Read caching is not disabled. The majority of the disk activity in Active Directory is disk reads, so that information will be cached to improve Active Directory performance. This parameter is not configurable.

VOLUME MANAGEMENT

Now that you understand the underlying technology and many of the new features and capabilities of Win2K file systems, it is time to discuss volume management. Volume management is the term for the architecture used in creating, deleting, and maintaining disk storage volumes. In the new Disk Management snap-in, Microsoft has improved on the functionality of the NT tool, Disk Administrator, with a simplified, more capable interface.

Before we take a look at this tool, let's look at the underlying architecture. A single Windows 2000 computer can simultaneously work with both basic and dynamic disks. It achieves this with a modified architecture that includes a separate component for each of these disk types: FTDisk and the ftdisk.sys driver, which manage basic disks, and the Logical Disk Manager (LDM) and the dmio.sys driver, which manage dynamic disks. As shown in Figure 5-8, they in turn interact with the upper layers: file systems, Disk Management, databases, and, indirectly, applications.

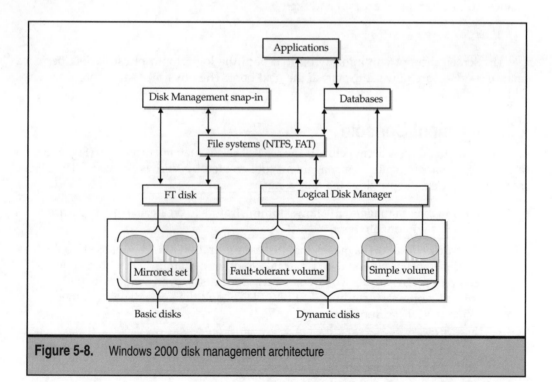

Figure 5-8. Windows 2000 disk management architecture

FTDisk

Much as it did in Windows NT, FTDisk manages the partitions and fault-tolerant volumes originally created using the MS-DOS, Windows, or Windows NT operating systems. The FTDisk component has been providing fault-tolerant support for all versions of Windows NT since its inception.

Logical Disk Manager (LDM)

The Logical Disk Manager (LDM) manages the new dynamic volumes of Windows 2000, providing better manageability and recoverability. It is key to providing much of the functionality of the Disk Management Console, described in the next section. With dynamic disks, volume configuration information is no longer stored in the registry. Disk configuration information is stored in a transactional database on each disk and replicated to all dynamic disks in a single computer, which enables LDM to control the recovery of mirrored or RAID-5 volumes. This makes the disk self-identifying, which means the dynamic disks may be transported between Windows 2000 systems. The receiving system can determine all volume configuration information, merging the databases transactionally with no loss or corruption of the configuration data.

One more note on logical disks: in the Win2K Performance Monitor, the logical disk object is not available by default. To enable the logical disk object and measure its performance, go to a command prompt and type:

```
diskperf -yv
```

The screen prompt will inform you that both the logical and physical disk performance counters are now set to start at the next boot. The physical disk counters are enabled by default.

Disk Management Console

Our interface to this new architecture is the MMC Disk Management snap-in (Figure 5-9), a complete, dynamic volume management tool created by Veritas Software. The Disk Management Console provides the following:

▼   **Online disk management** allows administrators to create, extend, or mirror volumes without a reboot.

■   **Self-describing disks** means that disk configuration information is stored on the device itself and then replicated to other dynamic disks in the same computer. This means we can move dynamic disks, even completely fault-tolerant volumes including SCSI IDs, LUNS, and the host adapter to other Windows 2000 computers.

■   **Simplified tasks** are manifested in the shortcut menus for tasks on a selected object and wizards to guide users through creating partitions and volumes and initializing or upgrading disks.

■ **Both local and remote management** of Windows 2000 client disks.

▲ **Delegation of administrative tasks** is available here, as elsewhere in Windows 2000.

The MMC Disk Management snap-in can be found at Start | Programs | Administrative Tools | Computer Management | Storage.

What Is Old?

As in other areas of this very complex system, with Disk Management, think "downlevel compatibility." Like NT's Disk Administrator, Disk Management supports primary partitions, extended partitions, RAID-0, 1, and 5; disk striping with parity; disk striping without parity; disk mirroring; and extended volume sets on basic disks. Disk Management can manage, repair, and delete all of these types of partitions on basic disks, but the only partition types it can create on basic disks are primary and extended partitions. You are limited to four primary partitions per disk.

What Is New?

Disk Management allows both local and remote management of disks. Plus, this function can be delegated to individuals or groups. The fanciest of the new stuff is reserved for the new dynamic storage. The volume types that Disk Management can create on dynamic storage include simple volumes, spanned volumes, mirrored volumes, striped volumes, and RAID-5 volumes. Fault-tolerant volumes can be created and rebuilt without a reboot. Volumes can be extended without a reboot.

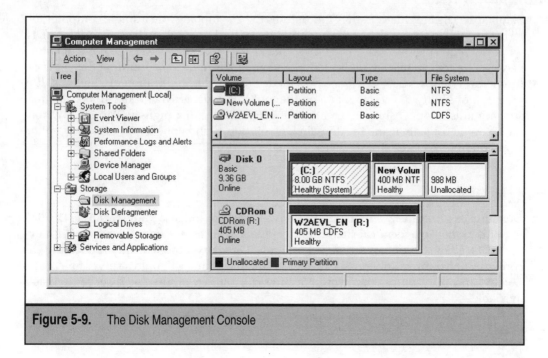

Figure 5-9.   The Disk Management Console

DISTRIBUTED FILE SYSTEM (DFS)

As administrators, we want our systems to appear to be stable and work in routine ways to the user, even while we are busy redesigning the network. When this work requires us to relocate network resources to which our users need to connect, we can give users a stable environment with the use of the Distributed File System (Dfs). Through Dfs, users see a single logical directory tree that appears to exist on a single server, when in reality, they are actually connecting to many different servers within the organization. The top level of this Dfs tree is known as the "Dfs root." The child nodes below it, represented as folders, are known as "Dfs links." Only one level of Dfs links is permitted under the Dfs root. When admins move resources, they only need to reconfigure the Dfs link or links to point to the new location. The user experience is unchanged.

Who can play this Dfs game? Dfs clients include Win2K clients, Windows 98, and Windows NT 4.0 by default. For Windows 95 clients, you must download the free Dfs client from Microsoft.

Dfs takes advantage of Windows 2000 Server security in the same way that standard File Sharing does, restricting access based on users, groups, and quotas. Windows 2000 supports two types of Dfs: standalone Dfs and domain Dfs. A domain controller can host two Dfs roots but only one of each type; a member server can host only one Dfs root—either domain or standalone; and a workgroup server can host only a standalone Dfs. Dfs is managed with the MMC Distributed File System snap-in.

Standalone Dfs

Standalone Dfs in Win2K, as in NT 4.0, stores the Dfs topology on a single computer, offering no fault tolerance if the computer that stores the Dfs topology fails. Standalone Dfs, while not requiring the Active Directory, creates the possibility of a single point of failure because the root cannot be replicated. Standalone Dfs allows for multiple data sources (replicas). Windows 2000 does not provide for automated replication of Dfs links. It is your responsibility to keep the data on the multiple sources synchronized. For this reason, administrators wishing to create a Dfs architecture in a high-availability environment should consider using the domain Dfs solution. Standalone Dfs is your only option if you do not have an Active Directory domain.

Domain Dfs

Domain Dfs stores the Dfs topology in Active Directory and also allows a single Dfs link to point to multiple identical shared folders (data replicas) for fault tolerance. With domain Dfs, all the topologies are stored in Active Directory, automatically replicating Dfs configuration information for all Dfs trees within the domain. Should a server fail, the topology, and all resources that were not physically stored on the failed server, remains available.

In addition to replicating the Dfs topology through Active Directory, shared folders can also be replicated for Dfs by the File Replication Service (FRS). This is done by assigning multiple shared folders on separate physical servers to the same Dfs link. Once configured, replication of multiple shares assigned to the same Dfs link can be totally automatic in a domain Dfs. Dfs balances the client requests among servers and reduces intersite network traffic. Dfs will direct the client computer to the share (data replica) that is physically closest to it (on its site). It also offers fault tolerance because if one of the servers hosting a Dfs share is not available, Dfs will direct the client to one that is available.

Dfs Replication

Automatic replication is available only for a domain Dfs. The Dfs root is replicated through normal Active Directory replication. To increase availability of data for clients and to improve performance, multiple shares can be assigned to the same Dfs link. Since administrators want identical information on each share represented by a single link, Dfs provides an independent replication topology powered by FRS. Once a second share has been assigned to a link, admins select an initial master share through the Replication Policy dialog box. This initial master copies its data to all other shares within the link. Once this first copy operation takes place, this function is no longer necessary because all shares now participate in the Dfs replication as multiple masters.

Setting Up a Dfs Root

From the Administrative Tools menu, open the Distributed File System console. In the left pane of the console, labeled Tree, right-click Distributed File System. On the context menu, click New Dfs Root. The Welcome to the New Dfs Root Wizard appears. Click Next.

In the Select the Dfs Root Type page, select the type of Dfs root and click Next. In the example, we have selected domain Dfs root. In the Domain Name box of the Select the Host Domain for the Dfs Root page, enter the domain name in FQDN form or browse for the domain. Click Next. Then, in the server name box of the Select the Host Server for the Dfs Root screen, enter the server name in FQDN form or browse for the server. Click Next.

In the Specify the Dfs Root Share page (Figure 5-10), enter the appropriate information, pointing to the directory and share on your root server. If you have pre-created the share, select Use an Existing Share and enter or select the share name. Or you can select Create a New Share and provide the path to the share and the share name. Click Next. In the Completing the New Dfs Root Wizard page, review the settings. If they are correct, click Finish.

Creating Dfs Links

To create a link, bring up the Dfs Console and highlight the root; right-click and select New Dfs Link. The Create a New Dfs Link screen appears (Figure 5-11). You must enter a name for the link, which is the name that the user will see. You also need to enter the path and name of the preexisting share, or you can browse to it. This is also the screen where you configure the length of time that the clients will cache the referral information. The default is 30 minutes. When complete, click OK.

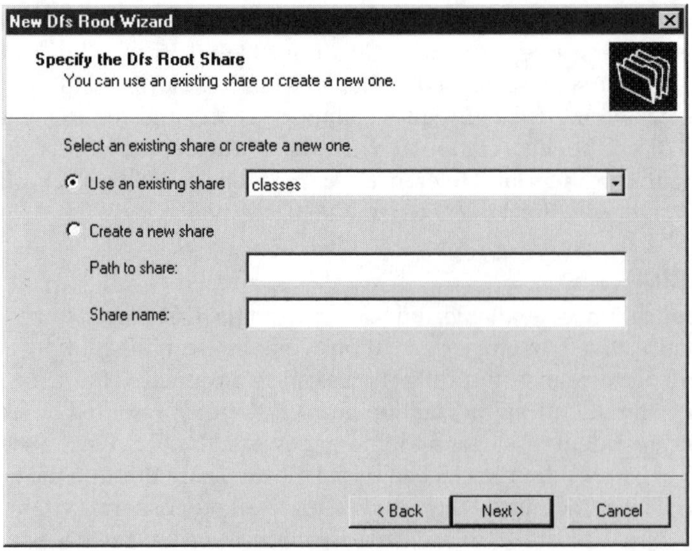

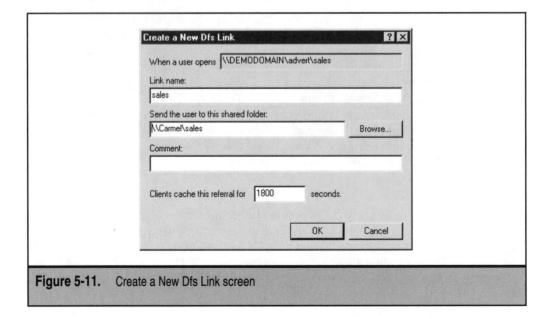

Figure 5-10. Specify the Dfs Root Share page

Figure 5-11. Create a New Dfs Link screen

Adding Data Replicas to a Domain Dfs Link

In the Dfs console, highlight an existing Dfs link, right-click, and select New Replica. The Add a New Replica screen appears, requesting the path of the additional share you wish to add to this link. Enter the path and choose automatic replication. Click OK. Assuming this is at least the second share in this Dfs link, the replication policy screen now appears. Even though you chose Automatic Replication, you must still enable each replica to participate in the Dfs replication topology. Highlight the desired replica and click Enable. Replication is not permitted between shares on the same server.

DISK UTILITIES

Several types of utilities are available, with Windows 2000 focusing on disk structure and file systems. In this section, we will focus on the master boot record utilities and several common programs used for disk maintenance.

MBR Utilities

Under the best of circumstances, Windows 2000 is immune from MBR or boot sector viruses because it accesses physical disks only through Protected mode disk drivers, whereas viruses usually depend on the BIOS INT 13h disk access routines of DOS, Win 3.*x*, and Win 9*x*. These viruses are not effective once Windows 2000 has started, which means that a machine that dual-boots between Windows 2000 and MS-DOS, Windows 95, or Windows 98 can become infected when one of these downlevel operating systems is booted up.

FDISK/MBR

This trusty old MS-DOS utility, fdisk/mbr, has proven effective in the past for overwriting MBR viruses because it overwrites a portion of the MBR but leaves the partition table intact. However, it is not even included with a Windows 2000 installation. Take this as your cue: Do *not* use this utility on a Windows 2000 computer.

AVBoot

A tool for detecting and removing memory resident, boot sector, and MBR viruses is included on the Windows 2000 Professional or Server CD in the \VALUEADD\ 3RDPARTY\CA_ANTIV folder. This utility must run from a bootable floppy disk, which you create with a batch file, makedisk.bat, located in the same folder on the CD. When you boot from this floppy disk, AVBoot scans memory and all physical disks to remove viruses.

Disk Maintenance Utilities

Despite the advances in hard disk technologies, today's disks still require maintenance by administrators. The complexity of the data, size of the files, and frequency of access have compounded problems inherent in the management of disk storage systems.

Defragmentation of Volumes

Because of the way in which most file systems, even NTFS, store data, pieces of files become scattered all over a volume. Disk fragmentation can creep up on you, causing active systems to experience a great deal of file fragmentation that manifests itself in slow performance on reads and writes. Such slow performance is your operating system taking more time to pick up all the pieces of a requested file before loading it into memory. Windows 2000 comes with a defragmentation utility, the Disk Defragmentation Tool, based on DiskKeeper from Executive Software. The utility allows for only local defragmentation; it cannot be run remotely. You might call it "defrag lite." It also cannot be automated from the command line or scripted, but it will defragment all three file systems supported by Windows 2000. Fully featured defragmentation utilities are available from third parties. In any case, defragmentation is an important administrative task; all servers and domain controllers should have a disk maintenance schedule. The frequency of disk maintenance will depend on the relative disk activity of the file writes on each server.

USING THE DISK DEFRAGMENTATION TOOL   Only an administrator or a member of the Administrators group can run the Disk Defragmentation Tool. You may also be prevented from using it if your computer is connected to an Active Directory network because Group Policy settings will apply. To run the Disk Defragmentation Tool, open Explorer, go to the Properties of a volume, and click on the Tools tab. Then click on Defragment Now, which will bring up the Disk Defragmenter window. Clicking on the Analyze button will generate an analysis of the defragmentation status of the selected volume. Upon completion of the analysis, the results will appear in the Analysis Display bar of the Disk Defragmenter window. The Analysis Complete dialog box will appear, with a recommendation on the need to defrag the volume. It will tell you that the volume does or does not need defragmenting. This Analysis Complete dialog box also provides a button labeled View Report, which is how you can view the report shown in Figure 5-1 earlier in this chapter. The Analysis Complete dialog box also has the Defragment button. Click it to start defragmentation. It may take several minutes on a large, highly fragmented volume.

DiskProbe

DiskProbe can be found on the Windows 2000 Professional or Server CD in the SUPPORT\TOOLS folder. Disk Probe can change the values of individual bytes in any sector, even on a dynamic disk. The problem with Disk Probe is that it cannot read the dynamic Disk Management database, so it cannot traverse the structure of a dynamic disk to enable you to find the sector you want to view or edit.

DiskMap

DiskMap is a Windows 2000 Resource Kit utility, installed with the Resource Kit tools. It can be used to display the layout of partitions and logical volumes on your disk. This utility cannot be used with dynamic disks because it cannot read the dynamic Disk Management database. Sample output from DiskMap follows:

```
Cylinders HeadsPerCylinder SectorsPerHead BytesPerSector MediaType
     935              128             63            512         12
TrackSize = 32256
CylinderSize = 4128768
DiskSize = 3860398080 (3681MB)


Signature = 0x08386f5a
 StartingOffset PartitionLength StartingSector PartitionNumber
*         32256      2146927104             63               1
   2146959360      1709309952        4193280               2
```

```
MBR:
          Starting              Ending         System Relative Total
  Cylinder Head Sector  Cylinder Head Sector    ID    Sector   Sectors
*        0    1    1         519  127   63     0x07        63  4193217
       520    0    1         933  127   63     0x07   4193280  3338496
         0    0    0           0    0    0     0x00         0        0
         0    0    0           0    0    0     0x00         0        0
```

SUMMARY

Windows 2000 has a significant number of enhancements in the area of disk administration, which should make the life of the average network administrator a little easier. While the major concepts are often straightforward, the implementation of the new features can sometimes be more complex. Like most things in life, with Windows 2000 disk administration, let's crawl before we walk. Try these new storage initiatives in your test environment first. Then stress them in the test forest. Hammer these servers and thrash these disks until you are satisfied that the new technologies work and work well in the scale of your environment. Every test I tried works flawlessly, but that doesn't mean yours will. Test it first, test it again, and then test it one more time. Then roll it out.

CHAPTER 6

Deploying and Configuring Essential Network Services in Windows 2000

C hapter 6 is not a detailed lesson on the entire topic of computer networking (I'm sure you've got enough books on that already) but rather a focused discussion of the key protocols and services that you must have to implement your Windows 2000 Active Directory network. We will not be going into detail through each layer of the OSI model but will reference it at times in this chapter. In fact, I will assume that you are familiar with many of the basic tenets of computer networking as we move forward in our discussion. For the most part, these topics will center only on the specific elements necessary for a successful Win2K implementation.

NETWORK TRANSPORT PROTOCOLS

The OSI model is shown in Figure 6-1, and we'll concentrate our discussions on level 3—the Network Layer. This layer supports the transport protocols that we use every day. Layer 1, the Physical Layer, is the wires, cables, hubs, repeaters, and network interface cards (NICs), while Layer 2, the Data Link Layer, defines the size and shape of the packets as they move across the wire. Layer 3 is, in essence, the language we speak across the network. All the participants in the network must speak the same language; otherwise, as it is in life, they cannot communicate. We call these languages *protocols*, a set of rules for communication. But when we don't adhere to the proper communication protocols, computers don't get angry or upset as humans do, they simply ignore the conversation as if it wasn't happening. The only communication that gets through must obey the rules of the protocol, or there is no response, no dialog, if you will. Each computer has selective listening. It "hears" some things but not others. Perhaps you might relate to this on the human side of your life.

There is so much to learn in the world of computer networking, and, the good news is, there are some wonderful resources to draw from. Check out these Web sites for great white papers and PDF files outlining network protocols:

▼ www.nai.com

■ www.net3group.com

▲ www.cisco.com

TCP/IP

The Transmission Control Protocol/Internet Protocol (TCP/IP) is a suite of protocols introduced to the Internet way back in 1983. It was created by computer scientists for one purpose—to run the Internet; that is why it is called the *Internet Protocol*. TCP/IP has undergone several revisions since its introduction. (We are currently running

DOD Model	OSI Reference Model		Microsoft TCP/IP	Devices
Application	Application		SMB NetBIOS Winsock API	G A T E W A Y S
	Presentation			
	Session		NetBIOS Frame	
Transport	Transport		TCP, UDP	
Internet	Network		IP, ICMP, ARP	Routers
Physical	Data-Link	LLC	NDIS	Bridges
		MAC		
	Physical			Repeaters

Figure 6-1.   The OSI Model

version 4—IPv4—on the Internet and just polishing the specifications on IPv6 to take us into the future.) Today, IP is still based on some intrinsically basic principles:

▼ Every host computer on the network must have a unique IP address.

■ Public addresses on the Internet are assigned by a central Internet authority.

■ Every network interface card (NIC) must have a unique hardware address known as a MAC (Media Access Control—OSI Layer 2) address.

▲ Devices known as *routers* allow administrators to segment the IP network for performance purposes.

Even today, no information moves across a TCP/IP network without a source address (the IP address of the sender) and a destination address (the IP address of the recipient). This addressing information is held in the packet header.

An IP packet (Layer 3) is a connectionless message similar to a letter in the postal service. You place a worldwide unique address and a return address on your letter and drop it in the mailbox. And, in the United States, it usually gets to the specified address. You have no idea how it got there, but because the address was correct, it arrived. If the letter is undeliverable, it is returned. An IP packet works the same way. It contains a destination address and source address. You send it off, and if the address is correct, it usually gets there. You have no idea the route it took. If it's undeliverable, it is returned.

A TCP packet (Layer 4) is a connection-oriented message similar to a telephone call. When you call your mother, you dial the number, it rings, and she picks up the telephone receiver. At that moment, a circuit is formed between your phone and your mother's phone. Even if your mother's phone is on the other side of the world, two wires are dedicated to you and your mother for the duration of the conversation. When you hang up, the wires are now free to be used by another caller. A TCP session maintains its connection with the machine on the other end until it hangs up. For example, you surf to a Web site, and the home page starts to appear on your browser, buttons begin to fill in on the left side, not necessarily in order, and the signature graphic is building in the center of the screen. This is all happening at the same time. It feels like a single session, but in reality, your browser and the Web server are establishing separate TCP sessions for each file that gets sent. Every button, every graphic, and the background are all separate TCP "phone" calls. Once the file has been retrieved, the browser "hangs up" until you ask for another file.

IP Addressing

An IP address has 32 bits divided into 4 octets of 8 bits each. Each 8-bit octet written in binary code translates into a decimal number from 0 to 255. Thus, we usually see IP addresses such as 192.168.2.200. IP addressing traditionally has been divided into classes—A, B, C, D, and E. Table 6-1 lists the IP address classes and provides additional information about IP addressing.

IP Address Class	First Octet	Number of Addresses	Default Subnet Mask
A	1–126	16,777, 214	255.0.0.0
	127	Reserverd for loopback testing	
B	128–191	65,534	255.255.0.0
C	192–223	254	255.255.255.0
D	224–239	Configurable for multicast only	N/A
E	240–255	Future use (IPv6)	N/A

Table 6-1. IP Addressing

This address class segmentation was originally created for the convenience of consistent subnet masks and router network identification. In today's IP networks (and in Win2K), we tend towards more custom subnet masking using the CIDR (Classless InterDomain Routing) notation (RFC 1519). For example, the IP address mentioned earlier of 192.168.2.200 is a class C address and would normally have a default subnet written as 255.255.255.0. Since 255 is the highest possible number that can be created by eight bits in binary code, all the bits must be set to 1. So in binary, 255.255.255.0 reads 11111111.11111111.11111111.00000000. There are 24 bits (count 'em) set to 1 so the CIDR notation for this address reads 192.168.2.200/24. You will see this notation when you create subnet objects to assign to additional sites in the Active Directory Sites and Services snap-in and when you create new scopes in the Win2K DHCP console.

Because of the explosive growth of the Internet, the number of addresses that are unassigned in the total theoretical pool of about 4 billion is currently zero. This means that all the possible addresses have already been given out to private companies and Internet Service Providers (ISPs). These ISPs will be happy to lease you one or more of their addresses for a reasonable monthly fee. Since you cannot participate in the Internet without an IP address, you receive a temporary one each time you dial in to your ISP from home. The IP address belongs to you only while you are connected. When you hang up, it's used for the next person who calls.

Many forward thinking organizations have many more IP addresses than they will ever need. In some cases, they have decided to actually give some of them back. They find that they no longer need thousands of addresses because of advancements in the technology of proxy servers and network address translation (NAT) routers.

A NAT router or proxy server operates around one simple concept—there is an outside world (the Internet) and an inside world (the company), and they divide and protect the inside from the outside (Figure 6-2). The outside world requires one (but only one) real live Internet-assigned IP address, but the inside world can operate under its own totally separate private IP addressing scheme, which then depends completely on the proxy or the NAT router to "translate" the inside private IP address to the outside world and vice versa.

Ports

As previously stated, TCP/IP is a suite of protocols, which means many separate and discrete protocols are listed under the unifying banner of TCP/IP. Each protocol has an identifying name and uses a specific port number to connect to another computer. Ports are like channels on your cable system. As you are watching TV, your set is receiving every channel all the time, but you are viewing only one. Even though lots of requests are streaming past the computer on the network, a specific network service "listens" on only one port. When it receives a correctly formed message using that port, it responds. For example, a Web server "listens" on port 80 for HTTP GET requests. When it "hears" one, it responds by downloading a Web page. Table 6-2 lists some of the reserved TCP/IP ports.

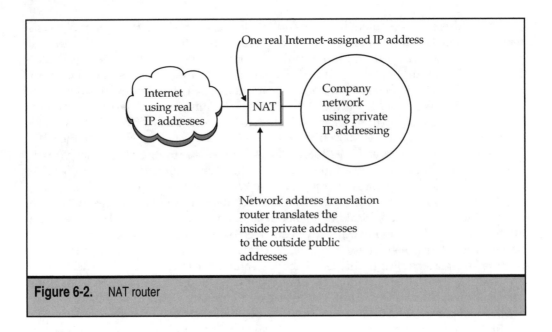

One real Internet-assigned IP address

Internet using real IP addresses

NAT

Company network using private IP addressing

Network address translation router translates the inside private addresses to the outside public addresses

Figure 6-2. NAT router

Essential TCP/IP-Related Services

In addition to the many protocols that make up the TCP/IP suite, a number of services define a TCP/IP network. Several of these services are critical to the success of your Windows 2000 Active Directory installation:

▼ **Domain Name Service (DNS)**   Provides computer name to IP address mapping for host computers and services

■ **Dynamic Host Configuration Protocol (DHCP) Service**   Allows the automatic assignment of IP addresses and key TCP/IP configuration parameters

▲ **Windows Internet Name Service (WINS)**   Proprietary to Microsoft and similar to DNS; provides computer name to IP address mapping for NetBIOS-based computers and services

In every case, these services either provide addresses to computers or translate a request for a name into an IP address. While many other services are in the world of TCP/IP, we will focus on these essential TCP/IP-related services for Windows 2000 in this chapter.

Required for Active Directory

It is possible (but unlikely) to run Win2K without TCP/IP. You can use other protocols on the network, but it is impossible to implement the Active Directory without TCP/IP. The AD also requires the DNS service to install and operate and strongly prefers DHCP, if at

Port Number	Type	Name	Description
20	TCP, UDP	ftp-data	File Transfer Protocol Data
21	TCP, UDP	ftp	File Transfer Protocol Control
23	TCP, UDP	telnet	Telnet
25	TCP, UDP	smtp	Mail, Simple Mail Transport Protocol
67	TCP, UDP	bootp	DHCP/BOOTP
68	TCP, UDP	bootp	DHCP/BOOTP
69	TCP, UDP	tftp	Trivial File Transfer Protocol
70	TCP, UDP	gopher	Gopher
79	TCP, UDP	finger	Finger
80	TCP, UDP	www	HTTP, World Wide Web
110	TCP, UDP	pop3	Post Office Protocol Version 3
119	TCP, UDP	nntp	Network News Transfer Protocol
137	TCP, UDP	netbios-ns	NetBIOS Name Service
138	TCP, UDP	netbios-dgm	NetBIOS Datagram Service
139	TCP, UDP	netbios-ssn	NetBIOS Session Service
161	TCP, UDP	snmp	Simple Network Management Protocol (SNMP)
162	TCP, UDP	snmptrap	SNMP Trap

Table 6-2.   Reserved TCP/IP Ports

all possible. Because downlevel clients don't recognize DNS, they require WINS in order to locate available NetBIOS resources. Once you create additional sites, the only way to associate a client computer to a site is by its IP address.

IPX/SPX

The Internetwork Packet Exchange/Sequenced Packet Exchange (IPX/SPX) protocol was developed in the early 1980s by Xerox. Today's network specialists know it as the default protocol for Novell NetWare. IPX/SPX has proven to be a very fast and secure protocol. Its addressing scheme is a numerical node address and a hexadecimal network address assigned by the NetWare client software on the workstation and during installation at the server. Novell still uses IPX today, but because of the dominance and pervasive influence of the Internet, they have been forced to enhance their NetWare 5.x product line to support native TCP/IP. Native IP means that the NetWare world no longer tunnels IP in an IPX packet. Microsoft's implementation of IPX/SPX is called NWLink, which stands for NetWare Link. This is how a Windows NT 4.0 or Win2K client can log onto a NetWare file and print server and participate in a NetWare NDS enterprise. Another occasion to use NWLink is when an NT 4.0 or a Win2K server is acting as an application server on a NetWare network. In this case, the Win2K server must receive and process requests from NetWare clients, which may be using only IPX/SPX as their protocol. IPX/SPX is a routable protocol, but at this time, most large enterprises are moving away from this protocol and toward the increased functionality and consistency of TCP/IP.

NetBEUI

The NetBIOS Extended User Interface (NetBEUI) protocol was developed by Microsoft and IBM around 1987 for use initially with OS/2 LAN Server and then later with Microsoft's LAN Manager product. NetBEUI was designed strictly for department-sized LANs in the late 1980s and early 1990s. Few envisioned the explosion of the Internet and the desire to tie organizations to it. For this reason, NetBEUI was implemented as a very fast, but very "chatty," broadcast protocol, which means that a NetBEUI packet does not contain destination or source addresses, and thus, every computer on the network has to "listen" for messages directed at it. With no destination or source address, NetBEUI is not routable. Therefore, by definition, it is limited to small, unrouted, nonswitched LANs.

AppleTalk

Developed originally as a way for Macintosh computers to share the expensive Apple LaserWriter printers in the 1980s, AppleTalk is still the transport used by many Macintoshes in a networked environment. Windows 2000 Server can install enhanced File and Print Services for the Macintosh, if desired, which is located in the Other Network Services category. File Services for Macintosh allows administrators to create Macintosh-accessible volumes on a Win2K NTFSv5 file system. Print Services for Macintosh allows Win2K printers to be used by Macintosh clients. Installing either File or Print Services for the Macintosh will automatically install the AppleTalk protocol on the Win2K Server.

DLC

The Data Link Control protocol was developed originally to talk to mainframes via special emulation software but has evolved into the default network protocol for many network interface printers. We are talking about printers that contain a network interface card and connect directly to the network, not to a PC. However, these printers must still use a print server service that is resident on a network computer, and in Microsoft network printing, the printers, of course, must be shared. The SMB share for each printer is held on the print server computer, as well as the print queue or spool for that printer. Therefore, it is necessary for the print server computer to "speak" directly to the printer. Since the printer "speaks" only DLC, the print server computer must also speak DLC. Therefore, administrators are required to install the DLC protocol only on the Win2K print server. It is not necessary for any other computer in the network to load the DLC protocol because these computers will spool their print jobs to the print server using the normal network protocols.

Installing Additional Protocols

TCP/IP is installed by default on every Windows 2000 computer. The steps for installing additional protocols are outlined in this section.

To install additional network protocols:

1. On the desktop, select My Network Places.

2. Right-click, and then select Properties. The Network and Dial-up Connections window appears.

3. Highlight the Local Area Connection you wish to configure and right-click.

4. Select Properties. The Local Area Connection Properties screen appears (Figure 6-3).

5. Click the Install button. The Select Network Component Type screen appears.

6. Highlight Protocol and click Add. The Select Network Protocol screen appears (Figure 6-4).

7. Select the protocol you wish to install and click OK.

8. Close the Local Area Connection Properties screen and the Network and Dial-up Connections window.

For those of you familiar with NT 4.0, the amazing part of the protocol installation is what you did not have to do. Windows 2000 does not require you to reboot when installing a new network client, service, or protocol. Very cool.

DOMAIN NAME SERVICE (DNS)

DNS was developed in 1989 in response to the growth of the Internet. The basic premise is simple—it's easier for humans to remember names than numerical IP addresses. Prior to DNS, the only way to address another host on the Internet was by its IP address. No wonder everybody thought the Internet was for nerds! Only nerds could remember IP addresses. The DNS holds a database of names and maps those names to IP addresses. Much like looking up a number in the telephone directory, you know the name of the person you want to call but not their phone number. You simply cannot call someone unless you know their phone number. The user knows the domain name of the Web site, www.microsoft.com, but not the IP address. On a TCP/IP network, packets do not move without a destination IP address. So our computer asks DNS for the IP address of the Web site. DNS responds to your request with the IP address of the Web server (see the section "How DNS Works," later in this chapter). The client then establishes communication.

DNS Naming

As shown in Figure 6-5, the Domain Name Service is a hierarchical naming structure where all names start at the root and move left from there. The first level under the root is

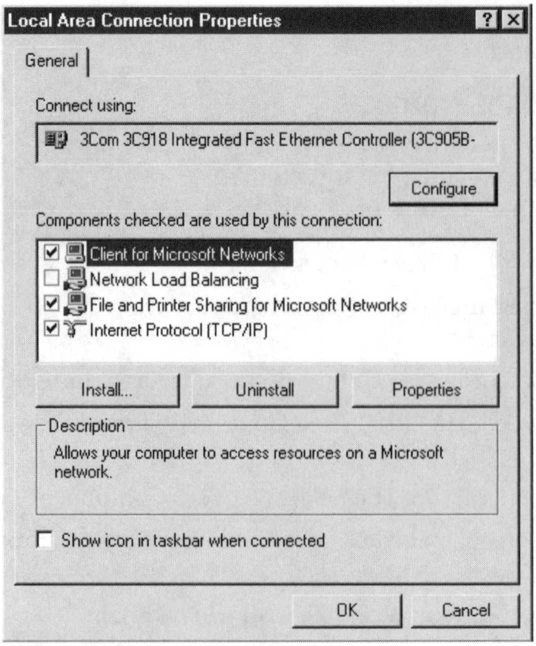

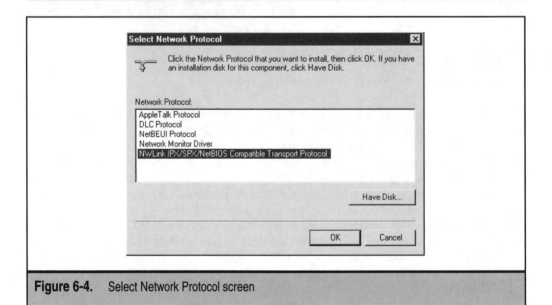

Figure 6-3. Local Area Connection Properties screen

Figure 6-4. Select Network Protocol screen

called the *first* or *top-level domain*. Six top-level domains traditionally were used to create a registered domain name:

- ▼ **com**   Commercial entities
- ■ **org**   Usually nonprofit organizations
- ■ **edu**   Educational institutions
- ■ **mil**   Military installations
- ■ **gov**   Government agencies
- ▲ **net**   Large Internet Service Providers

As the Internet has grown and more organizations have moved into the name registration business in accordance with ICANN (Internet Corporation for Assigned Names and Numbers) principles, more first-level domains have become available. In addition to those previously listed, there are also geographic top-level domain names, such as *us* for the United States, *ca* for Canada, *uk* for the United Kingdom, *de* for Germany, *fi* for Finland, and so on.

The next level in the hierarchy is the second-level domain. To insure that these names will be unique in the entire world, these names must be registered with one of the ICANN authorities. They are your company name, your Web site name, your Internet identity, and, increasingly, your corporate identity, such as microsoft.com.

Additional levels (third or fourth level) are ignored by most of the Internet DNS resolution process and apply only when the DNS request gets to the actual DNS server housing the information for the second-level domain name, such as www.microsoft.com.

How DNS Works

The Domain Name Service unflinchingly follows straightforward rules, which is why it continues to work perfectly for untold millions of Internet users every day. Every Internet server in the world of DNS has a Fully Qualified Domain Name (FQDN). The following illustration explains FQDN.

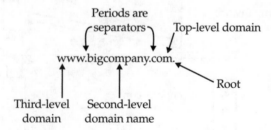

DNS is based on the principle of delegating authority. It resolves names from right to left. Every domain name has an invisible period at the end; that's the root. The root server knows only where the top-level domain servers are. Then we resolve the top-level names (com, org, net, edu, mil, gov). The top-level domain servers know only where the second-level domain servers are. The second-level servers know where the servers authoritative for specific domain names are located. Then the second-level domains registered with the Internet authorities are resolved. And, finally, a host name for the server containing the domain is resolved.

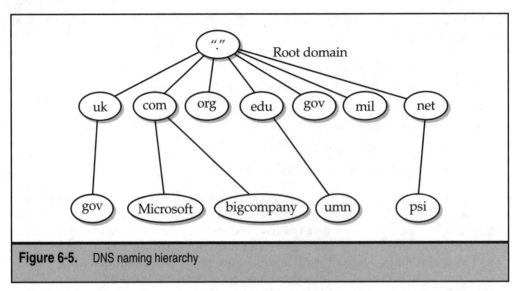

Figure 6-5. DNS naming hierarchy

Consider the actions generated in the next illustration when a home user on the Internet types **www.bigcompany.com** in the address box of their Web browser and presses ENTER.

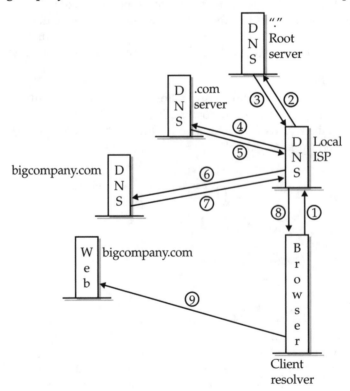

1. A client requests a name resolution for bigcompany.com from the DNS server at the local ISP.

2. The local ISP's DNS does not contain an entry for bigcompany.com, but it knows where to start the search and accepts responsibility for resolving the query. Basically, the first DNS server contacted says to the client, "Well I'll look for the address, but if I don't have it, I'll find out who does." So it looks in its own database first—no bigcompany.com. Then it contacts a root "." DNS server. There are 13 root servers worldwide at the present time. Their IP addresses are published.

3. The root DNS server responds with the IP address of a DNS server with authority over the .com domain.

4. The local ISP's DNS server contacts the .com server.

5. The .com server responds with the IP address for a DNS server that is authoritative for bigcompany.com.

6. The local DNS contacts the DNS that is authoritative for bigcompany.com.

7. The bigcompany.com DNS server responds to the local ISP's DNS server with the IP address of the server that hosts the bigcompany.com Web site.

8. The local ISP's DNS sends the IP address of the bigcompany.com server to the client.

9. The client sends the request directly to the bigcompany.com server because now it knows the IP address, establishes multiple TCP connections, and displays the Web page in its browser window. Every click to a new link that is not part of the bigcompany.com Web site repeats the entire process.

Selecting the DNS Infrastructure

The actual physical setup of a DNS server utilizes the concept of zones. Each zone is said to be "authoritative" for one or more domains. Traditional DNS servers contain zones that come in two flavors: primary and secondary. A primary zone is read/write and allows changes to be input directly. This is the zone where the admin makes the changes manually. For load balancing and redundancy, we may want the same DNS zone information housed on more than one server, but we do not want to have to manually copy the information to the other servers. For this reason, DNS comes complete with its own replication technology. A secondary zone is a read-only copy of the same information and receives all of its updates from the primary. This is a master/slave, one-to-many replication relationship, with the primary zone accepting changes and spreading those changes to the secondary zones through a process called *zone transfer* (similar in concept to the PDC/BDC replication topology in NT 4.0). A single DNS server can contain multiple zones; however, admins often place only one zone per server for fault tolerance and redundancy. While not technically correct (I'm nitpicking here), the admin slang refers to these as DNS primary servers and DNS secondary servers. For the sake of completeness, there is a third kind of DNS server called a *caching only* server, which runs the DNS service but contains no zones. Its only job is to hold information for a preset period of time and resolve DNS queries. It contains no DNS database. Windows 2000 fully supports the traditional primary and secondary zones. Microsoft has renamed the primary and secondary zone options in Windows 2000 to "standard primary" and "standard secondary" to differentiate them from the new AD-integrated zone type.

New in Win2K is the AD-integrated zone. As its name implies, an AD-integrated zone requires the Active Directory. This new AD-integration concept moves the DNS information out of the usual text file on the hard disk and into an object within the AD (the text file goes away). This object is then replicated along with the rest of the Active Directory to every domain controller in the domain using the normal replication cycle. Very cool. Each domain controller that the admin wishes to serve as a DNS server must then run the DNS service. The result is a fault-tolerant, dynamically updated, AD-integrated primary DNS zone—a multi-master DNS replication architecture. However, this strategy does not provide effective load balancing for the clients unless administrators correctly configure the DHCP scopes to manually load balance by rotating the order of the DNS server addresses across subnets.

Naming the First Active Directory Domain

Let's suppose that your organization, called Big Company, Inc., has a Web site named "www.bigcompany.com." You are now going to roll out Windows 2000 and the Active Directory. Because the root domain of the Active Directory forest can never change its name, the root domain name may be a subject of long discussion. After much political wrangling, it is decided that the name for our internal Active Directory domain will be "bigcompany.com", which is the same domain name as your Web site. Thus, you have a DNS problem. You can describe your solution like this: If someone from the Internet is seeking the name "bigcompany.com", you want them to find your Web site. If someone from the inside of your company seeks "bigcompany.com", you want them to find the Active Directory domain. How can you make this happen?

Create two zones named "bigcompany.com". Place one on the DNS server *outside* of your firewall and place the other on a separate (internal) DNS server *inside* your firewall. Block all DNS traffic (port 53) from crossing the firewall. The inside people will find the AD, and the outside people will find the Web site.

New DNS Elements in Windows 2000

New information is traditionally added to the DNS server by hand. An administrator sits down and types the information into a text file in a specific syntactical format, which is the only method for entering information into a traditional DNS database. The information in the DNS database is broken into zones, which consist of specific types of resource records. Table 6-3 defines the resource record types supported in a Windows 2000 DNS database.

Type of DNS Resource Record	Description
Start of Authority (SOA)	DNS server at the top of the authority for this domain.
Name Server (NS)	DNS server that is authoritative for a domain.
Host Address (A)	Computer name mapped to an IP address.
Alias (CNAME or canonical name)	Nickname or alias for an existing host or domain name.
IPv6 Host Record (AAAA)	Computer name mapped to a 128-bit IPv6 address. The IPv6 protocol stack is not supported in Win2K at this time.
Pointer (PTR)	Used in reverse lookups for address-to-name mapping.
Mail Exchanger (MX)	A pointer to a mail server.
Service Locator (SRV)	New in Win2K, enables a computer to locate a specific service.

Table 6-3.   Windows 2000 DNS Resource Record Types

Basically, DNS is designed to store names and numbers for computers. That's it. It is not mysterious. It does one thing and does it well. The traditional role of the DNS has to change in Windows 2000. The dynamic DNS service that ships with Win2K supports all of the following new requirements and recommendations:

▼ SRV resource records

■ Dynamic updates

■ Secure dynamic updates

■ Incremental zone transfer

▲ Negative caching

SRV RR (Service Location Resource Record)

The DNS server in Win2K must support SRV records as specified in RFC 2052. This allows a network service to register its location with DNS, which then responds to queries for that service with its location—an IP address. This is necessary because of the devolution of NetBIOS in the Win2K OS. With NetBIOS on the outs, network services can no longer register their locations only with WINS, a NetBIOS name server. These network services have to add themselves to a central database that is queried by non-NetBIOS Winsock-based (Windows Sockets) computers—in other words, dynamic DNS.

Figure 6-6 shows the records that the Windows 2000 Active Directory can't live without. In the details pane, we see the traditional DNS records, while in the left pane, we see the new types of SRV resource records designed to answer a number of client questions. Where do I log on (dc record)? Where is a specific domain (domains record)? Where is a Global Catalog server (gc record)? Where is the PDC Emulator (pdc record)? Where is the Kerberos KDC (tcp and udp records)? A Windows 2000 Active Directory network cannot exist with these SRV records. The implementation of SRV records is not user configurable.

Dynamic Updates (RFC 2136)

Microsoft strongly recommends support for dynamic updates as outlined in RFC 2136, so that Win2K client computers and servers, and the Win2K DHCP server, can automatically register newly booted machines and services with DNS. This means that no administrator has to enter the information manually; it's all automatic. The host and SRV records are added automatically when the Win2K system boots up and should be removed automatically when the system shuts down. An extension of the dynamic updates is the RFC 2137 specification for secure dynamic updates. This capability, which interfaces with the AD, is also recommended so that unauthorized computers and users are prevented from updat-

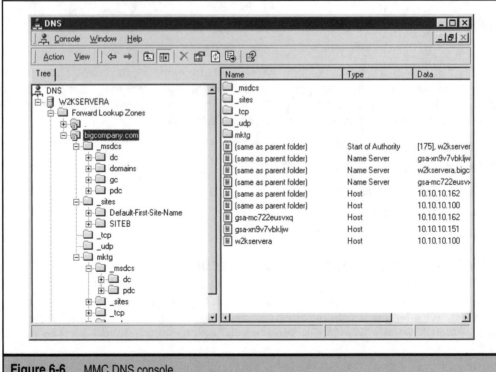

Figure 6-6.   MMC DNS console

ing the DNS dynamically. The secure updates option is available only on AD-integrated zones. The Win2K DNS service also includes a server aging/scavenging service that cleans up "stale" records that are left in the DNS database for over a specified period of time (seven days, by default). On a regular basis, the "scavenger" service checks each zone for records that have not been updated in the last seven days and then deletes them. Aging/scavenging is turned off by default; it must be enabled by administrators.

To configure the DNS zone properties, click Start | Programs | Administrative Tools | DNS. Highlight the zone you wish to configure and right-click. Select Properties. The Zone Properties window (Figure 6-7) appears. Notice the type of zone and the Change button. Press the Change button. The Change Zone Type screen appears (Figure 6-8). You may change the type of zone at any time, and rebooting is not required. In a standard primary zone, the default setting for Allow Dynamic Updates is No. Dynamic updates must be enabled by the administrator by selecting Yes. In an AD-integrated zone, the default setting for Allow Dynamic Updates is Only Secure Updates. Administrators must enable normal (nonsecure) dynamic updates by selecting Yes.

In addition, another factor involved in the dynamic update portion of the DNS is its new integration with the Win2K DHCP server. When a Win2K DHCP server gives a newly booted computer its IP address, the computer automatically registers its name and IP address with the dynamic DNS database. The DHCP server then automatically registers its reverse lookup (number-to-name mapping).

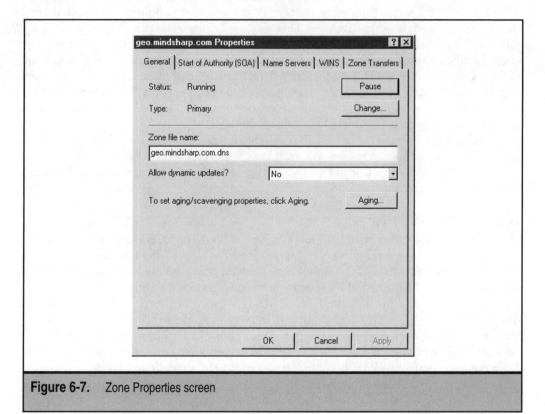

Figure 6-7.   Zone Properties screen

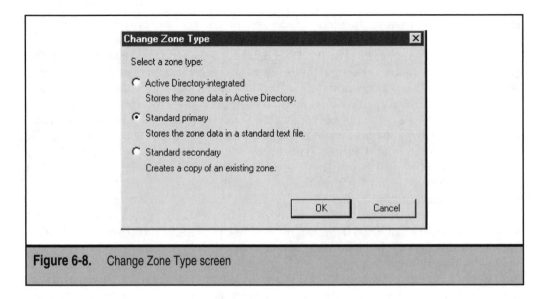

Figure 6-8. Change Zone Type screen

Incremental Zone Transfer IXFR (RFC 1995)

To improve DNS replication performance, Windows 2000 supports incremental zone transfer (IXFR) as defined in RFC 1995. This way, replication data traveling between standard primary and standard secondary zones in Win2K contains only the entries that have changed since the last update, not the entire zone file. The opposite of IXFR is AXFR (all or full zone transfer), which was the only zone transfer method until a couple of years ago. With AXFR, the entire zone database was transferred every time a change was made to the DNS. For this reason, most changes were performed by administrators at the end of the day, and most zone files were kept reasonably small.

Windows 2000 supports both AXFR and IXFR. If the secondary zone that is selected to receive the transfer supports the serial numbers required in RFC 1995, then the transfer will be incremental; if not, a full zone transfer will occur. This is not an administrator-configurable option.

DNS Resolver Cache

In DNS terminology, the client computer is the resolver. The DNS client service used by default in Win2K caches the successful query responses in its DNS resolver cache (RAM). However, the entries do not stay in the cache forever, but rather their length of stay is determined by the TTL (Time to Live) parameter received from the DNS server. If the client needs to contact a specific domain, it first checks its resolver cache to make sure it doesn't already know the IP address of the domain. If the domain name is in the cache, the client uses its cached information instead of performing another lookup. This can save significant time and increase the performance of a large network. To view the contents of the DNS resolver cache on a Win2K client, go to a command prompt and type:

```
ipconfig /displaydns
```

To erase the contents of the DNS resolver cache and force the client to request a new DNS lookup, go to a command prompt and type:

```
ipconfig /flushdns
```

This will force a flush of the DNS cache at that moment. It has no long lasting or permanent effects.

NEGATIVE CACHING   Windows 2000 supports negative caching in accordance with RFC 2308 at the client, which means that if a client has requested a DNS resolution and the result was negative—meaning the domain could not be found—the client caches the fact that it couldn't be found for five minutes, by default. Thus, if the same domain is queried within the next five minutes, no resolution will be attempted. The client will respond with the negative information from the cache. Negative caching is designed to reduce the load on DNS servers caused by multiple queries that are unsuccessful.

WINS Integration

It is possible to integrate the Win2K DNS with the WINS NetBIOS name resolution service (Figure 6-9). If this option is enabled, WINS is used for resolution if the DNS fails to resolve a domain name. Since the Windows Internet Name Service (WINS) is a Microsoft proprietary service, its addition to the Win2K DNS can cause problems if you attempt to integrate a Win2K DNS into an existing non-Win2K DNS structure. WINS records are incompatible with any non-Microsoft DNS server and can cause the non-Microsoft DNS to stop responding to queries. If you are using WINS integration in your Win2K DNS structure *and* you are integrating the Win2K DNS into a non-Microsoft DNS, be sure to check the Do Not Replicate This Record in the WINS tab of the zone properties. This will prevent it from corrupting the non-Microsoft DNS.

An Alternative to Win2K DNS

The big question on the minds of hundreds of UNIX administrators in existing organizations is "will my existing DNS structure have to be changed to install Windows 2000?" The answer is "it all depends." Windows 2000 Active Directory requires SRV records (RFC 2052), strongly recommends dynamic updates (RFC 2136), and would really like to have incremental zone transfers (RFC 1995), change notification (RFC 1996), and negative caching (RFC 2308). The Windows 2000 DNS supports all of these features. And so does the UNIX DNS, BIND 8.2.1. That's right, Win2K AD will run just fine on a network with a UNIX-based BIND 8.2.1 DNS server. To test the dynamic registration from a Win2K client, go to a command prompt and type:

```
ipconfig /registerdns
```

The A record for your computer should now appear in the DNS database whether it is Win2K or BIND 8.2.1.

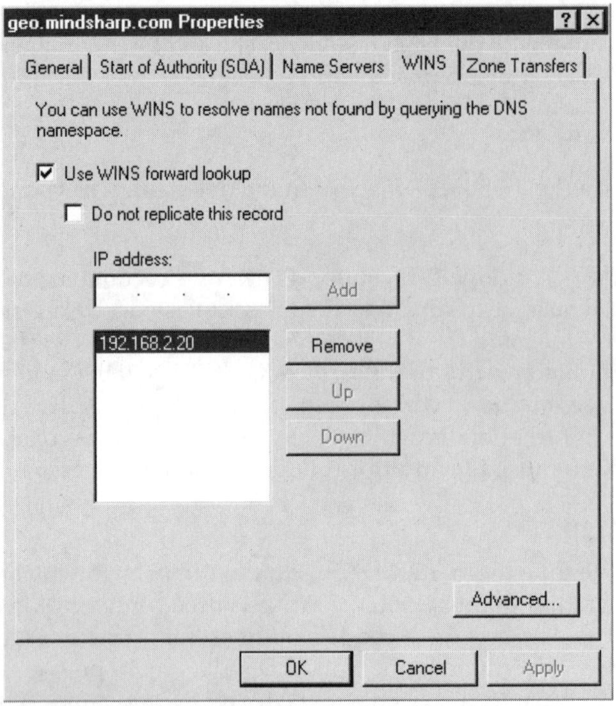

Figure 6-9. WINS integration

DYNAMIC HOST CONFIGURATION PROTOCOL (DHCP)

The Dynamic Host Configuration Protocol (DHCP) is a newer service than DNS. Declared a standard in 1993 in RFC 1533, DHCP is the successor to the boot protocol (BOOTP) used for many years in UNIX-based networks. DHCP expands on the capabilities of BOOTP in a number of ways. BOOTP simply assigned an IP address to a requesting client computer from a table of addresses; DHCP leases IP addresses to clients based on the parameters defined in one or more "scopes" in the DHCP server. Administrators can configure the length of the lease on a per scope basis. Ranges of IP addresses are entered during the scope creation process. The most important enhanced feature of DHCP is its ability to configure other common TCP/IP parameters on a per scope basis. The most common of these parameters include:

▼ DNS server IP addresses

■ WINS server IP addresses

▲ Name resolution node type (specifies the order of NetBIOS resolution)

These options are just 3 of the 57 possible scope options that can be configured on a DHCP-enabled client by the Windows 2000 DHCP server. These scope options range from setting time servers, to routing parameters, to encapsulation configuration. To see the entire list go to the DHCP console, open an existing scope, right-click on Scope Options and select Configure Options. Do not select options that you are unfamiliar with. Do not configure options at the DHCP server until you know exactly what will happen at the client who receives this configuration.

How DHCP Works

The client computer has had its network settings configured to obtain an IP address automatically, which means obtaining the IP address and any other TCP/IP options configured on the DHCP server scope. To begin the process, the computer boots up. As soon as the services start to load, the client computer broadcasts a Discover packet on port 67, which includes the MAC address of its network card for identification purposes. Every DHCP server running receives the broadcast and sends an Offer packet by broadcast on port 68. This packet includes an IP address that the DHCP server is willing to lease to the client. If there are multiple DHCP servers, the client could receive multiple offers. The client selects which offer it will accept (the first one) and broadcasts a Request packet on port 67 to the entire network, accepting one specific offer. This packet informs the selected DHCP server to reserve that address and respond, and it also informs all the other spurned suitors that they were not selected. The selected DHCP server responds still by broadcast with an Acknowledgment (ACK) packet on port 68. The client computer receives the ACK and configures its TCP/IP address and other parameters. This client is now a functioning computer on the network.

The DHCP server scope has a specific length of time that the client can maintain the IP address without renewing. A renewal is quite simple. No broadcasts need occur because both of the parties in the conversation now have IP addresses. The renewal is a directed Request packet and a directed ACK back from the DHCP server. It's quick and simple, with no muss or fuss. Renewals occur, by default, at every reboot of the client. Each time the lease is renewed, it starts over at the beginning of its lease duration. But what if the client isn't rebooted every day? At 50 percent of the lease duration, the client attempts a renewal with the same DHCP server. If that renewal attempt fails at 87.5 percent of the lease duration, the client starts broadcasting again looking for any DHCP server to respond with a new address. If that fails, at 100 percent of the lease period, the client resets its IP address to 0.0.0.0 and can no longer participate in the IP network. Administrators can manually force the release of the DHCP lease as well as forcing a renewal. At the DHCP client, go to a command prompt and type:

▼ `ipconfig /release` to release the IP address

■ `ipconfig /renew` to renew the IP address

▲ `ipconfig /all` to display the current configured TCP/IP settings

DHCP Relay Agent

In order for DHCP to function as described in the last section, organizations must have implemented routers that are compliant with RFC 1542. This standard specifies that when the broadcasts hit the router on ports 67 and 68, it will pass them on to the other subnets that it controls so that, theoretically, a single DHCP server could handle a large routed corporate network. If the routers are not 1542 compliant or if the router folks have blocked ports 67 and 68 for security and traffic purposes, there is still a way to use DHCP.

Install the DHCP Relay Agent service on a computer that is always running on each subnet and then configure it with the IP address of the DHCP server. The DHCP Relay Agent will receive the DHCP broadcast from the client, translate it into a directed packet, and send it on across the router to the DHCP server. And in reverse, the DHCP server sends a directed packet to the Relay Agent, which then translates it and broadcasts it back to the client. This allows DHCP to continue to function even when faced with a router that won't cooperate.

Server Authorization Requirements

New in Windows 2000 is the concept of authorizing servers. In the past, it was possible for "rogue" DHCP servers to pop up on the network and hand out duplicate IP addresses, causing no end of havoc. But in Win2K, if a DHCP server is not authorized to run in the Active Directory, the DHCP service will never start. To participate in the authorization process, the server must be running Windows 2000 and must belong to an Active Directory domain. The DHCP server could be a member server or a domain controller.

After installing the DHCP service with Add/Remove Programs, the server must still be authorized by the Active Directory. To authorize the DHCP server, click Start | Programs | Administrative Tools | DHCP. The MMC DHCP console screen appears. Highlight the word "DHCP" at the top of the console pane and right-click. Select Add Server. Enter the name of the server you wish to authorize. The server must be up and running and able to be reached from the DHCP console. You must authorize the server even if it's the same server you are sitting at running the DHCP console. Once the server is authorized, the DHCP service will start.

Another type of specialized Windows 2000 server, the Remote Installation server (discussed in detail in Chapter 2), must also be authorized. As with DHCP, the RI server must be part of the domain. The authorization process is identical to that in DHCP. Oddly, admins must use the DHCP console to authorize the RI server.

Can a non-Windows 2000 DHCP server be authorized? No, because it is not running Win2K, and it is not a member of the Active Directory domain. This means that these unauthorized servers can indeed dole out "bad" IP addresses and continue to cause problems. For this reason, it is recommended that you upgrade your DHCP servers to Win2K as quickly as possible.

Integration with DNS

By default, the Win2K DHCP is already integrated with the Win2K DNS service. This relationship is configured in the scope properties | DNS tab (Figure 6-10). By default, the

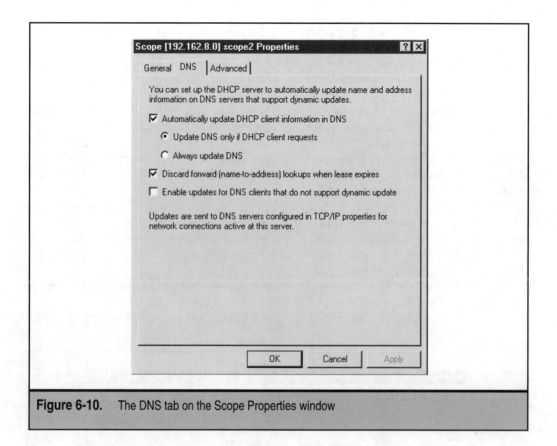

Figure 6-10. The DNS tab on the Scope Properties window

DHCP server updates the PTR records for the Win2K clients that have received their IP addresses from this DHCP server. The client automatically updates the host (A) record. Also by default, the DHCP server will remove those records (both A and PTR) when the client's lease expires, even if the client computer is not available.

Configuring Scope Options

DHCP scopes are not dissimilar in concept to zone files in DNS. Each DHCP server can contain as many scopes as you wish to configure. Each scope has a completely separate set of options and IP addresses. You can administer multiple scopes through a superscope. The scope is the fundamental building block of a DHCP server. It cannot function without at least one scope to administer.

Scopes

After installing the DHCP server service using Add/Remove Programs, in order for a DHCP server to be functional, it must contain at least one scope. To create a new scope, click Start | Programs | Administrative Tools | DHCP. The MMC DHCP console screen appears. Highlight the name of the server and right-click. Select New Scope. The Welcome screen for the New Scope Wizard appears. Click Next.

The Scope Name screen asks for a name for the scope, which is required and will only be seen by DHCP administrators. You may also provide a description for more clarity, if you wish. Click Next.

The IP Address Range screen appears, requesting a range of IP addresses to add to its pool for leasing to DHCP clients (Figure 6-11). Enter the IP addresses you wish to lease. You may enter a single subnet or multiple subnets, provided that they are contiguous. The wizard will force you to adjust your subnet mask to accommodate more than 254 addresses, or in Win2K, it will offer the option of creating a superscope (discussed in the next section). Click Next.

The Add Exclusions screen allows us to exclude specific ranges of IP addresses within the earlier range (a subset of the full range of addresses in the scope) that will not be used by DHCP. Enter a range of exclusions, if you wish, click Add, and then click Next.

The Lease Duration screen allows us to set the limits on the IP address client lease. The default is eight days. Click Next.

The Configure DHCP Options screen wants to know if we would like to configure the most common DHCP options now or later. The default is now. Click Next.

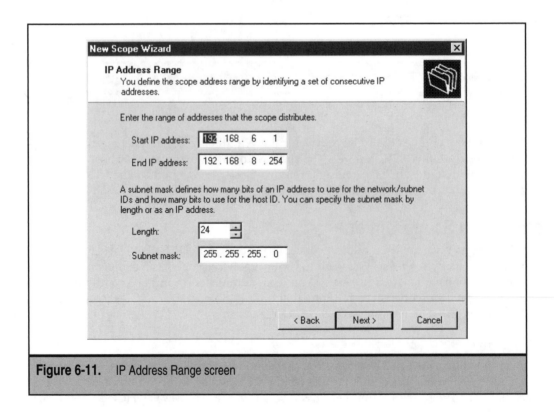

Figure 6-11.   IP Address Range screen

The Router (Default Gateway) screen wants the IP address of the router that connects us to the rest of the world. Enter the IP address. You may enter more than one and move them up or down in the priority list. Click Next.

The Domain Name and DNS Servers screen (Figure 6-12) needs to know the name of the parent domain and the name of the DNS server(s) and its IP address(es). In Win2K, you may enter up to 12 DNS servers. Enter all three pieces of information and then click Next.

The WINS Servers screen requests the name and IP address of the WINS server we would like to add to the scope. In Win2K, you may enter up to 12 WINS servers. This screen also lists a default node type of 0x8 (an H or hybrid node), which means it will attempt to use WINS first for its NetBIOS name resolution before reverting to broadcast. Add the desired information and click Next.

The Activate Scope screen wants to know whether to activate this scope now or wait until later. If you wish this DHCP server to begin leasing addresses immediately, then select now. If, on the other hand, you are configuring it for later deployment, select later. Click Next.

The Completing the New Scope Wizard screen appears. Click Finish. Your newly created scope now is shown in the left pane of the DHCP console. This scope, its configured options, and its range of addresses is now available for lease.

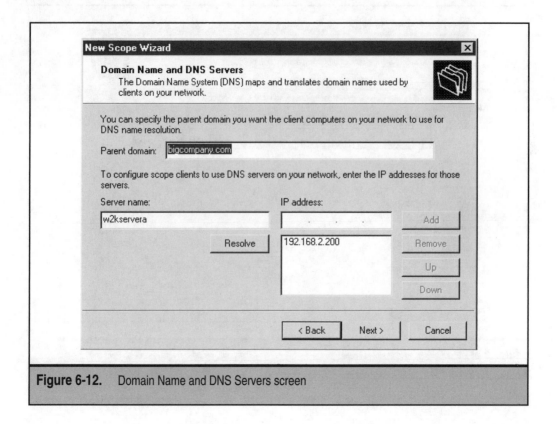

Figure 6-12.   Domain Name and DNS Servers screen

Superscopes

A *superscope* is simply an umbrella administration tool that oversees a number of existing scopes. Using the superscope, for instance, an admin can deactivate every scope within the superscope with a single click of the mouse. Always be careful when deactivating a scope because DHCP immediately begins a recall of all outstanding addresses, which could leave your entire enterprise without any networking capability.

To create a new superscope, click Start | Programs | Administrative Tools | DHCP. The MMC DHCP console screen appears. Highlight the name of the DHCP server and right-click. Select New Superscope. The Welcome to the New Superscope Wizard screen appears. Click Next.

The Superscope Name screen appears. Enter a name for the superscope. It will be seen only by DHCP admins. Click Next.

The Select Scopes screen (Figure 6-13) now tells us that you create a superscope by building a collection of existing scopes. Highlight all the scopes (SHIFT-click) you wish to be a part of this superscope and click Next.

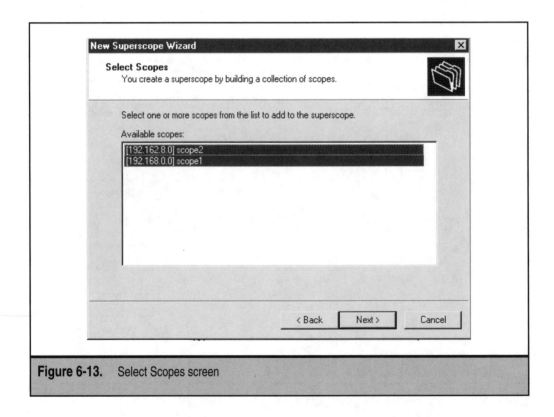

Figure 6-13.   Select Scopes screen

The Completing the New Superscope Wizard screen appears. This is your last chance to click Back and change your configuration. Click Finish.

Your new superscope now appears in the left pane of the MMC DHCP console. The scopes that are now a part of the superscope exist under it in the hierarchy.

Multicast Scopes

A broadcast in TCP/IP sends a message to everyone on the network using IP address 255.255.255.255. A multicast in TCP/IP is a single directed packet going to multiple recipients, with each recipient using an IP address in the class D range. This class D IP address is in addition to the IP address that the workstation already has. The purpose of multicast scopes is to assign the additional multicast addresses to specific clients. To create a new multicast scope, click Start | Programs | Administrative Tools | DHCP. The MMC DHCP console screen appears. Highlight the name of the DHCP server and right-click. Select New multicast scope. The Welcome to the New Multicast Scope Wizard screen appears. Click Next.

The Multicast Scope Name screen is requesting a name for this multicast scope. Enter a name and click Next.

The IP Address Range screen appears. Remember, in our earlier discussion of TCP/IP classes, that class D was reserved for multicast. Therefore, the addresses available for use here are 224.0.0.0 to 239.255.255.255. Enter a valid IP address range. Notice that the Time to Live (TTL) for multicast traffic defaults to 32 routers or hops. You may change the TTL setting here if you wish. Click Next.

The Add Exclusions screen appears, allowing us to enter any exclusions in the IP address range that we do not want used. Click Next.

The Lease Duration screen appears, informing us that the default lease duration for this multicast scope is 30 days. You may change it now if you wish. Click Next.

The Activate Multicast Scope screen wants to know whether we would like to activate this multicast scope now or later. The default is now. Click Next.

The Completing the New Multicast Scope Wizard screen appears, giving us one more chance to click Back and change our configuration. Click Finish.

The new multicast scope now appears in the left pane of the MMC DHCP administration console.

ClassID

New to Win2K and new to the IETF is the concept of classID in DHCP. This concept is still fairly theoretical at this point; this technology has not been implemented. There are two kinds of classID: vendor classes and user classes. The classID is a mechanism by which individual client computers can be set to be a member of a class. Let's say we create a vendor class on the DHCP console of classA. The vendor software running on the DHCP server would wait for computers to come and get their address from DHCP. If the computer identifies itself to be a member of classA. Then it may receive special hardware configurations from the vendor software.

WINDOWS INTERNET NAME SERVICE (WINS)

In the late 1980s, the only "name resolution" technology that Microsoft was using was called computer *browsing*. We know this service today as Network Neighborhood. It was and is a cumbersome and inefficient way to identify servers on a network, but it was the only way for quite some time. Its Achilles' heel became the IP router. Because browsing was designed originally to work with NetBEUI, it is broadcast-based, using the NetBIOS ports 137, 138, and 139. No one in charge of a router will leave these ports open, both for security reasons and because the broadcast traffic would negatively impact the network. Therefore, browsing couldn't go across an IP router. Also, as Microsoft started scaling NT to larger and larger IP networks, it became obvious that a name resolution service for the NetBIOS world was needed. Enter the Windows Internet Name Service (WINS).

NetBIOS name service was defined by RFC 1001 and 1002, but it really wasn't a product until WINS started shipping with NT. The concept is pretty simple. It's a NetBIOS version of dynamic DNS. One or more servers are designated as WINS servers, and the WINS service is installed using Add/Remove Programs. Each client computer is configured with one or more WINS server addresses (in Win2K up to 12). This is done manually by keying them into the client or through a DHCP scope. Once the client has the IP address of its WINS server, it dynamically registers its services with WINS when it boots up. When a WINS client needs to resolve a NetBIOS name, it sends a directed TCP/IP packet to the WINS server and requests resolution. If the WINS server has a record in its database for the name of the NetBIOS server requested, it responds with an IP address. If not, it just says no. Unlike DNS, the WINS service does not support recursive lookups.

WINS Replication Configuration

Like DNS, WINS also has its own replication architecture. Each WINS server can have multiple replication partners. Each partner replicates its entire database to the other. Partners can be configured as push (data is sent when a certain number of changes is reached) or pull (data is requested on a predetermined time schedule) or both. In Windows 2000 Microsoft recommends that all WINS servers be configured as push/pull, and that is the default. Multiple WINS servers should form a replication hierarchy as shown in Figure 6-14.

Windows 2000 Name Resolution

We discussed two separate forms of name resolution so far. Just who uses what kind of name resolution?

For names longer than 15 characters or names that contain a period (".") Windows 2000 clients will always use DNS first. If DNS fails to resolve the name, the Win2K client will "drop down" to NetBIOS and try to resolve the name using WINS. For names 15 characters or less with no periods in the name, Win2K will use WINS first and if that fails,

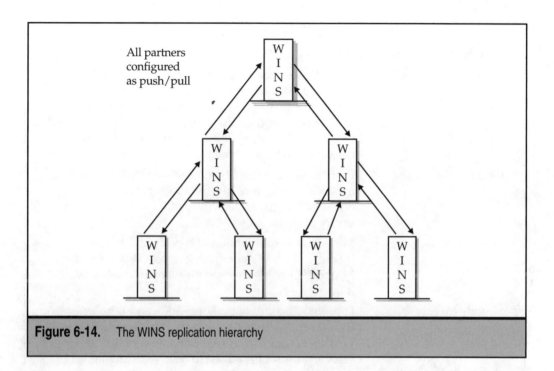

Figure 6-14.   The WINS replication hierarchy

it will then attempt resolution through DNS. Downlevel clients (Win 9x and Windows NT 4.0) configured as H-nodes (hybrid nodes) always try to resolve names using WINS first. If that fails, they issue a Name Query Request (broadcast) to locate the name. Table 6-4 describes the various node types associated with WINS.

Computers running Windows 2000 are B-nodes by default and become H-nodes when configured with a WINS server address in the TCP/IP properties.

WINS Proxy Agent

Similar to a DHCP Relay Agent, the WINS Proxy Agent allows older Microsoft operating systems that may be unaware of the existence of WINS to participate in the WINS structure. On each subnet, the WINS Proxy Agent is loaded onto a computer that will remain on all the time. The WINS Proxy Agent is then configured with the IP addresses of the WINS servers. It "listens" for name resolution broadcasts and translates them into directed packets to a WINS server. In reverse then, the WINS server communicates to the WINS Proxy Agent in a directed packet, and the Proxy Agent translates it into a broadcast for the older client operating system.

Node Type	Description
B-node (broadcast)	B-node uses broadcast NetBIOS name queries for name registration and resolution. B-node has two major problems: (1) Broadcasts disturb every node on the network, and (2) Routers typically do not forward broadcasts, so only NetBIOS names on the local network can be resolved.
P-node (peer-to-peer)	P-node uses a NetBIOS name server (NBNS), such as a WINS server, to resolve NetBIOS names. P-node does not use broadcasts; instead it queries the name server directly.
M-node (mixed)	M-node is a combination of B-node and P-node. By default, an M-node functions as a B-node. If an M-node is unable to resolve a name by broadcast, it queries a NBNS using P-node.
H-node (hybrid)	H-node is a combination of P-node and B-node. By default, an H-node functions as a P-node. If an H-node is unable to resolve a name through the NBNS, it uses a broadcast to resolve the name.

Table 6-4. WINS Node Types

SUMMARY

Many other network services are supported by Windows 2000, but an exhaustive look at networking was not the purpose of this chapter. We focused on the network services that you are most likely to implement and manage in a Windows 2000 Active Directory environment. Microsoft has come a long way since NT 4.0, and the superior quality of the network services shipping with Windows 2000 demonstrates Microsoft's commitment to industry standards and shows their willingness to admit that the proprietary nature of their previous efforts has outlived their original purposes. For all those geeks who said you can't do real networking with a mouse, I give you Windows 2000.

CHAPTER 7

Routing and Remote Access Technologies

Chapter 7 introduces many of the concepts surrounding Routing and Remote Access Service (RRAS) in Windows 2000. We'll focus on the most common configurations of RRAS as defined in its own configuration wizard. We also introduce Terminal Services in this chapter and explain a number of the details of Terminal Server installation and configuration.

ROUTING AND REMOTE ACCESS (RRAS)

RRAS, a separate service in Windows 2000, is installed by default on all Win2K computers, but it remains disabled until an administrator enables and configures it using the Routing and Remote Access Service (RRAS) MMC snap-in on Windows 2000 servers and Network and Dial-up Connections on Win2K Pro. Enabling RRAS creates a remote access server, which allows remote users to dial in to the RRAS server, be authenticated, and then be granted access to the local network as if they were sitting at a computer resident on the actual LAN. All the standard tools (for example, Windows Explorer) function normally over a RRAS connection. Normal client services such as File and Print Sharing, Web server access, and e-mail are also enabled with a remote access connection. Most commercial applications will work without modification over a remote access connection.

A remote access server can provide two basic types of connectivity: dial-up networking and virtual private networking.

Dial-up networking occurs when a client dials the phone number of one of the remote access server ports using a normal analog phone line (POTS) or an ISDN connection. The remote access server is configured to accept incoming connections. Whether the connection is by standard phone line or ISDN, the connection is temporary and can be broken at either end. This is the traditional use of a remote access server and supports mobile clients and most home-based employees or telecommuters. Dial-up networking is available to all Microsoft operating systems including DOS, Win 3.*x*, Win 9*x*, NT, and, of course, Win2K.

In contrast to dial-up networking, virtual private networking (VPN) creates secure, point-to-point connections across a private (LAN) or public (Internet) network. A VPN client uses special TCP/IP "tunneling" protocols (such as PPTP and L2TP) between the VPN client and the VPN server. A VPN connection requires a second IP address for both the client and the server. Using a TCP/IP tunneling protocol does not guarantee that the data will be encrypted. Data encryption must be enabled separately. VPN is available to all 32-bit Microsoft operating systems including Win 9*x*, NT, and Win2K.

Common Configurations

Let's begin by discussing each individual type of server that can be enabled by the RRAS service. There are five common configurations possible (Figure 7-1):

▼　Internet connection server

■　Remote access server

■　Virtual private network (VPN) server

- Network router
- Manually configured server (start with defaults and configure later)

Internet Connection Server

Selecting the Internet connection server option brings up a choice of selecting Internet Connection Sharing (ICS) or setting up a network address translation (NAT) router. If you choose the ICS option, the RRAS wizard informs you that this is not the right place for that option. Instead, you must go to the Network and Dial-up Connections folder accessible from the Start menu. I'll provide more information about this folder later in this chapter.

Selecting the NAT router option leads to another configuration question: select an existing network-based connection to the Internet or create a new demand-dial Internet connection. If your RRAS computer has two network cards and one is connected full time to the Internet (perhaps a CSU/DSU), then you can choose the LAN-based option; otherwise, if the RRAS computer is on the local network and will connect to the Internet through a phone or ISDN line, you'll have to select the demand-dial interface. Demand-dial is an easily understood concept. As its name suggests, it is an interface that will "dial on demand" by the system. When you select demand-dial interface, you access

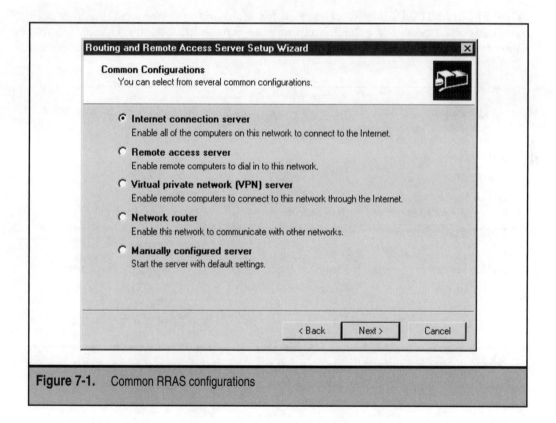

Figure 7-1.   Common RRAS configurations

the Demand-Dial Interface Wizard. You can choose to have the demand-dial interface over a modem/ISDN line or through a VPN. Be sure to enable a port to work with your modem or ISDN line if that is your selection.

NAT ROUTER   Network Address Translation (NAT), part of RRAS, provides the capability for a Win2K server to become a NAT router. NAT allows computers (hosts) on an internal private network to access computers on an external public network (the Internet). The internal computers can use a completely private addressing scheme, while the Internet will need at least one public unique registered address. The NAT router has the job of translating the internal network address to the external world, allowing two-way communication between the internal privately addressed network and the public Internet. NAT is fully configurable.

NAT provides a WINS proxy service (different from the normal WINS proxy agent) that allows the clients to believe that the NAT server is their WINS server. When the client sends a WINS query to the NAT server, it simply passes the request to the real WINS server in its own configuration. Client WINS registrations are simply dropped by the NAT server, which could cause problems with internal client name resolution.

NAT and ICS are compared in Table 7-1.

INTERNET CONNECTION SHARING   Designed for Mom-and-Pop-size small businesses or even networked homes (a SOHO environment—Small Office, Home Office), Internet Connection Sharing (ICS) is an idea whose time has definitely come. Let's say you've got

Type of Address	ICS Client Configuration	NAT Client Configuration
IP address assigned by service	192.168.*.*	192.168.*.*
Subnet mask	255.255.255.0	255.255.255.0
Default gateway (server IP address)	192.168.0.1 (ICS server)	192.168.0.1 (NAT server)
DNS server address	192.168.0.1 (ICS server)	192.168.0.1 (NAT server)
DHCP server	Provided by ICS server	Provided by NAT server
WINS server	None—mixed node	192.168.0.1 (NAT server) Client is hybrid node

Table 7-1.   Differences Between ICS and NAT

a small business with an ISDN connection to the Internet. You could install a Microsoft proxy server or a demand-dial NAT router, but that sounds expensive, will probably use additional hardware and software, and will definitely require more expertise than is possessed in most small businesses. Here comes Windows 2000 ICS to the rescue.

Any Windows 2000 computer, Server or Professional, is capable of ICS. The concept is quite simple, but, as with most of this technology, a couple of implementation details can get you. First, let's discuss the concept. Basically, ICS is a slimmed-down version of NAT. One user on one computer on a small internal network (the computer must have two interfaces—NIC to the LAN—and another external interface—modem, terminal adapter, or NIC) creates an outbound connection to the Internet (using the Network and Dial-up Connections folder, not the Routing and Remote Access MMC snap-in). This connection can use a dial-up phone line, Digital Subscriber Line (DSL), or ISDN. Then the user at that computer enables ICS (Figure 7-2). This computer's connection is now "shared" by the entire network. ICS is off by default, but checking the Enable Internet Connection Sharing for This Connection box also defaults to the on-demand dialing option being enabled as well. This means that if this computer is powered on but the Internet connection is not

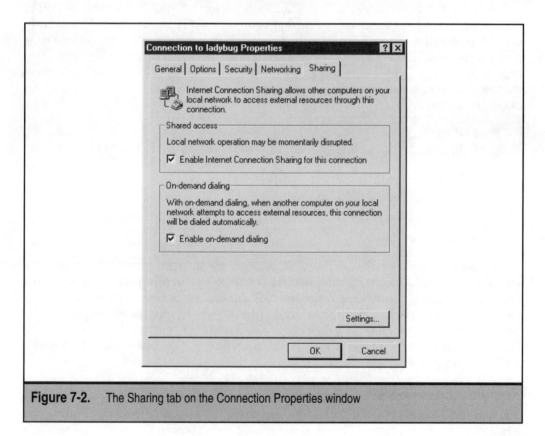

Figure 7-2. The Sharing tab on the Connection Properties window

active and another computer on the network wishes to access the Internet, this computer's external interface will dial it "on-demand." It is not difficult to imagine an incredible number of uses for this technology in a small business or in today's wired homes with "on-line" families.

Now let's discuss the implementation of ICS. Before we begin, it is important to note that NAT and ICS cannot both be run on the same computer because, while not the same service, they do use a number of the same system components. When ICS is enabled on the external interface (a modem or an ISDN connection), the computer hosting the connection will have its internal IP address changed to 192.168.0.1 with a class C subnet mask of 255.255.255.0. This may cause network access problems if static IP addresses were previously used. All the computers on the network must have their TCP/IP properties set to receive their IP addresses automatically, as if a DHCP server were on the network. The computer hosting the connection (the ICS server) now becomes a mini-NAT router (to perform the internal-to-external address translation) and a mini-DHCP server (to hand out class C IP addresses in the 192.168.0.0 subnet). The clients on the ICS network now look to 192.168.0.1 (the ICS server) for their DNS name resolution. ICS does not support WINS or the WINS proxy agent. The ICS clients perform NetBIOS name resolution as M-nodes or mixed mode clients. No further configuration is possible with ICS. If additional configuration is necessary for your environment, install an RRAS server as a fully configurable NAT router or purchase Microsoft Proxy Server 2.0. By clicking Start | Settings and then the Applications tab, you can enable specific applications for computers sharing this connection. The Services tab allows us to enable the following service requests to use this connection:

▼ FTP server

■ Internet Mail Access Protocol v3 (IMAP3)

■ Internet Mail Access Protocol v4 (IMAP4)

■ Internet Mail Server (SMTP)

■ Post Office Protocol v3 (POP3)

▲ Telnet server

ICS is an excellent solution for the wired home or the small business with less than ten workstations. The lack of bandwidth issue raises its ugly head pretty quickly when more than ten people are downloading files over a 56k dial-up line or single-channel ISDN connection. The computer hosting the connection (the ICS server) must be running Windows 2000, but the other computers on the network need only support Microsoft TCP/IP and DHCP. Windows 95, Windows 98, and Windows NT 4.0 will definitely interoperate with an ICS server connection.

Remote Access Server

The second selection in the Common Configurations list (available from the Routing and Remote Access Server Setup Wizard) is the remote access server. Remote access server is perhaps the most common usage of RRAS. This type of connection uses the new RRAS Policies to determine if a particular user can gain access from outside.

BASIC REMOTE ACCESS SERVER   A basic remote access server (RAS) is simply a server that allows remote access to a single machine, authenticated by that machine's local security account database (SAM). It does not require the Active Directory. In spite of the fact that this basic remote access server may be resident on a network, the connecting user cannot access the network. A remote access server could be a solution for someone wishing to dial in from home and connect just to their own computer in the office. This configuration is possible only on a workgroup server or a Windows 2000 Professional machine. The mission of basic remote access is to connect to a single computer, not the network.

To configure a Win2K machine to be a Basic Remote Access server, you do not run the Routing and Remote Access Server Setup Wizard; you simply create a new inbound connection using the Network and Dial-up Connections folder. Do not look for an RRAS management tool, because one doesn't exist. Remember, this option is designed for a single computer to connect to another.

ADVANCED REMOTE ACCESS SERVER   On a member server or domain controller, you have only one remote access server setup configuration type: the advanced remote access server. This configuration gives you the advanced Windows 2000 administrative features, such as remote access policies and Active Directory domain authentication. In the IP Address Assignment screen when you select Automatically Assign IP Addresses to Remote Clients, you are presented another choice. Will you use an existing DHCP server, or will the RRAS server generate the addresses? If the RRAS server has a static IP address assigned, a Routing and Remote Access warning message appears, cautioning you to make sure that the IP address of the RRAS server is "compatible" (in the same subnet) with the addresses assigned to remote clients via DHCP. Or you can specify a range of addresses from a static pool, much like NT 4.0 RAS. You must enter a range containing at least two addresses. Remember, selecting advanced remote access server adds the RRAS policies.

Virtual Private Network Server

A real private network can be defined as one in which you "own" the wire. Perhaps you don't own it, but you lease it for your use, and only your use, 24 hours a day, 7 days a week, 52 weeks a year. It's yours, and no one else can use it. It's your own private road between locations where only your car can drive. In a virtual private network (VPN), you "own" the information, but the wire is for the public to use. The obvious public network is the Internet, a heavily traveled public interstate highway where everyone can see everyone else's car.

In order to keep them from seeing inside the car, we employ special tunneling protocols and combine them with encryption schemes. To create a VPN server, you will need connections to the internal network and to the Internet. Once the configuration is complete (Figure 7-3), the VPN server contains 128 PPTP ports and 128 L2TP ports. Each Win2K client computer contains five PPTP ports and five L2TP ports by default.

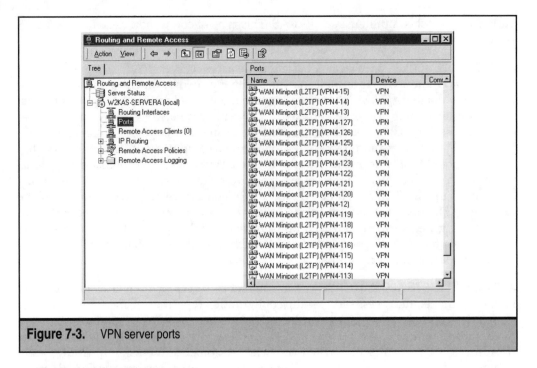

Figure 7-3. VPN server ports

POINT-TO-POINT TUNNELING PROTOCOL Point-to-Point Tunneling Protocol (PPTP) is a VPN technology that tunnels, or encapsulates, IP, IPX, or NetBEUI traffic inside of IP packets. One advantage of using PPTP over the Internet is that users can remotely run applications that are dependent upon particular network protocols.

LAYER TWO TUNNELING PROTOCOL Layer Two Tunneling Protocol (L2TP) provides encapsulation and tunnel management for any type of network traffic. We are talking about Layer 2 of the OSI model—that is, the layer below IP. L2TP uses IPSec in transport mode to provide the security for the L2TP tunnel packets. Table 7-2 lists the differences between PPTP and L2TP.

Category	PPTP	L2TP
Internetwork Protocol	IP	IP, Frame Relay, X.25, ATM
Header compression	No (6 bytes)	Yes (4 bytes)
Tunnel authentication	No	Yes (but not necessary when used with IPSec)
Encryption method	Built-in PPP	IPSec

Table 7-2. Comparison of PPTP and L2TP

INTERNET PROTOCOL SECURITY Internet Protocol Security (IPSec) begins with a normal TCP connection between two hosts; they mutually negotiate a shared secret key that encrypts the data in an IP packet. The keys have a limited lifetime and will be renegotiated if they expire before the end of the transmission. The two predefined security methods are the following:

▼ The Encapsulating Security Payload (ESP) provides data encryption, authentication, anti-replay, and integrity, making this method appropriate for higher security needs. ESP does not provide integrity for the header.

▲ Authentication Header (AH) protocol provides integrity, anti-replay, and authentication. This method is more appropriate for medium or standard levels of security.

Both AH and ESP can also be enabled using a custom security method to ensure integrity: Message Digest 5, MD5, which produces a 128-bit key, or Secure Hash Algorithm, SHA, which produces a 160-bit key. Both these security methods also provide Data Encryption Standard (DES) or triple DES (3DES) for confidentiality.

IPSec in tunnel mode can be used only in a point-to-point (router-to-router) scenario and cannot pass through a NAT router. Also, IPSec policies for computers can be set by Active Directory Group Policies.

Network Router

A network router is fairly straightforward device. There must be two network interfaces, and each interface must have a unique IP address on different subnets. In the Routing and Remote Access Service Wizard, we have a choice to configure one of the interfaces as a demand-dial connection now or later. Demand-dial configuration wants to know how we would like to handle the client addressing. Use an existing DHCP server and allow this server to generate the addresses (using NAT) or specify a range of addresses. Make your selections and then click Next. Miller Time. This one's simple.

Remote Access Policies

New in Win2K, Remote Access Policies are shared between Internet Authentication Service and Routing and Remote Access Service and cooperate with the Active Directory to provide secure access. Remote Access Policies are stored, per connection, on the RRAS server. They are not part of Group Policies, and they do not reside in the Active Directory. Each connection can have multiple RRAS policies. A connection attempt must meet the criteria of at least one RRAS policy, or it will be rejected. The three components of a Remote Access Policy are the following:

▼ **Dial-in Conditions** These must be met or a connection will be refused. They include:

■ Correct time of day

■ Correct day of week

■ Group membership

- Caller ID (phone number dialed from)
- Called ID (phone number dialed to)
- Framed protocol
- Type of service requested
- Tunneling protocol

■ **Permissions**   The Active Directory user account Remote Access permissions (Figure 7-4) can override the policy settings. If the AD Dial-in permissions specify an Allow, the user can always dial in no matter what. If the AD Dial-in permissions specify a Deny, the user can never dial in, no matter what. If the AD Dial-in permissions specify the Control Access Through Remote Access Policy, then the policy permissions will prevail.

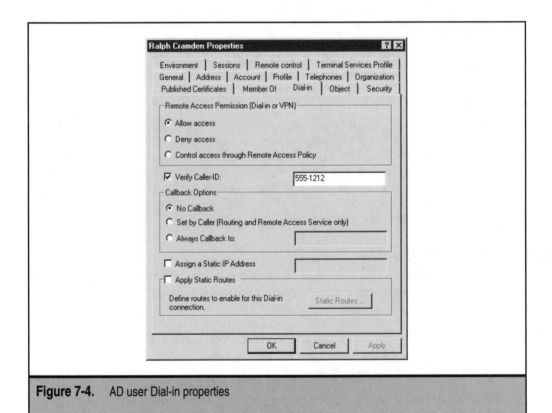

Figure 7-4.   AD user Dial-in properties

▲ **Dial-in profiles**   An extension of the policies discussed earlier in this section, dial-in profiles (Figure 7-5) hold the settings for authentication and encryption protocols that can be applied to each connection. If the connection settings don't match the user's dial-in settings or profile settings, the connection is denied. The following are some examples of these settings:

- IP address
- Authentication method
- Encryption level
- Maximum session time
- Disconnect if idle
- Date and time (again)
- Dial-in media

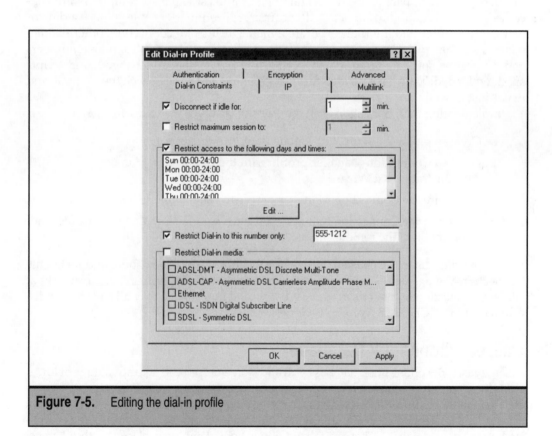

Figure 7-5.   Editing the dial-in profile

Multiple Remote Access Policies are allowed, but in some cases, can actually block each other if they are not carefully configured. The order in which multiple policies are applied is configurable by an administrator. It is important to note that the default Remote Access Policy installed with RRAS denies access to all connections. Microsoft implemented this feature to increase the default security. See Chapter 13 for a flowchart of how Remote Access permissions are applied.

CONNECTION MANAGER

With Connection Manager, organizations can automatically update phone book files located on the remote access client computer. Connection Manager actually automates the connection process by creating service profiles of preconfigured settings for remote access. These profiles can contain more than one access number. Consider this scenario: Field service and sales personnel are distributed nationwide for a Fortune 1000 company. Traditionally, these people are not technologists, at least as far as computers are concerned. Each is required to connect to the corporate headquarters at least once a day for news, information, and internal corporate e-mail. During that connection, other maintenance tasks take place in addition to the personnel's normal activities: phone numbers and connection software are updated, connection parameters are changed, and scripts are downloaded. They have no idea this is happening while they check their e-mail, and that is just as well.

Implementing the Connection Manager service involves the following steps:

1. Create a phone book file with Phone Book Administrator.
2. Create a Connection Manager profile with the Connection Manager Administration Kit Wizard.
3. Configure the Connection Manager profile to use the phone book database.
4. Distribute the Connection Manager software, Connection Manager profile, and phone book to the remote clients.

Step 4 brings us to the chicken and egg problem. You must distribute and install the Connection Manager software locally on each client before this rather cool idea works at all. The Connection Manager software is distributed in the same way all software is distributed: floppy, CD, SMS, Web, FTP, or network share.

Centralized Phonebook Database

In some cases, the phone book database will allow an enterprise to take advantage of lower cost special access numbers when remote users access the network. Business needs may dictate that the organizations access numbers will change from time to time. The dilemma is keeping the users up-to-date with the latest phone numbers. The answer is the centralized phone book database. This centralized phone book database is placed on the Connection Manager's phone book server and administered by Phone Book Administrator.

Connection Manager Profiles

As shown in Figure 7-6, service profiles are created by the Connection Manager Administration Kit (Start | Programs | Administrative Tools | Connection Manager Administration Kit). The rather lengthy profile creation wizard asks for a friendly name (the profile name) and an eight-character filename that will become the profile filename on the phone book server. You are given the opportunity to merge existing profiles into the new one, enabling you to update a profile without re-creating it from scratch. You can enter in the profile your own support phone number, which will appear in the logon dialog box.

Next, you can add a realm name. Windows 2000 does not require realms. RADIUS and IAS may require them under certain circumstances. For those familiar with Kerberos authentication, it requires realms. The Kerberos realm in Win2K is a domain. You must now add the existing dial-up networking entries (at least one) that you wish to associate with this service profile. You can also edit the parameters of the existing dial-up networking entry and add a script if you wish. You can also add VPN support for the profile, in which case you will be prompted for additional IP addresses for VPN use. You may now choose to specify preconnect actions, post-connect actions (like automatically downloading phone book updates), and disconnect actions. You may also specify any applications that you would like to run automatically while your users are connected. You now have the option to specify your own logon and phone book bitmaps.

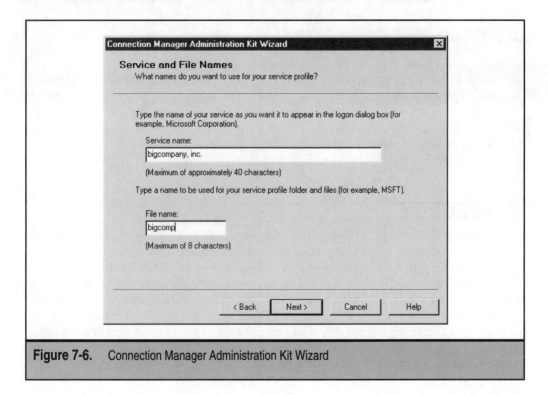

Figure 7-6.   Connection Manager Administration Kit Wizard

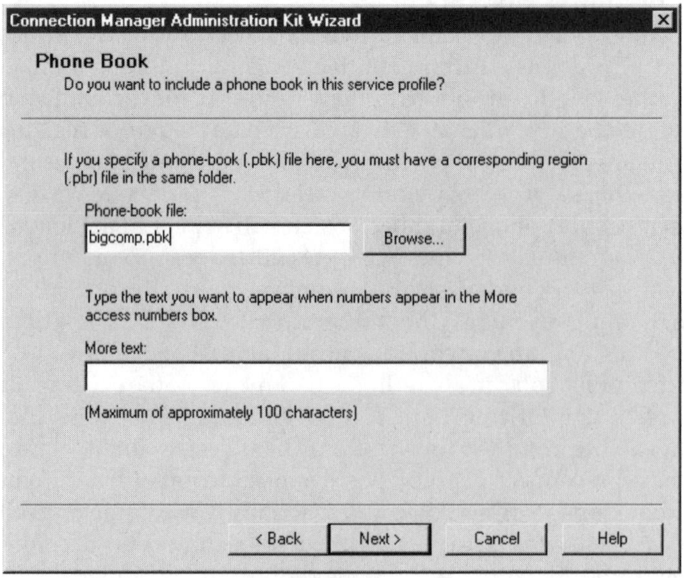

Figure 7-7.   Adding a phone book file to the service profile

As shown in Figure 7-7, you may now include a phone book file (.pbk) in your service profile or a phone book to be downloaded later (if you selected the post-connect action to download phone book updates). Then you can select custom icons and a shortcut menu if you wish. You can enter a custom help file for the profile. Upgrade the Client Connection Manager software to version 1.2 and include a license agreement. Add any additional files that will be needed. The wizard then builds the profile.

RRAS SECURITY

Most network environments feel compelled to provide some form of remote access connectivity for roaming users, remote sites, and much more so that information can be obtained from virtually anywhere, anytime, around the world. Unfortunately, providing remote access also can leave your network environment vulnerable to unauthorized access if proper security measures aren't taken. As a result, securing remote access connections into and away from your Windows 2000 network environment should be a high priority. In addition to the security measures already mentioned in this chapter, Windows 2000's RRAS includes many security features to help protect your network. These features include encryption, authentication, callback, VPN support, and much more.

Pre-Windows 2000 Compatible Access

The Windows 2000 Active Directory contains a Built-in Local group called the "Pre-Windows 2000 Compatible Access" group. The purpose of this group should be obvious from its name. Members of this group are granted access that bypasses many of the security elements of Win2K. The most common use for this group is to allow NT 4.0 RAS servers to continue to operate on a Win2K domain—specifically, to enable Win2K users to log on to the domain through an NT 4.0 RAS server.

The NT 4.0 RAS service connects to the NT 4.0 domain (SAM) database using NULL credentials, which is a no-no in the world of security. To plug this particular security hole, the Win2K Active Directory specifically prohibits any searching of its database by a user (or service) with NULL credentials. This prohibition will immediately eliminate NT 4.0 RAS servers from the Win2K network. To allow for migration, timing, and financial issues, Win2K provides the Pre-Windows 2000 Compatible Access group. During *dcpromo*, the Permissions screen gives us the option of choosing Pre-Windows 2000 Compatible Access. In reality, all this does is place the Everyone group into the Pre-Windows 2000 Compatible Access group. Now that you know this, you can place whatever groups you need in the Pre-Windows 2000 Compatible Access group. Your system is the most secure when this group is empty. So after upgrading your RAS servers, remove the Everyone group from the Pre-Windows 2000 Compatible Access group.

Remote Access Authentication Protocols

You can use several authentication protocols with remote connections. By default, RRAS uses MS-CHAP and MS-CHAPv2 authentication. Selected authentication methods are used by RRAS in the following order:

1. Extensible Authentication Protocol (EAP)
2. Microsoft Challenge Handshake Authentication Protocol version 2 (MS-CHAPv2)
3. Microsoft Challenge Handshake Authentication Protocol (MS-CHAP)
4. Challenge Handshake Authentication Protocol (CHAP)
5. Shiva Password Authentication Protocol (SPAP)
6. Password Authentication Protocol (PAP)
7. Unauthenticated access

The order of precedence is important because they range from the highest level of security to leaving the connection wide open for just about anyone to access. These authentication methods, shown in Figure 7-8, can be found within the RRAS Management Console by selecting the appropriate server in the right console and selecting Properties. Then, under the Security tab, select the Authentication Methods button. To use any of the authentication methods, you simply check the box beside them.

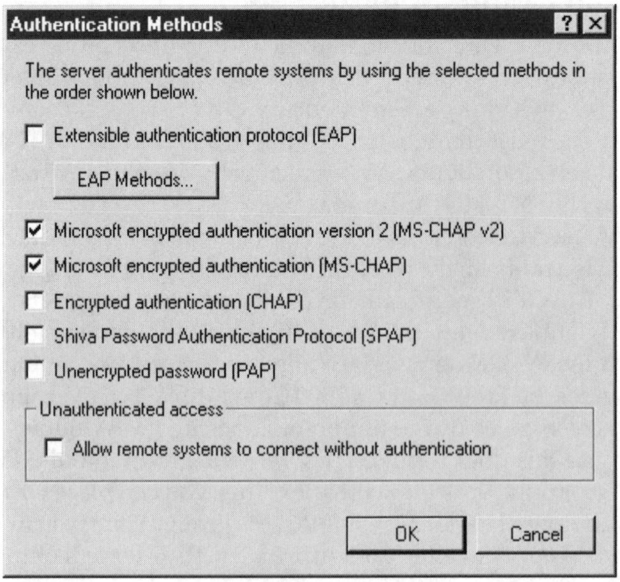

Figure 7-8. Remote access authentication methods

EAP

Extensible Authentication Protocol (EAP) is an extension to PPP that enables an arbitrary authentication method to be negotiated between the remote client and server. Once the link is established, the client and server negotiate on which EAP type of authentication mechanism will be used. These options include EAP-MD5 CHAP, EAP-TLS, Smart Cards, and more. After a decision is made, the client then uses the selected authentication mechanism to gain access to the RRAS server and network.

As the name implies, EAP is extensible, meaning that any number of EAP types can be added at any time. To see which EAP methods you're currently using, do the following:

1. Open the RRAS Management Console from the Start | Programs | Administrative Tools menu.

2. In the right console, right-click on a RRAS server and select Properties.

3. Under the Security tab, click the Authentication Methods button to display the Authentication Methods window.

4. Click the EAP Methods button to see the EAP methods that are currently installed.

EAP METHODS   Windows 2000 can support any EAP method types (for example, Smart Cards) as plug-ins, but it provides the following two EAP methods by default:

▼ **EAP-MD5 CHAP** is a required EAP method that retains many of the same attributes as CHAP but also sends the challenges and responses as EAP messages.

▲ **EAP-TLS (Transport Level Security)** is a certificate-based authentication method. This method is required if you're using Smart Cards. EAP-TLS is currently the strongest type of authentication, and it requires that the RRAS server be a member server in an AD domain. It provides mutual authentication (both client and server are authenticated), encryption, as well as secured private-key exchange.

CHAP

Challenge Handshake Authentication Protocol (CHAP) is probably the most common authentication suite of protocols in use today. Three versions of CHAP are supported by Windows 2000's RRAS, which are the following:

▼ **CHAP**, as an industry standard, is a challenge-response authentication protocol that supports one-way encryption of responses to challenges. The authentication process uses three steps to completion. First, the server challenges the client to prove its identity. Then, the client sends an encrypted CHAP message in response to the challenge. The server then verifies the response, and if it's correct, the client is granted access.

■ **MS-CHAP** is a modified, proprietary version of CHAP. The major difference between MS-CHAP and CHAP in Windows 2000 is that the user's password can be stored in a reversibly encrypted form.

▲ **MS-CHAPv2** is a stronger, more secure authentication method than the previous implementation of MS-CHAP. One of the most notable differences is that it no longer supports NT LAN Manager authentication (NTLM). Other differences are that it provides for a stronger mutual authentication, stronger initial data encryption keys, separate cryptographic keys used for sending and receiving data, and 128-bit encryption. MS-CHAPv2 is supported only on Windows 98 Second Edition and Windows 2000 systems.

SPAP

Shiva Password Authentication Protocol (SPAP) is a proprietary, yet still widely accepted, remote access solution. Clients using Shiva client software must be authenticated using SPAP. SPAP is a simple authentication method that encrypts passwords traveling across the link. Windows 2000 supports this authentication option only for backward-compatibility for Shiva clients that you may need to service. If you're not using Shiva products, it's best to use a more robust authentication mechanism.

PAP

Password Authentication Protocol (PAP) is actually a misnomer because it is the most insecure authentication method available today. Both the username and password are sent across the link in clear text. That's right—no encryption whatsoever. Anyone snooping the connection could easily grab and use the information to gain access to your network. As a result, using PAP for authentication is less than advisable.

Unauthenticated Access

Obviously, this option provides no degree of authentication for remote access. All I will say, though, is that you should never use this option unless you absolutely don't care about securing your environment. You're opening access to anyone and everyone who wants to connect remotely.

Callback

Callback means just what the name implies: a remote client dials the RRAS server and the client's credentials (username and password) are verified. Once the credentials are verified, the connection is dropped so that the RRAS server can call the remote client back. The number that the RRAS server calls can either be specified during the initial call, or you can require that RRAS call a specific number. The latter is the most secure method because it restricts remote connectivity locations that aren't originating from a designated location. Generally speaking, this option is truly beneficial when you're dealing with a remote access client who is dialing in from the same location most, if not all, of the time.

Caller ID

Caller ID (also known as Automatic Number Identification or ANI) is an extremely popular add-on feature provided by the local phone company. Many of you may have it on your phone systems at home and even on your cell phone. When someone calls you, their telephone number is displayed, which enables you to screen your phone calls, if you wish, and answer only the ones that you want to at the time.

Caller ID can also be used to verify that a remote client that dials into RRAS is calling from a specified number. If the client isn't calling from the specified number, the connection is denied and dropped. You sometimes may run into the problem where the phone company can't provide you with a caller's number because the plain old telephone systems (POTS) isn't equipped to handle caller ID in some places or the caller has blocked the number from being displayed. When the number can't be displayed, for whatever reason, the connection is denied. Therefore, check to make sure that the numbers will be revealed before you implement this solution.

Remote Authentication Dial-In User Service (RADIUS)

Specified in RFCs 2138 and 2139, the Remote Authentication Dial-In User Service (RADIUS) is designed as a large-scale, vendor-independent, distributed dial-in service. The key word here is *distributed*. The basic concept is that large and geographically diverse companies require distributed access but secure centralized authentication with a tracking or accounting mechanism for their employees all over the world. However, rather than lease high-speed lines and create their own private networks, they use an inexpensive and insecure public network—the Internet.

After attaching to the Internet, these companies connect to any RRAS server at the edge of their corporate intranets. The connection uses a VPN tunneling protocol to ensure the privacy of the communication. The RRAS server is functioning as the RADIUS *client*; the RADIUS client then forwards the remote client authentication request to the RADIUS *server* inside the corporate intranet that authenticates the login requests using IAS (Internet Authentication Service), and each employee's activity is logged.

Since the RADIUS specification is vendor independent, a Win2K RRAS server can function as a Win2K RADIUS server, a RADIUS client on another vendor's (non-Microsoft) RADIUS server, or both a RADIUS client and a RADIUS server simultaneously. To add the RADIUS server capability to an RRAS server, an administrator must install and configure IAS. This IAS installation is separate from enabling RRAS.

TERMINAL SERVICES

Based on technology from Citrix, Win2K Terminal Services could be a lifesaver for some installations. The concept is simple: Win2K is a mainframe. We change our distributed processing model into a centralized processing model (Figure 7-9). The clients connect to the central computer via terminal sessions. Client hardware requirements are minimal. All processing takes place on the central computer, and all applications run on the central computer. Sound familiar? It should. It's where we came from 20 years ago. What once was old is new again!

Windows 2000 Terminal Services ships with two modes: Remote Administration and Application Server. Each must be configured during the installation of the service. Once installed, the TS modes cannot be changed.

Terminal Services is very fast because the only data traveling across the network is keystrokes and mouse-clicks generated at the client and screen updates coming from the server. This makes Terminal Services an excellent dial-in solution because of the minimal traffic between the TS client and the server housing the Terminal Services. It's secure, too, with support for up to 128-bit encryption on the wire (40-bit encryption is also available for export limitations).

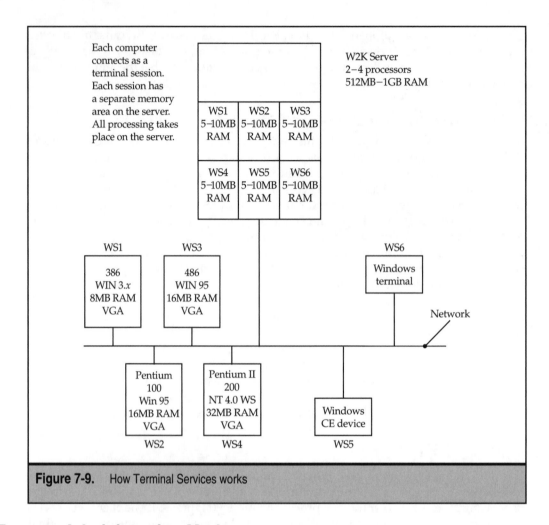

Figure 7-9. How Terminal Services works

Remote Administration Mode

Designed to assist administrators in managing and configuring servers and domain controllers from anywhere on the network, Remote Administration mode is one of the best ideas Microsoft has ever had (and it's about time). This feature really will enable us to effectively run an enterprise network. Without any additional cost, administrators can dial in to domain controllers or member servers or easily connect across the network to perform whatever administrative tasks they wish. These tasks include using all server administrative tools, the MMC, and remote software installation to these servers.

Licensing

In an all-Win2K environment, Remote Administration mode does not require any additional licenses. Win2K Terminal Services includes two free TS Client Access Licenses (CAL) and two free Win2K Server CALS as well. Separate licensing is required for accessing the server and then accessing Terminal Services. Each copy of Win2K Pro includes a free TS client access license but no free Win2K CAL.

Application Server Mode

This mode is one of the heaviest uses for a PC imaginable. Depending on what the users actually do on the systems, it may be possible to support up to 75 to 100 users on a single Terminal Server. But the hardware specifications are stiff: dual or quad Pentium III, with at least 1GB RAM. The TS Application Server mode should be installed only on a dedicated standalone server and never on a domain controller strictly for performance reasons. The payoff is reduced cost for the clients. All applications are loaded and run on this server. Application Server mode is approximately 30 to 40 percent slower when running 16-bit applications.

Licensing

Terminal Services Licensing is a separate installable (through Add/Remove Programs) service used only with the Terminal Services in Application Server mode. The Remote Administration mode does not require the Terminal Services Licensing service. Terminal Services Licensing ships on the CD with Win2K Server and Advanced Server.

Application Server Licensing requires the creation of a license server (it can be the same computer as the Terminal Server in small enterprises) and a one-time connection (you may use the Internet, Web, FAX, or phone) to the Microsoft Clearinghouse to activate the TS license that you've purchased. The Terminal Services licensing activation process works like this:

1. You provide your product number to Microsoft.

2. Microsoft runs an encryption algorithm on your product number.

3. Microsoft sends the results as an activation code.

4. You send the activation code back to Microsoft.

5. Microsoft runs another encryption algorithm on the previously encrypted activation code.

6. Microsoft sends you a license code corresponding to your previous activation code.

You have only 90 days after installation to activate the TS license. After that, if the License Server does not have a current activated license or the client does not present its own license, the Terminal Server(s) simply refuse connections.

A Terminal Services client computer must have one of the following licenses to connect to a Terminal Server:

▼ Terminal Services Client Access License (purchased TSCAL)

■ Terminal Services Internet Connector License (using Internet Application Service Providers—ASPs)

■ Built-in License (included with Win2K Pro)

▲ Temporary License (clients can connect during the 90-day "grace period" after a TS installation)

Prior to Win2K, Microsoft did not require activation of the licenses for NT 4.0 TSE, but the Citrix WinFrame product and MetaFrame add-on did require license activation directly from Citrix. If this activation experiment by Microsoft is a success, look for license activation to become a normal part of the BackOffice product suite.

Application Compatibility Issues

A significant number of application compatibility issues involve the Windows 2000 Terminal Services. Microsoft has tested a large number of applications on the new Win2K Terminal Services platform and has identified specific changes in the locations of files or settings for the client sessions that can get these applications running successfully on Win2K Terminal Services. After the Win2K Server installation, you will find a number of application-compatibility scripts for the express purpose of modifying existing application parameters to run with Terminal Services.

TERMINAL SERVICES APPLICATION COMPATIBILITY SCRIPTS In most cases, these scripts are command scripts (CMD), which are simply batch files designed to create new directories, copy files to new directories, and set new environment variables for legacy downlevel applications attempting to run on a Windows 2000 server using Terminal Services Application Sharing mode. The actual scripts themselves contain the most valuable documentation on when and how they should be deployed. They do not run automatically. Use Notepad or any text editor to read or modify the TS application compatibility scripts. In all cases, they will be run after the Win2K Server installation using Terminal Services installed in Application Sharing mode. The legacy applications for which Win2K includes scripts are listed in Table 7-3.

On the installed Win2K Server in the \WINNT\APPLICATION COMPATIBILITY SCRIPTS\INSTALL folder, we find 27 application compatibility scripts and 4 installation keys. Also in the same folder is a \TEMPLATE subfolder containing 13 installation keys that may be needed by other scripts.

Program Name	Script Filename
Corel Perfect Office 7.0 32-bit	coffice7.cmd
Corel Perfect Office 8.0 32-bit	coffice8.cmd
Microsoft Exchange Client 5.5	winmsg.cmd
Lotus SmartSuite 97 32-bit	ssuite97.cmd
Lotus SmartSuite 9.0	ssuite9.cmd
Microsoft Office 4.3	office43.cmd
Microsoft Office 95	office95.cmd
Microsoft Office 97 SR1	office97.cmd
Microsoft Project 95	msproj95.cmd
Microsoft Project 98	msproj98.cmd
Netscape Communicator 4.0	netcom40.cmd
Netscape Navigator 3.0	netnav30.cmd
Microsoft Outlook 98	outlk98.cmd
Peachtree 2000	pchtree6.cmd
Microsoft SNA Server 3.0	mssna30.cmd
Microsoft SNA Client 4.0	sna40cli.cmd
Microsoft SNA Server 4.0	sna40srv.cmd
Microsoft Visual Studio 6.0	msvs6.cmd

Table 7-3. Terminal Services Application Compatibility Scripts

In the \WINNT\APPLICATION COMPATIBILITY SCRIPTS\LOGON folder, we find 8 additional application compatibility scripts covering the startup parameters of these applications. Also in the same location is a \TEMPLATE subfolder containing 13 additional scripts to be used in starting legacy applications.

In the \WINNT\APPLICATION COMPATIBILITY SCRIPTS\UNINSTALL folder, we find 17 additional uninstall scripts for the express purpose of uninstalling login scripts pertaining to specific applications.

Terminal Services application compatibility scripts may be executed on the Terminal Server itself or the client computer, or they may involve a logon script. Check the documentation in the actual script for details.

TS Clients

On the client side, Windows 2000 supports both 16-bit (Windows for Workgroups 3.11) and 32-bit (Win 9*x*, NT, Win2K) Windows clients, as well as Windows CE handheld devices. For additional clients, you must purchase the Citrix MetaFrame add-on service, which is discussed later in this chapter. Every computer that wishes to connect via Terminal Services requires the TS client software to be installed on the local machine. To create the Terminal Services client installation disks, click Start | Programs | Administrative Tools | Terminal Services Client Creator; the Create Installation Disk(s) screen appears.

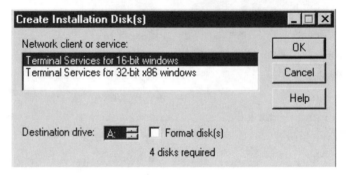

You will need four floppy disks to create the 16-bit TS client (for Windows for Workgroups 3.11) but only two floppies for the 32-bit TS client. After creating the installation diskettes, you can install the TS client on a Win2K computer by inserting the first floppy disk and running setup.exe.

It is also possible to install the TS client from a network share. The source files for the TS client are stored in the %SYSTEMROOT%\SYSTEM32\CLIENTS\TSCLIENT folder on the Terminal Server. Administrators can simply share that folder, connect to the share from the client computer, and run setup.exe from there.

By today's standards, the hardware required by the TS client is pretty small potatoes. (Dan Quayle, can you give me a hand here?) The Terminal Services client hardware requirements are listed in Table 7-4.

Citrix MetaFrame

Citrix Systems was the original developer of the Terminal Server concept back in the NT 3.51 days. They licensed the source code for NT 3.51 from Microsoft and then re-wrote the OS kernel to support multiple simultaneous sessions. Microsoft recognized the

Operating System	RAM	Processor	Video Card
Windows 2000	32MB	Pentium	VGA
Windows NT 4.0	16MB	486	VGA
Windows 98	16MB	486	VGA
Windows 95	16MB	386	VGA
Windows for Workgroups 3.11	16MB	386	VGA
Windows CE 3.0	Vendor	Vendor	Vendor

Table 7-4.   Terminal Services Client Hardware Requirements

wisdom of this technology and made significant changes in the NT 4.0 architecture to take advantage of the terminal session concept. Then Microsoft proceeded to license back some of the Citrix technology, which resulted in NT Server 4.0, Terminal Server Edition. NT 4.0 TSE was built around a separate proprietary kernel that was not the standard ntoskrnl that shipped with standard NT 4.0 Server, which caused a separate Service Pack schedule and occasional incompatibilities between normal NT 4.0 Server and the Terminal Server editions. When NT 4.0 TSE was shipped, as part of their licensing agreement with Microsoft, Citrix could sell only an add-on product to the TSE called MetaFrame. But this is the recent past.

In Windows 2000, Terminal Services are no longer a separate kernel but rather a standard service that can be loaded like any other network service. Citrix continues to market the add-on MetaFrame product to ride on top of the Win2K Terminal Services. MetaFrame provides a significant number of additional features over and above the Win2K Terminal Services product. When you add MetaFrame to a Win2K Terminal Server, you receive all of the capabilities of the Win2K TS as well as the enhanced functionalities of MetaFrame. One additional note that might be interesting is that in every comparison or test of the Microsoft Remote Display Protocol (RDP) versus the Independent Computing Architecture (ICA) protocol, ICA wins on nearly every account, especially speed. Also important to note is that Microsoft Product Support will not support Citrix MetaFrame or the ICA protocol. They will send you directly to Citrix for support. Table 7-5 lists some of the additional capabilities available with MetaFrame.

Category	Windows 2000 Terminal Services	Additional Capabilities Provided by Citrix MetaFrame
Clients	WfW 3.11, Win 9x, NT, Win2K	Win 3.1, DOS, Macintosh, Unix, Linux, Browser
Client devices	PCs, Win CE–based terminals	Macintosh, Handheld PCs, NC, Windows terminals, network terminals, set tops
Multimedia support	No	Yes
Transport protocols	TCP/IP	IPX/SPX, NetBEUI
Connection types	LAN, WAN, RAS Dial-up	Direct Serial, Direct Dial-up
Local device support	Local printer, local client print spooler	COM port redirection, local drive mapping
Shadowing	One-to-one	One-to-many, many-to-one, cross-server
Protocol	Remote Display Protocol (RDP), which is ITU T.120	Independent Computing Architecture (ICA)

Table 7-5.   Terminal Services versus Citrix

SUMMARY

One could easily write an entire book about the subjects touched on in this chapter. My intent was to introduce many of the elements in Windows 2000 Remote Access, a vast area indeed and a moving target. I believe that many of these services will continue to be enhanced as Windows 2000 becomes well-established in the marketplace. This specific area of technology seems to advance at a much faster pace than most. Perhaps it's because we've become so mobile, or maybe it's the barrage of security issues that make it into the mainstream press. Whatever the reason, it causes the remote access arena to constantly advance. And I'm sure that Windows 2000 will advance right along with it.

CHAPTER 8

Active Directory Basics

C hapter 8 focuses on the basic building blocks of Microsoft's Active Directory, its foundation, and its structure. The intensive detail of Active Directory implementation is reserved for Chapter 9 with configuration reserved for Chapter 10. In this chapter, we'll introduce new terminology that will be a part of all future Microsoft network administration. If you are new to the concept of a logical directory of objects, you may have to read parts of this chapter more than once to fully comprehend the key elements of the Active Directory and how they relate to one another. However, if you have previous experience with X.500 directory services in UNIX, AS/400, Banyan, or Novell, many of the conceptual elements introduced here will not seem foreign to you. As usual, however, Microsoft has put a unique twist on its implementation of the X.500 directory service, so much of the material in this chapter will be new to you even if you have experience with X.500 directory services.

The Active Directory is Microsoft's first real attempt to create a single enterprise-wide directory service. It's what sets Windows 2000 apart from all other operating system products, including NT, which is also made by the folks in Redmond. Without the Active Directory, Windows 2000 would simply be a nice upgrade to a reasonably good OS (NT); with the Active Directory, Win2K is a revolutionary platform on which an organization can base its network administration, security, and application development architecture for the next decade.

UNDERSTANDING DIRECTORY SERVICES

Directories of every kind surround us. We can't live without them. We need directories to find things. For as long as there have been things to remember and things to locate, we've had some kind of directory. And the more things we need to remember, the more help we need finding them.

Common Directories

The most common directory today is, of course, the telephone directory, which is divided into two major divisions, or domains, the White Pages and the Yellow Pages. Within each domain is a different organizational structure. In the White Pages, people and businesses are listed in alphabetical order and, therefore, are sorted by letter. In the Yellow Pages, each object (each business) is listed in alphabetical order within a function. We've accepted this directory and its organizational structure without thinking twice about it. If we're too lazy to look in the telephone book, we can even call Information Services and pay someone else to look up a person or business in their directory.

The leading Web directory is Yahoo!, a directory of Web sites organized by category or function. In fact, a good portion of Web sites are really nothing more than directories with links that point to other Web sites. Each one of us has a personal directory of friends and family in the form of an address book or personal digital assistant. Our e-mail client software includes a directory of e-mail addresses. Hundreds of numbers are programmed into our cell phones. The list of directories that we use daily goes on and on.

As the sheer volume of data, names, and numbers that we need to retrieve increases, the need for directory services skyrockets. And every directory should be designed so that information is easy to find. Finding information is, after all, the purpose of a directory. The information must be held in a format that allows for quick retrieval.

X.500 Directory Services

Computers need directories, too—directories like the X.500 Directory Services. Especially computers on a network. The bigger the network, the more desperately it needs a directory service. An enterprise-wide computer network can contain thousands of users, groups, computers, and printers, each of which is defined as a unique object in a directory database. With thousands or even millions of objects to store and retrieve, a single, enterprise-wide directory of these objects becomes essential.

But how to create an enterprise-wide directory? Where to begin such an overwhelming task? Even a colossus like Microsoft could feel a little like the Lone Ranger. Fortunately, there is already a worldwide standard for such a directory: X.500 Directory Services. First defined in 1989 by the CCITT (Comité Consultatif International Télégraphique et Téléphonique), X.500 Directory Services were further refined and updated in 1993 by the ITU-T (the International Telecommunication Union, the successor organization to the CCITT). The concept is simple; the initiative is bold: Create a set of rules that, if implemented correctly, will eventually allow for a vendor-independent directory of every computer, user, group, printer, server, volume, and file system in every department in every company in every country in the entire world.

World -> Country -> Corporation -> Department -> User

That's right, every object in the entire world! And this bold initiative was undertaken before the Internet hit its current popularity.

Commercially Available Directory Services

All commercially released directory services follow the ITU-T X.500 specifications exactly, right? I'm afraid not. Several vendors have already shipped successful directory services, but none are completely faithful to X.500. Banyan's StreetTalk was the first technically viable and commercially successful directory service that really addressed the needs of the modern networked enterprise. But the StreetTalk technology actually pre-dated most of the X.500 specifications. Banyan was by far the dominant player in enter-prise networking in the late 1980s and early 1990s. StreetTalk's niche was centralized administration and network management of distributed enterprises connected by wide area networks.

Banyan faded quickly in the stretch as Novell, the local area networking leader, in an effort to expand its LAN-based, smaller network focus to meet the needs of larger enter-prises, introduced NetWare Directory Services (NDS) in 1993. Novell's NDS moved the LAN giant away from its server-centric architecture to the network-centric world of X.500 Directory Services. NDS, the most widely used directory service in today's corpo-rate environment, is the product that has stayed the closest to X.500 specifications.

By introducing the Active Directory in Windows 2000, Microsoft has moved away from the somewhat server-centric model of domains in NT (where the only updateable object database in the domain is the PDC's). The AD promises to be the one to beat in the new millennium. Microsoft's Active Directory is "X.500-like," which is Microsoft's way of saying, "We looked at X.500 and we liked the concept."

While not exceptionally faithful to the X.500 specifications, the Active Directory in-cludes features and functionality beyond the imagination of the original X.500 creators. The Active Directory allows Windows 2000 to scale up to millions of objects with a single point of access. The AD includes fault tolerance and security. Because the AD supports LDAP v3, it is interoperable with Exchange 5.5 and Novell's NDS. Its schema is extensible to allow the creation of future products and applications. In Windows 2000, Microsoft tries to use existing industry standards much more than it has in the past.

What Microsoft is really attempting to do is to beat Novell at its own game. While Ac-tive Directory provides a reliable, network-centric administrative model for the enter-prise of the next five years, a new paradigm (buzzword alert!) is being created for directory-enabled applications. Microsoft's COM+ (Component Object Model) allows developers to leverage the power of an enterprise-level directory service to create and de-ploy applications (using COM objects) of unprecedented functionality in a distributed environment while keeping developmental resources to a minimum. Each of Microsoft's infrastructure products (Exchange, SQL, SMS) will also maximize the capabilities of the AD in future releases. Windows DNA (Distributed interNet Applications Architecture) is positioned to link, not just with Microsoft technology, but with a heterogeneous mix of future products from other vendors as well. This way, a seamless integration between fu-ture networks and databases and the capabilities of the intranet/Internet can be achieved. In other words, Microsoft is positioning Windows 2000 and the Active Direc-tory as the base platform for all of its future products and development efforts.

Meta-Directories Could Be the Ultimate Answer

Microsoft recently acquired ZOOMIT, a major provider of meta-directory technology. A *meta-directory* is a directory of directories. (The following illustration shows a meta-directory structure.) In a multi-vendor directory services environment, the meta-directory reads all the existing vendor-specific directories within an organization, copies all the necessary data into a higher-level "meta" directory, and keeps the data current by synchronizing with all the other directories. Using this new enterprise identity-management product, the user or administrator interacts only with the meta-directory and never directly updates the vendor-specific directories. The ship date for ZOOMIT is scheduled for four to six months after Win2K.

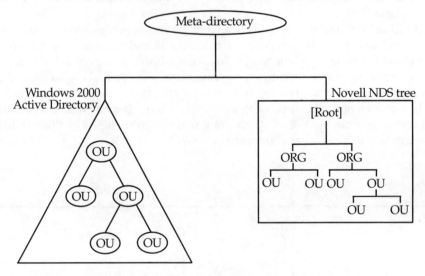

Here's a quote from Microsoft's July, 1999 press release: "ZOOMIT's technologies will enable customers to use Active Directory to manage identity data, such as account information, passwords, configurations and access rights, stored in heterogeneous directory services throughout the enterprise. Microsoft also will enhance Active Directory to become the industry's first comprehensive enterprise identity-management platform by adding support for many popular applications and network services that store identity information in places other than directories."

Could this be the once and future single sign-on?

Let's look more closely at the Windows 2000 Active Directory.

INTRODUCING THE WINDOWS 2000 ACTIVE DIRECTORY

The Active Directory (AD) is a database of all the objects within the enterprise. (Remember, in this chapter we stick to the conceptual and structural issues of Microsoft's AD. I save the nitty-gritty, under-the-hood stuff for Chapters 9–12.) Objects come in two basic types: objects that can contain other objects, cleverly named *container objects*; and objects that cannot contain other objects, named *leaf objects*. The name "leaf objects" comes from the X.500 concept of taking a tree and turning it upside down so that the roots are at the top and leaf objects are attached to the branches at the bottom. As shown in Figure 8-1, the "tree" concept of describing objects is the same concept that has been used for twenty years to describe file-system directories, but in a file system directory the root is at the top (volume), from which it branches into folders, subfolders (containers), and, finally, into listing files (leaf objects).

This built-in hierarchy that spreads from a single root is very different from the NT 4.0 domain model. In NT 4.0, all domains are created equal, and communication between domains is provided by trust relationships. In fact, as shown in Figure 8-2, the NT master domain model, in which you create a master accounts domain and one or more resource domains with one-way trusts to the master, is an attempt to create a hierarchy in a flat model. In fact, two of the three possible NT domain models that involve more than one domain create a hierarchy. Microsoft has long realized the benefits of a hierarchical domain structure, but it has taken the company a while to ship it.

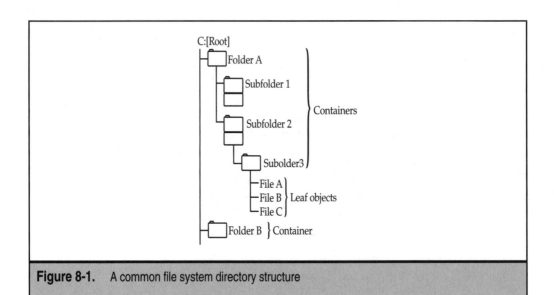

Figure 8-1.   A common file system directory structure

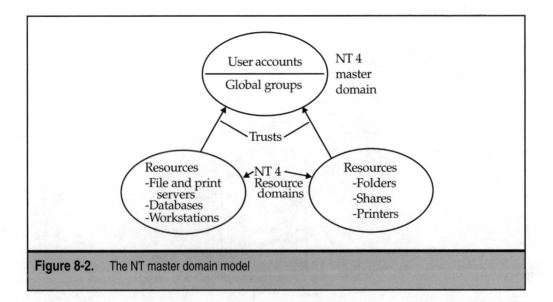

Figure 8-2.   The NT master domain model

In the Windows 2000 Active Directory, the container objects are domains, containers, and organizational units (OUs). The leaf objects are predefined as follows: users, groups, contacts, computers, shared folders, and printers. Figure 8-3 shows a Win2K domain with containers, OUs, and leaf objects.

All Active Directory objects have attributes associated with them. Each object's attributes are specific to the type of object. All objects and their attributes are defined in the schema. After we place all our enterprise objects in a logical database, the database instantly becomes the only way in which to create, modify, delete, manage, secure, and locate these objects. And there really isn't a way to go back. Can you say "paradigm shift"?

Let's start our in-depth discussion of Active Directory by looking at the basic building blocks of the logical AD structure: the forest that contains one or more domains, the domains that each contain a number of containers and organizational units. Then we'll populate the OUs with leaf objects.

The Forest

The forest is the full enterprise, the entire Active Directory, the whole shooting match. Each Active Directory contains a single forest, and that one forest contains all the domains, trees, organizational units, and leaf objects in the company. The forest defines the outside boundaries, the perimeter, the edges of the Windows 2000 Active Directory. Using an indexing capability called the Global Catalog, all objects within the forest, even objects from different domains, can be located quickly. The forest structure also allows for easy movement of leaf objects within the forest. By sharing a common schema or template, all objects of the same type (object class) within the forest share the exact same

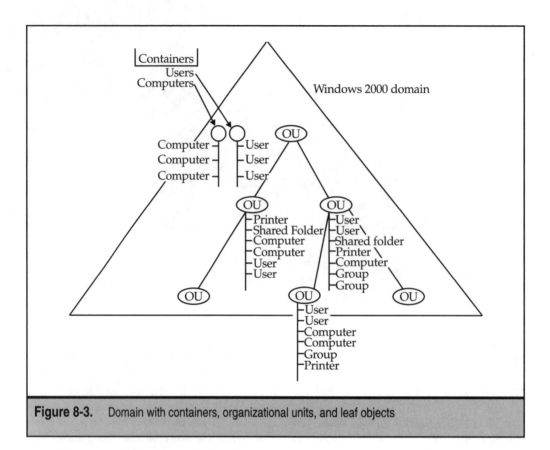

Figure 8-3. Domain with containers, organizational units, and leaf objects

attributes or properties. The schema defines these objects and their attributes, which, through replication, is exactly the same on each domain controller in each domain in the entire forest.

Domains

Domains are container objects that exist within our single forest. Domains contain AD containers and organizational units (OUs), as shown in Figure 8-4. A domain is the most basic building block of the Active Directory. You cannot have an Active Directory without at least one domain and one domain controller. The first Windows 2000 server promoted to domain controller begins the entire AD structure with the first or "root" domain in the forest. This first domain controller houses all the necessary elements to create and manage additional domains in the AD.

Domains are a security boundary. For instance, a member of domain admins in one domain cannot by default administer another domain, even a child domain in the same tree. AD object security inheritance also stops at the domain boundary. All AD objects

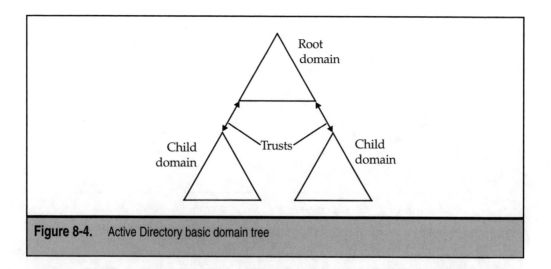

Figure 8-4.   Active Directory basic domain tree

have access control lists (ACLs) similar, in concept, to NTFS file-system ACLs. Each object is assigned a list of permissions to determine who can access it and what level of access will be granted. By default, these permissions flow down from the domain itself to the OU hierarchy within the domain and then to each leaf object. But Active Directory permissions do not flow from one domain to another.

A domain is also a replication boundary. Objects created within the domain on one domain controller will be replicated automatically to all other domain controllers in the domain. Objects that exist in one domain are not replicated to domain controllers from a different domain.

Finally, a domain is the boundary for the application of policies. Group policy objects (GPOs) can be assigned to a site, a domain, or an OU. The application of these GPOs flows from the domain down through the OU hierarchy to specific users or computers. But group policy inheritance stops at the edge of the domain. By default, group policy object inheritance does not flow from one domain to another.

Each domain has a unique DNS name in the forest (bigcompany.com). When a child domain is created under a parent or root domain, its name is unique but also includes the entire name of the parent (mktg.bigcompany.com) in accordance with DNS naming rules.

We can place additional (child) domains under the first (root) domain to form a domain "tree" (see Figure 8-4, which shows a basic domain tree). The Active Directory will automatically create two-way, transitive trusts (communication travels in either direction and can pass through one domain to get to another) between the parent and every child domain in the tree. As shown in Figure 8-5, there can be more than one tree of one or more domains in our AD forest. Each tree gets its own root domain and its own unique name. (Even a single domain is a tree and a single tree is a forest—a really small forest.) The Active Directory also automatically creates two-way, transitive trusts between the first root domain and all other root domains in the forest.

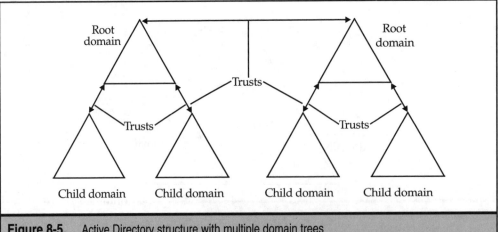

Figure 8-5. Active Directory structure with multiple domain trees

Organizational Units (OUs)

Organizational units (OUs) are logical container objects. Only one OU, the Domain Controller's OU, is created automatically by the system when the AD for each new domain is created. Additional admin-created organizational units can contain other OUs and any and all leaf objects. The OU is the primary unit of administration in the Active Directory. There are three primary reasons to create additional OUs:

▼ To allow for the delegation of administrative tasks. Win2K even provides the Delegation of Control Wizard to simplify this task, allowing domain admins to elect certain users or groups to perform specific tasks on designated objects with assigned permissions.

■ To simplify security administration by creating a departmental subdomain by which admins can grant access permissions at the OU level that will trickle down to the leaf objects within it.

▲ To allow for a hierarchical application of group policies. A single policy granted at a single, top-level OU will, by default, affect every object in the entire OU structure within the domain. (For more on Group Policies, see Chapter 12, "Managing Clients in the Active Directory.")

Containers

An AD "container" is a system-created, OU-like structure for holding leaf objects that are required by the system. Administrators cannot create, delete, or rename these containers.

By default, three AD containers are viewable in the MMC (Active Directory Users and Computers): Builtin, Computers, and Users. Figure 8-6 shows the default containers.

The system requires Builtin to hold the local groups retained from NT 4.0 and assign them specific user rights (some changeable, some not) to perform system tasks. If an NT 4.0 PDC is upgraded to Win2K, the eight built-in local groups appear in the Active Directory Builtin container. When a computer joins a domain, the AD places its object by default in the Computers container, although admins can move it later. Starting from the initial promotion to DC, the Active Directory requires a number of default users and groups to operate effectively; these user and group objects are placed by default in the Users container. Containers have an ACL similar to OUs, but group policies cannot be applied directly to containers.

Using a downlevel tool (NT 4.0 User Manager for Domains) to create users or groups in a mixed-mode domain places the users or groups in the Users container. Upgrading an NT 4.0 PDC places the users and global groups from the NT SAM database in the Users

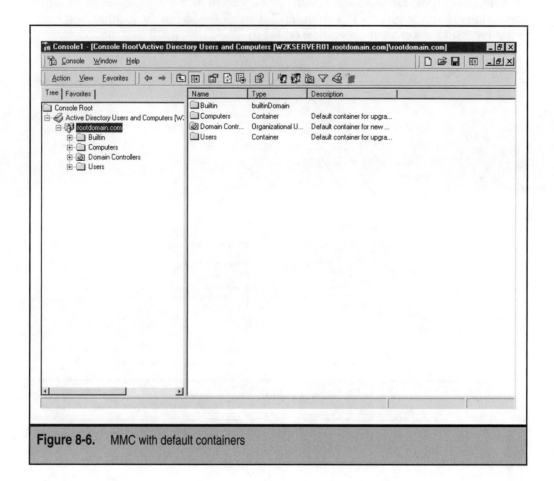

Figure 8-6. MMC with default containers

container and the built-in local groups in the Builtin container. (More detailed information on containers is available in Chapter 10.)

Leaf Objects

A leaf object cannot contain other objects. The predefined leaf objects in the Win2K Active Directory are users, contacts, groups, computers, printers, and shared folders. Leaf objects are placed in the OUs for administrative and security purposes and to facilitate the application of group policies. Figure 8-7 shows leaf objects within a domain.

You may be confused by the fact that a group cannot contain other objects. Obviously, a group has members—users and other groups. But, as far as the Active Directory is concerned, a group is a leaf object with a multi-valued attribute called *members*. When a user becomes a member of a group, the name of that user object is added to the members attribute of that specific group. The effective limit is 5,000 members per group.

Each object type, called an *object class*, has a different number of properties or attributes: printers have 29, groups 12, computers 7, users 55—you get the picture. Additional object types and object attributes can be added to the AD by modifying the schema.

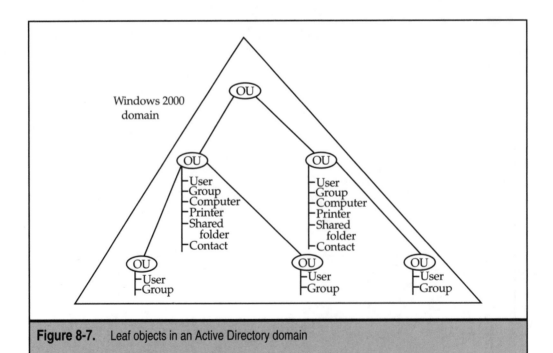

Figure 8-7. Leaf objects in an Active Directory domain

Shared Folders and Printers are Unique in the AD

In most cases, the Active Directory leaf object is the only representation of a specific entity. For example, the AD user object "John Smith" *is* the domain user account for John Smith. But in the unique case of shared printer and shared folder objects, the leaf object is not the only representation. A network printer in Windows 2000 is created exactly as it was in NT 4.0: The printer is installed and then "shared" by admin at the print server so that the entire network can use it. In nearly the same way, a folder that resides on a server is "shared" for the entire network to see and use. Downlevel clients that are not AD-aware, can still see the shared folders and printers using NetBIOS.

Access control lists exist in both cases to control which users and groups can access the resource and what level of access they can achieve. By default in Win2K, neither the shared printer nor the shared folder is part of the Active Directory. They simply advertise their presence the same way they did in LanMan, through the good old tried-and-true Server Message Blocks (SMBs). A Win2K administrator may decide to publish some network printers and shared folders in the Active Directory by creating an AD object. That way, anyone in the entire enterprise with proper permissions can find and use these resources. In these cases, the published AD object is simply a pointer to the already existing printer or shared folder. After they are published in the AD, these resources become available to the entire enterprise through the Global Catalog.

The Schema

The *schema* is the template for each object created in the AD. The schema, which is copied to each domain controller in the forest, contains the detailed definition of each object class and its attributes or properties. For example, suppose one AD object class is "user." The schema defines exactly what information can be stored about a user (i.e., First name, Last name, Street address, Telephone, E-mail, and Employee ID). The number and types of attributes differ for each object type (a group doesn't have a phone number, computers don't have last names, users don't have a list of members).

New object classes and attributes can be added to the schema if you have the proper permissions. The schema can only grow larger because additions to the schema can never be deleted. If you later decide that you don't need an additional object class or attribute, you can deactivate it in the schema. Doing so stops new instances of the object from being added and the actual object or attribute is no longer replicated to other DCs, but it doesn't delete it from the schema.

Remember that the schema, the underlying structure of the AD, is not connected to the user interface (UI) in any way. Adding a new object or property to the schema does not automatically update the UI. You need to look into additional display specifiers to pull that off. Because most changes to the schema also require changes to the user interface (UI), this will more likely occur when installing a new directory-enabled application. (For more information on modifying the schema, see Chapter 10, "Managing and Configuring the Active Directory.")

ACTIVE DIRECTORY'S PHYSICAL STRUCTURE

So far, everything we've talked about (forests, trees, domains, and OUs) in the AD has been logical in nature and has borne no relationship to the network infrastructure. In essence, we've built an ideal universe of objects, we've structured the objects, and we've organized them. We've moved them around until it's starting to feel good. Now we must introduce our nice, perfect, sheltered, logical world to the cold, hard reality of the network infrastructure. Cables and routers and bandwidth…oh my!

Sites

The concept of sites allows the logical structure of the Active Directory to be integrated with the physical structure of the network. With multiple sites, the logical structure of the enterprise lies on top of the physical and permits the admin to make adjustments in the logical structure that reflect the physical connectivity capabilities. This way, the logical design and physical layout work in sync. Figure 8-8 illustrates a domain structure with multiple sites.

Sites are new in Windows 2000, but they will look familiar to Exchange administrators from NT 4.0. Sites are manually defined within the AD as one or more well-con-

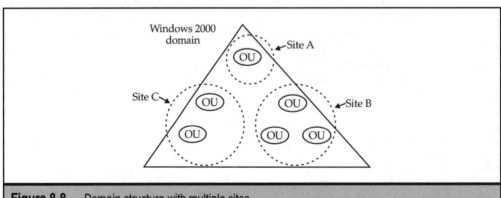

Figure 8-8. Domain structure with multiple sites

nected IP subnets. "Well-connected" means a reasonably fast and reliable connection. "Reasonably fast" means anything from 128Kbps in a small company, to 1.5Mbps (T-1) in a medium-sized firm, to 10Mbps or even 100Mbps in a large organization. "Reliable" means the connection stays up most, if not all, of the time. In other words, a site contains the computers that are nearby or connected with high-speed links. A good rule of thumb is that connections within a site should be 10Mbps or faster with 98 percent uptime.

By default, the entire forest has only one site (Default-First-Site-Name). Unaffected by the logical structure of the AD, a site can contain more than one domain, and a domain can contain more than one site. All new domain controllers are automatically added to the default site. Administrators must manually create and configure additional sites. DCs are moved onto new sites by the admins—nothing automatic here. Sites are used by the DNS to direct user logon requests to the closest domain controller. They also control domain replication by allowing admins to configure and schedule how often DCs replicate the AD over slow links. (For more information on sites and replication, see Chapter 10, "Managing and Configuring the Active Directory.") And, by using local rather than remote resources, sites improve response to most users' queries or searches and to directory-aware applications.

Domain Controllers (DCs)

Unlike NT 4.0, a Win2K domain controller (DC) is created *after* the installation of the server. After the Win2K server is completely installed, it is promoted to the status of domain controller by using the *dcpromo* utility. It should be noted that this means that the Active Directory runs as part of the security subsystem in the User mode (Ring 3) of the processor, not as a service in Kernel mode (Ring 0) of the OS. This allows any Win2K server to be promoted to a DC and any DC to be demoted to a member server. By extension, then, a Win2K DC can "switch" domains without a reinstall of the OS. To do so, it is demoted to a Win2K server and then promoted to a DC in a different domain.

When a Win2K domain controller is initially installed, it is running in mixed mode. Mixed mode assumes that one or more NT 4.0 BDCs are still present in the domain that require NT 4.0-style replication (one PDC to many BDCs). When all DCs in the domain have been upgraded to Win2K, admins can switch to native mode which disables NT 4.0 style replication and adds group functionality. (For more information on mixed vs. native mode, see Chapter 9, "Implementing the Active Directory.")

Every domain requires at least one domain controller. For fault tolerance, redundancy, and load balancing, most domains should contain a minimum of two DCs. The Win2K Active Directory employs a multi-master replication scheme. Gone are the days when only the NT 4.0 PDC could accept the (SAM) directory updates. In the Win2K Active Directory, all DCs are equal and can accept changes at any time. Each DC automatically replicates changes made directly to it to every other DC in the domain. The first DC to receive a change (the originating write) replicates that change with all other DCs from the same domain (and within the same site) within fifteen minutes of the change. DCs from one domain do not replicate AD objects with DCs from other domains.

Domain controllers also contain a number of additional AD components that are involved in under-the-hood administration. Some DCs house the Global Catalog. All DCs house the shared system volume (sysvol, which is used in the file replication service). Replication *between domains* is limited to the schema, domain naming, and global catalog partitions.

Sysvol and the File Replication Service (FRS)

Each domain controller contains the shared system volume designated by default as sysvol. This volume, which must be NTFSv5, contains a number of files that are used by the Active Directory but it does not contain the Active Directory itself. The shared system volume is replicated on a multi-master basis between all the domain controllers in the same domain. Therefore, any file or data replica placed on sysvol on any DC is automatically replicated to all DCs in that domain. The replication engine for the shared system volume is neither the normal Win2K domain replication, nor the directory replication service (LMrepl) from NT 4.0, which no longer functions in Win2K. Instead, the replication engine for the shared system volume is the new file replication service (FRS). Installed automatically on DCs, the only configuration option for the FRS is the ability to alter the time of day when file replication can take place. The FRS fires up automatically and simply works. By default, sysvol contains a scripts folder for logon scripts and NT system policy files, and a policies folder for the Win2K group policy template files.

Global Catalog Servers

Finding objects in a single domain environment is relatively easy because every DC in the domain contains a complete copy of all the objects in that domain. But what if you have more than one domain? Each domain controller has a complete copy of the objects in its own domain but no knowledge whatsoever of objects in other domains. That's where the Global Catalog (GC) comes in. The GC resides only on domain controllers and holds a copy of every object in the entire forest, but with a limited set of properties for each object. Only the properties deemed to be "searchable" are included in the GC. Actually, each global catalog server can access a "full replica" (all objects and all attributes) of the objects in its own domain and a "partial replica" (all objects, but only a few attributes) of the objects located in the other domains in the forest.

Admins can add searchable properties to the GC by modifying the schema. But modifying the schema should not be done on a whim, because it increases the *forest-wide* replication of the Global Catalog. To search for objects using the GC, simply click Start, click Search, and select Printers or People, and you're off. You can also search for objects by bringing up the Active Directory Users and Computers MMC snap-in, right-clicking a domain, and selecting Find. The Global Catalog also contains the Universal groups and their membership lists, as well as the names but not the members of all the Domain Local and Global groups in the forest.

By default, there is only one Global Catalog for the entire forest, on the first domain controller installed. Microsoft recommends one GC per site. Admins can add the Global Catalog to any domain controller by using the Microsoft Management Console. Remember that GC replication is forest-wide and happens at the same basic intervals as normal, domain-wide replication among the DCs. One GC per site is enough as long as the sites are properly configured.

DEVELOPING A DOMAIN NAMING STRATEGY

Obviously, carefully deciding what to name the domains in an Active Directory is important. Careful planning becomes doubly important when you realize that the very first name you implement—the root domain of the forest—cannot be changed without starting over again from scratch.

Hierarchical Namespace

In NT 4.0, the domain structure was "flat" and all domains were basically equal. Figure 8-9 shows an NT master domain model. In fact, the NT 4.0 master domain model was an attempt to impose a hierarchy on a situation where there really wasn't a master of any kind.

The X.500 directory service concept is hierarchical in nature. Earlier we saw how a root domain grew into a tree of domains with the addition of one or more child domains. We also saw how more than one tree could grow into a forest. But we never discussed how these domains would be named or how the domain naming rules work.

The names of domains within the Win2K Active Directory forest follow the specification set down by the Internet's Domain Name Service (DNS). DNS is based on a hierarchical naming structure. According to DNS rules, if a domain is "under" another domain,

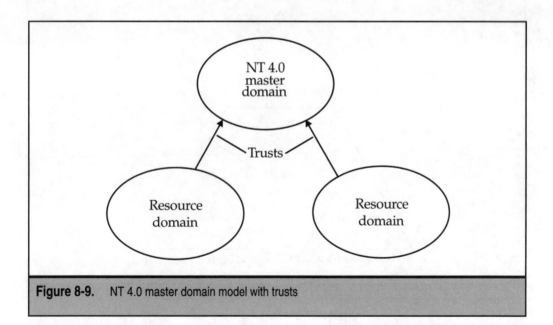

Figure 8-9.   NT 4.0 master domain model with trusts

its name is part of the first, or root, domain. (See Chapter 6, "Network Services," for more information on how DNS works.)

Consider a fictitious corporation called BigCompany, Inc. BigCompany has registered the second-level domain name "bigcompany.com" with the Internet authorities and hosts a Web site named "www.bigcompany.com" whose purpose is to teach the public about BigCompany and sell the company's products. BigCompany is planning its internal Win2K Active Directory domain naming strategy and has decided to use the AD root internal domain name "bigcompany.com", as in Figure 8-10, which shows the Active Directory with DNS naming structure. BigCompany decided to use its Internet domain name "bigcompany.com" because the management felt that it would be less confusing for its employees and vendors. (See Chapter 6 for information on using the same domain name both inside and outside your company.) BigCompany also decided to create separate domains for the Marketing and Production divisions. The marketing child domain would therefore be called "mktg.bigcompany.com", and the production domain under "bigcompany.com" would be named "prod.bigcompany.com". These three domains now form an Active Directory tree and a DNS contiguous namespace.

If two other domains were created under Marketing to represent the United States and Europe, their names would be "us.mktg.bigcompany.com" and "eu.mktg.bigcompany .com", as shown in Figure 8-11. We are still in the same AD tree and the same contiguous DNS namespace.

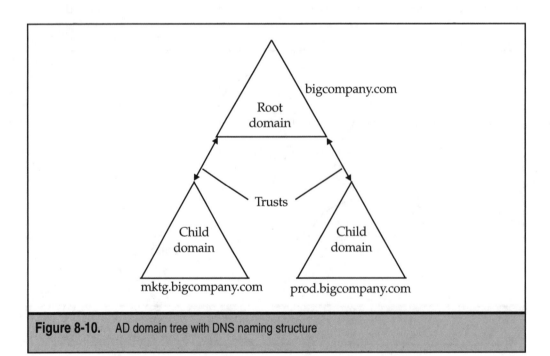

Figure 8-10. AD domain tree with DNS naming structure

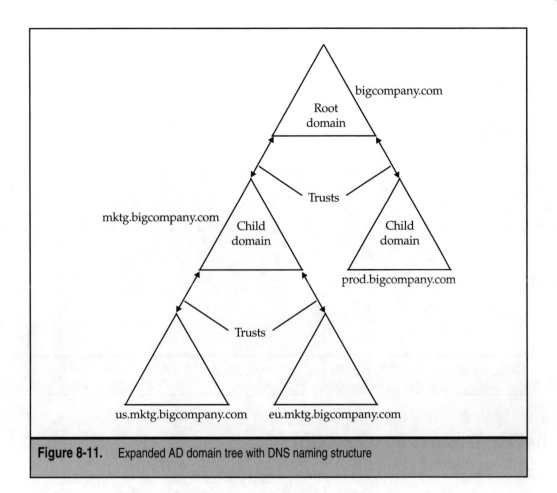

Figure 8-11. Expanded AD domain tree with DNS naming structure

If BigCompany, Inc. acquired another company, Widgets'r'Us, and wanted to maintain it under a separate internal name, a new root domain would be created (widgetsrus.int). If separate child domains were needed for the United States (us.widgetsrus.int) and Europe (eu.widgetsrus.int), our forest would look like Figure 8-12.

The new widgetsrus.int root domain begins a new DNS namespace that is not contiguous with bigcompany.com. However, the two child domains, us.widgetsrus.int and eu.widgetsrus.int, are part of the contiguous DNS namespace widgetsrus.int. Note also that the first-level domain *int* is not a standard Internet first-level domain name (com, org, edu, gov, mil, net). These standard names are only required when a domain name is public and the authoritative DNS server for a domain name is visible on the Internet. If a domain name and its authoritative DNS server are completely internal, you can use whatever first-level name strikes your fancy. And it doesn't even have to be three letters long.

The OU structure of each domain has no impact whatsoever on the DNS naming of the domains. However, OUs do have an impact on the LDAP naming and addressing.

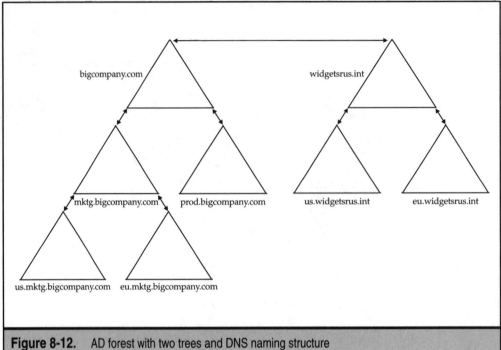

Figure 8-12.   AD forest with two trees and DNS naming structure

The Domain Name Service (DNS)

The Domain Name Service (DNS) was developed in 1989 and has been running success-fully on the Internet and most TCP/IP networks ever since. Its primary purpose is name resolution, the mapping of names that humans know to IP addresses that routers know so that data packets can move from point to point. DNS is a kind of electronic telephone book on steroids. The Win2K Active Directory cannot exist and will not install without access to a supported DNS Server. If the Windows 2000 Active Directory Installation Wizard (*dcpromo*) does not see a supported DNS server, it offers to create one during the DC promotion.

In Windows 2000, DNS is responsible for all name resolution. If the internal Win2K DNS cannot resolve a name, it reverts to using NetBIOS name resolution procedures by way of an updated version of the Windows Internet Name Service (WINS). Because Microsoft (and everyone else) would like to stop resolving names with WINS, let's all try real hard to use DNS.

Active Directory Design

We've talked about all the things you *can* do with Active Directory; now let's talk about what you *should* do. The KISS principle still works in Active Directory design—Keep It Simple, Stupid!

Domains

Unless you have a very good reason, don't go beyond a single domain. Remember, a domain can hold a million objects. You can delegate administrative control through OUs. You can handle the WAN connectivity problems using sites. If you're upgrading your existing NT 4.0 master domain model, think seriously about a single domain in which the NT 4.0 resource domains become one or more OUs in the new Win2K model. If you must add domains, don't go beyond three or four levels deep for performance and complexity of administration. Consider the DNS naming context as you plan your domain structure.

Trusts

Figure 8-13 shows a Win2K domain tree trusted by an NT domain. All the Win2K trusts are bidirectional and transitive. They are created automatically when each domain is created and cannot be deleted. The most common trusts that an admin may have to create are trusts between the new Win2K domain and an existing NT 4.0 domain that has not yet been upgraded. These will be nontransitive, unidirectional, NT 4.0-style explicit trusts. As in NT 4.0, a separate trust must be established for each domain. The transitive trusts of Win2K are not backward-compatible.

Another possible type of trust that an admin might wish to create is a cross-link trust between two Win2K domains down in the domain tree, as shown in Figure 8-14. A cross-link trust increases performance by allowing communication between domains (LDAP referrals) to take a shorter path. Any trust between two Win2K domains can be transitive.

Organizational Units (OUs)

After the domain structure, choosing the organizational unit structure is the most important design decision for the Active Directory. Figures 8-15 through 8-20 illustrate some possible OU structures. Because most businesses, even large ones, require only a single domain for the entire enterprise, the design of the OU structure becomes the pivotal element of the AD design. OUs can be organized by object (users, computers, groups, printers, domain controllers), by function (finance, marketing, sales, production), by geography (New York, Chicago, Los Angeles), or by nearly any combination of the aforementioned.

Figure 8-15 displays a simple OU layout where the administrator has created an organizational structure by type of AD object. A fair assumption here would be that this domain and all of its OUs exist in a single physical location.

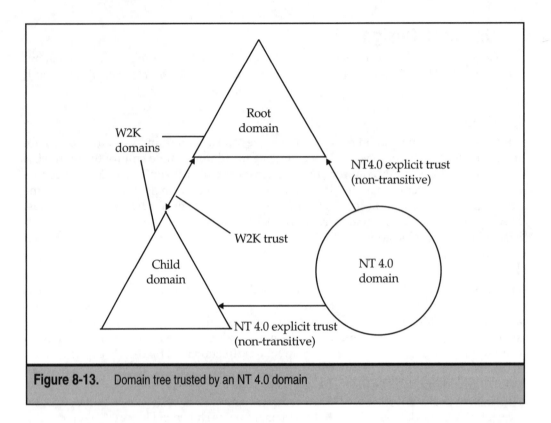

Figure 8-13. Domain tree trusted by an NT 4.0 domain

Figure 8-16 shows an OU structure more reflective of a corporation organizational chart. This could easily be expanded into more divisions or functional business units, departments and sub-departments.

Figure 8-17 illustrates a strictly geographical approach. This structure adds the advantage that geography is usually far less fluid than org charts, functional re-designs, and business process re-engineering thus providing a more stable OU strategy.

In Figure 8-18 we see a combination strategy. Here we store objects in their own OUs but then group those OUs under a specific corporate function. The assumption here would be separate administrators for, at least, each functional OU.

Figure 8-19 combines the geographic strategy with function. Each functional business unit has its own OU but these are then grouped under a central regional OU. Because of the large distances involved we would certainly deploy separate administrative teams for each geographical OU.

Figure 8-20 shows another combination example. This time each object type is resident in its own OU and these are then grouped by geographic region. Again we'd need separate admins for each regional center.

These are but a few examples of different OU hierarchical structures that can be deployed with the Win2K Active Directory. The driving force in the design process needs to

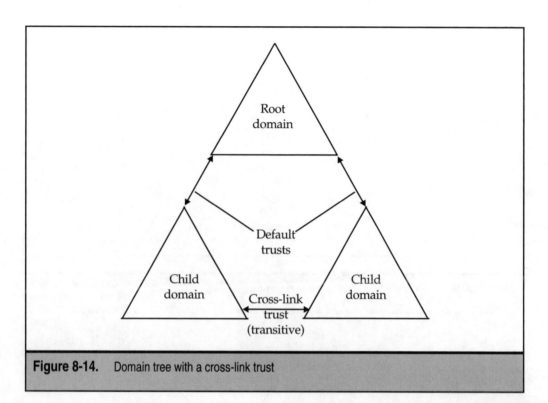

Figure 8-14.   Domain tree with a cross-link trust

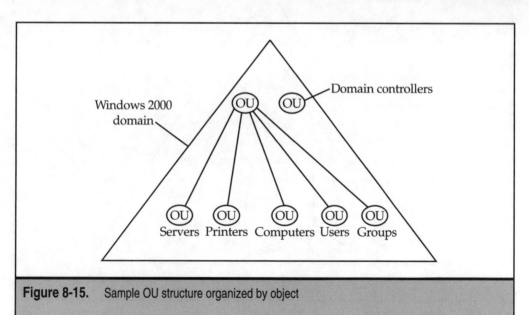

Figure 8-15.   Sample OU structure organized by object

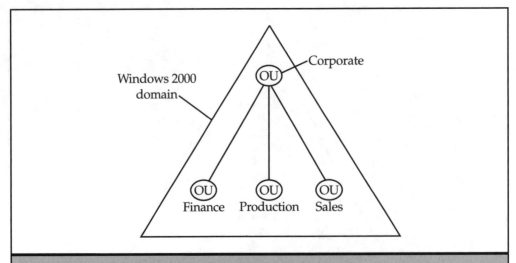

Figure 8-16. Sample OU structure organized by function

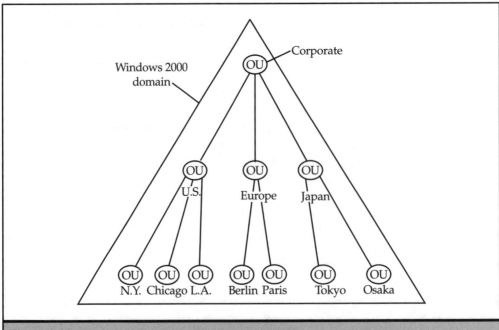

Figure 8-17. Sample OU structure organized by geography

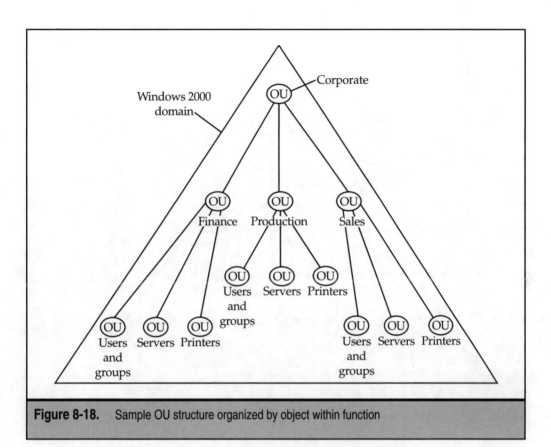

Figure 8-18. Sample OU structure organized by object within function

be ease of administration. We are not being totally self-serving here. The end-users often don't even know what OU they reside in. OUs determine how we can delegate control throughout an organization and provide the hierarchical framework for the application of group policies. These two factors are the most important consideration at the OU design level. Most organizations can be accommodated by OU structures no more than three or four levels deep.

Sites

This is the place where we use logical AD elements (sites, subnets, site links, site link bridges) to configure the existing physical limitations of our network infrastructure. The primary purpose of sites is to control domain replication over slow or unreliable network links. Their secondary purpose is to speed up responses to queries and logon requests. Use sites sparingly. Remember, if you choose to create additional sites, Microsoft recommends one DC, one GC (in a multi-domain forest), and one DNS server per site for performance reasons.

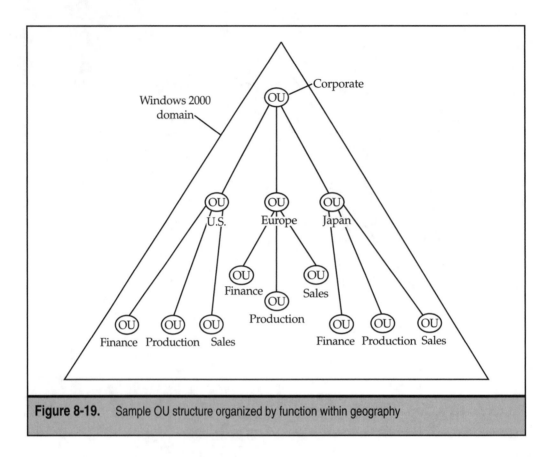

Figure 8-19.   Sample OU structure organized by function within geography

Before they start designing and planning for a Windows 2000 Active Directory, it is essential that those responsible have an in-depth understanding of the Active Directory and its components, TCP/IP, DNS, DHCP, and physical network management. Allot a significant amount of time for developing and testing the design and then testing the implementation plan before you rollout the Win2K Active Directory into the production environment.

ACTIVE DIRECTORY FAQS (FREQUENTLY ASKED QUESTIONS)

Any discussion of the Active Directory generates lots of questions. Hopefully, I've answered some in this chapter but no doubt many will remain. I've added a few of the most frequently asked questions (FAQs) here. The AD is large and multi-faceted, and I believe we'll all be learning more and more about it for quite some time.

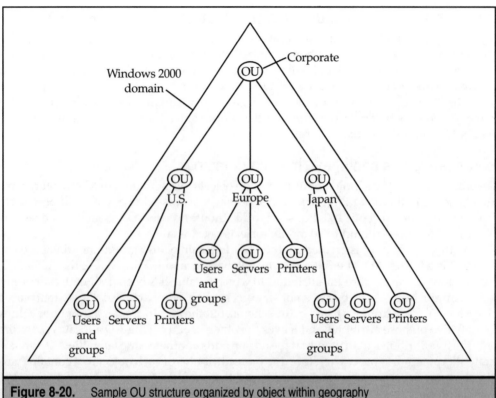

Figure 8-20.   Sample OU structure organized by object within geography

What is the recommended way of setting up an AD?

Unless you have a specific reason for creating more than one domain, stick with a single domain for your entire enterprise. A single domain greatly simplifies administration and increases performance. Use OUs for delegating administration, preferably no more than three or four levels deep.

What are the reasons for creating additional domains within a forest?

Autonomous divisions in a company that require separate names also require separate domains. Domains are also a security boundary. If two areas of a company have different domain-level security policies, you need a separate domain for each area. Domains can represent geopolitical boundaries as well. If you wish to administer DCs in certain areas of a company in a different language, you need more than one domain. Additional domains may be required due to network infrastructure or connectivity problems. If the WAN link between two locations is slow or unreliable and you expect these conditions to persist, you might need to create more than one domain.

Do I have to use the standard Internet first-level domain names?

No. This is strictly a DNS issue. The first-level domain from the Internet (com, org, edu, gov, mil, net) works just fine on both external and internal domains. If your Win2K domain name is *strictly* internal and will never be viewed on the Internet by anyone outside your company, you can create any first-level domain of any length. For example, you could use bigcompany.local, bc.internal, bc.int, microsoft.msft, or msft.corp. Shorter names are always better. Make sure that the proper entries are updated in the internal Win2K DNS and you're ready to roll.

How many users can I have in each domain?

Theoretically, an AD can hold about 10 million objects per domain, but Microsoft recommends no more than a million objects per domain for this release. One million objects translates roughly to about 100 thousand to 200 thousand users per domain. Lab tests at Microsoft have been run up to 10 million objects per domain.

The theoretical limit is created by the ESE (Extensible Storage Engine) database engine that is used for AD. The ESE limits its database size to 17TB. Because the Active Directory only allocates space for attributes to which a value has been assigned, estimating the maximum number of objects is not an exact science. For instance, let's say that a user object has 55 or so attributes listed in the schema, but the admin creates a user with values for only five of those attributes and leaves the other 50 empty; the AD allocates space for only the five attributes with values. If the admin adds another value later, the AD dynamically allocates more space. Therefore, the more attributes of each object that contains values, the more space each object consumes, and the fewer the total number of objects that are theoretically possible.

How do I locate objects in the domain? In the forest?

Users can search the entire forest for a specific object by using the Global Catalog (using port 3268). Click Start, click Search, select the type of object and the Global Catalog (Find) interface appears. Users can't "find" objects that they are prohibited from viewing. In other words, if the user does not have at least Read permission to an object, it will not be displayed in the search results. A more comprehensive LDAP query (using port 389) is possible by using the Advanced button in the Find dialog box and focusing on a specific domain. This search mechanism includes every attribute of each object in the domain.

How many domain levels can I have in a single domain tree?

LDAP has a limit of 64 levels, including all domains, OUs, and leaf objects. Microsoft recommends no more than ten levels deep at this time. The question becomes moot because DNS limits the length of a single domain name to 255 characters, including periods, with a 63-character limit between periods. Pity the fool who has to maintain the DNS entries for a 255-character domain name. Type very slowly.

How many trees can I have in an AD forest?

Theoretically, the number is unlimited. Each additional tree adds administrative and security complexity, as well as additional trusts and increased replication traffic.

How many OUs can I have in each domain?

The LDAP limit of 64 levels applies. Recommendation: Go no more than ten levels deep to maintain acceptable logon performance when applying multiple group policies. Shallow OU structures (three to four levels) perform better than deep ones. Group policies are applied only to the first 31 levels.

What are some good reasons for creating additional OUs?

OUs are the primary unit of administration in the AD. You can delegate administrative duties to local admins. The OU structure should reflect the administrative strategy of the organization. Group policies are applied directly to the objects within the OUs, so designing an OU structure for the optimum application of group policies is essential.

Can I merge two existing forests into one?

Not in this release. Microsoft has announced support for "prune, graft and merge" within twelve months of the release of Win2K.

Can I move a domain from one tree to another within the same forest?

Not in this release. Microsoft has announced support for "Prune, graft and merge" within twelve months of the release of Win2K.

Can I move OUs within the same domain?

Yes. Using the MMC Active Directory Users and Computers snap-in, you can simply highlight the OU that you wish to move, right-click, select Move, select the target location and click OK. The OU is now moved on the DC you were connected to. Wait until replication completes with all DCs in the domain before attempting to add or remove objects from the moved OU.

Can I move users, groups, and OUs between domains in the same forest?

Yes. Using the MOVETREE command, users, groups, and OUs may be moved between domains in the same forest.

Can I move computers between domains in the same forest?

Yes. By using the NETDOM command, computers may be moved between domains in the same forest.

How do I connect an NT 4.0 domain to a Win2K forest?

Use the NETDOM utility to create an NT 4.0-style explicit (nontransitive, single-direction) trust between your NT 4.0 domain and one domain in the forest. These same explicit trusts can connect two Win2K domains as well to save on network traffic and increase performance.

If the Active Directory isn't on sysvol, where is it?

By default, the Active Directory itself is a file called ntds.dit in the \WINNT\NTDS folder. By default, several database log files are also present in the same folder.

Microsoft recommends placing the ntds.dit on a separate physical drive from the log files for performance reasons.

Does this \WINNT\NTDS folder have to be NTFS?

No, but it should be. There is no logical reason why an admin would not want the Active Directory and its log files to reside on a secured volume. Sysvol must be formatted NTFSv5.

Must I configure additional sites?

No. Additional site configuration is solely a function of your network infrastructure and your desire to exercise control over domain replication. If your network is well connected with high-speed links, you can maintain the entire AD with a single site.

Are there specific requirements to run Active Directory on a Win2K server?

Microsoft's absolute minimum requirements are as follows:

- ▼ TCP/IP is required for name resolution, AD site creation, and the automatic assignment of IP addresses.
- ■ DNS that meets BIND 8.2.1 or higher specs or is compliant with RFC 2052. RFC 2052 allows for the creation of SRV records (services) in the DNS.
- ■ The shared system volume must be formatted in NTFSv5 for FRS file-tracking purposes.
- ▲ Pentium, 133MHz, 256MB RAM, 700MB system volume, 500MB AD volume.

Microsoft's additional recommendations are as follows:

- ▼ NTFSv5 is highly recommended for the AD volume(s) that hold the NTDS.dit file and the log file, since you want, of course, a secure location for the Active Directory.
- ■ Win2K DHCP is highly recommended because it will dynamically update the reverse lookup zone of the DNS.
- ■ DNS supporting RFC 2136 (dynamic updates) and RFC 1995 (incremental zone transfers) is strongly recommended. Without dynamic updates to DNS, you

lose significant Win2K functionality (BIND 8.2.1). Besides, incremental zone transfers improve DNS performance and lessen network traffic.

- All Win2K Professional clients, which allow all the features of Win2K Server and Active Directory to "come alive."

▲ Pentium II, 400MHz, 256MB RAM, 1GB system volume, 1GB AD volume.

The real-world requirements are as follows:

▼ TCP/IP everywhere.

- NTFSv5 on all server and DC volumes.

- Win2K DNS, which is currently the only shipping DNS that supports all the functionality of Win2K.

- Win2K DHCP, which is currently the only shipping DHCP service that supports the dynamic integration with Win2K DNS.

- Two SCSI high-speed drives per large or busy domain controller to allow the AD file (ntds.dit) and the log files to be on different physical drives (spindles). This way, you get improved AD performance.

▲ Pentium III, 500MHz +, 512MB+ RAM, 2GB system volume, 4GB AD volume.

SUMMARY

The Active Directory is the pivotal piece of the new Windows 2000 operating system. It is the single element that differentiates Windows 2000 from all previous operating systems from Microsoft. It is large, complex, and at times, difficult to understand. Many of its relationships are so intertwined it's hard to know where to begin. The first time you begin to sense the full breadth of the product it can feel overwhelming. Not to worry. We are going to switch gears now and drill down to the practical level. The next chapter outlines the step-by-step creation of the Active Directory and its surrounding issues.

CHAPTER 9

Implementing the Active Directory

C hapter 9 focuses on the practical issues surrounding the installation of the Active Directory in Windows 2000. This chapter deals with the nuts-and-bolts issues of implementing the Active Directory as well as the step-by-step details of installing the AD on Win2K servers. You also find out how to upgrade existing NT 4.0 domains.

PREPARING TO INSTALL THE ACTIVE DIRECTORY

There are only two possible scenarios for creating the very first Windows 2000 Active Directory domain controller in an enterprise. You'll either be upgrading an existing NT 4.0 primary domain controller (PDC) or promoting a Windows 2000 workgroup server (not yet a member of a domain) to a domain controller.

In order to create a Windows 2000 domain controller you must start with a Windows 2000 server. A fresh installation of Windows 2000 entails installing the server OS first (Server or Advanced Server), and, when the server installation is complete (see Chapter 3), the administrator initiating the domain controller promotion (*dcpromo*). An upgrade from an NT 4.0 PDC consists of a Windows 2000 server OS upgrade followed *automatically* by a domain controller promotion. In either case, the steps for promoting the domain controller are identical. This chapter covers promoting the server to a Win2K domain controller and the installation issues involved.

The First Domain Controller in the Forest

The first domain controller can actually refer to several computers. The first domain controller in the forest, the first domain controller in a site, and the first domain controller in a domain. In some situations these may all be the same physical computer, and in others they could exist on separate machines. Each has its own significance. Let's start off with the big one—the first DC in the forest.

The first domain controller in the forest is the single most important computer in the entire enterprise. The numerous single master operations assigned to this computer and the number of other specialized roles it plays give this computer elite status. It is essential that the computer becoming the first domain controller in the forest contains enough RAM, disk space, and processor power to adequately maintain domain operations. In essence, if this single computer goes down, the entire Active Directory is down.

The first domain controller in the forest hosts two forest-wide operations masters, the domain-naming master and the schema master. In the entire forest, the *domain-naming master* is the only writeable copy with information about all the domains in the forest and their relationships with each other. The *schema master* is the only write-enabled copy of the schema in the forest. The schema is the template for all objects and properties in the Active Directory. All other domain controllers in the forest hold read-only copies of both the domain-naming and schema information. This information is updated through the normal replication process (discussed in Chapter 10).

In addition, the first domain controller in the forest hosts the first and only Global Catalog for the entire forest. Depending on the performance and site topology of your enterprise, additional domain controllers can be designated as Global Catalog servers at a later time. One more thing: As shown in Figure 9-1, the first domain controller in the forest is the first computer to form one end of each Kerberos transitive trust with each child domain under it and each additional root domain in the forest. It becomes the "root" domain of the forest and its name cannot be changed.

As the first DC in the forest is installed, the default site is also created. By default, there is only one site for the entire forest, and it's called Default-First-Site-Name. This name can be changed later if you wish. The *dcpromo* process also creates the DEFAULTIPSITELINK and associates it with the Default-First-Site-Name. Any DC added to the forest will automatically be placed in this site. If you elect to create additional sites in the future, you will need to move these DCs to their appropriate sites.

The First DC in a Site

The first DC in the forest is also the first DC in the Default-First-Site-Name. The first DC installed in a site becomes the Auto InterSite Topology Generator. Unlike other operations masters, this role will move automatically from one DC to another within the same site without human intervention. As its name implies, this DC controls the topology (which DC replicates with what other DC) during intrasite and intersite replication.

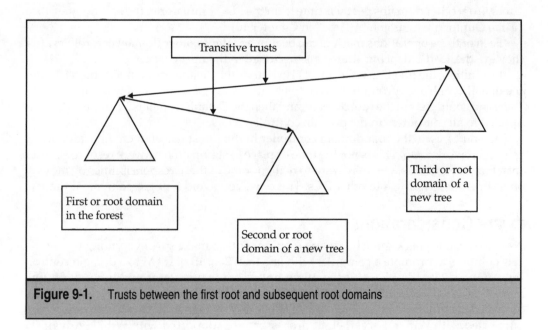

Figure 9-1. Trusts between the first root and subsequent root domains

The First DC in a Domain

The first DC in the forest is also the first DC in the root domain. The first domain controller in each domain hosts three domain-wide operations masters: the PDC Emulator, the RID master, and the Infrastructure Master. These operations masters exist on only one domain controller in each domain.

Each PDC Emulator operating in mixed mode serves in the following capacities:

▼ Serves as the PDC in NT 4.0 replication scenarios

■ Receives preferential password change updates

■ Acts as PDC for downlevel clients and downlevel administration tools

■ Serves as the Domain Master Browser for downlevel clients

■ Serves as the Time Master for its own domain

▲ Is the focus for changes in GPOs

The RID master allocates the ID numbers (SIDs) for each object created within the domain, while the Infrastructure Master keeps track of changes in group membership prior to replication.

Since the first domain controller in the forest is also the first domain controller in the first domain, it serves as the Time Master for the root domain. The Time Master for the root domain is the Time Master for the forest as well. All other Time Masters (PDC Emulators) from other domains get their time from the PDC Emulator in the root domain. (See "Time Out for a Discussion of Time" in Chapter 10).

Each of these operations masters can be moved later to other domain controllers after they exist. A load-balancing strategy is discussed in the next chapter.

In addition, the first DC in the forest also houses the default group policy objects. After the domain controller promotion is complete, the Default Domain Policy is applied to all users and computers in the root domain, and then the Default Domain Controllers Policy is applied to all computers in the domain controller's OU.

As you can see, the first domain controller in the forest has an incredible amount of important work to do. This is not the time or place to skimp on hardware resources. After installing several DCs, you may want to realign some of these responsibilities by moving some operations masters to other DCs. This way, you avoid a single point of failure.

Hardware Considerations

Now we need to check some hardware requirements to make sure everything will work. It is pointless to promote a computer with less than 256MB of RAM to a domain controller. After all, 256MB of RAM is the minimum recommendation from Microsoft for any Win2K Server. The processor should be a Pentium II or III (no Celerons, please). Processor speed should be no lower than 450MHz, preferably higher. Up to four processors are supported with Win2K Server; eight processors are supported with Win2K Advanced

Server. Busy domain controllers with a large number of objects in the Active Directory operate much more efficiently with two or more processors.

Disk space, I believe, is the biggest problem, especially for NT 4.0 to Win2K upgrades. The Windows 2000 base OS requires about 700MB of free space. The initial Active Directory installation (empty) requires about 250MB of free space. For the purpose of calculating disk space, let's round the 700MB for Windows 2000 and the 250MB for the AD installation to 1GB. You need 1GB of free space just to get the AD installed *without any objects!*

In an NT 4.0 to Win2K upgrade situation, the AD won't be empty. Rather, the upgrade process will create an AD user object for each NT 4.0 user, an AD group object for each NT 4.0 local and global group and each NT 4.0 built-in local group, and an AD computer object for each NT 4.0 computer that belongs to the NT 4.0 domain. The disk space required for these objects will vary depending on the number of objects in the NT 4.0 domain. After these objects exist in the Active Directory, you may populate many of the attributes by using the Exchange 5.5 Active Directory Connector. However, this will require even more disk space.

Microsoft recommends at least 1GB of space just for the Active Directory to allow for future growth and changes in the schema caused by directory-enabled apps, etc. (Microsoft and Compaq have conducted tests whose results show 100,000 users creating an AD of about 500MB. However, the first DC in the forest also houses the Global Catalog, which, depending on the eventual size of the forest, can nearly double the amount of disk space required.)

We're at roughly 1.7GB of disk space now. Throw in about 300MB for Service Packs, Support Tools and so on, and the rule of thumb (to be safe) is as follows: You'll use about 2GB of free space for the Win2K OS and the Active Directory on a Win2K domain controller. However, assuming 256MB of RAM, this does not take into account the paging file (another 256MB), the memory.dmp file if it bluescreens (another 256MB), and another 1GB just to be safe. That's 3.5GB on the OS partition. Double the RAM and you need another 500MB. Five gigabytes on the OS partition should be safe—for the time being, at least. New directory-enabled applications could throw these specs out the window in a hurry.

If your existing NT 4.0 PDC doesn't have 3.5GB of free disk space at a minimum on the boot partition where you're installing Win2K, you have a bigger problem. You need to select a new or existing BDC, increase the disk space on the boot partition, reinstall the NT 4.0 Server OS, and choose the BDC option for the current NT 4.0 domain during the install. When finished, promote the newly installed BDC to PDC, then upgrade the new PDC to Win2K. Since the Win2K Active Directory for each domain is replicated in its entirety to each domain controller in the domain (the Global Catalog is configurable), disk space requirements will be roughly identical for every BDC that gets upgraded to Win2K. So far, Microsoft's disk space recommendations have been painted very broadly. Let's drill down for a more specific look at Active Directory sizing.

AD Sizing

From an AD sizing perspective, allow approximately 3600 bytes for each security principal (User, Group, Computer) plus 100 bytes for each attribute or property of those objects that will contain a value. Security principals account for nearly all of the Active Directory size as well as its growth. Also allow about 1100 bytes for each object that is not a security principal (OUs, containers, domains, contacts, GPOs). All Active Directory objects are stored in a single file called the NTDS.DIT. DIT stands for Directory Information Tree and is derived from X.500 specifications.

In addition to the NTDS.DIT file, the Active Directory maintains a series of log files that both improve performance and protect the database from corruption. The log files are as follows:

▼ **EDB.log**   Active transaction log file.

■ **EDB*xxxxx*.log**   Created when EDB.log is full and circular logging is turned off. When the EDB.log fills up, it is renamed (i.e., EDB00001.log, EDB00002.log) and a new EBD.log is created.

■ **EDB.chk**   Checkpoint file provides a pointer for the data written to memory and the data written to the database. Simplifies recovery by pointing to where the system needs to restart.

■ **RES1.log**   Reserves 10MB at the end of the volume in the event that the volume fills.

▲ **RES2.log**   Same as RES1.log (for a total of 20MB reserved).

The Active Directory's NTDS.DIT file is roughly three times the size of all of its log files combined (depending on the level of activity). The ratio of disk space for each area should be allocated accordingly. Running out of disk space in either of these locations is very serious and will cause replication of the Active Directory to fail on that DC.

After the initial domain controller promotion (*dcpromo*) is completed and the AD populated with objects, simply checking the size of the NTDS.DIT file will let you guess reasonably what your future sizing requirements will be. If you accept the defaults during the domain controller promotion, you will find the NTDS.DIT file under the winnt\ntds folder. However, there is another NTDS.DIT under the winnt\system32 folder. That one is the original template from which your directory database gets created. Notice that the time-stamp is the same as for all other Windows 2000 distribution files. The template copy of the NTDS.DIT (\winnt\system32) may be deleted to conserve space.

AD Performance

So far in our discussion, we haven't mentioned performance-related choices. Microsoft specifically recommends (but does not require) that the Active Directory itself, which is the single file called NTDS.DIT, be placed on a separate drive spindle (separate physical hard drive) from its log files. The reasoning behind the recommendation is that these two areas are treated very differently during normal operation. The NTDS.DIT file is almost entirely read access, uses asynchronous writes, is multi-threaded, and is accessed randomly. By contrast, the log-file area experiences almost all write accesses, uses synchronous writes, is single-threaded, and is accessed sequentially. For performance reasons, the different type of disk access cries for two different physical hard drives so that the drive heads are not constantly being repositioned.

Inevitably, Microsoft's "separate spindle" recommendation leads to the question of whether we should use RAID technology or not. It is a well-known fact that load balancing across multiple disks (RAID 5) dramatically improves performance and reduces downtime because the impact of hardware failure is minimized. Other than cost, there is very little downside to RAID. It's fast, reliable, and efficient. Microsoft recommends (based on its testing) that *the most* effective use of RAID for high-performance domain controllers is hardware-based RAID 5 (disk striping with parity) for the NTDS.DIT, and hardware- or software-based RAID 1 (disk mirroring) for the logs. Additionally, Microsoft recommends that circular logging be turned on and, of course, that an ongoing AD backup strategy be developed.

Don't misunderstand. These are recommendations for maximum performance. Will a PII, 400MHz, single 6GB SCSI drive work for a few hundred users? Of course it will. In fact, it's more important to have multiple domain controllers than *the* ultimate domain controller. If your resources are limited, buy several normal-sized computers (for fault-tolerance) to serve the domain instead of one big, honkin' one.

Network Bandwidth

By now you are beginning to see that the Active Directory is a very busy place. Changes, updates, replication, queries, logons, and so on all take place across the network. Windows 2000 requires a fast network to excel in a medium to large company, the faster the better. "Fast" means 100Mbps to the desktop, if possible. At a minimum, 100Mbps on the backbone of a switched Ethernet environment with all domain controllers placed on the backbone and 10Mbps to each desktop. Can a small company be supported with a 10Mbps, 10BaseT network of a hundred or so users? Of course it can.

Windows 2000 is like a racehorse. Given a clean, open track and plenty of muscle, it will blow your hair back, but create any obstacle to speed and the horse will stumble. Windows 2000 requires a well-crafted network infrastructure with minimal bottlenecks and maximum bandwidth availability. If you believe that some or all of your current network infrastructure is becoming saturated or should be upgraded, then seriously consider performing the upgrade prior to or as part of your Windows 2000 installation. Microsoft has crafted Win2K to alleviate as many bandwidth issues as possible, but not all issues can be alleviated. By the way, if you're looking at new networking components (routers, smart hubs, and so on), make sure that they support the new DEN (Directory-Enabled Networking) features that allow a device to be configured and managed as an AD object. Check out www.cisco.com.

Domain Name Service (DNS)

The Windows 2000 Active Directory requires a DNS service that supports SRV records (RFC 2052). The Win2K Active Directory will not complete its installation until it locates or creates a DNS server running on the wire that supports SRV records. While it will technically work with a DNS that supports only SRV records, Microsoft recommends compliance with RFC 2136 (dynamic updates) and RFC 1995 (incremental zone transfer). Much of Win2K network functionality would be diminished without dynamic updates to the DNS. Currently, the only stable DNS server products that support RFC 2052, RFC 2136, and RFC 1995 are products that comply with BIND 8.2.1 or higher, which run on UNIX and the Windows 2000 DNS service.

If you choose the BIND 8.2.1 option, the DNS server must be accessible during the Active Directory promotion. It is essential that you check with the DNS service vendor to guarantee compliance with Windows 2000 and the Active Directory.

If you select the Win2K option, you have two installation choices:

▼ Install the Win2K DNS service on a separate Win2K workgroup server prior to the Active Directory domain controller promotion. This Win2K DNS server must be up and running on the wire during the domain controller promotion on another Win2K computer.

▲ Even though no compliant DNS server currently exists on the network, you may proceed with the domain controller promotion. When the Active Directory Installation Wizard cannot detect a compliant DNS server, it will offer to create one on the domain controller itself.

UPGRADING AN NT 4.0 DOMAIN

An NT 4.0 primary domain controller (PDC) contains the only write-enabled copy of the directory database (also called the Security Accounts Management Database, or SAM) in the NT 4.0 domain. NT 4.0 BDCs contain a read-only copy of the SAM database that they receive from the PDC through the normal synchronization/replication process. The SAM database contains all the domain users, passwords, groups, machine accounts, trusts, trust passwords, and so on in the entire domain. Losing access to the SAM is catastrophic. To keep things simple, I'm going to assume that your NT 4.0 domain model contains either a single domain or a single master domain (more complex migration strategies are covered later in Chapter 16). In either case, all the domain user accounts and the pertinent global group accounts from the entire enterprise are contained in this one domain and, by extension, on this one domain controller, the PDC. To upgrade an NT 4.0 domain to the Win2K Active Directory, you must upgrade the PDC first, then the BDCs.

Taking Precautions

The first step (as usual) is to cover yourself in case the whole thing blows up in your face. This involves using `rdisk /s` to update your NT 4.0 ERD (Emergency Repair Disk) for the PDC and BDCs, performing a full backup of the PDC (including the registry), and verifying that the data (and the registry) has actually been written to the tape.

The "BDC in the Closet"

One more precautionary step is necessary to ensure full recoverability in case of failure. I call this step the "BDC in the closet." First, using User Manager for Domains, create a brand new "dummy" domain user account to be used later for testing, and then select the "closet" BDC. At the BDC, force a synchronization (at the command line, type net accounts /sync and press ENTER) between the PDC and the BDC to be certain that the BDC contains the most recent updates and changes. Disconnect the selected BDC from the network and attempt to log on using the newly created dummy account. If the logon is successful, the synchronization worked. If you receive a message stating, "The policy of this computer does not allow you to log on interactively," the synchronization worked because it found the user account but the user was not granted the "log on locally" right.

If you receive a message that says, "The system could not log you on…" either you typed the username or password incorrectly or the synchronization failed. Try again. After you are certain that the latest information has made it to the BDC, perform an orderly shutdown of the BDC, turn it off, remove it from the network, and put it (either figuratively or literally) in the closet. After you've upgraded to Win2K, this BDC can be reconnected to the network from time to time and can continue to receive updates as long as the Win2K domain remains in mixed mode.

In the worst-case scenario, your Active Directory upgrade fails and, in the process, manages to corrupt the SAM database on the PDC, rendering it unusable. Then, to make matters even worse (this is an imaginary situation, you understand), all the SAM databases on all the other BDCs are corrupted as well through some mystical transference of bad replication karma. You're going down in flames (hope your resume is on a floppy at home). Your entire enterprise is now officially "hosed." Maybe you are about to experience an unplanned career interruption. (I am hard-pressed to even imagine a situation where this could occur, but we don't take these steps to protect us against things we can easily predict now do we?) You could attempt a repair by using the setup disks and the ERD. If that doesn't work, you could try to restore from a backup. If that fails, you're still covered. Take the BDC out of the closet, connect it to the network (making sure that no working PDC from the domain is up, but in our scenario the PDC died), fire up the "closet BDC," log on as the administrator, promote it to the PDC, and your enterprise has risen from the ashes. You've gone from goat to hero in one easy step. You still have lots of reinstalling of NT 4.0 BDCs to do to get your original configuration back, but your domain and your network is *not* down, just a bit slow.

Upgrading Existing NT Services

In a number of cases, specific services or applications that are running on the NT 4.0 PDC will be upgraded, and in some cases stopped, as a result of the Win2K upgrade. For example, if the NT 4.0 directory replication service (LMRepl) is running on the PDC, it is stopped automatically and the Windows 2000 *dcpromo* deletes it without giving any errors or warnings. LMRepl is completely incompatible with Win2K. Its functionality is replaced by the file replication service (FRS).

If your PDC is running the DHCP server service or the WINS server service, you may get error messages during the upgrade process as these services are being upgraded to the latest version of the Jet database. Relax. Simply click OK to continue. All database entries will remain intact.

If you are running BackOffice products on the PDC computer and the latest service packs have not been applied to them, you will be warned that the latest service packs are

Bridging the NT Directory Replication Service and Win2K File Replication Service

Many NT 4.0 installations use the directory replication service (LMRepl) to make sure that logon scripts and system policy files are replicated to every domain controller in the NT domain. This allows for consistent logon behavior and client configuration no matter what NT domain controller authenticates the client. In Windows 2000, LMRepl is not supported; its functionality is replaced by the shared system volume (sysvol) using the File Replication Service (FRS). FRS is autoconfigured so that every Win2K domain controller in the same domain has a replicated shared system volume with identical contents. Since NT 4.0 installations that depend on the LMRepl technology to distribute logon scripts and system policy files may wish to maintain this strategy during migration to Windows 2000, a "bridging" strategy must be developed between the two technologies, the NT 4.0 directory replication service (LMRepl) and the Windows 2000 shared system volume (sysvol). "Bridging" involves these steps:

1. Prior to the Win2K upgrade, realign the existing NT 4.0 LMRepl configuration. If your Export server is your PDC (a very common configuration), you need to move the Export server role to the BDC that is slated to be the last one upgraded to Win2K. Any NT 4.0 server can function as an Export server. Then, using Server Manager, re-point the current NT 4.0 Import servers to the new NT 4.0 Export server. Make sure that you test this new directory replication configuration before moving on.

2.   Upgrade the NT 4.0 PDC to a Win2K server and then a Win2K domain controller.

3.   Copy the existing NT 4.0 logon script(s) and system policy file(s) from the NT 4.0 Export server NETLOGON share (\%systemroot%\system32\ repl\import\scripts) to the Win2K NETLOGON share (\%systemroot%\ sysvol\sysvol\%domainname%\scripts). Once the logon script(s) and system policy file(s) reside on the shared system volume of a Win2K domain controller, the FRS will replicate them to the shared system volume on each Win2K domain controller in the domain. Each Win2K client will attempt to use a Win2K DC for authentication. These clients will receive their logon scripts via group policy settings.

4.   Create a batch file that will copy the logon script(s) and system policy file(s) from the NETLOGON share on a Win2K domain controller to the NETLOGON share on the NT 4.0 Export server. This batch file will basically "push" any changes made to the logon scripts on the Win2K domain controller to the NT 4.0 Export server, which will then, in essence, "push" the changes out to its Import servers. This batch file should be placed on the Win2K domain controller.

5.   Using the Task Scheduler on the Win2K domain controller, create a scheduled job to run the new batch file on a regular basis. You can run the batch file every few hours if you use the /D switch on the xcopy command. The /D switch will only copy files if they have changed. In this way, each downlevel client that authenticates to a BDC will receive updated logon scripts and system policy files.

6.   As the Active Directory OU structure takes shape, create group policy objects that apply logon scripts at each appropriate OU. Doing so will apply the same logon scripts to the new Win2K clients authenticating to the Win2K domain controllers as the downlevel clients authenticating to the NT 4.0 BDCs.

7.   When all domain controllers have been upgraded to Win2K, delete the scheduled job because all files are now being replicated by the FRS.

In a multi-forest enterprise it would be possible to use this same strategy and batch file to create consistent logon scripts across forest boundaries as well.

necessary for BackOffice operation with Win2K. It is recommended that the latest BackOffice service packs be applied prior to the upgrade. The safer route is to install the latest service packs and then stop the BackOffice services prior to the upgrade.

The SMS 1.2 (System Management Server) version of the network monitor cannot be used under Windows 2000. You will need either the version that ships with Windows 2000 or the full-blown network monitor from SMS 2.0, SP1.

DNS issues also come into play during the upgrade. If the PDC is hosting the DNS, you need to manually update the DNS to allow updates for the forward and reverse lookup zones during the Active Directory Installation Wizard.

Third-party services should also be stopped prior to the upgrade because there is no way of knowing how they will react to Win2K or affect the upgrade process. Any UPS signaling cable (serial cable into the COM port) should be disconnected prior to the upgrade.

In spite of Microsoft's truly impressive effort to make the upgrade as smooth as possible, the safest NT to Win2K upgrade path at the end of the day is simply to stop all nonessential NT services, BackOffice products, and third-party products. With that done, perform the Win2K upgrade and the subsequent domain controller promotion, and then start all the new services when the new Win2K domain controller is up.

Impact of dcpromo on NT 4.0 User, Group, and Computer Accounts

Whether you are upgrading an NT 4.0 PDC or promoting a Windows 2000 Workgroup server, the steps for promoting the domain controller are identical. The differences are found in what happens under the covers.

A fresh Win2K domain controller promotion adds the necessary default users and default groups as well as a single computer (itself) to containers and OUs in the Active Directory. Each new object is given a new SID for the domain and a new GUID for the Active Directory. Users and default global groups are placed in the Users container and what used to be called built-in local groups are placed in the Built-in container. Nothing is placed in the Computers container. The domain controller's own computer object is placed in the Domain Controllers OU.

In the case of an NT 4.0 PDC domain controller promotion, the promotion process is slightly more complex. In addition to adding all the necessary default users and default groups, as well as a single computer account (itself) to containers and OUs in the Active Directory, the existing NT 4.0 user, group, and computer accounts are migrated from the NT 4.0 domain to the Win2K Active Directory. The following happens in the promotion process:

▼ All NT 4.0 domain users become Win2K AD user objects and are placed in the Users container.

■ NT 4.0 global groups become Win2K Global security groups and are placed in the Users container.

■ NT 4.0 admin-created local groups become Win2K Domain Local security groups and are placed in the Users container.

- NT 4.0 built-in local groups (Administrators, Server Operators, Backup Operators, Print Operators, Account Operators, Users, Guests, Replicator) become Win2K Built-in Local groups and are placed in the Built-in container.

- All group memberships are maintained.

▲ Local existing domain computer accounts are placed in the Computers container and the domain controller's own computer object is placed in the Domain Controllers OU.

Each new object that is created is given a new SID for the domain and a new GUID for the Active Directory. Each existing NT 4.0 domain object (user, group, or computer) that is migrated during the NT to Win2K PDC domain controller promotion process receives a new GUID for the Active Directory. However, it retains its existing NT 4.0 SID for the domain so that access control will continue to function as before.

GUIDs, SIDs, Tokens, and ACLs

In NT 4.0, the security model for accessing resources (folders, files, shares, and printers) involves comparing an access token to an ACL. Here's how it works in NT 4.0: Each user and group is assigned a security ID (SID) as it is created. This SID is the method by which NT actually identifies the object. Since there is no mechanism for moving users or groups between domains in NT 4.0, the initial SID is the only SID an object will ever have. When a user logs on using his or her domain credentials and NTLM authentication, an access token is created on the computer where the user is logging on. The access token contains the user SID, the group SIDs of which the user is a member, and the user's rights on the local computer.

An access control list (ACL) is associated with each file and folder on an NTFS volume. The ACL contains a list of users and groups (SIDs) that can access the respective file or folder and what level of access they will be granted (Read, Write, Execute, Delete, Change Permissions, or Take Ownership). When you view the ACL of a folder or file, it appears to show a list of names (users and groups), but in reality it contains a list of SIDs. The ACL editor converts the SIDs to user and group names so that we poor humans can understand what's actually going on.

To gain access to a specific folder or file, the user, in essence, presents its access token. The Security Reference Monitor (an NT 4.0 Executive service) compares the SIDs on the access token with the SIDs on the ACL of the requested folder. If there's a match, the user is granted the access permitted on the ACL. If there's no match, access is denied.

In Windows 2000, the Active Directory assigns a GUID and a SID to each object. The GUID is a forest-wide ID that never changes; the SID is specific to the Win2K domain. In Win2K, the access token model for accessing resources is identical to that of NT 4.0. After the Win2K Kerberos logon, an access token is created just as it is in NT 4.0. The access token contains the SIDs, as before. Because these SIDs control whether a user can access a given folder or file, it is important that they not be changed. During an NT 4.0 PDC to Win2K upgrade all the existing NT 4.0 SIDs are maintained. By retaining the SIDs during an NT 4.0 PDC upgrade and *dcpromo*, Win2K assures the user of identical access capabilities after the Win2K upgrade. A user who logs on and works normally on an NT 4.0 domain on Friday arrives on Monday morning (after the Win2K upgrade), authenticates to a Windows 2000 domain controller, and continues working normally. The user can work normally because he or she can still access all the same resources in the exact same way as last week.

There are two differences between the NT 4.0 access token and the Windows 2000 Active Directory access token, both of which should remain transparent to any user:

▼   The token is created after a Kerberos authentication in Win2K (more on this in Chapter 13).

▲   Because in Win2K it is possible to move a user object from one domain to another in the Active Directory, an additional element—the SID history—has been added as a property of the user object and the access token. When a user is created in the Active Directory domain, he or she receives a domain SID as he or she would in an NT 4.0 domain, but in the Active Directory a user can be moved to another domain. When that move happens, the existing (old) SID moves to the SID History attribute of the user object and a new SID is assigned. The SID History attribute can hold up to 1023 SIDs (that's 1023 domain moves). At logon, the current user SID, current group SIDs, and all the SID History SIDs, are placed on the access token. When the Security Reference Monitor checks the token for a matching SID, it also looks at the SID History portion of the token. This ensures that the recently moved user will continue to receive the same resource access that he or she enjoyed before the object was moved. Under no circumstances is the Active Directory GUID ever changed.

Active Directory Names and Numbers

Each object in the Active Directory has seven names and three numbers associated with it. A thorough understanding of these names and numbers is not necessary to manage the Active Directory on a conceptual or even a planning level. However, administrators need to understand LDAP naming and syntax rules when they begin to write scripts that query or update the Active Directory.

The Distinguished name (i.e., DC=com,DC=bigcompany,OU=Sales,CN=John Smith) is the absolute LDAP path to the object in the Active Directory. Distinguished names are guaranteed to be unique. The Relative Distinguished name (RDN) (i.e., CN=John Smith) is sufficient to locate the object if your focus is in the Sales OU. Each RDN must be unique within the same container object. The Security Accounts Manager (SAM) Account name (BIGCOMPANY/jsmith), also known as the downlevel, or NetBIOS, name, is the method by which the object is identified when using a downlevel operating system like NT 4.0. The Active Directory Canonical name (jsmith/sales/bigcompany.com) uses a simpler syntax than the Distinguished name, as shown in Figure 9-2, and is the default name displayed by Win2K in the properties of each object.

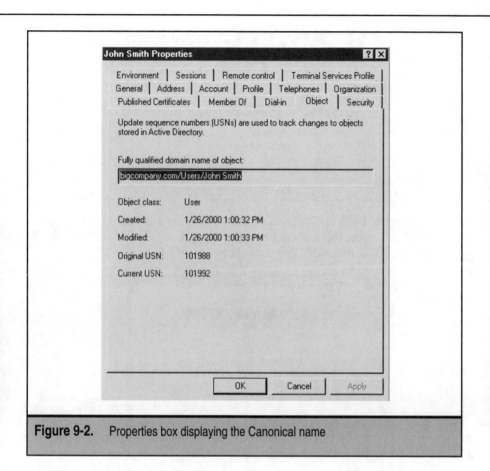

Figure 9-2. Properties box displaying the Canonical name

The LDAP Uniform Resource Locator (URL) is a concatenation of the DNS server's name and the Distinguished name of the object being located (i.e., LDAP: //dnsserver1.us.domain6.com/CN=John Smith/OU=Sales/DC=bigcompany/ DC=com). The Common name is contained within the Distinguished name. The DN (i.e., DC=com,DC=bigcompany,OU=Sales,CN=John Smith) contains the common names "Sales" and "John Smith."

Each AD object has three numbers associated with it: the globally unique identifier (GUID), the securityID (SID), and the relative identifier (RID).

The globally unique identifier (GUID) is a unique number assigned to the object and used for tracking and references throughout the entire forest. Following is an example of an object's GUID. The GUID for a specific object is guaranteed to be unique and will never change even if the object is moved from one domain to another within the forest.

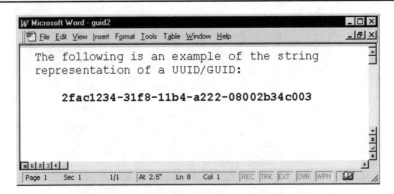

The SecurityID (SID) is assigned to each object on a domain-by-domain basis, similar to NT 4.0. In the following illustration, you see a SID and a RID in the Registry Editor. The SID is unique to the domain in which it was created.

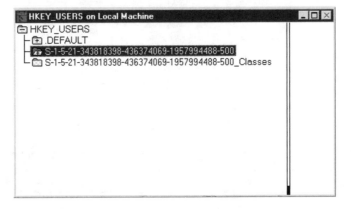

The last few digits of the SID are referred to as the relative identifier (RID). Most of the SID is identical for all objects within the domain, but each object has a unique RID. If a user is moved from one domain to another, it retains its GUID but receives a new SID/RID from the new domain. The old SID/RID is added to the SID-History attribute of the user and will be present on the user's access token after logon.

INSTALLING THE ACTIVE DIRECTORY

Now that you understand both the good and the bad about creating a Windows 2000 domain controller, let's push on. We'll begin from step one and take you through several popular scenarios.

The First Domain Controller Promotion (*dcpromo*)

Whether you are upgrading an NT 4.0 PDC or promoting a Win2K workgroup server, the steps are identical. Only the first screen in each procedure is slightly different.

After you complete the Win2K server OS upgrade on an NT 4.0 PDC, a reboot is required. Following the reboot, the system returns to the screen shown in Figure 9-3. Because the NT 4.0 computer was a PDC, you have no option. You must make this computer a Win2K domain controller.

When promoting a Win2K server, you would simply click the Start button, choose Run, type **dcpromo**, and click OK. The screen shown in Figure 9-4 appears.

Clicking the Next button in either screen takes you to the first decision you need to make, as shown in Figure 9-5. Since this is the very first domain, choose the Domain Controller for a New Domain option. We'll talk about the other options later in this chapter.

Click the Next button and another decision awaits you: Whether to create a new domain tree or join an existing one, as shown in Figure 9-6. Since this is the very first domain, it is also the very first domain tree. Therefore, select the Create a New Domain Tree option.

As shown in Figure 9-7, you'll make one more major decision about the shape and structure of your Active Directory: Do you want to create a new forest or join an existing one? Since you are creating the first domain in the first tree, you want, of course, to choose the Create a New Forest of Domain Trees option.

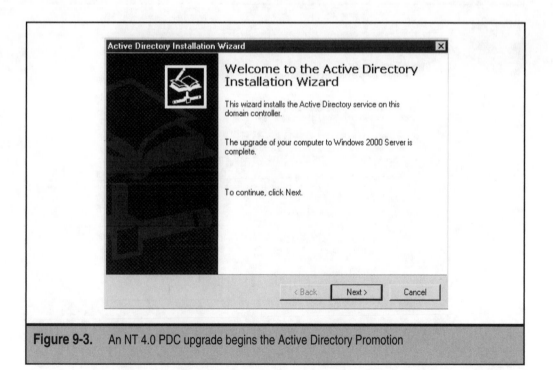

Figure 9-3.   An NT 4.0 PDC upgrade begins the Active Directory Promotion

Figure 9-4. The Active Directory Installation Wizard

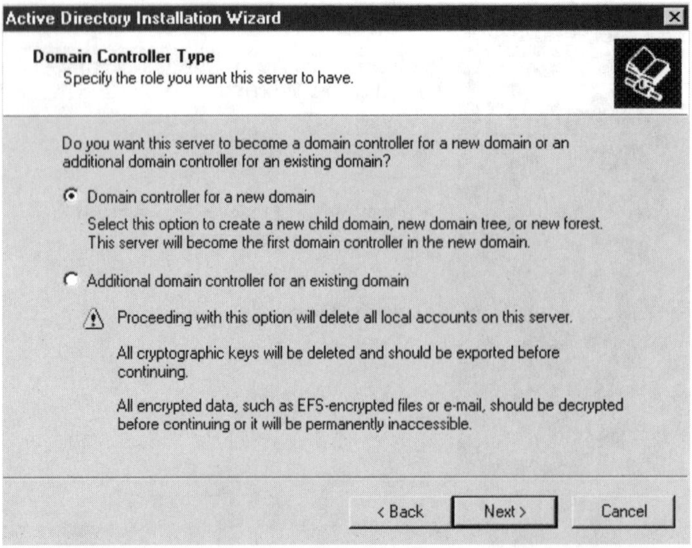

Figure 9-5. Active Directory Installation Wizard Domain Controller Type screen

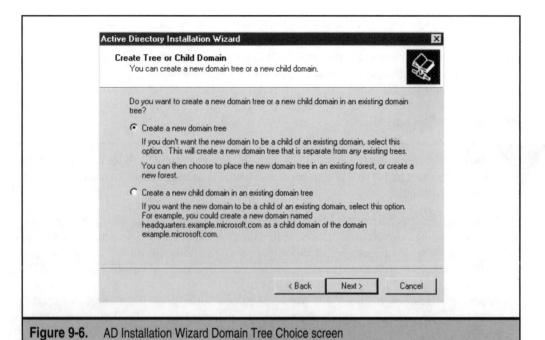

Figure 9-6. AD Installation Wizard Domain Tree Choice screen

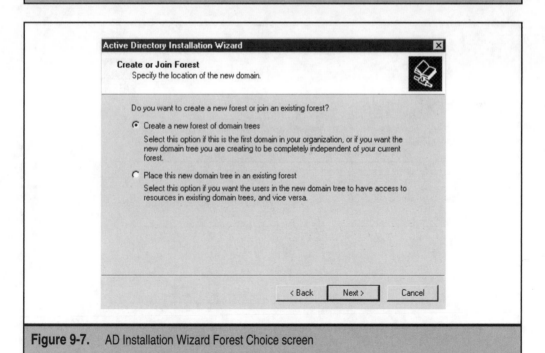

Figure 9-7. AD Installation Wizard Forest Choice screen

You've informed the AD Installation Wizard that you want to create a new domain. Now, as shown in Figure 9-8, the Wizard needs to know exactly what to call this puppy. The new domain name must comply with DNS naming rules as defined in RFC 1034. But if the domain is strictly internal and will never be seen or touched by the outside world (the Internet and its DNS servers), it need not follow Internet naming rules. This means that the first-level domain (usually com, org, net, gov, edu, or mil) can be anything you'd like it to be.

> **CAUTION:** Choose this first domain name carefully. You are about to name the root domain in the forest. This name cannot be changed without reinstalling the entire forest and the entire Active Directory in the enterprise.

So that downlevel clients (95/98/NT) can find the new domain, a NetBIOS version of the domain name is also created. The NetBIOS version allows for WINS and Browser registration. As shown in Figure 9-9, it defaults to a derivation of the DNS name that you provided, but you may change the name at this point to anything you like, as long as the name has fewer than 15 characters.

If you're upgrading from NT 4.0, this option does not appear. Regardless of the DNS name entered, the Win2K NetBIOS domain name is the existing NT 4.0 domain name.

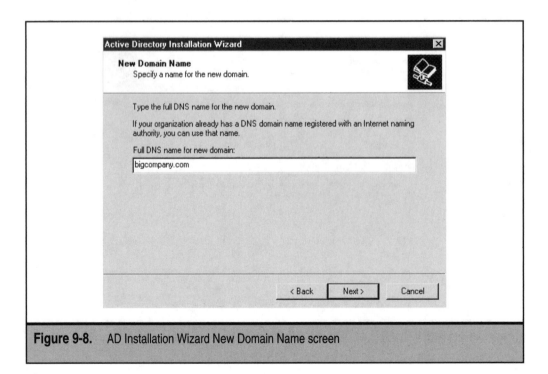

Figure 9-8. AD Installation Wizard New Domain Name screen

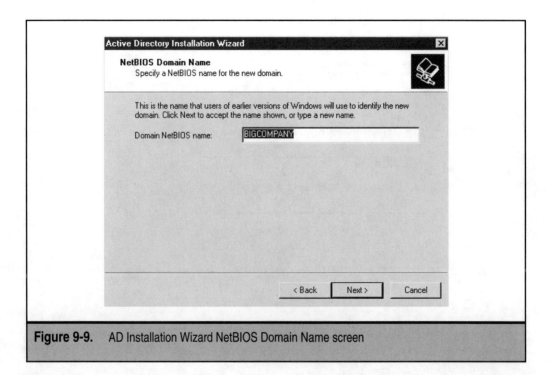

Figure 9-9.   AD Installation Wizard NetBIOS Domain Name screen

As shown in Figure 9-10, the AD Installation Wizard needs to know where you would like to physically store the two major elements of the Active Directory. At this point, keep in mind our earlier discussion of separate spindles, RAID 5, and so on. This is your opportunity to install the NTDS.DIT (Database location:) and the Log files (Log location:) on separate spindles or different physical hard drives. You can change these locations after the AD promotion by using NTDSUTIL, if necessary.

As shown in Figure 9-11, *dcpromo* now wants to know where you would like to place the shared system volume, the required volume that is auto-configured to replicate between all DCs in the same domain. It must be formatted with NTFSv5. The sysvol location cannot be changed after the DC promotion.

The AD Installation Wizard searches the network for a Win2K-compliant DNS server. Finding none, it asks if you'd like the Wizard to install and configure DNS, as shown in Figure 9-12. Yes is the recommended option.

As shown in Figure 9-13, the AD Installation Wizard now asks how you would like the permissions set on certain network services, specifically RAS, the Remote Access Server. Would you like them relatively weak, like RAS in NT 4.0, or much stronger, like RAS in Win2K?

If you are currently running NT 4.0 services on other NT 4.0 servers, particularly NT 4.0 Remote Access Service (RAS), you have a slight problem. The NT 4.0 RAS uses a special service account, LocalSystem, to log the service on. Unfortunately, LocalSystem logs

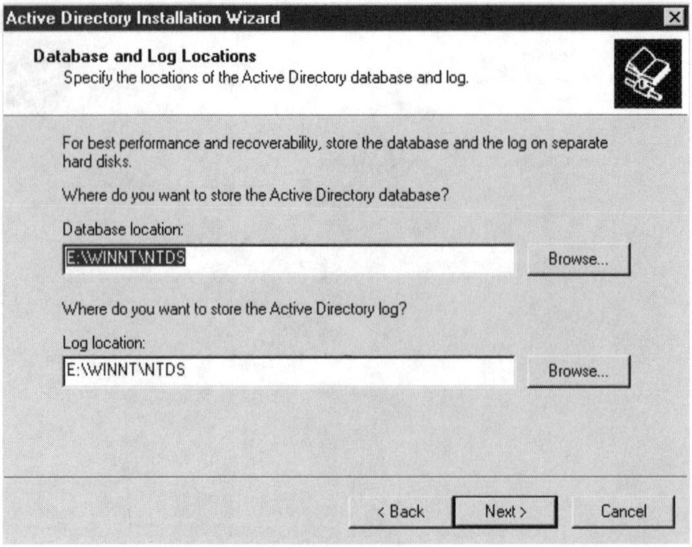

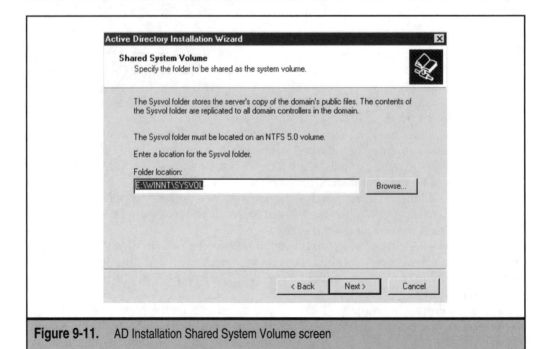

Figure 9-10.   AD Installation Wizard Database and Log Locations screen

Figure 9-11.   AD Installation Shared System Volume screen

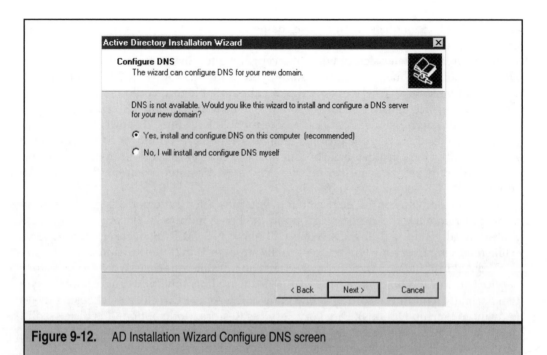

Figure 9-12. AD Installation Wizard Configure DNS screen

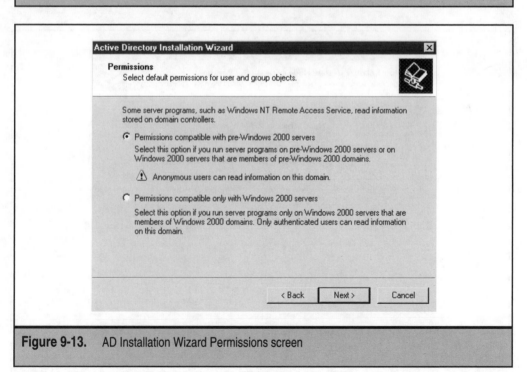

Figure 9-13. AD Installation Wizard Permissions screen

on with NULL credentials, with no user name or password. This form of logon allows anonymous users—really anonymous users—to authenticate and access files.

By default, Active Directory will not accept any querying of object attributes using a NULL session. This means that, by default, you cannot use an NT 4.0 RAS server on a Win2K Active Directory network because an attempted logon would need to query the user and group accounts. To enable the use of NT 4.0 RAS with the Active Directory, you can loosen the permissions (Permissions Compatible with Pre-Windows 2000 Servers). Doing so makes the Everyone group a member of the "Pre-Windows 2000 Compatible Access" Built-in local group which, by default, has Read permissions to any user or group object in the domain. For security purposes, Microsoft recommends upgrading your RAS servers to Win2K as quickly as possible.

After the domain controller promotion, you may alter these permissions by simply adding or removing the Everyone group in the Pre-Windows 2000 Compatible Access Built-in local group. Adding Everyone will allow NT 4.0 RAS (weaker) permissions, while removing Everyone will bring us to the stronger Win2K permission level.

The AD Installation Wizard now requests an administrator password for Directory Services Restore mode, as shown in Figure 9-14. If, at a later time, you cannot boot the system normally, you can restore a backup copy of the Active Directory by choosing the F8 (Advanced Startup Options), Directory Services Restore Mode option (it is discussed in detail in Chapter 15 on Recovery Options). When you start the computer in Directory Services Restore mode, you are prompted for an administrator password. On a DC, this

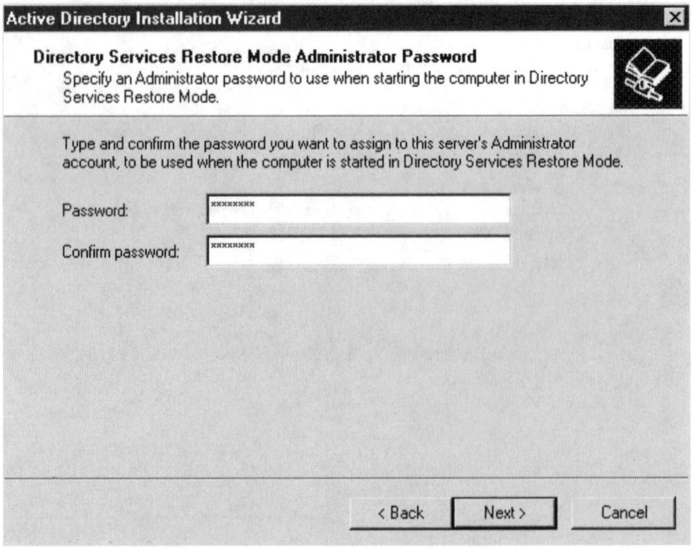

Figure 9-14. AD Installation Wizard DS Restore mode Admin Password screen

credential is *not* the same as the administrator password in the Active Directory, the domain, or the local SAM database; rather, it is a unique password that is stored separately in a mini-SAM database on this local computer and used solely for the purpose of authenticating an administrator in Directory Services Restore mode and the Recovery Console (see Chapter 15). The AD Installation Wizard is asking for this local, unique password in the screen shown in Figure 9-14. This password can be changed later in the DS Restore mode.

As shown in Figure 9-15, the next screen shows a summary of all the information that you've told the AD Installation Wizard. You've chosen to create a new forest, a new tree, and a new domain. In the figure, the name of the new forest and the new domain is bigcompany.com; the NetBIOS name is BIGCOMPANY. The screen tells where you chose to store all the AD files and states that the DNS service will be installed and configured on this computer. Check this screen carefully. This is your last chance to press the Back button and change the information.

Click the Next button and the AD Installation Wizard begins to create the Active Directory, as shown in Figure 9-16. Creating the AD takes at least five minutes and can take considerably longer in the case of an NT 4.0 PDC upgrade, because the Wizard must create Active Directory objects for each existing user, group, and computer account.

When the AD installation process is complete, you are informed what has been accomplished, as shown in Figure 9-17. Notice that the Active Directory is now installed on this computer and that it has been added automatically to the Default-First-Site-Name.

After the Active Directory installation is complete, the system must be restarted.

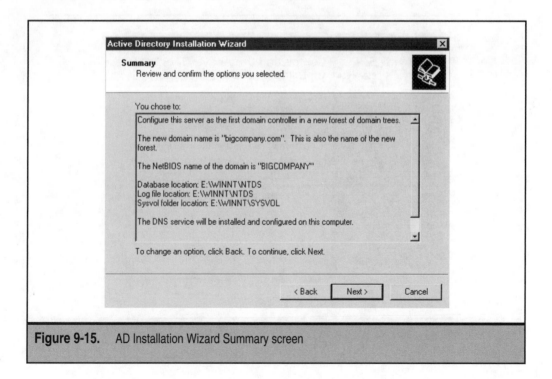

Figure 9-15. AD Installation Wizard Summary screen

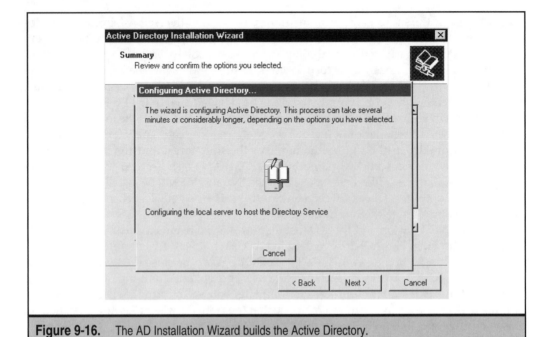

Figure 9-16. The AD Installation Wizard builds the Active Directory.

Figure 9-17. The AD Installation Wizard Completion screen

Promoting a Replica DC

Adding a second (or third or *n*th) domain controller to the same domain is relatively easy. In fact, it is conceptually quite a bit like adding a BDC to an NT 4.0 domain. You are simply adding another domain controller to a domain that already exists, so far fewer decisions need to be made. The process begins in the same way. First we see the Welcome screen. Click Next.

The first and only crucial decision you have to make comes on the next screen, as shown in Figure 9-18. Are you starting a new domain or joining an existing one? Select the second option, Additional Domain Controller for an Existing Domain.

Please note the word of caution that accompanies the Additional Domain Controller for an Existing Domain option: *Proceeding with this option will delete all local accounts on this server.* Because the local SAM database becomes inaccessible after the domain controller promotion, Microsoft believes that you won't need the local user accounts that you may have created while operating as a workgroup or member server. The only accounts left in the SAM after the *dcpromo* are Administrator, Guest, and the IUSR & IWAM accounts for anonymous access to IIS. If you demote the replica DC back to a member server, these are the only accounts that will exist.

Note this word of caution as well: *All cryptographic keys will be deleted and should be exported before continuing.* Cryptographic keys are assigned to a specific user. Only that user

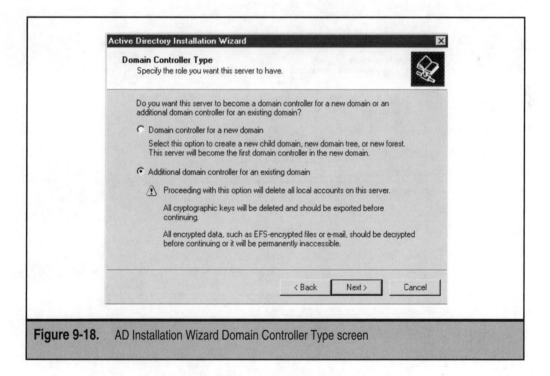

Figure 9-18. AD Installation Wizard Domain Controller Type screen

can utilize those keys. *dcpromo* is going to delete all the local users, so the keys aren't going to work anymore.

Finally, take note of the final word of caution: *All encrypted data, such as EFS-encrypted files or e-mail, should be decrypted before continuing or it will be permanently inaccessible.* Same reason. Only the local users can decrypt their files and e-mail. Once the local users and their keys are deleted, no one can decrypt the data.

Next, as shown in Figure 9-19, you have to identify yourself to the AD Installation Wizard as someone with the necessary group memberships and permissions to actually perform a *dcpromo*. You do not have to have an account in the domain that the computer is joining. Administrative privilege in the root domain is certainly sufficient.

Now, as shown in Figure 9-20, the AD Installation Wizard would like to know exactly what domain you are going to join as a replica DC. You must provide the exact DNS name for the Win2K domain; the NetBIOS name will not work.

As was the case with your first DC, you now have an opportunity to place the Active Directory database file (NTDS.DIT) and the AD log files, as shown in Figure 9-21. This is the screen where you can implement your "separate spindle" strategy. You can move these files later with NTDSUTIL.

As before, the wizard wants you to determine the physical location of the shared system volume, the volume that the FRS will automatically replicate with the other sysvols on all the other DCs in the domain. Figure 9-22 shows the Shared System Volume screen.

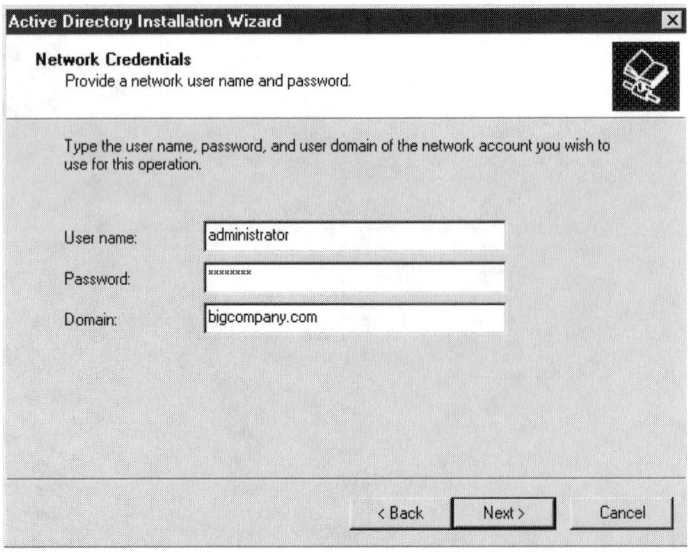

Figure 9-19. AD Installation Wizard Network Credentials screen

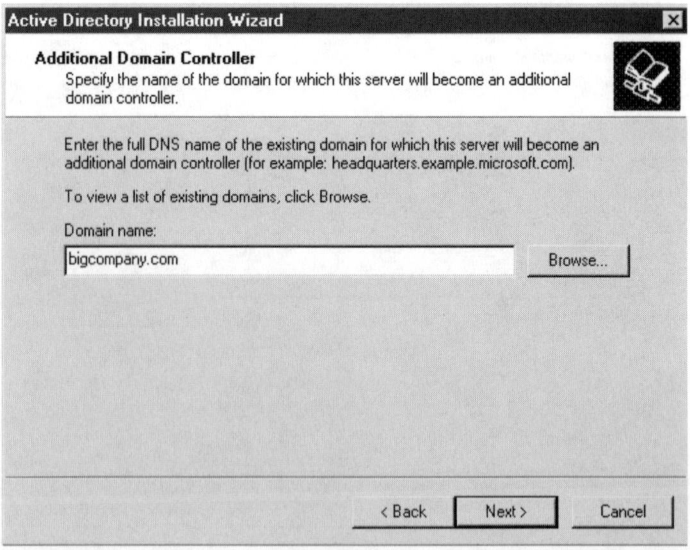

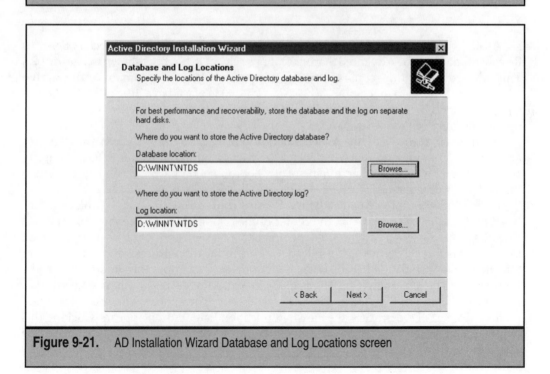

Figure 9-20.   AD Installation Wizard Additional Domain Controller screen

Figure 9-21.   AD Installation Wizard Database and Log Locations screen

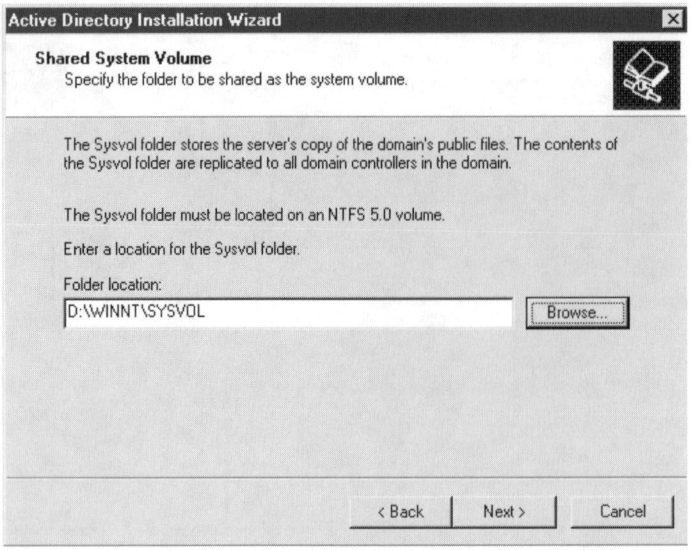

Figure 9-22.   AD Installation Wizard Shared System Volume screen

Again as before, the wizard needs an administrator password for the Directory Services Restore mode from the Advanced Startup Options screen (F8 boot), as shown in Figure 9-23. This password is *not* the same administrator password for the domain or the Active Directory; rather, it is a machine-based password that is placed in a little mini-SAM database on the local computer. It is used solely for the Directory Services Restore Mode boot option and the Recovery Console.

As shown in Figure 9-24, the AD Installation Wizard Summary screen is much shorter and simpler than the Summary screen for the first DC in the forest. In effect, it simply states, "I'm going to be another domain controller for bigcompany.com and here's where I'm going to put my stuff."

Figure 9-25 shows the AD Installation Wizard configuring the Active Directory. Notice that the animated pictures in the center of the dialog box are different from the pictures that you saw when you installed the first DC. You see information being transferred from the existing DC to the new replica DC. This replication process often takes longer than the initial installation because a number of objects may now exist and they must be transferred to create a new DC. The actual replication of current domain objects takes place near the end of the Active Directory promotion, after the AD has been installed. During this part of the process, the Finish Replication Later button appears. Clicking this button finishes the *dcpromo* process immediately, after which you are asked to reboot. The

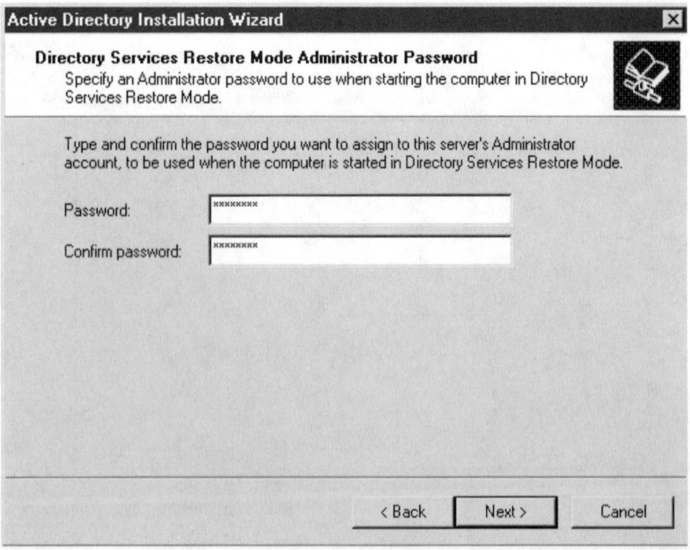

Active Directory Installation Wizard

Directory Services Restore Mode Administrator Password
Specify an Administrator password to use when starting the computer in Directory Services Restore Mode.

Type and confirm the password you want to assign to this server's Administrator account, to be used when the computer is started in Directory Services Restore Mode.

Password: ********

Confirm password: ********

< Back   Next >   Cancel

Figure 9-23.   AD Installation Wizard Directory Services Restore Mode Administrator Password screen

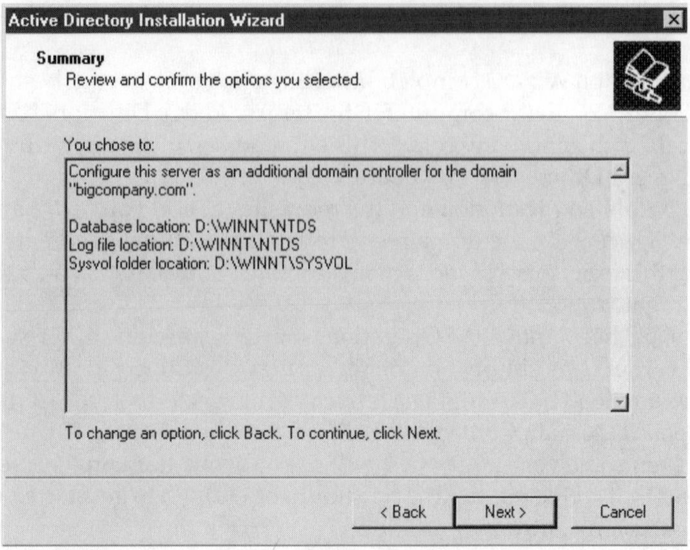

Active Directory Installation Wizard

Summary
Review and confirm the options you selected.

You chose to:

Configure this server as an additional domain controller for the domain "bigcompany.com".

Database location: D:\WINNT\NTDS
Log file location: D:\WINNT\NTDS
Sysvol folder location: D:\WINNT\SYSVOL

To change an option, click Back. To continue, click Next.

< Back   Next >   Cancel

Figure 9-24.   AD Installation Wizard Summary screen

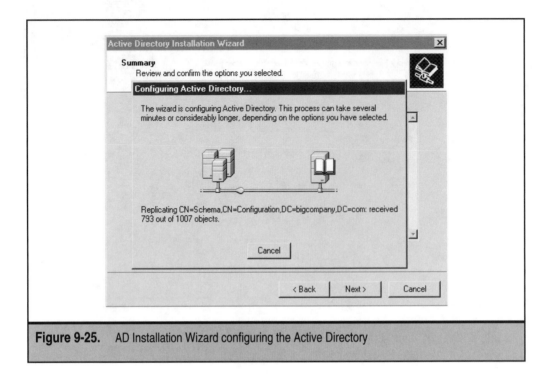

Figure 9-25. AD Installation Wizard configuring the Active Directory

AD data will then be added to the new DC during the normal domain controller replication process.

The AD Installation Wizard completion screen tells you what has been accomplished, as shown in Figure 9-26. In the computer in the figure, Active Directory has been installed for a domain called "bigcompany.com." This DC has been placed in the Default-First-Site Name, as will every DC created in the forest.

After the completed promotion and the requisite reboot, you now have two domain controllers. In Figure 9-27, the domain controllers are in the bigcompany.com domain. You can repeat this exact process for as many domain controllers as you believe are necessary for your organization.

The replica DC has none of the Operations masters and none of the special roles that we discussed earlier. It is simply another computer positioned to provide redundancy, fault-tolerance, and load balancing. The replica DC is affected by the Default Domain Policy and the Default Domain Controllers Policy. Since the vast majority of Windows 2000 installations, even some very large ones, will use only one domain with several DCs, the steps and issues that we've outlined so far should be enough to get started with an AD installation and domain controller promotion.

But we need to discuss two more scenarios before leaving the subject of installing the Windows 2000 Active Directory. The first scenario is the creation of a child domain within an existing domain tree. The second is the installation of a second root domain,

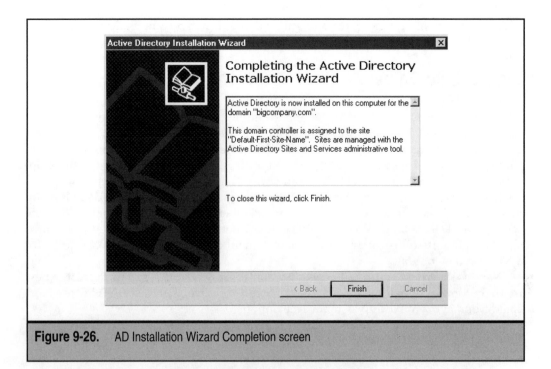

Figure 9-26. AD Installation Wizard Completion screen

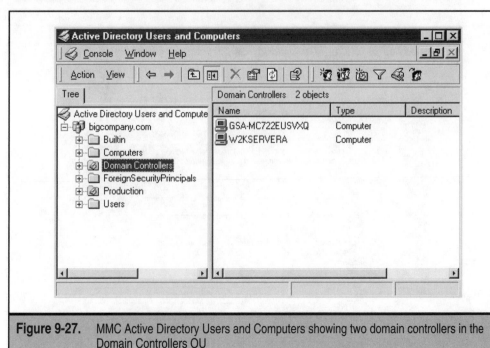

Figure 9-27. MMC Active Directory Users and Computers showing two domain controllers in the Domain Controllers OU

which entails creating a new tree and a new domain with a completely different DNS name in the same forest.

Creating a Child Domain

So far in our example, we have only a single domain with two domain controllers. But what if the Active Directory architects at our sample company, BigCompany, Inc., determine that a second domain must be created for the Marketing Dept. within the same tree under the main bigcompany.com domain? Of course, this will require another domain controller. And because it is the first DC in a domain, it will also have the three domain-wide operations masters: PDC Emulator, RID master, and infrastructure master.

It will serve as the time master for its domain and will be affected by the default group policies. The installation starts off the same as other installations. After the Welcome screen, the AD Installation Wizard wants to know if you want to create a new domain, as shown in Figure 9-28. You *are* creating a new domain, so select the Domain Controller for a New Domain option.

Next, as shown in Figure 9-29, *dcpromo* wants to know if you are going to create a new tree or become a child domain in an existing tree. Of course, you select the Create a New Child Domain in an Existing Domain Tree option.

As shown in Figure 9-30, the Wizard needs you to provide some network credentials. You need an account with sufficient permissions and group memberships to create a new domain.

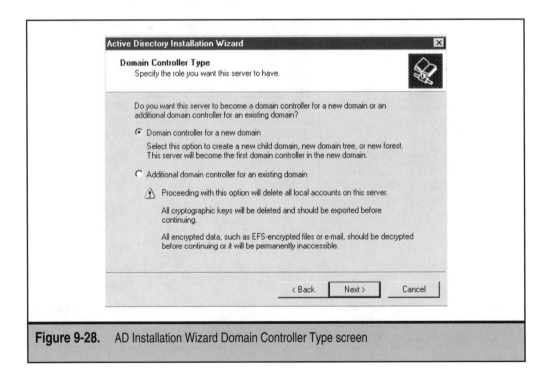

Figure 9-28.   AD Installation Wizard Domain Controller Type screen

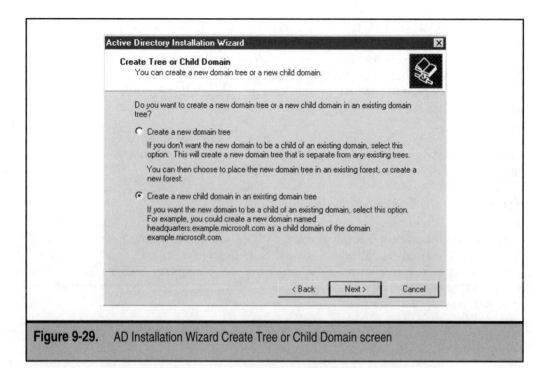

Figure 9-29.   AD Installation Wizard Create Tree or Child Domain screen

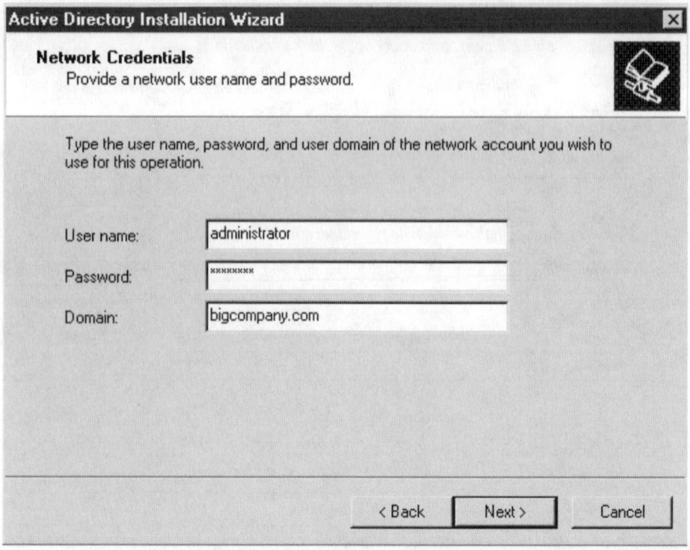

Figure 9-30.   AD Installation Wizard Network Credentials screen

The Credentials screen is the first that is completely different from any you've seen so far. As shown in Figure 9-31, you must fill in the DNS name of the parent domain under which you wish to create the child domain. You must fill in the name of the child domain as well. The Wizard builds the full DNS name on line 3 from the new child domain name on line 2 and the parent domain name on line 1. In order for this to work, DNS must be up and running, and the Domain Naming master (by default, the first DC in the forest) must be accessible.

From this point on, the *dcpromo* process does not differ from the previous examples. When the promotion process is complete and the new DC is rebooted, a new, fully functional child domain will exist in your domain tree.

Trusts

With the addition of a second domain, the concept of trusts enters the picture. Two-way, transitive trusts are created automatically, without admin intervention as part of the AD Installation Wizard, between all parent and child domains in the tree and between root domains in the forest. Assuming that he or she has Read permissions at least, a user located in the child domain mktg.bigcompany.com can see objects in the parent domain bigcompany.com, and vice versa.

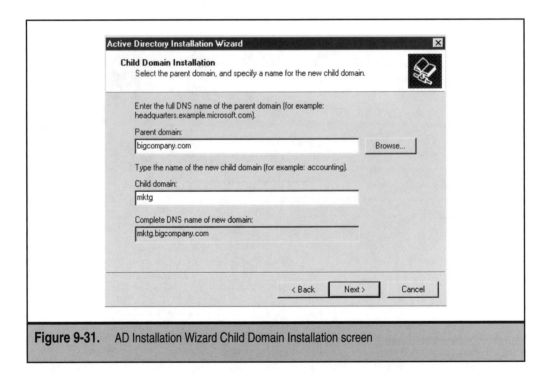

Figure 9-31.   AD Installation Wizard Child Domain Installation screen

Creating a New Domain Tree

The other scenario we need to discuss is the creation of a second tree within the same forest. A new tree means a new domain, a new DC, and a completely new DNS name. The DNS name of the new domain must be different from other DNS names currently in use in the forest. What's more, it must be unique within the DNS zones controlled by the enterprise.

The creation of a new tree starts off the same as always. After the Welcome screen, you are asked if you want to make this a replica DC or create a new domain, as shown in Figure 9-32. As usual, select the Domain Controller for a New Domain option.

Next, as shown in Figure 9-33, the Wizard asks whether we want to create a new tree or become a child domain in an existing tree. Select the Create a New Domain Tree option.

Next, *dcpromo* wants to know if you want to create a new forest or join an existing one, as shown in Figure 9-34. Select the Place This New Domain Tree in an Existing Forest option.

As shown in Figure 9-35, the Wizard requests your network credentials. Because you are creating a new tree, you must provide an account with administrative privileges at the root domain. The new tree establishes a trust with the root domain.

Now you need to enter the full DNS name of your new domain. In Figure 9-36, I entered **widgetsrus.int**.

From this point on in the *dcpromo* process, the screens are identical to the ones described previously in this chapter. After the process is complete and the new DC is rebooted, a new tree and a new domain, widgetsrus.int in my example, will be part of the

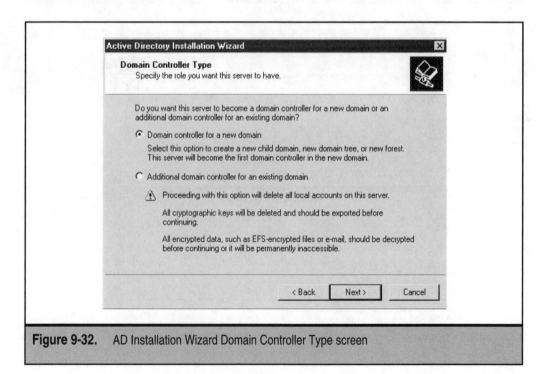

Figure 9-32.   AD Installation Wizard Domain Controller Type screen

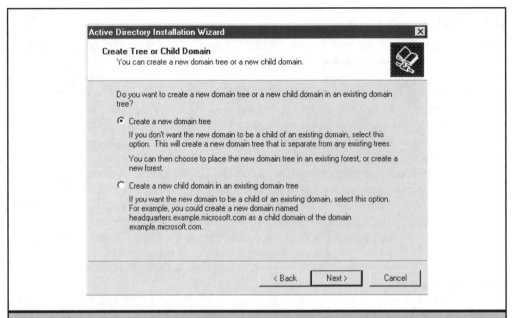

Figure 9-33. AD Installation Wizard Create Tree or Child Domain screen

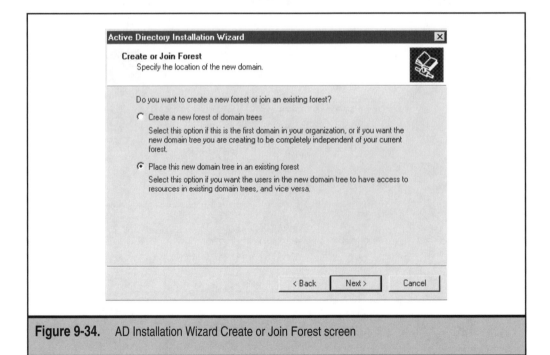

Figure 9-34. AD Installation Wizard Create or Join Forest screen

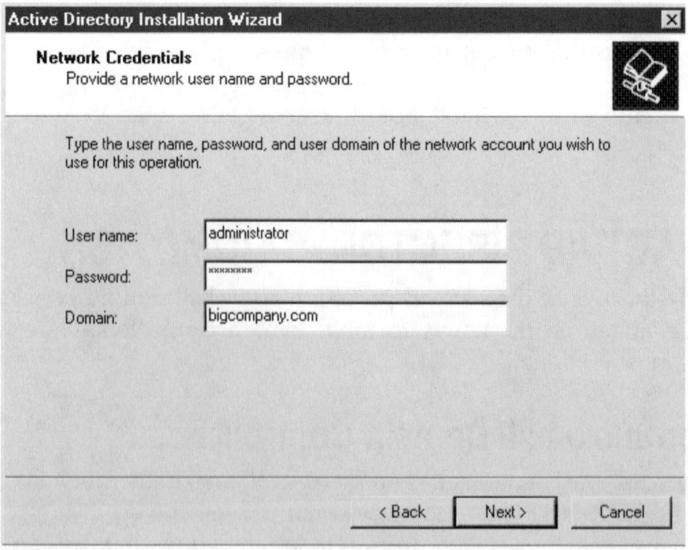

Figure 9-35.   AD Installation Wizard Network Credentials screen

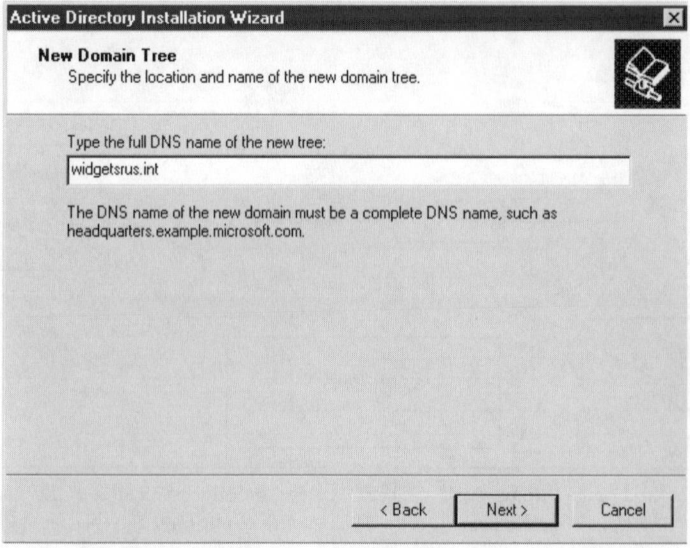

Figure 9-36.   AD Installation Wizard New Domain Tree screen

forest. In my example, a two-way, transitive trust will exist between bigcompany.com and widgetsrus.int.

Figure 9-37 shows the current structure of the sample Active Directory presented in this chapter.

Figure 9-38 demonstrates what it looks like in the MMC snap-in Active Directory Domains and Trusts.

AFTER THE ACTIVE DIRECTORY PROMOTION

As you would expect, once the *dcpromo* process is complete, a number of parameters and settings have changed on the newly-formed domain controllers. Here we chronicle a number of the most obvious.

Effects of *dcpromo* on all Domain Controllers

Certain changes are consistent on all domain controllers whether they are the first or last one installed in the forest. These changes occur during the *dcpromo* process. In many cases, the changes generate a screen prompt to let you know that they are happening.

The *dcpromo* Logs

The DCPromoUI.Log file contains every event that occurred during the *dcpromo* process beginning with the launch of the Active Directory Installation Wizard and continuing all the way to the end of the promotion process, whether the installation failed or succeeded. If the *dcpromo* failed, the log contains detailed error messages that appear immediately af-

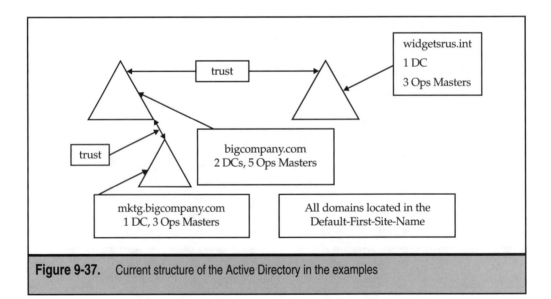

Figure 9-37.   Current structure of the Active Directory in the examples

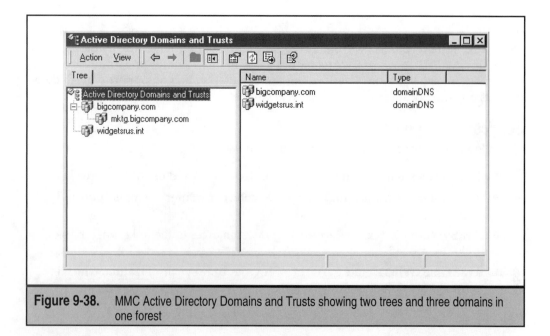

Figure 9-38.   MMC Active Directory Domains and Trusts showing two trees and three domains in one forest

ter the step that failed. These error messages can be extremely helpful in troubleshooting the reason for the failure.

The DCPromo.Log records a subset of the entries contained in the DCPromoUI.Log as well as the settings used for promotion. dcpromo entries include Site, the path for AD files, time sync, and the computer account information.

The Registry

dcpromo creates a new Registry key (HKLM\System\CurrentControlSet\Services\ NTDS). Parameters such as the path to the NTDS.DIT file and the Site with Which This DC Is Associated appear under the Parameters sub-key. ACLs on certain Registry keys are changed during *dcpromo* for additional security.

New Files

In addition to creating the Active Directory file itself (NTDS.DIT), *dcpromo* creates several log files:

▼   edb.log is the main AD log file.

■   res1.log and res2.log are simply there to reserve disk space and prevent the AD from crashing in case the disk gets full.

▲   edb.chk points to the spot in the log files that hasn't made it into the database yet.

Sysvol

The shared system volume (sysvol), the volume auto-configured for use by the file replication service (FRS), now exists. An identical copy of this volume appears on each DC in the same domain. The admin performing the installation had an opportunity to determine its physical location during the *dcpromo* process.

Services Configured

The following services are configured during *dcpromo*:

▼ **KDC (Key Distribution Center)**   Controls access and use of Kerberos keys

■ **ISM (InterSite Messaging)**   Provides control for InterSite replication and messaging

■ **TrkSvr (Link Tracking Services)**   Tracks changes to file links when files or links are moved

▲ **W32Time (Win32 Time Service)**   Provides time synchronization, which is required for Kerberos authentication

DNS Files

After the reboot that follows *dcpromo*, the NetLogon service will start and create a text file named NETLOGON.DNS in the \WINNT\system32\config directory. This file contains all the relevant DNS entries to be used by the DNS server. The NetLogon service uses this file to update the DNS server every time it (NetLogon) is initiated and at regular intervals thereafter. In Win2K, one way to make sure a given DC is registered with the DNS server is to stop and start the NetLogon service on the DC you wish to register. If you choose at a later time to change the DNS zones from Standard Primary to AD-Integrated, the NETLOGON.DNS text file will disappear because the DNS zone becomes an Active Directory object. The DNS zone and all of its entries are then saved in the Active Directory.

Default Containers

In the last chapter, we discussed the default containers in detail. Figure 9-39 shows all the default containers and the default users and groups in the Users container.

MIXED VS. NATIVE MODE

When the Active Directory is installed (*dcpromo*) it defaults to Mixed mode. Mixed mode is simply the "NT 4.0 Replication process mode." In other words, the assumption in Mixed mode is that you have upgraded an NT 4.0 PDC to Windows 2000 and that NT 4.0 BDCs still remaining in the domain still require replication of changes in the domain database. Mixed mode is required for the NT 4.0 BDCs from the upgraded domain to receive updates through the NT 4.0 PDC/BDC domain replication process.

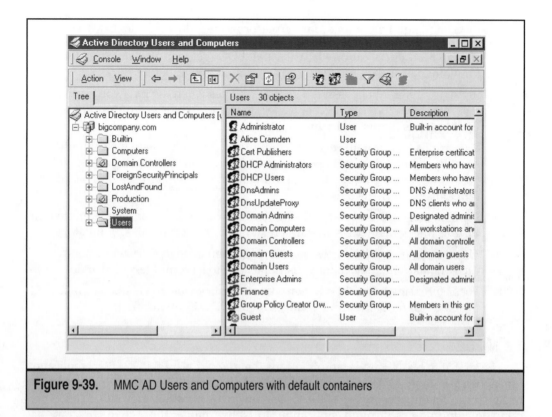

Figure 9-39.   MMC AD Users and Computers with default containers

Mixed Mode

Mixed mode gets a bad rap by admins who basically don't understand what's going on. Some admins assume that if something or other (such as DNS) doesn't work in Win2K, it doesn't work because the domain is running in Mixed mode. Nothing could be farther from the truth. Mixed mode is designed to continue updating the remaining NT 4.0 BDCs that are still functioning as logon servers for downlevel (Win 9x and NT) clients as well as Win2K client computers. Mixed mode has nothing to do with DNS, logons, DHCP, or the myriad other things it gets blamed for. It simply mimics the NT 4.0 replication behavior for BDCs and the NT 4.0 domain update behavior for clients.

Because the Win2K Mixed mode is basically the NT 4.0 Mimic mode, one way to explain it is to cover the duties of the PDC Emulator in Mixed mode. (The PDC Emulator and all other FSMO/Operations Masters are covered in Chapter 10.) The Win2K Mixed mode PDC Emulator serves as the PDC for existing NT 4.0 BDC synchronization, for downlevel client password changes, and for the creation of objects using downlevel tools. It also replicates in a multi-master process with any other Win2K DCs that have joined the domain.

The PDC Emulator (Operations Master) performs the following roles in Mixed mode:

▼ PDC in NT 4.0 replication scenarios. (All BDCs get their updates from the PDC Emulator just as they got their updates from the PDC before.)

■ Receives preferential password change updates when the password is changed on a Windows 2000 domain controller. This is called the out-of-band password update and is discussed in this chapter.

■ Acts as PDC for downlevel client computers (when changing the computer account name), for users logged on to downlevel boxes (when changing their password), and for admin tools (admin on an NT 4.0 BDC uses User Manager for Domains to create a user).

■ Domain Master Browser (the Computer Browser service has always elected the PDC as the Domain Master Browser, and now it elects the PDC Emulator).

■ Time Master (in a Win2K network, time is distributed to the PDC Emulators for each domain, and they, in turn, distribute time to all computers in their domain).

▲ Focus for changes in GPOs (when a Group Policy Object is created or modified, the GPO editor makes those changes on the PDC Emulator first).

Native Mode

The switch to Native mode simply means that the old NT 4.0 PDC/BDC replication functionality is gone. All DCs should be running Windows 2000 before the switch to Native mode. If, for any reason, NT 4.0 BDCs remain on the network, they will no longer receive domain updates through replication. In Native mode, the Active Directory has additional group functionality (these functions are discussed later, but only two items are removed from the list of PDC Emulator duties).

PDC Emulator has the following roles in Native Mode:

▼ Receives preferential password change updates when the password is changed on a Windows 2000 domain controller (an out-of-band password update)

■ Acts as PDC for downlevel clients and admin tools

■ Domain Master Browser

■ Time Master (for its domain)

▲ Focus for changes in GPOs (if the PDC Emulator is not available, System prompts for another DC on which to focus)

Switching to Native Mode

This one-time-only, irreversible domain-wide event is incredibly simple and, really, quite anticlimactic. To switch to Native mode, log on as the domain administrator. In the MMC, Active Directory Users and Computers, right-click the domain name and select Properties. The domain Properties sheet appears, as shown in Figure 9-40, with the General

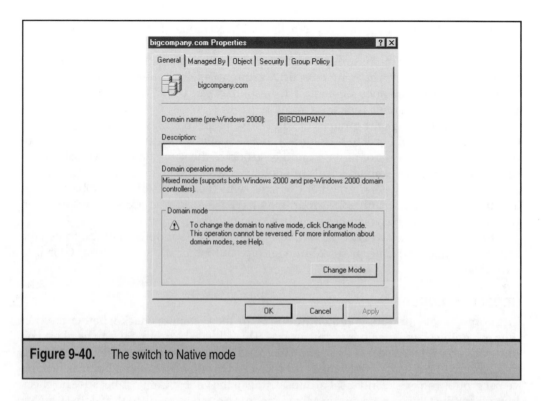

Figure 9-40.   The switch to Native mode

tab selected. In the lower-right corner, click the Change Mode button. A warning message informs you that this is a permanent change and, if you continue, the domain cannot be reset to Mixed mode. If you click Yes, the domain is changed to Native mode. This change will now be replicated to all other DCs in the domain.

Changes in Group Behavior

Native mode opens up substantial new functionality to the security groups housed in the Active Directory.

Universal groups are enabled. In Mixed mode, these groups cannot be created, but in Native mode they become an option. Universal groups can have members from any domain in the forest and can be applied to resources in any domain in the forest. Because Universal groups can have members from any domain, they reside in the Global Catalog.

A completely new capability is the ability to nest groups of the same kind. In Native mode, a Domain Local can be a member of a Domain Local group, and a Global can be a member of another Global group. Why nest groups? Because, for replication performance purposes, Microsoft recommends that a single group have no more than five thousand members. You see, all attribute updates must be completed as a single transaction. Because group memberships are stored as a single multi-value attribute, a change to the group membership will result in the whole membership list having to be updated (replicated) in a single transaction. Microsoft has tested and supports group memberships of up to five thousand members.

When an AD security group was created in Mixed mode, that was it. You could not modify its group type (Security or Distribution) or its group scope (Domain Local or Global). But in Native mode, group type and scope can be changed after the fact. Be careful, however, if you are changing a Security group to a Distribution group because unwanted loss of permissions or denials to resources can occur due to the fact that a Distribution group cannot appear on an ACL.

You can also change the group scope in Native mode, but only in one direction. You can change a Domain Local to a Universal or a Global to a Universal as long as the Domain Local or Global is not nesting another group of the same type. Universal groups cannot be changed to Domain Locals or Global because, first, Universal groups can potentially contain members from other domains (which is impossible for Global groups) and because, second, a Universal group may have been granted access to resources in multiple domains (which is impossible for Domain Local groups).

If the domain that switched to Native mode was the root domain of the forest, the Schema Admins and Enterprise Admins groups automatically switch from Global to Universal.

Impact on Logons

The normal behavior during authentication is for the system to check whether the user who is logging on is a member of any groups. This allows the group SIDs to be placed on the user's access token so that he or she can access resources. When a domain is in Mixed mode, logons do not attempt to check for Universal group membership because no Universal groups can exist. Universal groups reside in the Global Catalog. Because no check is made for the Universal groups in Mixed mode, no query is made to the Global Catalog server. This same behavior is true in a single domain forest as well.

In Native mode with a multi-domain forest, the authentication system has to check the Universal groups to see whether the user logging on is a member. Therefore, the system must query both the Active Directory of the authenticating domain *and* the Global Catalog server wherever it may be. This means that multi-domain, Native-mode logons can take noticeably longer than Mixed-mode or single-domain logons, especially if a Global Catalog server is not present on the client's site.

"Greenfield" Windows 2000 domains

If you are not upgrading your existing NT 4.0 domain to Windows 2000 but you are instead starting from scratch or a "green" field, the switch to Native mode is a non-event. You have no existing NT 4.0 BDCs to worry about, so you may switch at any time. In most cases, switching to Native mode as soon as you have completed the first *dcpromo* probably makes sense. There is absolutely no reason to wait.

In fact, you can install a domain directly into Native mode by changing the setting ntMixedDomain=1 in the schema.ini file in \WINNT\SYSTEM32 to ntMixedDomain=0 before performing *dcpromo*. After the domain controller promotion, the domain is in Native mode.

SUMMARY

While this chapter may not cover every conceivable Active Directory configuration, I believe that the examples it presents address the needs of the vast majority of small to medium-size corporations, as well as some large, multinational enterprises. Because the Win2K Active Directory can scale to fit nearly any size business, I believe that a single domain will be used in 80–90 percent of the installations of Win2K and the Active Directory.

In the next chapter, we'll drill down into our AD installation and configure OUs, sites, and replication. We'll also examine the recommendations and guidelines for the placement of the Operations masters for additional safety and performance.

CHAPTER 10

Managing and Configuring the Active Directory

Chapter 10 focuses on key strategies for managing and configuring the Active Directory in Windows 2000. It's always a good idea to know where you're going before you leave on a trip. Knowing where you're going on the way to a fully installed Active Directory is no different. Prior to designing and implementing an AD structure, understanding the true advantages and disadvantages of different designs is essential. That understanding comes with a detailed knowledge of how to successfully manage and configure the AD. A few of the topics we will cover here are creating and managing container objects, strategies for the proper placement of domain controllers and operations master roles, creating sites, and configuring replication for performance.

MANAGING THE AD CONTAINER OBJECTS

Now that you've installed the Active Directory (Chapter 9) and learned the basics about the various tools at your disposal for managing the Active Directory (Chapter 4), it's time to look into creating the individual container objects that make up the AD. This is where the strategies you learned earlier regarding OU structure, delegated administration, and Group Policy inheritance come into play.

The actual creation of the AD objects is very simple. The hard part is deciding where to create the objects, which objects to put where, and how to organize objects.

Domains

Domains are the primary building blocks of the Active Directory. It is impossible to have an Active Directory without at least one domain. In most cases, a single domain is all that is needed to support the entire enterprise. With a capacity for over 1 million objects and the ability to delegate administrative control to the OUs, there are few reasons to create additional domains.

Creating Domains

All of Chapter 9 is devoted to creating domains. The only way to create a Win2K Active Directory domain (using the UI) is by running *dcpromo*, the Active Directory Installation wizard, which is discussed in great detail in Chapter 9.

Modifying Domains

The domain properties are few but powerful. As shown in Figure 10-1, the General tab lists the DNS and NetBIOS name for the domain and allows you to enter an optional description. Most importantly, however, the General tab is where you execute the one-time, irreversible switch from Mixed to Native mode (see Chapter 9).

To switch modes, click the Change Mode button to bring up a confirmation screen, and then click Yes. Be careful, because even though this option is only available to Domain Admins, it is far too easy to execute inadvertently. Switch the domain to Native mode only after all DCs in the domain are running Windows 2000. Do not play "what-if" games here!

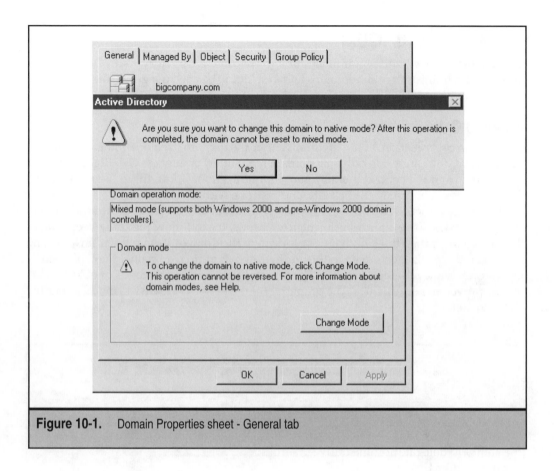

Figure 10-1.   Domain Properties sheet - General tab

After switching to Native mode, your NT 4.0 BDCs, if they exist, will no longer receive domain replication updates.

Deleting Domains

Domains can only be deleted in two ways:

▼ Run *dcpromo* on each DC in the domain to remove the Active Directory by demoting the DC back to a Win2K server. To completely delete the domain, be sure to check This Server Is the Last Domain Controller in the Domain when you run *dcpromo* on the last DC.

▲ Invoke the NTDSUTIL command line utility and select Metadata Cleanup.

Remember: After removing a domain in any fashion, checking the DNS database for possible inconsistencies is imperative. Depending on the circumstances, you may need to manually edit the DNS zone to bring it into sync with the new reality.

Organizational Units (OUs)

OUs are the primary unit of administration in the Active Directory. With OUs, you can now create administrative subdomains and in so doing be able to segment the various administrative areas under different policies and different administrators.

Creating OUs

To create an organizational unit, highlight either the domain itself or another OU. An organizational unit can reside only in a domain (container) or another OU. Right-click and select New from the context menu. Choose Organizational Unit, fill in the name of the OU, as shown in Figure 10-2, click OK, and be done with it.

Technically, there is no limit to how many levels of OUs you can create (LDAP will stop you at 64). However, for performance reasons, try to follow the three-deep rule of thumb: No more than three domain levels deep in the domain structure within a tree, no more than three OU levels deep in the OU hierarchy within a domain. Microsoft recommends only ten levels deep for OUs. The OU structure can be hundreds of objects wide without affecting performance. The properties of the new OU are easy to modify after the OU is created.

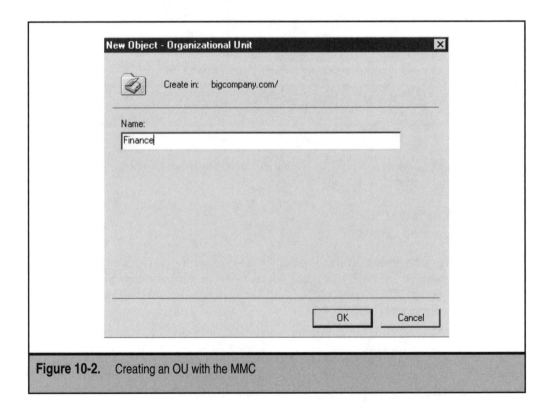

Figure 10-2. Creating an OU with the MMC

Modifying OUs

When the MMC View menu is set to Advanced Features, you see five tabs when you right-click an OU and choose Properties, as shown in Figure 10-3:

▼   **General tab**   Allows you to add a description of the OU and address information

■   **Managed By tab**   Documents the user account that is responsible for managing this OU

■   **Object tab**   Displays AD system information about the OU object

■   **Security tab**   Allows for changes to the ACL of the OU and determines who can perform what task on the OU object (discussed in detail in Chapter 14)

▲   **Group Policy tab**   Links the OU to group policy objects (discussed in detail in Chapter 12)

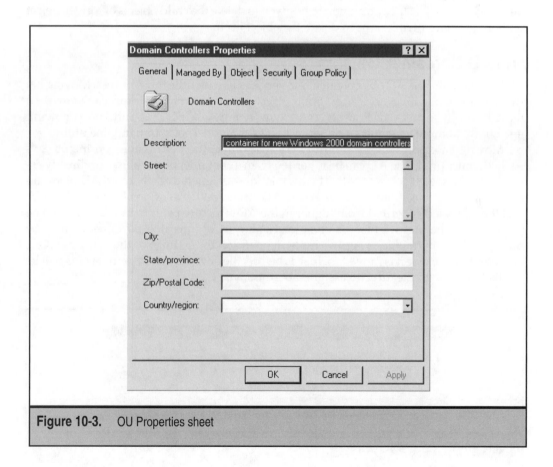

Figure 10-3.   OU Properties sheet

Deleting OUs

To delete objects, the user performing the deletion needs either Full Control on the object ACL or, at least, the Read and Delete permission. System-generated containers and OUs cannot be deleted.

Any admin-created OU may be deleted. Simply right-click the OU and select Delete or press the Delete key. When you see the standard "Are you sure?" dialog box, click the Yes/No confirmation notice. If the OU contains objects, clicking Yes brings up yet another notice, as shown in Figure 10-4, to warn you that this object contains other objects, and then you are asked whether you want to delete them, too. Because an OU can contain users, groups, computers, printers, shared folders, and even other OUs that can total hundreds or even thousands of objects, deleting an OU can have dire consequences indeed. Be sure you know which OU you are deleting and why. Admins have a habit of getting far too comfortable clicking OK to warnings that they don't have time to read. But the warnings are there to keep you from inadvertently making a huge mistake.

The Domain Controllers OU, which is created during the *dcpromo* process, cannot be deleted. It is possible for permission to be given to delete the child objects of a given object without granting permissions to delete the object itself.

Moving AD Container Objects

Within a domain, the AD objects can move very easily with little muss or fuss. Moving between domains is a little more dicey. Some objects, such as domains, simply can't move. To move between domains, OUs, users, and groups require a Win2K Support Tool command line utility. Computers require a different Win2K Support Tool command line utility.

Moving an object will, in almost every case, affect the permissions on the object's ACL. Permissions in the AD can be inherited from a container object above or directly assigned to the specific object itself. The permissions assigned directly to an AD object always stick with it as it moves through the AD structure. Permissions listed on the ACL that the AD object inherited from higher in the AD structure prior to moving will not be present after the move. In fact, a completely new set of inherited permissions may be present. Which permissions apply simply depends on the settings of the container (OU, domain) that the object is moved to. Just as before, the new, inherited permissions will be applied along with the directly assigned permissions.

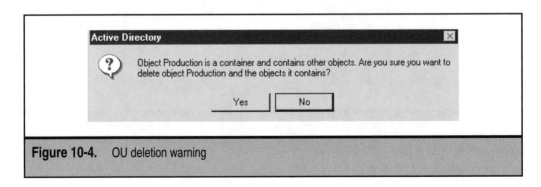

Figure 10-4.   OU deletion warning

Moving Objects within a Domain

Within the same domain, the MMC provides the easiest and simplest means of moving nearly any object. Right-click the object you wish to move and select Move from the context menu. The list of possible container objects appears. Choose the container to which you want to move the object, click OK, and click Done. It may take as long as 15 minutes for the change to replicate to all domain controllers on the site.

If the object is a container object such as an OU, all the objects it contains move with it. If the object is a group, its members don't move but they still remain members.

Moving a DC Between Domains

In NT 4.0, it was impossible to move a domain controller from one domain to another without a complete reinstallation of the operating system. If you must move a domain controller to a different domain, a process in Windows 2000 allows you to do it.

Assuming that there are other DCs in both the source and target domains to maintain the existing Active Directory, you must first run *dcpromo* on the DC you wish to move and remove the Active Directory. Then you reboot. When the now member server comes back up, run *dcpromo* again, but this time point to the "new" domain. When *dcpromo* completes its work, you will have successfully moved a Win2K DC from one domain to another. Moving computers is discussed in Chapter 12.

Moving OUs Between Domains

It will be nice in the future to be able to use the mouse to point and click your way through the process of moving OUs between domains, but not with this initial release. To perform an OU move between domains, you need the Win2K Support Tools command line utility MOVETREE. Assuming a DC named server1 in bigcompany.com and a DC named server2 in mktg.bigcompany.com, the syntax for moving the OU named MKTG from bigcompany.com to the domain mktg.bigcompany.com and renaming it SALES looks like this:

```
movetree /start /s server1.bigcompany.com /d
server2.mktg.bigcompany.com /sdn OU=mktg,DC=bigcompany,DC=com
/ddn OU=sales,DC=mktg,DC=bigcompany,DC=com /u
bigcompany\administrator /p mypasswd
```

Pardon the word-wrap, but that's all one command. This command, as written, would use the administrator credentials from bigcompany.com to execute the OU move and rename without any additional prompts or checking.

THE DEFAULT CONTAINERS

During the *dcpromo* process, several default containers are created within the domain. These containers are essential to the operation of Active Directory and they cannot be deleted, renamed, or moved. A container is different from an OU in that a GPO cannot be directly applied to it. One of the default containers listed is the Domain Controllers OU. It is included here because it is created automatically during *dcpromo*.

Builtin

Builtin houses the eight Builtin local groups that you recognize from an NT 4.0 domain controller, plus one additional group: Pre-Windows 2000 Compatible Access, as shown in Figure 10-5. If you upgrade an NT 4.0 PDC, the eight NT 4.0 local groups transfer directly to the Win2K AD Builtin container. Managing groups is discussed in detail in Chapter 11.

Computers

In an NT 4.0 PDC upgrade, all the existing computers' domain accounts end up in the Computers container. After the NT upgrade, while still in Win2K mixed mode, if a downlevel tool such as Server Manager creates a computer account, the account is created in the Computers container. In Win2K, computer accounts created at the client will be placed in this container. Computer objects are not required to remain in the Computers container, but the system simply needs a place to put them by default.

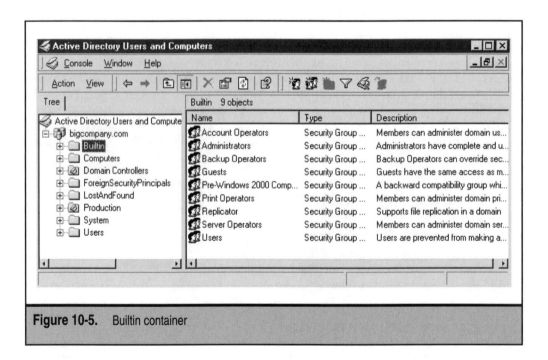

Figure 10-5. Builtin container

Blueprints for the Future

From its basic design concepts to its in-depth management details, the Windows 2000 Active Directory engenders emotions ranging from intense awe and stupefied wonder to abject confusion and overwhelming terror. We should probably spend most of our time somewhere in the middle. While the AD is very complex and difficult to comprehend initially, it remains complex but no longer mysterious with study and time. With a little patience, we can understand how it really works, and we can use this knowledge to make our enterprises run more smoothly and efficiently. The Active Directory is in your future. It's not a matter of *if*, it's a matter of *when*. After reading about the Active Directory and studying its ins and outs, and its do's and don'ts, use these blueprints to confirm your AD understanding and check your design and management assumptions. See if what you thought was true is really true. You just might surprise yourself.

The blueprints in this section are drawn from topics in several chapters in this book covering Windows 2000 Active Directory.

Win2K Active Directory Domain Tree

Windows 2000 Root Domain

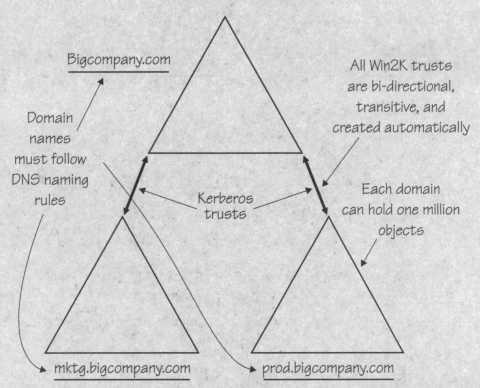

Bigcompany.com

All Win2K trusts are bi-directional, transitive, and created automatically

Domain names must follow DNS naming rules

Kerberos trusts

Each domain can hold one million objects

mktg.bigcompany.com

prod.bigcompany.com

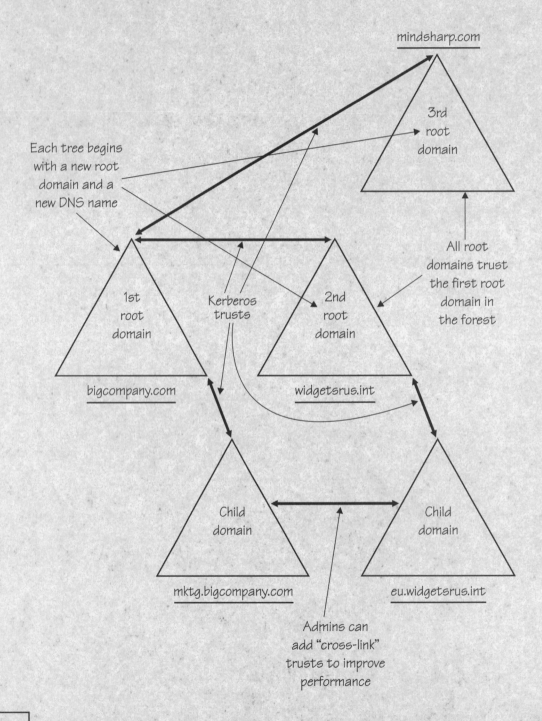

mindsharp.com

3rd root domain

Each tree begins with a new root domain and a new DNS name

1st root domain

bigcompany.com

Kerberos trusts

2nd root domain

widgetsrus.int

All root domains trust the first root domain in the forest

Child domain

mktg.bigcompany.com

Child domain

eu.widgetsrus.int

Admins can add "cross-link" trusts to improve performance

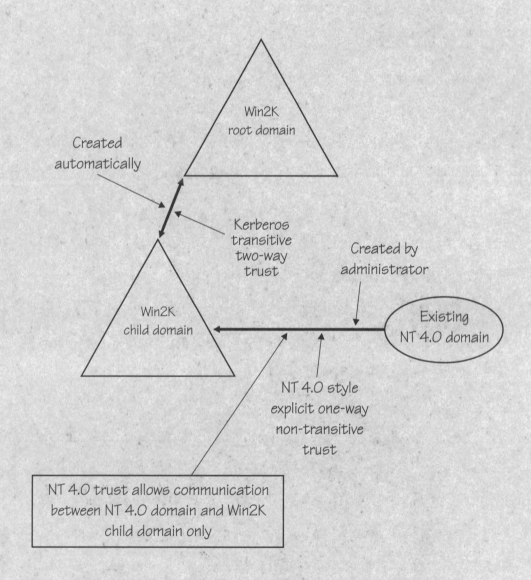

Win2K
root domain

Created
automatically

Kerberos
transitive
two-way
trust

Created by
administrator

Win2K
child domain

Existing
NT 4.0 domain

NT 4.0 style
explicit one-way
non-transitive
trust

NT 4.0 trust allows communication
between NT 4.0 domain and Win2K
child domain only

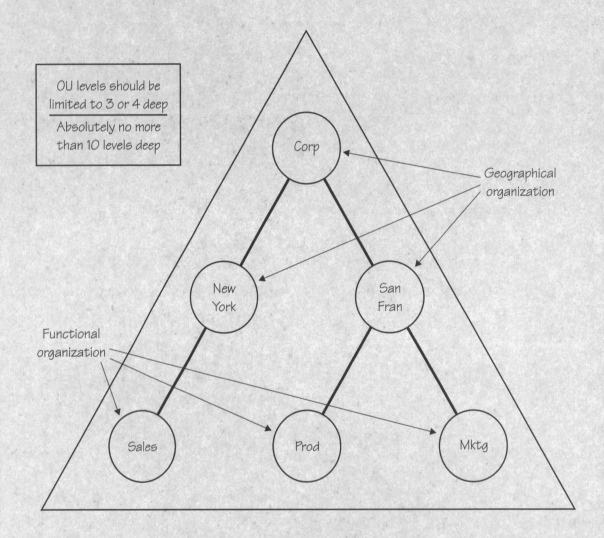

OU levels should be limited to 3 or 4 deep

Absolutely no more than 10 levels deep

Geographical organization

Functional organization

Corp

New York

San Fran

Sales

Prod

Mktg

bigcompany.com

OU structure organized first geographically then by function

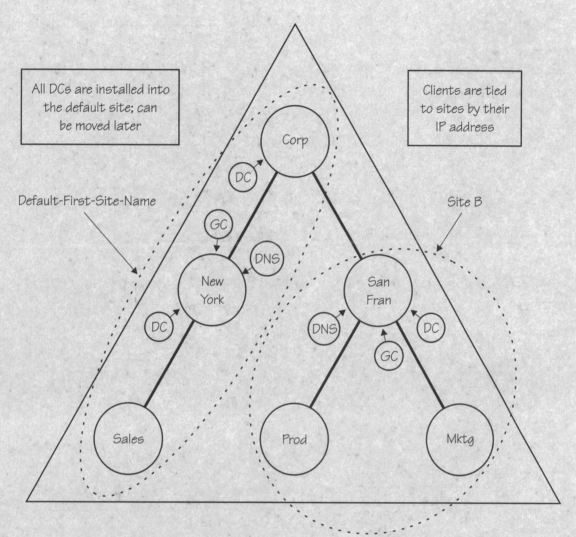

All DCs are installed into the default site; can be moved later

Clients are tied to sites by their IP address

Default-First-Site-Name

Site B

Corp

DC

GC

DNS

New York

DC

San Fran

DNS

DC

GC

Sales

Prod

Mktg

bigcompany.com

For improved performance and fault-tolerance, each site should contain a domain controller (DC), A global catolog server (GC), and a DNS server (DNS)

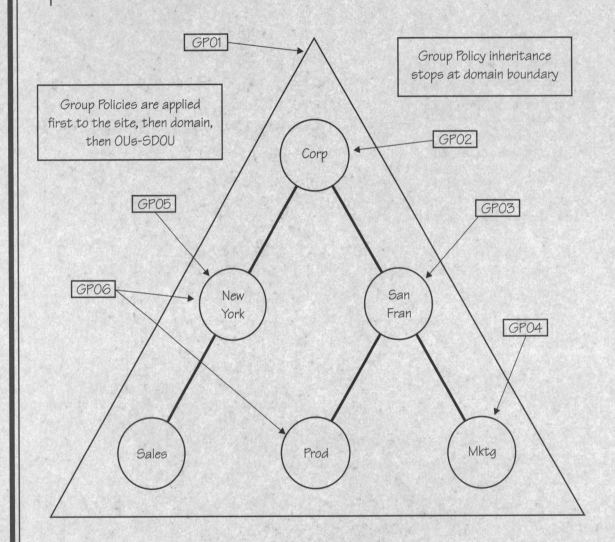

GP01

Group Policy inheritance
stops at domain boundary

Group Policies are applied
first to the site, then domain,
then OUs-SDOU

Corp

GP02

GP05

GP03

GP06

New
York

San
Fran

GP04

Sales

Prod

Mktg

bigcompany.com

Sales OU GPOs applied = GP01, GP02, GP05, GP06
Prod OU GPOs applied = GP01, GP02, GP03, GP06
Mktg OU GPOs applied = GP01, GP02, GP03, GP04

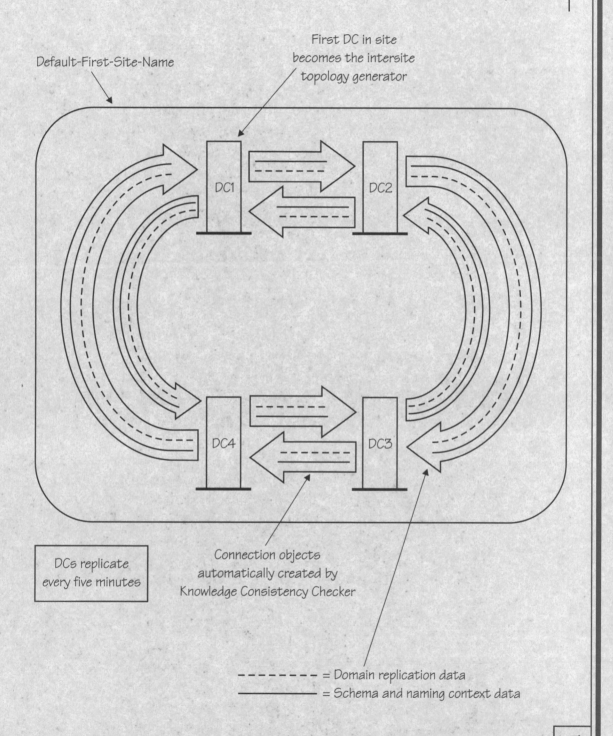

First DC in site
becomes the intersite
topology generator

Default-First-Site-Name

DC1

DC2

DC4

DC3

DCs replicate
every five minutes

Connection objects
automatically created by
Knowledge Consistency Checker

- - - - - - - - = Domain replication data
———————— = Schema and naming context data

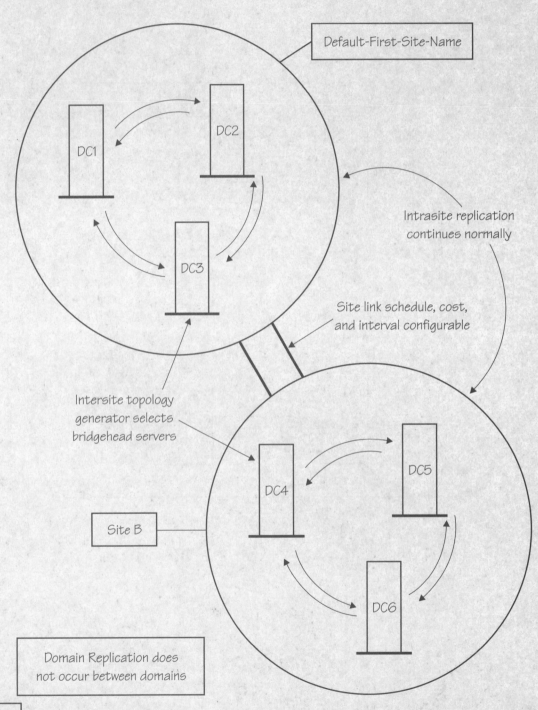

Default-First-Site-Name

DC1

DC2

DC3

Intrasite replication
continues normally

Site link schedule, cost,
and interval configurable

Intersite topology
generator selects
bridgehead servers

DC4

DC5

DC6

Site B

Domain Replication does
not occur between domains

ForeignSecurityPrincipals

The ForeignSecurityPrincipals container holds the system-populated dynamic groups such as Anonymous Logon, Batch, Creator Group, Creator Owner, Dialup, Enterprise Domain Controllers, Proxy, Restricted, Self, Service, System, Terminal Server User, Authenticated Users, Interactive, Network, and Everyone. Membership of these groups is completely controlled by the operating system and dynamically updated on a real-time basis.

Users

In an NT 4.0 PDC upgrade, all existing NT 4.0 domain user accounts migrate to the Win2K Users container. In addition, all NT 4.0 global groups will find themselves there as well along with the NT 4.0 admin-created local groups from the PDC.

In all Win2K Active Directories, the Users container holds all the users and groups by default, no matter what type or scope they may be, as shown in Figure 10-6. Users and groups may be created in any other container.

Domain Controllers OU

In an NT 4.0 PDC upgrade and a clean AD installation, the computer accounts for all domain controllers in the domain are placed in the Domain Controllers OU. These DC computer accounts should not be moved without due consideration. The primary reason they are placed in the Domain Controllers OU is to make them subject by default to the limitations applied by the Domain Controllers OU Default Policy. Moving these objects to another container removes these protections and may expose the DCs to unwanted risks.

With the MMC, View, Advanced Features checked, two more default containers appear: Lost and Found and System.

Lost and Found

The Lost and Found container is simply a place for the Active Directory to place objects that have no home. Its correct status is empty. Here's how an object can find itself homeless: Imagine a company where two network admins received two different instructions. One deleted the Sales OU, and, five minutes later, the other created a user Bob in the OU Sales. These instructions were carried out, it so happened, in two different buildings. Oops! Active Directory begins its normal replication and deletes the OU, as it was told to do. Then it creates the Bob user, gets momentarily confused, shrugs, and places user Bob with all its properties in the Lost and Found container. Bob exists, but he can't log on or be assigned any group memberships, resources, and so on until he is moved to a working container.

Admins should check the Lost and Found container periodically to make sure it is empty. If it is not empty, you may need to move the object(s) there to another container.

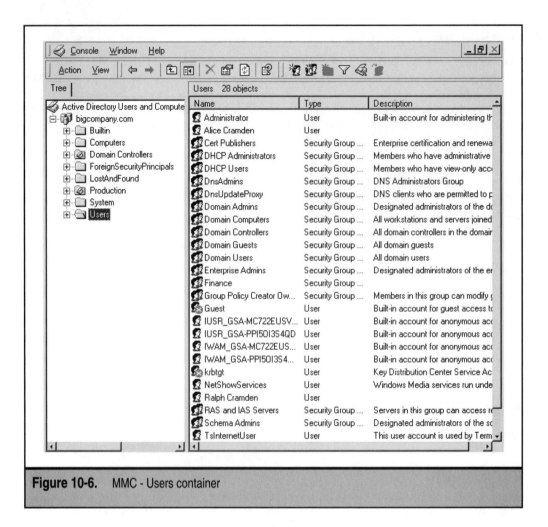

Figure 10-6. MMC - Users container

System

As shown in Figure 10-7, the System container holds all sorts of system-related goodies, including the classStore of the Default Domain Policy, the current Dfs Configuration, the File Replication Service parameters and schedule, link tracking folders, IPSec policies, DNS zone listings, Group Policy Containers, RAS and RADIUS Access checks, and settings for RPC and Winsock services.

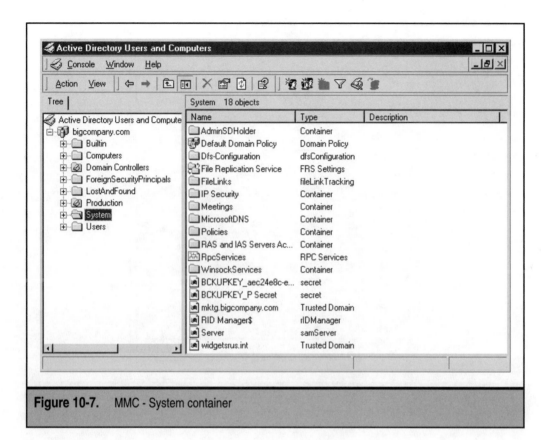

Figure 10-7.   MMC - System container

Configuring the File Replication Service (FRS)

This is the only user interface in Win2K to configure the file replication service (FRS). On the MMC View menu, check Users, Groups, and Computers as containers. Double-click the System container in the console pane. Highlight File Replication Service in the console pane. In the details pane, right-click Domain System Volume (SYSVOL share) and select Properties.

As shown in Figure 10-8, the Replica Set tab gives admins the ability to exclude folder and files from replicating. To do that, admins enter extensions or wildcards that would waste bandwidth and disk space. The Change Schedule button allows you to configure the times when file replication is available between domain controllers (or other subscribers to the FRS). By default, the FRS operates 24x7. Do not alter this setting unless you're comfortable with the ramifications. Limiting the FRS replication availability can seriously affect Group Policy updates.

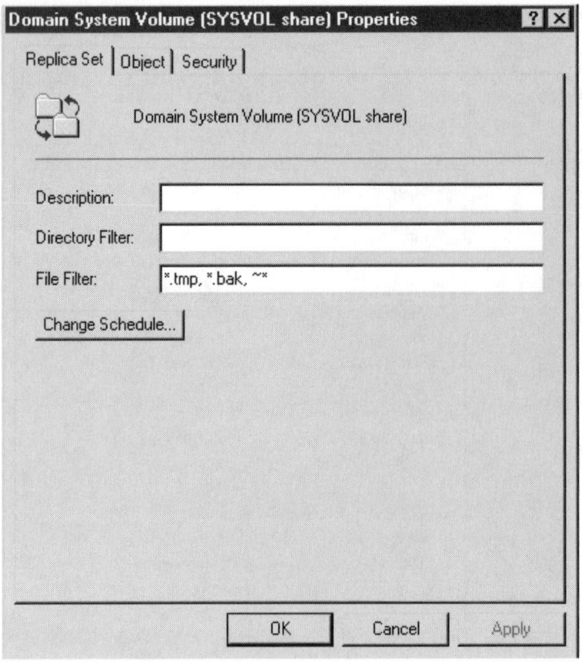

Figure 10-8. SYSVOL Properties

CONFIGURING AD REPLICATION

The Windows 2000 Active Directory uses *multi-master replication*. This means that, unlike NT 4.0, every domain controller has a write-enabled copy of the domain database, which is good and bad. The good news is that a Win2K Professional workstation doesn't have to go looking around for a PDC just to change a password. The bad news is that every Win2K DC in that same domain needs to get a copy of that new password—and make it snappy.

The primary strategy that admins can use to manage domain replication is the creation and proper configuration of sites. The primary tool for creating and configuring sites is the MMC Sites and Services snap-in.

How AD Replication Works

In spite of the fact that we constantly talk about replication in terms of a domain, the truth is that replication is simply one domain controller updating another domain controller with the latest information. The difference between NT 4.0 and Win2K is that, in NT 4.0, there was a single master (PDC) from which all updates flowed. In Win2K, however, updates can flow in any direction from any DC. As a result, admins have to deal with a number of new terms, new concepts, and new situations.

▼ **Update Sequence Number**   Each domain controller has a current Update Sequence Number (USN) that represents the current state of its directory database. The USN changes when a change to the AD is made directly at that DC (an originating write) or when the DC receives updates from a replication partner (a replicated update). In both cases, the USN, a 64-bit number, is incremented by 1 each time a change is made or received. Because DCs are created at different times, the USN of one domain controller may be substantially different from that of another DC. The USN is used to determine whether a DC has the latest updates from its replication partners. Using USNs to determine updates avoids problems that can occur when time is the determining factor in directory updates.

■ **High-watermark vector**   The *high-watermark vector* (HWV) is a value that each DC maintains for its replication partners. The HWV contains the highest known USN for each of its replication partners. The purpose of the HWV is to make sure that only changes the DC doesn't have from a specific partner are checked for updated information. For example, DC1 has a HWV for DC2 of 2764. DC1 contacts DC2 to initiate replication and sends the HWV of 2764 for DC2 in the message. DC2 has a current USN of 2766. DC2 checks only the changes represented by USN 2765 and 2766 to see if they contain any up-to-dateness vectors that DC1 does not contain.

■ **Up-to-dateness vector**   The *up-to-dateness vector* (UTDV) is a value that each DC maintains in a table for every other DC in the domain. The UTDV is the highest USN received from a specific DC that contained an originating write. The UTDV is used to determine whether a given DC is up-to-date and therefore does not need to receive this update because it has already received it from another replication partner. For example, DC5 has a UTDV for DC7 of 6276 that it received from DC4, one of its replication partners. DC5 contacts DC6 to initiate replication and sends the UTDV of 6276 for DC7 in the message. DC6 checks its own UTDV for DC7 and sees that it is also 6276. DC6 does not send any updated data for DC7 to DC5 because DC5 is already up-to-date. In this way a given change is not sent to the same DC twice. It stops being propagated around the domain unnecessarily. This is also known as *propagation dampening.*

■ **Resolving Conflicts**   Conceivably, the same attribute of the same AD object could be changed on two different DCs at about the same time. To resolve such conflicts, Active Directory attaches a "stamp" to the value being replicated. The stamp contains three elements: the version number of the attribute, which begins as 1 and increments by 1 each time the attribute is changed by an originating write; the originating time of the change on the originating DC; and the GUID of the originating DC. Conflicts are resolved first by version number. The highest version number always wins. If the version numbers are the same (and the values are different), then the later (most recent) time wins. If both writes happened within the same second, then the originating DC breaks the tie arbitrarily by selecting the highest GUID.

▲ **Repadmin**   None of these parameters are configurable by an admin, but there is a way to view what's happening. Using the Win2K Support Tool repadmin from the command line reveals an under-the-hood look at domain replication.

Sites

Sites are manually defined within the AD as one or more well-connected IP subnets. As previously discussed, "well-connected" means a reasonably fast and reliable connection. "Reasonably fast" means anything from 128Kbps in a small company to 1.5Mbps (T-1) in a medium-sized firm to 10Mbps or even 100Mbps in a large organization. "Reliable" means that the connection stays up most if not all of the time. In other words, a site contains the computers that are nearby or connected with high-speed links.

A good rule of thumb is that connections within a site should be 10Mbps or faster with a 98 to 99 percent uptime. Sites need to be so well connected because domain replication is not configurable within a site. Each DC must replicate with the other DCs in its domain. The Knowledge Consistency Checker (KCC), a service running on every Win2K domain controller, decides how best to replicate the DCs within a site (intrasite).

By default, the entire forest has only one site (Default-First-Site-Name). Unaffected by the logical structure of the AD, a site can contain more than one domain, and a domain can span more than one site. All new domain controllers are automatically added to the default forest site (Default-First-Site-Name). There is nothing automatic about the creation of sites. Administrators must manually create and configure all additional sites. The DNS uses sites to direct user logon requests to the closest domain controller. Sites also control domain replication because they allow admins to configure and schedule how often DCs replicate the AD over slow links. And, by using local rather than remote resources, sites improve the response time to most users' queries and searches and directory-aware applications. Dfs is also site-aware.

Sites work differently for domain controllers and clients. Admins must manually place domain controllers on a site. The IP address or IP subnet of the DC doesn't matter because it has been designated by the administrator to cover that site. The address of the appropriate domain controller is known by the Active Directory and will respond to logon requests emanating from that site/subnet. The IP address of the client, however, does matter. When the client computer contacts the DNS server to ask for the address(es) of the domain controller(s) in its domain, the DNS server provides a list of DCs and addresses, and the client sends a kind of "ping" to each DC. The client selects the DC that responds to the "ping" first. As the client logon progresses, the selected DC monitors the IP address of the incoming request from the client computer and checks its Active Directory to see if—based on the client's IP address—it is responsible for "covering" the client's site. If not, the DC forwards the client logon attempt to a DC that is responsible for the client's site, and the process continues. After successfully logging in, the client then caches the domain controller information (in its registry) so that subsequent requests need not repeat the DC discovery process. If no DC has been designated to "cover" a site, the client logs in to the original DC that responded to the "ping" first (it must be "close" or it wouldn't have been first).

TIP: While not officially required, it is highly recommended that each site in a multi-domain enterprise contain at least one domain controller, one Global Catalog server (also a DC), and a DNS server for name resolution (could also be a DC). In a small site, all three of these tasks could be placed on the same computer, as shown in Figure 10-9.

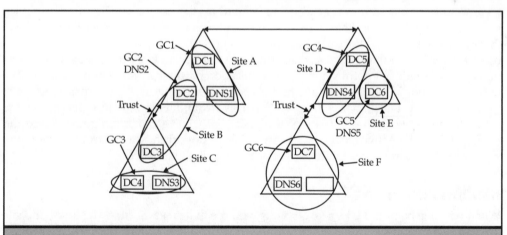

Figure 10-9.   Multiple domains with multiple sites; each site with a domain controller, Global Catalog server, and DNS server

Every logical element of the site topology is created and configured manually. After the admin, working in the Active Directory, completes the tasks in the following list, then and only then does Win2K and the KCC take over and decide how replication should be configured.

▼ Create a new site.

■ Create a new subnet object in the AD.

■ Associate the new subnet object with the new site.

■ Move the DC(s) onto the new site.

■ Create/modify a site link object to connect the new site with an existing site.

▲ Configure the site link object with a replication protocol, interval, schedule, and cost.

NT 4.0 Replication vs. AD Replication

In NT 4.0, replication occurred directly between the PDC and each BDC. The PDC was the only write-enabled copy of the SAM database—a single master. For that reason, all changes no matter how small (say, a user changing a password) had to happen at the PDC. If the PDC was unavailable, users couldn't change their passwords. By default every five minutes when the PDC was updated, it checked for changes in its SAM and sent out notifications to the BDCs to come and get the new info. The BDCs responded and downloaded the updates. The BDCs received all their changes directly from the PDC and the PDC only. The unit of replication in NT 4.0 was an object. In other words, if a user changed his or her password, the entire updated user object with all of its properties was sent to each BDC.

In Windows 2000, replication occurs on a multi-master basis, as in Figure 10-10, which shows the replication topology within a site. Replication on a multi-master basis means that every domain controller can accept updates and write them to its local copy of the Active Directory. After that, each DC checks its own Active Directory for updates every five minutes and sends out notifications to its replication partners to come and get them. The unit of replication in Win2K is an attribute. When a user changes his or her password, only the ID of the object (GUID) and the updated attribute (and its version number) are sent to the DC's replication partners. To help administrators achieve maximum performance and manageability, the Active Directory gives admins the opportunity to control and configure replication by creating sites, multiple site links, and site link bridges.

Replication and the KCC

When you step back and take a larger view, you see that creating sites, site links, and site link bridges is simply a method of informing the Knowledge Consistency Checker (KCC) of the physical situation of the network so it can "do its thing." The KCC automatically configures replication between domain controllers (DCs) within a site (intrasite). By default, the KCC assumes that the entire AD is well connected (entire forest, one site) with fast links for a fairly simple replication topology.

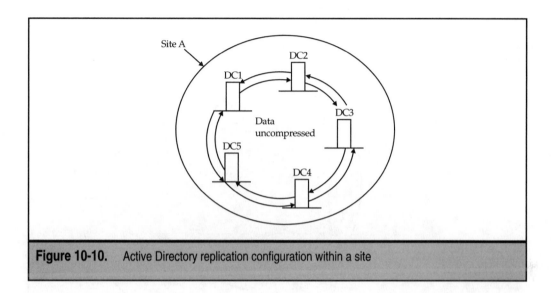

Figure 10-10. Active Directory replication configuration within a site

The KCC continues to operate in this manner and configures replication based on the single-site assumption. It does so, I should say, until an admin changes the rules. Admins change the rules by creating additional sites and configuring the links between them to better reflect the network reality.

The KCC's prime objective is to make sure that every DC is in sync with every other DC in the domain. And, using the concept of multi-master replication, the KCC strives to achieve this loosely synchronized state in three or fewer hops (a hop, in this case, involves Win2K DCs only, not routers). The KCC designs, implements, and manages the Active Directory replication topology automatically. The KCC also reacts to changes (DC goes down, new DC comes up, and so on) and automatically reconfigures the entire replication topology within fifteen minutes.

The replication topology is implemented by using connection objects. Figure 10-11 shows a replication topology with connection objects. Connection objects exist between two DCs and define which DC replicates with other DCs. In other words, connection objects exist between replication partners. The KCC automatically creates all the connection objects it needs (and deletes the connection objects it no longer needs). It creates connection objects, first, to replicate the new or changed domain objects to all DCs within the local domain, and, second, it creates additional connection objects as needed to replicate the configuration and schema changes to all DCs in the entire forest. The KCC also uses existing connection objects to partially replicate changes (all objects, limited attributes) to the Global Catalog servers throughout the enterprise.

Within a site, the KCC simply takes care of replication automatically. The traffic is uncompressed on the assumption that, this being a single site, there is plenty of network bandwidth.

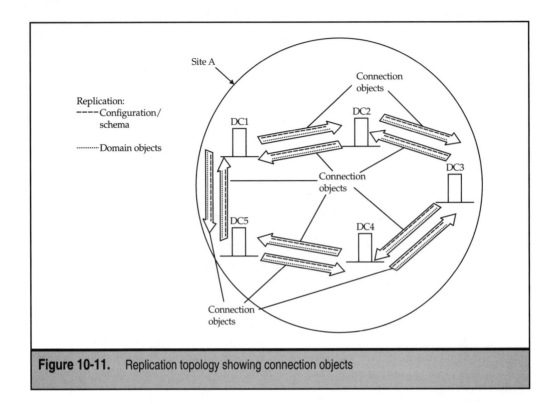

Figure 10-11.   Replication topology showing connection objects

An admin can implement only one option to affect replication within a site: he or she can manually create a connection object between two DCs. This will guarantee that, no matter how the KCC configures replication, the two DCs with the manual connection object will always be replication partners. Although the normal operation of the KCC is to create or delete connection objects as DCs are added or removed from the site, the KCC will work around any objects that admins created. The KCC will not delete or duplicate connection objects created by an administrator.

For intrasite (within a site) replication, the KCC uses the RPC over IP (RPC encapsulated in IP) protocol to send uncompressed data between each DC on the site. In this case, the KCC is lessening the load on each domain controller's CPU at the expense of slightly increased network traffic—another reason why DCs within a site must be well connected. Replication between sites (intersite) that are within the same domain is configured manually, with the KCC setting up the connection objects and selecting the bridgehead servers. Figure 10-12 demonstrates replication between two sites.

A site link is created in the Active Directory as a logical representation of the network connection between the two sites. In configuring the site link, admins can determine how often replication should occur (interval), what times of day are eligible for replication (schedule), and the cost of replication (an arbitrary number between 1 and 32,767 that represents the speed of the network link between sites *in relation to* the speed of other links). Intersite replication between DCs of the same domain also uses RPC over IP to send compressed data (10 to 15 percent of its original size) between the bridgehead servers on each site. Here, the KCC is lessening the network traffic at the expense of the CPU load on the bridgehead servers. Admins can configure intersite replication between DCs from different domains to use either the RPC over IP protocol or the Simple Mail Transfer Protocol (SMTP). SMTP utilizes a more network-efficient but less timely method (asynchronous, store and forward) that takes advantage of the fact that port 25 (SMTP) may already be open on most routers and firewalls. In a secure environment, TCP port 25 (SMTP) may be remapped to avoid firewall exposure.

A site link bridge is not necessary in a fully routed or switched network environment. The bridge, in essence, is a method of logically specifying the routes that replication will follow—a logical router.

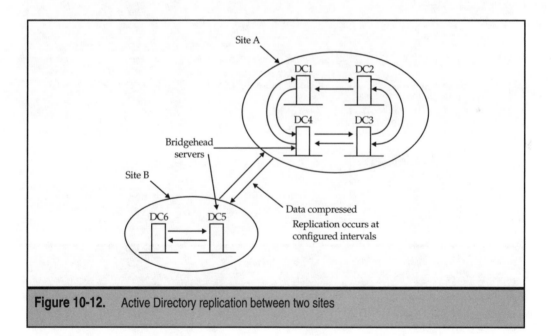

Figure 10-12.   Active Directory replication between two sites

Connection Objects

Connection objects define which DCs are replication partners in the multi-master replication scheme. To manually create a connection object, expand the MMC Active Directory Sites and Services snap-in, which is shown in Figure 10-13. Expand Sites, expand Default-First-Site-Name, expand Servers, expand the selected server, and highlight NTDS Settings. The current connection objects appear in the details pane. Notice that each was automatically generated by the KCC.

Right-click on the NTDS Settings option of the selected server and then choose New Active Directory Connection. The Find Domain Controllers screen appears, as shown in Figure 10-14. Select the DC with which you want to create a connection object and click OK.

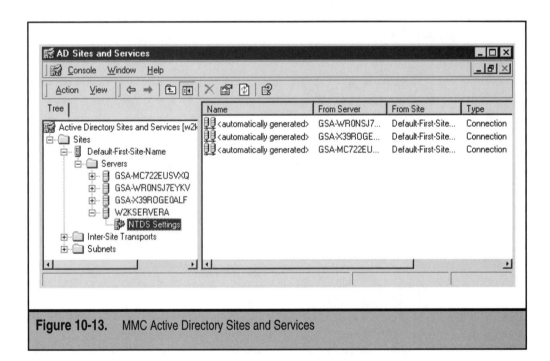

Figure 10-13.   MMC Active Directory Sites and Services

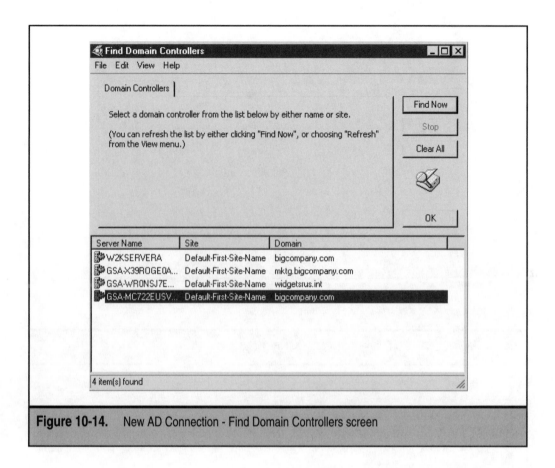

Figure 10-14. New AD Connection - Find Domain Controllers screen

The New Object - Connection screen appears, as shown in Figure 10-15. Here you can enter a meaningful name for the connection object to assist in documentation and troubleshooting later on.

Click OK and the Connection object is created, as shown in Figure 10-16.

Whether they are created automatically or manually, connection objects carry all replication traffic in both directions. The Schema partition and the Configuration partition are replicated together between domains. The domain information and the Global Catalog are replicated together. The Global Catalog, of course, may need to replicate between domains as well.

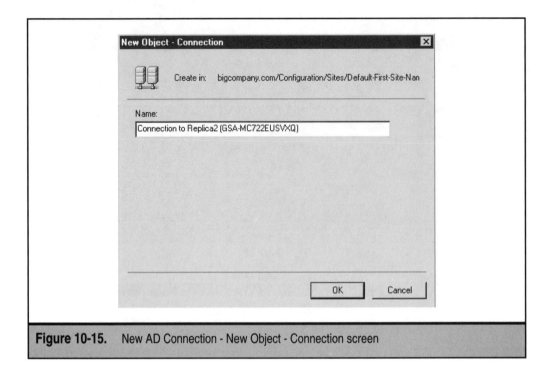

Figure 10-15. New AD Connection - New Object - Connection screen

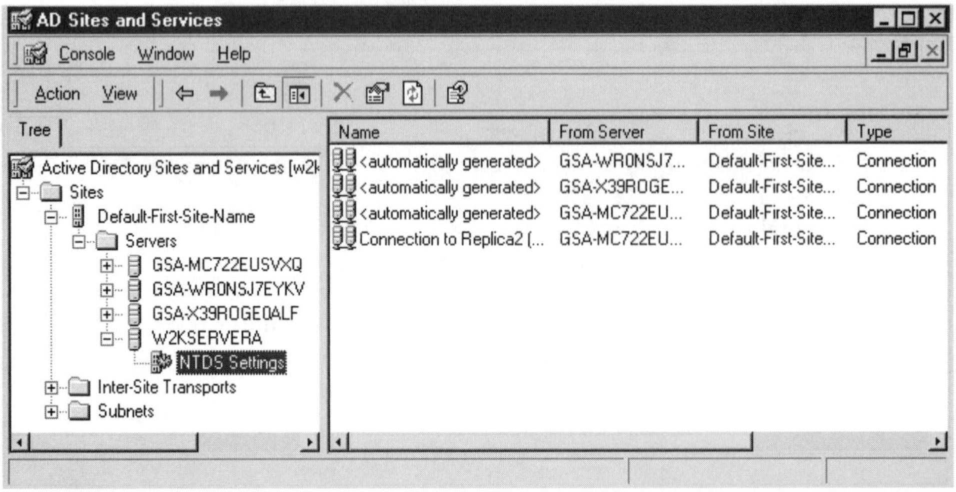

Figure 10-16. MMC AD Sites and Services—with admin-created connection object

Intrasite replication is based on a notification and a pull scenario. By default, each DC checks every five minutes to see whether any changes were made to its domain database, either through direct change or through replication from another DC. If DC1 sees that there are changes, it sends a notification to its direct replication partners noting the USN (version number) of its database. If the replication partner (DC2) hasn't received domain updates for the USN from DC1, it requests that all the changes it has not yet received be sent. The same goes for each successive replication partner until there are no more changes to be sent and every DC's data is the same (the system has reached convergence). In an active domain, convergence may only occur at night. In an international domain with DCs spread around the world in many time zones, convergence may never occur.

To alter the default five-minute replication interval for intrasite replication, go to the following registry key on each DC within a site:

```
HKLM\SYSTEM\CurrentControlSet\Services\NTDS\Parameters
```

Then notice the value:

```
Replicator notify pause after modify (secs):REG_DWORD:0x12c
```

The value 0x12c is hexadecimal for 300. Three-hundred seconds equals five minutes. Change the value to the desired interval.

Multiple Domains on a Site

So far our discussion has centered around a configuration of one site and one domain, which probably suffices for 80 to 90 percent of all Win2K Active Directory installations. But what if your enterprise has two domains on a single site. "No problem," says the KCC. Replication is handled, once again, automatically by the KCC. It automatically creates the necessary connection objects to achieve full replication between the DCs of each domain as well as the connection objects for interdomain replication. Thank heaven for the KCC or you'd have to do all this manually.

Creating Additional Sites

Remember that the entire forest by default exists in a single site called Default-First-Site-Name. All DCs are installed into this site even if additional sites were created. Check the InstallSiteName value in the registry entry:

```
HKLM\SYSTEM\CurrentControlSet\Services\NTDS\Parameters
```

If the enterprise's network infrastructure must contend with many physical locations that are connected by relatively slow WAN links (T1, F/T1, or ISDN), you undoubtedly need to create additional Active Directory sites to control replication. Here is your opportunity to create a logical vision of the physical network. Your logical vision, to be manually configured by the admin, will accomplish two goals: Allow the Active Directory and the KCC to maximize the available bandwidth, and minimize the impact of replication on normal business-related traffic across the WAN links. After the admin starts creating more sites, a number of other objects must be created as well, and then they must be linked to fully accomplish the task and achieve the desired result. You'll need to create another site (object), a subnet (object), and a site link (object). Then you'll need to associate them with the correct sites.

To create a new site, open the MMC Active Directory Sites and Services snap-in, right-click Sites, and choose New Site. The New Object - Site screen appears, as shown in Figure 10-17.

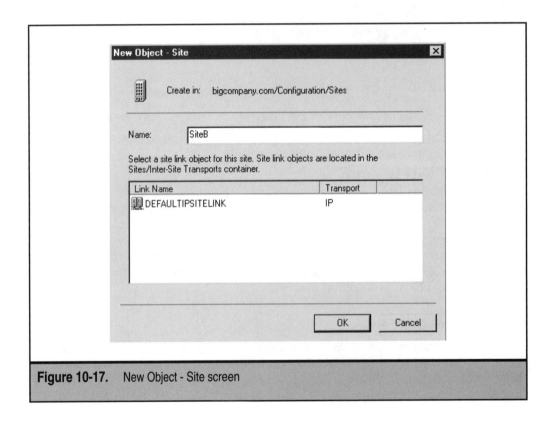

Figure 10-17. New Object - Site screen

You must now enter a name for the new site. Notice that the DEFAULTIPSITELINK is already associated with this site and configured to use RPC over IP. RPC over IP is your only option with the same domain. You must select it to move forward. If other site links exist, they will also be displayed. Click OK, the Site is created, and you see the site creation confirmation screen shown in Figure 10-18. The site creation confirmation screen offers a few short-but-to-the-point instructions for completing the process.

Your next step is to create a subnet to associate with your new site. In the MMC AD Sites and Services snap-in, expand Sites, and expand Subnets. If this your first additional site, no subnets currently exist. Right-click Subnets and choose New Subnet. The New Object—Subnet screen shown in Figure 10-19 appears.

Enter the subnet address and the subnet mask that you wish to associate with your new site. Notice that your entries are translated into CIDR (classless interdomain routing) notation. More information on CIDR is available in RFC 1519. Next highlight the site you wish to associate with this subnet. Click OK and the new subnet is created and associated with the site, as shown in Figure 10-20.

Obviously, a subnet (object) can be associated with only one site.

So, let's see now... You've got two sites, Default-First-Site-Name and SITEB. They are linked together using the DEFAULTIPSITELINK. SITEB is associated with subnet 192.168.1.0/24. Are you done? Not quite. Next you should move a DC onto the site.

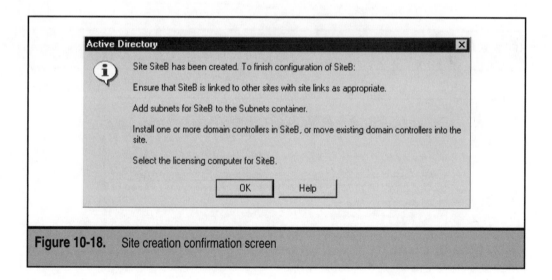

Figure 10-18.   Site creation confirmation screen

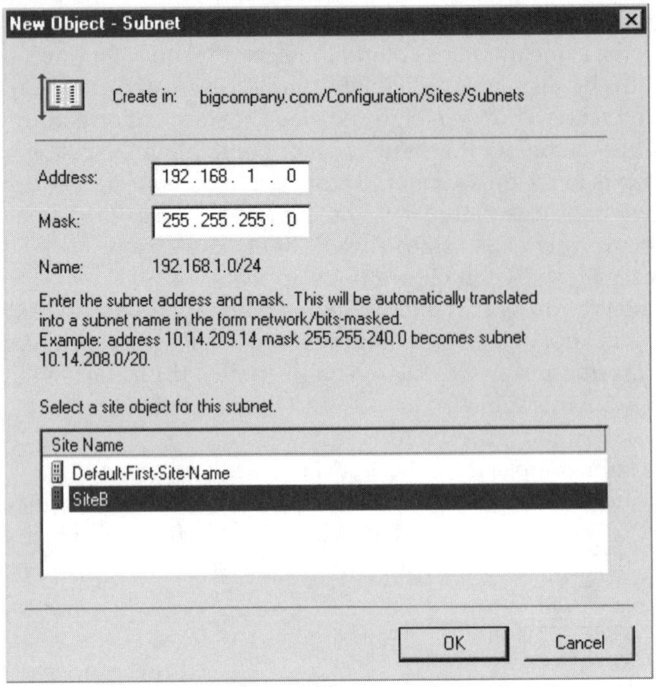

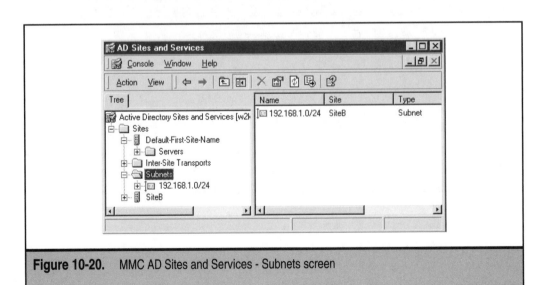

Figure 10-19. New Object - Subnet screen

Figure 10-20. MMC AD Sites and Services - Subnets screen

In the MMC, expand the AD Sites and Services snap-in, expand Sites, expand Default-First-Site-Name, and expand Servers. Then right-click the DC that you wish to move to the new site and select Move. The Move Server screen appears, as shown in Figure 10-21.

Select the site that should contain the DC and click OK. The DC is now moved to that site, as shown in Figure 10-22.

You have now created a new site, associated it with a subnet, linked it to another site, and moved a DC onto it. Miller Time! No more heavy lifting. Have a brewski while this new information makes its way through the rest of the enterprise.

Clients and Sites

As you have just seen, you moved a DC onto a site. But the DC's IP address does not need to match that of the subnet that is associated with the site. Sites treat DCs and client workstations in a completely different manner. DCs are moved onto a site to provide "coverage" for the range of client IP addresses associated with the site. Client computers initially don't really know which site they're a part of, but they do know their IP address. In the case of more than one site, when the client computer attempts to log on, it contacts a DNS for a DC. The client computer then contacts the DC, which looks up the client's site in the Active Directory or the name of the site closest to the client. If this DC doesn't cover that site, it refers the client to a DC that does. The client then updates its site information in the DynamicSiteName registry entry in

```
HKLM\SYSTEM\CurrentControlSet\Services\Netlogon\Parameters
```

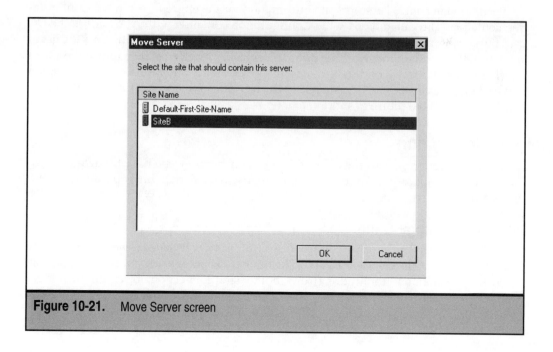

Figure 10-21. Move Server screen

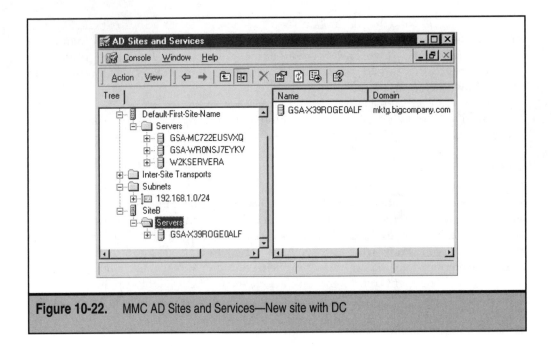

Figure 10-22.   MMC AD Sites and Services—New site with DC

Each domain controller stores site information for the entire forest in the Configuration container (you can only view the Configuration container with ADSI Edit). The DC uses the site information to check the IP address of the client computer against the list of subnets in the forest. In this way, the domain controller ascertains the name of the site in which the client is located or the site that is the closest match, and returns this information to the client. The client then "remembers" which DC logged it on last time and the information is used in the future to shorten logons.

Intersite Replication

Earlier in this section we covered intrasite replication, but now you have two sites. Within those two sites, replication occurs in the manner discussed earlier, but replication *between* the two sites (intersite) requires additional work.

Intersite Topology Generator

One domain controller per site assumes the role of *Intersite Topology Generator* (ISTG). By default, the first DC in a site is the ISTG. The Intersite Topology Generator is responsible for creating the inbound replication (from another site) connection objects on the bridge-head servers in its own site. If the ISTG becomes unavailable, a new DC is chosen for the role after 60 minutes. How is the new ISTG role owner chosen? By selecting the DC that is capable of utilizing the current intersite transport (IP) that has the lowest GUID. Pretty arbitrary, but there has to be a process.

Configuring Site Links

Each site link contains three configuration settings: Cost, Interval, and Schedule. To configure a site link, start in the MMC, expand the AD Sites and Services snap-in, expand Sites, expand Inter-Site Transports, and highlight IP. The DEFAULTIPSITELINK object appears in the details pane. Right-click the DEFAULTIPSITELINK object and select Properties. The DEFAULTIPSITELINK Properties dialog box shown in Figure 10-23 appears.

The General tab allows you to enter a description that other admins can make use of and informs you which sites are and which aren't linked to this site link (at least two must be linked). Near the bottom of the Properties dialog box, you can configure the Cost, configure the Replication interval, and schedule replications.

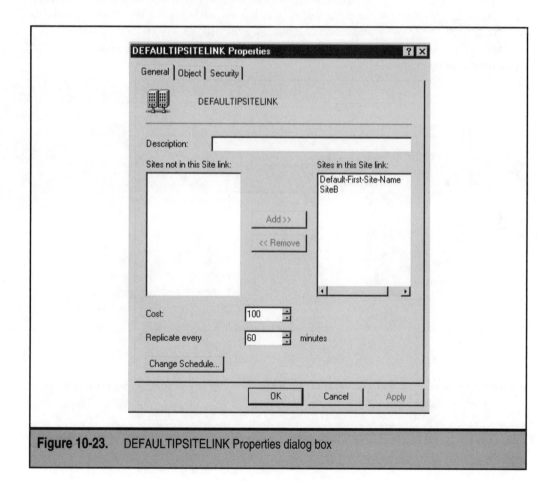

Figure 10-23.   DEFAULTIPSITELINK Properties dialog box

The Cost is an arbitrary number between 1 and 32767. It is designed to reflect the network speed of the link *in relation to* the speed of other site links. If there is more than one route between the two sites, the KCC will use the cost information to compute the most desirable route for replication. The lower the cost, the faster and more desirable the route. The default number is 100. It is important not to set the number to 1, because, as networks get faster, you will need somewhere to go. If there is only one site link between sites, the KCC will use that link no matter what the cost.

The Interval (Replicate every) setting determines how often replication cycles occur. Make sure that the interval does not conflict with the schedule. For example, if you accept the default interval of every 3 hours but leave only a 2-hour time window for replication, there will be no replication. The Active Directory is depending on you to configure this correctly. No error-checking mechanism will catch a mistake here.

Press the Change Schedule button and the Site Link Schedule dialog box shown in Figure 10-24 appears. You can now configure, in 1-hour segments, when during the week the site link is available for intersite replication. Figure 10-24 shows replication available from midnight to 6:00 A.M. and noon to 2:00 P.M. every day. Care should be taken when multiple time zones are involved so that replication is scheduled to take place during the same hours on each end.

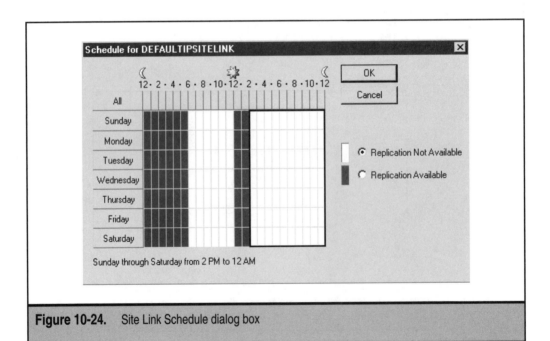

Figure 10-24.   Site Link Schedule dialog box

Bridgehead Servers

Those familiar with Exchange will recognize the term bridgehead server. A *bridgehead server* in Win2K is the DC from each site that the Intersite Topology Generator decides is the one to replicate with the other site. Either the KCC selects a bridgehead server on each site to complete the replication or the admin selects a bridgehead server manually. To configure bridgehead servers, start from the MMC, expand the AD Sites and Services snap-in, expand Sites, expand the selected Site, expand Servers, right-click on the desired DC, and select Properties. The Server Properties sheet shown in Figure 10-25 appears.

To make this the preferred bridgehead server, highlight IP in the Transports Available box and click Add. The IP moves to the Preferred Bridgehead Server box. Click OK and the server becomes the preferred bridgehead server for this site using the RPC over IP intersite transport. If a preferred bridgehead server is configured, the ISTG will always choose the preferred one to host the inbound replication connection objects.

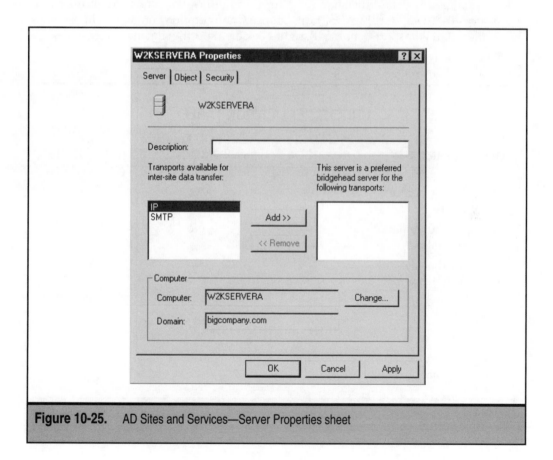

Figure 10-25. AD Sites and Services—Server Properties sheet

Site Link Bridges

In a fully routed or switched network, site link bridges are not needed. They basically allow an admin to create a "logically routed" network of sites and site links.

Urgent Replication

In NT 4.0 as well as Win2K, a number of system-related events trigger what is known as *urgent replication*. When urgent replication is triggered, the DC does not wait the standard five minutes to check for changes but rather begins an immediate replication cycle. Furthermore, when the urgently replicated change reaches each successive DC, it continues to be "urgently replicated" until all DCs in the domain are updated. When an urgent replication event is triggered, all pending replication events at each DC are replicated as well. Table 10-1 lists the events that trigger an urgent replication.

By default, urgent replication occurs only within a site, never between sites. It is possible to change this default behavior and turn on notification (urgent replication) between sites. To do so, start in ADSI Edit, choose Configuration container, choose Sites, choose Inter-Site Transports, choose IP, right-click on a specific site link object, and select

URGENT REPLICATION TABLE			
System Event Triggering Urgent Replication	W2K DC to W2K DC [Either Mode]	W2K PDC Emulator to NT 4 BDCs [Mixed Mode]	NT 4 Domain [NT 4 PDC to NT 4 BDCs]
Changing the account lockout policy	No	No	Yes
Changing the domain password policy	No	No	Yes
Changing the password on a machine account	No	No	Yes
Newly locked out accounts	Yes	Yes	Yes
Changing an LSA secret	Yes	Yes	Yes
Interdomain trust password changes	No	Yes	No

Table 10-1. Events that Trigger Urgent Replication

Properties. Under Select a Property to View, choose Options. In the Edit Attribute textbox, enter **1**. Click Set and then click OK. Urgent replication will now function across the site link. Be careful, however, because this setting increases the network traffic between sites.

Out-of-Band Password Changes

When a password change is made at any Win2K DC, the DC attempts to establish a secure RPC connection with the PDC Emulator of the user's domain to immediately inform it of the new password. This is outside the normal replication process, or "out-of-band." If the connection is established, the PDC Emulator is updated immediately and a second originating write at the PDC Emulator is created that halves the time it takes for full domain replication. If for whatever reason the connection cannot be established, no further out-of-band attempt is made to update the PDC Emulator and it receives the password update within the normal replication cycle.

The reason for this behavior, which is the same in Mixed and Native mode, makes a lot of sense. In Figure 10-26, UserA's password was changed on DC3 two minutes ago. DC3 immediately executed an out-of-band password update to DC1, the PDC Emulator. DC1 and DC3 now have UserA's new password. Suppose UserA logs off and attempts to log on again. This time the authenticating DC is DC2, which contains the old password. However, before rejecting UserA's logon attempt, DC2 contacts the PDC Emulator (DC1) to see if DC1 has the password that User A submitted during the logon. DC1 *does* have the correct password, so DC2 accepts the logon by UserA. In another three minutes or so, DC2 receives the new UserA password through normal replication.

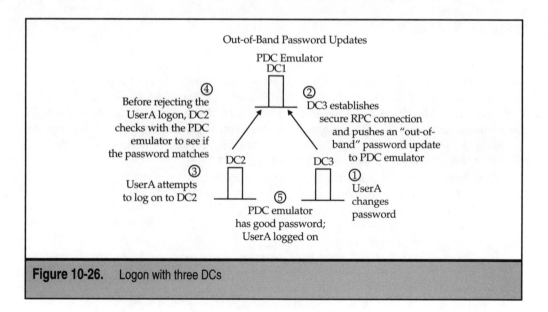

Figure 10-26.   Logon with three DCs

Out-of-band password updates occur within a site and between sites. Out-of-band updates between sites ignore the Site Link schedule for allowable replication times that the administrator set. Whenever a password is changed on any DC, the originating DC attempts a secure RPC connection to the PDC Emulator. But what happens if the PDC Emulator (the target of the out-of-band update) is located across a WAN link? Wouldn't this cause a lot of extra network traffic that you prefer not to have? Yes, it would. The original DC will try to establish a connection with the PDC Emulator even over a slow WAN link, but you can solve this problem by editing the Registry on each Win2K DC. To edit the Registry, go to the following Registry key:

```
HKLM\System\CurrentControlSet\Services\Netlogon\Parameters\
```

Next, add a REG_DWORD value of `AvoidPdcOnWan`
Set the data to 1.
Now the out-of-band behavior will continue on the local network, but not over the WAN link.

FSMO ROLES AND PLACEMENT

The Operations Masters were originally called FSMOs (Flexible Single Master Operations) and the term persists in several places in Win2K. Don't be surprised if you see it. The name is synonymous with Operations Master, role owner, and token holder. As you begin to implement your Win2K Active Directory, keep in mind the following rules with regard to FSMO placement.

Operations Masters

Although all the replication of existing AD objects is multi-master, certain elements of the Active Directory exist only on a single computer. These Operations Masters can reside only on domain controllers. There are five Operations Masters in all: the per-forest Schema and Domain Naming (Configuration) Operations Masters; and the per-domain PDC Emulator, RID Master, and Infrastructure Operations Masters. By default, the first domain controller in the forest houses all five Operations Masters as well as the Global Catalog. The first domain controller in each new child domain contains the three per-domain Operations Masters: PDC Emulator, RID Master, and Infrastructure.

The *Schema Master* holds the only write-enabled copy of the schema and controls all updates and changes to the schema. There can be only one Schema Master in the entire forest. To modify the schema, you must have access to the Schema Master, belong to the Schema Admins Global/Universal group, and enable schema modification. (See "Editing the Schema" later in this chapter.)

The *Domain Naming Master* (also known as the Configuration Master) holds the only write-enabled copy of the naming configuration for the forest and controls the adding and deleting of domains in the forest. This computer is responsible for maintaining all domain and trust relationships in the forest. There can be only one Domain Naming Master in the entire forest.

Time Out for a Discussion of Time!

Time out for a brief discussion about time in the Windows 2000 Active Directory. Win2K synchronizes the time on all DCs using something called Simple Network Time Protocol (SNTP). It works like Network Time Protocol (NTP), but with a slight difference. When NTP sends the time from one computer to another, it actually attempts to adjust for the amount of time spent in transit over the wire, but SNTP doesn't do that. SNTP assumes that the network will get the time there in much less than a second. And since time is not *that* crucial to Win2K, the second or so assumption is good enough. The following illustration demonstrates how time is updated in Windows 2000.

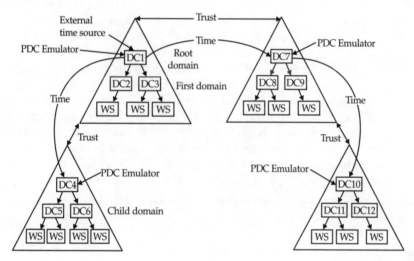

Time is not a life-and-death issue in the Active Directory, but it is still quite important. Time is used in the Kerberos logon process of each computer. If the time on the client computer is more than five minutes off the domain controller (either slow or fast), Kerberos refuses the authentication. Time zones are not a factor because Win2K is completely time-zone aware. Time is also one of the factors used to resolve replication conflicts between domain controllers. If a DC receives an update for a given property from two different replication partners and the version numbers are the same but the values are different, the DC takes the update with the later time stamp.

There is a single source for time in the Active Directory: the PDC Emulator of the first root domain. Here's how it works:

▼ Win2K clients and member servers get the time from the DC they use for logon.

■ The DCs get their time from the PDC Emulator in their domain.

■ The PDC Emulators get their time from the PDC Emulator in the (first) root domain.

▲ The root domain PDC Emulator gets its time internally or from a third party—automatically or manually reset.

To adjust any computer's time source from a command prompt, type: **net time /setsntp:<computer to be used as time source>**.

Unlike Novell's NDS, time is not *negotiated* between DCs in Windows 2000. Here's how the Win2K SNTP works: The client connects to its logon DC once each "period" for a time-check. The initial period is eight hours. If the client's time is behind the DC's time, time on the client is immediately set to the DC's time. If the client's time is ahead of the DC's time, the client's clock is slowed over the next twenty minutes to align the two times, unless the client's time is more than two minutes out of sync, in which case the time is simply reset immediately.

If the client time is off from the DC's time by more than two seconds but less than two minutes, the interval check period is divided in half. This process is repeated at the next interval check until either the client and DC time remain within two seconds of each other or the interval check period is reduced to the minimum setting of 45 minutes. If synchronization is maintained within two seconds, the interval check period is doubled at each check, up to the maximum period of eight hours.

To adjust the settings of the Windows Time service (W32Time), use the command line utility w32tm. Type **w32tm /?** for help with syntax.

Each Win2K domain must have one domain controller that acts as the *PDC Emulator*. In Mixed mode, the PDC Emulator performs the master/slave replication scenario with the NT 4.0 BDCs, as is the case with NT 4.0 (see "Mixed vs. Native Mode" in Chapter 9). For downlevel clients, the PDC Emulator is the Domain Master Browser and the PDC. The PDC Emulator provides the SIDs to all new objects created by downlevel clients because all new SIDs must continue to come from the PDC, as they did in NT 4.0. In either mode, the PDC Emulator receives preferential out-of-band password changes to diminish the impact of incomplete replication on user logons. The PDC Emulator also serves as the Time Master for the domain, and, by default, the Group Policy editor always focuses on the PDC Emulator when changing GPO policy settings.

One domain controller in each Win2K domain plays the role of *RID Master*. A RID is the number at the end of an object's SID (Security ID). The SID is the unique domain "serial number" for each object in the domain. The RID Master role can be transferred to other DCs in the domain. The RID Master allocates a block of 500 RIDs to each Win2K domain controller within the domain so that each DC can create new AD domain accounts and still maintain a unique SID/RID for each domain object. When a specific domain controller has used 80 percent of its available RIDs, it requests another block from the RID

Master. The RID Master sends another block of 500 RIDs to the requesting DC and marks those numbers (RIDs) as no longer available within the domain.

Every domain must also have a DC in the role of *Infrastructure Master.* The Infrastructure Master is charged with updating the group-to-user, group-to-group references when group memberships change in other domains. See "Maximizing Domain Performance" later in this chapter.

Eliminating Single Points of Failure

By design, every FSMO is a single point of failure for its specific function. Specific functionality will be lost if an FSMO is down. For the forest, for example, no Schema Master means no changes can be made to the schema; no Domain Naming Master means that no new domains or trusts can be added to the forest. For the domain, no PDC Emulator means no downlevel replication or new object creation in Mixed mode and no downlevel client password changes; no RID Master eventually means that no objects can be added to the domain; no Infrastructure Master means that cross-domain group memberships will not be up-to-date.

Dealing with FSMO failure involves four steps:

1. Document which Operations Masters currently exist on which computer. This will allow you to respond knowledgeably in case of a problem.

2. Spread out your risk. In the last chapter, you learned that the first DC in the forest houses all five of the Operations Masters and the Global Catalog. The first DC in a domain houses the PDC Emulator, RID Master, and Infrastructure Master. These situations should not be allowed to persist after installation. Place these functions on different DCs if at all possible.

3. Designate other DCs as "standby" operations masters. Doing so is not an official designation (no GUI tool does it), but it is important in the network recovery plan. A standby operations master should have a direct connection object with the primary operations master.

4. Become familiar with the Directory Services Restore mode and the NTDSUTIL command to recover (seize the master) from a FSMO failure. (Detailed information about recovering from the failure of an Operations Master is found in Chapter 15.)

By default, the Global Catalog also exists on only a single domain controller, the first DC in the forest. We have discussed creating additional GCs on each site for performance purposes, but creating addition GCs also provides higher availability and fault-tolerance in case of a DC failure. Let's follow this rule of thumb: If possible, there should be more than one GC in a multi-domain forest even if there is only one site. The GC is far less important in a single domain forest because each DC contains a complete copy of every object in the forest already.

Maximizing Domain Performance

Early testing has resulted in a number of domain controller/FSMO Do's and Don'ts. Never have a Global Catalog on the Infrastructure Master. Always have a Global Catalog on the bridgehead server. Separate the PDC Emulator from the RID Master in a very active domain. Let's look a little closer at these rules.

A Universal group can contain references to members in other domains. Included in these references are the names of the members. The Infrastructure Master periodically updates these references. It checks for discrepancies between what it knows about the names of security principals in other domains and what a current domain controller in the domain where the security principal (group) resides knows. It then replicates the knowledge it gained to all other DCs in its domain. Because a Global Catalog server already has accurate current knowledge of all objects in the entire forest, it detects no discrepancy and therefore never updates the other DCs in its domain. The updated objects are placed in the ForeignSecurityPrincipals container, and each of them represents a cross-reference to an object in another domain. This only affects multi-domain environments, so if you have a single domain forest, just ignore this. Observe this rule: the domain infrastructure master should never be located on a Global Catalog server, but the domain infrastructure master should have a direct connection object to a Global Catalog server, preferably in the same Active Directory site.

In a multi-site, multi-domain enterprise always place a Global Catalog on each bridgehead server designated to replicate between sites. Doing so significantly reduces the latency (delay) involved in multi-domain replication between sites. Because Global Catalog information is replicated along with domain data and because you should have configured a Global Catalog server on each site. Faster, more accurate searches for clients on both sites result when each bridgehead server also houses the Global Catalog.

In very active, very busy domains, separate the PDC Emulator from the RID Master. Do so strictly for performance purposes to reduce the load on each.

By default, the schema master and domain naming master operations masters are on the same domain controller, the first DC in the forest. They should remain on the same DC as they are seldom used and should be heavily secured. The two most demanding functions on a single DC are the PDC Emulator and the Global Catalog. Separate these, if possible, as well.

As mentioned earlier, it is better to have several passable domain controllers than one great big, honkin' DC. Now you are beginning to see why. Anyone for Intel stock?

Cross-Link Trusts

A cross-link trust is an admin-created trust. Making use of the NETDOM utility, an admin can create a one- or two-way transitive trust between any two Win2K domains. The purpose of such a trust in a Win2K forest is primarily to enhance the performance of

LDAP queries, LDAP referrals, and interdomain replication of the Global Catalog and the Schema and Naming Context partitions.

The command to create a two-way trust between doma.com and domb.com would look like this:

```
netdom trust /d:doma.com domb.com /add /uo:administrator@doma.com
/po:admpasswda /ud:administrator@domb.com /pd:admpasswdb /twoway
/verbose
```

As written, this command uses the credentials of the two domain administrators to establish a two-way transitive trust between the two domains. Verbose simply tells us what's happening.

EDITING THE SCHEMA

I include this section with some trepidation but in the interests of full disclosure. I do not recommend or encourage editing the schema—quite the opposite. Remember: After an object or property is added to the schema, it can never be deleted. Objects within the schema can be deactivated, but never deleted. Deactivating a schema object prevents any new instances of that object from being added to the AD and removes the current instances of the object from the replication process.

Schema Manager

In addition to the tools and snap-ins mentioned so far, another tool called the Active Directory Schema Manager ships with Windows 2000 Server. By default, this MMC snap-in does not appear on the list of available snap-ins. After it is invoked, it permits the direct editing of the schema, the template for all objects in the entire forest. In order to make the Active Directory Schema snap-in available you must first register the .dll with the operating system. Go to a Command prompt and type the following:

```
regsvr32 schmmgmt.dll
```

You should receive a message telling you that the registration was successful. As shown in Figure 10-27, the Schema Manager snap-in is now available to the MMC. You may now add it to any console in Author mode. Installing the Win2K Support Tools also registers the Schema Manager snap-in.

CAUTION: The Schema Manager snap-in is not a tool for experimentation. You can do irreparable harm to your Active Directory and, by extension, your entire enterprise with this tool. If you have no reason to edit the schema, simply don't do it.

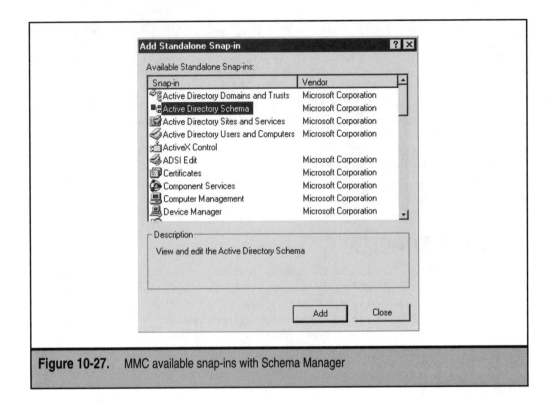

Figure 10-27. MMC available snap-ins with Schema Manager

Schema Locks

Because modifying the schema can cause many unwanted problems, Microsoft has inserted three "schema locks" to make it difficult to make those changes accidentally. First, the Schema Master, usually the first DC in the forest, must be online and available. Second, the user who attempts to access and change the schema must be a member of the Schema Admins security group in the root domain of the forest. Third, a value must be inserted into the registry of the Schema Master domain controller at:

```
HKLM\System\CurrentControlSet\Services\NTDS\Parameters
```

Add the value Schema Update Allowed as a REG_DWORD with a value of 1. This can also be done by checking The Schema May Be Modified on This Domain Controller box under the Operations Master menu item in the context menu of the Schema Manager snap-in, as shown in Figure 10-28.

Most changes to the schema will not come from direct editing but rather will result from the installation of a "directory-enabled" application. These applications, from Microsoft, from third-party vendors, or homegrown, will be the single greatest factor in the future well-being of your Active Directory–based enterprise. For instance, the next version of Microsoft Exchange Server, to be called Exchange 2000, contains up to 1800 additions and modifications to the Win2K schema. Microsoft recommends installing the schema changes separately (the `/schemaonly` switch) from the rest of the Exchange installation so that normal replication can take place prior to installing Exchange. Directory-enabled applications exploit the true power of the Active Directory but will push our current hardware and network resources to the limit.

CAUTION: Because new AD objects and properties in the schema increase domain sizes and possibly enterprise replication traffic as well, admins are advised to determine exactly what the ramifications of installing that new "latest and greatest" directory-enabled application are before they slap the CD in the drive. The potential for disaster is great. Only the registry of a single machine was at risk in NT 4.0. With the Win2K schema, we're talking irreversible changes to the basic template of the directory database of all the objects in the entire enterprise. The only conceivable means of recovery is to restore the Schema Master from tape before it has a chance to replicate. In short, the consequences of not thinking and planning ahead are not very pretty at all.

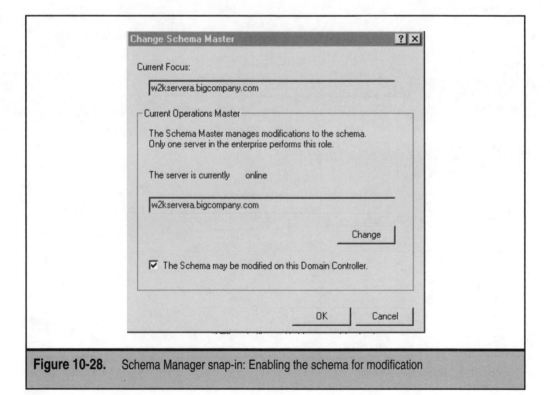

Figure 10-28.   Schema Manager snap-in: Enabling the schema for modification

TIP: Install new directory-enabled applications on a test network with a separate test forest (imperative) to determine the impact such programs will have in your environment.

SUMMARY

When you say the words "manage the Active Directory," you are really saying, "Manage the enterprise." The Active Directory is large and complex, but Microsoft has done an admirable job of making sense of it all. Even after a reasonable period, most admins won't be experts at every AD element. Rather, they will focus on or specialize in one section until they feel comfortable enough to move on. The learning curve is fairly steep. New concepts mix with old ones to form a single enterprise management system called the Active Directory. Trying to employ every aspect of the technology in the first week causes problems. Take it slow. Test each move, each addition, and each new element on a nonproduction network before you roll it out. And if you take away only one thing from this entire chapter, let it be this: Don't edit the schema unless you have to. And watch out for developers who are licking their chops to make changes in the schema by the hundreds. The devil is in the details and the schema is one detail over which network admins must be vigilant.

CHAPTER 11

Managing the Common Active Directory Objects

C hapter 11 focuses on the common objects used nearly every day in the Win2K Active Directory. This chapter discusses creating, modifying, configuring and deleting users, groups, printers, and shared folders. It explains how to locate objects anywhere in the enterprise. You also learn a few of the AD search-capability "gotchas."

THE SAM VS. THE ACTIVE DIRECTORY

You were introduced to the security account management database (SAM) in NT 4.0. On NT 4.0 workstations, Member servers, and Workgroup servers, the SAM database held a particular computer's local users and local groups. These local users and groups were managed by the User Manager utility. On NT 4.0 domain controllers, the SAM held all the domain user accounts, local groups on the DCs, and the domain's global groups. These domain users, local groups, and global groups were managed by a utility called User Manager for Domains. There were no "local" users on the NT 4.0 domain controllers because there was only one SAM per computer. All users in the DC-based SAM were domain users.

In Win2K, a SAM database is once again on all Win2K Professional workstations, Member servers, and Workgroup servers. It holds each specific computer's local users and local groups. The local SAM is managed by an appropriately titled MMC snap-in called Local Users and Groups, which can be found on Win2K computers under Computer Management, System Tools. The local groups on a Win2K non-DC are the same groups that you know from NT 4.0: Administrators, Backup Operators, Guests, Power Users, Replicator, and Users. In addition, service-related groups are installed, depending on which network services are loaded and running on the Member server. Figure 11-1 shows the local groups on a Win2K Member server. So far, it feels as though you're running NT 4.0, but a number of things change when a Win2K Server is promoted to a domain controller.

As a result of the DC promotion, all but four local user accounts are deleted from the local SAM. The remaining accounts are as follows: Administrator, Guest (disabled), IUSR_MACHINENAME (IIS), and IWAM_MACHINENAME (IIS). That's it. The Active Directory Installation Wizard warns you that accounts will be deleted. It explains, right on screen and in no uncertain terms, that files encrypted by these users will no longer be retrievable if they are left encrypted.

When *dcpromo* is complete, the DC's local SAM is no longer reachable. The SAM is still there, but *dcpromo* has disabled it. The thinking here is: why would you need to access a local account on a domain controller? What if the AD is damaged and the network is down? How would you log in to repair the system? You'd use either Directory Services Restore mode or the Recovery Console (more on this subject in Chapter 15). If you attempt to use the Local Users and Groups MMC snap-in on a DC, it fails. The local SAM is not reachable.

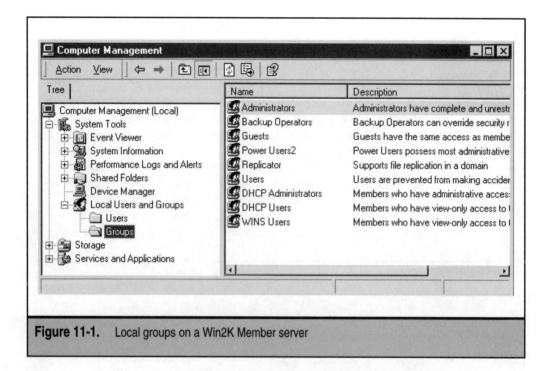

Figure 11-1.   Local groups on a Win2K Member server

If later on you decide to demote the domain controller and make it a Member server, the local SAM is again reachable by means of the Local Users and Groups snap-in. But only the four users discussed earlier remain after the demotion.

MANAGING AD USERS

More so than any other domain-management task, Active Directory administration time will be spent administering and configuring user accounts. The MMC does a good job of consolidating the myriad screens that you needed in NT 4.0 to manage users and set account and password policies into a cohesive management tool. Perhaps the most important lesson to be learned from NT 4.0 is that user administration and management never involves a single element. Even with a consolidated tool, you must know many facets to effectively manage the AD users.

Creating AD Users

If the domain was upgraded from an NT 4.0 PDC, all the user accounts from the NT 4.0 domain have already been created and currently reside in the Users container of the

Active Directory. Any new users created after the upgrade by a downlevel tool such as User Manager for Domains will also find themselves in the Users container.

Creating new Win2K users is quite simple. Right-click the container or OU where you want to place the user object, choose New, and choose User on the context menu. You see the New Object – User screen shown in Figure 11-2. Complete the First Name and Last Name text boxes (initials are optional). Notice that the full name is updated based on what you typed in the First and Last Name text boxes, but the User Logon Name remains blank. Complete the User Logon Name field and, using the down-arrow if necessary, select a domain. The *user logon name* (also known as the UPN, or user principal name) is used to log on to the domain, and, when combined with the domain name, must be unique within the entire enterprise (forest). The pre-Windows 2000 user logon name fills in automatically, but you can change it to a name up to twenty characters long.

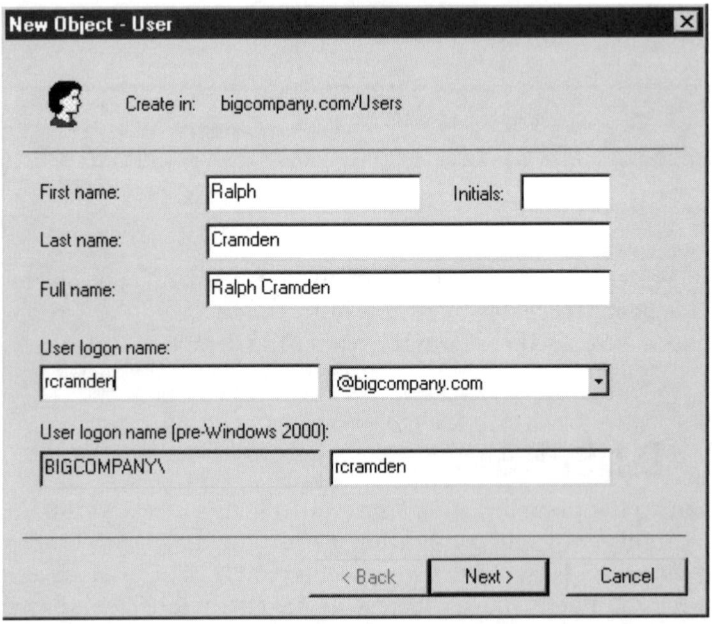

Figure 11-2. Creating Users – New Object – User screen

"Pre-Windows 2000" means NetBIOS. For logons to be successful from pre-Windows 2000 (Win 9*x* and NT) computers, which only speak in NetBIOS, a NetBIOS name is necessary for both the domain and the user account. Logons from Win2K computers to Win2K domain controllers do not use NetBIOS.

Click Next and the Password screen shown in Figure 11-3 appears. Set and confirm the user password and select other password options if you so desire. Requiring new users to "change password at next logon" is a good idea because it ensures privacy. But, unlike NT 4.0, this option is not checked by default.

Click Next and the summary screen shown in Figure 11-4 appears. Here, you get one last chance to change your mind. If you are satisfied with the entries, click Finish and the user is created.

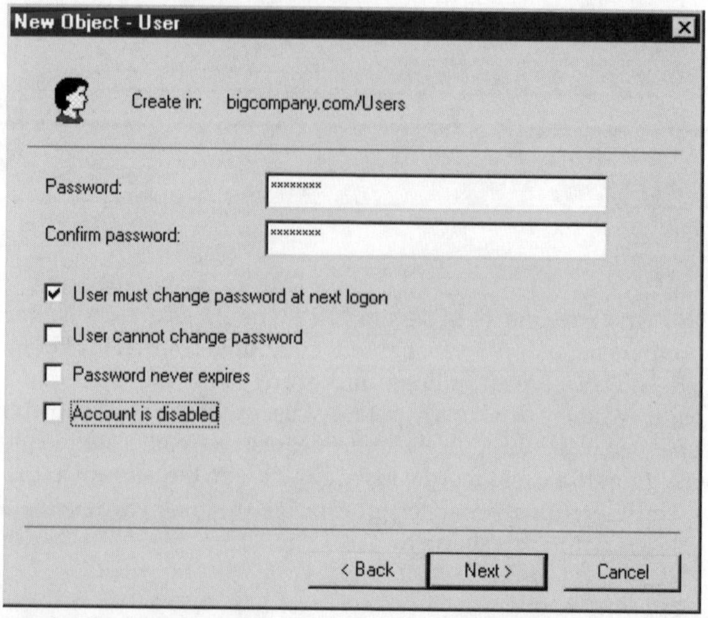

Figure 11-3. Creating Users – Password screen

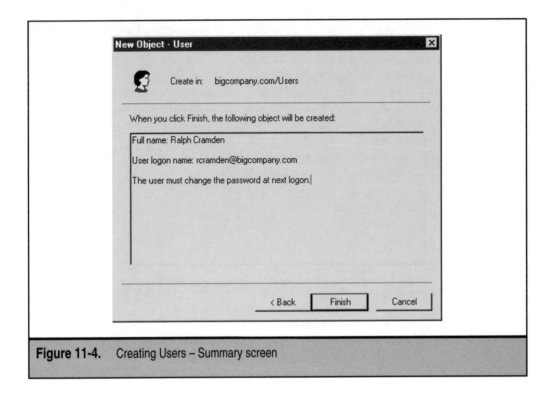

Figure 11-4. Creating Users – Summary screen

Those of you who have created users in NT 4.0 might ask, "Just wait a darn minute! Where's the group memberships? What about logon time restrictions? How about dial-in permissions?" Relax. They are all still here and so are plenty more, I might add. Microsoft felt that, because there are now so many potential user properties, as shown in Figure 11-5, you shouldn't have to wade through the entire set just to create a simple user account. To add properties settings to a user account, just right-click on the account in the MMC and select Properties. The User properties sheet appears. It is discussed in detail in "Modifying an Object's Properties" later in this chapter.

Copying Users

Configuring all the properties of a single user can be a time-consuming task. In NT 4.0, you created user templates to resolve this problem, and the same is true now. Simply create a new user account, designate it as a template, configure a separate template account for each type of user you need to create, and copy templates to create each new user.

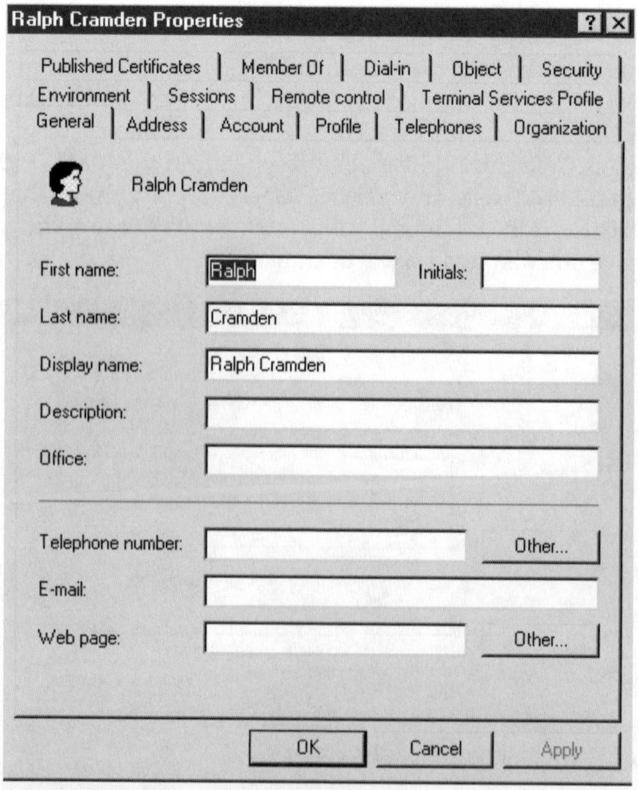

Figure 11-5. User Properties sheet

Some properties *do* copy to a new user object, including these: group memberships, the profile path, logon hours, and account options. But many user-specific properties *don't* copy to a new user object, including these: name, logon name, password, address, telephones, certificates, dial-in permissions, and organization information.

With user templates, marking the template account as disabled to prevent unwanted logons is always recommended. Reflecting Win2K's more secure outlook, the Account disabled option *does* copy to a newly created user. Disabled user accounts are displayed in the MMC details pane, where a red circle enclosing a white "X" appears over the icon. This is a significant change from NT 4.0, where a *disabled* template would produce a *nondisabled* (enabled) account automatically.

Creating an Additional Domain Suffix

For management purposes and to ensure that UPNs (user principal names) are unique, you can create more suffixes for the drop-down box beside the User Logon Name text box in the New Object – User entry screen. Note the "@additionalsuffix.com" in the following illustration. To create additional suffixes, start in the MMC, right-click Active Directory Domains and Trusts, and choose Properties. The only tab that appears is the UPN suffixes tab. Enter the additional suffix text you wish to use, click Add, and click OK. You can have an unlimited supply of suffixes.

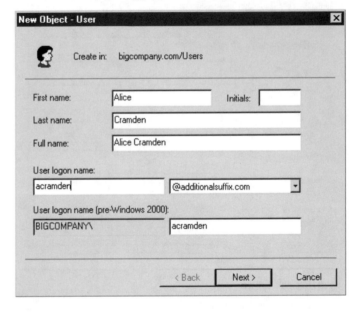

Because templates are disabled, each new account created by copying from a disabled template remains disabled as well until an admin individually enables it. The accounts can be created and configured but still remain disabled until the admin is ready for them. You can also select multiple user accounts in the MMC details pane. As shown in the following illustration, open the User Object context menu, right-click, and select Enable Account to enable all newly created user accounts at once. Unlike NT 4.0, admins cannot select multiple accounts and change most of their properties all at once. And it is still impossible to change individual user properties by group membership. A number of these shortcomings could be resolved by an aggressive and targeted use of group policies.

Utilizing Scripts to Create AD Users

It is also possible (and in many cases preferable) to add users via a script. Following is a sample script to add a single user. It prompts you to enter the username and password you wish to create and loops back to the beginning so you can continue creating additional users until you click Cancel. You must be logged on as a user account capable of creating users.

```
'Script to add user to Users container
On Error Resume Next

'Bind to the Active Directory and get the current domain
set dse = GetObject("LDAP://RootDSE")
set domain = GetObject("LDAP://" & dse.Get("defaultNamingContext"))

'Bind to the Users Container
set cnUsers = domain.GetObject("container", "CN=Users")

varName = Inputbox("Enter the Name of the User to Create")

do while varname <> ""
     varPassword = Inputbox("Enter the Password of the User")
```

```
'Check if user already exists
strName = cstr("cn=" & varName)
set oUser = cnUsers.getobject("user", strName)

'If user is not found error will occur

'Otherwise update password and SAM name
if err then
      set oUser = cnUsers.create("user", strName)
      wscript.echo "Creating New User"
else
      wscript.echo "Updating User Account"
end if

'Turn off error handling so user will receive any new errors
on error goto 0

'Set the down-level name required for using with NT DC's
oUser.put cstr("sAMAccountName"), cstr(varName)

'Enable the account
oUser.put "userAccountControl", "0020"

'Create the user account
ouser.setinfo

'Set the password
oUser.SetPassword varPassword

'Clean up object
set oUser = nothing

      varName = Inputbox("Enter the Name of the User to Create")
loop
wscript.echo "Finished User Maintenance"
```

Using Downlevel Tools to Create AD Users

You may continue to use downlevel tools such as the NT 4.0 User Manager for Domains or Server Manager to create objects in an upgraded NT domain, if desired. All user and group objects created with these downlevel tools are placed in the Users container of the AD domain. After the object has been created using the downlevel tool, you can modify its attributes by means of the MMC Active Directory Users and Computers snap-in. If a user at a downlevel workstation (Win 9x, NT 4.0) changes his or her password in a Win2K domain, the PDC Emulator processes it normally (as the user expects) and the end-user experience is unchanged. The Directory Services add-on client (dsclient.exe) allows downlevel clients to change their password at any Win2K DC, but this is transparent to the user.

Modifying an Object's Properties

Before we begin our discussion of modifying the properties of the users, let's discuss the several Property tabs that appear on nearly every object. The Properties sheet for an object is always accessed the same way: right-click on the object and select Properties.

The General Tab

Nearly every object will display a General tab on the Properties sheet. The General tab always contains information that describes the object. It may also contain status, location, or address information. In a number of cases, it displays configurable parameters that do not appear anywhere else.

The Managed By Tab

Domain, OUs, and groups display the Managed By tab. From the tab, admins can view the object in the MMC to see what user account is responsible for the management of these objects. This tab is for documentation purposes only.

The Object Tab

When View, Advanced Features is checked in the MMC, the Object tab appears. Nothing can be configured or changed on the Object tab. It displays the following AD-related information: object class, object creation date and time, object last-modified date and time, the original USN of the object when it was created, and the current USN of the object. This information can come in handy when you are troubleshooting.

The Security Tab

Let's step back and take a look at the concept of a Security Principal. A Security Principal is an object in the AD that can be granted access to another object. In NT 4.0, the only Security Principals were users and groups. In Windows 2000 we add one more—computers. Therefore, in Win2K, you can grant users, groups or computers access to a shared resource.

Modifying AD Users

On the Account tab, admins will find most of what they remember from NT 4.0: Logon Hours (time restrictions), Log On To (workstation restrictions), account lockout, and expiration settings, as shown in Figure 11-6.

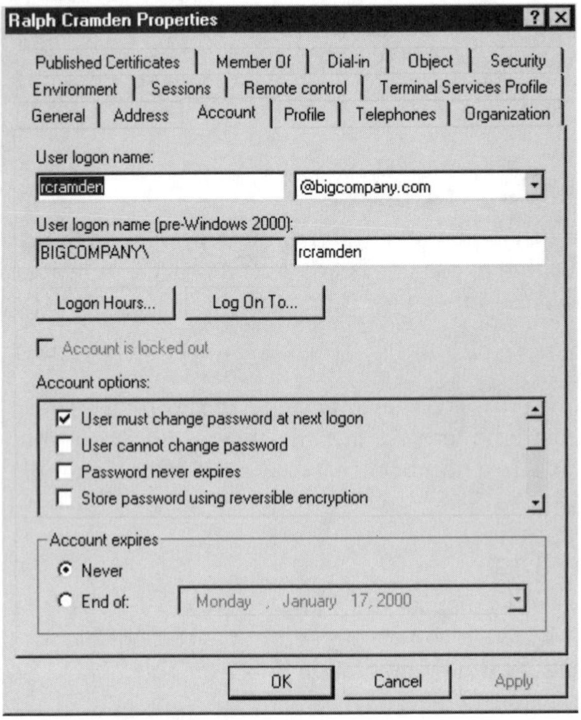

Figure 11-6. MMC – User Properties – Account Tab – view 1

In the lower half of the Account tab is the Account options list, as shown in Figure 11-7. Some of these checkboxes are familiar from NT 4.0: User Must Change Password at Next Logon, User Cannot Change Password, Password Never Expires, Account Is Disabled (not shown). The rest are new and require some explanation. The Store Password Using Reversible Encryption option actually weakens the password storage algorithm because the norm is to store the password using One Way Encryption Format (OWF) or irreversible encryption. The option is unchecked by default and should remain unchecked.

The Smart Card Is Required for Interactive Logon option requires the user to log on interactively at any machine in the forest using a smart card; all other interactive logon attempts will be refused.

The Account Is Trusted for Delegation option allows this account to have X.509 certificates or permits users from non-Windows Kerberos realms to be mapped to this account (we're talking UNIX here, a Win2K Kerberos realm is a domain). This means that users entering your network with specific certificates or credentials will be treated as if they were this account and will be granted or refused access to resources as if they were this account without actually authenticating to Win2K. Name mapping is similar in concept to the Anonymous User in IIS being mapped to the IUSR_MACHINENAME.

The Account Is Sensitive and Cannot Be Delegated option prevents the account from accepting delegation or name mapping.

The Use DES Encryption Types for This Account option represents another weakening of the encryption schemes. Data encryption standard (DES) uses 56-bit keys instead of the North American standard 128-bit keys. DES might prove useful for an international company whose personnel travel outside of the U.S. frequently or for long periods of time. Microsoft recently announced that, because of changes in the U.S. government encryption export regulations, Windows 2000 will be the first platform shipped internationally with 128-bit encryption.

The Do Not Require Kerberos Preauthentication option once again serves the name mapping concept where this user is acting as a surrogate for another user with a certificate.

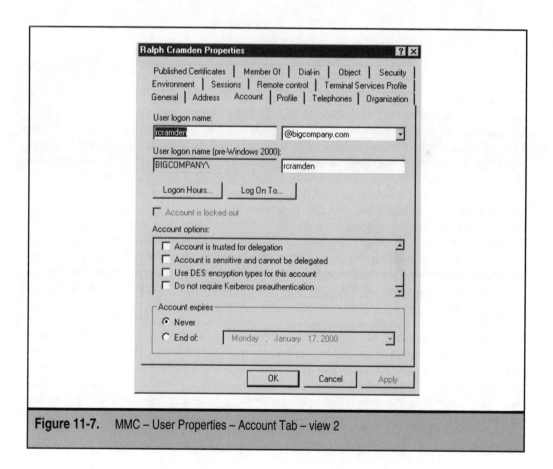

Figure 11-7.   MMC – User Properties – Account Tab – view 2

Unlike NT 4.0, admins cannot reset an AD user's password from anywhere on the Properties sheet. Instead, admins must right-click the user object in MMC Active Directory Users and Computers and work from the context menu as shown next. Users can still change their own passwords at any time by pressing CTRL+ALT+DELETE.

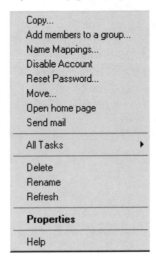

User profile and Home folder settings are on the Profile tab. Don't use the Profile tab for logon script settings because they conflict with the logon script settings in Group Policy. Use the script settings in Group Policy only. If this user intends to log on using Terminal Services, going to the Terminal Services tab and pointing to a different profile location for use with Terminal Services is recommended. The Environment, Sessions, Remote Control, and Terminal Services Profile tabs are only present if Terminal Services has been installed. Dial-in permissions are on the Dial-In tab (covered in detail in Chapter 7). Group memberships can be found in the Member Of tab. The General, Address, Telephones, and Organization tabs are pretty self-explanatory. A sign of the times, you can list multiple home phone numbers (in addition to multiple fax numbers and mobile numbers), but only one address. I guess everybody's gotta live somewhere. The Published Certificates tab lists all the X.509 certificates published for this user account. The Object tab specifies pertinent AD information about the user object. There is no Managed By tab for user accounts.

As shown in Figure 11-8, the Security tab presents the access control list (ACL) of the user object. It spells out who (users or groups) can access, modify, or delete the object. Notice the SELF user, a system account that represents the actual user. SELF can read the object; change password, mail, phone, Web, and personal information; and read all the other info about the account. Without SELF and the default permissions applied, a user would not be able to log on or change even the most basic information about his or her own account.

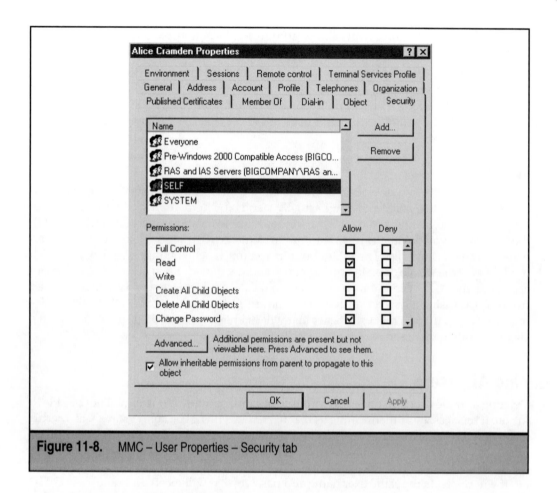

Figure 11-8.   MMC – User Properties – Security tab

Setting User Policies

To set parameters such as password length and account lockout in Win2K, you configure a Group Policy object to apply to a specific OU and the users within that OU. We'll discuss group policies in detail in the next chapter, but several bear mentioning here:

▼   Password Policy is the group policy setting by which the following are configured: password history, maximum password age, minimum password age, minimum password length, password filtering (NT 4.0 passfilt.dll), and reversible encryption. Only applicable at the domain level.

■   Account Lockout Policy determines Account lockout duration, Account lockout threshold, and when to reset the lockout counter. Only applicable at the domain level.

■ Logon and Logoff Scripts allows admins to place multiple script files that are executed in a specific order when the user logs on, and, if desired, logs off.

▲ Folder Redirection can point some of the most common folders—Application Data, Desktop, My Documents, My Pictures, and Start Menu—to a server-based location. This is done to protect the data from being lost when the server is backed up nightly. The user does not know that these folders are being redirected.

krbtgt

The default built-in account krbtgt is unique among all the built-in users. It is always disabled and cannot be enabled. Krbtgt actually stands for Kerberos Ticket Granting Ticket (TGT). When the client is given a TGT in Kerberos authentication (a subject of Chapter 13), the TGT is encrypted with the Key Distribution Center's (KDC's) secret key. The KDC is always a domain controller. The krbtgt built-in account is actually the secret key by which the TGTs for the whole domain are encrypted and decrypted. Because krbtgt is a domain account in the AD, it is present on every DC in the domain. This way, a TGT that is issued from one DC (using the secret key housed in the krbtgt account) is valid at all DCs in the domain. A TGT is used to request a ticket that will establish an encrypted session between a client computer and a server.

Deleting AD Users

Deleting a single user also presents a number of ramifications. The user will not be able to log on. If services are authenticating as that user, they will not be able to start. X.509 certificates and non-Windows Kerberos accounts that are mapped to that user account will no longer be able to function. If this user account was used to encrypt (EFS) files on the NTFS file system, only the Data Recovery Agent can now decrypt the files.

If you re-create the same user name and password, it will receive a brand-new GUID and a brand-new SID. Although the account and password are the same as before, the new account will be unable to access resources until it is placed in appropriate groups that already have access to resources.

Utilizing Scripts to Delete AD Users

Often you want to delete a large number of users at once. The most efficient method of doing that is to create a script. A sample user deletion script follows. The script prompts you to enter the name of the user you wish to delete. Just enter the user name and BAM! Gone. You must be logged in as a user capable of deleting users to run the script.

CAUTION: There are no confirmations in this script, so be careful.

```
'Script to delete users from Users container
on error resume next

'Bind to the Active Directory and get the current domain
Set dse = GetObject("LDAP://RootDSE")
Set domain = GetObject( "LDAP://" & dse.Get("defaultNamingContext"))

'Bind to the Users Container
set cnUsers = domain.GetObject("container", "CN=Users" )

varName = Inputbox("Enter name of user to delete")

do while varname <> ""
        'Check if user already exists
        strName = cstr("cn=" & varName)
        set oUser = cnUsers.getobject("user", strName)

        'If user is not found error will occur
        if err then
                wscript.echo "User Not Found"
        else
                cnUsers.delete "user", strName
        end if

        varName = Inputbox("Enter name of user to delete")
loop
```

MANAGING AD GROUPS

In nearly every other network operating system, specifically UNIX and NetWare, there is only one kind of group—a group. That may sound silly but it's true. In NT 4.0, there were two kinds of groups—local and global.

An NT 4.0 local group could be thought of as a "machine" group because it tended to exist in the local SAM database of one computer (the exception being the domain controllers, which all had the same SAM database and, hence, the same local groups). The local group could only be granted permissions to resources on the same computer that housed the group. The local group could accept members (users and global groups) from other NT computers and even other (trusted) domains.

An NT 4.0 global group is more accurately thought of as a domain group. It exists only in the SAM database of the NT domain controllers. It can contain only domain users from its own domain. However, it can be a member of any local group in its own domain or any trusting domain. This may seem a little confusing, but most NT 4.0 admins have come to grips with it by now.

Just when you thought it was safe to go back in the water, here comes...*dun-dah-dun-dah-dun-dah*...Active Directory with two *types* of groups and three *scopes* of group influence.

AD Group Type, Scope, and Strategy

The Active Directory has two types of groups: Distribution and Security. It has three scopes or levels of influence: Domain Local, Global, and Universal within each type. A few strategies on how to deploy them are discussed later in this section.

Group Type

A Distribution group is designed to replace the concept of Exchange 5.5 Distribution Lists in the upcoming Exchange 2000. Exchange 2000 forsakes its own Active Directory in favor of complete integration with the Windows 2000 AD. A Distribution group cannot function as a Security Principal, cannot be granted access to resources, and will not appear on its members' access tokens. A Distribution group is used solely to distribute mail.

A Security group is the type of group you're used to from NT 4.0. It functions as a Security Principal, it can be granted access to resources, and it will appear on its members' access tokens. In addition, a Security group can be used to distribute mail.

Group Scope

A Domain Local group resides in the Active Directory, can be granted permissions to resources only on computers within its own domain, can belong only to groups from its own domain, and can have members from any domain. A Domain Local group is similar in concept but not the same as a local group in NT 4.0. In Native mode, a Domain Local group may be nested in another Domain Local group, can be a member of a Universal group, and can be changed to a Universal group.

A Global group resides in the Active Directory, can be granted permissions to resources in any domain, can belong to groups from any domain (and Universals), and can have members only from its own domain. A Global group is very similar to Global groups in NT 4.0. In Native mode, a Global group may be nested in another Global group, can be a member of a Universal group, and can be changed to a Universal group.

A Universal group (Native mode only) resides in the Global Catalog, can be granted permissions to resources in any domain, cannot belong to any other group, and can contain members from any domain. This is a brand-new functionality.

Group Deployment Strategies

If your enterprise contains but a single domain, you can modify the NT 4.0 A-G-L-P model into A-G-DL-P. User **A**ccounts are placed in **G**lobal groups, which are placed in **D**omain **L**ocal groups, which are the only ones granted **P**ermissions. Domain user accounts with like needs are placed in a Global group. At the resources (Shared folders and Printers), Domain Local groups are granted appropriate permissions. Then, to connect the two sides of the equation, place the Global groups into the Domain Local groups and you're cookin' with gas. In a single domain forest, Universal groups are basically irrelevant.

In a multi-domain enterprise, Universal groups are both necessary and useful. But because a Universal group and its members all reside in the Global Catalog, you must take steps to keep the GC replication to a minimum. The recommendation is that a Universal group only contain Global groups. The Global-groups-only strategy will keep the membership of the Universal group static. And because replication only happens when something changes, the strategy reduces inter-domain replication traffic. When a user logs on in a multi-domain Native mode enterprise, each Universal group is checked to see if the user is a member of the group in order to update the user's access token. To facilitate quick logons, be sure that there is a Global Catalog server (that houses the Universal groups) on each site.

Here is an example of a good implementation of a Universal group: suppose three groups of managers from three different domains all need read and write access to three SQL databases located one in each domain. You place each domain's managers in a Global group and have each domain's Global group join a single Universal group. Then you grant read and write access at each SQL database to the single Universal group. All three managers, one from each domain, now have read and write access to each SQL database.

A Flaw in the AD Group Object Design

As shown in Figure 11-9, the switch to Native mode also opens up the capability of nesting the Domain Local and Global groups. Why nest groups? Because, in my humble opinion, there is a flaw in the object design that can affect an admin in several ways. First, the flaw…

An AD group object has a single multi-valued attribute called Members that lists all the members of the group. Remember that AD replication is performed by attribute. Therefore, the Members attribute must be replicated every time a single user is added to or removed from a group's Member list. That means that the entire list of members is replicated every time a change is made to the group. One other issue: each attribute replication must be completed as a single transaction, and if the Member list gets too big, that isn't possible. To address both of these issues, Microsoft has conducted extensive testing and determined that 5000 members should be considered as the limit for a single group. If you need a group of more than 5000, simply nest multiple groups under a "top-level" or "container" group.

This same design flaw causes another situation that can impact admins. Let's assume that two different admins on two different domain controllers are changing the membership of the same group at roughly the same time. The Sales Group has 20 members. AdminA adds 6 users to the Sales Group and, a minute later, AdminB removes 3 different users from the Sales Group. Now the Sales Group should have 23 members. However, five minutes later, after replication, the Sales Group has 17 members, all the original members less the 3 removed by AdminB. The 6 users added by AdminA are nowhere to be found. Why?

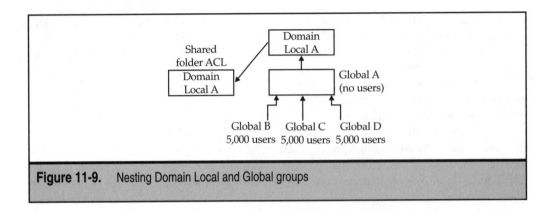

Figure 11-9.   Nesting Domain Local and Global groups

When two admins update the same attribute on the same object at almost the same time, a replication conflict results. Following the rules of replication conflict resolution (see Chapter 10), the AD checks the version number of the Members attribute on each update (remember that replication is by attribute, so conflicts are by attribute). The version numbers are the same. Next, the AD checks the values. The values are different. So the tie-breaker becomes the time-stamp. AdminB removed 3 users one minute after AdminA added 6. Because both updates occurred within the same replication cycle (and have the same version number), AdminB wins and the Sales Group has 17 members. In about fifteen minutes, AdminA can go back in and add the 6 users to make everything work as it should.

As an admin, what must you do to avoid this problematic situation? Develop a procedure whereby only one admin does group membership changes. Even that's not enough. Make sure that the single admin follows a simple but foolproof procedure. Do all your adds in one sitting. Wait thirty minutes for replication. Do all your removes in one sitting. This is a very simple procedure that will guarantee optimal database integrity.

Creating AD Groups

If you upgraded from an NT 4.0 domain, all of your existing groups have already been migrated to the Active Directory with their membership lists intact. You'll find all of your global groups in the Users container, the built-in local groups in the Builtin container, and any local groups that admins created in the Users container.

Creating new groups is an easy task. In the MMC, select the OU or container where you want to place the group, right-click, and choose New, Group. The New Object – Group dialog box shown in Figure 11-10 appears. Enter the name of the group (the pre-Windows 2000 name automatically appears as well). Choose the Group scope, Domain Local, Global, or Universal (in Mixed mode the Universal group option is not available). Next, choose the Group type, Security or Distribution. Unless the group you are creating is to be used solely for distributing mail in Microsoft Exchange 2000, keep the default choice, Security. A Security group can be granted permissions to other objects and can even be used to distribute mail. Click OK and the group is created.

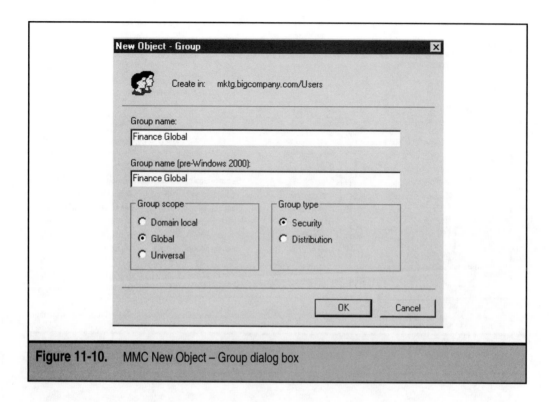

Figure 11-10.   MMC New Object – Group dialog box

Exploring the Builtin Local Groups

The Builtin container houses the eight Builtin local groups that you recognize from an NT 4.0 domain controller as well as one additional group: Pre-Windows 2000 Compatible Access, as shown in Figure 11-11. If you upgrade an NT 4.0 PDC, the eight NT 4.0 local groups transfer directly to the Win2K AD Builtin container. Builtin groups can never be deleted.

Account Operators is empty by default and is mostly used to accommodate backward-compatibility from NT 4.0 upgrades. Its members can still administer domain user and group accounts.

Administrators is still the king of the hill when it comes to local domain administration. By default, the domain administrator user, the Domain Admins global group, and the Enterprise Admins global/universal group are all members. The Builtin Administrators group can manage nearly every task in the local domain.

Backup Operators is empty by default. Its members can still override existing security for the sole purpose of backing up or restoring files.

By default, the members of Guests are Domain Guests, Guest user (disabled), IUSR & IWAM from IIS, and TSInternetUser from Terminal Services.

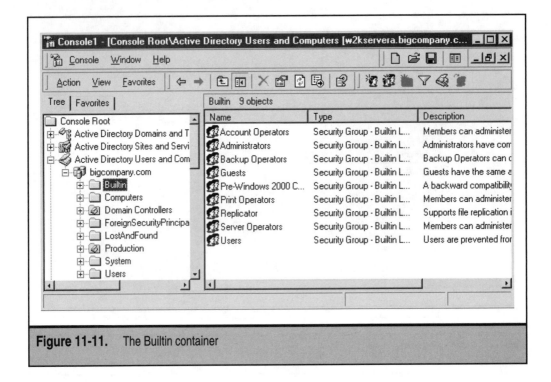

Figure 11-11. The Builtin container

The Pre-Windows 2000 Compatible Access group was created to do just what its name implies: provide access to downlevel users and computers. Its primary purpose at this time is to allow an NT 4.0 RAS server to exist on a Win2K domain. Remember the question shown in Figure 11-12 asked during *dcpromo* about Permissions? If you chose to accept pre-Windows 2000 permissions, the Everyone group appears here as a member. If not, the membership is empty.

The Print Operators group has no members by default. Its members can administer domain printers.

The Replicator group has no members by default. It supports the File Replication service between DCs in a domain.

The Server Operators group has no members by default. Its members can administer domain servers and shares.

The Users group has three members by default: the system-generated Authenticated Users group, the system-generated INTERACTIVE group, and Domain Users. Because the Domain Users group contains all domain user accounts, every user in the domain is indirectly a member of the Builtin Users group. Through default permissions, members of the Users group are prevented from making accidental or intentional system-wide changes. Therefore, Users can run Win2K certified applications, but not most legacy applications.

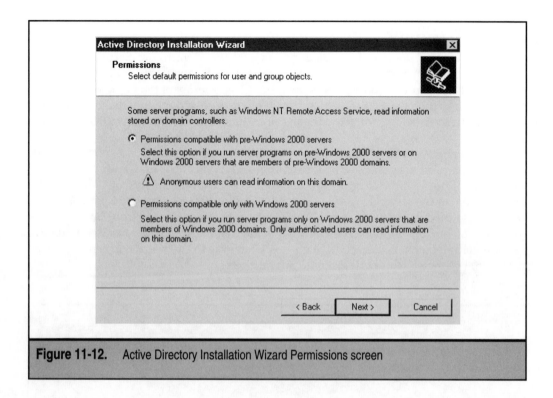

Figure 11-12.   Active Directory Installation Wizard Permissions screen

Understanding the Key AD Groups

Enterprise Admins is the granddaddy of administrative groups. It is located only in the Root domain of the forest. In Mixed mode, it's a Global group. In Native mode, it automatically converts to a Universal group. It is automatically placed in the Builtin Local Administrators group in every domain in the forest. A Domain Admin from the child domain can remove it from the local Administrators group, thus removing the EA's administrative power over the child domain.

Schema Admins is a very exclusive group indeed. Located in the root domain, only the local Administrator of the root domain is a member by default. In order to edit or modify the schema in any way, you must be logged on as a member of the Schema Admins group. Like the EA, Schema Admins is a Global group in Mixed mode; in Native mode, it is a Universal group.

Domain Admins is similar in scope to the Domain Admins group in NT 4.0. It automatically becomes a member of the local Administrators group of every computer that joins the domain. This gives Domain Admins administrative privilege by default over every computer within its domain.

Modifying AD Groups

Groups, of course, possess the standard Managed By, Object, and Security tabs. The Members tab lists all current members of the group (any Security Principal can be a member) and allows you to add or remove members. The Members tab is the only place to view the group membership. The Member Of tab lists all groups to which the group in question currently belongs. It provides an opportunity to add or remove this group as a member.

As shown in Figure 11-13, the General tab allows you to alter the pre-Windows 2000 (NetBIOS) name of the group, write a description, and enter an e-mail address. In Mixed mode you cannot alter the Group scope or Group type. Admins are welcome to add notes at the bottom of the screen to assist others in managing this group on the network.

In Native mode, however, you are free to change the Group scope from Domain Local to Universal, or from Global to Universal, as shown in Figure 11-14, provided you have not nested the Domain Local or Global groups. Changing to Universal is a one-way street; you cannot change a Universal group to anything else.

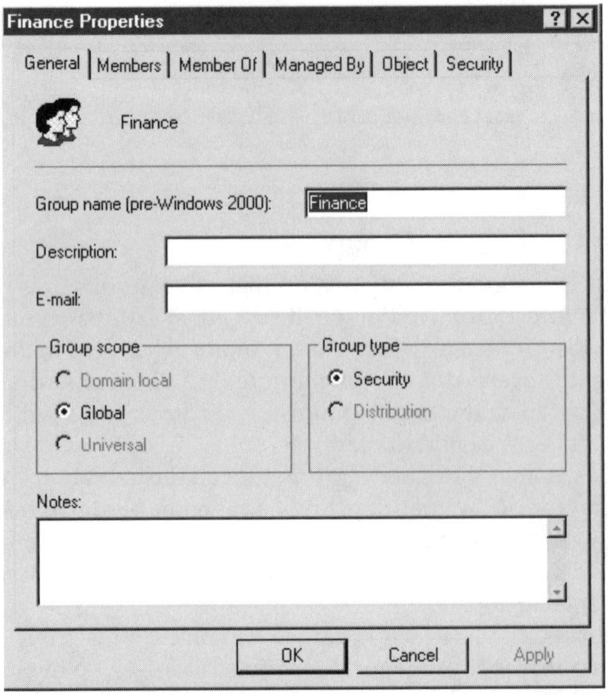

Figure 11-13.   Group Properties – General tab – Mixed mode

Finance Properties   **? X**

General | Members | Member Of | Managed By | Object | Security |

Finance

Group name (pre-Windows 2000):   Finance

Description:

E-mail:

┌─ Group scope ─────────────┐ ┌─ Group type ─────────────┐
│ ○ Domain local   │ │ ● Security   │
│ ● Global   │ │ ○ Distribution   │
│ ○ Universal   │ │   │
└───────────────────────────┘ └───────────────────────────┘

Notes:

                OK   Cancel   Apply

Figure 11-14.   Group Properties – General tab – Native mode

In Native mode, you can also change the Group type. Changing from Distribution to Security presents no real consequences or loss of functionality, but going the opposite direction from Security to Distribution can lead to problems, as the confirmation warning screen shows in the following illustration. A Distribution group is not a Security Principal. If you have granted or denied permissions using this group, those permissions or denials will no longer be in force.

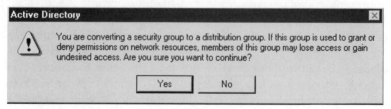

Active Directory   X

You are converting a security group to a distribution group. If this group is used to grant or deny permissions on network resources, members of this group may lose access or gain undesired access. Are you sure you want to continue?

                Yes   No

Unlike NT 4.0, the Windows 2000 Active Directory now allows you to rename groups at any time. To do so, right-click the group name in the details pane of the MMC and select Rename. The renaming functionality is available in both the Win2K SAM and AD-based groups.

Moving Users and Groups Between Domains

Moving user and group objects between domains requires a Win2K Support Tool command line utility called MOVETREE. Assuming a DC named server1 in bigcompany.com and a DC named server2 in mktg.bigcompany.com, a sample syntax to move UserA from the Users container in bigcompany.com to the Users container in mktg.bigcompany.com looks like this:

```
movetree /check /s server1.bigcompany.com /d
server2.mktg.bigcompany.com /sdn
CN=userA,CN=Users,DC=bigcompany,DC=com /ddn
CN=userA,CN=Users, DC=mktg,DC=bigcompany,DC=com /u
bigcompany\administrator /p *
```

As written, this command prompts for the **bigcompany.com** administrator password, performs a test run of the object move, confirms that the move works, and moves the user account. Check the Win2K Support Tools help for more detail on this utility.

Deleting AD Groups

Deleting a group does not delete the objects that are currently listed as members. However, deleting a group might affect which access permissions or denials these objects currently have on existing resources. For example, UserA has access to FolderB. This access is granted because UserA is a member of Group C. Group C appears on the Access Control List of FolderB, but UserA does not. If Group C is deleted, its SID no longer appears on UserA's access token. Now UserA no longer has access to FolderB. UserA won't know this until he or she logs off and then logs back on and attempts to access FolderB.

MANAGING SHARED FOLDERS AND PRINTERS

Shared folders and printers present a different way of looking at an Active Directory object. In all other cases—users, groups, OUs, and so on—the object in the Active Directory is the only representation of the entity involved. In other words, a user object *is* the user as far as the AD is concerned; a group object *is* the group; and so on.

However, Shared Folder objects, rather than the actual NetBIOS share, are a means of publishing a pointer in the Active Directory to a NetBIOS share. Once published, a user with the Global Catalog and the Find command can locate the Shared Folder object. Downlevel clients with the directory services add-on (dsclient.exe) can locate the object using the Global Catalog or Find command. At the same time, downlevel, non-AD-aware clients can also find it by using the old-fashioned computer browser mechanism.

The same is true of AD Printer objects. These objects contain a pointer to the NetBIOS share name for the printer. The printer object can also be located by AD-aware clients using the Global Catalog and the Find command. Downlevel clients can attach to the printer as before using the computer browser in My Network Places.

Microsoft has created a scenario that is tilted toward migration and backward-compatibility here. In future releases, look for another way of publishing these resources without the use of NetBIOS.

Publishing Shared Folders in the Active Directory

In the MMC Active Directory Users and Computers, choose the organizational unit where you would like the Shared Folder object to appear, right-click, and choose New, Shared Folder. The New Object – Shared Folder box shown in Figure 11-15 appears. Fill in the name that you want to be seen in the Active Directory. Then complete the network path with the UNC name (*server**share*) of the pre-existing shared folder on a Win2K, NT, or other Microsoft OS-based computer. The AD Shared Folder object now appears in the MMC under the OU.

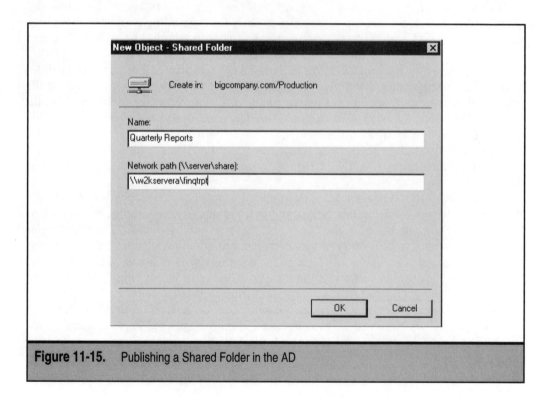

Figure 11-15. Publishing a Shared Folder in the AD

Please note that before a Shared Folder object can be created in the AD, the actual NTFS folder must be shared in the exact same way you did it in NT 4.0. In Windows Explorer, right-click the folder you wish to share, and choose Sharing. Click the radio button next to share this folder, type the share name, set the permissions if necessary, and click OK. The folder is now shared using the traditional SMB (Server Message Blocks) sharing protocol. Or, if you prefer, type the following at the command line:

```
net share sharename=drive:path
```

Publishing Shared Printers in the Active Directory

Printers are published in the Active Directory in two different ways, depending on where they are located. If the printer is connected to an NT 4.0 or Win 9x computer or if its printer share is managed by a downlevel computer, create the printer object by selecting the OU where we would like it to reside, right-clicking, and choosing New, Printer. The New Object – Printer box appears. Enter the network path of the already existing pre-Windows 2000 print share (*server**printshare*) and click OK. The printer object appears under the selected OU.

On the other hand, if you are creating a printer on a Win2K computer, you must use the Printers folder from Control Panel, or click the Start button, choose Settings, and choose Printers. The basic setup is very similar to NT 4.0: open the Add Printer Wizard, click Next, choose Local vs. Network printer, and choose whether you want Plug and Play to locate and identify your printer. Click Next, choose a Printer Port (usually LPT1:), click Next, and select the manufacturer and model of your printer (both port and printer selection are unnecessary if PnP worked). Click Next, pick a local display name for the printer, and, if more than one printer is installed, decide whether this is the default printer. Click Next and select shared or not shared. If you select shared, you must provide a share name to be seen by all downlevel users on the network. Click Next and enter a location to assist in finding the printer when searching the AD and Global Catalog. Click Next and test the printer. Click Next, read the summary screen, and click Finish to create the printer.

While still in the Printers folder, right-click the newly created printer and choose Properties. Click the Sharing tab. Notice the share name. Just below the Shared As text box is a checkbox called List in the Directory. It is checked by default. *The status of this box is what determines whether the printer you created will be published in the Active Directory.* If it is checked, users will be able to search the AD and use the Global Catalog to locate the printer. If it is not checked, the printer can only be found by conventional (NetBIOS) means, as shown in Figure 11-16. To locate a printer in Win2K using downlevel methods, on the desktop click My Network Places | Entire Network | Entire Contents | Microsoft Windows Network | Domain Name | Name of the Computer Hosting the Printer Share and, finally, the list of shares hosted on this server appears, including our long lost printer.

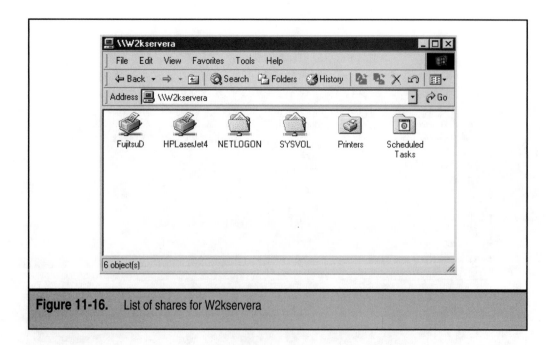

Figure 11-16. List of shares for W2kservera

Unfortunately, even if List in the Directory is checked, the printer object is still not visible by default in the MMC Active Directory Users and Computers. To see the printer object you've created, you must first choose Users, Groups, and Computers as Containers on the MMC View menu. Highlight the computer object where the printer was created in the console (left) pane. The printer object you just created is then displayed in the details (right) pane, as shown in Figure 11-17.

Permissions on Shared Folders and Printers

One final note about both the AD Shared Folder and Printer objects: each has a Security tab and an Access Control List. Users and groups that have been granted permissions on these ACLs have permission to the *AD object*, not the actual folder share or the actual printer share. Access permissions to the share are granted directly at the resource itself. And in the case of a Shared Folder, you even have a third set of permissions to manage: the NTFS Folder permissions, as shown in Figure 11-18. In other words, a user could search and find a Shared Folder object because he or she had permission to read the object in the AD. The same user, however, could not access the actual folder because he or she was not present on both the share ACL and the NTFS folder ACL.

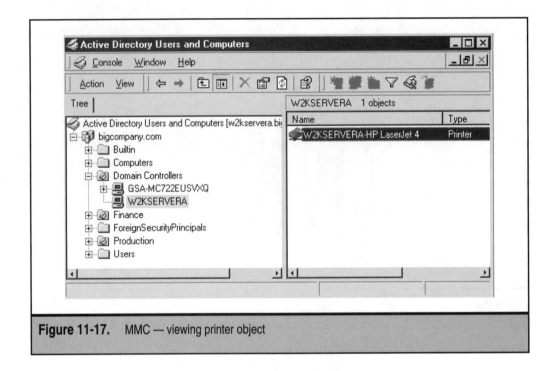

Figure 11-17. MMC — viewing printer object

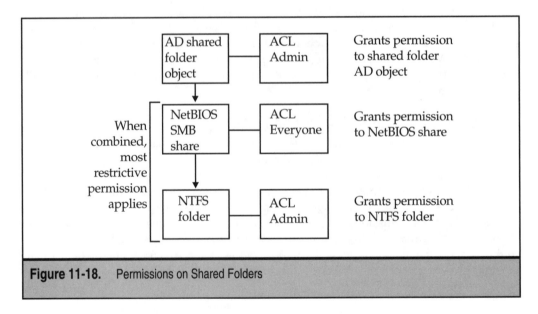

Figure 11-18. Permissions on Shared Folders

LOCATING AD OBJECTS

With the potential for millions of objects in the Active Directory, finding a specific user in a list of other users could be nearly impossible—like finding the proverbial needle in a haystack. So, instead of leaving you awash in a sea of LDAP, Microsoft has created several simple, yet effective ways of locating AD objects.

Locating Users with the Global Catalog

The Global Catalog is the number one tool for searching the Active Directory. It is the tool with which most end-users will actually interface. And because its interface was designed for end-users, launching it is easy. To find a user, click the Start button, choose Search, and choose For People. The Find People box shown in Figure 11-19 appears.

The first time a user gives the Find People command, the Search – Find People dialog box offers to search the Address Book. To look in the Active Directory (Global Catalog), click the down-arrow in the Look In box and choose Active Directory, as shown in Figure 11-20. This setting is retained in each user's personal settings. Notice that you can also use a number of Internet services to search for people, assuming you are connected to the Internet.

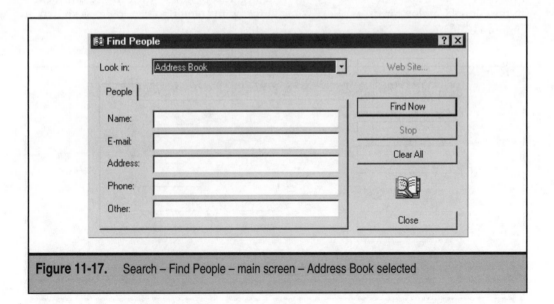

Figure 11-17. Search – Find People – main screen – Address Book selected

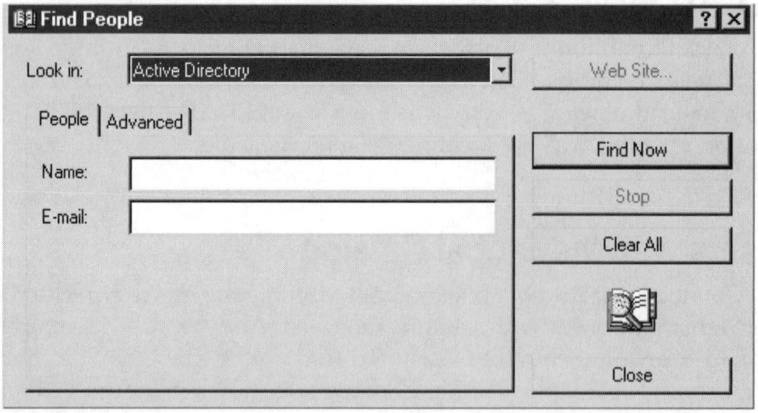

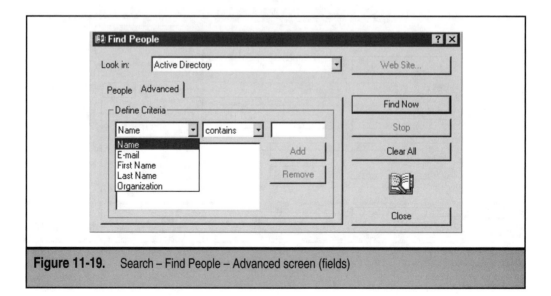

Figure 11-18. Search – Find People – main screen – Active Directory selected

The People tab gives you the ability to search by account name or e-mail address only. Click Advanced for additional search options, as shown in Figure 11-21.

Your first task is to choose which field to search in the Active Directory. Your choices are Name, E-mail, First Name, Last Name, and Organization. These are the fields indexed in the Global Catalog for users. Next you can throw in some Boolean logic, as shown in Figure 11-22.

Figure 11-19. Search – Find People – Advanced screen (fields)

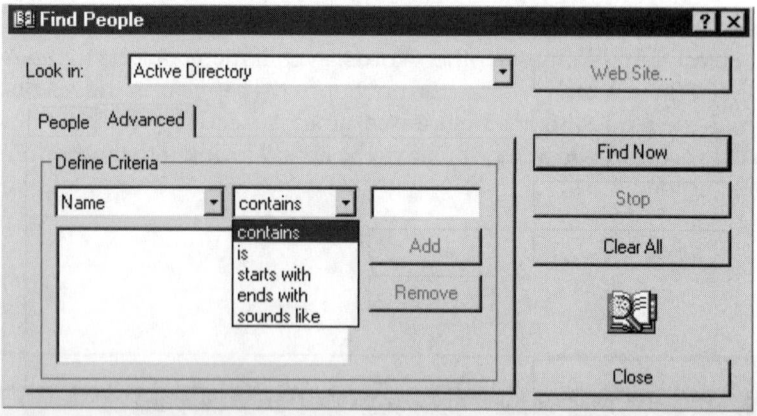

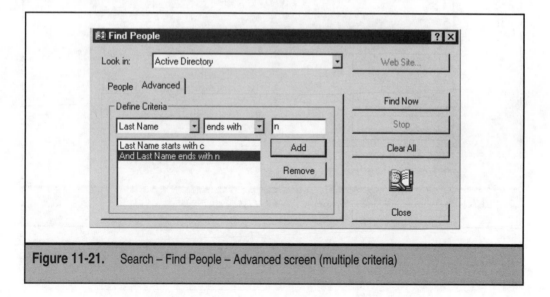

Figure 11-20.   Search – Find People – Advanced screen (Boolean operators)

Depending on how sure you are of the spelling of the user's name or other data, you can use operators such as Contains to search for a string of letters or Is to search for exact matches. If we are literally guessing at a name, use the wildcards such as Starts With or Ends With or even Sounds Like to try to locate the user. You can even combine searches, as shown in Figure 11-23, by defining one search criteria, clicking Add, and then defining a second criteria, clicking Add, and clicking Find Now.

Figure 11-21.   Search – Find People – Advanced screen (multiple criteria)

As shown in Figure 11-24, the Global Catalog will return all Active Directory entries that meet the search criteria, provided that the user performing the search has permission to read the object that is found. In other words, even if many objects in the Active Directory meet the defined search criteria, the only ones that appear in the results box are objects for which the requesting user possesses, at least, Read permission.

Once a user account is located, you have the ability to add it to the Address Book with the click of a button.

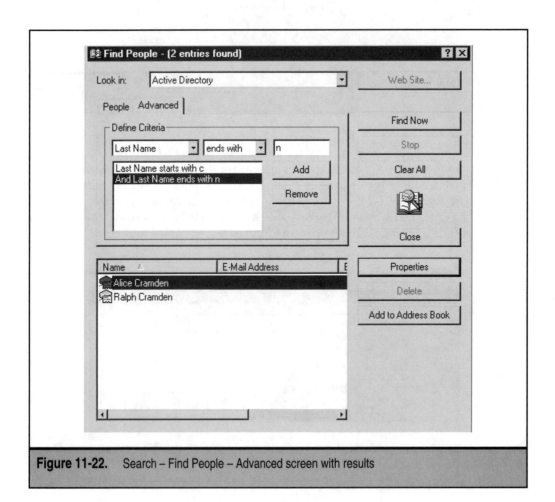

Figure 11-22.   Search – Find People – Advanced screen with results

Locating Printers with the Global Catalog

Microsoft has decided that the average end-user needs to find other users (people) and printers. As with users, finding printers is easy. Click the Start button, choose Search, and choose For Printers. The Find Printers dialog box shown in Figure 11-25 appears. Notice that the default entry in the In textbox is Entire Directory, a Global Catalog search. It is important to remember when you search for printers that you are performing a search for the AD Printer object, not the printer share itself. The user must have Read permission to the object for it to display in the results panel. If you wish to see the printer share, go to My Network Places.

The Printers tab allows you to search by Name, Location, and Model. The name and location were entered when the printer object was created. The model is the print driver that was selected. The Features tab shown in Figure 11-26 will still generate a Global Catalog search.

The Features tab presents some options that are configurable on the Printer Object Properties sheet and others that are specific to the print driver that is selected. You can search with these options: Can Print Double-Sided, Can Staple, and Can Print Color.

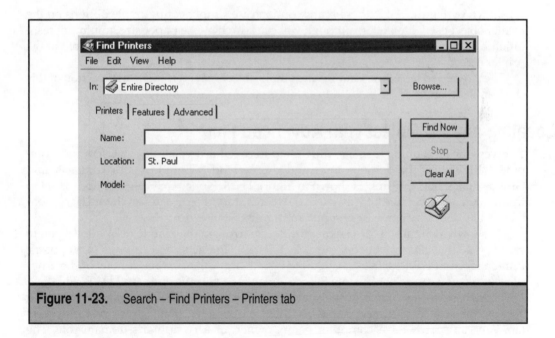

Figure 11-23.   Search – Find Printers – Printers tab

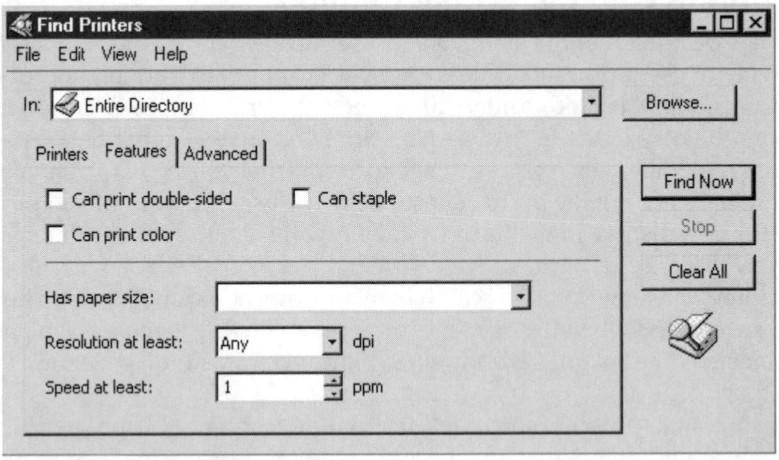

Figure 11-24. Search – Find Printers – Features tab

As shown by Figure 11-27, these search options are simply configurable options on the printer object itself. However, although you can search by the paper size, minimum resolution, and speed, these are functions of the print driver and cannot be configured at the printer object.

The Advanced tab of the Find Printers dialog box is covered in the next section of this chapter. Read on.

Locating any AD Object with Advanced Find

To access the Find utility, use the MMC snap-in called Active Directory Users and Computers. Right-click the domain name and choose Find. The Find Users, Contacts, and Groups dialog box appears, as shown in Figure 11-28. Notice that the In textbox is set to the domain name because that is where the search started. You can search for Users, Contacts, and Groups by name or description from this dialog box.

As shown in Figure 11-29, clicking the down-arrow in the Find textbox allows you to search for any AD object. You can select Users, Contacts, and Groups; Computers; Printers; Shared Folders; OUs; or Remote Installation Clients. And, if none of these options work, you can select Custom Search and enter a specific query in LDAP syntax.

These basic tabs are fairly straightforward as long as you always remember that you are searching for an AD object, not its NetBIOS or downlevel name. From the Computers tab, you can search for a computer name, owner, or a computer's domain role. The Printers tab was discussed earlier. From the Shared Folders tab, you can search by name or keywords. Remember that you are searching for the Shared Folder AD object, not the

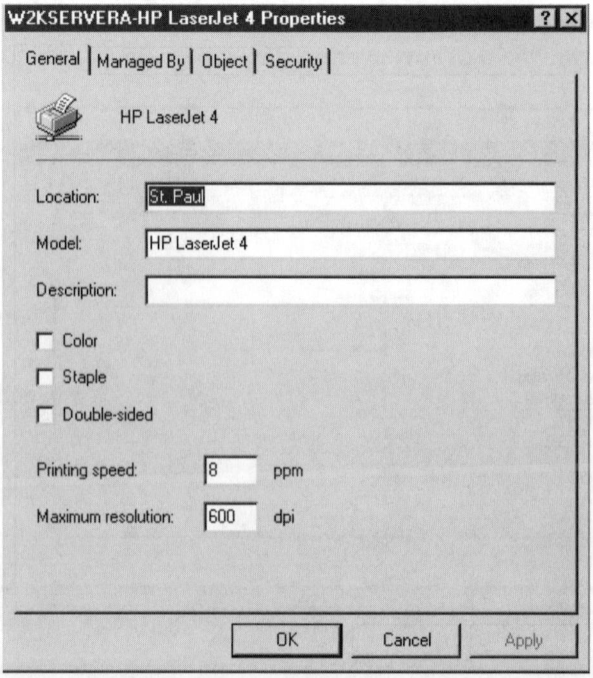

Figure 11-25.   MMC – Printer Properties – General tab

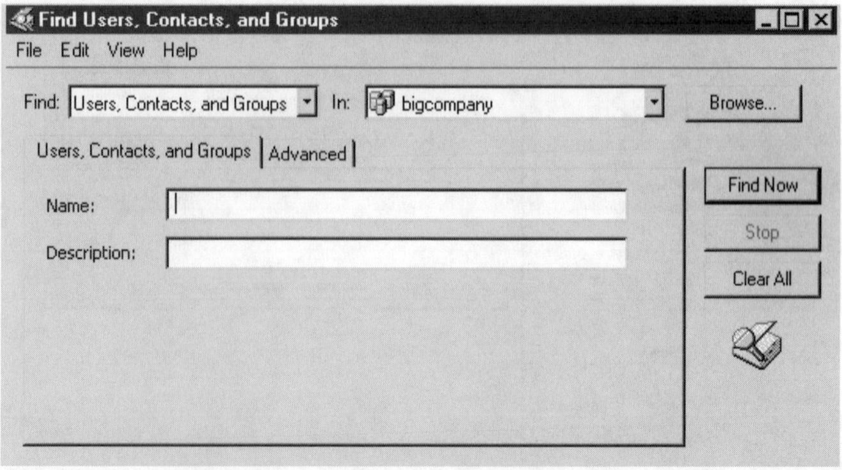

Figure 11-26.   Find Users, Contacts, and Groups dialog box

actual shared folder itself. Search for an OU by name. Remote Installation Clients can be located by GUID and Remote Install server. Custom Search allows us to perform a Boolean search on any field of any object in the AD, as shown in Figure 11-30.

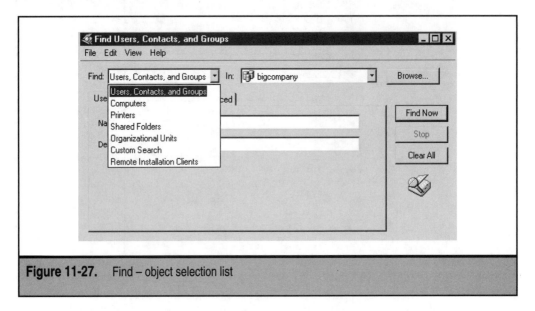

Figure 11-27.   Find – object selection list

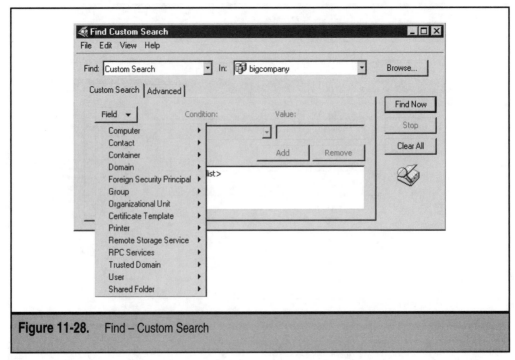

Figure 11-28.   Find – Custom Search

The Find, Advanced tab is where things start to get interesting. Once an object has been selected, a click on the Field down-arrow displays every AD property of the selected object. (It is possible for an object to have properties that do not display, if an object is not configurable or if searching in the UI doesn't make sense. For example, the SIDHistory property of a user object is not displayed. However, you can use the Custom Search, LDAP query to search for it. Heavy geek points for this one!) Figure 11-31 shows the user properties displayed in the Advanced tab when Users is selected. Notice the arrows as they roll off the screen. This total property display is repeated for every object class.

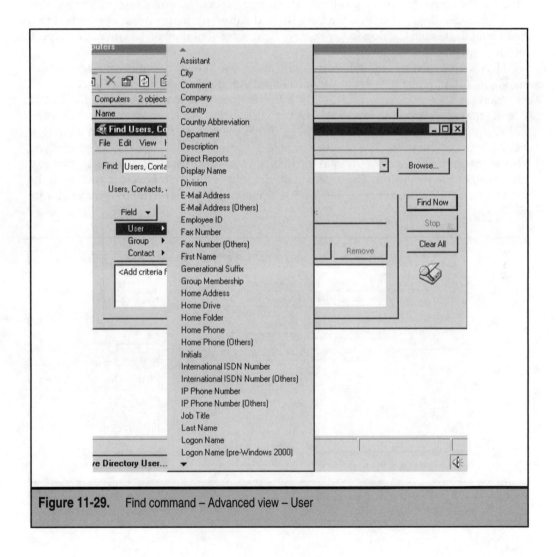

Figure 11-29. Find command – Advanced view – User

Now comes the really confusing part. Take a look at the In: textbox on the top of the screen. It defaulted to the domain because that is where the Find utility was invoked. If you click the down-arrow, you can select different domains if they exist, OUs (by clicking the Browse button), or the Entire Directory option, as shown in Figure 11-32. The Entire Directory option is the Microsoft secret code word for "use port 3268 to search the Global Catalog for a match with the search criteria entered." All options apart from Entire Directory are Microsoft secret codes for "use port 389 to perform an LDAP query against a domain for a match with the search criteria entered." "So what?" you ask. "They both find what I'm looking for, right?" Wrong.

One quick aside here. Remember that the Global Catalog contains an entry for every object in the forest. However, to allow for fast replication and quick response to queries, the Global Catalog contains only a very limited subset of the properties of each object. Searching the Global Catalog for a property it does not contain will, as you might expect, produce no matches. *Nada.* Goose egg.

Here's the problem: whether you choose the Entire Directory option or a specific domain, the full range of properties for each object still displays so you can select a search criterion (as shown in Figure 11-31). In other words, what you selected in the In box doesn't matter as far as the property selection display is concerned, so you can select any object property you wish in searches. Even if the object and property exist in the AD, if your search criteria contains a property that is not present in the Global Catalog and you choose the Entire Directory option in the In box, you will *not* locate that object when you click the Find Now button. The search will yield no results. However, if you leave the search criteria alone and choose the Specific Domain option in the In box, you *will* locate

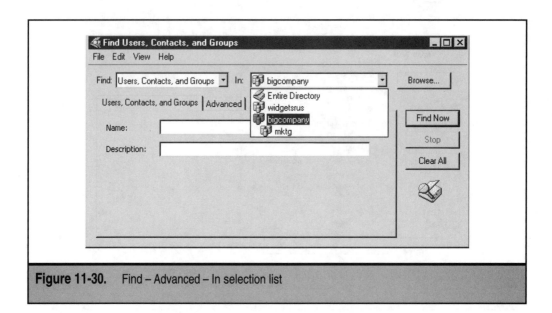

Figure 11-30.   Find – Advanced – In selection list

the object after you click the Find Now button. The reason is simple. In the first search you are using the Global Catalog (using port 3268). It does not contain the object property, there was no match to the search criteria, so the object is not found. In the second search, you are using LDAP (using port 389) to look in the entire AD of a given domain that, of course, contains all properties of all domain objects. Therefore, the object is found. This all makes sense once you get your arms around it, I guess. But I find this confusing, not just to users, but to admins who tend to believe what they see on the screen. By the way, the Help program is no help here.

One more item we haven't mentioned. Can a user find an object that he or she doesn't have permissions to see? Short answer: No. Whether the user is searching the Global Catalog or a specific domain and has entered a search criteria which will yield an existing AD object, the search results will not display an object to a user without Read permission to that object.

DELEGATING CONTROL

Since a domain can include tens of thousands of users, hundreds of groups, and shared folders and printers, the concept of delegating some or all the administrative work to someone else sounds particularly attractive.

One of the coolest new capabilities afforded by the Active Directory is the ability to delegate administrative control. In a large organization, each area or department in the company could have its own network admin—perhaps not a Win2K guru, but someone capable of handling the day-to-day tasks of user administration, password resets, group memberships, printer setup, and so on. Microsoft has provided the ultimate tool for delegating administrative chores: the Delegation of Control Wizard. In spite of its nice, logical GUI interface, the Delegation of Control Wizard in reality simply automates the changing of permissions on AD objects, albeit many objects at one time.

Using the MMC Active Directory Users and Computers snap-in, you can delegate control at the site, domain, and OU levels. Most of the time, you delegate control to an OU. Right-click OU and choose Delegate Control, click Next on the Welcome screen, and add the users or groups to which you want to delegate. Click Next and the Tasks to Delegate screen appears, as shown in Figure 11-33.

You can select one or both of the common tasks. Or, if you prefer, you can create a custom task to delegate, as shown in Figure 11-34.

Once you have selected the object type(s), you must select the permissions you want to delegate, as shown in Figure 11-35.

A summary screen appears. Click Finish and you're done. Delegating control of a site or domain requires taking the same steps in the Delegation of Control Wizard. It's quick, it's easy, and it's fun! There's just one problem, and it could be a big one: there is no "Undelegate Control Wizard." That's right, if you change your mind and want to remove the administrative control you just delegated, you must access each object that was changed and remove the permissions manually. Bummer.

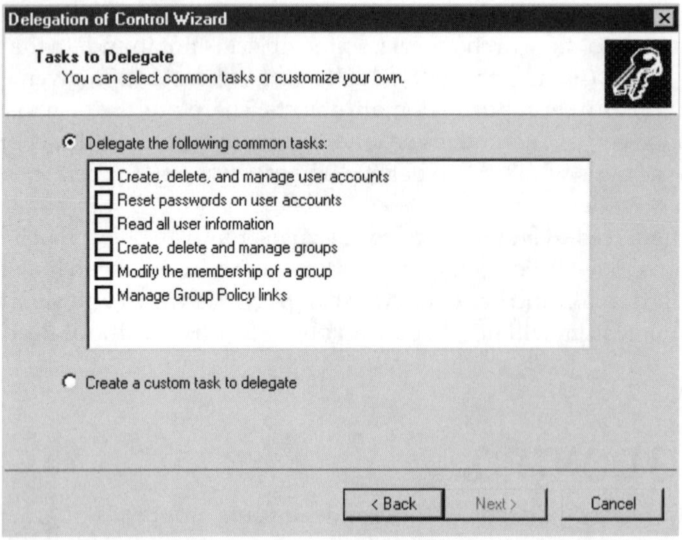

Figure 11-31. Delegation of Control Wizard – Tasks to Delegate screen

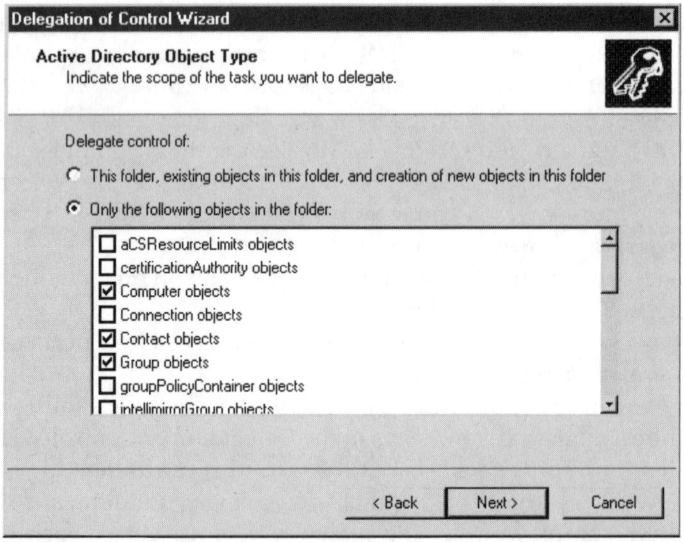

Figure 11-32. Delegation of Control Wizard – Custom Task – AD Object Type

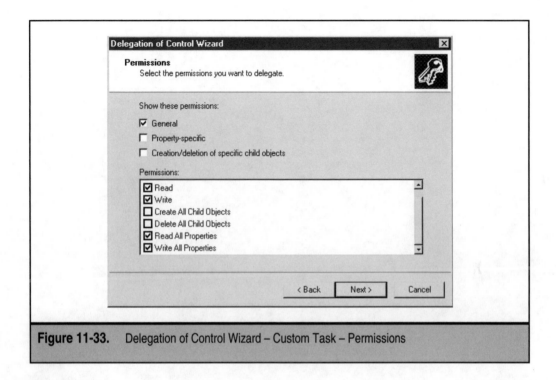

Figure 11-33.   Delegation of Control Wizard – Custom Task – Permissions

SUMMARY

Effectively managing the common AD objects is not difficult as much as it is challenging in terms of procedures and planning issues. The Active Directory Users and Groups MMC snap-in has a simple, straightforward interface that suffices for small to medium-size enterprises. Scripting user maintenance tasks and configuration options is the order of the day in larger enterprises. In any size organization, the key administrative and management initiative for the desktop is the application of Group Policies. And that is a topic we will discuss in detail in the next chapter.

CHAPTER 12

Managing Clients in the Active Directory

Chapter 12 focuses on creating, managing, and modifying computer accounts, as well as the management of the workstation environment through the application of Group Policies. Group Policies promise to be the future of client administration in tomorrow's corporate environment. They provide one of the two major drivers for the design of the OU structure in the Active Directory model.

MANAGING AD COMPUTER ACCOUNTS

As in NT 4.0, you get an opportunity to join a domain or remain in a workgroup when you install a Win2K Professional (or Server) operating system. If you choose to remain in a workgroup, obviously no domain account is created for the computer. However, you can create a domain account for the computer later and join the domain quite easily. It is important to note that computer accounts can only exist for a machine running an operating system that supports its own local database of accounts—in other words, NT and Win2K. Windows 95 and 98 don't get to play this game at all. No computer accounts are possible for Win 9*x* computers.

Creating Computer Accounts/Joining AD Domains

If you ever created a computer account in NT 4.0, you will be right at home, because the exact same concept applies in Windows 2000. You can pre-create the account either at the domain controller first and then join the computer to the existing account, or you can create the account from the joining Win2K computer itself as long as you have administrative privilege to create the computer account. As shown in Figure 12-1, if you wish for downlevel (NT 4.0) computers to join the Win2K domain using this computer account, you must fill in the Pre-Windows 2000 Computer Name box and check the Allow Pre-Windows 2000 Computers to Use This Account check box in the New Object – Computer screen. Checking the box will allow an NT 4.0 workstation to join the Active Directory domain using the pre-created computer account.

Click Next, and, depending on the computer you are using to create the computer object (whether or not RIS is installed), you may see a screen that asks you to decide whether this is a "Managed" computer. Click OK for now (Chapter 2 offers more about managed computers in the section "Remote Installation Services"). Finally, the summary screen appears. Click Finish to create the computer account.

After a computer account is created in the Active Directory, a user with administrative or delegated privileges can add the computer to the domain. Or, similar to NT 4.0, with domain administrative privilege you may also join a domain and create a computer account from the Win2K client computer itself, as shown in Figure 12-2. In either case, right-click My Computer, select Properties, and click the Network Identification tab. The current workgroup vs. domain status of the computer is displayed. To change the status and join a domain, click the Properties button near the center of the box. You see the Identification Changes box, which displays the Computer name and the current membership status of this computer. In this case it belongs to the workgroup named WORKGROUP.

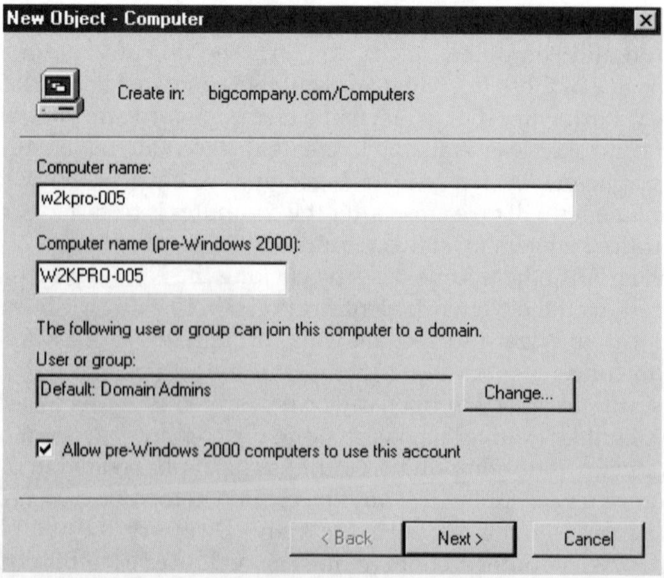

Figure 12-1.   Creating a computer account using the MMC

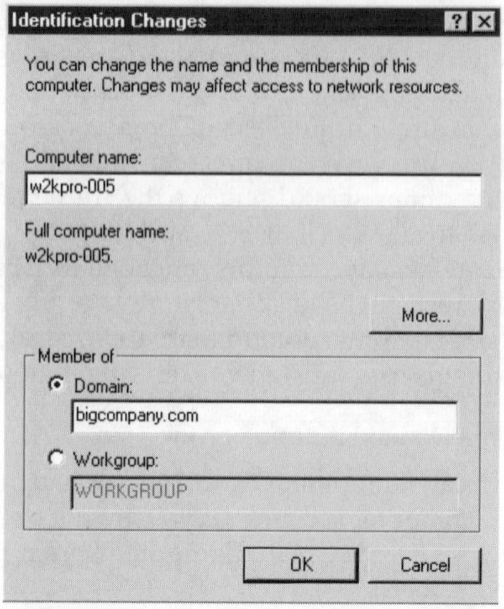

Figure 12-2.   Joining a domain from the Win2K Professional workstation

Click the radio button next to Domain, enter the full domain name, **bigcompany.com**, and click OK. You are prompted to enter the name and password of a domain account with privileges to add computers to the domain. The domain admin account always works, but this is one of those tasks that an administrator can delegate using the Delegation of Control Wizard. Enter the correct name and password and click OK. Assuming a Win2K domain controller was available to create the account, a Network Identification success message appears: "Welcome to the bigcompany.com domain." Click OK and you are told that the changes will take affect after the computer is restarted. Changing the domain or workgroup membership status requires a reboot.

You can also perform these same tasks by clicking the Network ID button instead of the Properties button on the Network Identification tab. Clicking the button launches the Network Identification Wizard so you can walk through this process if you aren't really sure what's happening.

Both of the scenarios I just described can be performed by a user located on an NT 4.0 workstation or standalone server who is creating the computer account on a Win2K Active Directory domain. If no computer account has been pre-created in the Active Directory, the new computer account will always be created in the Computers container. If the computer account has been pre-created in the Active Directory, the new NT 4.0 computer will find and use that computer account (it must have the same NetBIOS name) no matter what OU it may be in. The procedure is the same as performing these operations from Win2K Professional workstations.

Who Can Create AD Computer Accounts?

In the Default Domain Controllers OU Security Policy (choose Computer Configuration | Windows Settings | Security Settings | Local Policies | User Rights), the Authenticated Users group is present on the Add Workstations to Domain user right. Therefore, any user who can successfully authenticate can add a workstation to a domain. In NT 4.0, only members of the Administrators and Server Operators groups were given this privilege. Each domain user (non-privileged account) can only add ten computer accounts to the domain. I believe that admins should remove the Authenticated Users group from this policy unless they plan to allow each user to add his or her own computer to the domain (some large organizations may want this functionality). Interestingly, to remove a computer account, a user must still have administrative privilege.

To clarify this whole add computer accounts situation, consider this: In order to add a workstation to the domain, the user must meet one of the following conditions:

▼ Be a member of the Domain Admins group.

■ Be assigned the Create Computer Objects permission in the OU where you wish to create the computer account. (If you are not pre-creating the computer account in a specific OU, the Create Computer Objects permission must be in the Computers container.)

- ■ Possess the Add Workstations to Domain user right through your dynamic membership in the Authenticated Users group (10 workstation limit).

- ▲ Possess the Add Workstations to Domain user right through a direct assignment to a user or group account.

Modifying Computer Accounts

Figure 12-3 shows the Properties sheet of a computer object. The Managed By and Object tabs were discussed in the last chapter, and the Security tab is discussed in detail in Chapter 14. The Member Of tab allows admins to add this computer to an existing security group. We're not used to placing computers in groups, but it's a good thing. How many times have you wanted the capability of computer groups when applying NT 4.0 system policies? This new facility will come into play as well when you must choose how to filter Group Policies within an OU. Using a computer group, admins can apply a Group Policy object to some computers within an OU but not to others.

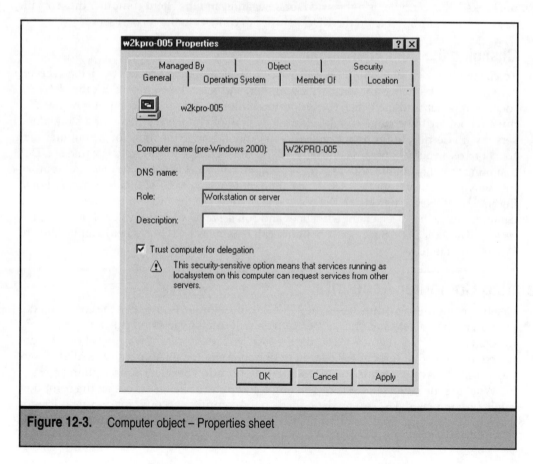

Figure 12-3.   Computer object – Properties sheet

The Operating System tab automatically displays the current version of the OS and Service Pack level of the member computer. This information is obtained by querying the member computer in real time; it is read-only in this tab. The Location tab, for documentation purposes only, allows you to manually enter a location for the computer; this field is not searchable in the Global Catalog. Admins half a world away can look at the object in their Active Directory, know where the computer is located, and, by looking in the Managed By tab, know who is responsible for it. The General tab displays the DNS name and pre-Windows 2000 (NetBIOS) name of the computer as well as its current role in the network, but these names cannot be changed from here. If you wish, you can add a description for this computer.

Notice the Trust Computer for Delegation check box. When you connect to a computer that must connect to another computer to get the information you need, Kerberos authentication allows the first computer to obtain, for the session between the first and the second computer, a session ticket from the KDC (Key Distribution Center) *on your behalf*. That is what happens when the Trust Computer for Delegation check box is checked. If the box is unchecked, the computer is not trusted for delegation and the client computer must obtain a session ticket for itself from the KDC in order to connect to the second server.

Changing the Computer Name

To change the computer name for a Win2K Professional, member, or standalone server, start from the Desktop, right-click My Computer, and select Properties. Click the Network Identification tab and then click the Properties button to change the computer name. You must reboot for the change to take effect. You cannot change the name of a standalone server with Certificate Services installed. You cannot change the name of a computer that functions as an active domain controller. If you must change the computer name of a DC, assuming that it is not the only DC in the domain, you must first run *dcpromo* and remove the Active Directory from the server. Be careful not to demote a DC that is currently housing an active Operations Master. Reboot and then complete the procedure above. When the computer name has been changed, reboot and run *dcpromo* again to restore the Active Directory. The NETDOM Support Tool utility can rename NT 4.0 BDCs before upgrading to Win2K and the AD.

Deleting Computer Accounts

Deleting computer accounts using the MMC is quite simple: Right-click the computer object you wish to delete and choose Delete. You will receive the standard "Are you sure?" message. Click Yes and you will receive the "Are you really sure?" warning about this object containing other objects. All computer objects contain the IASIdentity (RADIUS) service object. DCs also contain the NTFRS (File Replication Service) Subscription object.

What are the adverse effects of deleting a computer? The resources on the computer might be eliminated. Users who depended on the computer account for group policies or as their security principal on other objects might lose access. If the computer is "trusted for delegation," other computers might not be able to access resources on the network.

The NETDOM Win2K Support Tool command line utility can also be used to remove a computer from a domain.

Moving Computer Accounts

Thanks to binary image copying, or "cloning" as I like to call it, the concept of physically moving a computer seldom happens in many corporate environments. But that doesn't hold true for every organization and it certainly doesn't hold true for computer objects within an Active Directory. In fact, the AD computer object could be moved several times without the user who uses that computer even knowing it.

Moving Computers Within a Domain

Moving computers within a domain is easy. From the MMC Active Directory Users and Computers snap-in, highlight the computer object you wish to move, right click, and select Move. The domain and its container objects appear. Select the container where the computer should now reside, click OK, and you're done. In the details pane (the right side) of the MMC, normal Windows "list grabbing" technology applies, so you can move many computer objects at once by SHIFT-clicking or CTRL-clicking.

Moving Computers Between Domains

Moving AD computer objects between domains is a little more complicated. The NETDOM Win2K Support Tool command line utility allows for the movement of workstations or servers (not DCs) from one Win2K domain to another. The tool proves an excellent one for moving machines from what are now NT 4.0 Resource domains to an OU in the upgraded Win2K Master Domain. To move a computer named w2kpro-ws1 from the Computers container in bigcompany.com to an OU called Production in mktg.bigcompany.com, the command looks like this:

```
netdom move /d:mktg.bigcompany.com w2kpro-ws1 /uo:w2kpro-
ws1\administrator /po:localadminpswd
/ud:administrator@mktg.bigcompany.com /pd:domadminpswd
/ou:production /verbose
```

As written, this command will move the computer w2kpro-ws1 from the bigcompany.com domain to the Production OU in the mktg.bigcompany.com domain. And, in doing so, it will tell us everything it's doing on-screen (/verbose). The old computer account in the previous domain (bigcompany.com) is not deleted, but it is disabled in a Win2K domain. Check the Win2K Support Tools help file for more detailed information.

Client Interaction

As in NT 4.0, all NT/Win2K computers in a domain must have a computer account in the domain, in Win2K, the Active Directory. As the computer is booting, it must identify itself to the AD before it can be fully functional in the domain. There seems to be a lot of confusion in the trade press over the question of how the client computer authenticates in

Native mode and in Mixed mode. But there is no difference at all. Let's look at the computer logon process in Win2K.

The Computer Logon Process

The computer logon process is as follows:

1. The Win2K client computer needs to locate a DC. To facilitate its logon, the client uses a local copy of the NetLogon service.

2. The client computer sends the domain to which it belongs (it's in the registry) to its own Netlogon service.

3. The Netlogon service on the client uses the domain information to look up a domain controller in one of two ways:

   ■ For a DNS name, Netlogon queries DNS to read the SRV and A records from DNS. If you upgraded your PDC first, Win2K client computers will probably belong to a DNS domain.

   ■ For a NetBIOS name, Netlogon performs a domain controller discovery by using WINS. If a Win2K client computer is logging on to an NT 4.0 domain or if the DNS does not respond, WINS is used.

4. The Netlogon service sends a kind of "ping" to the IP addresses of the computer(s) that registered the domain controller service. It received these addresses either from DNS or WINS. For NetBIOS domain names, the datagram is a mail-slot message. For DNS domain names, the datagram is an LDAP UDP search.

5. Each available domain controller responds to the client's "ping" to indicate that it is currently operational and returns its pertinent identifying information.

6. The client Netlogon service selects the domain controller that responds first. (Not exactly selective…)

7. The client Netlogon service caches the domain controller information in its registry so that subsequent requests will not repeat the discovery process. Caching the information will speed up subsequent logons significantly.

Win2K clients will default to using DNS resolution to locate DCs, which will tend to give them Win2K domain controllers because the NT 4.0 BDCs don't register with DNS. NT NetBIOS clients will always use WINS to find a DC and the first ones in the WINS database will be the NT 4.0 BDCs.

Even if no NT 4.0 BDCs or NT 4.0 Servers are on the network, the NetBIOS downlevel clients will still use WINS to locate a DC. WINS will respond with the IP addresses of the existing Win2K DCs. Windows 2000 domain controllers run NetBIOS for this very reason: backward-compatibility. The NetBIOS clients will receive a downlevel NetBIOS response from the Win2K DCs that they can understand and process. The computer logon process will be completed and the end-user experience will be unchanged.

Logging On Using Kerberos Authentication

A detailed discussion of Kerberos authentication is reserved for Chapter 13, which looks at Authentication and Identification, but several factors are worthy of special note.

Win2K interdomain trusts use the Kerberos protocol to authenticate with other domains. Therefore, in an all-Win2K forest where all domains are Win2K, Kerberos authenticated two-way, transitive, trusts exist between every parent and child domain. But suppose you have an NT 4.0 Master Domain model with two Resource domains, you've upgraded only the PDC in each domain to Win2K, and you have seven BDCs to go. Must you wait for every DC in every domain to be upgraded before you can take advantage of transitive trusts? No. Transitive trusts are in place as soon as the PDC of each domain has been upgraded to Win2K. Either Windows 2000 clients or downlevel (Win 9*x* or NT) NetBIOS clients can use transitive trusts for interdomain authentication and resource access. Pass-through authentication will function normally in *both* directions.

Kerberos authentication is based on a ticket-granting service. This service runs on the KDC (Key Distribution Center), a service on every Win2K domain controller. Win2K clients will always attempt to use Kerberos as their authentication protocol. Downlevel clients will always use NTLM as their authentication protocol because Kerberos is not supported even with the new Directory Service client extensions. The Directory Service client extensions *do* create the capability for a new, more secure authentication method for Win 9*x* downlevel clients called NTLMv2. NTLMv2 has been available for authentication between NT 4.0 clients and servers since Service Pack 4. (See more on this in Chapter 13.)

If for any reason a KDC is not available to authenticate a Win2K client, the clients will revert to NTLM and attempt to log on to any DC that responds to their Netlogon requests. While this situation is unlikely to occur, it can cause a significant problem if the registry has been changed to allow only NTLMv2 authentication.

MANAGING LEGACY CLIENTS

Most of us have networks with Windows 95, Windows 98, and NT 4.0 Workstations on the desktop. In most cases, an NT domain or three handles file and print services, e-mail, application servers, and so on. Some people have the same desktop environment but with Novell NetWare servers that handle the file and print services. Now that Win2K has shipped, you are forced to consider them all as legacy systems.

DOS and Windows 3.*x*

This book hasn't paid much attention to DOS, Windows, and Windows for Workgroups. And most of you know why. Because DOS is dead! Really. I read it in a magazine five years ago. And Win 3.*x* is dead, too. Nobody uses this stuff any more, right? Wrong, although I think IT managers everywhere tried to use Y2K as a means of getting rid of a lot of it.

Well, in case you're one of those fortunate few who still use this stuff, here's the skinny: A DOS or Win 3.*x* client can still log on to a Win2K domain using the same NetBIOS network client software that they've always used. By default, Win2K fully supports the LAN Manager authentication protocol used by DOS and Win 3.*x*. It's no better or worse than it was before. But one question is really puzzling me: If you're still running DOS or Windows 3.*x*, why did you buy this book? Aha! Because you want to run your 16-bit, single-tasking, legacy DOS applications capable of using 1MB of RAM on a processor with single-digit clock speeds on a highly sophisticated, multitasking, 32-bit operating system that can take full advantage of 4GB of RAM and run at 500MHz. Stop! Just don't do it! Keep your legacy OS running on your legacy hardware until you are ready to upgrade your legacy apps, and then switch to Win2K. Otherwise, you're wasting an incredible amount of money.

Windows 95 and 98

Differences in the way that Win2K clients and NetBIOS clients interact have nothing to do with the two domain modes but everything to do with the Active Directory. By default, no pre-Windows 2000 client (Win 9*x*, NT) can see the Active Directory. Therefore, any function that depends on the AD is precluded from a pre-Windows 2000 client operating system. But, that said, a standard Win 9*x* computer can log on to a Win2K domain with no changes at the client computer whatsoever. By default, Win2K fully supports the LAN Manager authentication protocol that is used natively by Win 9*x*.

DSCLIENT.EXE

To mitigate the negative impact and limited functionality of the legacy NetBIOS clients until all the workstations in the domain are upgraded to Win2K, Microsoft has developed the Directory Services extension for Windows 95 and 98. The service enables legacy client platforms to take advantage of some of the features that the Windows 2000 Active Directory provides. The DS client extension for Win 9*x* includes the following capabilities:

▼ Ability to log on to a Domain Controller "closest" to the client (site affinity)

■ Ability to change a password on any Win2K Domain Controller instead of the PDC

■ Allows scripting to the Active Directory

■ Provides a Dfs client for access to Windows 2000 distributed file system

■ Allows a user to change personal information properties on his or her AD user object (e.g., phone #, address)

▲ Takes advantage of the improved authentication features available in NTLMv2

The Directory Services client extension has the following limitations:

▼ No Kerberos support for Win 9*x* clients

■ No Group Policy support

▲ No IPSEC/L2TP support

The Windows 95/98 version (dsclient.exe) ships on the Windows 2000 Server CD in the \CLIENTS\WIN9X folder. Execute it from the Win 9*x* computer you wish to upgrade.

Windows NT 4.0

Calling NT 4.0 a "legacy" operating system seems odd, but with all the incredible advances in Win2K, I'm afraid "legacy" is the right term. Remember that you've been patching this baby since the fall of 1996. It's old, folks. It's a legacy OS. Windows NT 4.0 is the only thing you could point to from Microsoft and say "business-related OS" without rolling on the floor laughing.

Let me be clear: An unchanged NT 4.0 Workstation or Server can log on to a Win2K domain without any modifications whatsoever. In either Mixed or Native mode, Win2K fully supports the NTLM authentication method that all computers use natively. And that was going to be the end of the story.

For a substantial portion of the development period of Windows 2000, Microsoft steadfastly declared that there would be *no* Directory Service client for NT 4.0 computers. Their reasoning was simple: You obviously have enough horsepower in your hardware to run NT 4.0, so it will probably run Win2K Professional just fine. Worst case is you might have to add a little RAM. We can only give NT so much functionality without completely gutting it and turning it into Win2K. The NT 4.0 to Win2K upgrade is a couple of clicks and you're done. So what's your problem?

And, basically, Microsoft is right. Microsoft was more than adamant on this point. But the company simply bowed to pressure from the market to present every possible upgrade option to the customer and remove every possible objection to a full and ubiquitous acceptance of Win2K.

Proof that Microsoft started late on the NT 4.0 Directory Services client extension is the fact that it does *not* ship with the Windows 2000 product. The promised NT 4.0 client extension will ship with either NT 4.0 Service Pack 7 or Win2K Service Pack 1, which is due in June 2000.

USING GROUP POLICIES TO MANAGE THE WORKSTATION ENVIRONMENT

For the past five years, Microsoft has dreamed of providing a workable method of administering the distributed workstation environment and the users on those workstations from a central location. Microsoft's dream spawned technologies such as Win 95/98 and NT 4.0 system policies, the Zero Administration Kit, and large enterprise products such as Systems Management Server (SMS). But the solutions that were provided never totally fulfilled the dream. Good steps were taken but not always completed. We seemed to be sitting outside the Promised Land looking in. Win2K Group Policies is another step closer to the dream of total remote administration. And coupled with a few other Win2K technologies and a new version of SMS, I think we might have made it. Figure 12-4 demonstrates specifically how Group Policies are applied.

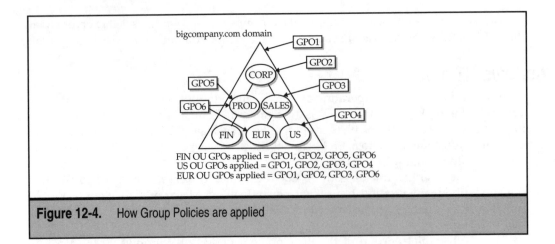

Figure 12-4. How Group Policies are applied

Group Policy Inheritance

Group Policies are applied first *at* the site, then the domain, then OU, then OU, then OU (SDOU-OU-OU), and on down the OU hierarchy. Group Policy inheritance stops at the domain boundary. Group Policies do not by default flow from domain to domain. The settings embodied in the Group Policy object (GPO) are applied *to* domain users and computers, not to sites, domains, OUs, and, strange as it may sound, groups. The term Group Policies stemmed from the concept of grouping all the policies together in one object, which is still possible, just not recommended. Therefore, when you hear "Group Policies," you need to think of "group" as a verb or an action, as in "to group together." Sorry for the digression but it just drove me crazy so I had to find out.

Local Policies

Each computer can have a set of local computer and user policies that reside on that computer. The Local Policy shortcut from Administrative Tools will allow you to configure only the computer portion of the local policy. In the order of GPO processing, the local policy runs first, then the inherited policies, then the directly linked policies, then the No Override policies. The chances of policies applied at the local level running on a computer in an Active Directory domain being overwritten are extremely high. On the other hand, if the computer is a standalone server or laptop and no domain authentication is involved, the local policies are the only policies that apply.

Default GPO Inheritance Behavior

Policies applied directly to the site will affect all computers and users on that site, regardless of the domain to which they belong or the OU where their object is located. Policies applied directly to the domain will affect all users and computers within that domain, regardless of the site they are in or the OU that contains their object. Policies applied directly at a specific OU will affect all computers and users in that particular OU and all computers and users in the OUs below it. As stated earlier, Group Policy inheritance stops at the domain boundary.

Blocking Group Policy Inheritance

It is possible to alter the default behavior by blocking the inheritance of Group Policies from above. To do so, a domain can be configured to block GPO inheritance from a site. An OU can be configured to block GPO inheritance from the domain or an OU above it in the hierarchy. When the Block Policy Inheritance option is checked on the Group Policy tab of a domain or OU, as shown in Figure 12-5, all GPOs from its parent containers are blocked. The only Group Policy settings that will apply at this domain or OU are the settings contained in a GPO that is directly applied at the container. Block Policy inheritance also means that inheritance for child OUs further down the hierarchy begins at the domain or OU that has blocked GPOs from above. In other words, inheritance is blocked for the entire downstream hierarchy of OUs. By default, administrators have the permissions necessary to block inheritance, but this capability can be delegated if desired.

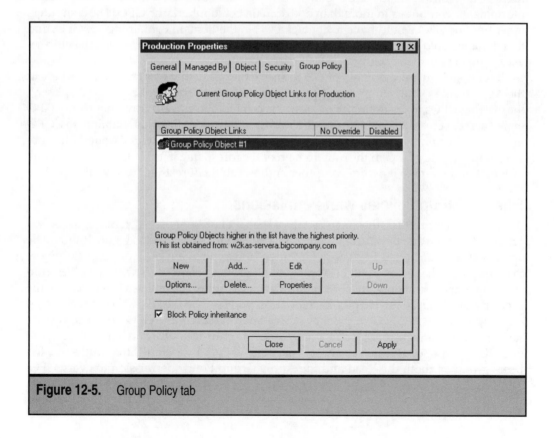

Figure 12-5.   Group Policy tab

No Override Always Wins

In many cases, a high-level administrator may wish to create a Group Policy that will always be applied to the entire domain. For example, he or she may always want to run a specific logon script for every user in the domain. In this example, OU administrators have been given complete power over the GPOs applied at their OU and the ability to block inheritance (not a good plan, as I'm sure any admin would try not to do this, but you know how politics are). Not knowing whether the OU administrators have blocked inheritance, the high-level admin can flag a policy with the No Override option. This way, the policy will be applied to every child container no matter what else is happening. In reality, what happens is that the No Override policy is added to the GPO processing list for every client, and it places itself at the top of the list so it will execute last. See "GPO Processing Order" later in this chapter for more details.

Linking GPOs

When a GPO is applied directly to a container, it is said to be linked to that container. Linking a GPO to a site can have negative performance implications because the GPO actually resides on a domain controller in a single domain. Because a site can contain multiple domains, computers in more than one domain could inherit the GPO. The computers inheriting the GPO would have to contact a DC in the domain containing the GPO, and that domain could be located in a different site across a slow WAN link, which could severely impact the logon performance of client computers.

It is possible to link a domain or OU to an existing GPO that was created elsewhere in the AD forest. As shown in Figure 12-6, click Add in the Group Policy tab to display all the existing GPOs in the entire forest. Admins can link the current container to any GPO in the forest or create a new GPO. In other words, admins can link this container to a GPO in another domain in what amounts to the possibility of a forest-wide Group Policy object. Simply create a GPO in the root domain of the forest, flag it as No Override, and link every other domain to it. Every computer and user in the forest will receive that policy.

Filtering Group Policies with Permissions

As shown in Figure 12-7, the Security tab of the GPO presents an ACL of the users and groups who can read, modify, or delete this Group Policy object and to whom it should be applied. The Security tab is where you "filter" the application of Group Policies. Now that you know that a GPO will be applied to all users or computers within a given container, imagine a situation where the admin wants to apply the policies to just *some* of the users in an OU, not all the users. To achieve this, you remove the Allow for a specific user or group from the Apply Group Policy or Read permission of the GPO. In effect, you are saying, "Even though this Group Policy is applied to this OU and your object is in this OU, this policy doesn't apply to you personally." By default, the Authenticated Users group has both the Read and the Apply Group Policy permission to every GPO.

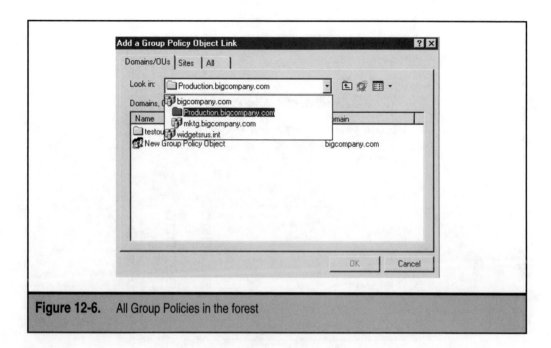

Figure 12-6.   All Group Policies in the forest

Admins are "disabling" the GPO for the one user or group and making its application impossible because they don't have the Apply Group Policy or Read permission for this GPO. This "filtering" functionality allows you to apply policies at a much more granular level. The No Override policy also does not get applied because the user or group does not have the proper permissions for GPO application.

Loopback Processing Mode

In a pure Win2K environment, the GPO settings for a computer are applied normally when the computer starts up and the GPO settings for a user are applied when the user logs on. If any policy settings conflict, the user wins because his or her settings were written last. But what about the situation of a special-use computer such as one found in a bank lobby or a touch-screen demo where you want the computer settings to prevail no matter who logs on. In the Group Policy Editor Computer Configuration | Administrative Templates | System | Group Policy folder, you find the User Group Policy Loopback Processing Mode policy. Here, you can replace or merge the User settings with user settings contained in the computer GPO. Doing so, in effect, rewrites the computer policies after the user policies are applied. So the computer's policies win.

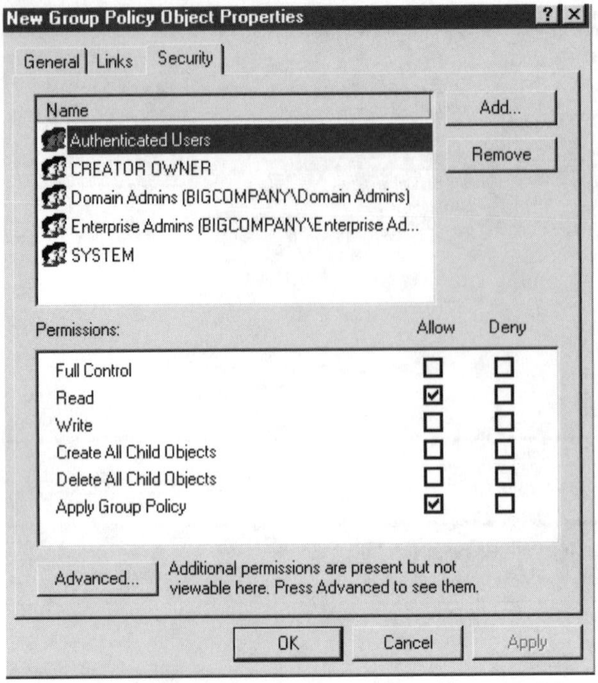

Figure 12-7. GPO Security tab

One Glaring Exception

There is one almost incredible exception to the GPO inheritance rules. Certain policies exist that only GPOs linked directly to a domain can apply. The reason is simple: because the settings specified can only logically apply at the domain level. However, this presents an unbelievably confusing situation for network administrators. Here's the problem: The Group Policy user interface allows an admin to set these same policies at all levels—site, domain, and OU. When setting these policies at the OU level, an admin *who believed the user interface* would think that he or she was setting security policies separately for each OU—policies that perhaps were more stringent than those set at the domain. This cannot be true, however, because the Account Policies can only apply to a domain. Therefore, when applied to an OU, these policies (Password Policy and Account Lockout Policy) are completely *ignored* by the system. That's bad enough, but to make matters worse there is no error message. No little warning box with a yellow triangle appears. There is no notification of any kind. You are simply supposed to magically understand that the Account Policies are only applied at the domain level. Now, I guess, you do understand.

Following are specific policies that appear in the user interface at an OU-linked GPO but are applied only at the domain level:

▼   Account Policies

   ■   Password Policy

   ■   Account Lockout Policy

These two policies are also available from the Domain Security Policy and the Domain Controller Security Policy shortcuts in the Administrative Tools menu. When you set these policies from the Domain Controller Security Policy (OU) shortcut, they are ignored. When you set them from the Domain Security Policy (domain) shortcut, they are applied. Account Policies (Password Policy and Account Lockout Policy) are the only known exceptions to the GPO inheritance rules.

Disabling the GPO

The Group Policy tab Options button allows us to configure two link options. No Override (discussed earlier) prevents other GPOs lower in the OU structure from writing over the settings made by this GPO. Disabled turns off this entire GPO at this container (OU). The GPO will not be applied to this OU and all OUs beneath it. Disabling the entire GPO enables the GPO to apply its settings down to a specific point in the OU hierarchy and then stop without having to block inheritance for *all* policies from above.

DISABLING PORTIONS OF THE GPO   On the OU properties sheet, the Properties button brings up a separate Properties sheet for the Group Policy object itself, as shown in Figure 12-8. The General tab contains the usual identifying information but also includes two configurable options:

▼   Disable Computer Configuration Settings should be checked if a Group Policy
    object contains only settings under the User portion of the object.

▲   Disable User Configuration Settings should be checked if the GPO contains
    only settings under the Computer portion of the object. Microsoft recommends
    disabling unused portions of the GPO to improve logon performance.

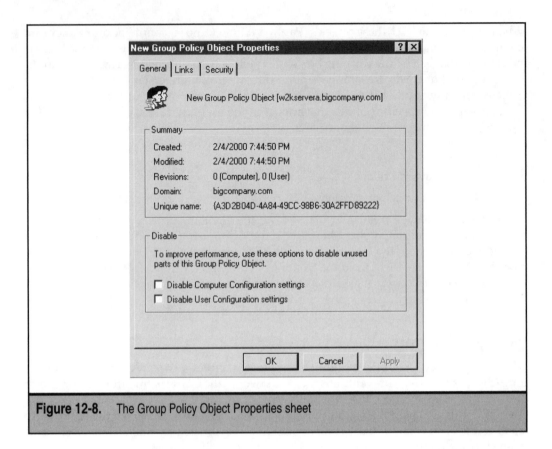

Figure 12-8. The Group Policy Object Properties sheet

GPO Processing Order

On the OU properties sheet with Group Policy selected, all the GPOs linked to this OU are listed, as shown in Figure 12-9. The Up and Down buttons control in what order the GPOs will be processed at this OU. Based on the familiar principle of "Last Write Wins," the first GPO in the list receives the highest priority, so it will be processed last; the second in the list will be processed next to last; and so on. Inherited GPOs from higher in the hierarchy are processed before the directly assigned GPOs. As discussed earlier, any local policies present on the computer itself are processed first.

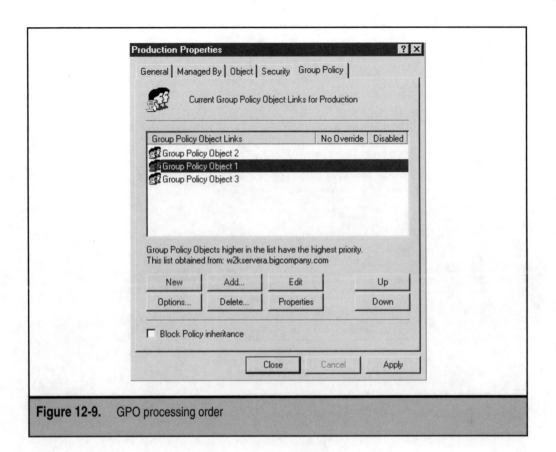

Figure 12-9.   GPO processing order

Periodic Refresh Cycle

Group Policies will always be applied when a computer starts up (startup scripts and Computer Settings only) or a user logs on (logon scripts and User Settings only). But you can also specify that Group Policies be processed periodically. To provide rudimentary load balancing, the periodic interval is set by default to every 90 minutes for non-DC computers and all users with a randomized offset of up to 30 minutes. You can change the default values by using the Group Policy Refresh Interval For... setting in Administrative Templates | System | Group Policy, as shown in Figure 12-10. Look under both the Computer and User Configuration areas. By default, the background refresh of Group Policies is enabled.

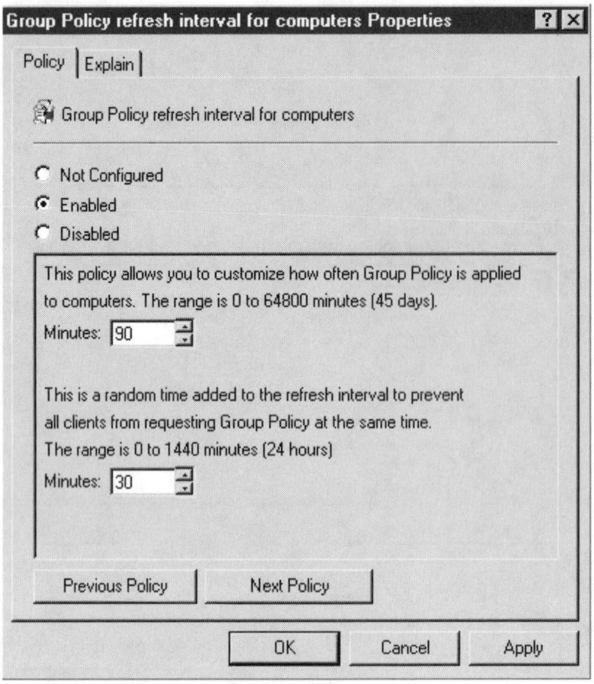

Figure 12-10. Group Policy Refresh Interval for Computers

For domain controllers, the default refresh interval is every 5 minutes with no randomized offset. In all the above cases, the settings will alter the registry of the client computer, a further demonstration that all group policy application is initiated (pulled) by the client, not pushed by the DC.

To disable the periodic refresh of Group Policies completely, in Computer or User Configuration | Administrative Templates | System | Group Policy, select Disable Background Refresh of Group Policy. If you enable this policy, the system waits for the user to log off before updating both the computer and user policies. (That's right: You have to enable the Disable setting in order for it to be disabled. Disabling the Disable setting enables it. Or you could just not configure it to ignore the Disable setting and thereby enable background refresh. Is this a great industry or what?) If you specifically disable this policy, updates are applied with each periodic refresh. If you do not configure this policy at all, updates are applied with each periodic refresh.

To avoid conflicts between the timing of certain events, software installation and folder redirection processing occurs only when computers start up and users log on, not on a periodic basis. Processing these policy sections periodically would produce undesirable results because users on client computers might be working with these elements as a

Group Policy attempts to change or remove them. As shown in Figure 12-11, admins can choose whether other types of policies can be applied during periodic background processing. The default setting for most policies is Apply During Periodic Background Processing (On).

SECEDIT COMMAND LINE TOOL   To force the security policy to refresh on a client computer, admins can use the secedit command line utility. The syntax looks like this:

```
secedit /refreshpolicy {machine_policy | user_policy} [/enforce]
```

machine_policy refreshes the security settings for the local computer.

user_policy refreshes the security settings for the logged-on user account.

/enforce refreshes the security settings even though the GPO has not changed.

The command to refresh the security settings for a computer reads like this:

```
secedit /refreshpolicy machine_policy /enforce
```

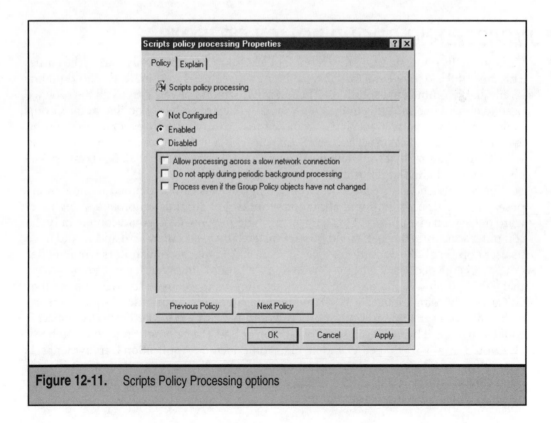

Figure 12-11.   Scripts Policy Processing options

It is important to remember that this command affects the security settings only. No other Group Policy is refreshed with this command.

Win2K Group Policies vs. NT 4.0 System Policies

Which computer or user receives what kind of policy depends solely on whether the computer or user account is located on a server running NT 4.0 or Win2K. In a Mixed mode domain, system policy will be applied if an NT 4.0 BDC authenticates, but Group Policy will be applied if a Win2K DC authenticates. Avoiding these types of inconsistencies is an excellent reason to upgrade all your NT 4.0 BDCs very quickly and switch to Native mode.

More specifically, if a Win2K computer is authenticated by an NT 4.0 BDC, the computer section of the NT 4.0 system policies is applied. The Win2K Group Policy is applied if a Win2K DC authenticates the Win2K computer account. In Mixed mode, if an AD user account is authenticated by an NT 4.0 BDC, the user section of the NT 4.0 system policies is applied. The Win2K Group Policy is applied if a Win2K DC authenticates the AD user account. Admins cannot configure this behavior. Group Policies can only apply to Win2K computers and users. Therefore, when a downlevel client (Win 9*x*, NT 4.0) is authenticated by either a Win2K DC or an NT 4.0 BDC, the downlevel client receives its appropriate system policy (Win 9*x* – config.pol; NT 4.0 – ntconfig.pol).

ADMINISTERING GROUP POLICY OBJECTS

Unfortunately, understanding the technology of Group Policies is only part of the battle. This area of the Active Directory, like so many other things in Win2K, has no right answers, just recommended solutions. The folks in Redmond have given us all the rope we need to either lasso the bulls in the china shop or hang ourselves. Looking at the Group Policy technology, you can see that it would be possible to configure every desired setting in a single Group Policy object and apply that one object to the entire domain and be done with it. And I'm sure that some smaller organizations just might do that. But I can't possibly recommend it for larger or more diverse enterprises.

The recommended approach to Group Policy objects can be defined as single-purpose. Single-purpose GPOs will allow for simplicity of administration and straightforward delegation of authority. For example, a single-purpose GPO could contain only the computer security settings. It could be administered by the security staff and would have its user portion disabled to improve performance. All other administrators would either not possess the necessary editing permissions or would simply agree not to mess with that GPO. Admins would also agree not to configure any security settings in any other GPOs. Another single-purpose GPO might contain only the Application Deployment assignments for users. Its computer portion would be disabled for better performance. It could be managed by the Desktop/Workstation or End-User Computing group. Nobody else would mess with that GPO and no one would include Application Deployment settings in any other GPO. You start to get the picture. Once the various functions were separated, admins could also decide to which container objects and even groups they should be applied at a much more granular level.

CREATING GROUP POLICY OBJECTS

The easiest way to create or modify Group Policy objects is in the MMC Active Directory Users and Computers snap-in. Simply highlight the domain or OU where you want to create or modify the GPO, right-click, and select Properties. Click on the Group Policy tab. Six major options appear near the bottom of the dialog box. If you wish to create a brand-new GPO, click New. A New Group Policy object appears. To configure it, click Edit. If you wish to add a link to an existing GPO somewhere else in the forest, click Add. To edit an existing GPO, click Edit. To delete an existing GPO, click Delete. You are prompted as to whether you want to delete the link to the GPO or the GPO itself. Click OK or Cancel. The Options button gives you two choices: No Override (to make this GPO always win) and Disabled (to turn this GPO off at this container). The Properties button allows you to disable only part of the GPO, view the links that this GPO possesses, and set the ACL on exactly who can do what to this GPO. The Security tab is also where you filter the application of this GPO.

Who Can Create or Modify Group Policy Objects

To set Group Policy for an Active Directory container, you must have a Windows 2000 domain controller installed, and you must have read and write permission to, first, access the Shared System volume of domain controllers (sysvol) and, second, modify permissions to the AD container object. These permissions can be obtained by appropriate group membership or through the Delegation of Control wizard.

Group Policy Storage Locations

Group policy objects are made up of two components: the Group Policy container, which holds the version and status information, and the Group Policy template, which stores the actual policy settings. The Group Policy containers are stored in the Active Directory, specifically in the System container | Policies folder. Each Group Policy container is listed by its GUID. The Group Policy templates are stored separately on the Shared System Volume. Specifically, you can locate them at \%SYSTEMROOT%\SYSVOL\sysvol\ %domainname%\Policies. Because the Group Policy information is stored in two different locations, these locations can be out of sync from time to time during the replication cycle. When this occurs, the computers or users affected by these policies will continue to receive (during periodic processing of policies) the last GPOs that were applied successfully until they are again successfully synchronized.

DC Options

When a GPO is edited, it "focuses" on a specific DC to receive its changes. Which DC becomes an important decision. Since a GPO is an Active Directory object like any other, it can only be updated on one DC, and then the altered GPO will be replicated to the rest of the domain normally. To avoid the potential conflicts that might occur when two admins are editing the same GPO on two different DCs, point all the admins to the same DC for editing the GPO. Please remember that some DCs may be across slow WAN links.

There are two methods available to set the DC options for Group Policy. The manual method is to use the Group Policy MMC snap-in, where the administrator can set domain controller options by using the DC Options dialog box. To select a domain controller for GPO editing, open the Group Policy MMC snap-in and select DC Options from the View menu. The Options for Domain Controller Selection dialog box shown in Figure 12-12 appears. Here, you can specify a DC to use for editing the Group Policy object.

The available choices for the Options for Domain Controller Selection dialog box are:

▼ **The One with the Operations Master Token for The PDC Emulator**   This is the default and by far the best option. It forces the Group Policy MMC snap-in to use the same DC to update the settings no matter where the GPO is edited from. Choosing this option will go a long way toward preventing the data loss that can occur when two admins are making changes to the same GPO on different DCs. This is the strongly recommended option.

■ **The One Used by the Active Directory Snap-Ins**   This option uses the DC that the Active Directory MMC snap-in tool is currently using. It enforces no controls.

▲ **Use Any Available Domain Controller**   This is the least desirable option, in most cases, because it allows the Group Policy snap-in to pick any available DC, most likely a DC on its own site close by.

All of these manual options can be overridden by a group policy setting. The setting is available in the Group Policy MMC snap-in | User Configuration | Administrative Templates | System | Group Policy folder.

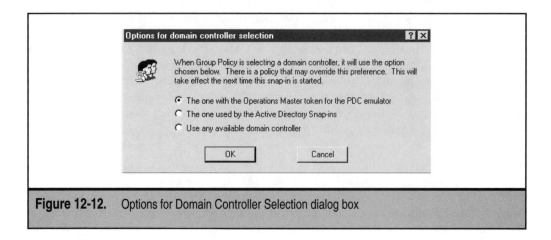

Figure 12-12.   Options for Domain Controller Selection dialog box

Group Policy Editor

The Group Policy editor is both an MMC standalone snap-in and an extension of the MMC Active Directory Users and Computers snap-in. When editing a Group Policy object (GPO), you can change any of the 629 built-in settings as well as a myriad of user-configurable options. The best news is that each one of the 629 built-in settings comes with a one page explanation of exactly what it does on the Explain tab, as shown in Figure 12-13. Group policies are divided into five major areas:

▼   Administrative Templates

■   Security Settings

■   Scripts

■   Folder Redirection

▲   Application Deployment

A detailed explanation of each major category follows.

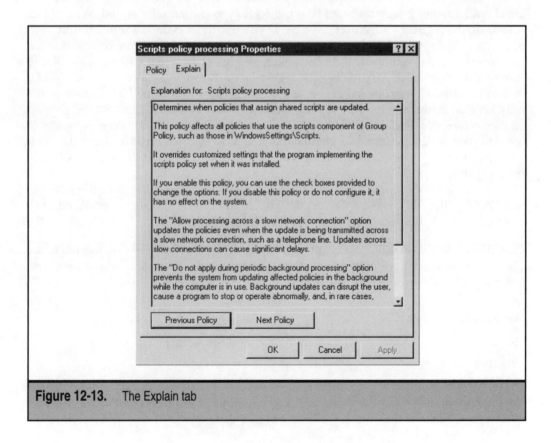

Figure 12-13.   The Explain tab

Administrative Templates

Administrative templates are ASCII text files that require basically the same type of .adm syntax that is used in NT 4.0/95/98 system policies. The purpose of administrative templates is to alter the workstation/server registry to achieve the functionality (or lack of functionality) that the administrator desires. Usually, administrative templates are used to lock down a workstation in a manner similar to that of the NT 4.0 Zero Administration Kit (ZAK). As in NT 4.0, a few standard templates ship with Win2K, but you can, of course, always roll your own. However, the Win2K default administrative templates include most of the functionality from the NT 4.0 templates (winnt.adm, common.adm), as well as many additional settings for disk quotas, group policies, network connections, printers, and so on. The separate templates for users and computers reflect the two major portions of the workstation's registry.

TATTOOING THE REGISTRY   One large difference between the NT 4.0 system policies and the Win2K administrative templates is that registry changes implemented by the Win2K Group Policy are removed automatically if the Group Policy is removed. When an NT 4.0 system policy implemented a change in the workstation registry, the change remained in effect until another policy reversed it or the registry was manually edited. We call this "tattooing the registry." In Win2K, as long as you use the standard administrative templates that ship with Win2K, the changes in the workstation registry are removed when the Group Policy is removed. If the admin creates his or her own custom .adm files (a common practice in NT 4.0), the Win2K registry is "tattooed" just as it was with NT 4.0 system policies. This is not the end of the world. It simply means that administrators must keep on their toes with the use of custom .adm files in Win2K. Admins must depend on themselves, not the system in this case, and understand the negative consequences of being too busy to document what might happen. This is especially true in an organization with high mobility where administrators are being moved to other departments within the company.

According to Microsoft, any policy setting that is not stored in either the HKLM\ SOFTWARE\Policies registry key or the HKLM\SOFTWARE\Microsoft\Windows\ CurrentVersion\policies registry key will "tattoo" the registry.

COMPUTER CONFIGURATION   As shown in Figure 12-14 and in the following table, the Computer Configuration settings will affect the computer section of the client's registry. In the registry editor you can see it as HKEY_LOCAL_MACHINE (HKLM).

Windows Components	Settings
NetMeeting	1 built-in setting
Internet Explorer	8 built-in settings
Task Scheduler	7 built-in settings
Windows Installer	13 built-in settings

Windows Components	Settings
System	
Logon	12 built-in settings
Disk Quotas	6 built-in settings
DNS Client	1 built-in setting
Group Policy	16 built-in settings
Windows File Protection	4 built-in settings
Network	
Offline Files	17 built-in settings
Network and Dialup Connections	1 built-in setting
Printers	13 built-in settings

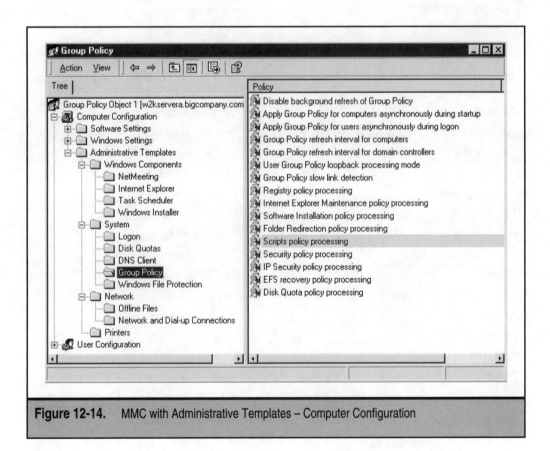

Figure 12-14.   MMC with Administrative Templates – Computer Configuration

USER CONFIGURATION   As shown in Figure 12-15 and in the following table, the User Configuration settings will affect the user section of the client's registry. In the registry editor you can see it as HKEY_CURRENT_USER (HKCU).

Windows Components	Settings
NetMeeting	14 built-in settings
Application Sharing	7 built-in settings
Audio & Video	6 built-n settings
Options Page	5 built-in settings
Internet Explorer	30 built-in settings
Internet Control Panel	6 built-in settings
Offline Pages	11 built-in settings
Browser menus	16 built-in settings
Toolbars	3 built-in settings
Persistence Behavior	5 built-in settings
Administrator Approved Controls	12 built-in settings
Windows Explorer	20 built-in settings
Common Open File Dialog	3 built-in settings
Microsoft Management Console	2 built-in settings
Restricted/Permitted snap-ins	29 built-in settings
Extension snap-ins	26 built-in settings
Group Policy	12 built-in settings
Task Scheduler	7 built-in settings
Windows Installer	4 built-in settings
Start Menu & Taskbar	24 built-in settings
Desktop	10 built-in settings
Active Desktop	11 built-in settings
Active Directory	3 built-in settings
Control Panel	3 built-in settings
Add/Remove Programs	10 built-in settings
Display	9 built-in settings
Printers	5 built-in settings
Regional Options	1 built-in setting

Windows Components	Settings
Network	
Offline Files	12 built-in settings
Network and Dial-up Connections	19 built-in settings
System	10 built-in settings
Logon/Logoff	14 built-in settings
Group Policy	6 built-in settings

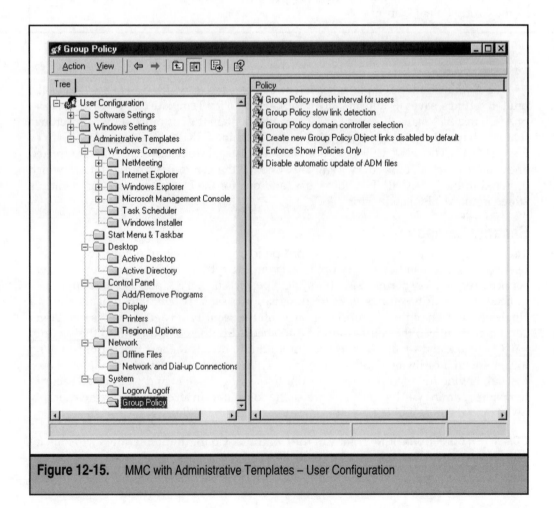

Figure 12-15.   MMC with Administrative Templates – User Configuration

Win2K Administrative Template Files
Incompatible with Legacy Systems

The basic file format of the Registry.pol files in the Win2K Group Policy Template is different from the administrative templates (.adm files) used in NT 4.0 and Win 9x. System policy files created by the NT 4.0 and Win 9x System Policy Editor(s) using NT 4.0 and Win 9x administrative templates can be applied only to the operating system on which they were created. The NT 4.0 System Policy Editor produced a binary file in contrast to the Registry.pol file created by Administrative Templates section of the Win2K Group Policy snap-in, which is a text file with embedded binary strings. The upshot is that the Registry.pol file cannot be viewed or edited outside the Group Policy snap-in.

The Administrative Templates section of Group Policies, which contains a total of 454 built-in settings, saves its information in the Group Policy Template on Sysvol in the form of ASCII text files named Registry.pol. These files contain the customized registry settings that you have configured to be applied to the Machine (HKEY_LOCAL_MACHINE) or User (HKEY_CURRENT_USER) portions of the registry. Two Registry.pol files are created and stored in the Group Policy Template, one for the Computer Configuration, which is stored in the \MACHINE subdirectory, and one for the User Configuration, which is stored in the \USER subdirectory.

Security Settings

The security settings area covers password policy, account lockout policy, audit policy, user rights assignments, security options, event log settings, restricted groups, system services, registry key permissions, file system permissions, IPSec policies, and public key policies. The security settings allow for the creation of security templates that alter, with a single application of the appropriate policy, all the security-related elements of a target computer. In effect, the settings amount to sheep-dipping computers into the security vat. One dunk and—*poof!*—it's secure. Important to note is the fact that admins will no longer spend inordinate amounts of time executing checklists of post-installation tasks. Instead, having invested the time up front to develop detailed and well-tested security templates, admins will be able to secure all the computers in an entire department simply by turning them on and letting the computers log on to the domain.

COMPUTER CONFIGURATION   Many of the Computer Configuration settings will look familiar from NT 4.0. The group policy or local policy area is the only place where these settings can be configured, as shown in the following table.

Account Policies (See "One Glaring Exception" earlier in this chapter)	Settings
Password Policy	6 built-in settings
Account Lockout Policy	3 built-in settings
Local Policies	
Audit Policy	9 built-in settings
User Rights Assignment	34 built-in settings
Security Options	40 built-in settings
Event Log	
Settings for Event Logs	13 built-in settings
Restricted Groups	User-configurable settings
System Services	67 built-in settings
Registry	User-configurable settings
File System	User-configurable settings
Public Key Policies	
Encrypted Data Recovery Agents	User-configurable settings
Automatic Certificate Request Settings	User-configurable settings
Trusted Root Certification Authorities	User-configurable settings
Enterprise Trust	User-configurable settings
IP Security Policies on Active Directory	3 built-in settings

USER CONFIGURATION   Only one setting here deals with certificates issued to the user.

Public Key Policies	
Enterprise Trust	User-configurable settings

The Security Settings group policies contain a total of 175 built-in settings plus a number of user configurable settings.

Scripts

Under the scripts policy, there are four new areas to place files in script format: Machine Startup and Shutdown scripts under the Computer Configuration folder, and User Logon and Logoff scripts under the User Configuration folder. More than one script file can be placed in each of the four areas. The scripts will be executed in the order in which they appear in the Group policy object. The syntax of these scripts can be any language that the Windows Script Host supports.

You should also be aware that there is a Group Policy setting called Maximum Wait Time for Group Policy Scripts found in Computer Configuration | Administrative Templates | System | Logon. This policy limits the total amount of time that these scripts applied by Group policy are allowed to finish running: startup, logon, logoff, and shutdown. If the scripts have not finished running when time expires, the system stops processing scripts and sends an error to the system log. By default, Win2K lets the combined set of scripts run up to 600 seconds (ten minutes), but you can use this policy to adjust the interval.

COMPUTER CONFIGURATION   These scripts will be applied when a computer is booted up or shut down with the shutdown command:

Scripts	Settings
Startup	User-configurable settings
Shutdown	User-configurable settings

USER CONFIGURATION   These scripts will be applied when the user logs on or logs off respectively:

Scripts	Settings
Logon	User-configurable settings
Logoff	User-configurable settings

By design, all settings within the scripts policies are user-configurable.

Folder Redirection

Folder redirection does exactly what its name implies: It redirects a specific local folder on the user's workstation computer to another path on a remote server. The interesting element here is that the user does not know that the folders are really on the server. All the folders appear as if they were stored locally. The only local folders eligible for redirection are Application Data, Desktop, My Documents, My Pictures, and Start Menu. Folders are redirected based on the user's membership in an Active Directory security group but cannot be limited to a single specific user account. A redirected folder can also be used in conjunction with offline folders.

USER CONFIGURATION   Because only users can access folders, there is no folder redirection for computers. Users in a specific group will get their folders redirected.

Application Data	User-configurable settings
Desktop	User-configurable settings
My Documents	User-configurable settings
My Pictures	User-configurable settings
Start Menu	User-configurable settings

OFFLINE FOLDERS   When a Win2K Professional workstation connects to a remote shared folder, the concept of offline folders comes into play. Here's the scenario: A user getting ready to go on a trip is sitting at a Win2K laptop that is connected to the network. The user knows he or she will need certain files on the laptop that normally reside on the server. The user has a drive letter mapped to that folder. The user does nothing. He or she executes a shutdown, leaves, boards an airplane, turns on the laptop, goes to Windows Explorer, sees that the mapped drive is still visible, opens the mapped drive, and sees the folder with the files in it. The user makes changes in the files. Upon returning to the office, the user hooks up to the network and *BAM!* The files are synchronized up to the server. Too good to be true? On the contrary, this is a normal Win2K operation.

Here's how it works: The drive mapping is performed normally. While at the Win2K Pro laptop, you open Windows Explorer, simply right-click the folder that you always want on your laptop, and select Make Available Offline, as shown in Figure 12-16. If there are subfolders, a confirmation screen asks if the subfolders should be made available offline as well. You confirm the selection and *BAM!* That folder will always be available on your laptop until you tell it not to be available.

The user only performs this action one time per folder. It's a "set and forget" function. Offline folders are enabled by default in Win2K Professional. You can adjust the settings for Offline folders in Windows Explorer | Tools | Folder Options | Offline Files tab. Synchronization settings can be adjusted or synchronization can be forced from the Desktop | Start | Programs | Accessories | Synchronize shortcut. Offline folders can be used in conjunction with a Group Policy specifying redirected folders to create a nearly user-proof desktop environment.

But what happens if the user updates the file on the road while, back at the office, a co-worker changes the copy on the server? The Synchronization Manager is smart enough to notice. It will display a warning and present the user with the choice of overwriting or renaming the file. You can see why I call this feature the "briefcase that works."

For the true nerds reading this, the offline file cache is located on the workstation in a well-hidden folder named %SYSTEMROOT%\CSC (client-side caching). It is possible to move this cache, but, because you can't see it, you must use the Win2K Resource Kit tool called cachemov.exe to execute the move.

Application Deployment

The Application Deployment folder allows Windows Installer-based (.msi) application packages to be assigned to users or computers, or to be published to users. Assigned application packages appear as shortcuts on the Programs menu even before they are installed.

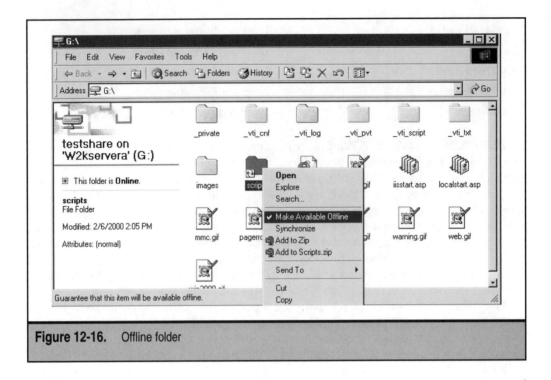

Figure 12-16. Offline folder

The assigned application installs automatically when the user invokes it. When an application is assigned, it also becomes resilient, or self-healing. Suppose, after the application is installed, a user deletes a file that the assigned application needs in order to run (say, a user cleaning the hard drive decided to delete all files ending in .dll because they are never used). The Windows Installer remembers where the deleted files were originally installed from (the installation point must remain an active UNC share), copies the files to the local workstation, and launches the application *without presenting an error message to the user*. Published application packages appear in the Add/Remove Programs section of the Control Panel and the user can install them when desired.

COMPUTER CONFIGURATION Computers can only have the software applications assigned to them. Applications cannot be published to a computer.

| Software Installation | User-configurable settings |

USER CONFIGURATION Users can have applications deployed by group policies either assigned or published to them.

| Software Installation | User-configurable settings |

THE WINDOWS INSTALLER SERVICE   The full functionality of the Windows 2000 Application Deployment features can only be realized if the client is running Win2K, Active Directory is installed on a Win2K DC, Group Policies are configured, and the application has a native msi installer package to assist in the remote installation. "Where can I get one of those msis?" you say. Bad news: They come from the software vendor. Good news: Any software vendor who wants the "Runs with Windows 2000" logo on its box has to provide msi installer packages that include the capability for a total (and successful) remote uninstall. The problem, of course, is that no msi installer packages come with existing software applications; only new versions have them. Office 2000 ships complete with msi installer packages, as does Win2K itself (Support Tools, Resource Kit).

These msi packages use the Windows Installer service to accomplish the impossible feat of performing hands-off application software installations. The applications install under the security context of the Windows Installer service, which logs on as a local system account on the client computer. A normal user with no elevated privileges whatsoever can preside over an installation that requires both the file system and the registry to be updated. If you wish, you can extend these elevated privileges to a user to all applications outside of the Group Policy Deployment. To do so, look in the Computer Configuration | Administrative Templates | Windows Components | Windows Installer folder for the Group Policy setting. Another Group Policy setting in the same location allows admins to completely disable the Windows Installer service. It is important to note that the Windows Installer service is running by default on every Win2K client computer. The client performs the installation so the client needs the service.

The native msi functionality also allows for automated upgrades to software packages that have been installed by the Windows Installer. When you add the new package, you tell the policy what existing application you are upgrading (say, Word 97) and what type of upgrade you wish to perform: required (mandatory) or optional. A mandatory upgrade replaces the old application with the new one (say, Word 2000). An optional upgrade, on the other hand, isn't really an upgrade at all. The system installs the new version of the application but leaves the old version on the client computer.

A similar concept applies to the automated removal of applications that the Windows Installer service installed. Admins can deploy a forced or an optional removal of an existing software application. Depending on the policy setting, a forced removal deletes the installed application when the client computer starts up or the user logs on. An optional removal does not remove the application from the client computer. Rather, the application is removed from the list of deployed applications. Users who have it installed can continue to use it, but there will be no new deployments of the application.

REPACKAGING EXISTING APPLICATIONS   Hopefully, new applications and new versions of existing applications will ship with a native Windows Installer package in the months ahead. But what about the existing applications you already have? Is there a way to automate their installation onto a Win2K client? Yes. It's called "repackaging." The repackaging process involves two networked computers and a third-party repackaging tool from Veritas Software called WinINSTALL LE that ships with Win2K Server.

The first computer is the reference computer. Here you will install Win2K Professional and the application that you are repackaging. The second computer is basically your camera computer. You will use it to take multiple snapshots (before and after the application is installed) of the reference computer during the repackaging process. The steps for repackaging are as follows:

1. Install Win2K on the reference computer. Do not install any applications. Do not install the application to be repackaged.

2. Install WinINSTALL LE on the camera computer. You'll find the file swiadmle.msi on the Win2K Server CD in the \VALUEADD\3RDPARTY\ MGMT\WINSTLE folder. After the WinINSTALL LE installation, share the wininstall folder (\Program Files\VERITAS Software\Wininstall). You'll need at least 250MB of free space in this folder to hold the temporary files that are created by this process.

3. On the reference computer, quit all applications, including screen savers and anti-virus software. Using a command prompt, run the Discover Wizard (discoz.exe) from the share point on the camera computer. Follow the instructions to take a snapshot (the before snapshot) of the reference computer. You'll have to specify a location and filename for the eventual package.

4. When the Discover Wizard is finished with the before snapshot, install the application to be repackaged on the reference computer. (Do not repackage any applications that install Internet Explorer. These will conflict with the version of IE that is installed automatically by Win2K.)

5. On the reference computer, launch the newly installed application. Configure the application options that you want installed in the repackaged version. Create shortcuts. This is your one and only shot to get this app set up just the way you want. Now's your chance to avoid unnecessary administrative effort and troubleshooting calls later on.

6. Restart the reference computer to be absolutely certain that the changes are written to the registry.

   After the reference computer restarts, run the Discover Wizard again across the network from a command prompt on the reference computer. You will be asked if you want to take a new Before snapshot or an After snapshot. Click Take an After Snapshot. Ignore any warnings about paths. The Discover Wizard creates three files and places them in the folder specified for the Before snapshot:

   An .msi file: The Windows Installer package
   An .nai file: For internal WinINSTALL purposes
   A .reg file: For making the necessary registry changes

7. Test the package by installing it on a third computer. Make sure all aspects of the installed application function according to plan.

This package is now finished. If you wish to use the same reference computer for another package, I recommend a complete reinstallation of Win2K Professional to avoid the complications that vestigial registry entries from incomplete application uninstalls can cause. Don't try to get too fancy here. One application per package is the recommended best practice.

These repackaged applications will not install in the same way as the native .msi packages. Group Policy Software Installation cannot be used to deploy repackaged applications. Admins must place the .msi package either in a script or on the RunOnce list (HKLM\SOFTWARE\Microsoft\Windows\CurrentVersion\RunOnce) in the registry of the client computer.

As compared to native .msi packages, with repackaged applications there is a significant reduction in the overall functionality provided:

▼   Applications cannot be published or assigned; they are simply installed

■   No resiliency or self-healing functionality

▲   The user might need to be involved in the installation

CLIENT CONNECTIONS OVER SLOW LINKS

An authorized user logging on to a network using a remote access dial-up connection is a very common situation. Depending on the user's connection media, remote access connections can occur at speeds as slow as a 14.4Kbps or as fast as a 768Kbps, 1Mbps (on a DSL line), or even faster. Remote access will continue to grow as more organizations shift to full- or part-time telecommuting to save money and retain staff. The question for network administrators is: "Do you want the system to respond differently to clients when the connection speed is considered slow?" And here is a second question for administrators: "Exactly what is considered slow?"

Slow Link Detection

By default, Win2K detects "slow links" between the user's computer and the remote server. Slow link detection is enabled separately for Group Policies and User Profiles. And, within Group Policies, it is enabled separately for computers and users.

Group Policy Application over Slow Links

The default definition of "slow link" is 500Kbps for Group Policies. This definition is separately configurable in the Administrative Templates | System | Group Policy folder under Computer Configuration and User Configuration. You can disable slow link detection for Group Policies in the same location. When disabled, all links will be considered "fast" for Group Policy processing.

When Group Policy detects a slow link, the system must decide whether or not to apply policy over the slow link. The Security Policy and Administrative Templates will always be applied no matter what the speed of the link.

The default settings for what policies will be applied across a slow link are as follows:

Group Policies Applied over a Slow Link	Default Setting
Security Policy	ON (and cannot be turned off)
Administrative Templates	ON (and cannot be turned off)
Registry Policy	OFF
Internet Explorer Maintenance Policy	OFF
Software Installation	OFF
Scripts	OFF
Folder Redirection	OFF
IP Security Policy	OFF
EFS Recovery Policy	OFF
Disk Quota Policy	OFF

For all but the Security Policy and the Administrative Templates, a separate policy is provided for toggling each of these settings to ON or OFF in the Administrative Templates | System | Group Policy folder under Computer Configuration.

User Profiles Download over Slow Links

Similar to NT 4.0, a local copy of the user's profile is stored under the %SYSTEMROOT%\ Documents and Settings folder for each user that has ever logged onto a computer. Administrators can either allow the local profile to be used (the default behavior) or establish a roaming profile on a server. The admin then points the user account to the location of the roaming profile in the Profile tab of the user account Properties. Depending on the user, the profile can become quite large. By default, the profile size is unlimited, but it can be limited in the User Configuration | Administrative Templates | System | Logon folder. Because the default size is already configured at 30MB, admins must decide whether a roaming profile should be downloaded to the client computer over a slow link.

Operating under an independent set of rules, the default definition of "slow link" for user profiles is 500Kbps for IP connections or 120 milliseconds for SMB connections. The definition is configurable only under Computer Configuration in the Administrative Templates | System | Logon folder. If the link is determined to be slow, the local copy of the user's profile is used. You can turn off slow link detection for user profiles by enabling the Do Not Detect Slow Network Connections policy. If this setting is enabled, all connections will be considered "fast" for user profile downloads and the entire user profile will be downloaded. From this same location in the GP Editor, you can also set a policy to delete the cached (local) copy of the roaming profile. However, do not enable this setting if you are using slow link detection. If you enable the setting, there will be no local copy of the user profile for the system to use if the link is determined to be slow and either the roaming profile or the default profile settings will be loaded.

SUMMARY

Entire books could easily be written on the topics covered in this chapter. And I'm sure they will be. My goal has been, with regard to client computer administration, to introduce you to many of the features and some of the pitfalls of the functionality provided by Windows 2000. This area contains much of the promise of Windows 2000. However, its biggest downside is the necessity for an all-Win2K Active Directory world on the network. For most of us, that is a year or two away at least. But the planning for these elements should begin now as you lay out the structure for your Active Directory. Remember that the OU structure is in place for two primary reasons: delegated administration and the application of Group Policies. An in-depth understanding of Group Policies will clarify many of the decision points during the Active Directory design process.

CHAPTER 13

Windows 2000 Authentication and Identification

For many, security is an extremely complex and intimidating subject. In order to safeguard your Windows 2000 environment, you need to be familiar with the various security-related technologies that are directly integrated with Win2K. There are also multitudes of other choices to help protect your investment, all of which will be discussed shortly.

Security is a paramount concern to keep sensitive, personal, financial, and mission-critical information safe and private. Microsoft has been under tremendous public pressure to provide a secure, enterprise-level operating system. Windows NT provided a solid security infrastructure for many, but, over time, more and more security risks were exposed. However, to their credit, as those security risks were uncovered, Microsoft responded quickly and responsibly by providing security patches and service packs to safeguard NT systems. Many of the security schemes that were longed for in Windows NT have made their debut in Windows 2000.

The Windows 2000 security infrastructure builds upon and strengthens the NT 4.0 security model. In fact, one of the primary design goals for Win2K was to provide the highest level of security for your environment. In order to achieve this, Microsoft launched a Web site during the beta stages using a Win2K server running IIS on the Internet and asked everyone to try and hack the server. Only the system's internal security mechanisms were used to protect the server from intrusion, the idea being to test Win2K's built-in security and attempt to uncover any possible vulnerability. Despite attacks, the server was reportedly never actually penetrated. Now, Windows 2000 has an unprecedented level of security to protect your network environment.

This chapter is intended to uncover the security mechanisms used in Windows 2000 and to examine the necessary steps required to strengthen your Win2K environment. Other security measures that can be used in conjunction with Windows 2000's built-in capabilities are also discussed in this chapter.

SECURITY ESSENTIALS

Before you begin securing your environment, you must realize that you'll never completely prevent unauthorized access no matter which technologies, including operating systems, you use. As the saying goes, "Where there's a will, there's a way." If someone really wants to get into a system, he or she can eventually find a way. Given enough time, money, technology, and commitment, intruders will get in. The best thing you can do is to make unauthorized access as difficult as possible or at least not worth the hassle. The more effort you put into securing your environment, the less likely is the chance that your information will be compromised, modified, or completely destroyed. It's also important to remember to weigh the risks against the value of the information.

Another important thing to remember is that you can have all the security technologies at your disposal, but they're only as good as your implementation of them. Not implementing them at all leaves you vulnerable to the outside world. Inform your users about the security mechanisms currently in place and the proper procedures that they must follow. Proper implementation of system-wide security and user awareness, together with ongoing vigilance on the part of the security administrator, can provide you and your users with a highly functional yet secure network environment.

Evaluation

The cost of securing your systems versus the value of the information is an important issue to consider. A good place to start is to determine the monetary value of the information. If the information was destroyed, altered, or stolen, how much would it cost you?

Determining a monetary value for some types of information is extremely difficult, if not impossible. For example, if you're responsible for securing a hospital's data, how would you calculate the value of patient records?

On the other extreme, you may conclude that your information is not very important and therefore not worth the effort to secure. In this case, instead of thinking in terms of the information not being of value, consider what the costs would be if your network infrastructure was compromised or destroyed. How much time and effort would be needed to rebuild the corporate infrastructure? What would be the impact on the company's reputation? Would the publicity surrounding a security breach negatively impact sales? What is the bottom line? The company's future?

The biggest thing to remember is securing your resources. If you can at least strike a balance between the cost of securing your Win2K environment and the value of your information, you're headed in the right direction. Fortunately, Windows 2000 equips you with a variety of security mechanisms by which you can create a solid security infrastructure without incurring additional costs.

Security Standards

All products tell you what their important features are and list the standards that they support. What's imperative is examining how they measure up to other products and how well they support those standards. Looking at how products compare and how well they support standards is especially important when you're reviewing security features and/or products. Comparing a product to measurement standards is one way of evaluating how well it protects the network environment. This is similar to how industry benchmarks, such as the TPC-C and TPC-D, analyze a system's performance characteristics.

C2

Issued in December, 1985, the United States Department of Defense Trusted Computer System Evaluation Criteria (TCSEC), also known as the Orange Book, *is* one of the most notable and widely used security certifications in the industry. Several government-rated security levels are outlined in the Orange Book, which is part of the larger Rainbow Series, so-called because each book is known by a different color. The most popular security level in the PC world is the C2 Security Level. C2 is a baseline security measurement that is applied to operating systems on standalone PCs. If your computer is connected to a network, it can't be truly C2-certified.

The primary tenets of the C2 security level are discretionary access control, object reuse, identification and authentication, audit, strong internal technical architecture, and detailed security-related documentation. To learn more about the TCSEC, check out this Web site: www.radium.ncsc.mil/tpep/library/tcsec/index.html.

Several other security levels for networked computers are basically interpretations of the Orange Book levels, including the Red and Blue Book interpretations.

The C2 evaluation process is very strenuous and usually quite time-consuming (NT 4.0 took three years to be evaluated). A standalone NT 4.0 server was evaluated at the E3/F-C2 level and an NT 4.0 server implementation has recently been awarded C2 certification.

In a C2 evaluation, the internals of the operating system are torn apart and the basic system integrity is examined. Then the tools and procedures are scrutinized for flaws. Finally, the documentation is examined both from the standpoint of a network administrator and a developer. After the evaluation is complete, the system is said to be "evaluated at the C2 level." This simply means, "We looked at it real hard and *if* you implement it correctly, it will be pretty secure."

C2 certification means that a C2-evaluated operating system (such as NT 4.0) has been installed and implemented in a production environment with specific hardware. A team of experts visits the site and examines the implementation, the hardware, and every other aspect that affects security. Then the team certifies *this implementation, this site* as C2. If you use different hardware in the future, you may lose the certification. If you move equipment to a different room, you may lose your certification. If you alter your installation or monitoring procedures, you may lose your certification. If you install Windows 2000 (before it's evaluated), you may lose your certification. All this in spite of the fact that everyone knows your organization would be *more* secure with Win2K than NT 4.0. Such is the way of the DOD.

Windows 2000 is just starting the C2 evaluation process. Considering the fact that Windows 2000 only strengthens the NT 4.0 security model, it will no doubt be successful in getting the C2-level evaluation.

Common Criteria

Recently, the ISO (International Organization for Standardization) and the IEC (International Electrotechnical Commission) formed a Joint Technical Committee, the ISO/IEC JTC 1, to develop worldwide standards for information technology. In May of 1998, the committee published a document known as ISO/IEC 15408 that was adopted by the Common Criteria Implementation Board and republished under the title "Common Criteria for Information Technology Security Evaluation, version 2.0." Lest you think this Common Criteria fancy mumbo-jumbo is just the work of a couple of upstart security nerds, here is a list of the seven governmental agencies in the Common Criteria Project Sponsoring Organizations:

Common Criteria Project Sponsoring Organizations

Canada	Communications Security Establishment
France	Service Central de la Sécurité des Systèmes d'Information
Germany	Bundesamt für Sicherheit in der Informationstechnik
Netherlands	Netherlands National Communications Security Agency
United Kingdom	Communications-Electronics Security Group
United States	National Institute of Standards and Technology
United States	National Security Agency

Not too shabby, eh? The goal of developing and disseminating this document is summed up in one sentence from the "Scope" section of the document: "By establishing such a common criteria base, the results of an IT security evaluation will be meaningful to a wider audience." Currently, every security evaluation criteria and certification is specific to the country in which it was made. As our world continues to shrink, the Common Criteria allows an international, common IT security framework to be developed that will eventually set minimum standards for worldwide IT security. Because it excludes networks, the Orange Book does not really allow for the flexibility that is needed in today's ultra-connected IT environments. The Rainbow Series and the Orange Book were pioneers in the area of IT security standards. But the concepts envisioned in 1985 and even the subsequent revisions (the last revision/interpretation of the Orange Book was 1991, two years before NT 3.1 shipped) have been eclipsed by the rapidly changing realities of ubiquitous LANs and the Internet. The Orange Book is where we've been, and standing on the shoulders of its predecessors, the Common Criteria is where we are going. To learn more about the Common Criteria, check out this Web site: http://csrc.nist.gov/cc.

New Security Features for Windows 2000

Throughout this book, you've seen just how different Windows 2000 is from previous Windows NT versions. Active Directory (AD) alone makes Win2K radically different from Windows NT. You would think that Windows 2000's security model is a complete overhaul of its predecessor's, but it really isn't. Instead, Win2K builds upon most of NT 4.0's security model.

It is also true that some of the security features of previous versions have been replaced with greater levels of protection. The most notable example is NT LAN Manager (NTLM) authentication being upgraded to NTLMv2 for downlevel clients and completely replaced by the industry standardized Kerberos, v5 for Win2K clients.

The many new features that Windows 2000 introduces to help protect the corporate environment include:

▼   Access control for all objects in the AD

■   Central storage of security policy and account policy information

■   Using Kerberos version 5 for Win2K authentication but supporting multiple authentication methods for backward-compatibility reasons

■   Kerberos, v5 two-way, transitive trust relationships

■   Automatic updating and synchronization of all security policy and account information across domain controllers (DCs)

■   Encryption of data that is transmitted over the network

■   Encryption of data that is stored on disk

▲   Smart card support

Top Security Recommendations

Various steps can be taken to secure a Windows 2000 environment. The steps that you take will vary from environment to environment. The ten suggestions I present here aren't the only ones that you should take. Many security-related suggestions are given throughout this chapter.

1. Use alphanumeric (complex) passwords.

2. Monitor powerful group memberships.

3. Limit the number of users with Administrator privileges.

4. Keep up-to-date with the latest security technologies and concerns at Microsoft's Security Web site (www.microsoft.com/security/), and, if you are really interested in this topic, check out www.ntbugtraq.com.

5. Keep up-to-date with service packs and hot fixes.

6. Place servers in secure, access-controlled rooms.

7. Upgrade downlevel clients to Windows 2000 to enable them to use Kerberos instead of NTLM authentication. Upgrading downlevel clients also enables you to use a variety of other security-related features (i.e., encryption, group policies, and so on) that can only be used with Windows 2000. If upgrading downlevel clients is not possible, add the dsclient.exe to the downlevel (Win 9x) client and enable NTLMv2.

8. Use NTFS on all partitions and encrypt sensitive data with EFS.

9. Enable auditing (logon validations, security changes, and so on).

10. Secure remote connections by using extensible authentication protocol (EAP), callback, caller ID, or virtual private networking (VPN) technologies. See "Securing Remote Access" later in this chapter for more information.

AUTHENTICATION

Before you can start using Windows 2000 and network resources, you must log on to either the local computer or the domain to get authenticated and verify who you say you are. Logging on is similar to going to a bar or a nightclub in your youth. In the doorway, you must present some form of identification that proves you are over the age of 21.

The authentication model that Windows 2000 supports provides two types of authentication:

▼ **Interactive logon** Confirms the user's identification to the user's local computer or to the domain.

▲ **Network authentication** Confirms the user's identification to any network resource or service that the user is attempting to access.

Windows 2000 supports five different protocols to support authentication, including LM, NTLM, NTLMv2, X.509 v3 public key certificates for public key infrastructure (PKI), and Kerberos version 5. Kerberos is used as the default authentication protocol for Win2K. LM is the default authentication protocol for Win 9x. NTLM is the default authentication protocol for NT 4.0. After you've added the dsclient.exe to Win 9x or NT 4.0 machines to make them AD-aware, you can implement NTLMv2 for a more secure authentication protocol.

NOTE: Windows 2000 uses NTLM for interactive logon authentication. Kerberos and PKI are used strictly with network authentication. If the user is logging in directly to his or her local computer, there is no need for a challenge-response protocol of any kind. Win2K simply hashes your password and checks it against the corresponding hash in the SAM database. If it matches, the user is authenticated.

Downlevel clients such as NT 4.0 and Win 9x (without the Directory Services client software) are not aware of the existence of the Active Directory. Therefore, the client determines which authentication protocol is to be used. For instance, when a user on NT 4.0 (without the Directory Services client software) tries to log on, he or she can only authenticate with NTLM because NT 4.0 doesn't recognize the Kerberos protocol. The converse is true for network authentication as well. If the server that holds the resource (resource server) isn't capable of understanding Kerberos (an NT 4.0 BDC), the client (a Win2K Professional workstation) also must use the recognized authentication protocol, in this case NTLM.

LAN Manager (LM)

For those of you who were not in this industry in the late 1980s, LAN Manager was the first attempt by Microsoft at local area networking. It was not an enterprise solution by any means, but many of the elements we use in today's NT 4.0 were conceived and implemented in LAN Manager. The particular element that we will focus on here is the LM authentication protocol.

From a security standpoint, LM authentication is the weakest of all the protocols that Win2K supports because the algorithm stores passwords in seven-character chunks. For that reason, passwords longer than seven characters can be attacked in seven-character chunks. The storage algorithm limits the effective password strength to only seven characters drawn from the set of uppercase letters, numbers, and punctuation characters. No lowercase alphabetic characters are used in LM. And, as we all know, many end users don't even use more than the alphabetic characters in their childrens' names in passwords.

"So let's eradicate this incredibly weak authentication method from the face of the earth," you say. All right, you paint the signs while I organize a sit in on the Microsoft campus. After all, Win2K computers don't need the LM authentication. Even NT computers don't need it. However, DOS, Win 3.*x*, and Win 9*x* computers can't log on to an NT or Win2K server/domain without it. That's right—all your Win 9*x* clients still use the LM authentication protocol by default. Worse than that, all your NT 4.0 clients also send LM authentication (in addition to their native NTLM) across the wire in the misguided notion that they may be authenticating to a Win 9*x* box that functions as a "server" or the antiquated notion that they might actually be authenticating to a LAN Manager server. Both situations send chills down the spine.

A standard installation of Win 9*x*, using the LM authentication protocol, can log on to a Win2K domain in either Mixed or Native mode. To remove the LM protocol and increase the security on your network, you have two options:

▼ Upgrade all your Win 9*x* computers to Win2K, which will use Kerberos.

▲ Add the dsclient.exe software to the Win 9*x* clients and enable NTLMv2. Read on.

NTLM Authentication Protocol

In contrast to LM, NTLM authentication takes advantage of all fourteen characters in the password (in a single chunk) and also allows for lowercase letters. Therefore, even though an attacker listening in on the NTLM authentication protocol can attack it in exactly the same way as the LM protocol, the brute force attack will take far longer to succeed. If you have implemented strong passwords, cracking a password can take weeks or even months of computing time. On the other hand, if a password is not strong enough, a dictionary attack can find it in a matter of seconds. NTLM passwords are encrypted with DES (Data Encryption Standard), a 56-bit encryption technique from RSA (www.rsa.com).

"Strong" Passwords

One way of getting a "strong enough" NTLM password is to make it at least eleven characters long and make at least four of those characters uppercase letters, numbers, or punctuation marks. Thus, even if the remaining seven characters are lowercase, more than DES's key space of $7.2*10^{16}$ possible combinations will be created, and the password will not appear in the cracker's dictionaries.

For years, Windows NT systems have relied on NTLM for authentication. Now, as is the case with LM, NTLM is only supported in Win2K for backward-compatibility with downlevel NT clients. NTLM authentication is used only in the following scenarios:

▼ Downlevel NT computers authenticated by Win2K domain controllers

■ Downlevel NT computers requesting resources from Win2K servers

■ Downlevel NT computers requesting resources from NT servers

■ Windows 2000 computers logging on to servers that are running NT 4.0

▲ Windows 2000 computers requesting resources in NT 4.0 domains or resources on an NT 4.0 computer in a Win2K domain

NOTE: A common misconception is that when you switch to Native mode in Windows 2000, you turn off LM and NTLM authentication. The myth is that LM and NTLM are only supported in Mixed mode, not Native mode. This is *not* true. LM, NTLM, and NTLMv2 authentication are fully supported for downlevel clients in both Mixed and Native mode.

The Logon Process

As with NT computers, the logon process is also mandatory with Windows 2000 computers. Whether a user is accessing resources on the local machine or in a domain, the process is different for Windows 2000 computers.

The user must provide security credentials to gain access to resources. A user logging on locally to a Win2K machine must supply a user name and password that is then validated by the machine's local SAM database. Logging on to a domain is much like logging on to the local machine, except the domain controller validates the account instead of the local machine.

In NT 4.0, either a PDC or one of the BDCs in the domain handles the user's request to log on to the domain. In a Windows 2000 domain, the domain controllers (DCs) act as if they're either a PDC (a Windows 2000 Flexible Single Master Operation server or an operations master) or, most likely, a BDC. It is essentially a race between the controllers to determine which processes the request. Typically, the BDC wins the race simply because it usually is not as busy as the PDC and can consequently respond to the request more quickly. The client machine accepts the first response, and the winner (PDC or BDC) begins processing the request. Processing may involve loading user profiles, logon scripts, and drive mappings. After a user is logged on to the domain, the user can access resources (with proper access permissions) within the domain. The NetLogon Service performs this entire process.

NETLOGON SERVICE   With regards to user authentication, the NetLogon Service has three responsibilities: discovery, secure channel setup, and pass-through authentication.

▼ **Discovery**   This process occurs during machine initialization. As the machine starts up, the NetLogon Service tries to locate a domain controller for the specified domain. More specifically, it looks for a machine that responds to the name *DOMAINNAME*<1C>. Domain controllers go through this process as well, except they search for domain controllers in all trusted domains.

- **Secure channel setup** A secure communications channel is established between an NT machine and the domain controller by a series of challenges and responses that they issue to and from each other. This verifies the validity of machine accounts and ensures a secure channel between the two machines. This channel is then used to pass user identification information.

▲ **Pass-through authentication** Pass-through authentication takes place when a user requests a service or attempts to connect to a resource where the user cannot be authenticated by a domain controller in the domain in which the user is logged on. The computer that is asked to provide a resource sends the user's request to the destination's domain controller for authentication. The same logon process occurs when a user with proper accesses privileges logs on to a domain controller, except the user can log on only to the domain. Users cannot log on to a domain controller locally, because domain controllers do not store a local SAM database in addition to the domain SAM database.

Disadvantages of NTLM

As I said earlier, Windows 2000 NTLM is used only for backward-compatibility with downlevel clients. Using NTLM has several disadvantages (they are mentioned shortly), but most of them can be summed up in one major disadvantage: NTLM weakens the Windows 2000 security model. The only way to stop using NTLM authentication is to upgrade all downlevel computers to Windows 2000 to enable the use of Kerberos, or, at least, to install the Directory Service client software on Win 9x computers. Then edit the registry on the Win 9x and NT 4.0 computers to enable the use of NTLMv2.

Following is a list of disadvantages to using NTLM:

▼ NTLM doesn't support mutual authentication (only Kerberos does), which makes it possible for a server to impersonate a network resource or service and trick the client into supplying secure information.

■ The NTLM authentication process forces passwords to be transmitted across the network. Therefore, anyone using a network sniffer (or easily downloadable programs) can jeopardize security by grabbing passwords and other sensitive information.

■ NTLM Trusts are non-transitive, difficult to manage, and limited in scalability.

■ Compared to Kerberos, NTLM is a relatively slow authentication mechanism.

■ Kerberos grants a ticket that expires at a specific time; until expiration, no further authentication is needed. NTLM must re-authenticate the user every time a resource is accessed.

■ NTLM forces the server hosting the resource to assume responsibility for a successful authentication. Kerberos places this responsibility completely with the client.

▲ NTLM is a Microsoft proprietary authentication protocol.

NTLMv2 Authentication Protocol

Recognizing the crucial need to improve security, Microsoft scrapped the entire NTLM authentication concept in Win2K. Kerberos is the only authentication protocol that is needed on an all-Win2K internal network. However, for many of us, a total Win2K world could be years away. Happily, while we plan the inevitable migration to Win2K, the folks at Redmond have created a much more secure middle ground called NTLM version 2 for use with downlevel clients today. Win2K computers support NTLMv2 natively. For existing Win 9*x* clients, the only way to move up to NTLMv2 is to install the dsclient.exe software that ships on the Win2K Server CD. This add-on will also make clients AD-aware. As for NT, you can make sure that all of your NT 4.0 clients and servers are currently running Service Pack 4 or higher. NTLMv2 was initially released as part of NT 4.0, SP4. Service Pack 4 does not make your NT 4.0 machines Active Directory-aware.

In NTLMv2, the space for a password-derived key is now 128 bits instead of the 56 bits for NTLM. One hundred twenty-eight bits makes brute-force password cracking practically impossible, if the password is strong enough. In use with NT 4.0, if both client and server are using SP4, the enhanced NTLMv2 session security is negotiated between them. It provides separate keys for message integrity and confidentiality, and client input into the challenge to prevent chosen plain text-attacks. It also makes use of the HMAC-MD5 algorithm (see RFC 2104) for message integrity checking.

Two registry keys are used to implement and control NTLM and NTLMv2. To choose which variant of the LM, NTLM, and NTLMv2 each computer will use, edit the following registry key:

```
HKLM\System\CurrentControlSet\Control\LSA
```

Find or add the REG_DWORD value: LMCompatibilityLevel
By default, the value is set to 0 (zero). Here is a list of possible options:

▼ **Level 0**   Send LM response and NTLM response; never use NTLMv2 session security.

■ **Level 1**   Use NTLMv2 session security if negotiated.

■ **Level 2**   Send NTLM authentication only.

■ **Level 3**   Send NTLMv2 authentication only.

■ **Level 4**   DC refuses LM authentication.

▲ **Level 5**   DC refuses LM and NTLM authentication (accepts only NTLMv2).

If you are going to use NTLMv2, the system clock on the client and server should be within 30 minutes of each other. Otherwise, the server will think the challenge from the client has expired.

To choose the minimum security to be negotiated for applications using the NTLM Security Service Provider (SSP) on a client computer, edit the following registry key:

```
HKLM\System\CurrentControlSet\control\LSA\MSV1_0
```

Find or add the REG_DWORD value: NtlmMinClientSec
By default, the value is set to 0 (zero). Here is a list of possible options:

▼ **0** No minimum level

■ **0x00000010** Message integrity

■ **0x00000020** Message confidentiality

■ **0x00080000** NTLMv2 session security

▲ **0x20000000** 128-bit encryption

These settings come into play if the computer is functioning as a client. For a server, use the same registry key but a different value NtlmMinServerSec with the same settings options. It is permissible to add the settings for a client and a server on the same computer since one computer can function both as a client and a server.

NOTE: Use caution when changing these settings because it is very easy to prevent legitimate users from authenticating by deploying these changes too quickly and without testing. A lot more information concerning NTLMv2 is in the Microsoft Knowledge Base.

Public Key Infrastructure (PKI)

So far I've acknowledged the fact that Windows 2000 supports both NTLM and NTLMv2 authentication protocols for interactive logons. Users with accounts in the Windows 2000 domain or local computer can log on if they're given the proper access rights (i.e., they must be allowed to log on to the domain or local computer). But what happens if a user account doesn't exist on the local computer, domain, or trusted domain? Put simply, users are denied the ability to log on and are unable to use any resources.

Believe it or not, this is a growing problem for many companies mainly due to e-business and e-commerce. Whether information is being transferred from business to business (B2B) or business to customer (B2C), methods must be in place by which information can be securely transferred without having to create accounts in Windows 2000 computers or Active Directory domains. Besides, would you really want to create user accounts for anyone coming in from the Internet?

Public key security, also known as public key infrastructure (PKI), can be used to solve these dilemmas. PKI enables the identity of the sender and receiver to be verified to be sure that they are indeed who they say they are. And after the identity has been verified, the data can be sent in an encrypted fashion in order to discourage abuse, and, hopefully, eliminate security breaches. If you've ever worked with secure Internet-based e-mail such as the Pretty Good Privacy (PGP) or S/MIME, you'll see the similarities with PKI.

Public-Key Cryptography

Windows 2000's PKI uses public-key cryptography, which, put simply, is the science of protecting data. Cryptographic algorithms combine data (*plaintext*) and an *encryption key* to generate encrypted data (*ciphertext*). It's virtually impossible to reverse-engineer ciphertext. The only way to transform the data into something that is useable is to use a *decryption key*.

In PKI terminology, the keys mentioned above are two separate keys developed as a key pair to work together. The encryption key is called the *public key* and the decryption key is called the *private key*. As their names imply, the public key is freely available to anyone who wishes to have it, but the private key is kept secret. Preferably, only one individual has access to the private key. It's also important to note here that each key serves a single purpose. In other words, the public key can't decrypt information and the private key can't encrypt messages.

Most of us have purchased a product over the Internet. Internet purchases are one of the most commonly used implementations of public key cryptography in today's world. Let's say you've selected a few Win2K books (published, of course, by Osborne/McGraw-Hill) and placed them in your virtual shopping cart. Now we're ready to check out. Because checking out involves the transmission of your name, address, and credit card information across the Internet, the vendor's Web site now establishes a "secure" connection using the Secure Sockets Layer (SSL) or Transport Layer Security (TLS) technology on port 443 to encrypt the transaction. Remember that to encrypt the data on your end before it goes across the wire, you must possess the public key of the vendor. When did you get it? When you clicked the Checkout Now button. Where is it? It was sent to your computer's Internet browser as a *cookie*, a certificate that contains the vendor's public key. When you submit your order, the data is encrypted using the certificate obtained from the vendor (in your browser, look at Certificates | Authorities) and the vendor's public key. The e-commerce site receives the encrypted data, decrypts it with its private key, enters it into its database, and, in a few days, you get the books ordered. The vendor who issued the public key is the only entity that can decrypt the data. The insecurity involving Internet credit card transactions is not that the credit card number travels across the wire—the wire is secure. Rather, the security breach is possible after the data has been stored in the vendor's database. Vendors' databases are where a number of well-publicized exploits have occurred. Unfortunately, the security "eye" has been looking at the wrong ball.

The Certificate Authority

Both the public and private keys in PKI are stored in the certificate authority (CA). The CA is responsible both for issuing and signing certificates. A certificate is a digitally signed agreement that binds the value of the public key to a specific private key, which can represent a user or service.

Certificates typically hold the following information:

▼ The public key value

■ The name of the user or service

■ The certificate's validity period, which is the length of time the certificate is valid

- ■ The CA's identifier information
- ▲ The digital signature

The CA acts as a middleman between the two entities that wish to exchange information securely. It verifies the validity of the digital certificate so that you know you're communicating with the user or service that you intended to communicate with initially. In an Internet book purchase, the CA is probably Verisign, a trusted Internet Certificate Authority in business to do nothing but issue and verify the authenticity of digital certificates. In Windows 2000, you create and manage certificates through Certificate Services (installing Certificate Services is described in the following section). A Win2K server or domain controller becomes the CA on the Windows 2000 network.

With all this in mind, consider another simple example that illustrates how public and private keys work in Win2K. In this example, I'm assuming that Grant wants to send Andrew a secure message and that Windows 2000's Certificate Services has already created key pairs for both parties. Grant writes the message first and then encrypts it using Andrew's public key (that he freely obtained). Now only Andrew can decrypt the message. The message is then sent to Andrew, who, upon receiving it, uses his private key to decrypt and read the message. In this simple example, notice that neither Grant nor Andrew had to exchange passwords over the network. All they had to do was establish a trust with the CA.

NOTE: CAs can trust one another to form a certification hierarchy that can extend the security infrastructure boundary beyond your imagination. If CAs trust each other, their users (or services) can trust each other as well.

Installing Certificate Services

Windows 2000 Certificate Services is required for using digital certificates. Before you install the service, I highly recommend thoroughly planning how to fit PKI into your Windows 2000 network infrastructure. There are simply too many options and configurations to ignore.

To install Certificate Services, do the following:

1. Double-click Add/Remove Programs in the Control Panel.

2. Select Add/Remove Windows Components to display the Windows Components Wizard.

3. Check the Certificate Services check box. If you see a warning message, read it carefully before clicking Yes. Click Next to continue.

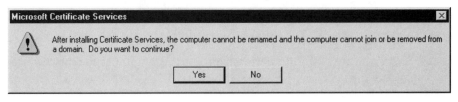

4. Choose any one of the following four choices for the Certificate Authority Type, as shown in Figure 13-1:

- **Enterprise Root CA**   This is a top-level CA in a certification hierarchy and it requires the Active Directory. It signs its own certificates and publishes them to other CAs in the enterprise through the Active Directory.

- **Enterprise Subordinate CA**   This CA obtains its certificates from the Enterprise root CA and therefore also requires the Active Directory. Must be a domain controller or member server.

- **Stand-Alone Root CA**   The primary difference between this CA and an Enterprise root CA is that the standalone CA (as its name implies) doesn't require the Active Directory. Therefore, it doesn't have to be a part of the domain. However, it will use AD if it's installed on a DC.

- **Stand-Alone Subordinate CA**   Similar to the Enterprise subordinate CA, it obtains its certificates from the standalone root CA. It does not require AD.

5. You can optionally select Advanced options to configure the Certificate Authority that you choose in Step 4. These options include key length, hash algorithms, and cryptographic service provider (CSP). The CSP is used to generate the key pair and perform the cryptographic operations on behalf of the CA. If you are unsure what to select, do nothing and accept the defaults.

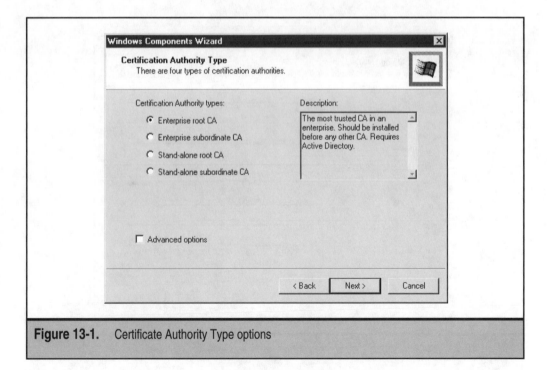

Figure 13-1.   Certificate Authority Type options

6. Fill in the appropriate information to identify the CA, as shown in Figure 13-2. In addition, you can specify how long the CA is valid. Click Next to continue.

7. The next step is to specify where to store the configuration data, database, and log files. If you're unsure where to store them, I recommend keeping the defaults. Click Next to continue.

NOTE: You may be prompted to stop the Internet Information Service (IIS) before proceeding. Make sure that you have your Win2K Server installation files ready, too.

8. Click Finish to complete the installation.

After the installation is complete, you can use the Certificates or Certification Authority MMC snap-ins shown in Figure 13-3 to manage digital certificates, as shown in Figure 13-4. Users and administrators can use the Certificates snap-in, but, in order to use the Certification Authority, you must have administrative privileges.

Kerberos

Kerberos version 5 is the default network authentication protocol used in Windows 2000. It's an industry standard developed by the Massachusetts Institute of Technology (MIT) and is described in Request for Comments (RFC) 1510.

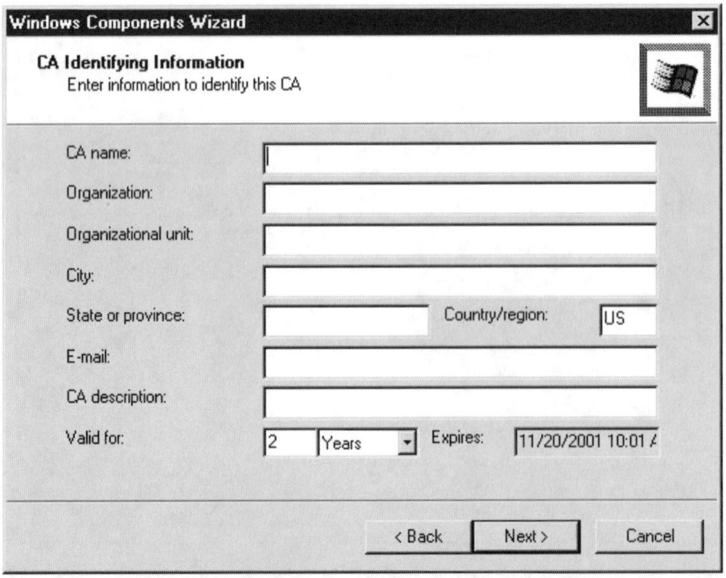

Figure 13-2. Identifying the CA

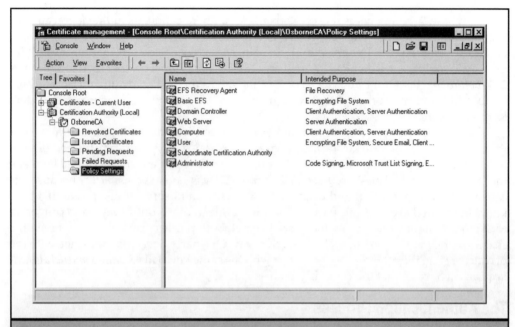

Figure 13-3. Certificates and Certification Authority MMC snap-ins

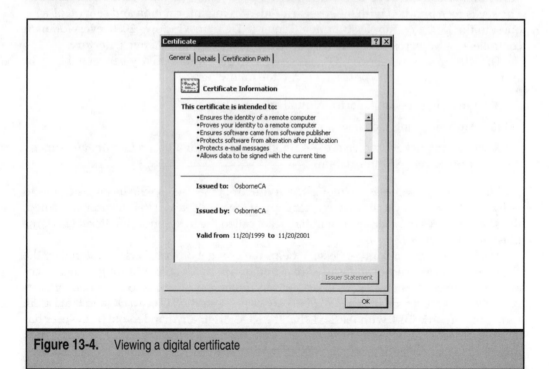

Figure 13-4. Viewing a digital certificate

Many Win2K components rely on Kerberos for authentication, including logon authentication and trust relationships between domains. As an integral part of AD, the server side of Kerberos runs on each DC in a Win2K domain, and its client side service runs on all Windows 2000 computers. Downlevel Win 9*x* and NT 4.0 clients must be upgraded to Windows 2000 before the client computer can recognize and use Kerberos-based authentication. There is no add-on client software that will make any downlevel client operating system Kerberos-aware.

Kerberos uses cryptographic techniques similar to PKI, but the primary difference is that Kerberos uses private key (also known as *shared-secret*) cryptography instead of public-key cryptography. In this scenario, the same secret (the private key) is shared between the client and server. The shared-secret, or private, key is said to be *symmetric* because it is capable of both encryption and decryption. The client and server must prove that they know the shared-secret. Both parties don't trust one another until they have proven to each other that they both know the shared-secret. Both parties prove that they know the shared-secret in a simple but highly effective way: One party encrypts a message with the private key and the other party decrypts it with the same key. This is called *mutual authentication*; each trusts that the other is who it says it is.

The Authentication Process

A client using Kerberos first types in his or her password and attempts to log on to the Windows 2000 domain. Behind the scenes, the password is *hashed*. Hash means to generate a number using encryption and the user's password. The hash now becomes a *key*. The key is then bundled with other security-identifying information and sent off as a request to the Kerberos Key Distribution Center (KDC). In Windows 2000, every domain controller is a Kerberos KDC. Therefore, Kerberos requires the Active Directory.

The KDC, a service on every DC, serves as a trusted intermediary between the client and server. Its primary purposes in life are the following:

▼ Providing session keys for mutual authentication

■ Authenticating the client and server

▲ Granting tickets, which are essentially vouchers for a user's identity and other security-related information

When the KDC receives the request, it verifies that the user is who he or she claims to be by matching the key to its own master copy of the user's key. After the user is verified, the KDC provides the user with an initial ticket called the ticket-granting ticket (TGT), as illustrated in Figure 13-5.

The TGT is a special kind of ticket; it helps the user get other tickets. It is stored by the client (in the client's cache) and is used to get other tickets for authenticating with services and resources on the network. More specifically, when a user wants to use a network service or resource, the user's Kerberos client service presents the TGT to a DC and that DC, in turn, compares the TGT with the TGT that the KDC originally handed out. If the user has appropriate access privileges, the user is presented with a session ticket (ST). This ST, when presented to the service or resource, enables the user to make use of the service or resource.

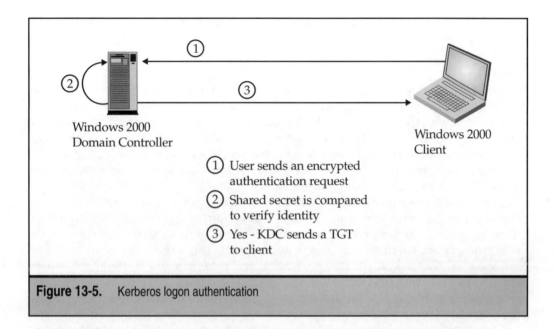

Figure 13-5.   Kerberos logon authentication

If the Kerberos authentication process fails for any reason, the Win2K client attempts to use the cached credentials stored in its registry from previous successful logons by this particular user from this particular computer. Cached credentials store (in the client's registry) the user name, password, domain information, and access token that were used in the last ten previous successful logons. If the cached credentials logon authentication is successful, the user has access only to this local client computer. Since the user does not possess a current TGT from the Key Distribution Center, he or she cannot access any network resources. Under no circumstances does a Win2K to Win2K logon ever use the NTLM protocol.

Kerberos Trust Relationships

The Kerberos protocol is responsible for establishing two-way, transitive trust relationships between domains. Because each domain has its own KDC, the way in which a user gains access to resources in other domains is changed slightly. Two domains can enable authentication across domain boundaries simply by sharing an inter-domain key. In Windows 2000 this happens automatically when two domains establish a trust relationship.

In the simplest scenario, let's say you have two domains (bigcompany.com and mktg.bigcompany.com) and a user named "Amy" in one domain is trying to access a resource in the other domain. Amy resides in mktg.bigcompany.com and I'll assume that she's already been granted a TGT from her domain.

The KDC in her domain has no authority over the KDC in the bigcompany.com domain, and, more than likely, the KDC has no idea about the resource that Amy is trying to use. So her KDC finds the KDC for bigcompany.com and passes a referral ticket to her. Her Kerberos client service then sends a request to obtain a TGT for the bigcompany.com domain. As soon as Amy receives the other TGT, she can use it to get a session ticket for the desired resource in the bigcompany.com domain.

Smart Cards

Windows 2000's support for smart cards further strengthens its commitment to high-security standards. Smart cards replace traditional password authentication methods with a stronger, more effective method. Smart card technology is composed of a physical smart card, a personal identification number (PIN), and the smart card reader on a Windows 2000 computer. Think of smart cards as high-tech, ATM bankcards. As technology progresses, you can expect the simple PIN number to be replaced by biometric devices such as fingerprint readers and retina scanners.

Smart card support is an extension to the Kerberos authentication protocol. As I explained earlier, Kerberos uses shared-secret cryptography, but the smart card implementation is a public key extension much like the one used in PKI. A smart card contains the public and private keys used to encrypt and decrypt. The private key is never shared (only the user, not the KDC, has the key) and is never stored anywhere but on the smart card. The Win2K extensions to the Kerberos protocol permit initial authentication to the domain using public key certificates rather than conventional shared-secret keys. This enhancement allows Kerberos to support interactive logon with a smart card.

A user initiates the logon process by inserting the smart card into the smart card reader. The system then requests a personal identification number (PIN). The user types a PIN. Windows 2000 uses the PIN to access the card (the user authenticates to the card) and all necessary cryptographic operations are performed within the smart card. If the user types in the correct PIN and has the appropriate access rights, he or she is logged to the system using the public key certificates from the smart card.

NOTE: Before you begin using smart cards, you must install a smart card reader as well as Certificate Services for Windows 2000. Refer to "Installing Certificate Services" earlier in this chapter for more information.

SECURING REMOTE ACCESS

Now that information can be obtained anytime from virtually anywhere in the world, most network environments feel compelled to provide some form of remote access connectivity to roaming users and remote sites. Unfortunately, if proper security measures aren't taken into account, providing remote access can leave a network environment vulnerable to unauthorized access. As a result, securing remote access connections into and away from your Windows 2000 network environment should be given a high priority. In addition to the security measures already mentioned in this chapter, Windows 2000's Routing and Remote Access (RRAS) includes many security features to help protect networks. These features include encryption, authentication, callback, VPN support, and much more.

Pre-Windows 2000 Compatible Access

The Windows 2000 Active Directory contains a Builtin Local group called Pre-Windows 2000 Compatible Access whose purpose should be obvious from its name. Members of this group are granted access that bypasses many security elements of Win2K. The most common use of this group is to allow NT 4.0 RAS servers to continue to operate on a Win2K domain. Specifically, the group allows Win2K users to log on to the domain through an NT 4.0 RAS server.

The NT 4.0 RAS service connects to the NT 4.0 domain (SAM) database using NULL credentials—a no-no in the world of security. To plug this particular security hole, the Win2K Active Directory specifically prohibits any user (or service) with NULL credentials from searching its database. This will immediately eliminate NT 4.0 RAS servers from the Win2K network. To account for migration, timing, and financial issues, Win2K provides the Pre-Windows 2000 Compatible Access group. During *dcpromo*, the Permissions screen gives you the option of choosing Pre-Windows 2000 Compatible Access. In reality, all this does is place the Everyone group into the Pre-Windows 2000 Compatible Access group. Now that you know this, you can place whatever groups you need in the Pre-Windows 2000 Compatible Access group. Your system is the most secure when this group is empty. So, after upgrading your RAS servers to Win2K, remove the Everyone group from the Pre-Windows 2000 Compatible Access group.

Remote Access Authentication Methods

Several authentication methods can be used with remote connections. By default, RRAS uses MS-CHAP and MS-CHAPv2 authentication. Selected authentication methods are used in the following order of precedence:

1. Extensible authentication protocol (EAP)
2. Microsoft Challenge Handshake Authentication Protocol version 2 (MS-CHAPv2)
3. Microsoft Challenge Handshake Authentication Protocol (MS-CHAP)
4. Challenge Handshake Authentication Protocol (CHAP)
5. Shiva Password Authentication Protocol (SPAP)
6. Password Authentication Protocol (PAP)
7. Unauthenticated Access

The order of precedence is important because methods differ. One offers the highest level of security, while another leaves the connection wide open for almost anyone to access. The authentication methods, which are shown in Figure 13-6, can be found within the RRAS management console by selecting the appropriate server in the right console and selecting Properties. Then, under the Security tab, click the Authentication Methods button. To use an authentication method, simply check the box beside its name.

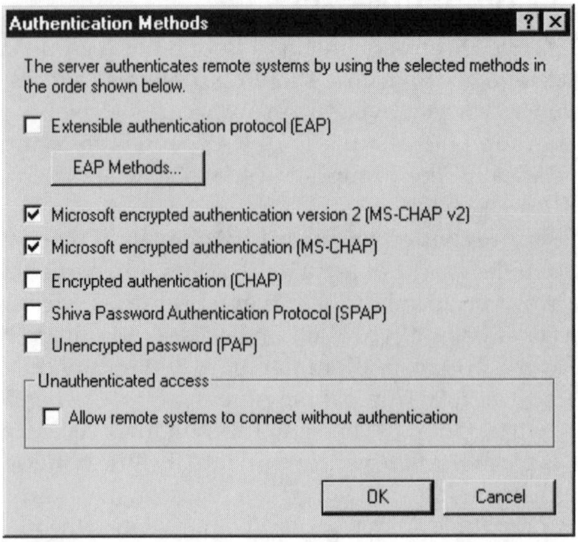

Figure 13-6.   Remote access authentication methods

EAP

EAP, an extension to PPP, allows an arbitrary authentication method to be negotiated between the remote client and server. After the link is established, the client and server negotiate which EAP type of authentication mechanism will be used. Mechanisms include EAP-MD5 CHAP, EAP-TLS, Smart Cards, and more. After a decision is made, the client uses the authentication mechanism that was selected to gain access to the RRAS server and network.

As the name implies, EAP is extensible, meaning that any number of EAP types can be added at any time. To see which EAP methods you're currently using, do the following:

1. Open the RRAS management console by clicking the Start button and choosing Programs | Administrative Tools menu.

2. In the right console, right-click a RRAS server and select Properties.

3. Under the Security tab, click the Authentication Methods button to display the Authentication Methods window.

4. Click the EAP Methods button to see the EAP Methods that are currently installed, as shown in Figure 13-7.

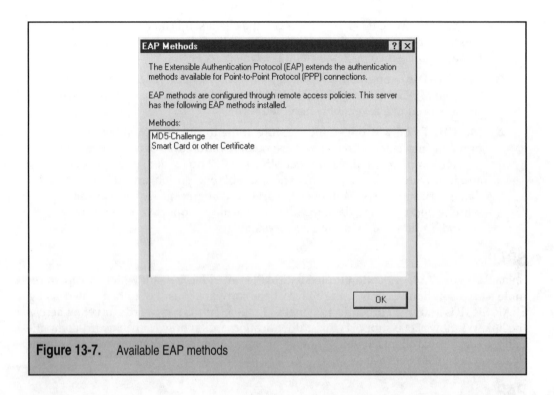

Figure 13-7. Available EAP methods

EAP METHODS Windows 2000 can support any EAP method type (e.g., Smart Cards) as plug-ins, but it provides the following two EAP methods by default:

▼ **EAP-MD5 CHAP** is a required EAP method that retains many of the same attributes as CHAP but also sends the challenges and responses as EAP messages.

▲ **EAP-TLS (Transport Level Security)** is a certificate-based authentication method. This method is required if you're using Smart Cards. EAP-TLS, currently the strongest type of authentication, requires that the RRAS server be a member server in an AD domain. It provides mutual authentication (both client and server are authenticated), encryption, and a secured private key exchange.

CHAP

CHAP is probably the most common authentication suite of protocols in use today. Actually, three versions of CHAP are supported by Windows 2000's RRAS:

▼ **CHAP**, as an industry standard, is a challenge-response authentication protocol that supports one-way encryption of responses to challenges. The authentication process entails three separate steps. First, the server challenges the client to prove its identity. Second, the client sends an encrypted CHAP message in response to the challenge. Third, the server verifies the response. If the response is correct, the client is granted access.

■ **MS-CHAP** is a modified, proprietary version of CHAP. The major difference between MS-CHAP and CHAP in Windows 2000 is that the user's password can be stored in a reversibly encrypted form.

▲ **MS-CHAPv2** is a stronger, more secure authentication method than the previous implementations. The most notable differences between it and the previous implementations are that MS-CHAPv2 no longer supports NTLM and it provides mutual authentication, 128-bit encryption, and stronger initial data-encryption keys. Moreover, separate cryptographic keys are used for sending and receiving data. MS-CHAPv2 is only supported on Windows 98, Second Edition and Windows 2000 systems.

SPAP

Shiva Password Authentication Protocol (SPAP) is an older, yet still widely accepted remote access solution. Clients using Shiva client software must be authenticated using SPAP. SPAP is a simple authentication method that encrypts passwords traveling across the link. Windows 2000 supports this authentication option only for backward-compatibility to serve Shiva clients. If you're not using Shiva products, use a more robust authentication mechanism than Shiva.

PAP

Password Authentication Protocol (PAP) is a misnomer—it is the most insecure authentication method available today. Both the user name and password are sent across the link in clear text. That's right. No encryption whatsoever. Anyone snooping the connection can easily grab and use the information to gain access to your network. As a result, using PAP for authentication is less than advisable.

Unauthenticated Access

Obviously, the Unauthenticated Access option provides no degree of authentication for remote access. I will say, though, that you should never use this option unless you absolutely don't care about securing your environment. With this option, you're opening access to everyone who wants to connect remotely.

Callback

Callback means just what the name implies. A remote client dials the RRAS server and the client's credentials (username and password) are verified. After the credentials are verified, the connection is dropped so that the RRAS server can call the remote client back. The number that the RRAS server calls can either be specified during the initial call or, if you want, RRAS can call a specific number. The latter of the two is the most secure method because it prevents calls from remote connectivity locations that haven't been designated as such. Generally speaking, this option is truly beneficial when you're dealing with a remote access client who is dialing in from the same location most, if not all, of the time.

Caller ID

Caller ID (also known as Automatic Number Identification, or ANI) is an extremely popular add-on feature provided by local telephone companies. Many of you may have it on your phone systems at home. Someone calls you and a telephone number is displayed so you can screen phone calls and answer only the ones that you want to answer.

As shown in Figure 13-8, Caller ID can be used to verify that a remote client that dials into RRAS is calling from a specific number. If the client isn't calling from a specific number, the connection is denied and dropped. Sometimes you run into the problem of a

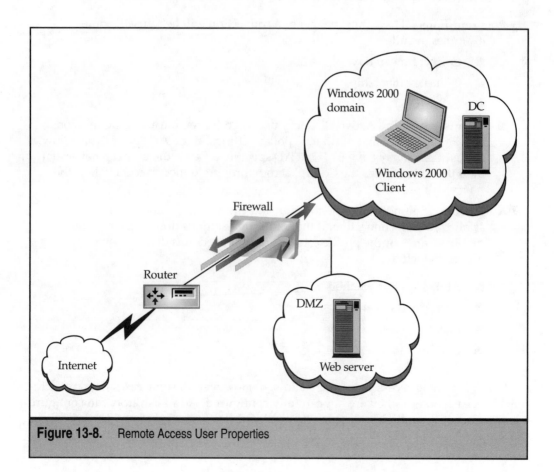

Figure 13-8. Remote Access User Properties

telephone company not being able to provide callers' numbers because the plain old telephone systems (POTS) isn't equipped to handle caller ID or the caller has blocked the number to keep it from being displayed. When a number can't be displayed for whatever reason, the connection is denied. Therefore, check to make sure that the numbers will be revealed before you implement this solution.

Remote Access Policies

New in Win2K, remote access policies are shared between IAS (Internet Authentication Service) and RRAS and cooperate with the Active Directory to provide secure access. Remote access policies are stored, per connection, on the RRAS server. They are not part of Group Policies and they do not reside in the Active Directory. There can be multiple RRAS policies for each connection. A connection attempt must meet all the criteria of at least one policy or it will be rejected. There are three components of a remote access policy:

▼ **Conditions** These must be met or a connection will be refused. Some examples include:

- Correct time of day

- Group membership

- Caller ID

■ **Permissions** The Active Directory user account remote access permissions (see Figure 13-8) can override the policy settings. If the AD specifies an Allow, the user can always dial in. If the AD specifies a Deny, the user can never dial in. If the AD specifies the Control access through Remote Access Policy, the policy will prevail.

▲ **Profiles** Settings for authentication and encryption protocols must be applied to each connection. If the connection settings don't match the user's dial-in settings or the profile settings, the connection is denied. Some examples include:

- Authentication Method

- Encryption Level

- Maximum Session Time

- Dial-in Media

Multiple remote access policies are allowed. However, in some cases they can actually block each other if they are not carefully configured. Administrators can configure the order in which multiple policies are applied. The flow chart in Figure 13-9 shows how the Remote Access Policies are applied.

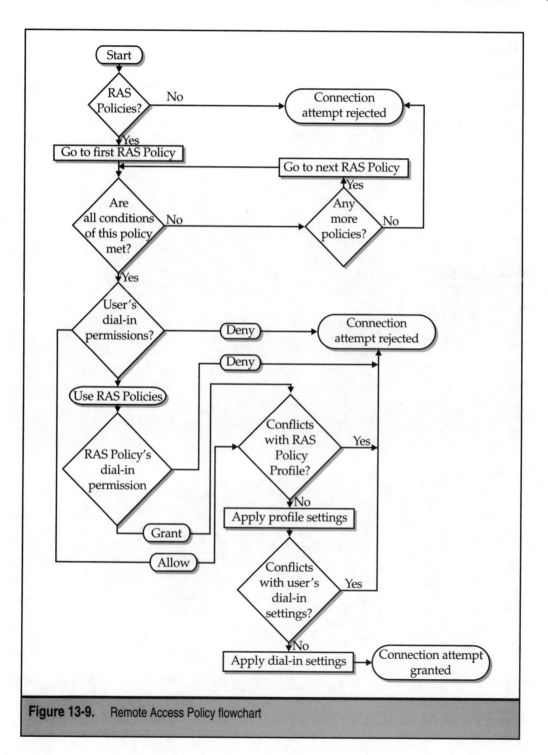

Figure 13-9.   Remote Access Policy flowchart

SUMMARY

Entire books have been written about security in general and NT security in particular. The subject feels nearly endless. Many of the concepts are complex and much of the implementation of those concepts is challenging as well. This chapter focused on the issue of authentication and general security issues as well. Chapter 14 concentrates on the security issues involving the Active Directory, users, groups, resource access, and auditing.

CHAPTER 14

Implementing Windows 2000 Security in the Enterprise

Chapter 14 gets into the specifics of applying Windows 2000 and Active Directory security in today's corporate environment. While understanding security concepts and corporate security policies is essential for most network administrators, the devil is in the details. In this chapter, we'll go deeper into the individual security enhancements in Windows 2000 and how to make them work.

INTEGRATING ACTIVE DIRECTORY AND SECURITY

The Win2K Active Directory (AD) is tightly integrated with security. In fact, if you look at Figure 14-1, you'll see that it's impossible to separate the two because AD fits within the security subsystem rather than being its own independent subsystem. The advantages are enormous and will be explained throughout this chapter.

The Windows 2000 security architecture lends itself to more flexibility than the NT 4.0 model. In Windows NT 4.0, you were rather limited by the Security Accounts Management Database (SAM). For example, NTLM trusts were established in only one direction, and the scope of assigning security rights was limited to a few levels. Now, however, you're dealing with a distributed Active Directory service that enables you to have much more diversified control over your network environment. You have new features such as organizational units (OUs) and delegated administration that you didn't have before.

Active Directory Objects and Security

As you know, AD stores all Windows 2000 network objects and their associated attributes. These objects (users, groups, computers, printers, and so on) are protected through the use of authentication and access control mechanisms.

Because of the tight integration of AD and security, you can control access to an object as a whole or down to the attribute level. For example, for the user account Amy Sigrist, you can either allow access to all of her attributes or define a particular group (such as HR) to be able to modify only certain attributes such as her address, department name, and e-mail address.

In addition, the AD/security integration also enables the inheritance of security rights among most, if not all, AD objects. Inheritance is when an object receives similar properties from the object above it in the AD hierarchy. Inheritance never crosses domain boundaries.

Object Identities

Although all objects in the AD can be found using a distinguished name, they are also given other unique identities, the security identifier (SID), and the globally unique identifier (GUID). AD uses these two unique identifiers internally instead of the object's name because unlike an object name, GUIDs never change and SIDs seldom do.

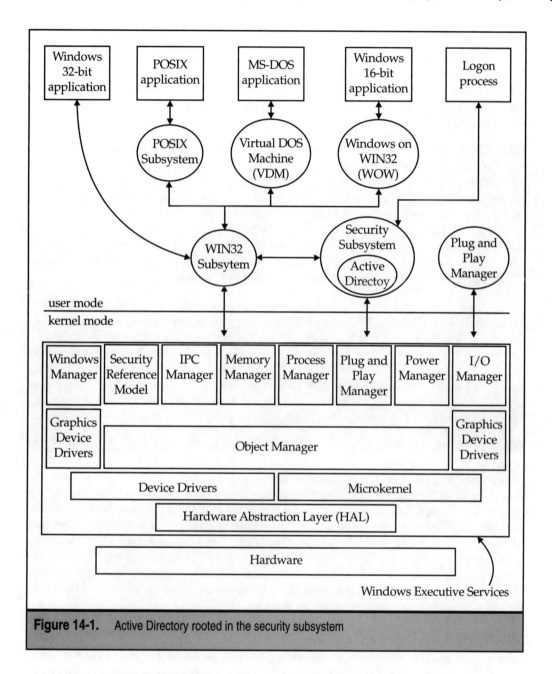

Figure 14-1. Active Directory rooted in the security subsystem

SID   As with NT 4.0, a Windows 2000 SID identifies a security principal (user, group, or machine account) within a domain. SIDs are generated by the domain when a new domain object is created. The domain is a boundary for the SID. If the object moves to a different domain, it receives a new SID.

The same limitations in the NT 4.0 implementation still apply in Windows 2000. A SID is limited to a single domain, and duplicate SIDs can cause significant security-related problems such as when cloning computers. (See Chapter 2 for a discussion of sysprep.exe.)

SID HISTORY   Unlike NT 4.0, in Windows 2000, you can easily move objects from one domain to another. But even though the object has moved to a new domain and received a new SID, its access to shared resources is unchanged. This is possible due to a new object attribute called the SID History. When an object is moved to a different Win2K domain and assigned a brand new SID, its old SID is placed in the SID History.

Since the SID History contains one or more SIDs for each domain (the limit is 1,023) that the object has resided in, any security rights from the older domain membership is still a part of the object. This simplifies administration and helps bypass some of the limitations of the SID. Refer to the section "Access Tokens," below.

GUID   In addition to an object's distinguished name and SID, every object in the Active Directory has a GUID. A GUID is a 128-bit number that is guaranteed to be unique. Although it is similar to a SID, there are a couple of major differences. First, neither administrators nor the AD itself can ever change a GUID. Also, a GUID stays permanently attached to the object for the duration of its life no matter where the object moves. In other words, the only boundary for the GUID is a Windows 2000 forest; it is guaranteed to be unique no matter how many domains you have in the tree or forest or how many times the object moves.

ACCESS TOKENS   In Win2K, when a user authenticates either to the local machine SAM or to the Active Directory domain, they receive an access token on the computer where they are logging on. This token contains their user SID, the SIDs of any groups that the user belongs to, the user's rights and privileges on this local computer where they are logging in, and (here's the new part) all the SIDs present in the SID History attribute of their user object. When the user wishes to obtain access to an object, the Security Reference Monitor service checks the SIDs on the object's ACL and then compares them with the SIDs on the access token. If there is a match and the user's permissions allow the level of access requested, the user is in. If not, access is denied. If the user object was moved, this allows the user to access the same resources that they were able to access before the object was moved without any intervention by the administrator.

Modifying the Object Properties

Before we begin our discussion of modifying the properties of Active Directory objects, let's discuss several of the tabs that appear on the Property sheet of nearly every object. The Property sheets for an object are always accessed the same way: right-click on the object and select Properties.

THE GENERAL TAB   Nearly every object will display a General tab on the Properties sheet. It always contains information on the description of the object. It may also contain status, location, or address information. In a number of cases, it displays configurable parameters that do not appear anywhere else.

THE MANAGED BY TAB   Domains, OUs, and groups display the Managed By tab. This allows administrators viewing the object in the MMC to see what user account is responsible for the management of these objects. This is for documentation purposes only.

THE OBJECT TAB   In the MMC, when View | Advanced Features is checked, the Object tab appears. There is nothing configurable or changeable on the Object tab. It displays the AD-related information:

▼ Object class

■ Object creation date and time

■ Object last modified date and time

■ The original USN of the object when it was created

▲ The current USN of the object

This information can come in handy when troubleshooting problems.

THE SECURITY TAB   Before we discuss the Security tab in detail, let's step back and take a look at the concept of a *security principal*. A security principal is an object in the AD that can be granted access to another object. In NT 4.0, the only security principals were users and groups. In Windows 2000, we add one more—computers. Therefore, in Win2K, you can grant resource access to users, groups, or computers. No discussion of security principals is complete without addressing the issue of OUs.

In Novell's NDS (NetWare Directory Services), an OU is also a security principal and can be granted direct access to other objects within the NDS structure or folders in the file system. This access automatically flows to all objects within the OU as well. This simplifies the management of permissions significantly.

In Windows 2000, an OU is not a security principal, and the equivalent functionality can be implemented only by creating groups that match the OU structure and maintaining their membership to mirror the OU membership. Despite Microsoft's claims that their way is better because users have different roles in the same OU, it's not. Tracing the permissions is difficult because of inheritance, and moving objects will create administration nightmares, especially if we attempt to match the OU membership with a group membership. From the network administrator's point of view, Novell got this one right. Microsoft missed an important opportunity to excel.

To see the Security tab on the Object Properties sheet, you'll also need the MMC, View | Advanced Features checked. The Security tab actually contains three screens, which display in increasing levels of complexity and allow an increasing level of granular control. The top half of the opening screen displays a list of all the users and groups that have specific permissions granted directly to this object and the users and groups that have permissions granted to objects above this one in the hierarchy that are being inherited by this object. The bottom half contains a "short list" of possible permissions granted for this type of object. It is not a complete list but rather the most commonly used permissions. When a user or group is highlighted in the top half, its permissions to this object are displayed in the bottom half. As shown in Figure 14-2, permissions granted directly to this object display as white boxes with a check mark inside.

Permissions that have been inherited from objects higher in the hierarchy display as gray boxes with a check mark inside.

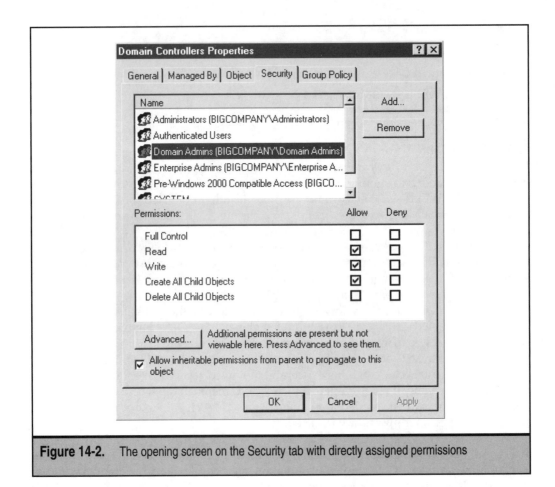

Figure 14-2.   The opening screen on the Security tab with directly assigned permissions

Static vs. Dynamic Inheritance of AD Permissions

Microsoft has always favored static inheritance. Even the NT 4.0 NTFS file system used a fairly unsophisticated implementation of static inheritance. Each folder and file included an access control list (ACL). When you made a change to the ACL of a folder, you had the opportunity to copy this ACL (in its entirety) to the files below (check box on by default) and, using a separate check box, to the folders and subfolders below (off by default). The problem was that it was impossible, without using command-line tools like CACLS or XCACLS, to "interweave" or add the changes we'd made into the ACL settings. It was all or nothing if you wished to stay in the GUI. The ACL that you created completely erased the old one and replaced it with the ACL you had edited. (BTW, CACLS ships with Win2K, and XCACLS is still in the Win2K Resource Kit.)

Static inheritance became more and more problematic as our permissions strategy became more granular and specific. Other than the command-line tools, there was no fix.

In the Active Directory, Microsoft implements a very sophisticated form of static (Create Time) inheritance. Each child object has an ACL attached that contains the summary of all access permissions that are either directly granted to the object or inherited from its parent objects. The Active Directory recomputes the child object's access permissions automatically when a parent object's permissions are changed. Then only the change to the parent object's ACL is propagated between replica domain controllers and global catalogs. The child object access permissions are then recomputed on each domain controller locally—a quick, painless, and non-network-intensive operation.

Microsoft has designed this form of static inheritance to optimize the Active Directory for Read (versus Write) access. The Active Directory recomputes access control settings only once (at the time a parent object's ACL is changed), rather than on every read operation. In addition, the impact on bandwidth usage in WAN environments is minimal.

Novell's NDS implements dynamic (Read Time) inheritance of object access rights. This means that to access an object directly, I must first go up the NDS hierarchy to the container where the access rights are directly assigned in order to discover if I have the access rights for this object. Based on Novell's concept of partitioning, it is conceivable, though highly unlikely, that the object that contains the permissions that I must find is not present on the same server, thus creating more network traffic as I search for objects on up the NDS hierarchy.

Microsoft got this one right. What percentage of the time do we change the permissions in the Active Directory (far less than 1 percent) versus the percentage of time we spend accessing (reading) AD objects (far more than 99 percent)? Doh! Optimizing the AD for better read performance makes sense to me. Microsoft is trading a couple of seconds in a write operation performed every once in a while for the least possible amount of time in a read operation performed hundreds or thousands of times a day. Provo gets the razzberries now! Thumbs up to Redmond.

Unlike NT 4.0, the permissions in Win2K are displayed with either Allow or Deny. An Allow checked means that the user or group has that permission at this object. A Deny checked means that the specific user or group is denied that permission under any circumstance. Even if the user is a member of another group that has an Allow for that permission, the user is denied. In NT 4.0, we had a No Access permission, which locked a user or group completely out of a folder or file no matter what other permissions they might possess for that resource. The Win2K Deny is like a No Access operating independently for each permission. In other words, if a directly assigned Deny conflicts with an inherited Allow, or vice versa, the Deny always wins. But only for that specific permission, not the entire object. Full Control—Allow grants Full Control to the object. Full Control—Deny prohibits any access to the object whatsoever. If neither box is checked, the user or group is not granted the specific permission but could receive it by inheritance if it was granted in an ACL higher in the AD structure.

Near the bottom of the opening screen is a check box to Allow inheritable permissions from parent to propagate to this object. This is checked by default. In other words, AD object and property permissions are inherited in the AD hierarchy by default. Unchecking this box brings up a warning and a choice (see Figure 14-3). You can either take the existing inherited permissions and transform them into directly assigned permissions (the Copy button), delete the inherited permissions from the object and be left with only the directly assigned permissions (the Remove button), or Cancel out of here and return to the default (checked) status.

Just below the Permissions display box is the Advanced button. Click it and the "second" Security screen appears, the Advanced view (shown in Figure 14-4). Notice the three tabs across the top. These should "feel" familiar to NT 4.0 administrators; the look is different, but the functions are basically the same. The Permissions Entries box summarizes each separate ACE (Access Control Entry) on this object. The Auditing tab lists each user and group that will be audited (generate an entry in the Security log) when accessing this object. The Owner tab displays the current owner and allows you to take ownership of the object if you have the user right or the permission to take ownership. Change owners by highlighting the new owner in the Change Owner To box and click Apply.

Both the Permissions tab and the Auditing tab have the Allow Inheritable...from Parent to Propagate to This Object check box. They both work the same way described earlier. It is important to note that these inheritance tabs function independently of each other. You can block the inheritance of permissions from the parent at this object, while at the same time retaining the default inheritance of auditing entries.

Both the Permissions and the Auditing screens contain the View/Edit button. Click it, and our "third" and most detailed, granular screen appears (Figure 14-5). Notice the Object and Properties tabs at the top of the screen. The Object tab displays the object permissions either granted or inherited for the specific user or group displayed in the Name text box.

Click the Apply Onto down arrow (Figure 14-6), and you see just how granular the security control can be. While this may initially appear complex, it solves a myriad of problems from the NT 4.0 time frame. Most of us have inadvertently copied over permissions in the NTFS file system because we didn't realize that the ACL from above replaced the

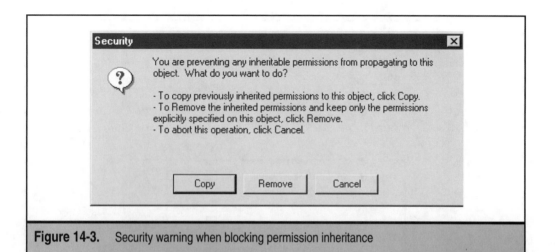

Figure 14-3.   Security warning when blocking permission inheritance

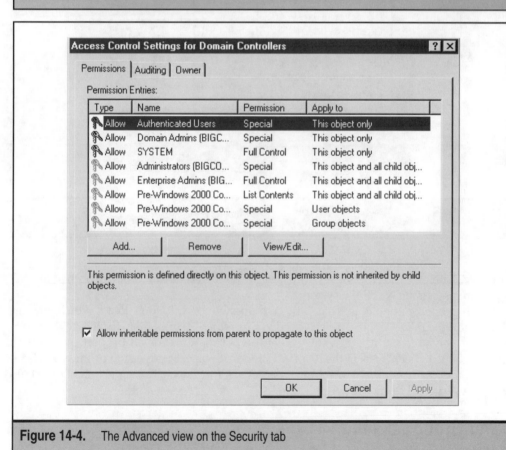

Figure 14-4.   The Advanced view on the Security tab

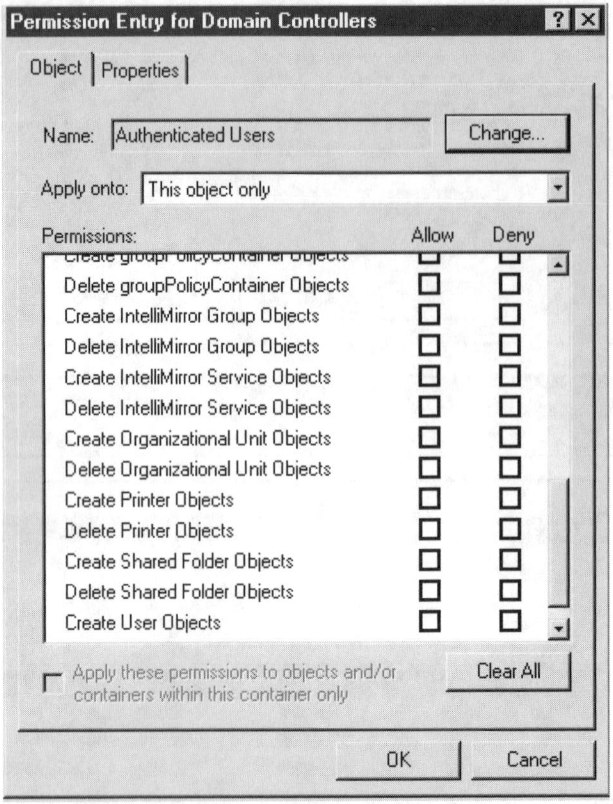

Figure 14-5. The Object tab Detailed Permissions view for an OU object

entire ACL below. The Apply Onto functions of Win2K solve that problem both in the AD structure and in the NTFS file system.

Each property of an object has only two possible permissions: Read, which enables the user or group to see that property, and Write, which enables them to change the property. For convenience, it is possible to set the permissions for all properties with one mouse-click. A check mark in the Read All Properties object permission produces a check mark in the Read permission of every property of the object. The same behavior occurs with the Write All Properties permission.

User and Group Accounts

Like other AD objects, user and group accounts can be protected with access rights. The functionality behind user accounts hasn't (and probably never will) changed from NT

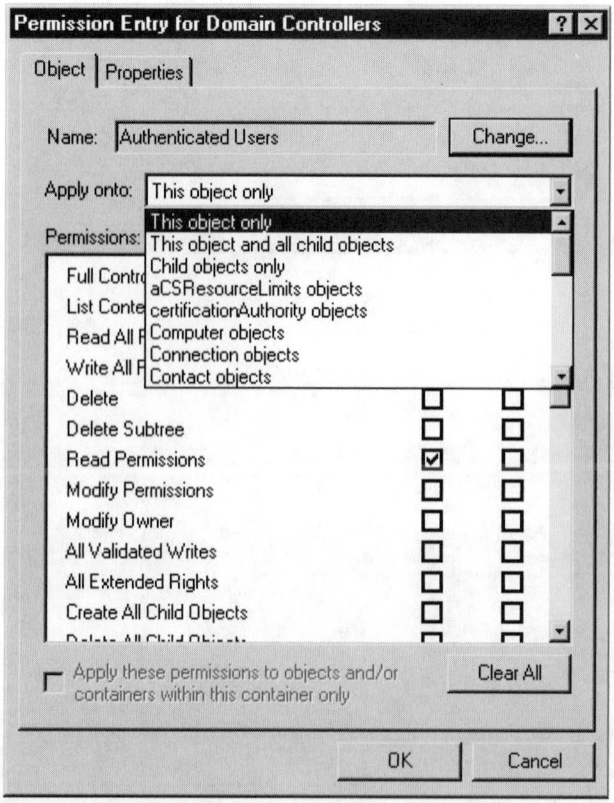

Figure 14-6.   The Apply Onto list on the Object tab

4.0. Users are still allowed to log directly onto a computer or across the network to a domain and access local and remote resources.

There are numerous security-related configuration options to choose from for user accounts, as follows:

▼ **Group membership**   Assign which groups the user account is a member of (see Figure 14-7). You can also specify the primary group that the user is affiliated with. All users must have a primary group.

■ **Remote access dial-in or VPN permissions**   This gives you the option to allow or deny access for remote connections, and you may also set callback options as shown in Figure 14-8.

■ **Logon hours**   Used to specify the time of the day in which the user can log on.

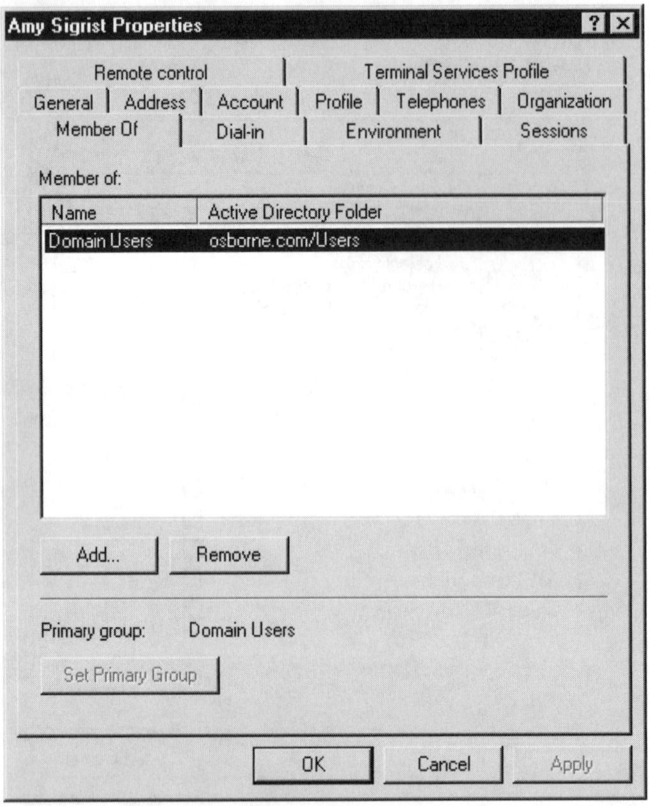

Figure 14-7. Group membership assignment

- ■ **Workstation restrictions** Used to specify the name of the computer(s) where the user can log on.

- ▲ **Account Expiration** Sets a date after which the account is automatically disabled.

Groups

A group is a collection of user accounts that can be used to help simplify administration including configuring security options. For instance, instead of configuring several user accounts with the ability to log on after business hours, you can create a group, add the appropriate users, and then assign the rights in one fell swoop.

GROUP TYPE A Distribution group is designed to replace the concept of Distribution Lists in the upcoming Exchange 2000. Exchange 2000 forsakes its own Active Directory in

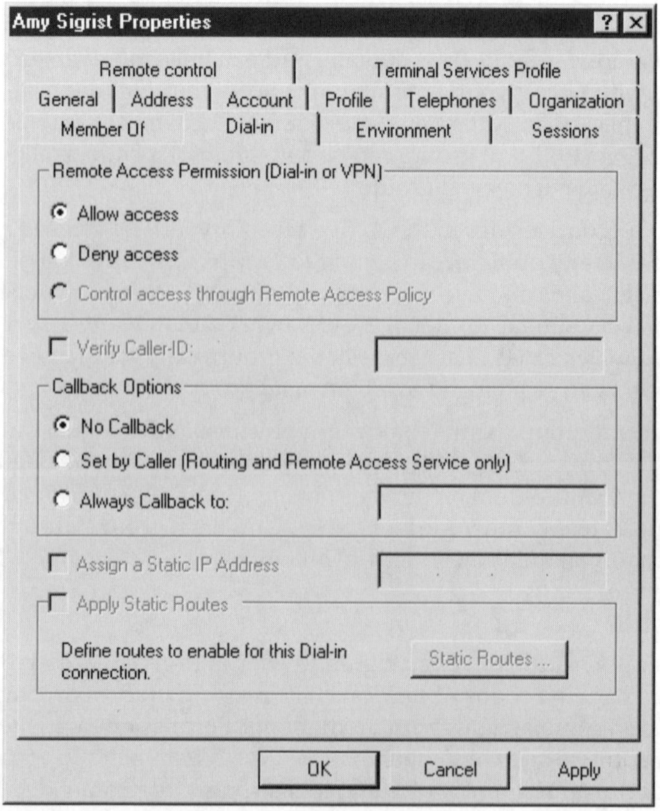

Figure 14-8. Remote access security options

favor of complete integration with the Windows 2000 AD. A Distribution group cannot function as a security principal, cannot be granted access to resources, and will not appear on its member's access tokens. A Distribution group is used solely to distribute mail.

A Security group is the type of group we are used to seeing in NT 4.0. It functions as a security principal, it can be granted access to resources, and it will appear on its member's access tokens. In addition, a Security group can be used to distribute mail.

GROUP SCOPE In addition to the two types of Win2K Active Directory groups discussed earlier, each type must have one of three possible scopes. The scope of a group will determine its capabilities and its restrictions in the Active Directory forest. In some cases, but not all, the scope of a group may be changed after it has been created. This is also the one place in the AD where native mode *does* make a significant difference, as you will see in the following list.

▼ A **Domain Local** group resides in the Active Directory, can be granted permissions to resources only on computers within its own domain, can belong only to groups from its own domain, and can have members from any domain. The Domain Local group is similar in concept, but not identical, to a local group in NT 4.0. In Native mode, a Domain Local group may be nested in another Domain Local group, can be a member of a Universal group, and can be changed to a Universal group.

■ A **Global** group resides in the Active Directory, can be granted permissions to resources in any domain, can belong to groups from any domain (and Universals), and can have members only from its own domain. The Global group is very similar to Global groups in NT 4.0. In Native mode, a Global group may be nested in another Global group, can be a member of a Universal group, and can be changed to a Universal group.

▲ A **Universal** group (Native mode only) resides in the Global Catalog, can be granted permissions to resources in any domain, cannot belong to any other group, and can contain members from any domain. A Universal group cannot be changed to any other kind of group. Universal groups are a brand new functionality in the Win2K Active Directory.

Account Rights

As an administrator, you can assign rights to user and group accounts that authorize them to perform certain actions or tasks such as backing up files or logging on to a machine locally. Don't confuse rights with permissions. Permissions apply to specific objects whereas rights apply to specific actions.

From an administrative point of view, it is strongly recommended that you define rights with groups rather than users. Using groups makes it easier to keep track of the rights that you assign, and it ensures that everyone that needs a specific capability has it.

There are two types of user rights: privileges and logon rights. On member servers they can be managed through the Local Users and Groups MMC snap-in, while on domain controllers they require the Group Policy MMC snap-in, as illustrated in Figure 14-9.

PRIVILEGES   The following list shows the privileges that can be assigned to a user or group:

▼ Act as Part of the Operating System

■ Add Workstations to Domain

■ Back Up Files and Directories

■ Bypass Traverse Checking

■ Change the System Time

■ Create a Pagefile

■ Create a Token Object

■ Create Permanent Shared Objects

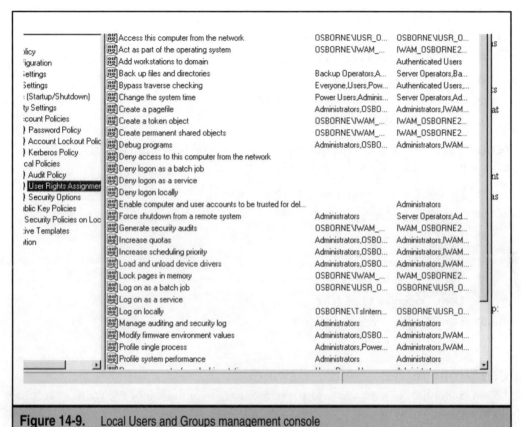

	Access this computer from the network	OSBORNE\IUSR_O...	OSBORNE\IUSR_O...
blicy	Act as part of the operating system	OSBORNE\IWAM_...	IWAM_OSBORNE2...
iguration	Add workstations to domain		Authenticated Users
iettings	Back up files and directories	Backup Operators,A...	Server Operators,Ba...
Settings	Bypass traverse checking	Everyone,Users,Pow...	Authenticated Users,...
: (Startup/Shutdown)	Change the system time	Power Users,Adminis...	Server Operators,Ad...
ty Settings	Create a pagefile	Administrators,OSBO...	Administrators,IWAM...
count Policies	Create a token object	OSBORNE\IWAM_...	IWAM_OSBORNE2...
} Password Policy	Create permanent shared objects	OSBORNE\IWAM_...	IWAM_OSBORNE2...
} Account Lockout Polic	Debug programs	Administrators,OSBO...	Administrators,IWAM...
} Kerberos Policy	Deny access to this computer from the network		
cal Policies	Deny logon as a batch job		
} Audit Policy	Deny logon as a service		
} User Rights Assignmer	Deny logon locally		
} Security Options	Enable computer and user accounts to be trusted for del...		Administrators
blic Key Policies	Force shutdown from a remote system	Administrators	Server Operators,Ad...
Security Policies on Loc	Generate security audits	OSBORNE\IWAM_...	IWAM_OSBORNE2...
ive Templates	Increase quotas	Administrators,OSBO...	Administrators,IWAM...
tion	Increase scheduling priority	Administrators,OSBO...	Administrators,IWAM...
	Load and unload device drivers	Administrators,OSBO...	Administrators,IWAM...
	Lock pages in memory	OSBORNE\IWAM_...	IWAM_OSBORNE2...
	Log on as a batch job	OSBORNE\IUSR_O...	OSBORNE\IUSR_O...
	Log on as a service		
	Log on locally	OSBORNE\TsIntern...	OSBORNE\IUSR_O...
	Manage auditing and security log	Administrators	Administrators
	Modify firmware environment values	Administrators,OSBO...	Administrators,IWAM...
	Profile single process	Administrators,Power...	Administrators,IWAM...
	Profile system performance	Administrators	Administrators

Figure 14-9. Local Users and Groups management console

- Debug Programs
- Enable User and Computer Accounts to be Trusted for Delegation
- Force Shutdown from a Remote System
- Generate Security Audits
- Increase Quotas
- Increase Scheduling Priority
- Load and Unload Device Drivers
- Lock Pages in Memory
- Manage Auditing and Security Log
- Modify Firmware Environment Values
- Profile a Single Process

- ■ Profile System Performance
- ■ Replace a Process-Level Token
- ■ Restore Files and Directories
- ■ Shut Down the System
- ■ Take Ownership of Files or Other Objects
- ▲ Unlock a Laptop

LOGON RIGHTS   The following list shows the logon rights that can be assigned to a user or group:

- ▼ Access This Computer from the Network
- ■ Log On as a Batch Job
- ■ Log On as a Service
- ■ Log On Locally
- ■ Deny Access to This Computer from the Network
- ■ Deny Logon as a Batch Job
- ■ Deny Logon as a Service
- ▲ Deny Logon Locally

Use Strong Alphanumeric Passwords

Logon credentials (usernames and passwords) are usually one of the weakest security links in your Windows 2000 network environment. They are usually one of the first things hackers try to determine because they are the easiest to find.

For starters, most companies use some form of an employee's name. For example, the user Margaret Flanagan, probably uses "margaret", "margaretf", or "mflanagan" as her username. It's also very common for the user's e-mail address to also be the username (and we all have business cards with our e-mail addresses on them, right?). The list can go on almost indefinitely, and unfortunately, there's not too much you can do about hackers finding out your username.

As a result of the ease of getting a username, it's imperative that you use strong, alphanumeric passwords. Passwords aren't always as easy to determine, but chances are, a seasoned hacker will be able to determine it in no time. If the password isn't one of the common ones like birthdays, family members' names, or default passwords, the hacker can use various "dictionary attack" programs and other utilities to guess passwords.

To strengthen passwords, policies governing what is allowed need to be established. It's also important to have users understand the ramifications of weak passwords. The following is a list of guidelines that you should consider using:

1. Passwords must be a minimum of six characters long (11 characters is best for NTLM).

2. Passwords may not contain your username or any part of your full name.

3. Passwords must be made up of characters from three of the four classes shown in Table 14-1.

4. Users should keep passwords secret (that is, don't write them down or disclose them in any other way—see the section "Social Engineering," on the following page).

5. Users should never reuse passwords.

6. Exercise and enforce password rotation on a regular basis (for example, every month or every quarter).

7. Enforce account lockouts.

8. Set expirations on temporary accounts.

9. Disable or remove unused user accounts.

Password Filtering

Beginning in NT 4.0, SP2 password filtering could be enabled. It involved adding a file named PASSFILT.DLL to the \%SYSTEMROOT%\SYSTEM32 folder and then editing the registry to enable it. All passwords changed by the user were passed through the "filter" to see if they complied. The default password complexity filter implemented points 1, 2, and 3 from the previous section. If the password met the criteria, it was changed. If not, the user received the world's strangest error message and immediately called the help desk. For this reason, not too many installations implemented this technology.

The same password filtering technology and the same complexity parameters as NT 4.0 have been implemented for Win2K as a Group Policy at the Domain level. It is disabled by default. You can implement it by clicking Administrative Tools | Domain Security Policy | Security Settings | Account Policies | Password Policies | Passwords Must Meet Complexity Requirements, then select Enabled and click OK. The policy will be implemented in the entire domain within 90 minutes.

Character Class	Example
Uppercase letters	A, B, C...Z
Lowercase letters	a, b, c...z
Numbers	0, 1, 2, 3...9
Nonalphanumeric symbols	`~!@#$%^&*()=+,"<>.?\	[]{}

Table 14-1. Character Classes for Passwords

Social Engineering

One of the most effective hacking tools available has absolutely nothing to do with keyboards, phone lines, or cryptography. It is the ability to manipulate, cajole, and generally deceive—people. Why spend days trying to crack a password when you can get most of them by simply asking for them? It is essential that the end user community be educated, then nagged, wrist-slapped, and more if they reveal their password to anyone. It is the most prevalent security breach in today's corporate environments.

Security Policies/Settings

Security policies (also known as *security settings*) give you yet another option to define security configuration parameters. They are applied through the use of Group Policy objects (GPOs) that enable centralized management and control of security for your Windows 2000 network environment. For more information on Group Policies, refer to Chapter 12.

Windows 2000 computers have specific security areas (see Figure 14-10) where security policies can be applied through the GPO. The following are security areas that can be configured:

▼ **Account Policies**   Contains settings for password, account lockout, and Kerberos policies

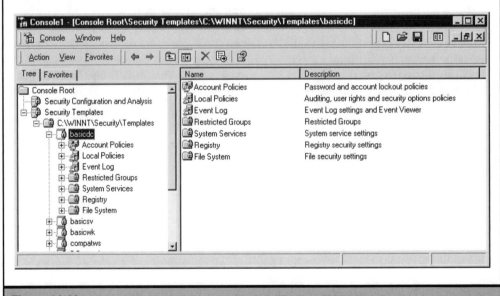

Figure 14-10.   Security areas that can be defined on Windows 2000 computers

- ■ **Local Policies**   Contains settings for auditing, user rights assignment, and security options (see Figure 14-11)

- ■ **Event Log**   Includes manageable Event Log settings

- ■ **Restricted Groups**   Used to control the membership of Windows 2000's built-in groups for the local computer

- ■ **System Services**   Allows you to control various configuration parameters on the local computer's system services

- ■ **Registry**   Security settings for the local computer's registry including auditing keys, permissions to keys, and much more

- ▲ **File System**   Used to configure security settings (permissions) for files, folders, and shares

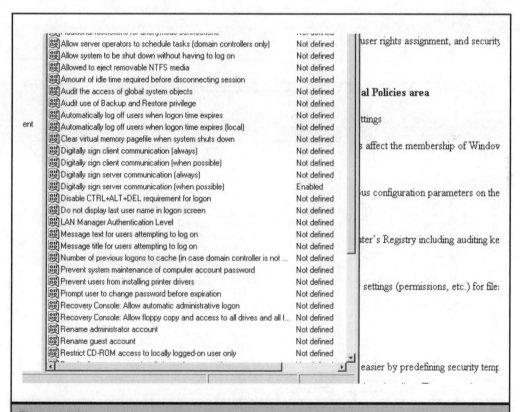

Figure 14-11.   Other security options within the Local Policies area

Security Templates

Microsoft has tried to make your life a little easier by predefining security templates that can be used to configure the security areas mentioned earlier. These security templates represent a collection of security settings that you can apply through the GPO.

Security templates are stored, by default, in the %SYSTEMROOT%\SECURITY\ TEMPLATES folder, and each one is saved as a text-based .inf file. These templates can be managed using the Security Templates MMC snap-in. As you can see in Figure 14-12, there are several predefined security templates. Each one organizes security policies depending on the type of computer that it's being applied to and what role that computer is playing in the network. For instance, you probably wouldn't want to apply one of the basic security templates to a DC, and you wouldn't want to apply the DC security template to a Windows 2000 Professional client machine.

You're not limited to only using the predefined security templates. You can easily create your own. Using the Security Templates snap-in, simply right-click on the security templates path (for example, %SYSTEMROOT%\SECURITY\TEMPLATES) and select New Template. Once you give the template a name, Windows 2000 builds the default security areas for you. Then you can define each of the security areas of your choice.

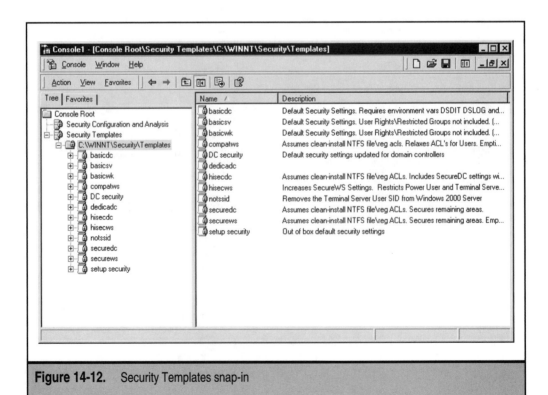

Figure 14-12.   Security Templates snap-in

Registry Security

The registry is a database containing static and dynamic information about your Windows 2000 computer. It is separated into a set of files found in %SYSTEMROOT%\SYSTEM32\CONFIG directory. Since the registry is comprised of these files, you are able to set access permissions just like you would with ordinary files, directories, or printers. If your system partition is using NTFS, you can modify the permissions on those files. By default, Administrators and the SYSTEM have Full Control while Server Operators and Authenticated Users have List Folder Contents rights to these files as illustrated in Figure 14-13. For more information on setting file permissions, see the section "Securing the File System," later in this chapter.

The Registry Editor (regedt32.exe) also has an internal security mechanism to prevent users from modifying the registry. The default security permissions for most registry keys are listed in Table 14-2.

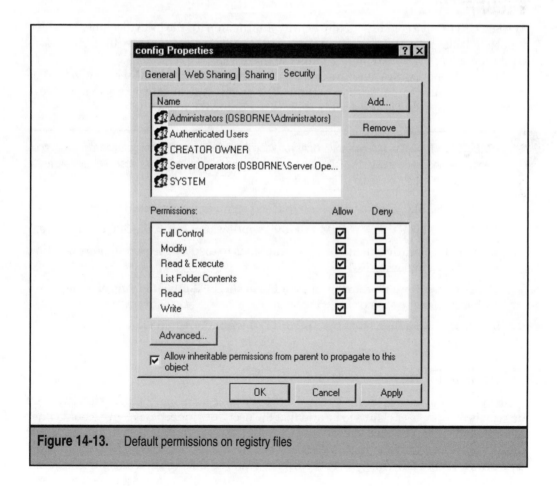

Figure 14-13.   Default permissions on registry files

User or Group	Read Access	Full Control Access
Administrators	√	√
Authenticated Users	√	
CREATOR OWNER		
Server Operators	√	
SYSTEM	√	√

Table 14-2.   Default Registry Security Permissions

SECURITY Hive

The SECURITY hive contains all the security information for the local machine. This hive is not available for modification by default even to administrators. Only the SYSTEM security context is allowed to make changes to this hive.

In order to modify this key, you must either log on as the SYSTEM security context or change the default Administrators settings. The easiest way to gain access to this hive is to change the default Administrators settings, by doing the following:

> **CAUTION:**   It is highly recommended that you keep the default security configuration to prevent accidental unauthorized access. The following steps should be followed only if it's absolutely necessary to allow the hive to be modified by administrators.

1. Start REGEDT32 by typing it on the Run menu or Command Prompt.
2. Open the HKEY_LOCAL_MACHINE window and select the SECURITY hive.
3. From the Security menu, select Permissions to display the permissions window as shown in Figure 14-14.
4. Select the Administrators group and then check Allow Full Control in the Permissions section of the window.
5. Click OK and then open the SECURITY hive as shown in Figure 14-15.

AUTHORIZATION

Authentication of user accounts determines that a user who logs on to a Windows 2000 domain is who the user claims to be and that the user does indeed have an account either in the domain or in a domain that is trusted. After the user is authenticated, however, AD must provide an additional layer of security to determine what objects the authenticated user can view and use. This type of security is achieved through access control.

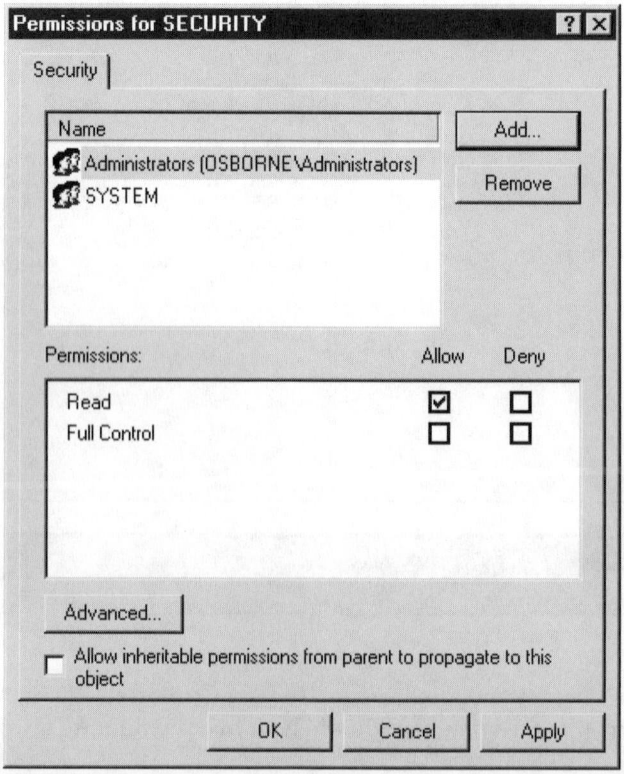

Figure 14-14. Setting permissions on the SECURITY hive

As with Windows NT and various other operating systems, Windows 2000 uses access control (also known as *authorization*) methods to allow or deny access to objects, such as files, shares, and printers. It authorizes access to these resource objects on a computer or on the network through the use of security descriptors, which are sets of information containing a list of who can access the objects.

A security descriptor includes the following information for every securable object:

▼ **The object's owner** This is the user who created the object and who has privileges to change permissions on that object.

■ **An access control list (ACL)** The ACL is maintained by the object's owner (typically the Administrator account) and determines who can see the object and what actions can be performed on that object. Windows 2000 enforces these permissions that are set by the owner whenever a user or process requests access to the object. So if the user or process doesn't have the privilege

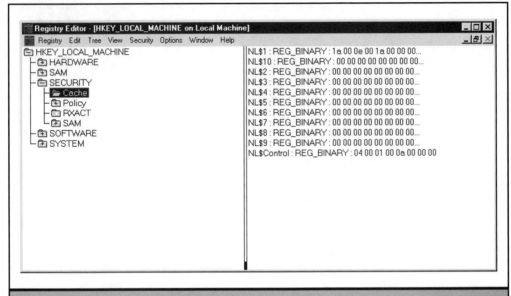

Figure 14-15. Viewing the SECURITY hive

to use the object, it's denied access. The names of users, groups, and computers that we wish to audit are held in a separate ACL called the system ACL (SACL).

■ **Access Control Entry (ACE)** An ACE is a single entry within the ACL.

▲ **Auditing information** Once enabled, the auditing information (in the SACL) contains which objects and events to monitor based on access by specific users, groups, or computers. Auditing is disabled by default.

NOTE: Unlike Windows NT, Windows 2000's access control is very granular due to the object-oriented and distributed nature of AD. This means that you can configure access control security in greater detail and depth.

Printer Security

After creating and then sharing a printer object, you can configure appropriate access to that printer. There are three basic levels of permissions (print, manage documents, and manage printers) for printers but, as with many AD objects, you can assign permissions in greater detail if you so desire.

By default, the Everyone group has access to print to the printer. This means that everyone, not just authenticated users, can print to this printer, and as a result, this may or may not cause a security problem in your environment. It depends on how tightly you want to control access. For tighter control over printer access, I recommend removing the Everyone group and replacing it with the Authenticated Users group to ensure that only those who log on to the domain have access. Also, administrators, print operators, and server operators on a domain controller have Manage Printer permission.

Table 14-3 lists the capabilities of the different permission levels.

To redefine printer permissions, do the following:

1. Open the Printers folder from the Start | Settings menu.

2. Right-click on the printer that you want to configure permissions for and select Properties.

3. Select the Security tab, and for each group, you can define the appropriate permissions as shown in Figure 14-16.

4. Optionally, you can add or remove groups by clicking the Add or Remove buttons, respectively.

Securing the File System

Giving access to files and folders can be split into two ways. First, you can share a folder and assign specific share permissions to gain access. You can also establish access control on the files or folders themselves.

Permission Capabilities	Print	Manage Documents	Manage Printer
Print documents	√	√	√
Pause, resume, restart, and cancel the user's own document	√	√	√
Connect to a printer	√	√	√
Control job settings for all documents		√	√
Pause, restart, and delete all documents		√	√
Share a printer			√
Change printer properties			√
Delete printers			√
Change printer permissions			√

Table 14-3.   Printer Permissions and Capabilities

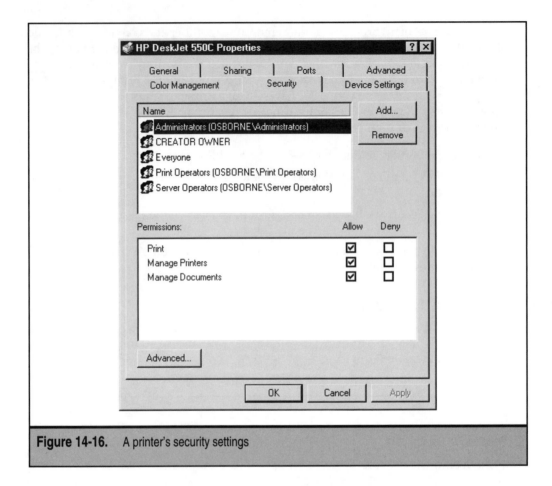

Figure 14-16. A printer's security settings

The two access control methods work in conjunction with one another. If you use both file and share access control methods, the more restrictive ACL takes precedence. For instance, if you set share permissions as read-only and the files have change control, then you'll only have Read-Only access. You benefit from the access control methods working nicely together because it tightens down who has access to files on your system.

NOTE: If you're using any other file system besides NTFS (for example, FAT, FAT32, CDFS), the only available access control method you can use is through shares.

NTFS

To protect data on a system, NTFS is the file system of choice (it is also strongly recommended for many services such as Active Directory and required for the Shared System

Volume [sysvol]). NTFS is the only file system supported by Windows 2000 that allows you to set permissions on files and folders.

File permissions include Full Control, Modify, Read & Execute, Read, and Write while folder permissions add one more permission to the list, which is List Folder Contents. Table 14-4 lists the permissions and which actions are associated with them.

SETTING NTFS PERMISSIONS   To configure file permissions, do the following:

1. Open Windows Explorer from the Start | Programs | Accessories menu.

2. Select the files or a group of files that you want to set permissions for. Then right-click and select Properties.

3. Select the Security tab, and for each group, you can define the appropriate permissions as shown in Figure 14-17.

4. Optionally, you can add or remove groups by clicking the Add or Remove buttons, respectively.

Action	Full Control	Modify	Read & Execute	Read	Write
Traverse Folder/ Execute File	√	√	√		
List Folder/Read Data	√	√	√	√	
Read Attributes	√	√	√	√	
Read Extended Attributes	√	√	√	√	
Create Files/Write Data	√	√			√
Create Folders/Append Data	√	√			√
Write Attributes	√	√			√
Write Extended Attributes	√	√			√
Delete Subfolders and Files	√				
Delete	√	√			
Read Permissions	√	√	√	√	√
Change Permissions	√				
Take Ownership	√				
Synchronize	√	√	√	√	√

Table 14-4.   NTFS File and Folder Permissions with Associated Actions

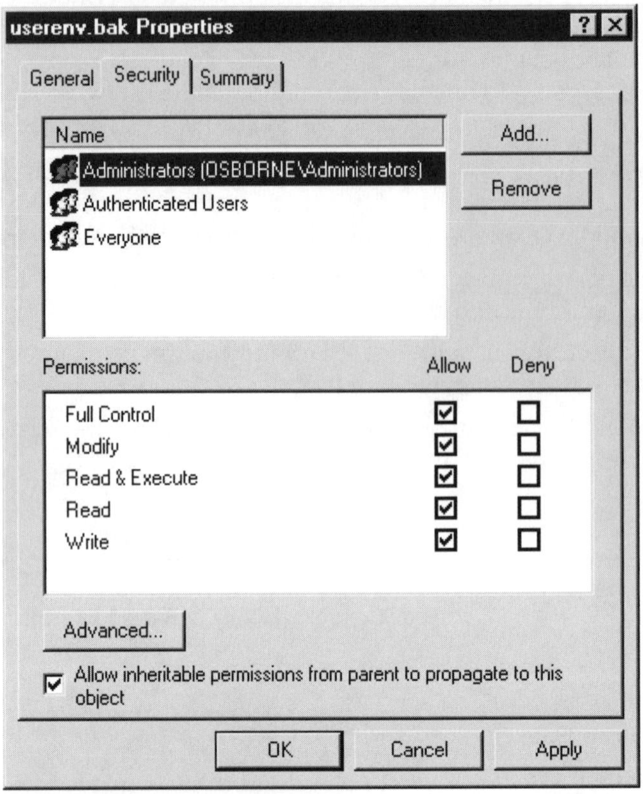

Figure 14-17. Setting NTFS file permissions

NOTE: The same steps can basically be applied when you're setting folder permissions. The differences are that you will be choosing the folder instead of individual files and you'll also have the ability to use the List Folder Contents permission.

Other than folders containing system-related files, by default, Windows 2000 sets the Everyone group as having Full Control on file and folder permissions. Microsoft probably decided to set permissions this way for convenience rather than disregarding security concerns for files and folders. In order to beef up your file and folder security, I strongly recommend that you remove the Everyone group and grant general permissions only to the dynamically updated Authenticated Users group. In addition, Win2K adds another dynamically updated group named ANONYMOUS LOGON. The system automatically traps connection attempts using NULL credentials and places them in this group. To protect your system, you need to place this group on the ACLs of the folders you wish to protect and set its access to Full Control—Deny. This will lock anyone attempting unauthorized access out of those folders.

EFS

The Encrypting File System (EFS) is an extra layer of protection against unauthorized access that allows you to encrypt files and folders on Win2K NTFS partitions using Data Encryption Standard (DES) 56-bit symmetric encryption. It is based on public-key cryptography, which is also used in PKI and somewhat in Kerberos authentication.

EFS is tightly integrated with NTFS so that files aren't just protected by the operating system's access control. In this way, if a hacker is lucky enough to compromise the NTFS permissions, they will then have to break the encryption in order to use the files or folders. The applications for EFS are endless. It can be used to prevent intruders from using MS-DOS-based utilities that read NTFS partitions, discourage laptop theft, and much more.

NOTE: The initial release of EFS supports only DES encryption, but you can expect that updates to Windows 2000 will most likely include updates for EFS, especially in light of the recent announcement that Windows 2000 will be the first operating system to include 128-bit encryption *worldwide*. It's also important to note that the initial release allows only the person who encrypted the file to open the file.

To encrypt a file or folder, do the following:

1. Open Windows Explorer from the Start | Programs | Accessories menu.
2. Select the files or folder that you want to encrypt. Then right-click and select Properties.
3. Under the General tab, click the Advanced button.
4. In the Advanced Attributes window, select Encrypt Contents to Secure Data.

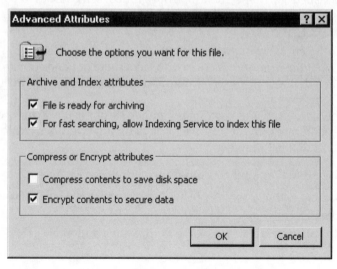

5. Click OK twice to close the Properties window. At this point, the Confirm Attribute Changes window appears and prompts you to decide on how you'd like to apply the encryption change.

Attempts by other users to read an encrypted file will result in an "Access Denied" message.

EFS can also be controlled from the command line using the cipher command. For example the command:

```
Cipher /E /S:secure /I /F
```

Will encrypt the \SECURE folder and all of its subfolders and continue to run even if there are errors.

DATA RECOVERY AGENT   Win2K provides a Data Recovery Agent for situations where the user who has used EFS to encrypt the files has left the company or the encryption keys are lost. By default, the Data Recovery Agent is the local administrator.

For your local computer, you can add Data Recovery Agents by using the MMC Group Policy snap-in focused on the local computer. Select Local Computer Policy | Computer Configurations | Windows Settings | Security Settings | Public Key Policies | Encrypted Data Recovery Agents. On the right side, you should see the Administrator account.

You can add Data Recovery Agents for a domain by using the MMC Active Directory Computers and Users snap-in; right-click on the domain whose recovery policy you wish to change and select Properties. From there, it's Group Policy | Select the Policy You Wish to Change | Edit | Computer Configurations | Windows Settings |Security Settings | Public Key Policies | Encrypted Data Recovery Agents. On the right side, you should see the Administrator account. To facilitate a domain Data Recovery Agent, Certificate Services must be running in the domain, and each domain Data Recovery Agent must have a valid certificate issued. Only specific users, not groups, can be Data Recovery Agents.

Share-Level Security

Share-level security enables you to control which users and processes can connect to the shared folder. What the user or process can do from there depends on the file and folder security you have defined. Share-level permissions include Full Control, Change, and Read access.

You can configure and manage shares either through the Windows Explorer or Shared Folders MMC snap-in (in this case, I'm using the Windows Explorer). To define share permissions, do the following:

1. Open Windows Explorer from the Start | Programs | Accessories menu.

2. Select the share that you want to set permissions for. Then right-click and select Properties.

3. Select the Sharing tab and click the Permissions button.

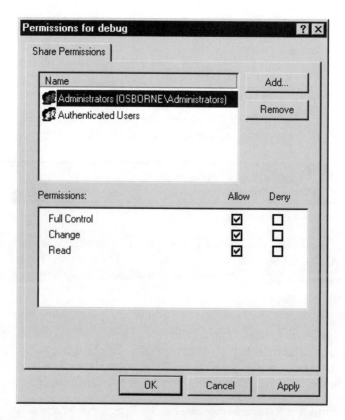

4. Configure the appropriate share permissions for groups or users.

5. You can optionally add or remove groups and users by using the Add and Remove buttons, respectively.

HIDDEN SHARES   In addition to shares that you can view from anywhere on the network, there are shares that are hidden. These shares are typically used for administrative purposes only and are denoted with the $ symbol. Table 14-5 lists the default hidden shares for Windows 2000.

You can create your own hidden shares for directories and printers by adding the $ to the end of the share name. Even though "out of sight is out of mind," you still are not completely secure. Therefore, after creating the hidden share, make sure that you set the appropriate permissions to the share as well as the files and any subdirectories.

Shared Folder Object Security

In addition to the NTFS permissions and share-level permissions, if the shared folder is published in the Active Directory, there is a third set of permissions: the permissions to the Shared Folder object itself. The purpose of publishing a Shared Folder in the AD is simply to allow the existing Active Directory search methods (Global Catalog and LDAP) to be

Hidden Share	Path
C$, D$, E$	Root of each partition
ADMIN$	%SYSTEMROOT%
IPC$	Temporary connection between servers
print$	%SYSTEMROOT%\SYSTEM32\SPOOL\DRIVERS

Table 14-5. Windows 2000's Default Hidden Shares

used in locating the folder. The Shared Folder object in the AD contains only a pointer to the existing UNC share. Users searching for the Shared Folder object must have Read permission to the object. By default, the Authenticated Users group has Read access.

Ownership

Whoever creates the object (for example, file, folder, or printer) is the object's owner. The only ones that can change access permissions on the object are the owner, the administrator, or a user with take ownership permission. For example, to take ownership of a file or folder object, do the following (assuming you have Administrator privileges):

1. Open Windows Explorer from the Start | Programs | Accessories menu.
2. Locate the file or folder you want to take ownership of.
3. Right-click the file or folder and then click Properties.
4. Select the Security tab and click the Advanced button.
5. Select the Owner tab and then click New Owner.
6. You can optionally take ownership on all of the subfolders by selecting Replace Owner on Subcontainers and Objects.
7. Click OK.

It is also possible to transfer ownership of the object. This can be done only indirectly, meaning that you can grant another user the Take Ownership permission; however you can't actually assign the ownership to another user.

AUDITING

In addition to securing resources, it's critical to monitor security events. Auditing is an important, yet often overlooked, facet of security. The importance of auditing comes from the fact that it can record possible security problems or security-related events, can be used to provide evidence of security compromises, and ensures accountability.

There are numerous ways to audit a Win2K system ranging from system-wide security events to monitoring individual security-related events for printers. The options determining just what events you can audit depend on the object that you're monitoring. All security-audited events can be viewed in the Security log within the Event Viewer.

The first and required step is to configure system-wide audit policies through the Local Computer Policy MMC snap-in or from the Group Policy snap-in for a DC. Once you've installed the snap-in, browse down the tree in the left pane (Computer Configuration | Windows Settings | Security Settings) and click on Audit Policy as shown in Figure 14-18. In the right pane, you'll see the following events that you can configure for auditing:

▼ Audit account logon events

■ Audit account management

■ Audit directory service access

■ Audit logon events

■ Audit object access

■ Audit policy change

■ Audit privilege use

■ Audit process tracking

▲ Audit system events

These events can be audited for success or failures.

Auditing Files and Folders

Auditing files and folders allows you to monitor various security-related events for specific users or groups. For example, you can configure auditing to watch for Authenticated Users creating folders and Administrators changing permissions.

To perform audits on files or folders, do the following:

1. Open Windows Explorer from the Start | Programs | Accessories menu.

2. Right-click on the file or folder you wish to audit and select Properties.

3. Select the Security tab and then click the Advanced tab.

4. In the Access Control Settings window, select the Auditing tab.

5. Click the Add button and then select a user, group, or computer to watch when accessing this file or folder. Click OK.

6. In the Auditing Entries window, specify the events that should be audited as shown in Figure 14-19. Click OK to close the window.

7. Click OK twice to exit completely.

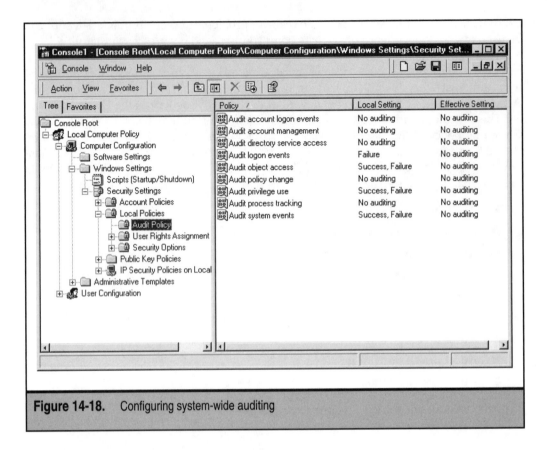

Figure 14-18. Configuring system-wide auditing

Auditing Printers

As with other objects, auditing printers is no exception. It allows tighter control and monitoring of your print processes. The major difference between auditing printers and other objects is what you can monitor.

The following printer events can be audited (successful or failed):

▼ Print

■ Manage printers

■ Manage documents

■ Read permissions

■ Change permissions

▲ Take ownership

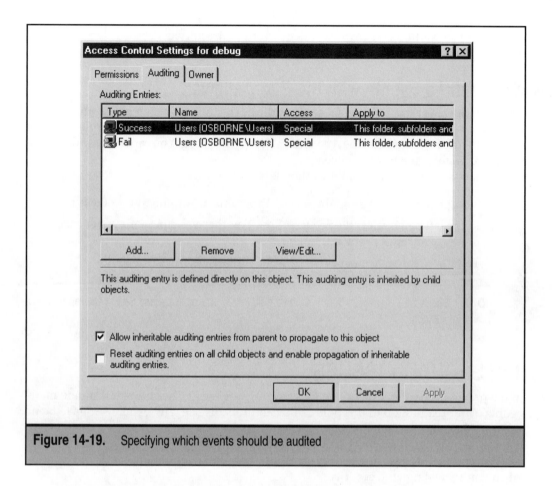

Figure 14-19.   Specifying which events should be audited

To perform audits on printers, do the following:

1. Open the Printers folder from the Start I Settings I Printers menu.
2. Right-click on the printer you wish to audit and select Properties.
3. Select the Security tab and then click the Advanced tab.
4. In the Access Control Settings window, select the Auditing tab.
5. Click the Add button and then select a user, group, or computer to watch when accessing this file or folder. Click OK.
6. In the Auditing Entry window, specify the events that should be audited. Click OK to close the window.
7. Click OK twice to finish.

You can set auditing on any object in the Active Directory using the exact same steps as setting auditing on a printer object.

Viewing Audited Events with the Event Viewer

As in Windows NT 4.0, when you enable auditing, the information from an audit policy or event gets populated into the Security Log of the Event Viewer. For example, failed or successful logon attempts can be recorded in the Security Log. You can then use the Event Viewer to analyze the recorded events.

To view the Security Log, do the following:

1. Select Event Viewer from the Start | Programs | Administrative Tools menu.

2. In the left pane, select the Security Log. You then see summaries of entries made by an audit in the right pane.

3. To view the details of an event, simply double-click on that event.

NOTE: Successful events are denoted with a gold key icon, while unsuccessful events appear as a gray padlock icon.

OTHER SECURITY ISSUES

In the previous chapter, I mentioned that security-related issues often intimidate many people. After reading up to this point, you can probably see why—there seems to be no end to what you must learn, on top of everything else you need to know about configuring and managing a Windows 2000 environment. Moreover, a lot is at stake (financial costs, corporate secrets, medical information, corporate reputation, and much more) when you're dealing with security.

Unfortunately, many other issues still have yet to be addressed when talking about security. Many of these concerns are outside of the scope of the built-in security measures within Windows 2000. However, they're still crucial to protecting your Win2K network environment.

Securing Your Connection to the Internet

The Internet is one of the most common ways that hackers try to gain unauthorized access to your Windows 2000 network environment. From a security point of view, the Internet is totally untrustworthy because you have no exercisable control over security measures being used. However, you do have the ability to control what comes into and out of your network infrastructure.

No matter how tightly you lock down your Win2K network, if you don't guard the border, you'll create more vulnerability than you'd ever imagine. Millions of people would have the opportunity to take a direct crack at your security implementation. I'm definitely not saying that Windows 2000 is an insecure operating system, but I am saying that the more you protect your gateway to the Internet, the safer your network will be.

Firewalls and Proxy Servers

Firewalls are blockades against unwanted intrusion that stand between your network and the rest of the world as illustrated in Figure 14-20. On the other hand, proxy servers such as Microsoft Proxy Server 2.0 have traditionally provided only performance enhancements (such as Web page and file caching) for your network but are now equipping themselves with firewall-class security mechanisms.

Different types of firewalls and proxies exist on the market, and I recommend that you research them in order to find out which one best suits your needs and budget. Many offer comparable features such as packet filtering, network address translation (NAT), support for a variety of protocols, security-related technologies, the use of a demilitarized zone (DMZ), and much more. Table 14-6 lists a variety of vendors that supply firewall security.

NOTE: A DMZ is created by the firewall to allow incoming Internet traffic but in a controlled manner. For example, Web servers are typically placed in a DMZ and only allow Web-based traffic (for example, HTTP).

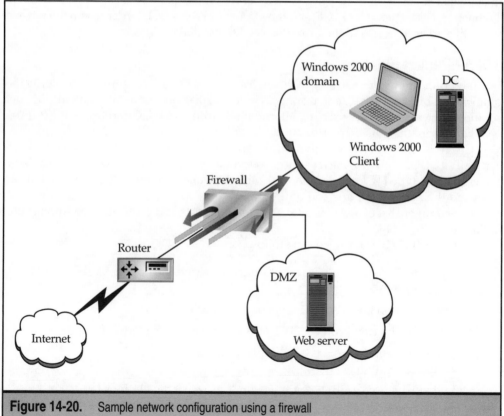

Figure 14-20.   Sample network configuration using a firewall

Company	Web Site
CheckPoint Software	http://www.checkpoint.com
Borderware	http://www.border.com
Network-1	http://www.network-1.com
NetGuard	http://www.netguard.com
Raptor	http://www.raptor.com
Microsoft	http://www.microsoft.com/proxy/

Table 14-6. Firewall and Proxy Vendors

It is important to note that Microsoft Proxy Server 2.0 requires an update (msp2wizi.exe) in order to run on a Win2K Server. The Update wizard is available on the Technet "Service Packs CD 3" CD and the Microsoft Web site. In order to run the wizard, you will also need access to the Proxy Server 2.0 installation files.

TCP/IP Packet Filtering

If you're connecting your network to the Internet, firewalls and/or proxies are highly recommended, but I also realize that some Windows 2000 environments can't afford such solutions. A viable, but less secure, alternative is to use Win2K to filter TCP/IP traffic coming in from the outside world.

TCP/IP filtering allows you to permit traffic coming into specific ports. These ports can be TCP, UDP, or both. Each service reserves a specific port number and also determines the port type (TCP, UDP, or both). Table 14-7 lists numerous TCP/IP-related services and their associate ports and port types.

For a complete list of all Windows 2000–related ports and protocols, see Appendix D at the end of this book.

To enable TCP/IP filtering, do the following:

1. Open the Network and Dial-up Connections folder from the Start | Settings menu.
2. Right-click on Local Area Connections and select Properties.
3. Select the Internet Protocol (TCP/IP) and click the Properties button.
4. In the Internet Protocol (TCP/IP) Properties window, click the Advanced button.
5. In the Advanced TCP/IP Settings window, select the Options tab.
6. Select TCP/IP filtering and select Properties.

Port Number	Type	Name	Description
20	TCP,UDP	ftp-data	File Transfer Protocol Data
21	TCP,UDP	ftp	File Transfer Protocol Control
23	TCP,UDP	telnet	Telnet
25	TCP,UDP	smtp	Mail, Simple Mail Transport Protocol
67	TCP,UDP	bootp	DHCP/BOOTP
68	TCP,UDP	bootp	DHCP/BOOTP
69	TCP,UDP	tftp	Trivial File Transfer Protocol
70	TCP,UDP	gopher	Gopher
79	TCP,UDP	finger	Finger
80	TCP,UDP	www	HTTP, World Wide Web
110	TCP,UDP	pop3	Post Office Protocol Version 3
119	TCP,UDP	nntp	Network News Transfer Protocol
137	TCP,UDP	netbios-ns	NetBIOS Name Service
138	TCP,UDP	netbios-dgm	NetBIOS Datagram Service
139	TCP,UDP	netbios-ssn	NetBIOS Session Service
161	TCP,UDP	snmp	Simple Network Management Protocol (SNMP)
162	TCP,UDP	snmptrap	SNMP Trap

Table 14-7.   Reserved TCP/IP Ports

7. In the TCP/IP Filtering window, click Permit Only for TCP, UDP, or both as illustrated in Figure 14-21. You'll notice that the Enable TCP/IP Filtering (All Adapters) check box is checked now. If you don't want filtering to be applied to all adapters, then uncheck this option.

8. Click the Add button and then type in the port number for the port type you selected. Click OK when done.

9. Click OK four times to completely exit.

The disadvantage to manually configuring TCP/IP filtering is that you have to know the specific ports that you'll need to permit, which is difficult even for those experienced with TCP/IP. If you decide to use filtering, just be prepared to spend a lot of time troubleshooting connectivity problems.

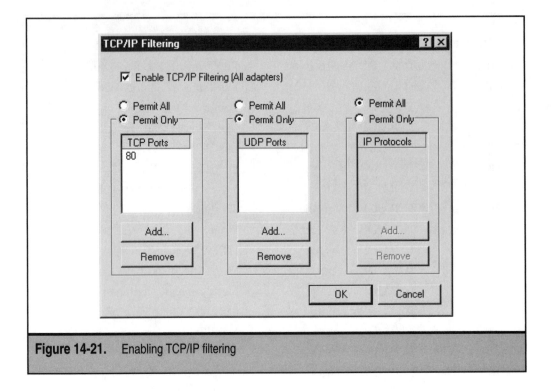

Figure 14-21.   Enabling TCP/IP filtering

Anti-Virus Solutions

Surprisingly, virus attacks have received notable attention only since the outbreak of the Michaelangelo virus a few years ago. Now, they're becoming increasingly widespread and even more damaging. For this reason, your security plan must include a third-party anti-virus solution in order to protect against virus threats.

A virus is a piece of code that can self-replicate and is designed to affect your computer in some form or fashion without your knowledge or permission. The code could be malicious or benign, but in either case, it's unwanted.

Types of and Effects from Viruses

There are several different types of viruses including the following:

▼   Master boot record and boot sector (hides in the housekeeping portion of the disk)

■   Trojan horses (hides inside what appears to be a normal harmless program)

■   File infecting (latches on to executable files)

- Stealth (tries to hide itself)
- Polymorphic (changes its shape every time you boot your system)
- Macro (does not affect the OS but can really mess up your Word documents)
- ▲ Hoaxes (don't really exist; they're simply rumors that someone starts as a joke)

Unfortunately, the list goes on and on, and it's important that you protect your Windows 2000 network environment from them all. The effect of these viruses on your environment depends on the type of virus it is. For example, a Trojan horse is usually hidden within another program, and it can cause a considerable amount of damage (for instance, corrupting all files on the hard disk) to the system it infects. Other viruses may just constantly display annoying messages on the screen.

Some common problems caused by viruses include, but aren't limited to, the following:

- ▼ Boot failures
- Lost data
- Reduction in available system memory
- Slow system performance
- Changes to file time-stamps
- ▲ Reduction in disk space

Virus Remedies

In order to prevent virus infections or to bring a system back to good health, you'll need help from an anti-virus program. You can either buy a "shrink-wrapped" type of application or download shareware anti-virus applications. The applications' features vary, but you should look for the types of viruses they detect and how they detect them. For example, some scan the hard disks, stay resident in memory, and some allow you to schedule periodic scans. Table 14-8 lists a few companies that provide anti-virus software.

Company	Web Site
Cheyenne Computer Associates	http://www.cheyenne.com
Dr. Solomon's Software	http://www.drsolomon.com
IBM	http://www.ibm.com
McAfee Associates	http://www.mcafee.com
Symantec	http://www.symantec.com

Table 14-8.   Anti-Virus Software Companies

When installing many applications, you should stop any memory-resident virus "shielding" programs. You can restart them when the installation is complete.

> **NOTE:**   Most, if not all, anti-virus applications have regular updates from the Web containing application enhancements and newly defined virus signatures that allow for a greater number of viruses to be detected. At all costs, you should invest in an anti-virus solution that provides regular updates.

SUMMARY

In this chapter, we've barely scraped the surface on one of the deepest subjects in the world of IT—security. It is truly heartening to see the leaps that Microsoft has moved forward in the world of security since NT 4.0. It was difficult for me to recommend NT 4.0 to my clients as a truly secure enterprise network operating system given the security exploits that were made possible by the fundamental flaws in the authentication, remote access, and network security architectures. I am pleased to say that I have no such qualms about Windows 2000. It will stack up favorably against the competition and, indeed, may outclass several of the most popular operating systems running networks today.

CHAPTER 15

Backup Procedures and Disaster Recovery Tools

Chapter 15 chides you to remember that the mundane functions of backup and restore just might save your hide some day. When it comes to equipment failure, it's not *if*, it's *when*. I also focus on the disaster recovery options for the Active Directory and the Advanced Startup Options menu.

KEEPING YOUR SYSTEM UP-TO-DATE

As administrators, we know that our systems, especially our servers, should have the most recent Service Packs, hot-fixes, and patches available. These new files remove the security "holes" which permit the very public exploits that we hear about in newsgroups and even in the mainstream press. But they also fix the vulnerabilities quietly uncovered behind the scenes by Microsoft or one of their enterprise customers who would rather not have the news of the exploit spread around due to the risk of losing public confidence or damaging their corporate reputation or both. Most of us know someone who has gotten burned by jumping onto a hot-fix or Service Pack too quickly. Perhaps, it was just one BDC that had to be reinstalled because the Notes server couldn't boot.

So just when should we jump in? Like most complicated discussions, the answer is "It all depends." Only you can determine the risk-versus-hassle factor for your organization. If you run a highly secured environment and the latest exposure could cost your company big money or severely damage its reputation, then you need to hop on a test pilot right now. If, on the other hand, your network borders are well-protected by high-quality firewalls, you may be able to wait several months or even a year. Many conservative IT organizations never implement any hot-fixes at all and don't install one Service Pack until the next one is released. In this way, even though they haven't got the latest and greatest protection, they are assured that what they are installing works flawlessly. This strategy may get a boost from the fact that Microsoft has announced that Service Packs will be released more often (three to four times a year) and on a predictable schedule. Service Pack 1 for Win2K has already been scheduled for release in June 2000.

Service Packs

Service Packs were released for NT 4.0 when Microsoft felt like it. The schedule was unpredictable:

> NT 4.0 Released: August 1996
> NT 4.0 Service Pack 1: October 1996 (2 months)
> NT 4.0 Service Pack 2: December 1996 (2 months)
> NT 4.0 Service Pack 3: June 1997 (6 months)
> NT 4.0 Service Pack 4: October 1998 (16 months)
> NT 4.0 Service Pack 5: May 1999 (7 months)
> NT 4.0 Service Pack 6: October 1999 (5 months)
> NT 4.0 Service Pack 6a: December 1999 (2 months—a fix for SP6)

Because Win2K is language independent, Service Packs should now be able to be released worldwide at the same time. This has not been the case for NT 4.0. Organizations in countries other than the United States have had to wait months for NT Service Packs to be released in their language. Since Terminal Services is no longer a separate kernel, there will be no separate Terminal Server Service Packs with Windows 2000. Microsoft recently announced that the U.S. government has agreed to let Win2K be the first operating system to ship with 128-bit encryption worldwide—not quite worldwide because Microsoft won't include countries that the United States considers a terrorist threat. But this means that there shouldn't have to be separate Service Packs because of encryption strength either. NT 4.0 had different encryption settings for different countries depending on just exactly how much the U.S. government trusted them or their security measures. All of these developments will help us here in North America as well because thousands more users will be receiving, testing, and breaking these releases in a much shorter time frame than before. This will mean that Microsoft will be able to fix the existing problems, even the ones in Service Packs, much more quickly, and that's good for us all.

Slip-Streaming

In Windows 2000, Microsoft will also provide slip-streaming for the first time. All Service Packs traditionally have been applied to an existing installed system, and often had to be reapplied after the installation of server applications. This update had to be performed manually on every installed system, even those we were installing after the release of the Service Pack. Slip-streaming can change all that. In addition to the normal Service Pack update that we are used to getting with NT 4.0, Microsoft will also ship the new versions of the compressed installation files. We can simply copy these new compressed files to a network installation point, and each new Win2K computer that we install will already be running at the latest Service Pack level. We will still need the good ol' Service Pack update, however, because we may have to reapply it after installing certain software applications.

Hot-Fixes

Hot-fixes are a fact of life. With a system this large and this complex, countless things can go wrong. And plenty of folks are out there just dying to find them, too. Microsoft's high visibility in the press makes their products a prime target for the hacking community. Even before Windows 2000 was shipped, a hot-fix was available for a security vulnerability that impacted NT 4.0 Index Server and the Windows 2000 Indexing Service. Microsoft's critics were quick to jump on it as a sign of weakness in the Win2K operating system. I look at it from the complete opposite direction: since these types of nagging vulnerabilities are inevitable in a massively complicated product like Windows 2000, Microsoft should be congratulated for being Johnny-on-the-spot and patching the problem so quickly and publicly.

Let's go over a few important facts about hot-fixes. They are not regression tested, which means that they worked on the Microsoft systems but may not work on yours. The priority is to get them out on the Web site as quickly as possible once an operational bug or security vulnerability is uncovered. Service Packs are well tested, while hot-fixes are not. Hot-fixes must be installed in date and time-stamp order from the earliest to the latest. Later files may not work with earlier versions of certain other files. Hot-fixes always build on Service Packs. Each Service Pack will contain all the previous hot-fixes so the hot-fix list will move to a new directory with each new Service Pack, and no additional hot-fixes will be added to previous Service Packs.

The URL for accessing Win2K hot-fixes is not published at this time, but if it follows the form of the NT 4.0 products, you might try ftp://ftp.microsoft.com/bussys and have a look in the directory for Win2K or something close to that.

Web Sites

Many excellent Web sites, newsgroups, and e-mail newsletters can keep you up-to-the-minute with Windows 2000 news. Here are just a few:

▼ **www.microsoft.com/security**   Security bulletins on Microsoft products.

■ **www.winntmag.com**   Several e-mail newsletters that provide an excellent source of timely information.

■ **www.ntbugtraq.com**   *The* list to monitor if you want to be informed in real time about problems with Windows NT and Win2K. This site is monitored to keep the signal-to-noise ratio very high.

■ **www.sans.org**   Regular e-mail newsletter summaries of bugs and security issues.

■ **www.cert.org**   The U.S. government list of potential vulnerabilities.

▲ **www.ntsecurity.net**   The latest security news on NT and Win2K.

BACKING UP AND RESTORING YOUR DATA

Few functions are more important than backing up your data, but, like Rodney Dangerfield, backing up don't get no respect. We know that we must back up every server every night, and we usually create some kind of automated process to accomplish this. But workstations seldom if ever get backed up. Win2K domain controllers are a different animal. If the only information you are trying to protect is the Active Directory, then you really need to back up only one DC each night. The AD information is identical on every DC in the same domain.

The Windows 2000 Backup Utility (NTBackup) has been greatly enhanced over the NT 4.0 version. To launch the backup utility, click Start | Programs | Accessories | System Tools | Backup (or Start | Run and type **Ntbackup**). The Welcome screen (Figure 15-1) appears.

Backup Procedures

Backing up data is far less about technology and far more about procedures policies. First of all, your organization must have a plan, a backup strategy: parameters like Monday

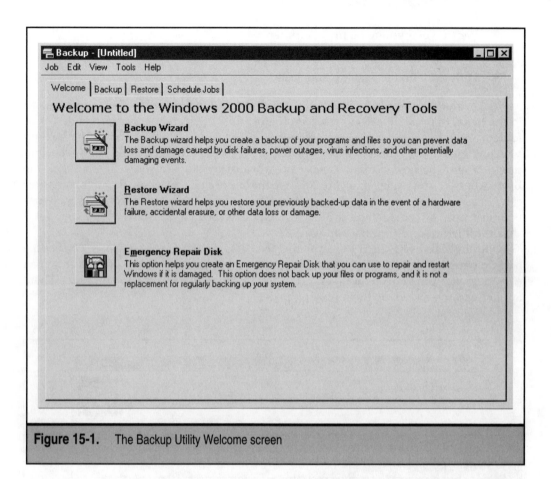

Figure 15-1.   The Backup Utility Welcome screen

through Thursday, we'll do a Differential, and Friday, we'll go with a Normal. Three copies of the backup media will be maintained with one copy off-site at all times. All backup logs to be printed out and included in the backup log book with time, date, who did it, backup set name, tape number, and so on. Back up each volume as a single entity, the restore will be faster. All storage media and devices will be stored in a controlled access room, not out in the hallway. All backup personnel will receive adequate training.

It is possible to use the binary image copying tools like Ghost or Drive Image Pro to back up the client workstation environment. If the policy of the organization is such that the user is not supposed to store any personal or important data on their desktop computer, then when there is a problem with the desktop, admins can bring down a sysprep image, and the system is back up and running.

The easiest way to start your Win2K backup is to use the Backup Wizard. From the Welcome screen or the Tools menu, select Backup Wizard and then click Next. Now you must decide what to back up. Three choices are presented as shown in the following list.

▼   Back up everything on my computer

■   Back up selected files, drives, or network data

▲   Only back up the System State Data

Make your selection and click Next. The second option requires further configuration in the Items to Back Up selection screen (Figure 15-2). Select the appropriate drives or folders and click Next. All three choices bring you to the Where to Store the Backup screen (Figure 15-3), which is where the big differences between the old NT 4.0 backup program and the new Win2K backup program really start to show. If you click the Browse button, you realize that you can store the backup on any media that this computer can see as a device, including floppy disks, Zip or Jazz drives, local volumes, network volumes, and, of course, tape drives. You can even search the Active Directory for a shared folder to store your backup on.

Clicking Next brings up the Completing the Backup Wizard screen, which verifies the backup parameters. Clicking the Advanced button brings up the Type of Backup screen (Figure 15-4), from which you first need to choose what type of backup you want. There are five choices, shown on the following page.

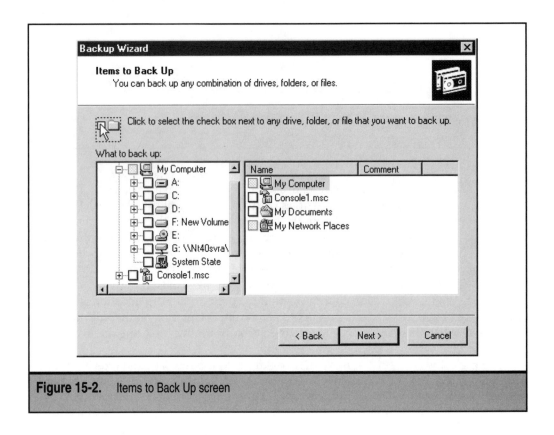

Figure 15-2.   Items to Back Up screen

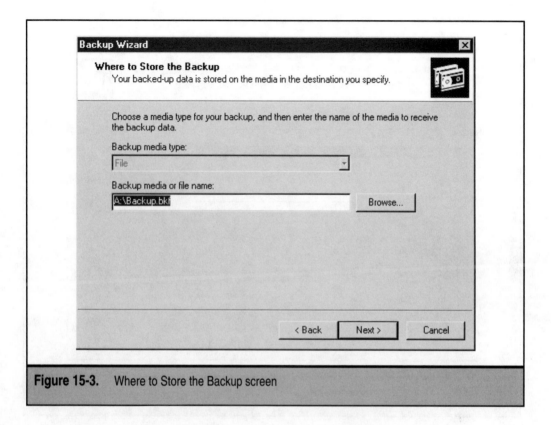

Figure 15-3. Where to Store the Backup screen

▼ **Normal** This option, the default, copies all selected files and clears the Archive attribute when complete. Sometimes called a "full backup." This backup takes the longest and is the shortest restore.

■ **Copy** Copies all selected files and does not clear the Archive attribute when complete. Simply copies all the files without messing with the archive bit. Longer backup, shorter restore.

■ **Incremental** Copies only files with Archive attribute on and clears the Archive attribute when complete. Copies only the files that have changed since the last normal or incremental backup. Shorter backup, longer restore.

■ **Differential** Copies only files with the Archive attribute on and does not clear the Archive attribute when complete. Copies only the files that have changed but lets the changes build on top of each other from day to day. Longer backup each day, shorter restore.

▲ **Daily** Copies only files that have a modified date matching today's date and does not clear the Archive attribute. Copies files that changed today regardless of anything else.

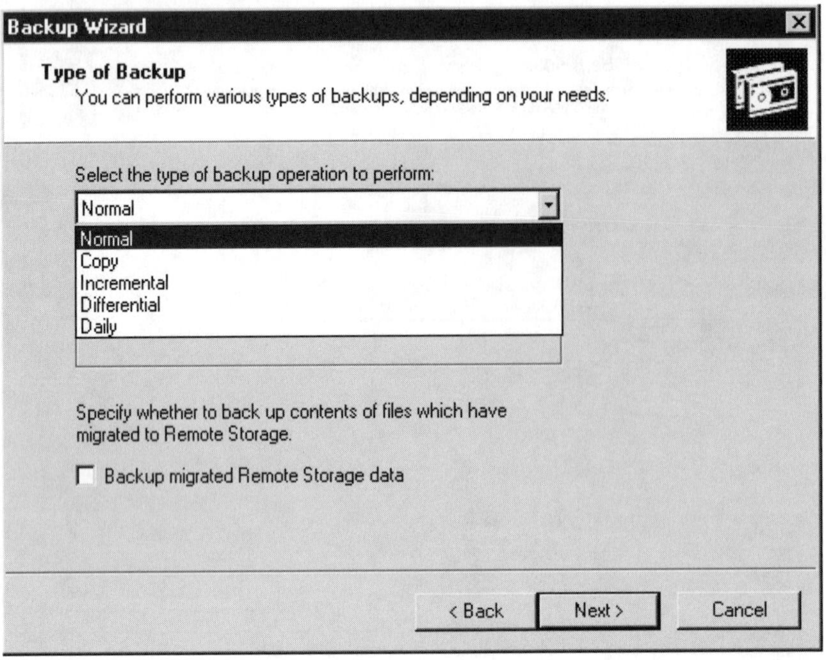

Figure 15-4. Type of Backup screen

In addition, one more setting is available on this screen: the check box next to Backup Migrated Remote Storage Data where you are answering the question, "Do you want to back up the contents of files that have been migrated to Remote Storage?" The default is unchecked or no. If you check this box, the Remote Storage device and media must be available during the backup process. When you've made your selections, click Next. The How to Back Up screen appears, asking whether you wish to verify data after backup. Verification will take extra time, but it helps to ensure a successful backup. If your hardware supports it, a check box asking whether you wish to use hardware compression appears. Hardware compression saves space on the storage media but limits you to restoring only from devices that support the same type of compression. Click Next.

The Media Options screen appears, asking if you'd like to append this backup data to the last backup on this media or write over it. Make your selection and click Next. The Backup Label screen appears, giving you an option to change the label on the backup you are about to perform. When you are satisfied with the label, click Next. The When to Back Up screen appears. You can run the backup right now or schedule it for later. You'll need credentials with the right to perform backups in order to create a scheduled job. You need to enter a name for the job and set the schedule and frequency of the backup and a number of other configuration and option settings. Click Next, and you are back to the Completing the Backup Wizard screen. Click Finish and, depending on your selections, either the backup begins, or the job is scheduled.

Backup and Restore Permissions

The Backup right does not give a user Read permission to the files but only the ability to copy those files to another medium. However, once the files are on the other medium, it is possible that they could be vulnerable. This is why the Backup and Restore rights are considered so powerful.

By default, the built-in local group Backup Operators has the right to back up and restore files. Also by default, this group has no members. In a high-security environment, it is probably better if no one belongs to the Backup Operators group, allowing admins to be the only group empowered with the ability to restore data. The back up files and directories user right can be granted to any user or group through Group Policies. It is always a good practice to separate the Backup right from the Restore right. In other words, the same people (except for Administrators) should be able to both back up and restore.

Restoring Your Data

When a server goes down, many things happen that are not technological. Workers can't work so they "pop" up out of their cubes or "prairie dog." Executives notice the unusual volume of conversation and look out of their offices to see all the "prairie dogs" chatting away. From past experience, they know that this can mean only one thing "the network is down." I call this "executive network monitoring." These are the times when the suits find their way to the server room to see if there is anything they can do to "help."

It is a truly strange phenomenon, but most administrators have the backup procedures documented to a "T" but are content to literally "wing" any potential restore armed with their considerable knowledge and experience. This is a bad idea—a very bad idea. First, you must understand that Murphy's Law says that hard drives will die only when the senior admin is training on the next crucial product in another city and the second admin is out sick. Second, because today's equipment is so reliable, we forget just how much pressure the person performing the restore is under. The best example I've heard is from the military. The hard drive dies in the server, the technician, a corporal, swaps it out and starts the restore from tape. The restore software presents a time to completion on the screen. A colonel comes in and demands to know what's wrong. The corporal explains and finishes with the fact that the restore will be complete in (reading the screen) 2 hours and 14 minutes. The colonel turns to leave and barks, "I want this thing back up in one hour, son. That's an order." "Yes, sir," answers the corporal, stifling his smirk.

The "Restore Bible"

All this brings me to the "Restore Bible." The restore procedures must be documented and tested. And not just documented—each individual step must be documented for dummies so that nearly anyone could perform a restore and (here's the one we don't like to admit) so that we have a fallback when we are under the gun. Pressure can make even the best of us temporarily incompetent. We need a framework, an outline, to get started. I call these documented restore procedures the "Restore Bible." Its procedures have been tested, practiced, and refined until a child could do a restore. These procedures are developed when things are working and calm and are tested periodically for accuracy and clarity. Tapes are verified on a weekly basis. Trial restore procedures are practiced by anyone who might be called upon to restore a system. Backup is not enough; you need the "Restore Bible."

WINDOWS 2000 ADVANCED OPTIONS MENU

Similar to Windows 9*x*, Windows 2000 now comes with the F8 option at startup. When you see the normal boot menu, simply press F8 to get to the Advanced Options menu. Adding this option has enabled Microsoft to clean up the cluttered NT boot screens for Win2K by removing the VGA Mode option from the boot menu and the Last Known Good option from the startup sequence. You'll find them both here in the Advanced Startup Options screen (Figure 15-5).

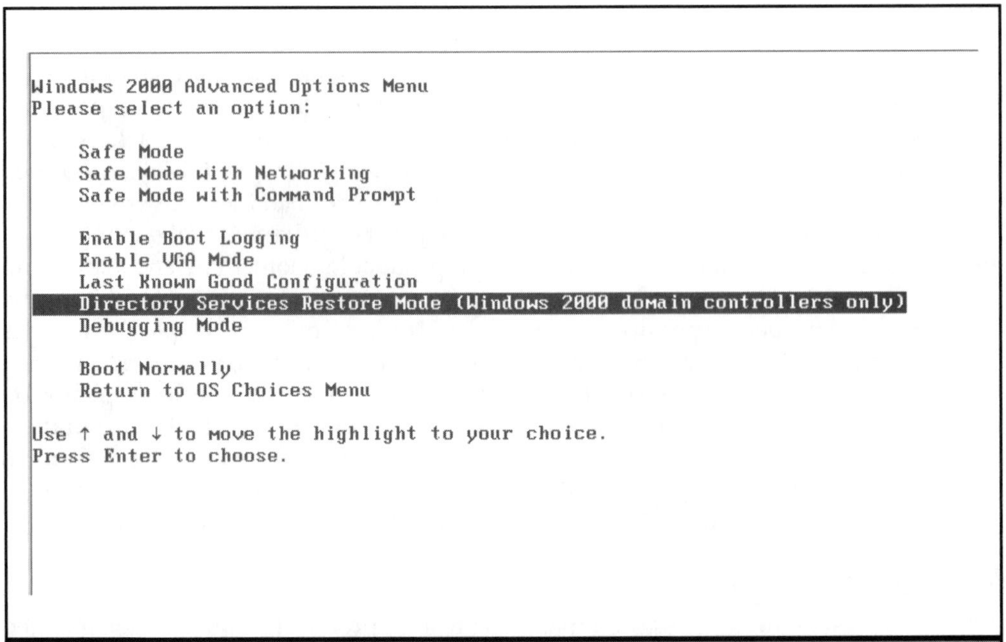

```
Windows 2000 Advanced Options Menu
Please select an option:

    Safe Mode
    Safe Mode with Networking
    Safe Mode with Command Prompt

    Enable Boot Logging
    Enable VGA Mode
    Last Known Good Configuration
    Directory Services Restore Mode (Windows 2000 domain controllers only)
    Debugging Mode

    Boot Normally
    Return to OS Choices Menu

Use ↑ and ↓ to move the highlight to your choice.
Press Enter to choose.
```

Figure 15-5.   Win2K Advanced Options screen (F8 bootup)

The first three options will boot the system into Safe mode, which means that the bare minimum of device drivers are loaded. Only the mouse, keyboard, CD-ROM, standard VGA drivers, and the Event log, Plug and Play, RPC, and Logical Disk Manager services are loaded. The Safe Mode with Networking option adds the networking drivers so the computer can participate in the network environment. Safe Mode with Command Prompt boots in Safe mode and brings up a Command Prompt window, which is the only option that can be run. You will not mistake the fact that you are in Safe mode; the screen wallpaper is black with the words "Safe Mode" appearing in all four corners of the screen. The video driver doesn't load so your resolution is probably back to 640×480; plus, you usually get a "Running in Safe Mode" warning after you log in.

Enable Boot Logging is similar to the old win /b from days gone by. It creates a file called ntbtlog.txt in the \%SYSTEMROOT% folder, which contains a beginning (start) for each device or service that the system attempted to load and an end (success) when each device or service was successfully loaded. The file is used primarily in the troubleshooting process of bootup problems because you can see the exact point where the boot failed and on what device or service.

Enable VGA Mode is the same concept we used in NT 4.0 when it showed up in the opening boot menu. VGA mode is used to repair problems with the video drivers or video devices. It is possible to install a new video graphics adapter, and for whatever reason, it doesn't work (wrong drivers, wrong parameters, and so on). However, we now have a problem: since the video doesn't work, how can we display the system so that we can repair or remove the offending item? Enter VGA mode. By selecting VGA Mode from the F8 Advanced Options menu, you are configuring the system with base video drivers, and no additional video drivers will load. This allows an admin to repair the problem and test it again. VGA mode works only from the F8 bootup menu, which means you must reboot between every attempt to repair the video problem.

Last Known Good Configuration works identically to the same option in NT 4.0. Win2K saves multiple complete copies of the configuration of the computer under the HKLM\SYSTEM registry key (CurrentControlSet, ControlSet001, ControlSet002, and so on). When a new device is added, only the CurrentControlSet is updated. Upon reboot, the system will, by default, load the CurrentControlSet. If this produces an error, you are notified by the familiar "One or more services failed to start" message, which will appear even if you haven't logged on. If you haven't yet logged on, you can restart the computer, this time pressing F8 and selecting Last Known Good Configuration. The previous configuration will load, presumably without the error. Now we can correct the parameters of the device or service.

But here's the catch: When does the CurrentControlSet become the Last Known Good? When the user successfully logs on, the CurrentControlSet registry key is copied to the ControlSet00x key, serving as the Last Known Good repository (same registry location—Select key). So what does this mean to you? Simple. Don't log on to a system where you've made a configuration change until you are sure that the system will boot without errors. Just wait a couple of minutes while the OS finishes loading all of its services to ascertain if all services loaded successfully. Most of us are busy, and we pounce on the keyboard the very second the CTRL-ALT-DEL logon box appears. Win2K is not finished loading services when the logon box appears; it is simply a result of the winlogon service being loaded. So back off for a minute or two; it could save you hours of time later when you don't have to reinstall.

Directory Services Restore Mode works only with Windows 2000 domain controllers and is discussed later in this chapter.

Debugging Mode starts Win2K in Kernel Debug mode, which allows a debugger to access the kernel for in-depth troubleshooting.

Boot Normally boots the system normally, and Return to OS Choices Menu takes you back one level to the original boot menu.

The Win2K Advanced Options menu is a great addition to Windows 2000 from both the user and the administrator's perspective. The users get a clean, uncluttered boot process, while the admins get all the necessary bootup troubleshooting tools in one central place within easy reach.

BACKING UP THE ACTIVE DIRECTORY

The easiest way to back up the Active Directory is to use the Backup Wizard. From the Welcome screen or the Tools menu, click Backup Wizard, click Next, then select Only Back Up the System State Data, select the backup media (you'll need something that can hold the entire AD), click Next, and finally, click Finish. The backup process begins. See Table 15-1 for details on system state data.

Backing Up System State Data

One of the NTBackup options available is System State Data. Table 15-1 outlines the various components of system state data that are backed up depending on which installation of Windows 2000 you are running.

The individual components of system state data cannot be backed up separately. Backing up the system state data must be performed as a local operation only. You cannot back up system state data on a remote computer. You can, however, schedule backups of system state data on remote computers.

When you back up the system state data, a copy of all your registry files is saved to the \WINNT\REPAIR\REGBACK folder. Backing up the system state data is similar to rdisk /s in NT 4.0, which saved your registry files to the \WINNT\REPAIR folder. In case of failure, these files can be used to repair your registry without performing a full restore of system state data.

You cannot restore the system state data on a domain controller while the Active Directory service is running. To restore system state data on a DC, you must reboot the DC and restart in Directory Services Restore mode (see the section by that name later in this chapter). Restoring the system state data on a non-DC computer is simply a matter of answering the prompts in the Restore Wizard.

	System		
	Win2K Domain		**Win2K**
Component	**Controller**	**Win2K Server***	**Professional**
Registry	X	X	X
COM+ Component Services Class Registration Database	X	X	X
System startup files	X	X	X
Certificate Services Database	X	X	
Active Directory	X		
Sysvol folder	X		

* Win2K Standalone or Member Server running Certificate Server

Table 15-1. System State Data

ACTIVE DIRECTORY—DISASTER RECOVERY OPTIONS

While we all wish that we didn't require a section on Active Directory backup and disaster recovery, none of us is naïve enough to think that that we'll never need it. Microsoft has done a reasonable job giving us the basic tools we need to recover from a failed domain controller. Look for more fully functional tools from third-party vendors and even from Microsoft before too long. The available tools are sufficient for the initial rollouts, but for a large distributed implementation of Windows 2000, we need to see more remote backup and recovery options.

Always remember that normal replication can be a backup and restore option. If other DCs in the domain are working properly, one option for a failed DC (assuming that no other data is needed) is to reinstall Win2K Server, then *dcpromo*, and allow replication to bring the new DC up-to-date. Replication is designed to supply redundancy to the Active Directory. Remember to check to see which Operations Masters were housed on the DC that failed. Recovery may involve more than just restoring some data; admins may be required to seize the Operations Master from another DC.

To restore a previous backup and "turn back the clock," making the backed up version "authoritative," you'll need to run NTDSUTIL from the DS Restore mode (F8 Advanced Boot Options), which is discussed later in this chapter.

Emergency Repair Disk (ERD)

As previously noted, your registry files are saved to your hard disk through the backing up of system state data, but they can also be saved to the same location by clicking that option when creating an Emergency Repair Disk (Figure 15-6). Checking the option to "Also backup the registry to the repair directory" is the only configurable option when creating the ERD. It is important to reiterate that, unlike the NT 4.0 rdisk /s option, no registry files are stored on the Emergency Repair Disk in Windows 2000 but rather on the hard disk in the \WINNT\REPAIR\REGBACK folder.

The Emergency Repair Disk contains only three files: autoexec.nt and config.nt (used for setting up the DOS environment for running 16-bit applications) and setup.log, which will allow for the reinstallation, from CD, of any system file that may be missing.

The easiest and, by far, the fastest method of beginning a repair of the operating system is to boot the computer from the installation CD. As in NT 4.0, once you receive the Welcome to Setup screen, one of the options is to press R for repair. It will take a good deal longer but you can get to this same Welcome to Setup screen if you boot the computer with the four setup floppies created by the MAKEBOOT command. (See Chapter 3 for more details on creating the setup floppies.)

Directory Services Restore Mode

I've already discussed the other options on the (F8) Advanced Startup Options menu so in this section, I will focus the discussion on the Directory Services Restore mode.

From the F8 menu, select DS Restore Mode and then Microsoft Windows 2000 Server (if necessary). The system proceeds to boot in Safe mode. Press CTRL-ALT-DEL to log on. Remember, this is *not* the normal domain or local Administrator password, but rather a separate and unique password used only here and in the Recovery Console. (For details, see the section "Using the Recovery Console," later in this chapter.) After logging on, you

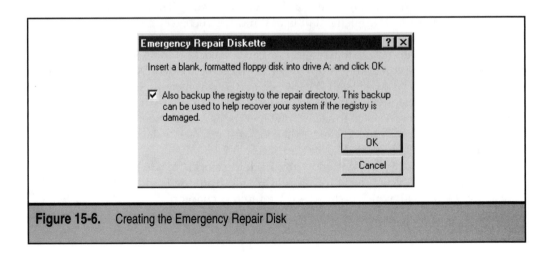

Figure 15-6. Creating the Emergency Repair Disk

will finally receive a "Windows is running in safe mode" warning (Figure 15-7); click OK. Safe mode means that the absolute minimum of device drivers and services have been loaded. If the administrator has logged on to this computer previously, the Administrator profile is used.

While in Directory Services Restore mode, admins use the normal NTBackup restore solution to restore the system state data to the local computer. If other DCs in the same domain are functioning properly, then reboot normally, and the standard replication process will bring this DC up-to-date. If, however, you wish to "turn back the clock" and force all domain controllers to replicate back to the level of the *restored* data, then you must use the NTDSUTIL Authoritative Restore option.

CAUTION: Before using the Authoritative Restore option, be certain you are clear on the ramifications of your actions. This option can cause deleted users to reappear, as well as recently created objects to disappear. Be careful. This is not a trivial event.

Authoritative Restore

The name "authoritative restore" is a little misleading. The actual restoring of the system state data is still performed by NTBackup or another backup/restore utility. After the data has been restored in Directory Services Restore mode, we can use the Authoritative Restore option of NTDSUTIL.

The Authoritative Rrestore option (Figure 15-8) in NTDSUTIL is available only when the domain controller is started in DS Restore mode; therefore, this DC does not have the Active Directory service running and is temporarily offline. What is really going to happen when the authoritative restore is run is that the version number of every object in the Active Directory, or a specified AD subtree, say an OU, on this domain controller (currently

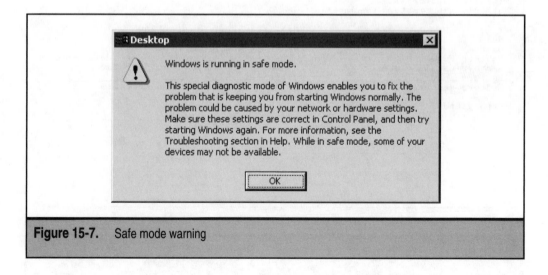

Figure 15-7. Safe mode warning

at the level of the just-restored data) is going to be incremented up by 10,000. The assumption here is that less than 10,000 changes have been made to the properties of this OU's objects since the backup was made. This means one simple thing to admins about to perform an authoritative restore: use a recent backup. In fact, significant problems can result if the backup tape is older than 60 days (the tombstone period). But who would restore a 60-day-old backup, right?

Once the data has been restored, the authoritative restore is run, and the object's version numbers have been changed, simply reboot normally. The DC comes up in its regular way. When the DCs in this domain contact each other for normal replication, the authoritatively restored DC will appear to have the most recent updates (highest version numbers), and the data on this DC will then be replicated to all the other DCs in the domain.

Note the options available in Figure 15-8. "Restore database" will increase the version numbers on every AD object by 10,000. "Restore database verinc %d" would be written:

```
restore database verinc 500
```

The number 500 in the example is a variable, allowing admins to choose the exact amount that they would like to increase the version number on each object in the AD. You could use 50,000 if you thought more than 10,000 changes had been made since the backup.

"Restore subtree %s" would be written:

```
restore subtree OU=sales,DC=bigcompany,DC=com
```

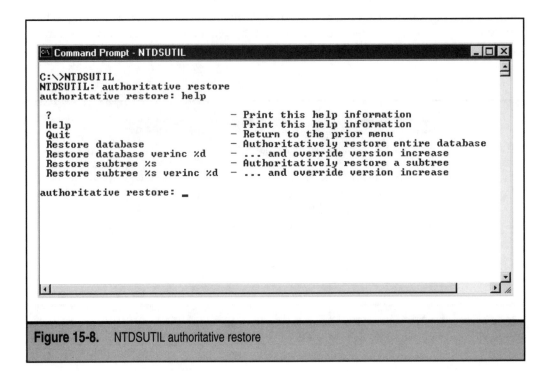

Figure 15-8.   NTDSUTIL authoritative restore

This increases the version number of every object located in the Sales OU and every object in every OU under the Sales OU by 10,000. The same verinc variable is also available for the subtree as well.

So when would we actually use the Authoritative Restore option? Well, let's try a scenario. Jim, an admin, is very distracted by a personal issue and is not paying any attention to what he is doing. He somehow manages to delete the Sales OU and all of its users and computers, answering OK to all the warnings, and then rushes off to an appointment outside the building. Upon his return, an hour later, all hell has broken loose. No one, absolutely no one, in the Sales department can access the system. The CEO has been down to the server room, and the network nerds are scrambling for sniffers and network monitors and thinking about when they last updated their skills inventory on techies.com. Jim, quietly suspecting that he could have caused the problem, brings up MMC Active Directory Users and Computers and looks for the Sales OU. It's gone. And its lack of existence has now been replicated to every other DC in the enterprise. Jim closes the door to the server room and starts paying very close attention to what he's doing. He reboots the DC, grabs last night's backup, restores just the system state data from tape, performs the authoritative restore on just the Sales OU, and reboots the DC again. When the DC comes back up, using the Sites and Services MMC snap-in, Jim starts forcing replication with each DC in the enterprise until all the Sales folks can log on normally within a few moments. Nobody knows why it broke or how it managed to fix itself. There is much shrugging and head-shaking going on. Acronyms dominate the hallway conversations. He'll wait a week to decide whether to tell anyone of his surreptitious repair.

The Authoritative Restore option is incredibly powerful and should be employed only after fully understanding its consequences.

Seizing the Operations Master

In a number of other places in this book, I have discussed the concept of the five Operations Masters. Two of them, the Schema Master and the Domain Naming Master, reside on only one DC in the entire forest. Three of them—the PDC Emulator, the RID Master, and the Infrastructure Master—reside on only one DC per domain. These domain controllers have special purposes within the forest/domain structure, and significant functionality may be lost if these DCs fail. It is possible to transfer the Operations Master roles, at any time, to other DCs using the MMC or NTDSUTIL, if the current role owner DCs are up and running.

You can transfer the Schema Master with the Schema Manager MMC snap-in. The Domain Naming Master can be transferred using the Active Directory Domains and Trusts snap-in. The remaining three operations masters (PDC Emulator, RID Master, and Infrastructure Master) may be transferred using the Active Directory Users and Computers snap-in.

But what happens when the DC holding one of the Operations Masters dies without warning? The functionality embodied in that Operations Master is no longer available to the Active Directory. Depending on which Operations Master went down, the implications can be quite serious.

Microsoft has created a method of moving an Operations Master to another DC, even if the original token holder is down. It's called "seizing the master" (Figure 15-9).

The DC used to perform the operation must be booted in DS Restore mode. To do so, go to the command prompt and type **NTDSUTIL**. A typical sequence to seize the Schema Master looks like this:

```
ntdsutil <enter>
roles <enter>
connections <enter>
connect to server w2kservera <enter>
quit <enter>
seize schema master <enter>
[The Role Seizure Confirmation box appears.
Click Yes to seize the role]
quit <enter>
quit <enter>
```

In this example, the Schema Master now resides on the server w2kservera. Every other Operations Master can be seized in the same manner.

Using the Recovery Console

The Recovery Console is a special command-line operating system that you can boot directly into. You can enter the Recovery Console by booting directly from the Windows

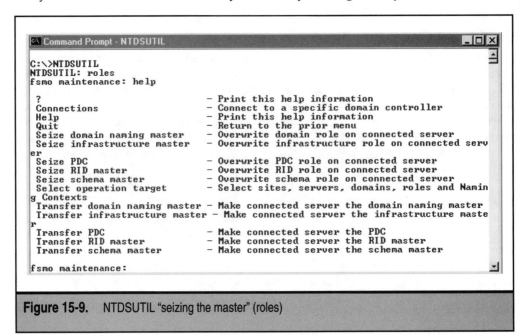

Figure 15-9. NTDSUTIL "seizing the master" (roles)

2000 Server CD (or using the four setup floppies) and choosing R for repair and then Recovery Console. Or you can install the Recovery Console in advance of a problem occurring on your system and access this special console any time you need to. For those of you with NT 4.0 Server experience, the Recovery Console feels like booting from the setup floppies, but instead of them asking for the ERD, it drops to a command prompt—most importantly, a command prompt that can read NTFS.

Installing the Recovery Console

To install the Recovery Console directly onto your system, place your Win2K Server CD in the CD-ROM drive. Choose Start | Run and type **x:\i386\winnt32.exe /cmdcons** (where x is the drive letter assigned to your CD-ROM drive). /cmdcons refers to the fact that the Recovery Console was known as the "Command Console" at an earlier time. A setup message appears asking if you're sure you'd like to install the Recovery Console. Click Yes, and the Recovery Console is installed. It requires 7MB of hard disk space. The Recovery Console will now appear as an option on the normal Boot (boot.ini) menu (Figure 15-10). Unfortunately, there is no administrative option to perform this installation during a normal installation, but it would be an excellent practice to install the Recovery Console on every single Win2K Server and domain controller in the enterprise *before something goes wrong*.

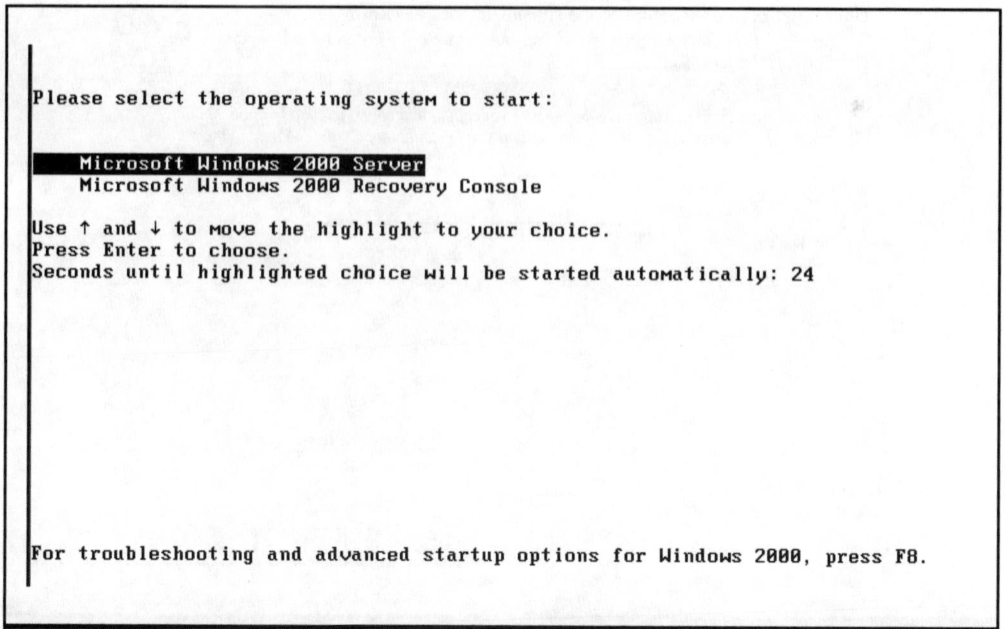

```
Please select the operating system to start:

    Microsoft Windows 2000 Server
    Microsoft Windows 2000 Recovery Console

Use ↑ and ↓ to move the highlight to your choice.
Press Enter to choose.
Seconds until highlighted choice will be started automatically: 24




For troubleshooting and advanced startup options for Windows 2000, press F8.
```

Figure 15-10. Win2K Bootup menu with Recovery Console option

Selecting the Recovery Console allows you to press F6 to install a third-party SCSI or RAID disk driver. The system prompts you to select a specific Win2K installation (even if there's only one) and then requests the Administrator password (see the next section). The Recovery Console does not give you access to the entire file system, but rather only to removable media (floppies and CD), the root of each volume, and the system-related folders of your Win2K installation.

Administrator Password

If you are using the Recovery Console on a Win2K Professional workstation or a member server, you will need to know the password of the local Administrator account. You will be prompted for it as you boot up. The domain administrator won't help you here because only the local Administrator account will work. You can always change the local Administrator password on a workstation or member server by pressing CTRL-ALT-DEL after logging in. However, if you are running the Recovery Console on a Win2K domain controller, you will need the Administrator password that you entered during *dcpromo* (see Figure 15-11).

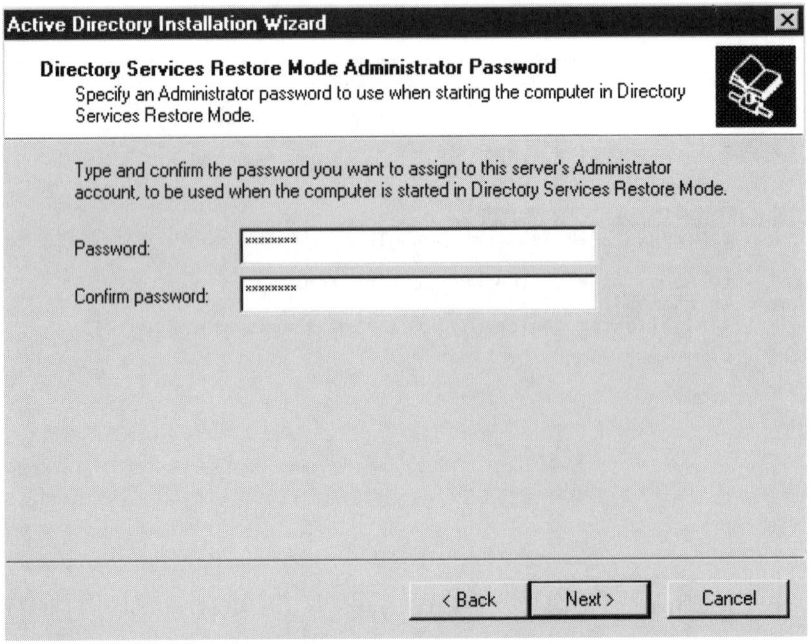

Figure 15-11.   AD Installation Wizard Administrator Password screen

This special Administrator password does not reside in the Active Directory since the Recovery Console is designed to be used at times when the machine has failed and cannot access the AD. It does not reside in the local SAM database, like the local Administrator password, because the local SAM is disabled on domain controllers and cannot be accessed. Instead, it resides in what I can only describe as a mini-SAM database of one account and one password. This one account and password is used to authenticate to the Recovery Console's logon command, which runs automatically at startup, and to log in to Directory Services Restore mode in the (F8) Advanced Startup Options discussed earlier. The password is stored locally on each DC so it is possible to have different DS Restore Mode Administrator passwords for every domain controller in the enterprise, Lord forbid!

It is only possible to change this special Administrator password on a domain controller from the Directory Services Restore mode. After logging in to DS Restore mode using the current Administrator password, press CTRL-ALT-DEL and simply change the password as you would any other.

Recovery Console Commands

A significant number of commands are usable in the Recovery Console. For DOS users, many of these commands will look familiar, but don't get too cocky. A number of the "old DOS" commands do not provide the full DOS-like functionality. To display a list of all the available Recovery Console command options, type **help** at the prompt, and the list will appear. The commands and their capabilities are briefly summarized in the sections that follow.

ATTRIB   Modifies file attributes such as Read-Only, Archive, System, Hidden, and Compression. Does not display attributes, but you can view attributes with DIR.

BATCH   Use this program to run a list of Recovery Console commands stored in a file. Takes a text file for input and has an optional text output file. Regular batch files with a .bat or .cmd extension do not work unless they follow the syntax of these special commands, and you need to run them with this command to execute.

CD OR CHDIR   Change Directory lets you view or change the directory/folder you are currently working in. This command allows you only into floppies, CDs, the root directory of each drive, and the system-related directories.

CHKDSK   Performs a chkdsk on your hard drive to look for errors and inconsistencies. Does a check only if the drive is flagged as "dirty"; use the /p option to make it check regardless of the flags. Option /r for recover is also available, although it can take a significant amount of time (could be 30 minutes or longer) because it reads and writes every byte of data on the drive to ensure it is consistent.

CLS   Clears the console screen you are viewing.

COPY   Copies a single file from an allowed location to another allowed location (floppies, CDs, the root directory of each drive, and system-related directories). The destination cannot be a floppy. This command automatically uncompresses files from the CD and asks if the file already exists. The command does not allow the use of wildcards.

DEL OR DELETE   Deletes one file at a time, with no wildcards supported. Lets you delete files only on floppies, the root directory of each drive, and system-related directories.

DIR   Displays files and directories (including system and hidden) in the current or specified directory and the file size, date, and attributes. The attributes shown also include compressed, encrypted, and reparse points (used for remote storage). Lets you only into floppies, the root directory of each drive, and system-related directories.

DISABLE   Use this command to view and change service startup parameters. *See also* listsvc and enable commands.

DISKPART   This utility accepts parameters to add or delete a partition based on device specifications (use the map command to view), or without parameters. It runs a DOS program that is similar to the partition management screen from the Win2K setup program. In order to make the partition usable, you must follow up with the format command.

ENABLE   Use this command to view and change service startup parameters. *See also* the listsvc and disable commands.

EXIT   Quits the Recovery Console and restarts the computer.

EXPAND   Expands a compressed file into a directory. This command also includes switch /f to use with wildcards. The destination can be the root directory of each drive and system-related directories; it cannot be floppies. The command asks if the destination file already exists.

FIXBOOT   This command writes a brand new boot sector to the hard drive of your x86-based machine.

FIXMBR   Fixes the Master Boot Record (MBR) on your x86-based machine. If it detects a nonstandard partition table, it asks before rewriting the MBR. This command might save you if you've got a boot sector virus.

FORMAT   Formats a partition FAT16, FAT32, or NTFS. Use diskpart to delete and create partitions. Use map to see current format.

HELP   Displays a list of all available commands.

LISTSVC   Lists the services and drivers on the system and their startup parameters. Use the enable and disable commands to modify the startup parameters.

LOGON   Displays all installed versions of Windows 2000 on the local computer and prompts you for the version you wish to log on to with the Administrator password. Runs automatically when the Recovery Console starts up. Remember, on a domain controller, this password is neither the Domain Administrator password nor the local Administrator password but rather the special Administrator password that resides in a little mini-SAM database for use with the DS Restore mode and the Recovery Console.

MAP   Shows physical device mappings (like C: NTFS \Device\Harddisk0\Partition1) in either device format or by ARC (Advanced RISC Computing—multi(0)disk(0)rdisk(0)partition(1) format).

MD OR MKDIR   Creates a directory. Works only on floppies and the system-related directories.

RD OR RMDIR   Deletes a directory and everything below it (much like deltree). Works only on directories located on floppies, the root directory of each drive, and system-related directories.

REN OR RENAME   Can be used to rename one file. Works only on files located on floppies, the root directory of each drive, and system-related directories.

SYSTEMROOT   Changes the current directory (generally, C:\WINNT) to the systemroot folder.

TYPE OR MORE   Displays a text file to the screen. Automatically shows one screen at a time.

SUMMARY

We've come a long way from the Emergency Repair Disk in NT 4.0. Microsoft has done an excellent job of providing simple, easy-to-use backup and restore functionality while maintaining the necessary flexibility to make it useful. Wow! An internal data backup tool that just might get used. And with regard to the Active Directory, the combination of the DS Restore mode, the Recovery Console, and NTDSUTIL provide admins with sufficient confidence to implement this new technology without going too far out on the limb.

CHAPTER 16

Migrating to Windows 2000

Chapter 16 focuses on migration strategy from a number of perspectives: planning the migration, managing the upgrade, selling the rollout, and, finally, implementing the technology. When technologists start to move forward with any large project, the potential for disaster is high—not because they don't understand the technology, but because they fail to understand the people using the technology. This chapter addresses both the people issues and the technology issues involved in a Windows 2000 migration.

OVERALL MIGRATION STRATEGY

Your first decision in the migration process may indeed be your most important. How do I start? Where do I begin? Well, first and foremost, since no upgrade happens without some degree of pain, you and those above you have to believe that upgrading to Windows 2000 at this time is a good idea. Everybody needs to be on board before you begin, which may seem obvious to you, but trust me, it is perhaps the most overlooked piece of the puzzle by many in IT. Then, you'll need a grand plan, a broad strategy as to how you are going to migrate. Something sweeping like "we'll do all the workstations and member servers first, and in six months, we'll switch to Active Directory and upgrade the DCs." Reality will adjust your time frame. Then comes a much more detailed project management tactical outline including timelines, phased rollout schedules, costs, projected impacts on operations and resource availability, additional training and support needs, and so on. Let's take a look at the key migration issues to be concerned about:

▼ **Minimal business disruption** We can all agree on this one. The organization cannot shut its doors while the geeks have their field day installing or upgrading new operating systems. Whatever upgrade strategy we employ must not disrupt the day-to-day operations of the enterprise.

■ **Data integrity** We must avoid at all costs putting the current systems and the data housed on them at risk during the migration. In today's business environment, the information housed on the local networks and internal servers is at least 50 percent of all the information that the enterprise needs to function—in some cases, much, much more. Every precaution must be taken to avoid corruption or loss of this prime corporate asset during the migration process.

■ **Marketing and communication** We may not consider this our personal strongpoint as technologists, but the lack of it has destroyed many a successful implementation of great technology. As nerds, we tend to go off in our own little world of bits, bytes, and nodes. Well, sitting at those nodes are users. And, for all the time we spend mocking them and insulting them behind their backs, they are the reason that we have jobs. A successful rollout will include marketing events: open houses, demonstrations, contests, and even prizes. And we must communicate clearly and often about exactly what a user or department can expect and the time frame. We must then check back with them a couple of days before we turn their lives upside down, so that they:

- Remember that we are coming.
- Are able to plan their efforts around us.

Companies invest heavily in technology to make users more productive. Therefore, the key to a successful migration is the users. Their perceptions and their successes.

- **"One touch"**   It is imperative when performing a large-scale rollout of this kind that the upgrades, especially the client upgrades, be designed around a "touch it only once" philosophy. If possible, automating or scripting such tasks both maximizes the utilization of scarce technical resources and ensures accuracy and consistency in what can be an incredibly repetitive and mind-numbing process.

- ▲ **Ready or not?**   If the enterprise isn't ready, don't do it! You may be ready. IT may be ready. Win2K is ready. But if you believe that the business units aren't ready. Stop! Now your job is to get them ready. Do everything within your power to help them get ready, but under no circumstances should you force a new operating system down their throats.

As we examine several migration strategies, we will use the preceding key upgrade issues as the drivers for our migration design.

Most IT organizations will undoubtedly fall into one or more of the following four categories:

- ▼ **If it ain't broke, don't fix it!**   *My company is running just fine with NT 4.0, thank you very much. I don't need all this high-falutin' Plug and Play and TCO, and my domain works great so you can keep your directory, I don't care how active it is! I can't wait until the next PC they order ships with Win2K preinstalled.* At this point, no one knows how long Microsoft will continue to support Windows NT 4.0, but I can assure you, they will not repeat Novell's mistake of continuing to support two network operating systems indefinitely.

- **Let's go for it now! Why not?**   This type of organization is peppered with gung ho network jockeys who can lead upper management around by the acronym. Damn the torpedoes! Full speed ahead! To hell with planning, give me the CD, and let's party like its 1999. (The year 1999 was kind of a party for IT vendors. Did you ever think you'd look back on Y2K fondly? Never have POs sailed through so smoothly.) This approach can lead to limited interruption of the business or worse. In the end, the production system and the workers who depend on it will be the guinea pigs and the training ground for these network admins.

- **We're ready. Win2K's ready**   A few hundred organizations, called Joint Development Partners (JDP) or Rapid Deployment Partners (RDP), have been working with Microsoft over the past two years during the key development and beta deployment phases of the Win2K product. These companies have been instrumental in recommending a significant number of the Win2K features and product changes that were implemented in the last two years. Many have had Win2K pilot programs up and running for over a year. They know the product well, they know it works, they know how it will work in their environment, and they have been planning for at least a year how to perform a successful rollout. These will be our early adopters, the subjects of the case study articles that we'll read about in the trade mags.

▲ **The rest of us** *Win2K looks exciting. I'm certainly going to upgrade…soon, but I'm not quite sure when. I'm on the ad hoc migration task force. We're looking into it. I've been to a class. I'm reading this book, aren't I?* The rest of this chapter is aimed at this group: those of us struggling to find a place that makes sense somewhere between the hype surrounding Win2K and the reality of our life and the well-being of our enterprise if and when we migrate to Win2K.

Workstations, Clients, and Servers First

Should I upgrade my clients first or my domains? Or should we just bite the bullet and do them all at once? This decision will be faced countless times by thousands of admins in the next 12 months. The decision point really comes down to the Active Directory. Does my organization need the advantages afforded to me by the Active Directory, such as a single domain, delegated administration, or remote configuration by policy, right now, or can we continue to operate nicely with our NT 4.0 domains for a while?

Another key factor is the reality that most current NT administrators know little or nothing about X.500 Directory Services in general and the Active Directory in particular. Why should they? The product was just released on Feb. 17, 2000. In this case, ignorance is not bliss. It is much easier to understand and comprehend the changes between NT 4.0 workstation and Win2K Professional than it is to explore the vast wonders of the Active Directory. I have seen a number of NT people who were lulled by the simplicity of Win2K Professional into thinking that the rest of Win2K must be simple too. That's like saying NT must be easy, right? It's Windows. Microsoft has been offering Active Directory classes based on the beta versions of the product for more than a year before the ship date of Win2K to alleviate the inevitable ignorance about a brand new product (perhaps even to many, a brand new paradigm), but classes based on the released product didn't start their phased shipment availability until just after the Win2K launch.

Now we enter the weird and nontechnical world of perception. If we are anxious for rapid acceptance of the Windows 2000 platform in our enterprise and we want our user community to be enthusiastic about the switch to Win2K, then we have to provide improvements that are tangible to them, not us—things that they can point to and say, "Yes, this is better, I like it, and it's cool." The payoff will be more visible when the workstations, as opposed to the DCs, are upgraded. End user systems should operate faster. Plug and Play will make new devices quicker and easier to install. Perhaps, especially if bundled with an Office 2000 upgrade, the apps will run much faster too. If you upgrade your file and print servers at the same time, you can offer offline folders to your Win2K users as well. The OS is rock solid. Fewer bluescreens, hangs, and reboots. In general, it will "feel" like it works better than 9*x* or NT, and, in reality, it *will* work better. (A recent survey of IT professionals indicated that they felt the *beta* releases of Win2K were twice as reliable as NT 4.0 and three times as reliable as Windows 98.) This scenario is opposed to the relatively invisible payoff offered by the activities (Active Directory) happening in the back room (domain controllers) where our biggest and loudest (shout it from the rooftops) claim to the customers will be "you shouldn't notice any difference," which will take tons of planning and flawless execution to achieve. Active Directory delivers a lot of steak, but Win2K Pro is the sizzle.

I believe that most organizations will choose the "workstations first" strategy for their Win2K migration. Some organizations may adopt a wait-and-see attitude toward the Active Directory. They'll wait and read the trade magazines to see if the early adopters were able to punch any holes in the bulletproof veneer of the Active Directory. The definition of "wait-and-see" differs widely from enterprise to enterprise. Some companies will wait a few months until the first Service Pack (due in June 2000) is released and then jump right onto the Active Directory. Others may heed the advice of the highly paid sages at the top IT consulting firms like the Gartner Group, who have been advising folks to wait until the second quarter of 2001 for any implementation of the Active Directory. With all due respect, what IT consulting firm has ever said, "We think it will be perfect the moment it's released, so we'll stand behind your decision to risk your enterprise on a one week-old operating system"? Consultants and consulting firms just aren't built that way.

The "workstations first/AD later" migration strategy has another major advantage: experience with the product. Industry experience, to be sure, will play a part, but playing a much bigger role in determining your comfort level is your own degree of hands-on Win2K product experience. A phased workstation rollout has the advantage of training the admins who will eventually be responsible for the system on the ins and outs of Win2K Professional at the expense of a relatively small number of workers in the enterprise. The phased approach also allows for a re-adjustment of the parameters and assumptions currently guiding the upgrade with an eye toward our key issues previously discussed.

We need to discuss one more item: the standalone and member servers in our current NT 4.0 environments. As far as the Active Directory is concerned, these servers behave as client computers just like the Win2K Professional workstations. There are very few reasons not to upgrade these servers right along with the clients. The shares will all work in the same way they did before, so there are really no issues at all for file and print servers. Both downlevel and Win2K clients can see and use the shared folders and printers on these servers. Application servers will take a little more attention. Some BackOffice versions are not supported on Win2K. Most will need additional Service Packs (the latest available) to run successfully on Win2K. Proxy Server 2.0 even needs a special wizard. In some cases, the network services upgrade just fine, but the database doesn't until after the first reboot. Chapter 3 discusses these server upgrade issues in detail.

Phased Rollout Approach

I may be at risk of preaching to the converted here, but I strongly believe that the phased rollout approach is the best way to implement any major changes to the corporate desktop environment. A phased project will minimize the impact of your planning mistakes or misconceptions about the product by affecting only a limited number of people. In addition, a phased rollout will maximize our learning potential as we change, adjusting our migration through the company.

▼ **Phase 1**   We should start by eating our own dog food. Upgrade the IT department first. We have knowledgeable users, which should help. We understand the obtuse twists and turns of computer technology, which also should help. We have little patience for incompetence and lack of forethought, which could prove to be a problem. Several advantages accrue from an IT department conversion. We learn what we did wrong among our peers, and we can keep the glaring issues "in the family," so to speak. Rollouts may start out being about technology, but they quickly become about reputation and, I'm afraid, politics. If an end user department suffers significant downtime or unplanned business interruption during the migration, every other department suddenly will want to be *last*.

■ **Phase 2**   So after our IT department migration, we step back, analyze, debrief, revise the migration plan, and move forward to the next area. This time we are looking for a technology-friendly department that is anxious to get the latest and greatest improvements (kind of a "be the first one on your block to own the decoder ring" philosophy) *and will work with us as a partner, side-by-side, to make sure the migration comes off without a hitch*. After this migration, step back again, analyze, debrief, revise the plan, and select the next department.

▲ **Phase 3**   We are looking for a normal end user department with relatively low visibility in the organization for this third phase. In this case, we are not going to get any special "help" from the department or its management, but by now, we know exactly the amount of cooperation to ask for because we've done this twice before. Once we've migrated this department, our "formula" should be complete and ready for prime time.

Notice that we started the rollout process by working "inside the IT family" and then re-grouped. We expanded to a technology-friendly environment where we would have a partner to help with the migration and then re-grouped again. And, finally, we adopted our more familiar "service provider" role but with a low visibility department to make sure that we had this process down pat. With these three phases under our belt, we should be able to successfully migrate just about anybody—do it right, do it well, do it in the shortest possible amount of time, and do it with minimum disruption. This phased approach is not connected with Win2K and can be adapted to fit nearly any major migration project.

Domain Controllers First

Of course, what we are really saying is convert the existing NT 4.0 domain structure to a Win2K Active Directory before upgrading the client machines. As we delve deeper and deeper into the technology, we must never forget that for the large capital outlay represented by a Win2K migration, a strong business case must exist. The questions are simple. Why are we moving to Windows 2000? Why isn't our current environment good enough? Does it give us a competitive advantage? What are the tangible benefits to the enterprise if we move to Win2K? The answers are discussed nearly everywhere in this book. The benefits are reduced TCO through Group policies and remote OS installation, consolidation of the administrative model through the Active Directory, more productivity and fewer support calls through remote application deployment, and so on. Once upper management is sold on the need for upgrading, we can move forward.

Since moving to the Active Directory requires planning by knowledgeable individuals, let's start with the term *knowledgeable*. Do the people involved understand the Active Directory and how it works? The only *accurate* sources for this detailed AD knowledge are Microsoft Official Curriculum (MOC) classes and newsgroups, and reading supplemental material like trade books, white papers, the Resource Kit documentation, and (believe it or not) the Win2K help files. In these early days, not all information is accurate. More classes from third-party vendors should be available soon. This theoretical or "book" knowledge comes with a price tag of time away from the job, as well as real training dollars. In addition, all the theoretical knowledge in the world won't help without some hands-on practice, so it is essential that several computers be set aside as a test environment for the Active Directory installation. While many network departments already have a test environment, I cannot overly emphasize the importance of a test forest implementation *prior* to the installation of the Active Directory in the production environment.

Now let's move on to planning. If your IT organization is centralized and can gently impose its will on the rest of the enterprise (you remember mainframes), then a small group of people can design an effective Active Directory structure in no time. If, on the other hand, your IT organization is more decentralized into separate sub-empires, then simple concepts like operating in a single domain may be nearly impossible to achieve. The administrators for each separate organization will inevitably jockey for control of their own IT infrastructure and its desktop environment. Negotiations become the key word, and multiple domains will almost certainly exist even in a medium-sized enterprise.

Exchange 2000

Exchange 2000 will be one of the major drivers of the rapid adoption of the Windows 2000 Active Directory. When Exchange 2000 ships, sometime in the second quarter of 2000, a substantially increased business case can be made for upgrading to the Active Directory.

As you know, Exchange 2000 requires Windows 2000 and the Active Directory in order to function. Many companies currently on Exchange 5.5 are eagerly awaiting the significant enhancements embodied in Exchange2K. These improvements include installable filing system, instant messaging, data conferencing, AD integration, routing groups, and bandwidth conservation, just to name a few. And those companies will be moving to the Win2K Active Directory soon after the Exchange2K release.

It is important to note that Exchange 2000 doubles the Active Directory database size of each user from approximately 4KB to 8KB and triples the size of each contact from 1.7KB to 5KB. Early testing by reputable sources indicates that a Windows 2000 AD with Exchange 2000 is at least 30 percent larger.

CURRENT NT 4.0 DOMAIN ARCHITECTURE

As we look at the different options for upgrading the current NT domain structure to the Win2K Active Directory, we will view each current NT domain model differently.

Single Domain

The most common NT 4.0 domain model installed today is the single domain model. By far, the easiest, quickest, most painless process to reach a Win2K DC is to upgrade your existing single NT 4.0 domain to a single Win2K Active Directory domain, which is almost a "no brainer." Go to the PDC (it must be the PDC), insert the Win2K CD, answer a few questions (see Chapter 3), go to lunch, and about an hour later, you've got a Win2K server. Continue with the Active Directory promotion using *dcpromo* (see Chapter 9). Answer a few more questions, the promotion happens, the SAM database migrates to the Active Directory, and then reboot. You're in business. A few services might need some tweaking, but in a couple of hours (start to finish), you've created your first AD domain controller. You can now proceed to upgrade the BDCs as well, being careful to keep one in the closet, just in case. When all the BDCs are upgraded and you feel confident that things are working well, you can switch to native mode. But before you switch, take your NT 4.0 closet BDC and reconnect it to the network. Let it replicate with the Win2K domain one final time and then put it back in the closet, just in case. When you switch to native mode, downlevel replication is no longer possible. All the existing NT 4.0 objects (users, groups, and computers) migrate to the new Active Directory domain. As discussed in earlier chapters, all the NT 4.0 objects retain the same SID as they move to the Active Directory. In this way, the same access token is created, and the same access control remains in place for shared folders and printers. I believe that 80–90 percent of the Win2K installations will use this model for migration. It's quick, easy, well-tested, and solid.

Single-Master Domain Model

The NT 4.0 single-master domain model (Figure 16-1) basically imposes a kind of pseudo-hierarchy on a flat domain architecture. One domain is declared to be the master domain, and all user accounts and global groups are placed in the master domain. The other domains are declared to be resource domains with a one-way trust to the master do-

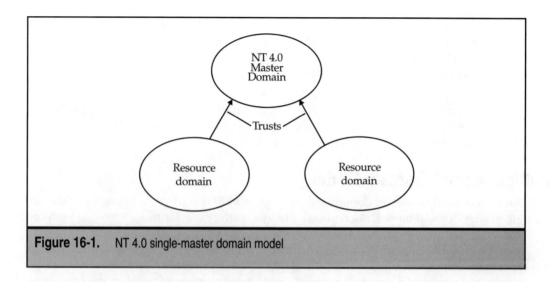

Figure 16-1.   NT 4.0 single-master domain model

main. The resource domains are supposed to hold workstations and servers but no users or global groups except the ones created by default during the NT 4.0 installation.

In upgrading the master domain model, the real question is "how do you want to handle the resource domains?" You have several options:

▼ Upgrade all the domains just as they are and leave the model alone. With this option, no objects are moved between domains, so all existing SIDs are retained.

■ Upgrade all the domains just as they are. When that process is complete, use NETDOM or the Domain Migrator to move the objects in the resource domains into new OUs created in the Win2K "master" (root) domain (Figure 16-2).

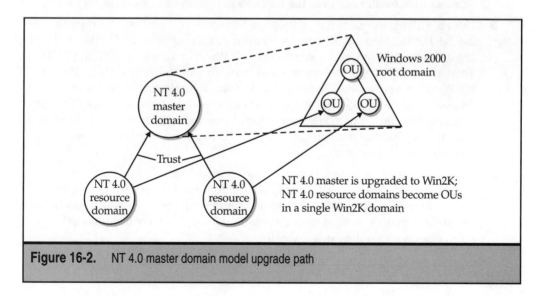

Figure 16-2.   NT 4.0 master domain model upgrade path

When all objects have been moved, delete the old "resource" domains, which will result in a single Active Directory domain. With this option, any user objects being moved will receive new SIDs from the Win2K "master" domain, and the old SIDs from the resource domains will be placed in SID History.

▲ Use NETDOM, Domain Migrator, or a third-party migration tool to move the objects from the resource domains to the master domain *before* the upgrade. Then proceed as if you were doing a single-domain upgrade. With this option, the original SIDs are retained during the upgrade.

Multiple Master Domain Model

An NT 4.0 multiple master domain model (Figure 16-3) is simply an expansion of the single-master domain model based almost always on the need for more accounts than one master domain could handle. The theoretical limit of an NT 4.0 domain is 40,000 objects. Most troubleshooting types (like me) feel that around 10,000 is the practical limit, though I personally know of domains with over 23,000 users. Each master domain in the multiple master domain model contains a subset of the total number of users in the enterprise. Each user account must appear in one, and only one, domain.

In upgrading the NT 4.0 multiple master domain model to the Active Directory, the most important question is "how many domains do we want when we are finished?" Since an Active Directory domain can contain up to one million objects or, roughly, 200,000 users, the size limits of NT 4.0 are no longer an issue. So, do we want to collapse all the master domains into one? If so, then the next question becomes a repeat from the single-master model: "How do you want to handle the resource domains?" Don't be surprised if politics rears its ugly head as you work on this one. You have several options:

▼ Upgrade all the domains just as they are and leave the model alone. All existing SIDs are retained in this model. The problem here is that you have to decide whether each master becomes the root of a new tree. This option is not ideal.

■ Upgrade all the domains just as they are and when this process is complete, use NETDOM, Domain Migrator, or a third-party migration tool to move all the objects in the other master domains into the Win2K root domain (Figure 16-4). Then move all the objects from the resource domains into new OUs created in the Win2K root domain. When all objects have been moved, delete the empty "master" and "resource" domains, which will result in a single Active Directory domain. With this option, any user objects being moved will receive new SIDs from the Win2K root domain, and the old SIDs from the previous domains will be placed in SID History.

▲ Create a brand new Active Directory root domain for administrative and domain naming purposes. Upgrade all the domains just as they are, being careful to place each existing master as a child under the new root and each resource domain as a child under a master. No objects have been moved, so all objects retain their original SIDs.

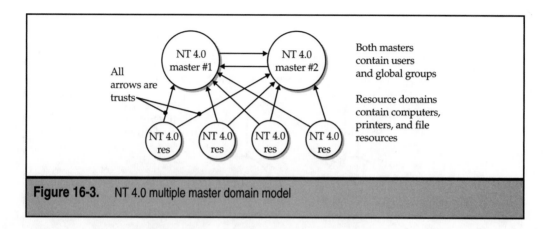

Figure 16-3.   NT 4.0 multiple master domain model

Complete Trust Model

The NT 4.0 complete trust domain model (Figure 16-5) exists, ironically, because of a lack of trust between business units in a decentralized environment. It also comes about when different business units implement the NT 4.0 domains at different times and basically

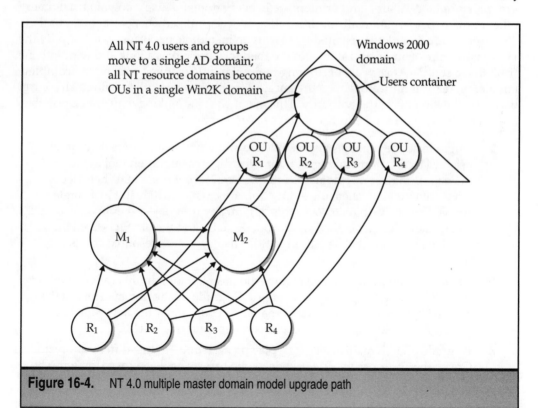

Figure 16-4.   NT 4.0 multiple master domain model upgrade path

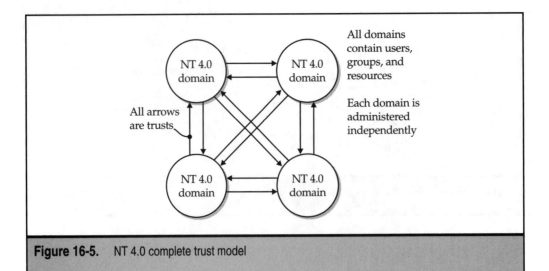

All domains
contain users,
groups, and
resources

Each domain is
administered
independently

All arrows
are trusts

Figure 16-5. NT 4.0 complete trust model

have to be "bolted on" to an existing domain structure. Its premise is simple: users, groups, computers, shares, and printers are in every domain. Every domain trusts every other domain. By definition all administration is decentralized on a per domain basis.

Upgrading a complete trust model presents an incredible opportunity to simplify the IT infrastructure of an organization, but the road to simplicity is a long and winding one (isn't that a song?). After years of running their own little empires with nearly complete autonomy, the administrators of each separate domain may be loath to relinquish control back to some kind of central authority. This major shift in thinking may not be possible, but it's probably worth the effort. You have several options:

▼ Upgrade all the domains just as they are and when that process is complete, use NETDOM, Domain Migrator, or a third-party migration tool to move all the objects in the other domains into the Win2K root domain. When all objects have been moved, delete the empty domains, which will result in a single Active Directory domain. With this option, any user objects being moved will receive new SIDs from the Win2K root domain, and the old SIDs from the previous domains will be placed in SID History so that resource access is unaffected.

■ Create a brand new Active Directory root domain for administrative and domain naming purposes (Figure 16-6). Upgrade all the domains just as they are, being careful to place each domain as a child under the new root. No objects have been moved so all objects retain their original SIDs.

▲ Upgrade each domain just as it is, placing each domain in a different forest. Create the appropriate NT 4.0–style explicit trusts between each domain. The major question here is "what have you gained?"

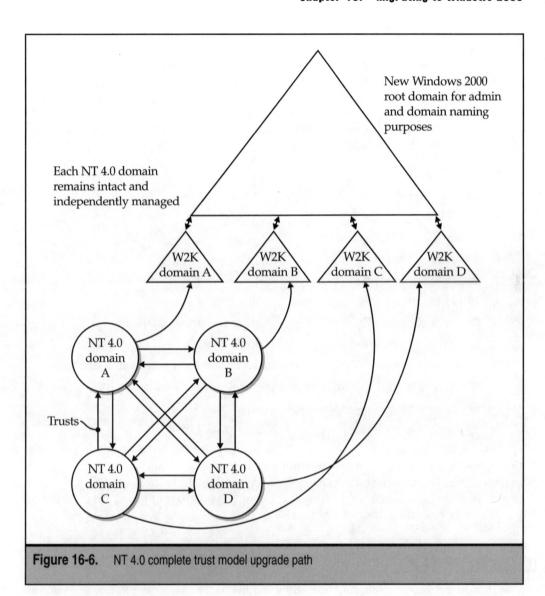

Figure 16-6.   NT 4.0 complete trust model upgrade path

Sites and Replication

Because of the addition of sites to the Win2K Active Directory, physical location and network topology no longer need to be a consideration in our logical AD design process. Our site structure will reflect the physical network topology. Even with a single domain, we can still maintain excellent replication performance within each of our several physical locations (sites), while at the same time, maximizing our bandwidth usage by controlling the amount of replication traffic that flows between each location across the WAN.

Domain Controllers

Migrating PDCs and BDCs does require some forethought and planning due to the large number of new roles that the Win2K DCs must play. Remember that the first DC in the forest (which, in an upgrade scenario, has to be our old PDC) has an incredible number of hats to wear simultaneously. This one machine not only holds a full copy of the Active Directory and serves as the Kerberos Key Distribution Center for Win2K authentication, but also executes the following additional roles:

▼   Schema Master

■   Domain Naming Master

■   RID Master

■   Infrastructure Master

■   Global Catalog

■   InterSite Topology Generator

▲   PDC Emulator—which performs the following tasks:

   ■   Serves as the PDC in NT 4.0 replication scenarios (mixed mode)

   ■   Receives preferential password change updates

   ■   Acts as PDC for downlevel clients and downlevel administration tools

   ■   Serves as the Domain Master Browser for downlevel clients

   ■   Serves as the Time Master for its own domain

   ■   Serves as the default focus for changes in all GPOs

The question becomes a simple one: "Does our current PDC have enough horsepower to become the first domain controller in our new forest?" See Chapter 8 for detailed information on hardware requirements for domain controllers. If the current PDC can't cut it, then it's time to go shopping. You cannot scrimp on resources for this machine. If you do, you'll simply be cutting your own throat.

MIGRATION TOOLS

Win2K is barely out the door, and already the third parties are lining up to help you migrate to Windows 2000 from NT 4.0 and NetWare. Individual machine upgrades may be quite easy, but a complete NT domain or NDS tree migration is a whole different ball game. Planning, testing, planning, testing, and more planning, and more testing, along with a great migration tool, will make for a successful upgrade and rollout, a well-performing network, happy users, and satisfied management.

One thing to keep in mind as you move forward in this world of migration tools: nearly every one of them requires that the domain be switched to native mode before migration can take place. I believe the major issue here is the SID History concept. Remember, in NT 4.0, that concept of moving objects between domains was nonexistent. Most of the migration tools discussed in the sections that follow are in the business of moving objects between domains. The movement of user objects causes the old SID to be placed in a new attribute on the user object called SID History. Read more about it in the section "Access Tokens," later in this chapter.

Microsoft Domain Migrator (DM)

Licensed from Mission Critical Software by Microsoft, Domain Migrator (DM) is an important addition to the Win2K toolkit. DM ships with Win2K Server as an MMC snap-in. It allows the migration of any and all objects from NT 3.51, NT 4.0, and Win2K domains in any combination or direction. Since it is included with all Win2K servers, check this one out before laying out the one-time cash and learning curve for third-party tools. Win2K's Domain Migrator should be able to handle most small- to medium-sized NT-to-Win2K migrations (say, up to 1,000 users or so).

Active Directory Connector (ADC)

Included with Win2K Server, the Active Directory Connector (ADC) provides ongoing, real-time synchronization of user and group objects between the Win2K AD and the existing AD running on Exchange Server 5.5 (requires at least SP2). Synchronization can be established in both directions, if desired. You can manage both "sides" from either side. Upgrading to Exchange 2000 obsoletes the ADC.

Systems Management Server (SMS 2.0)

The existing version of Systems Management Server (SMS 2.0) can package an upgrade of Win2K Pro to existing SMS 2.0 client workstations. Expect a future SMS release to have tighter integration into Win2K and the Active Directory.

Microsoft Directory Synchronization Services

In January 2000, Microsoft announced a licensing agreement with FastLane Technologies (www.fastlane.com) to include its DM/Consolidator data migration technology in the upcoming Microsoft File Migration Utility (MSFMU) for companies migrating from a Novell NetWare environment to Windows 2000. In addition, through integration with Microsoft Directory Synchronization Services (MSDSS), MSFMU can automatically assign an appropriate security access setting in Windows 2000 to each file it moves. Both MSDSS and MSFMU will be available in the upcoming release of Microsoft Services for NetWare version 5 (slated for Summer 2000). Stay tuned.

OnePoint EA

Mission Critical Software (www.missioncritical.com) offers a complete suite of systems administration and operations management software called OnePoint EA that is compatible with NT and Win2K. The component focused on Windows 2000 migration is the OnePoint Domain Administrator. One of the problems with the Mission Critical suite is that the strongest tool (Domain Migrator) was sold to Microsoft in June 1999. Mission Critical has had to rebuild its toolkit in the wake of that sale.

Domain Administrator features:

▼ Automated discovery and assessment of data

■ Automated Active Directory OU population

■ Automated migration to Windows NT 4.0 or Windows 2000 from NetWare

▲ Automated domain consolidation and reconfiguration

DM/Suite

FastLane Technologies (www.fastlane.com) also offers a suite of systems management and domain administration tools called DM/Suite. The component that focuses on migration to Windows 2000 is called DM/Manager, which is a mature product with a potential downside. It uses a proprietary scripting language called "final." Using this product could mean a steep learning curve prior to the migration with little payback after the migration. The DM/Consolidator product handles data migration.

FastLane DM/Manager capabilities:

▼ Automates any domain reconfiguration

■ Intuitive and step-by-step

■ Integrated with centralized management

▲ Automates iterative migration processes

DirectManage

Entevo (www.entevo.com) offers a suite of tools called DirectManage that offers "comprehensive directory management, before, during, and after Windows 2000." Entevo's migration tool specializing in comprehensive Windows 2000 migration is called DirectMigrate. The good news about the Entevo product is that it uses VBScript technology to automate the migration process. Many organizations already possess substantial expertise in Visual Basic so this could be a plus.

DirectMigrate 2000 capabilities:

▼ Support for all migration scenarios

■ Integral migration process management

▲ Comprehensive functionality

Enterprise Suite

Aelita Software Group (www.aelita.com) has a full-featured set of migration and management tools called the Enterprise Suite. It contains seven separate tools; those directly related to domain migration are:

▼ Virtuosity is a database-driven management utility that comprises comprehensive auditing, reporting, and domain cleanup tools.

■ Domain Migration Wizard helps move you from a multi-domain structure to a single domain, as well as create an Active Directory structure and test it in a controlled environment.

▲ Delegation Manager allows you to delegate administrative tasks on the network.

NAMING CONVENTIONS

The Active Directory requires us to rethink our naming strategy for computers and domains—no more nice little 15-character NetBIOS name for domains; now the name has got to be DNS compliant, which means no spaces, periods, or underscores in the machine or the domain name. The Active Directory might be considered the gateway into the new world, but new, by definition, means different. There are going to be some changes here.

One of our first decisions will be what to call our new domain, which is crucial because, in the currently released version of Win2K, you are unable to change the name of the root domain ever. In future releases, look for prune, graft, and merge Active Directory functionality, but that is a year or so after the launch, and this is now. Whatever name you choose now as you upgrade your PDC will be your domain name, so choose wisely. The original NetBIOS name of the domain (the domain name before we started the upgrade) will remain the same no matter what you may decide to use as a DNS name for Win2K. The NetBIOS domain name provides downlevel name resolution and authentication by downlevel clients.

The downlevel NetBIOS names of computers, users, groups, and domains are retained for downlevel authentication and NetBIOS interaction between servers. All Win2K servers and clients continue to support NetBIOS for backward-compatibility. In the case of brand new Win2K computers or users being added to the Active Directory, the downlevel NetBIOS name is generated automatically as the object is being created.

Name Resolution

In our new Active Directory world, the name resolution of computers (hosts) and services changes dramatically. To understand the new world, let's look at the old one.

DNS and WINS

In NT 4.0, the primary form of name resolution over TCP/IP was a proprietary solution called WINS. The Windows Internet Name Service (WINS) was created by Microsoft to address the problems associated with the computer browser service and the fact that its NetBIOS broadcast packets could not cross an IP router. To alleviate this inherent drawback, WINS appeared. We had to install the WINS service on one or more NT servers, and then we had to configure *each* client computer with the IP address of its primary and secondary WINS server or specify the settings in a DHCP scope. When a NetBIOS machine booted up, it registered the services running on it with WINS. When a client needed to locate a specific service on the network, it went to the WINS server in its configuration and asked for the IP address. WINS is more generically called a NetBIOS name server (NBNS).

The other major form of name resolution partially supported by NT 4.0 was DNS. The Domain Name System was developed in 1989 to handle name resolution on the Internet. So while Microsoft was stuck with NetBIOS and had to use WINS, the rest of the world was going with DNS for its name resolution. Traditional DNS does not register anything; its "database" is an ASCII text file of the names of computers coupled with their IP addresses. There are no records for services of any kind in traditional DNS. The text file has to be manually updated by the DNS administrators. Traditionally, DNS does not provide automatic registration or removal of computer names or IP addresses.

Along comes Windows 2000, and Microsoft dumps its dependence on the proprietary and limiting NetBIOS naming scheme in favor of—tada!—DNS. Now all Microsoft Active Directory names have to be DNS compliant, and DNS becomes the only name resolution you really need. But wait, Microsoft still needs to register its network services (domain controllers for logon, global catalogs for searching, Kerberos for authentication) somewhere so they expanded the role of DNS, and now Win2K DNS registers network services automatically just like WINS used to. Every Win2K client, server, and domain controller must be configured, either manually or automatically through DHCP, with the IP addresses of their DNS servers, or they will not function on the network.

Speaking of WINS, it is not dead yet. Every downlevel (Win 9*x* and NT 4.0) computer remaining in the Win2K domain still requires WINS to log on and locate any other services it may need. WINS cannot be removed from a Win2K domain until all computers have been upgraded to Win2K and until no applications are running that need to find data or services using WINS.

During a Win2K installation, WINS, DNS, and DHCP services are all upgraded (assuming that they are running). See Chapter 3 for details.

DHCP

While, strictly speaking, DHCP (Dynamic Host Configuration Protocol) is not part of the name resolution process, it does configure each of the client computers with the addresses where these services (DNS and WINS) can be found. And, by default, it configures the node type of each NetBIOS computer as well. Also in Win2K, after the client registers itself with the DNS, the DHCP service, now integrated with the Win2K DNS, registers the reverse lookup parameters with the DNS as well.

UPGRADING THE FILE SYSTEMS

Windows 2000 supports every file system that Microsoft has ever created: FAT16, FAT32, NTFSv4, NTFSv5, and Dfs (not a real file system). The only true "drop dead" requirement for the Win2K NTFSv5 file system is on domain controllers: the shared system volume (sysvol) on every domain controller must be formatted in NTFSv5. There are obviously a myriad of recommendations for better security on your system, but that is the only true requirement for NTFSv5.

NTFSv5

NTFSv5 is a much better file system than anything we've had before and promises to keep getting better over the next few years. It includes brand new features like the change journal and the indexing service to improve performance, increased levels of permissions to allow more granular security of resources, and the addition of mount points to allow for expansion of an existing volume.

NTFSv4 to NTFSv5

If you are upgrading an existing NT 4.0 computer with volumes currently formatted in NTFSv4, the Win2K upgrade process will automatically convert these volumes to NTFSv5 volumes without warning. A "may I upgrade your volumes" warning may be displayed in the beginning of the upgrade, but it is referring to your existing FAT volumes, not the NTFS volumes. Setup won't mention those volumes. It is still possible (but not recommended) to maintain a dual-boot configuration with NT 4.0 and Win2K, but you must first install Service Pack 4 or higher on your NT 4.0 installation before you install Win2K.

Permissions/ACLs Retained

Upgrading an existing NTFS volume retains the existing access control lists (ACLs) on each of the folders, files, and shares contained in the volume. The ACL Editor will look substantially different than the editor in NT 4.0 (Figures 16-7 and 16-8), but the actual permissions will remain unchanged.

Access Tokens

Each user and group account in NT 4.0 and Win2K has a security ID or SID assigned on a per domain basis. This SID is used in the access control decisions at each resource in the network—"Does this user have access to this resource?" When a user authenticates, they receive an access token that contains their SID, the SIDs of all the groups they belong to, and any rights or privileges that they may possess on the current machine. When a user

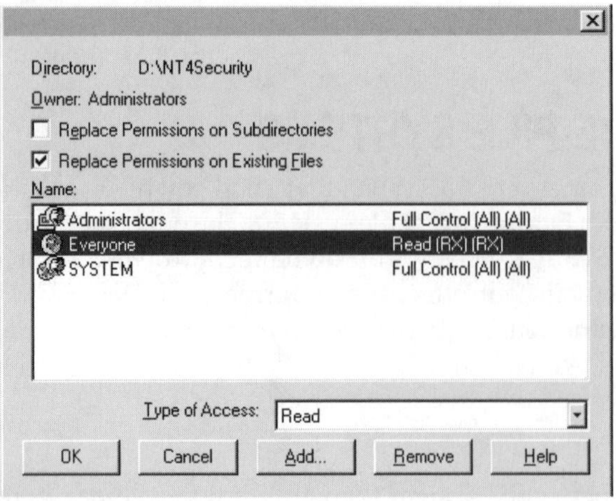

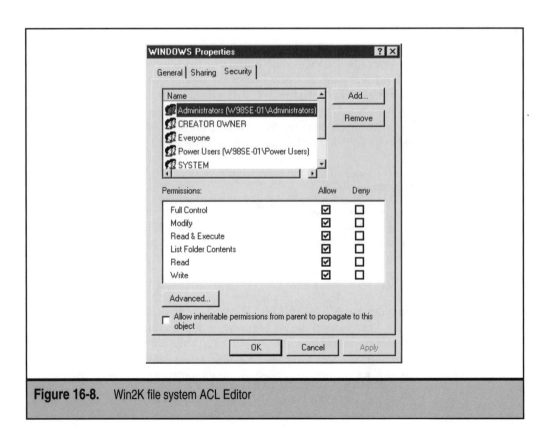

Figure 16-7. NT 4.0 file system ACL Editor

Figure 16-8. Win2K file system ACL Editor

attempts to access a folder, for instance, the ACL on the folder (resource) that lists the SIDs of the users and groups allowed access is compared with the SIDs on the access token; if there's a match, they're in. In a normal upgrade from a single NT 4.0 domain to a single Win2K domain, the user and group SIDs are unchanged, so user access to resources is also unchanged.

However, Win2K adds a new wrinkle. In NT 4.0, users could not be moved between domains so the user SID could never change. In Win2K, users *can* be moved between domains, and this introduces a new issue for admins: "How can I maintain seamless resource access for the user even though I know they'll be getting a new SID?" When a user is moved, from DomainA to DomainB in Win2K, they receive a new SID from DomainB. This new SID has never been used before so it cannot appear on any existing ACLs, which means that this user, if they have to depend on their new SID, will not be able to access any resources in the enterprise with the exception of access granted to generic groups like Authenticated Users. Win2K resolves this potentially thorny problem by creating a new attribute for the user object called SID History. In our preceding example, the user SID from DomainA is placed in the SID History attribute and added to the user's access token when they log on. In this way, the user's access to resources is unchanged after they move between domains.

FAT16, FAT32

FAT16 has been around since 1983, and it is still widely used today. All of the popular Microsoft operating systems support FAT16, and in many of the older systems, it was the only file system they supported. DOS, LAN Manager, Windows 3.*x*, and Windows 95 (before OSR2) supported FAT16 and only FAT16. Later versions of Windows 95 and any version of Windows 98 also supported FAT32. FAT16 has a 2GB volume size limitation, while FAT32 can handle volumes up to 2TB (terabytes). Volumes in Win2K being formatted as "FAT" will default to FAT16 below 2GB and FAT32 above 2GB. It is important to note that neither FAT16 nor FAT32 include any security functionality whatsoever.

NT 4.0 has always supported FAT16 but never supported FAT32. As previously stated, Win2K supports all existing Microsoft file systems. There is one caveat with Win2K's support of FAT32: even though the FAT32 specification calls for a maximum volume size of 2TB and even though you could theoretically create such a volume using Windows 98, the maximum FAT32 volume size that Win2K can create is 32GB. This size isn't exactly shabby, given that most of the FAT32 volumes we create will be on Win2K Professional workstations, but it is a design limitation imposed by Microsoft to force network administrators to use the far more secure NTFSv5 file system. It is Microsoft's contention that network files should be secured, and I wholeheartedly agree.

Converting FAT to NTFSv5

As in NT 4.0, it is possible to install or upgrade the Win2K operating system on a FAT16 or FAT32 boot partition. NT 4.0 and Win2K include a convert utility that allows for the conversion of FAT volumes to NTFS. When converting the volumes, all the existing data is retained. There are at least two problems with converting FAT volumes to NTFSv5.

First, the cluster size created by converting a FAT volume to NTFS is 512 bytes versus a 4KB cluster generated natively in NTFS (see Chapter 5 for more information). This makes native NTFSv5 much more efficient and, in some cases, actually faster. Because NTFS stores less housekeeping information about the physical location of files and because the indexing service is maximized for use with the new Change Journal, file searches can be blindingly fast.

Second, and a much more serious problem, the default security permissions do not get applied when converting the boot partition from FAT to NTFS. This means that, after you've converted the boot partition from FAT to NTFS, the access permissions for the entire volume are set to Everyone Has Full Control just as they were before the conversion. Win2K provides a method for applying the permissions after the conversion.

To apply default security to a Win2K server NTFS boot partition:

1. Log on as Administrator.

2. Go to a command prompt and type:

```
Secedit /configure /db c:\winnt\temp\tmp.mdb /cfg
c:\winnt\inf\defltsv.inf /areas filestore
```

Pardon the word wrap; the preceding is a single entry. Assuming that Windows 2000 Server is installed in the C:\WINNT directory, this command will apply the default NTFS permissions to the C:\WINNT and Program Files folders only. No other folders are affected. For Win2K servers, I strongly recommend that this option be executed for any NTFSv5 boot partitions that have been converted from FAT.

SECURITY

Now that we have moved from our NT 4.0 domain objects living in the SAM database that resides in the registry of the PDC and BDCs into a whole new world of Active Directory objects located in a much larger separate database, we need a different take on security. We are not concerned just with limiting access to files, folders, and registry keys anymore. In Win2K, we now have to secure every object in the Active Directory structure, which could prove to be an overwhelming task except that Win2K does provide reasonable Active Directory security by default. A positive change in security philosophy seems to have taken place as well. The concept of a wide open system with holes that have to be plugged has given way to a pretty tight ship with varying levels of options to make it a lot tighter. As we all know, that wasn't the case with Windows NT 4.0.

AD Security

The Active Directory security model operates primarily by the principle of inheritance. Theoretically, you could go to the top of the domain, set permissions to objects and properties at that level, and let them trickle down to every single AD object within the domain. Inheritance stops at domain boundaries. Few, if any, organizations could live with this model, however. We need a little more access over here, a little less over there, and none at all here, here, and here. The Win2K AD security model is up to the task and then some. Throughout the life of NT 4.0, we've been asking for more granularity in granting and applying access permissions and more granular ways of locking out intruders. Be careful what you ask for, you just might get it. See Chapters 13 and 14 for detailed information about the Windows 2000 authentication technology and the Active Directory security model.

Default AD Security

Let's look at the default Active Directory security set on the domain as an example of the granular complexity of AD security:

Everyone (this object only):

Read All Properties

Enterprise Domain Controllers (this object only):

Replicating Directory Changes

Replication Synchronization

Manage Replication Topology

Administrators (this object only):

Replicating Directory Changes

Replication Synchronization

Manage Replication Topology

Administrators (this object and all child objects):

List Contents

Read and Write All Properties

Delete

Read and Modify Permissions

Modify Owner

All Validated Writes and All Extended Rights

Create All Child Objects (Computer, Contact, Group, Group Policy, OU, Printer, Shared Folder, User)

Add GUID and Add or Remove a Replica DC in the domain

Change PDC Emulator

Authenticated Users (this object only):

> List Contents
>
> Read All Properties
>
> Read Permissions

SYSTEM (this object only):

> Full Control

Domain Admins (this object only):

> Same as Administrators listed previously

Enterprise Admins (this object and all child objects):

> Full Control

Pre-Windows 2000 Compatible Access group:

> List Contents (this object and all child objects)
>
> Read All Properties (user and group objects only)
>
> Read Permissions (this object only)

Migrating File System Permissions

It is important to note that any discussion of file system security must start with the caveat that all volumes must be formatted in NTFS to have security applied. FAT16 and FAT32 have no security functionality. In Win2K, more of the NTFS permissions are exposed to the users—a total of 14 in all, each permission with a discreet Allow or Deny permission. This allows for a more detailed security approach.

Default System Files Permissions (Standalone or Member Servers)

As you can see in the following illustration, the default security on the system files for a standalone server is a significant improvement over the NT 4.0 defaults, but the group Everyone continues to stay where it's not wanted. The group Everyone is unnecessary and insecure and should be deleted from this ACL. The Power Users group is still a judgment call. If you actually place users in that local group on a server, then perhaps it's necessary, but if you don't use it, remove it from this ACL.

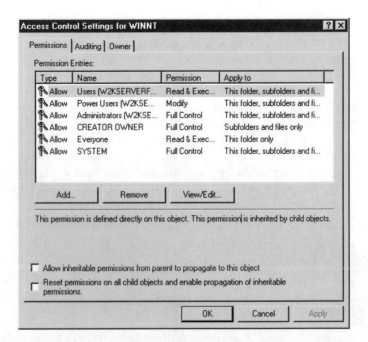

Notice the check box at the bottom of the screen to Allow Inheritable Permissions from Parent to Propagate to This Object. It is unchecked (off) at this system folder. The system files and subfolders should not be receiving permissions from above. If inheritance were enabled, security could possibly be relaxed, and crucial system files could be deleted or corrupted with viruses. On the other hand, security could be altered so that even the Administrators wouldn't have access, and logons could potentially fail. When the member server is promoted to a domain controller, the only change is that the Server Operators group replaces the Power Users group.

Default Security for Active Directory Files

The Active Directory itself and its logs are in the \WINNT\NTDS folder. Security is tight here; only Administrators and SYSTEM have Full Control, and no one else is present on the ACL. This is excellent protection for the AD files. The SYSVOL folder is also well protected by default with Administrators, SYSTEM, and Creator Owners at Full Control and Authenticated Users and Server Operators at Read and Execute.

A-G-L-P Becomes A-G-DL-P

In NT 4.0, Microsoft espoused the concept of A-G-L-P. User Accounts go into Global groups, which are placed into Local groups on the resource computer and granted Permissions: A-G-L-P. The closer you examined the concept, the more you realized it made much more sense in a multi-domain environment where the groups were crossing trusts than it did in a single-domain environment where no trusts were involved. Things have changed substantially in Windows 2000.

If your Active Directory enterprise contains but a single domain, you can modify the traditional NT 4.0 A-G-L-P access permission model (User Accounts are placed in Global groups, which are placed in Local groups, which are the only ones granted Permissions) into A-G-DL-P: User Accounts are placed in Global groups, which are placed in Domain Local groups, which are the only ones granted Permissions. Domain user accounts with similar needs are placed in a Global group. At the resources (shared folders and printers), Domain Local groups are granted appropriate permissions and placed on the ACLs. Then, to connect the two sides of the equation, place the Global groups into the Domain Local groups, and you're in business.

CLIENT MIGRATIONS

Because Win2K is fully backward-compatible with the older legacy Microsoft operating systems, administrators have a number of client options as they move into the wondrous world of Windows 2000:

▼ Do nothing. Upgrade the servers and domain controllers in the back room. Work out the kinks in your Active Directory structure. The clients will keep logging on the same way they did before. The users won't even know you've upgraded. This may also be necessary if one of the mission-critical applications in your organization is incompatible with Win2K. You may just have to spend your time leaning harder on the software vendor.

■ Add the Directory Services client to Win 9x. It's quick and painless. (Maybe the users could install it? OK, bad idea. How about a logon script?) Once it's installed, users can search the AD (Win 9x), and you can strengthen the logon security in Win 9x and NT 4.0.

▲ Migrate all your Win 9x and NT 4.0 clients to Windows 2000 Professional. The only caveat here is application compatibility. Test it. Test it. Test it. If you don't, it's gonna come back and bite you in the…you know where! If the apps fail the tests, see the first bullet in this list.

Windows 95/98 Clients

From the first day of a Windows 2000 enterprise, Windows 95 and Windows 98 users can log on to the servers and domain controllers using the exact same methods they use right now. Win 9x clients aren't required to upgrade in order to do basically what they've always done. However, we are not upgrading to Windows 2000 so we can do what we've always done. We want more. And to get the full functionality of the Windows 2000 Active Directory and Group policies, we'll have to upgrade our legacy clients, maybe not tomorrow, but soon…very soon.

Directory Services Client

Windows 2000 provides a Directory Services client (dsclient.exe) that ships with the Server CD. You find it in the \CLIENTS\WIN9X folder. You must execute this file on the Win 9x computer you wish to upgrade. The DS client extension for Win 9x includes the following capabilities:

▼ Ability to log on to a domain controller "closest" to the client (site affinity)

▲ Ability to change password on any Win2K domain controller instead of the PDC

■ Allows scripting to Active Directory

■ Provides a Dfs client for access to Windows 2000 distributed file system

■ Allows the user to change personal information properties (for example, phone number and address) on their AD user object

■ Takes advantage of the improved authentication features available in NTLMv2

The Directory Services client extension for Win 9x has the following limitations:

▼ No Kerberos support for Win 9x clients

■ No Group policy support

▲ No IPSEC/L2TP support

The dsclient.exe file is about 3MB so it won't fit on a floppy, but the installation only takes about 60 seconds. Double-clicking on the file brings up an installation wizard with only four screens: the Welcome screen, the Ready to Install screen, the Installation screen, and the Completed screen for a total of two Nexts and one Finish. After the installation, you must restart the Win 9x computer. After restarting, the bootup or logon processes are not noticeably different. In fact, you might find yourself thinking that the installation didn't work. If you're like me, you're looking for the ON switch or a new client to install from the Control Panel | Network icon—but dsclient is an add-on not a replacement. As shown in Figure 16-9, simply click Find on the Start menu and then People, and you realize that you are suddenly, but seamlessly, able to search the Active Directory for objects from Windows 98 just as if you were running Win2K.

Migrating Windows 9x to Windows 2000 Professional

Microsoft is to be congratulated on the clarity and simplicity of the Win2K Professional upgrade process. Not only is it clear and straightforward, but minimal user involvement is compressed to the first few minutes of the upgrade. Then you just step out of the way, and let the Win2K setup program take over. After the first Win2K upgrade you perform, you will never want to go back to NT.

Boot into Windows 95 or 98 and insert the Win2K Professional CD. The autorun will display some self-explanatory prompts. A new element does appear, however, with the

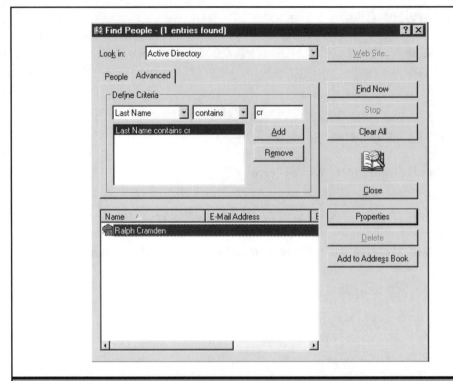

Figure 16-9. Searching the Active Directory from Windows 98 with the Directory Services
client installed

Provide Upgrade Packs screen. Setup tells us that some existing programs may need upgrade packs to work with Win2K. These upgrade packs are obtainable only from the software manufacturer of the application. Upgrade packs may contain updated replacement
files and scripts for installing them. If there is going to be problem with your workstation
rollout, it will be with applications that are incompatible with Win2K, not with the operating system itself. If you have any question about application compatibility, check
Microsoft's compatibility Web site at www.microsoft.com/windows2000/upgrade/
compat/search/default.asp.

As the Web site tells us, applications are classified according to which of the three levels of testing they have passed:

▼ **Certified:** meets all the Windows 2000 Applications Specification standards.

■ **Ready:** ISV-tested for Windows 2000. ISV (Independent Software Vendor) will
   provide product support for the application running on the final version of
   Windows 2000.

▲   **Planned:** ISV has committed on paper to testing and delivering a true Windows 2000–compatible version of the application.

You should rigorously test *all* of the applications that may be currently running on your user desktops on a Win2K Pro pilot machine before beginning your rollout. Beware of those sneaky little applications like WinZip, Adobe Acrobat, fax services, or virus shields running in the background. Implement your own application-compatibility testing program and stick with it before purchasing new applications to run on the Win2K Professional desktops.

After a few more screens, the Upgrade Report screen appears. Near the bottom of the report, Setup gives you the bad news (if any) that some hardware devices or applications may not be compatible and, in some cases, that your Recycle Bin won't be saved and you'll lose your deleted files. From this screen, you can also print the report for later use or save the report as a text file.

The Ready to Install Windows 2000 screen appears, informing you that Setup now has all the necessary information to install Win2K Pro. This is the last human interaction needed. Without another keystroke or mouse-click, your fully-installed and completely capable Windows 2000 Professional workstation is ready 30 to 40 minutes later.

Windows NT Clients

In contrast to Windows 9*x*, Win2K offers no Directory Services client for NT 4.0 to allow for searching the Active Directory. As previously stated, a Directory Services client was never in Microsoft's plan for Windows 2000. However, in late 1999, Microsoft announced that a DS client for NT 4.0 would be developed but not by the Win2K launch date. It will be shipped in Service Pack 7 for NT 4.0.

One of the additional features afforded to the Win 9*x* client by the Directory Services client add-on is the vastly more secure authentication protocol—NTLMv2. This new authentication protocol increases the logon security significantly. Ironically, NT 4.0 has been able to use this improved authentication method since Service Pack 4, but it was a pointless exercise since Win 9*x* was still using the incredibly old and insecure LAN Manager (LM) authentication protocol. If Win 9*x* was on the network, logons were insecure. Now that we have a method for using NTLMv2 with Win 9*x*, we can improve our logon security by moving all downlevel clients to NTLMv2, assuming, of course, that we are going to wait to upgrade them to Win2K, which uses the most secure Kerberos protocol for authentication.

The migration process from Windows NT 4.0 Workstation to Windows 2000 Professional is simple and straightforward.

Migrating NT 4.0 Workstation to Windows 2000 Professional

Once again, the folks from Redmond have opted for clarity and for efficient use of the installer's time. An experienced installer could spend five minutes or less at each computer to execute the upgrades. The only thing that is vastly different is the application-compatibility sections: Win 9*x* has them, but NT 4.0 does not.

From an NT 4.0 workstation, insert the Windows 2000 Professional CD. Autoplay brings up some of the same prompts we've seen before. The wizard screens are self-explanatory, and we'll click through them quite quickly. The Welcome to the Windows 2000 Setup Wizard screen. Do you want to upgrade? Yes. Upgrade your existing install or opt for a clean install? Upgrade. Do you accept the terms of the License Agreement? I accept. Please enter your product key? Enter slowly.

Assuming that your NT 4.0 installation is at Service Pack 4 or higher and that the network settings in NT 4.0 have been previously configured, then correctly entering the product key is the last human interaction needed to complete the upgrade. It's completely automatic from there on out.

After the upgrade is complete, the system restarts automatically and returns in a fully-installed version of Windows 2000 Professional. Total elapsed time for the upgrade is approximately 50 minutes.

SUMMARY

Let the migration stories begin. We'll read about the great successes, the incredibly huge companies going with a single-domain model, or the forest of 17 domains worldwide with monitored replication, 38 Global Catalog servers, and 250,000 users. We'll also read about the failed rollouts with business downtime—horror stories that were almost certainly caused by unbelievably poor planning and incompetence. Have you ever wondered why the exact same technology works beautifully at one organization, while another one just can't seem to keep their network up? I wonder why that is. The most important migration story is yours. Make sure it falls into the successful category.

APPENDIX A

Windows 2000 Support Tools

One piece of good news is that, unlike previous versions of NT, the best Windows 2000 support tools ship on the Server CD. These tools initially were going to be in the Win2K Resource Kit to be purchased separately, but Microsoft wisely determined that the tools were so indispensable that the new OS couldn't ship without them. You must install the Support Tools separately after the OS is up and running, but at least you didn't have to buy them. You'll find them in \SUPPORT\TOOLS. Double-click on either 2000rkst.msi or setup.exe to bring up the Win2K Support Tools Setup Wizard. The Support Tools take up about 18MB of well-deserved disk space. You will need these tools to manage a Win2K network and Active Directory.

Each of the Support Tools comes with some kind of help. If the tool is GUI, then clicking Help will get you to expanded explanations and syntax examples. If the tool uses the command line, then typing a **/?** after the command will bring up a list of all the possible options for that command.

ACLDIAG.EXE   Allows you to view Active Directory ACL entries, showing *effective* permission for either the users or groups based on directly assigned permissions or those applied through inheritance. Can also be used to check or fix Delegation of Control Wizard permissions. Output can be tab delimited for import into a database.

ADSIEDIT.MSC   An MMC snap-in that connects to Active Directory using LDAP. This snap-in displays AD from a object-class-attribute standpoint, similar to the way you view a Site Server Metabase (for membership) or Exchange Administrator in raw mode. As its name suggests, it also allows admins to edit Active Directory data.

APCOMPAT.EXE   When installing a legacy application on a Windows 2000 machine, use this program to "fool" the setup program installing the application by returning a different operating system (remember setver.exe from DOS 6). You can run this tool as a GUI or command-line program. It will "lie" to the setup program, informing it that Windows 2000 is really Windows 95 or Windows NT, SP4, for example. This allows installation of legacy applications that know nothing of Win2K.

APMSTAT.EXE   APM (Advanced Power Management) features from the registry (detected at startup) and in the BIOS of the computer are included in the report created by this tool. Even though APM was replaced by ACPI (advanced configuration and power interface), this command-line tool still reports on this information and can tell you if the computer is running in ACPI mode.

BROWSTAT.EXE   You can use this command-line utility, similar to the NT 4.0 Resource Kit program (browmon), to view browsing information on your network. Includes statistics about browsing, finding Browse Masters, and backup browsers.

CLONEPR.DLL AND RELATED SCRIPTS: CLONEBB.VBS, CLONEGGU.VBS, CLONELG.VBS, CLONEPR.VBS   Use these scripts to duplicate objects (User, Local Group, and Global Group) from a separate forest or Windows NT 4.0 domain to a Windows 2000 Active

Directory domain with the security principal retaining its old SID as part of its SID History, allowing it to retain its associated permissions and resource access. *See also* movetree.exe for operations within a forest.

DCDIAG.EXE   An end user command-line reporting tool, it reports on connectivity, trusts, replications, and other network functions. *See also* netdiag.exe.

DEPENDS.EXE   This tool is useful for programmers or admins with conflicting installations of software (a Microsoft hot-fix wants to replace a critical .dll, for example). This GUI utility can show the .ocx, .sys, .dll, and .exe files a particular program requires to run correctly, displaying the minimum required files and versions, and even missing files.

DFSUTIL.EXE   This command-line tool allows you to view information about Dfs (distributed file system—a logical file structure that points to a series of actual servers and file shares). You can use the tool to troubleshoot, maintain, and clean up the metadata about a Dfs root.

DNSCMD.EXE   View and modify Windows 2000 DNS servers with this command-line utility. It can force replication, add RRs (Resource Records—like an A record for a UNIX host), and even create a new zone.

DSACLS.EXE   Use this command-line tool as the Security tab on most Active Directory objects, letting you manipulate the security attributes on the objects' ACL. acldiag.exe offers more information and better output formatting options.

DSASTAT.EXE   This command-line Active Directory tool can be used to view capacity information, such as the number of objects and megabytes per server, but can also compare replicated objects and determine if a domain controller has a consistent image of a domain partition or a Global Catalog partial partition.

DSKPROBE.EXE   A low-level GUI disk drive utility, dskprobe.exe can be used to view or modify individual sectors on the hard drive.

DUMPCHK.EXE   Similar to the NT 4.0 Resource Kit version, this command-line utility verifies that a crash dump file was created, for example, when a STOP error (BSOD) occurs. It can also provide basic analysis of the dump file without having to use the debugger.

FILEVER.EXE   This handy command-line utility displays the version information of executable and dynamic-link libraries (DLLs). It returns the binary build of a program or hot-fix. This operation can be performed on a local or remote computer.

GFLAGS.EXE   A GUI tool to modify the registry setting for certain programming functions. It can modify flags that reflect kernel memory, allow the display of certain handles, and provide other settings.

KILL.EXE Much like the NT 4.0 Resource Kit version (and the UNIX program of the same name), this command-line program can end a process on a Windows 2000 box by its process name or its PID (process ID). Use tlist.exe or Task Manager to obtain a PID or process name.

KSETUP.EXE Used with tools like ktpass.exe, this tool updates a client for use with an MIT Kerberos server and assists the client in finding the correct Kerberos realm. It can also set up the account mappings between the local accounts and the Kerberos accounts. This can affect Windows 2000 domain membership.

KTPASS.EXE Used with tools like ksetup.exe, this tool can configure services and Kerberos settings for interoperability with Unix services that may require a "keytab" file with a secret key to work correctly.

LDP.EXE Yet another tool to view Active Directory with LDAP (see adsiedit.msc). This tool allows you to view metadata-like replication information and security descriptors.

MEMSNAP.EXE This command-line tool creates a log file that is a snapshot of the memory resources used by all running processes.

MOVETREE.EXE Move Active Directory objects (users, groups, and OUs) between domains within the same forest with this command-line tool. Given the complex nature of Active Directory, not all objects can be moved. Certain things like GPOs linked to the OU retain their links after the OU is moved, and the user accounts retain their SIDs (in the SID history) after the move. Computer accounts can be moved within the forest but require the NETDOM utility. Other things such as built-in groups and policies are not moved and will need to be re-created in the new domain. *See also* clonepr.dll for similar operations between forests or between a Win2K AD domain and an NT 4.0 downlevel domain.

MSICUU.EXE New with the Windows Installer is a database of the programs that are installed via this new service. If you have a problem with the Installer and want to reinstall an application, you'll need to remove the registry entries pertaining to that application. Use this GUI-based tool to clean up those registry entries. It only cleans the registry and doesn't delete files. *See also* msizap.exe for a command-line version.

MSIZAP.EXE New with the Windows Installer is a database of the programs that are installed via this new service. Use this command-line tool to clean up the registry entries, if you have a problem and want to reinstall an application. Only cleans registry and doesn't delete files. *See also* msicuu.exe for a GUI version.

NETDIAG.EXE This command-line tool is intended for broad usage because it performs many tests without user input (like pinging the loopback, a DNS test, and an IP security test). Designed for easy scripting and usage with WMI (Windows Management Instrumentation).

NETDOM.EXE Upgraded considerably from the NT 4.0 Resource Kit, this powerful domain and trust relationship tool has lots of new functionality. It can view and reset connections, verify workability, establish or remove trust relationships (Kerberos two-way, one-way, and so on), and add/remove/move computers to domains while retaining security descriptors. This tool can even rename a domain.

NLTEST.EXE   Use this command-line tool in an integrated Windows 2000 Active Directory and Windows NT 4.0 Directory Services environment for things like checking the status of a secure channel, verifying trust relationships, and monitoring domain synchronization.

PMON.EXE   Improved from the NT 4.0 Resource Kit, this command-line utility provides a command-line Task Manager, displaying running processes with CPU time, memory usage, priority, and other details.

POOLMON.EXE   If pool tagging is enabled, this tool allows you to view kernel memory tags, such as total paged and nonpaged bytes; it's commonly used to find memory leaks. Use with gflags.exe to set pool tagging.

PPTPCLNT.EXE AND PPTPSRV.EXE   Use these tools to verify connectivity flowing between two PPTP hosts over TCP port 1723. Does not test the functionality of a PPTP server or client, just the routers in between the client and the server. Will not run on Windows 95.

PVIEWER.EXE   A GUI-based tool that displays currently running processes and allows you to change priority and kill processes on remote computers.

REG.EXE   A command-line tool that, using simple text files, is great for scripting changes to registry entries. Expanded heavily from the NT 4.0 Resource Kit version, it can now be used to compare remote registries, save and restore sections, and other functions.

REMOTE.EXE   A remote console command tool that works both as a server and a client component. This utility does no security checks. *See also* wsremote.exe.

REPADMIN.EXE   A command-line replication tool, it allows you to force a replication (either between two DCs or sync all) and view connection information and even the status of the USN for a property. Intended to be used to diagnose replication problems.

REPLMON.EXE   This GUI tool allows you to view Active Directory replication in a visual format, displaying connection objects and showing which domain controllers are in specific roles. It can also monitor history, transports, performance, status, and even force replication. It works with COM so you can also script its functionality with VBScript.

RSDIAG.EXE   Use this command-line utility to display diagnostic information about Remote Storage databases in a text file. Works with rsdir.exe.

RSDIR.EXE   A command-line tool to display the Remote Storage information for a directory, allowing you to diagnose problems and recover data.

SDCHECK.EXE   Use this command-line tool to display the ACLs on Active Directory objects, showing the hierarchy and inheritance.

SHOWACCS.EXE   This utility shows access to NTFS files, registry, file shares, printer shares, and local groups (with or without built-in local groups). It can output into a comma-separated value (.csv) file for easy input into a Excel spreadsheet or an Access database. Works in conjunction with sidwalk.exe and sidwalk.msc.

SIDWALK.EXE   This command-line program runs in conjunction with showaccs.exe, and it is used to go through the registry, NTFS files, shared folders, and printer shares, using a .csv file as its input. It is used to delete or replace SIDs with newly mapped SIDs to allow you to map over resources during migration or even between forests.

SIDWALK.MSC   A snap-in for the MMC that is used to map the SIDs of computers migrating from an NT 4.0 resource domain or server resources between domains. Uses a .csv file for its configuration input and allows you to delete or replace the SIDs of the resources in the target domain.

SNMPUTILG.EXE   A GUI utility to query/set SNMP parameters by a host's IP address for basic SNMP operations. It also supports saving the data to a .csv file or to the clipboard.

TLIST.EXE   Similar to tlist.exe in the NT 3.5 and NT 4.0 Resource Kits, this command-line utility lists all the running processes and their PIDs (process IDs) on the operating system.

WINDIFF.EXE   A graphical comparison utility, this program is slightly updated from the NT 4.0 Resource Kit and still compares files and directories. Configurable display shows differences or similarities of folders or files. When comparing directories, you can drill down to see the exact differences between text files, for example.

WINREP.EXE   Dr. Watson on steroids, this end user GUI reporting tool prompts for a problem description, expected results, and steps to reproduce the problem. Also captures system information. When complete, the entire report, plus the system info, is saved as a .cab file.

WSREMOTE.EXE   A remote console command tool that works both as a server and a client component. Much like the one in the NT 4.0 Resource Kit, you simply start it on a machine as the server with a unique ID (you can start multiple versions at once with different IDs), and then you simply connect to this "server" using wsremote on the client specifying the ID to which you want to connect. One advantage to this tool is that if you start the "server" side from your logged on user session and then connect to it from a client, the two command prompts are synchronized so you can see exactly what is going on from both computers.

APPENDIX B

Windows 2000 Command-Line Utilities

Microsoft has committed to making Windows 2000 fully scriptable by Service Pack 1, which is a major commitment when you remember that NT 4.0 had no scripting tools except a third-party utility call Kixstart on the NT 4.0 Resource Kit. Because of this commitment, Microsoft has expanded the number of command-line utilities that ship with Win2K and expanded the options on many of the existing commands, all the while retaining many of our old favorites from DOS and Win 3.*x*. This appendix provides a list of the command-line utilities in Windows 2000.

A

APPEND   Allows programs to open data files in other directories using a search path; similar to using the path statement to find executables.

ARP   Views and clears the local ARP (Address Resolution Protocol) cache.

ASSOC   Changes filename extensions from a command line.

AT   Command-line program for running programs at a specific time.

ATMADM   Acquires and displays ATM Call Manager statistics.

ATTRIB   Displays and modifies the file attributes system: archive, hidden, and read-only.

B

BATCH COMMANDS   A command following the && symbol runs only if the command preceding the symbol succeeds. A command following the | | symbol runs only if the command preceding the symbol fails. The & symbol separates multiple commands on a command line. Parentheses ( ) group commands. The escape character ^ allows typing command symbols as text. A semicolon ; or a comma , separates parameters.

BREAK   Use within a batch file to control CTRL/C behavior.

BUFFERS   A config.nt file setting that controls rudimentary disk caching.

C

CACLS   Use to view or edit file ACL (Access Control Lists) from a command line.

CALL   Starts another batch file from within a batch file, returning control to the original batch file when finished.

CHCP   Changes the code page if dealing with a different language (Full-screen mode only).

CHDIR (CD)   Changes the working directory.

CHKDSK   Scans a drive for errors immediately, or if the drive is in use, flags drive so check occurs during next bootup. Add the /f flag for remedial checks (5–10 minutes), the /v flag to read each sector (45+ minutes).

CHKNTFS   Controls the scheduling of autochk, the NTFS volume scanner.

CIPHER   Views or set the EFS (Encrypting File System) properties for a file.

CLS   Clears screen of text in a command window.

CLUSTER   Used to set parameters for Microsoft Cluster Service.

CMD   Starts a Win2K 32-bit character-mode shell, the command prompt.

CODEPAGE   Sets the codepage for running multilingual programs. *See also* CHCP.

COLOR   Changes the color within a command prompt window.

COMP   Compares text files or a group of text files.

COMPACT   Views or modifies the compression status of files and folders.

CONVERT   Converts a FAT16 or FAT32 drive to NTFS. Changes the cluster size to 512 bytes.

COPY   Copies one or more files to a destination directory. Does not copy directories.

COUNTRY   A config.nt command for changing the character set.

D

DATE   Sets or views the date of the system.

DEL (ERASE)   Deletes one or more files.

DEVICE   A config.nt command used to load device drivers for physical or logical devices.

DEVICEHIGH (DH)   A config.nt command used to load device drivers into upper memory blocks.

DEVINFO   An OS/2 config.sys command, listing the information on each device.

DIR   Lists files and directories on-screen.

DISKCOMP   Used to compare the contents of two floppy disks.

DISKCOPY   Used to do a sector-by-sector copy of two floppy disks.

DISKPERF   Toggles disk performance counters on or off for use with performance monitor. Diskperf –yv turns on the logical disk counters in Win2K.

DOS   A config.nt command used to load a portion of DOS itself into the High Memory Area (HMA).

DOSKEY   Lets you keep a command history and create macros.

DOSONLY   A config.nt command that alters the behavior Win2K allows in command.com command prompts.

DRIVEPARM   A config.nt command that alters the internally stored drive parameters. Win2K and the MS-DOS subsystem do not take action for this command.

E

ECHO   Turns on or off the display of information to the screen from within a batch file.

ECHOCONFIG   A config.nt command used to display messages from the processing of the config.nt and autoexec.nt commands when an MS-DOS subsystem becomes active.

EDIT   A character-based text editor.

EDLIN   A single-line command-line text editor.

ENDLOCAL   Used within a batch file for environment variable control.

EVNTCMD   Displays SNMP (Simple Network Management Protocol) events.

EXE2BIN   Converts executable (exe) files to binary format.

EXIT   Quits the current command interpreter.

EXPAND   Uncompresses compressed Microsoft distribution files (that is, cab files).

F

FC   Compares two text files and displays the difference.

FCBS   A config.nt command that controls the number of file control blocks that can be in use for DOS applications.

FILES   A config.nt command that controls the number of file handles that can be available for DOS applications.

FIND   Searches for a text string in a file.

FINDSTR   Searches for a string in multiple files.

FINGER   Connects to a Finger server and displays relevant information.

FOR   Used within a batch file to process a loop for a specified number of times.

FORCEDOS   Used for programs not recognized by Win2K as DOS applications; causes the operating system to open the application in an MS-DOS virtual machine.

FORMAT   Places the logical file system structure on a disk.

FTP   Sets up a File Transfer Protocol session to an FTP host.

FTYPE   Displays or modifies the file extension type.

G

GOTO   Used within a batch file to jump to a label within the file.

GRAFTABL   Shows extended character set in graphics mode.

H

HELP   Displays a list of popular commands and a short description.

HOSTNAME   Displays the TCP/IP host (computer) name.

I

IF   Used within a batch file to provide conditional capability.

INSTALL   A config.nt command that loads a memory-resident program into memory before the shell is loaded.

IPCONFIG   Used to view the TCP/IP configuration of a machine. For DHCP, /release will release the current IP address, /renew will renew a previous DHCP lease, /registerdns will register the client with the DNS server, while /flushdns will erase the client's resolver cache.

IPXROUTE Used to view and modify the IPX/SPX NwLink networks and routing tables.

IRFTP Sends files over an infrared link.

L

LABEL Changes the label associated with a mounted volume.

LASTDRIVE A config.nt command that defines the logical drive table for a real-mode session.

LOADHIGH (LH) Loads a program into upper memory blocks.

LPQ Accesses the TCP/IP printing queue.

LPR TCP/IP printing command.

M

MEM Used to display the amount of used and free memory in your DOS virtual machine.

MKDIR (MD) Creates a new folder or directory.

MORE Displays information on-screen one screen height at a time.

MOUNTVOL Used to create, delete, or list the existing volume mount points.

MOVE Used to move files and rename files and directories.

N

NBTSTAT Displays and purges local and remote NetBIOS name caches.

NET A powerful utility that can start/stop services, map drives, display shares, connect to printers, and perform other useful functions.

NETSH Provides a scripting interface for configuring and monitoring Win2K. Several subcontexts exist within this command.

NETSTAT Displays TCP/IP statistics such as open connections and port numbers.

NSLOOKUP A standard DNS query tool, it can look up interactively or one record at a time. Can look up SRV records.

NTCMDPROMPT Runs the Win2K command interpreter after running a DOS memory-resident program. *See also* dosonly.

P

PATH   Displays and modifies the search path used when launching a program from a command line.

PATHPING   Combines and enhances the ping and tracert capabilities with additional information.

PAUSE   Used within a batch file to temporarily halt execution.

PAX   A POSIX command that starts the Portable Archive Interchange utility.

PENTNT   The fix for the Intel Pentium floating-point division error.

PING   Used to see if another TCP/IP host will respond to a basic ICMP message.

POPD   Used within a batch file to change the current directory to the directory stored by pushd.

PORTUAS   Merges a LAN Manager 2.*x* user accounts database into a Windows 2000 user accounts database (SAM).

PRINT   Sends a text file to a printer via LPT1.

PROMPT   Changes the look of the command prompt.

PUSHD   Used within a batch file to save the current directory; use popd to restore this directory.

Q

QBASIC   Loads a Basic language interpreter; required by MS-DOS edit.

R

RCP   A remote copy command provided with the TCP/IP stack.

RECOVER   Attempts to recover information from a bad disk. The operative word here is *attempts*. Do not use this command.

REM   Remark; used as a comment in a batch file.

RENAME (REN)   Renames files and folders.

REPLACE   Replaces files in the destination directory with files in the source directory with the same names. Will also add unique files from source directory to destination directory.

REXEC   Used over TCP/IP to run a command on a remote computer.

RMDIR (RD)   Removes a directory.

ROUTE   Used to view or modify the TCP/IP routing table on the local machine.

RSH   Used over TCP/IP to run a command on a remote computer within an RSH service shell.

RUNAS   New secondary logon service that will enable you to run a program in a different security context than the logged on user. Recommended for administrative tools. You must know the password of the secondary user.

S

SET   Used to view or modify environment variables.

SETLOCAL   Used within a batch file to keep variables local to the current shell.

SETVER   Used to "lie" to DOS applications about the current version of the operating system. Win2K uses apcompat.exe for the same purpose.

SHELL   A config.nt command used to define the source name and location of the command interpreter and the size of the space used to store environment variables.

SHIFT   Moves the position of a command-line parameter used in executing a batch file.

SORT   Sorts text input; you can specify column number and ascending/descending.

STACKS   A config.nt command used to configure the number of stacks (open processes in DOS) and the size of each stack.

START   Starts up a program in a new window, and you can specify the base priority that program will run at.

SUBST   The local map drive command; used to map a drive to a directory.

T

TCMSETUP   Used to configure or disable a telephony client.

TFTP   Transfers files to and from a remote computer running the Trivial File Transfer Protocol.

TIME   Used to change or view the system time.

TITLE   Changes the window title for the cmd.exe window.

TRACERT   A TCP/IP utility that will send a ping to the destination (takes a hostname or IP address for input) and displays the time for each hop along the path to the destination.

TREE   Displays the file system directory structure from a command line.

TYPE   Used to display the contents of a text file.

V

VER   Displays the OS version.

VERIFY   Used to turn on or off the verification of file copies in a command prompt.

VOL   Displays information about a disk such as volume label.

W

WINNT   The DOS-based Windows 2000 Setup program executable.

WINNT32   The 32-bit Windows 2000 upgrade program executable. Can also be used to install Recovery Console (/cmdcons).

X

XCOPY   Copies files and directories; new and improved—now comes with 25 options.

APPENDIX C

Windows 2000 Resource Kit Tools

The Windows 2000 Resource Kit does not ship with the product, but it contains a number of utilities you cannot live without. Any major installation that is serious about implementing and managing a successful Win2K network must have a copy of the Win2K Resource Kit. It may be optional to Microsoft, but it is not optional for Win2K administrators. The utilities listed in this appendix are, for the most part, available only by obtaining the Win2K Resource Kit. If you happen to be a Microsoft "Technet" subscriber, a full copy of the Windows 2000 Resource Kit CD with all the utilities and documentation shipped in the January 2000 issue of "Technet."

A

ADDIAG.EXE   Software installation diagnostics. Gives information about user accounts, system status, Windows Installer applications, and Active Directory.

ADDUSERS.EXE   Adds, deletes, or outputs user accounts specified in a file. Can also be used to modify certain properties, even Terminal Services properties.

APIMON.EXE   Used for program debugging and troubleshooting DLL usage.

APPSEC.EXE   Controls authorized applications that Terminal Services users are allowed to run and the location they can run from.

ASSOCIATE.EXE   Sets up a file extension mapping to a program.

ATANLYZR.EXE   Tool to look for registered AppleTalk devices.

ATMARP.EXE   This tool enables you to view information about ATM (Asynchronous Transfer Mode) and the ARP/MARS/MCS-related information about the Windows 2000 machine acting as an ATM server on the network.

ATMLANE.EXE   Used to monitor the LANE (LAN Emulation client) that is installed with ATM on a Windows 2000 machine.

AUDITPOL.EXE   Sets the audit policy of a machine from a command line.

AUTOEXNT.EXE   This tool enables you to configure a batch file named autoexnt.bat to run during system startup without requiring a logon.

B

BROWMON.EXE   Used to view the master/backup browsers of workgroup browsing (Network Neighborhood).

C

CACHEMOV.EXE   Use this command to move the storage location for offline folder storage.

CCONNECT.EXE   Monitors and tracks the number of concurrent connections a computer has connected; also monitors and tracks information about the client computers.

CHKLNKS.EXE   Checks links (shortcuts) on the machine to make sure they point to something that exists; otherwise, it provides a list of "dead" links.

CHOICE.EXE   Used within a batch file to provide the same features as the old DOS batch command function of the same name.

CLEARMEM.EXE   This tool clears up memory by forcing pages out of RAM and clears the file cache.

CLIP.EXE   This command tool redirects the STDIN to the clipboard so you can paste it elsewhere.

CLIPPOOL.EXE   Enables you to share a common clipboard across multiple computers; places an icon in the system tray next to the clock.

CLIPTRAY.EXE   Enables you to have multiple clipboards by storing blocks of text in files; it resides in the system tray next to the clock and then presents you with a list.

CLUSREST.EXE   A cluster tool to fix the registry after one of the two cluster servers has been backed up; fixes the quorum disk part.

CLUSTOOL.EXE   A cluster utility tool to back up, restore, and migrate resources on your cluster servers.

COMPRESS.EXE   A companion to expand.exe, this tool can compress one or more files.

COPSLPM.EXE   This tool enables you to control the ACS (Admission Control Service) policy server by installing the COPS (Common Open Policy Service) LPM (Local Policy Module) server.

CON2PRT.EXE   Allows the user to disconnect all existing connections to NT printers and connect to new NT printers.

CPUSTRES.EXE   Used to create a multithreaded load with configurable priority level settings to test your CPU.

CREATFIL.EXE   Use this tool to create an artificial file of any size to fill up a hard drive.

CTRLIST.EXE This tool gives a list of all the Performance Monitor objects and counters on a system.

CUSRMGR.EXE This command-line tool gives some of the same functionality, such as renaming a user or setting a password, as the local users and groups MMC snap-in.

CVU\CLUSTSIM.EXE The cluster verification utility file that tests the shared SCSI drives.

CVU\SETUP.EXE Sets up the cluster verification utility.

CVU\WPCVP.EXE The main cluster verification utility file that has the verification codes.

D

DEFPTR.EXE Use this tool to change the default printer.

DELPROF.EXE This tool can delete a user profile either locally or remotely on Windows 2000 or Windows NT.

DELRP.EXE Deletes a directory or file and any associated reparse points (used with remote storage where files are placed on backup tapes when unused).

DELSRV.EXE Use this tool to remove an installed service.

DH.EXE Displays the heap; used to view user and kernel memory usage to spot memory leaks.

DHCMP.EXE Compares two heap dumps that were grabbed from dh.exe.

DHCPLOC.EXE This tool finds DHCP servers available from the machine where it is running and can beep or send an alert.

DHCPOBJS.EXE Use this tool to enhance the functionality of the DHCP server by extending what you can do from a command line or remotely.

DIRUSE.EXE Used to display the amount of space utilized by a directory and its subdirectories. This command is useful in a batch file to see which directories are growing and which ones are utilizing the most space.

DISKMAP.EXE Displays lots of detail about how your hard drives are configured but does not work with dynamic disks.

DISKPAR.EXE On a multiple disk system, this tool can realign the starting sector for a possible increase in performance.

DISKUSE.EXE   This tool reports the amount of space used on a disk by each user per directory, subdirectories, and even the whole disk.

DMDIAG.EXE   Disk Manager diagnostics is a tool to report all kinds of disk and storage related information.

DOMMON.EXE   Domain Monitor, used to verify secure channels and trusts.

DRIVERS.EXE   Command-line tool that can list loaded drivers and version information.

DRMAPSRV.EXE   A terminal services utility to configure net share and net use access.

DSSTORE.EXE   Directory Services Store is a utility that can do things such as list certificates and validate certificates in PKI locations or on Smart Cards.

DUMPCFG.EXE   More disk configuration information can be dumped with this utility, and it can dump the disk signature.

DUMPEL.EXE   Command-line tool to dump the event log to a text file.

DUPFINDER.EXE   This GUI tool finds duplicate files and shows size, date, and language information.

DUREG.EXE   Use this tool to estimate the size of your registry, find strings, and look at how much data is being stored in each hive or even on a subkey level.

E

EFSINFO.EXE   This tool displays information about the EFS (Encrypting File System) such as the certificate used to encrypt the file.

ELOGDMP.EXE   Dumps information from an event log (much like dumpel.exe), and you can query for specific events either locally or remotely.

EMPTY.EXE   Empties the working set of virtual pages of memory a process is using while running.

ENUMPROP.EXE   Displays properties on any AD object like the security descriptor, SID, GUID, and so on.

EXCTRLST.EXE   Another tool to allow you to view all the Performance Monitor counters, but with this tool, you view the DLLs that are registered in the registry.

EXETYPE.EXE   Use this program to tell you if a program is compiled to run for DOS or OS/2 so you can troubleshoot the proper subsystem.

EXPAND.EXE　Used with compress.exe, this tool can expand (or uncompress) files and is useful for a lot of the system files from Microsoft that are compressed using the Microsoft format.

EXTRACT.EXE　Use this tool to extract the various .cab files that you receive from Microsoft or applications packaged with Microsoft programs like VB.

F

FCOPY.EXE　A file copy and compression tool that uses MSMQ (Microsoft Message Queue) so it can transmit files in 32KB segments that MSMQ will guarantee delivery of.

FCSETUP.EXE　The Setup program for fcopy.

FILESPY.EXE　This tool enables you to monitor local and network drive activity for file I/O operations.

FINDGRP.EXE　Use this tool to find all the group memberships for a given user.

FLOPLOCK.EXE　Use this tool to control the locking/unlocking of access to the floppy disk drive.

FORFILES.EXE　Used within a batch file to select multiple files for batch processing.

FREEDISK.EXE　This tool checks for free disk space, returning a 0 if there is enough and a 1 if not; thus, trapping on the ERRORLEVEL in a batch file is all that is necessary.

FSPYINST.EXE　Installs filespy.sys service.

FSPYUNIN.EXE　Uninstalls filespy.sys service.

FTEDIT.EXE　Use this utility to modify the fault-tolerant disk sets by writing to the SYSTEM hive of the registry.

G

GETMAC.EXE　Displays the MAC addresses for each installed adapter and the binding order.

GETSID.EXE　Displays SID information.

GETTYPE.EXE　This tool tells you what type of OS you're running and if it is a DC, a workstation, and so on.

GLOBAL.EXE   Displays the members of a global group.

GPOLMIG.EXE   Use this tool to migrate system policies in NT 4.0 to Windows 2000 Group Policy.

GPOTOOL.EXE   This tool can check the health of a GPO (Group Policy object), making sure it is replicated and consistent.

GPRESULT.EXE   Use this tool to list all the applied GPOs (Group Policy objects) to a specific computer and user and the last time they were refreshed.

GRPCPY.EXE   This tool copies groups from one domain to another by adding users of the same names.

GUID2OBJ.EXE   Allows you to map a GUID to a DN (Distinguished Name) in AD.

H

HEAPMON.EXE   Another tool to allow you to view the operating system heap information.

HTMLFLTR.EXE   Cleans unneeded comments and white space from html files.

HTTPCMD.EXE   A command-line http client that allows you to view the returns from the http server.

HTTPMON   Provides immediate monitoring of Web servers.

I

IASPARSE.EXE   This tool can be used to read the log files for the IAS (Internet Authentication Service) and remote access.

IFILTTST.EXE   Works with the ifilttst.ini to test for compliance with the Ifilter specification.

IFMEMBER.EXE   Use as a conditional in a batch file to determine if a user is a member of a specified group.

IISHOSTSVC.EXE   The IIS Host Helper service registers IP header strings as NetBIOS names to allow the usage of WINS to access the Web server.

INSTALER.EXE   Use this tool to watch over application setup programs; it creates an .iml file with changes and can undo what the setup program does including registry changes.

INSTSRV.EXE   Service installer; takes an executable file and registers it as a service on the system.

INTFILTR.EXE   Used on an SMP (Symmetric Multi-Processing) system to set hard affinity for network or disk usage.

INUSE.EXE   If you are an administrator, enables you to replace system files that are locked because they are in use.

IPSECPOL.EXE   Use this tool to apply an IPSec security policy to a machine from the command line and/or a batch script.

J

JAVAREG.EXE   Java registration tool so Java classes are registered in the same way as COM components.

K

KERBTRAY.EXE   This GUI utility sits in the system tray and enables you to view the Kerberos ticket information such as the time left.

KERNPROF.EXE   Use this tool to view the counters and information regarding the kernel of the operating system, and on SMP machines, you can view information for each processor.

KIX32.EXE   A logon script processor and enhanced scripting language, Kixtart can conditionally display information, map drives, start programs, and so on. Other Kixtart commands include: kixplay.exe, kxrpc.exe, and xnet.exe.

KLIST.EXE   View and delete Kerberos tickets in the current logon session with this tool.

L

LEAKYAPP.EXE   Use this program to slowly use up more and more of your system RAM. This is useful in simulating the behavior of poorly written applications and determining if the remedies that you have implemented really are working.

LINKD.EXE   Use this tool to link an NTFS 5.0 directory to an object, device, or directory.

LIST.EXE   Display and search text in text files; doesn't load the entire file in memory so it is more efficient than other programs of this nature.

LOCAL.EXE   Display the members of a local group with this tool.

LOGEVENT.EXE   Use this tool to make entries to the event log on a local or remote system; it's handy to use in a batch file to report success or failure.

LOGOFF.EXE   Use within a batch file to log off the current user session.

LOGTIME.EXE   This program tracks how long a command takes to execute and stores this information in a logtime.log file.

LSREPORT.EXE   Used to track the licensing key packs installed on Terminal Services servers.

LSVIEW.EXE   This GUI tool shows all the Terminal Services servers in your domain.

M

MCAST.EXE   Use this tool to send multicast packets or listen on a specific address.

MCOPY.EXE   A command-line tool that can be used in place of the copy command in a batch file. Creates a log file during the copy operation. *See also* mtc.exe.

METAEDIT.EXE   Used to work with the IIS metabase, this tool works like regedit for the registry.

MIBCC.EXE   A Windows 2000 SNMP MIB database compiler.

MOVEUSER.EXE   Changes the security profile of a user to another so you can move it from one domain to another.

MSINFOSETUP.EXE   Use this program to set up Windows 2000 to read previous versions of system information.

MTC.EXE   This command-line tool can be used in place of xcopy in a batch file. Creates a log file during the copy operation. *See also* mcopy.exe.

MTFCHECK.EXE   Tape format verification tool that verifies the MTF (Microsoft Tape Format).

N

NETCLIP.EXE   This GUI tool will enable you to view the contents of the clipboard of another computer on the network.

NETCONS.EXE   This command-line tool replaces "net use" and displays all the network connections.

NETSET.EXE   Use this tool to install and configure networking components from a batch file.

NETSVC.EXE   This handy tool will enable you to start/stop/pause/continue/query a service running on the machine. *See also* sc.exe.

NLMON.EXE   A command-line tool to view and test trust relationships; it's dependent on the browser service.

NOW.EXE   Much like the VB function of the same name, this tool can be used in a batch file to report the current time.

NTFRSUTL.EXE   Dumps the internal tables, thread, and memory information for the ntfrs service. Runs on both a local as well as a remote server.

NTIMER.EXE   This tool times how long a process takes to execute, showing time in both User Mode and Kernel Mode.

NTRIGHTS.EXE   This tool gives you the ability to grant or revoke user rights.

O

OH.EXE   Open Handles display, showing which files are open and which program has them open.

OIDGEN.EXE   This program creates unique OID (Object Identifier) numbers to be used for extending the AD schema.

OLEVIEW.EXE   A GUI tool to allow you to browse all the registered COM classes on your computer.

P

PATHMAN.EXE   This tool can modify the system and user paths.

PERFMON4.EXE The old Performance Monitor from NT 4.0 is now replaced by a System Monitor MMC snap-in.

PERFMTR.EXE Performance Meter is a command-line version of Performance Monitor.

PERMCOPY.EXE This program copies share and file permissions from one share to another.

PERMS.EXE Displays the user's access permissions to files but does not show the effect of group memberships.

PFMON.EXE Page Fault Monitor is a tool to track the hard and soft page faults resulting from a process.

PLAYBACK.EXE An IIS tool, this program records activity on an IIS server to be repeated later.

PSTAT.EXE Process and thread status from a command line; this tool shows detailed information about everything running on your system.

PTREE.EXE With Process Tree, you can view the process tree and inheritance and kill processes locally or remotely.

PULIST.EXE Displays running processes, their PIDs, and the user contexts they are running in. Tlist appears to be absent from this resource kit, so this tool comes closest to that functionality.

Q

QGREP.EXE A similar tool to grep in UNIX, this tool can be used to search for a text string.

QIDLE.EXE Queries a Terminal Server usage for idle time.

QOSTOOLS

    qtcp.exe Use these tools to set the Quality of Service TCP/IP priority traffic settings.

    tpc.exe This tool enables you to work with the RSVP feature, to set up QoS sessions and test them.

    tsinstl.exe Installs timestmp.sys.

QSLICE.EXE A little graphic utility to view processor usage by process in a bar graph.

QUICKRES.EXE Adds a little GUI enhancement to change screen resolutions quickly.

QUIKTRAY.EXE A little utility to enable you to configure applications to show up in the system tray so you can launch them.

R

RASLIST.EXE Displays RAS server announcements from the network.

RASSRVMON.EXE RAS Server Monitor can be used to give you greater detail of the RAS server on a server, port, summary, or individual connection basis.

RASUSERS.EXE Lets you list at a domain level all the users who have been given access to dial-in. On Windows 2000 RAS, be sure to take the RAS policy and profile into account.

RDPCLIP.EXE This Terminal Server utility allows you to copy and paste between the server and client.

REDUCER.EXE Works as an event tracing tool to break down the trace logs into detailed information.

REGBACK.EXE Used with regrest.exe, this tool can make a backup of the registry or just a particular hive. Use it within a scheduled batch script to create many backups of your system's registry with complete flexibility.

REGDMP.EXE Displays or dumps the contents of the registry to the command prompt, or the contents could be re-directed to a file.

REGFIND.EXE Used to search for a text string within the registry.

REGINI.EXE This tool can modify the registry, taking a text file for input.

REGREST.EXE Used with regback.exe, this tool can restore a particular registry hive even while machine is running (takes effect after reboot).

REMAPKEY.EXE Allows you to remap the keyboard keys so that, for example, the 9 key becomes the Z key. Takes effect for logon screen and command prompts.

RKILL.EXE Client to rkillsrv.exe from a command line.

RKILLSRV.EXE Service to allow clients (rkill.exe and wrkill.exe) to connect to enumerate and kill processes.

ROBOCLI.EXE Tool for testing Terminal Server connections from the TS client.

ROBOCOPY.EXE   This tool enables robust file copy. It's a nice file copying program that can duplicate a folder structure (deleting files on destination to match) and has configurable retries, logging, and other useful features.

ROBOSRV.EXE   Stress testing tool for Terminal Server.

RPCDUMP.EXE   Dumps the RPC endpoints mapped on a machine to use for troubleshooting.

RPINGC.EXE   RPC ping to test for RPC connectivity on Windows 2000, NT, 98, 95 machines.

RPINGC16.EXE   RPC ping to test for RPC connectivity on Windows 3.1 clients.

RPINGDOS.EXE   A ping in which you can select your network protocol.

RPINGS.EXE   RPC ping server component for Windows 2000 and NT.

RSMCONFIG.EXE   Removable Storage Manual Configuration Wizard can be used to set up the robotic library changes that the auto-configuration cannot set up.

RSM_DBIC.EXE   Removable storage integrity checker looks at the database for inconsistencies.

RSM_DBUTIL.EXE   This removable storage database utility is a GUI tool to manage the database by checking integrity, backup, and by searching the database.

RUNAPP.EXE   Runs an application. Running it by itself will cause a session logoff.

S

SC.EXE   Service Control, much more verbose than using net stop/start. Use this tool to view the current status of a service, and also to start, pause, continue, and stop services.

SCANREG.EXE   A command-line registry search tool to locate a string.

SCLIST.EXE   Handy command-line utility to list all the services configured on a system and their current states (for example, running, stopped, and so on).

SENDFILE.EXE   An IIS Web server performance comparison tool that works with a Web stress testing tool.

SETEDIT.EXE   Similar in appearance to System Monitor, this tool has editable instance names.

SETSPN.EXE   Use this command-line tool to manage the SPN (Service Principal Names) for the directory service account.

SETUPMGR.EXE   Much like the tool in the NT 4.0 Resource Kit, this wizard assists you in creating an unattend.txt or winnt.sif file to be used to automate the installation of Windows 2000. (See Chapter 2.)

SETX.EXE   A command-line tool to set environment variables as a batch operation from registry keys or a text file. It can work on both user variables or system variables.

SHOWACLS.EXE   This command shows the file permissions on a folder or file. It shows "effective permissions" for a user by enumerating the local and global group memberships and will use those SIDs.

SHOWGRPS.EXE   This tool lists all the groups a user belongs to.

SHOWINST.EXE   Displays text files associated with an installation name.

SHOWMBRS.EXE   This tool shows all the names of the members of a group.

SHOWPERF.EXE   This GUI tool dumps the raw performance data so you can look at the stuff that may not show up in System Monitor.

SHOWPRIV.EXE   This tool displays all the users and groups granted a particular privilege.

SHUTDOWN.EXE   Use this command to shut down a server from a command line. Can perform an optional reboot, and shut down programs by killing them by using a /c.

SIPANEL.EXE   Soft input panel allows you to use a pen as a primary input device and provides handwriting recognition.

SLEEP.EXE   Used within a batch file to make it stop running for a number of seconds.

SMCLIENT.EXE   The Service Monitoring Client is required to run smconfig.exe.

SMCONFIG.EXE   Service monitoring tool.

SNMPMON.EXE   A SNMP Monitor tool to be used to view SNMP MIB variables across multiple nodes.

SNMPUTIL.EXE   This tool enables you to get SNMP information from a host.

SOON.EXE   Uses the AT scheduler service to start a program after a specified number of seconds.

SRVANY.EXE   Use this utility to configure an application to run as a service rather than a user process.

SRVCHECK.EXE   This tool lists all the shares and ACLs on a machine from a command line.

SRVINFO.EXE   Displays a few statistics about a server, its disk configuration and usage, the currently logged on users, services status, and other useful information.

SRVINSTW.EXE   This wizard aids you in installing a services and device drivers.

SRVMGR.EXE   Server Manager from NT 4.0, this tool can be used only on NT 4.0 SAM databases; it's not AD aware.

SU.EXE   Used to switch user security context to start a new process, this tool requires suss.exe to work.

SUBINACL.EXE   Use this command to replace an ACE (Access Control Entry) on an ACL with another user SID. For example, you can use this command when a user has moved between domains, and you want to replicate their file permissions.

SUSS.EXE   Server component to su.exe.

SVCACLS.EXE   Service ACL editor to control access to control services on a system.

SVCMON.EXE   A service monitoring tool, this tool uses a polling interval to monitor whether a service has stopped or started, and it can then send an notification e-mail.

SYSDIFF.EXE   Used to automate the installation of many workstations by capturing a before and after snapshot of the OS.

SYSPREP.EXE   Used to remove machine-specific information before using a third-party imaging tool. When the system is rebooted after running this tool, a mini-Setup program runs.

T

TAKEOWN.EXE   Use this tool to clean up the installation of Windows 2000; it cleans files without formatting the drive.

TCCOM.EXE   The traffic control COM server.

TCMON.EXE   You can use this tool to monitor tccmon.exe to control the traffic flow between two computers.

TEXTVIEW.EXE   This tool enables you to quickly view text files with basic editing and searching capabilities.

TIMEOUT.EXE   Used in batch files much like sleep, this command awaits input or continues after a certain time period designated in seconds.

TIMETHIS.EXE   Used to measure how long a process takes to execute.

TIMEZONE.EXE   Use this utility to change the time zone start and end dates.

TLOCMGR.EXE   Use this tool to manage telephone locations and settings.

TOP.EXE   Shows the top processes for resource usage using the CPU.

TOTLPROC.EXE   This tool displays the total memory usage and processor time on a SMP machine.

TRACEDMP.EXE   Creates a trace log dump file of event trace log items in a user-readable format.

TRACEENABLE.EXE   This tool can modify the registry to turn RAS/RADIUS tracing on/off.

TRACELOG.EXE   This tool turns event trace logging on/off; used with tracedmp.exe to view results.

TSREG.EXE   Terminal Services client registry editor for things like the bitmap cache size.

TSVER.EXE   Terminal Services version monitor to control which clients can connect.

TYPEPERF.EXE   View Performance Monitor counters from a command line with this tool.

TZEDIT.EXE   Use this tool to modify time zone entries in the Control Panel.

U

UNDOINST.EXE   Removes the installation name.

UPTIME.EXE   Displays system uptime in hours, minutes, and seconds.

USRMGR.EXE   User Manager for Domains from NT 4.0.

USRSTAT.EXE   This handy tool lists the user's name and last logon time for the entire domain.

USRTOGRP.EXE   Used to add a list of users in a text file to a specified group.

V

VADUMP.EXE   Used to view the working set of memory a process has; use clearmem.exe to flush out this memory.

VFI.EXE   This tool can list file information like path and date; it's useful for understanding setup program modifications.

W

WAITFOR.EXE   Used in a batch file to wait for a network signal or a pre-determined number of seconds.

WHERE.EXE   This tool can find files and display date and size information.

WHOAMI.EXE   Displays the current security context of the command session.

WINSCHK.EXE   This tool checks the names and versions in a WINS database and can monitor replication activity.

WINSCL.EXE   Use this tool to manage WINS, things like monitoring activities and initiating a replication.

WINSTA.EXE   Terminal Server GUI tool to monitor the status of all the users connected and provide statistics like domain and IP address.

WPERF.EXE   Another GUI tool that displays Performance Monitor data in a different way.

WRKILL.EXE   Client to rkillsrv.exe from a GUI window.

X

XCACLS.EXE   Much like cacls.exe from the regular OS command line but with many, many more options; used to view or edit the file ACLs on an NTFS file system.

APPENDIX D

Protocols and Ports Used by Windows NT or Windows 2000 Services

After scouring dozens of white papers, books, articles, and the entire Internet, (yeah, right!) this is the most exhaustive list of Windows NT and Windows 2000 ports and protocols I could compile. The information is current and derived from a myriad of public sources and some private discussions with folks in the know.

As we are continually forced to secure our networks with increasing granularity, the knowledge of which port must be open on a firewall to accomplish a specific task can be invaluable. As always, please test these assumptions in your own environment before rolling it into production.

PORT	TCP/UDP	FUNCTION DESCRIPTION
20	TCP	File Transfer Protocol (FTP) Data
21	TCP	File Transfer Protocol (FTP) Control
23	TCP	Telnet
25	TCP	Simple Mail Transfer Protocol (SMTP)
42	TCP	Windows Internet Name Service (WINS) Replication
53	TCP	Domain Name Service (DNS) Name Resolution
53	UDP	DNS SOA Record Transfer
67	UDP	Dynamic Host Configuration Protocol (DHCP) Server (port also used for BOOTstrap Protocol—BOOTP)
68	UDP	Dynamic Host Configuration Protocol (DHCP) Client (port also used for BOOTstrap Protocol—BOOTP)
69	TCP/UDP	Trivial File Transfer Protocol (TFTP)
70	TCP/UDP	Gopher
79	TCP/UDP	Finger
80	TCP	Internet Information Services (IIS) Web Publishing Service using Hypertext Transport Protocol (HTTP)
88	TCP/UDP	Kerberos
102	TCP	Message Transfer Agent (MTA)—X.400 over TCP/IP (Exchange)
110	TCP	Post Office Protocol v3 (POP3)
119	TCP	Network News Transfer Protocol (NNTP)
123	TCP	Network Time Protocol (NTP)/Simple Network Time Protocol (SNTP)

PORT	TCP/UDP	FUNCTION DESCRIPTION
135	TCP	**Location Service**
		Replication
		Remote Procedure Call (RPC)
		RPC EndPoint (EP) Port Mapper
		WINS Manager
		DHCP Manager
		Exchange Client/Server Communication
		Exchange Administration
137	UDP	**NetBIOS Name Service**
		Logon Sequence
		NT 4.0 Trust Authentication
		NT 4.0 Secure Channel
		Pass Through Validation
		Browsing (Share Name Lookup)
		Printing
		WINS Registration
138	UDP	**NetBIOS Datagram Service**
		Logon Sequence
		NT 4.0 Trust Authentication
		NT 4.0 Directory Replication
		NT 4.0 Secure Channel
		Pass Through Authentication
		NetLogon
		Browsing
		Printing
139	TCP	**NetBIOS Session Service**
		NetBIOS over TCP/IP (NBT)
		Server Message Blocks (SMB)
		File Sharing and Printing
		Logon Sequence
		NT 4.0 Trust Authentication
		NT 4.0 Directory Replication
		NT 4.0 Secure Channel
		Pass Through Authentication
		NT 4.0 Administration Tools
143	TCP	Internet Messaging Access Protocol (IMAP4) (Exchange)
161	UDP	Simple Network Management Protocol (SNMP)

PORT	TCP/UDP	FUNCTION DESCRIPTION
162	UDP	Simple Network Management Protocol (SNMP) traps
179	UDP	Border Gateway Protocol (BGP)
389	TCP	Lightweight Directory Access Protocol (LDAP)
443	TCP	HTTPS (HTTP over TLS/SSL) Transport Layer Security (TLS) is backward compatible with Secure Sockets Layer (SSL)
445	TCP/UDP	SMB Direct Host / Microsoft Directory Services
464	TCP/UDP	Kpassword (Kerberos)
465	TCP	SMTP (SSL)
500	UDP	Internet Protocol Security (IPSec), ISAKMP, IKE
507	TCP	Content Replication Service/Content Deployment (Site Server)
531	TCP	Internet Relay Chat (IRC)
522	TCP	Internet Locator Service (ILS) (NetMeeting)
593	TCP/UDP	HTTP-RPC-EPMAP (remap of RPC using Web protocol)
636	TCP	LDAPS (LDAP over TLS/SSL)
691	TCP/UDP	Microsoft Exchange Routing
750	TCP/UDP	Kerberos Authentication
751	TCP/UDP	Kerberos Authentication
752	UDP	Kerberos Password Server
753	UDP	Kerberos User Registration Server
754	TCP	Kerberos Slave Propagation
888	TCP	Login and Environment Passing
993	TCP	IMAP4 (IMAPv4 over TLS/SSL)
995	TCP	POP3 (POP3 over TLS/SSL)
1025	TCP	Directory Replication
1109	TCP	POP3 with Kerberos
1433	TCP	Microsoft SQL Server Session (TCP client)
1434	TCP/UDP	Microsoft SQL Monitor
1477	TCP/UDP	Microsoft SNA Server
1478	TCP/UDP	Microsoft SNA Base

PORT	TCP/UDP	FUNCTION DESCRIPTION
1503	TCP	NetMeeting T.120 or Terminal Services Remote Display Protocol (RDP)
1512	UDP	WINS (Windows Internet Name Service)
1645	TCP	RADIUS Authentication (*See also* 1812)
1646	TCP	RADIUS Accounting (*See also* 1813)
1701	UDP	L2TP Traffic
1723	TCP	Point-to-Point Tunneling Protocol (PPTP) Control Channel
1731	TCP	NetMeeting Audio Call Control
1745	TCP/UDP	Remote Winsock
1755	TCP/UDP	NetShow
1801	TCP/UDP	Microsoft Message Queue (MSMQ)
1812	TCP	RADIUS Authentication (*See also* 1645)
1813	TCP	RADIUS Accounting (*See also* 1646)
2053	TCP	Kerberos de-multiplexor
2105	TCP	Kerberos encrypted rlogin
2382	TCP/UDP	Microsoft OnLine Analytical Processing (OLAP)
2383	TCP/UDP	Microsoft OnLine Analytical Processing (OLAP)
2393	TCP/UDP	Microsoft OnLine Analytical Processing 1 (OLAP 1)
2394	TCP/UDP	Microsoft OnLine Analytical Processing 2 (OLAP 2)
2504	TCP/UDP	Windows Load Balancing Service (WLBS)
3020	TCP/UDP	Common Internet File System (CIFS)
3268	TCP	Global Catalog query
3269	TCP	Global Catalog query with LDAP over TLS/SSL
3343	UDP	Microsoft Cluster Net (heartbeat)
3389	TCP	Remote Display Protocol (RDP—used in Terminal Services)

APPENDIX E

Windows 2000 Pertinent and Current RFC List

As Microsoft begins to require the TCP/IP protocol and because Windows 2000 uses Internet-based standards for nearly all of its services, an understanding of the original Internet Engineering Task Force (IETF) documents that defined the standards can be beneficial.

The Internet was founded on the principle of everyone working together to make the network a better place. That's why Internet standards are first issued as RFCs (Requests for Comments). After several years of discussion, the RFC might become a proposed standard and then, finally, a standard. These decisions are made by the IETF, the governing body for all Internet and TCP/IP standards.

The list in this appendix is the result of both formal and informal research and, as you might imagine, has grown through time. If you wish to obtain the actual RFCs listed, simply point your browser to www.rfc-editor.org.

X.500 and Active Directory

LDAP, Lightweight Directory Access Protocol (RFCs 2251–2254, 2256)

Representing Tables and Subtrees in the X.500 Directory (RFC 2293)

Using Domains in LDAP/X.500 Distinguished Names (RFC 2247)

Naming Plan for Internet Directory-Enabled Applications (RFC 2377)

Network Services

Dynamic DNS (RFCs 822, 1034, 1035, 1183, 1779, 1886, 1995, 1996, 2052, 2136, 2137, 2181, 2308, 2535)

WINS (RFCs 1001, 1002)

NTP v3 (RFC 1305)

SNTP (RFC 2030)

DHCP (RFCs 1533, 1534, 2131, 2132, 2241, 2322)

Bootp Relay Agent (RFC 1542)

Security

Kerberos (RFC 1510, 1964)

Internet X.509 Public Key Infrastructure Operational Protocols - LDAPv2 (RFC 2559)

Routing and Remote Access

CIDR (RFC 1519)

EAP (RFC 2284)

RADIUS (RFCs 2138, 2139)

Mobile IP [RADIUS] (RFC 2508, 2509)

RIP (RFC 2453)

OSPF (RFC 2328)

IPSec (RFCs 1825, 2401–2412)

PPTP (RFC 2637)

L2TP (RFC 2661)

BAP (RFC 2125)

PPP (RFCs 1661, 1962, 2153)

MS-CHAP (RFC 2433)

MS-CHAPv2 (RFC 2759)

Private IP Addressing (RFC 1918)

Network Address Translation (NAT) (RFC 1631)

INDEX

B

D

N

▼ O

V

W

X

  Y

 Z